McDOUGAL LITTELL

*L*ITERATURE

AND LANGUAGE

· GOLD LEVEL ·

BOY WITH A PLASTIC JACKET   1983   Daniel Quintero
Courtesy, Marlborough Gallery, New York.

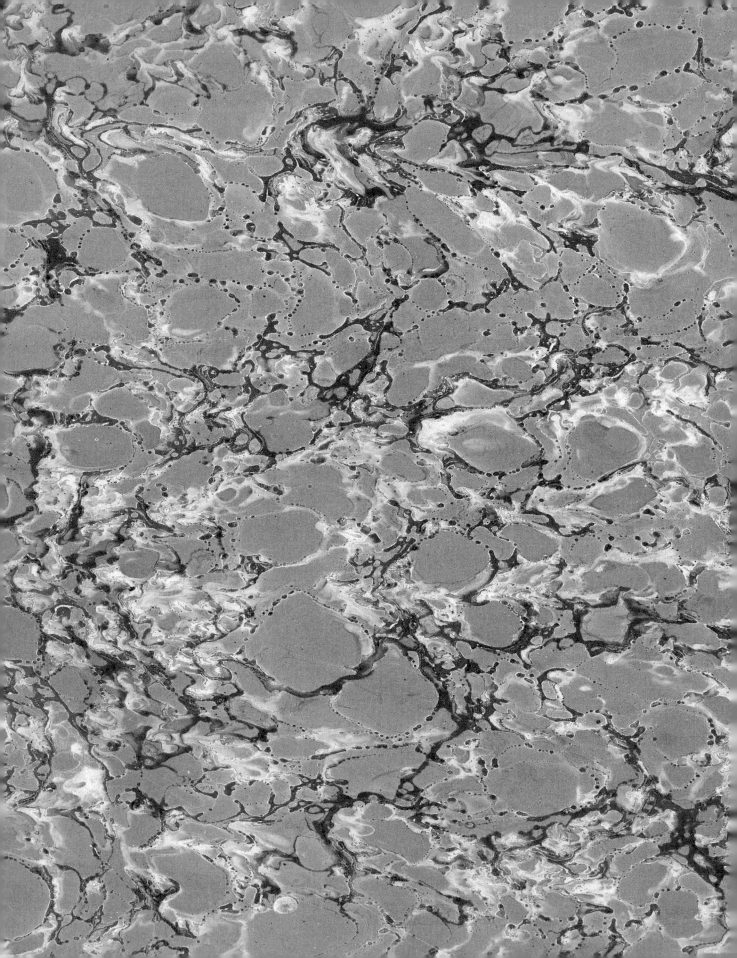

McDOUGAL LITTELL

*L*ITERATURE
AND LANGUAGE

Gold Level

Senior Consultants

Arthur N. Applebee
State University of New York at Albany

Andrea B. Bermúdez
University of Houston—Clear Lake

Susan Hynds
Syracuse University, Syracuse, New York

Judith A. Langer
State University of New York at Albany

James Marshall
University of Iowa, Iowa City

Donna E. Norton
Texas A&M University, College Station

McDOUGAL LITTELL INC.
A Houghton Mifflin Company

Evanston, Illinois
Boston   Dallas   Phoenix

Acknowledgments

F. E. Albi: "Street Corner Flight" by Norma Landa Flores, from *Sighs and Songs of Aztlan*. Copyright © 1975 by F. E. Albi and J. G. Nieto. Reprinted by permission of F. E. Albi, editor.

Ricardo E. Alegría: "The Three Wishes," from *The Three Wishes: A Collection of Puerto Rican Folktales*, selected and adapted by Ricardo E. Alegría, translated by Elizabeth Culbert. Copyright © 1969 by Ricardo E. Alegría. Reprinted by permission of Ricardo E. Alegría.

Arte Publico Press: "Petals," from *Chants* by Pat Mora (Houston: Arte Publico Press-University of Houston), copyright © 1985. Reprinted by permission of the publisher.

Susan Bergholz Literary Services: "Eleven," from *Woman Hollering Creek* by Sandra Cisneros. Copyright © 1991 by Sandra Cisneros. Published in the United States by Vintage Books, a division of Random House, Inc., New York, and simultaneously in Canada by Random House of Canada Limited, Toronto. Originally published in hardcover by Random House, New York. Reprinted by permission of Susan Bergholz Literary Services, New York.

Beyond Words Publishing, Inc.: Excerpt from an interview with Harriett Starleaf Gumbs, from *Wisdomkeepers: Meetings with Native American Spiritual Elders* by Harvey Arden and Steve Wall (Beyond Words Publishing, Inc.), copyright © 1990. Reprinted by permission of the publisher.

BOA Editions, Ltd.: "The 1st," from *good woman: poems and a memoir, 1969-1980* by Lucille Clifton. Copyright © 1987 by Lucille Clifton. Reprinted by permission of BOA Editions, Ltd., 92 Park Avenue, Brockport, NY 14420.

Art Buchwald: "Love and the Cabbie" by Art Buchwald. Copyright © The Washington Post Company. Reprinted by permission of the author.

Cambridge University Press and Eric and Tessa Hadley: "Yhi Brings the Earth to Life," from *Legends of Earth, Air, Fire and Water* by Eric and Tessa Hadley. Copyright © 1985 by Cambridge University Press Reprinted by permission of Cambridge University Press and the authors.

Arthur Cavanaugh: "Miss Awful" by Arthur Cavanaugh. Copyright © 1987 by Arthur Cavanaugh. Reprinted by permission of the author.

CBS Radio and LaVonne Crutchfield: *A Shipment of Mute Fate* by Les Crutchfield. Copyright © 1953 by the Columbia Broadcasting System, Inc. All rights reserved. Reprinted by permission of CBS Radio, a division of CBS, Inc., and the Estate of Les Crutchfield, LaVonne Crutchfield, administrator.

Continued on page 743

Cover Art
BOY WITH A PLASTIC JACKET (detail) 1983 Daniel Quintero
Courtesy, Marlborough Gallery, New York.
Background photograph © David Muench.

ISBN: 0-8123-8039-8

Copyright © 1994 by McDougal Littell Inc.
Box 1667, Evanston, Illinois 60204

4   5   6   7   8   9   10 - DWO - 97   96

Senior Consultants

The senior consultants guided conceptual development for the *Literature and Language* series. They participated actively in shaping prototype materials for major components, and they reviewed completed prototypes and/or completed units to ensure consistency with current research and the philosophy of the series.

Arthur N. Applebee
Professor of Education, State University of New York at Albany; Director, Center for the Learning and Teaching of Literature; Senior Fellow, Center for Writing and Literacy

Andrea B. Bermúdez
Professor of Multicultural Education; Director, Research Center for Language and Culture, University of Houston–Clear Lake

Susan Hynds
Associate Professor and Director of English Education, Syracuse University, Syracuse, New York

Judith A. Langer
Professor of Education, State University of New York at Albany; Co-director, Center for the Learning and Teaching of Literature; Senior Fellow, Center for Writing and Literacy

James Marshall
Associate Professor of English and Education, University of Iowa, Iowa City; Executive Secretary, High School Task Force, National Standards Project for English Language Arts K-12.

Donna E. Norton
Professor of Children's Literature, Texas A & M University, College Station

Senior Writer

The senior writer participated in the conceptual development of the series and wrote all the lessons for the literature selections in this text.

Lisa DeSloover Herzog
Educational Materials Specialist, Urbana, Illinois

Writers

Mary Seymour Milici (Workshops)
Educational Materials Consultant, Haydenville, Maryland; formerly Project Editor at National Evaluation Systems, Amherst, Massachusetts

Wordworks (Language Handbook)
Educational Publishing Services, Gloucester, Massachusetts

Multicultural Advisory Board

The multicultural advisors reviewed literature selections for appropriate content and made suggestions for teaching lessons in a multicultural classroom.

Andrea B. Bermúdez, Professor of Multicultural Education; Director, Research Center for Language and Culture, University of Houston–Clear Lake
Alice A. Kawazoe, Director of Curriculum and Staff Development, Oakland Unified School District, Oakland, California
Sandra Mehojah, Project Coordinator, Office of Indian Education, Omaha Public Schools, Omaha, Nebraska
Alexs D. Pate, Writer and columnist on multiculturalism, literature, and teaching; Adjunct faculty member, University of Minnesota and Macalester College

Manuscript Reviewers

The following educators reviewed prototype lessons and tables of contents during the development of the *Literature and Language* program.

Cheryl S. Archiable, Teacher, Shroder Paideia Middle School, Cincinnati Public Schools, Cincinnati, Ohio

William A. Battaglia, Teacher/Chairperson, Herman Intermediate School, Oak Grove School District, San Jose, California

Joanne Robertson Bizarro, Literature Teacher, St. Kevin's School, Catholic Diocese of Brooklyn, Flushing, New York

Martha W. Christian, Secondary English Department, Curriculum Specialist, Consultant, Southwestern Middle School, Southwestern Central School District, Jamestown, New York

Margaret J. Cummings, Language Arts Department Chairperson, William Chrisman High School, Independence Schools, Independence, Missouri

Kathleen Forslund, Principal, Aquinas Middle School, La Crosse, Wisconsin

Lorraine Gerhart, Reading Teacher, Chairperson and Team Leader, Elmbrook Middle School, Elmbrook Schools, Elm Grove, Wisconsin

Deborah Lynn Moeller, Teacher and Language Arts Department Chairperson, Attucks Middle School, Broward County Schools, Hollywood, Florida

Josephine Scott, Supervisor of Multicultural Education, Northgate Center, Columbus Public Schools, Columbus, Ohio

Elaine G. Sherman, Administrative Specialist, Secondary English and Reading, Division of Curriculum and Instruction, Clark County School District, Las Vegas, Nevada

Martha T. Stewart, Teacher and Chairperson of Language Arts, Turrentine Middle School, Burlington City Schools, Burlington, North Carolina

Sandra Childress Stringer, Principal, Lincoln Elementary School, Evanston District 65, Evanston, Illinois

Joel A. Turetzky, Ed.D., Teacher and Chairperson, Department of English, Raleigh Egypt Junior High School, Memphis City Schools, Memphis, Tennessee

Richard Wagner, Language Arts Curriculum Coordinator, Paradise Valley School District, Phoenix, Arizona

Virginia L. Woodley, English Department Chairperson, Brixner Junior High School, Klamath County School District, Klamath Falls, Oregon

Student Board

The student board members read and evaluated selections to assess their appeal for sixth-grade students.

Max Alper, Chute Middle School, Evanston, Illinois   **Danielle Anthony,** Chute Middle School, Evanston, Illinois   **Christopher Brown,** Chute Middle School, Evanston, Illinois   **Taryn S. Friedin,** Vanderhoof Elementary School, Arvada, Colorado   **Aryn A. Lane,** Swope Middle School, Reno, Nevada   **Guillermo Lona,** King Middle School, Kansas City, Missouri   **Christopher Lynch,** I.S. 285, Brooklyn, New York   **John Monroe Myers,** Old Trail School, Bath, Ohio   **Melissa O'Donnell,** Nathan Hale Elementary School, Carteret, New Jersey   **Erik Phillips,** Greenspun Junior High School, Henderson, Nevada   **Stephanie Rocker,** Indianola Elementary School, Selma, California   **Alejandra Rodriguez,** Lincoln Junior High School, McAllen, Texas   **Janell Thompson,** Powell Junior High School, Jackson, Mississippi   **Jennifer A. Wideman,** Chute Middle School, Evanston, Illinois

Contents

Unit One

WITH OPEN EYES

Unit Two

RISING TO THE CHALLENGE

Unit Three

FACE TO FACE

Unit Four

IN AND OUT OF CONTROL

Unit Five

WHAT MATTERS MOST 432

Unit Six

THEMES IN WORLD FOLKLORE — 534

Handbook Section

READER'S HANDBOOK

WRITER'S HANDBOOK

LANGUAGE HANDBOOK

Contents Overview

INTRODUCING
*L*ITERATURE
AND LANGUAGE

Literature and Language is different from other books you have used in two important ways. First, it is organized to help you tie together your study of the language arts—literature, writing, and language. The literature, chosen for its appeal to your life, serves as the starting point for all your learning. Students like you helped to select the stories, plays, articles, and poems that appear in this book (see their names on page vi). You'll find stories that have been favorites for many generations, as well as works by current writers.

Second, as you use this book, you will find that it does not present a "right" way to understand a story or to write a paper. Instead, it requires you to think for yourself. It asks you to form your own opinions and make your own decisions.

Unit Organization

All the parts of this book fit closely together. If you look at the Table of Contents, on pages vii–xviii, you will see that the book is divided into six units. Each unit is organized around a theme, such

2

as "Rising to the Challenge" or "Face to Face," that connects to your life and the world around you. To narrow the focus of these broad themes, each unit is further divided into two subunits. For example, "Rising to the Challenge" is divided into "Promises to Keep" and "Expect the Unexpected."

After the literature selections in each subunit, you will find a Writer's Workshop, a Language Workshop, and a third workshop that varies in content. These workshops are based upon the literature selections, so that all the parts of the subunit work together.

Organization of the Literature Lessons

Each literature lesson follows a carefully designed pattern, described below.

EXPLORE: *Before You Read* An **Explore** page, marked by a green band at the top, appears before each selection. Its three parts prepare you for reading.

• **Examine What You Know** provides an activity or discussion question based on your own experiences to help you get into the selection.

• **Expand Your Knowledge** gives you useful background information about the selection.

• **Enrich Your Reading** or **Write Before You Read** provides a specific reading or writing activity to help you better understand the literature you are about to read.

3

Reading the Selection Useful words that you should add to your vocabulary are underlined in the selection. These words are defined in a blue box at the bottom of the page where they first appear. Other difficult words and phrases are defined in footnotes, which appear beneath a black line at the bottom of the page.

EXPLAIN: After You Read
You'll find one or two **Explain** pages at the end of the selection, marked by a red band at the top. This section starts with discussion questions about the literature. The questions, which have no "right" or "wrong" answers, help you develop your own ideas and interpretations.

After the discussion questions, a literary concept is presented to help you become aware of literary techniques and their importance. In addition, writing activities give you another way of thinking about the literature. Finally, a vocabulary practice is provided if the selection includes vocabulary words.

EXTEND: Beyond the Reading This page, marked by a purple band at the top, gives you creative ways to display your understanding. These **Options for Learning** allow you to show what you have learned in many different ways such as group projects, dramatics, art, storytelling, and debates. An author biography also appears here.

Literature-based Workshops

Three workshops appear at the end of each subunit.

Writer's Workshop Each Writer's Workshop guides you through an entire writing assignment closely related to the literature and theme of the subunit. Clear instructions, helpful hints, optional suggestions, examples from literature, and models of student writing will help you write your own compositions.

Language Workshop Each Language Workshop focuses on skills that are related to your work in the Writer's Workshop as well as other writing that you do.

Related Skills Workshop The third workshop gives you additional tips in reading, vocabulary, or speaking and listening.

Reading on Your Own

Two pages at the end of each unit suggest novels that tie in with the unit theme. The plot summaries of these novels will help you choose books to read on your own.

Handbook Section

At the back of the book, you'll find three reference handbooks to round out your language-arts studies—a **Reader's Handbook,** a **Writer's Handbook,** and a **Language Handbook.**

Strategies for
READING

When you are so "into" a book that you forget about the world around you, you are an active reader. Active readers not only step into the actions, times, and places of stories and poems but also become more involved in the issues and events they read about in magazines, newspapers, and textbooks. To become a more active reader, try the strategies below. They describe the kinds of thinking good readers engage in as they read.

- **Questioning** Ask questions about what is happening in the selection. Also, make mental notes about words or statements that confuse you, but don't get sidetracked. Things may get clearer as you read further.

- **Connecting** Think of similarities between what is described in the selection you are reading and what you have experienced, heard about, or read about.

- **Predicting** Try to figure out what will happen next and how the selection might end.

- **Reviewing** Stop occasionally for a quick review of what you understand so far. Then draw conclusions about what is "between the lines," that is, what is suggested but not stated directly.

- **Evaluating** Form opinions about what you read, both during and after reading. Develop your own images of, and ideas about, characters and events.

The reading model on the next page shows how one reader used these strategies while reading the story "The Pudding Like a Night on the Sea." Of course, your thoughts would be different from these, since you think in your own way. You might have different questions, and you would make different connections based on your own experiences.

The Pudding Like a Night on the Sea

ANN CAMERON

▶ What a funny title. What does it mean?
(Questioning)

I'm going to make something special for your mother," my father said.

My mother was out shopping. My father was in the kitchen, looking at the pots and the pans and the jars of this and that.

"What are you going to make?" I said.

"A pudding," he said.

My father is a big man with wild black hair. When he laughs, the sun laughs in the windowpanes. When he thinks, you can almost see his thoughts sitting on all the tables and chairs. When he is angry, me and my little brother, Huey, shiver to the bottom of our shoes.

▶ I know someone just like that.
(Connecting)

"What kind of pudding will you make?" Huey said.

"A wonderful pudding," my father said. "It will taste like a whole raft of lemons. It will taste like a night on the sea."

Then he took down a knife and sliced five lemons in half. He squeezed the first one. Juice squirted in my eye.

"Stand back!" he said, and squeezed again. The seeds flew out on the floor. "Pick up those seeds, Huey!" he said.

Huey took the broom and swept them up.

My father cracked some eggs and put the yolks in a pan and the whites in a bowl. He rolled up his sleeves and pushed back his hair and beat up the yolks. "Sugar, Julian!" he said, and I poured in the sugar.

He went on beating. Then he put in lemon juice and cream and set the pan on the stove. The pudding bubbled, and he stirred it fast. Cream splashed on the stove.

"Wipe that up, Huey!" he said.

Huey did.

It was hot by the stove. My father loosened his collar

▶ The father is bossy.
(Reviewing)

and pushed at his sleeves. The stuff in the pan was getting thicker and thicker. He held the beater up high in the air. "Just right!" he said, and sniffed in the smell of the pudding.

He whipped the egg whites and mixed them into the pudding. The pudding looked softer and lighter than air.

"Done!" he said. He washed all the pots, splashing water on the floor, and wiped the counter so fast his hair made circles around his head.

"Perfect!" he said. "Now I'm going to take a nap. If something important happens, bother me. If nothing important happens, don't bother me. And—the pudding is for your mother. Leave the pudding alone!"

He went to the living room and was asleep in a minute, sitting straight up in his chair.

Huey and I guarded the pudding.

"Oh, it's a wonderful pudding," Huey said.

"With waves on the top like the ocean," I said.

"I wonder how it tastes," Huey said.

"Leave the pudding alone," I said.

"If I just put my finger in—there—I'll know how it tastes," Huey said.

And he did it.

"You did it!" I said. "How does it taste?"

"It tastes like a whole raft of lemons," he said. "It tastes like a night on the sea."

"You've made a hole in the pudding!" I said. "But since you did it, I'll have a taste." And it tasted like a whole night of lemons. It tasted like floating at sea.

"It's such a big pudding," Huey said. "It can't hurt to have a little more."

"Since you took more, I'll have more," I said.

"That was a bigger lick than I took!" Huey said. "I'm going to have more again."

"Whoops!" I said.

"You put in your whole hand!" Huey said. "Look at the pudding you spilled on the floor!"

"I am going to clean it up," I said. And I took the rag from the sink.

"That's not really clean," Huey said.

"It's the best I can do," I said.

▶ What does that mean?
(Questioning)

▶ Oh, oh. I have a feeling something bad will happen.
(Predicting)

▶ That's where the title comes from.
(Reviewing)

FAMILY by Varnette P. Honeywood © 1992.

"Look at the pudding!" Huey said.

It looked like craters on the moon. "We have to smooth this over," I said, "so it looks the way it did before! Let's get spoons."

And we evened the top of the pudding with spoons, and while we evened it, we ate some more.

"There isn't much left," I said.

"We were supposed to leave the pudding alone," Huey said.

"We'd better get away from here," I said. We ran into our bedroom and crawled under the bed. After a long time we heard my father's voice.

"Come into the kitchen, dear," he said. "I have something for you."

"Why, what is it?" my mother said, out in the kitchen.

▶ They're trying to cover up the damage. I've done that. *(Connecting)*

▶ They've eaten most of the pudding. They're in big trouble. *(Reviewing, Evaluating)*

▶ The father is going to be furious. *(Predicting)*

Under the bed, Huey and I pressed ourselves to the wall.

"Look," said my father, out in the kitchen. "A wonderful pudding."

"Where is the pudding?" my mother said.

"WHERE ARE YOU BOYS?" my father said. His voice went through every crack and corner of the house.

We felt like two leaves in a storm.

"WHERE ARE YOU? I SAID!" My father's voice was booming.

Huey whispered to me, "I'm scared."

We heard my father walking slowly through the rooms.

"Huey!" he called. "Julian!"

We could see his feet. He was coming into our room.

He lifted the bedspread. There was his face, and his eyes like black lightning. He grabbed us by the legs and pulled. "STAND UP!" he said.

We stood.

"What do you have to tell me?" he said.

"We went outside," Huey said, "and when we came back, the pudding was gone!"

"Then why were you hiding under the bed?" my father said.

We didn't say anything. We looked at the floor.

"I can tell you one thing," he said. "There is going to be some beating here now! There is going to be some whipping!"

The curtains at the window were shaking. Huey was holding my hand.

"Go into the kitchen!" my father said. "Right now!"

We went into the kitchen.

"Come here, Huey!" my father said.

Huey walked toward him, his hands behind his back.

"See these eggs?" my father said. He cracked them and put the yolks in a pan and set the pan on the counter. He stood a chair by the counter. "Stand up here," he said to Huey.

Huey stood on the chair by the counter.

"Now it's time for your beating!" my father said.

Huey started to cry. His tears fell in with the egg yolks.

► They are making things worse by lying.
(Evaluating)

► The father is mean.
(Reviewing)

"Take this!" my father said. My father handed him the eggbeater. "Now beat those eggs," he said. "I want this to be a good beating!"

"Oh!" Huey said. He stopped crying. And he beat the egg yolks.

"Now you, Julian, stand here!" my father said.

I stood on a chair by the table.

"I hope you're ready for your whipping!"

I didn't answer. I was afraid to say yes or no.

"Here!" he said, and he set the egg whites in front of me. "I want these whipped and whipped well!"

"Yes, sir!" I said, and started whipping.

My father watched us. My mother came into the kitchen and watched us.

After a while Huey said, "This is hard work."

"That's too bad," my father said. "Your beating's not done!" And he added sugar and cream and lemon juice to Huey's pan and put the pan on the stove. And Huey went on beating.

"My arm hurts from whipping," I said.

"That's too bad," my father said. "Your whipping's not done."

So I whipped and whipped, and Huey beat and beat.

"Hold that beater in the air, Huey!" my father said.

Huey held it in the air.

"See!" my father said. "A good pudding stays on the beater. It's thick enough now. Your beating's done." Then he turned to me. "Let's see those egg whites, Julian!" he said. They were puffed up and fluffy. "Congratulations, Julian!" he said. "Your whipping's done."

He mixed the egg whites into the pudding himself. Then he passed the pudding to my mother.

"A wonderful pudding," she said. "Would you like some, boys?"

"No thank you," we said.

She picked up a spoon. "Why, this tastes like a whole raft of lemons," she said. "This tastes like a night on the sea."

▶ Oh! The father is *not* whipping the boys!
(Reviewing)

LEMONS   by Varnette P. Honeywood   © 1992.

▶ It's pretty smart how the writer uses whipping and beating in two ways.
(Evaluating)

▶ The father taught his sons a good lesson. They won't forget it.
(Evaluating)

WITH OPEN EYES

To look at any thing,

If you would

know that thing,

You must

look at it long.

John Moffitt

SUMMER SONG   Rod Frederick
The Greenwich Workshop.

$\mathscr{S}$EEING THE LIGHT

Have you ever had the experience of suddenly seeing a familiar object in a new light? It was as if you had new eyes or were seeing the object for the very first time. The title of Unit One, "With Open Eyes," suggests the simple act of seeing. Sometimes we can look directly at something but fail to really "see," or understand it. Perhaps becoming too familiar with a thing or situation blinds us. Once in a while, though, something happens that causes us to "see the light"—to see clearly what is true.

As you read the following selections, you will discover how certain characters finally "see the light" and how their new understanding affects them.

Elements of *FICTION*

When you read a story, you are reading a work of fiction. **Fiction** is writing that comes from an author's imagination. Although the author makes the story up, he or she might base it on real events.

Fiction writers write either short stories or novels. A **short story** usually revolves around a single idea and is short enough to be read at one sitting. A **novel** is much longer and more complex. In this textbook, the fiction selections that you will read are short stories. However, at the end of each unit you will find recommendations for novels that you can read on your own.

*U*nderstanding Fiction

Character **Characters** are the people, animals, or imaginary creatures that take part in the action of the story. Usually, a short story centers on events in the life of one person or animal. That person or creature is the **main character.**

Generally, there are also one or more **minor characters** in the story. Minor characters sometimes provide part of the background for the story. More often, however, minor characters interact with the main character and with one another. Their words and actions help to move the plot along.

Setting The **setting** is the time and place in which the story happens. The time may be the past, present, or future; day or night; and any season. The place where the action of the story occurs may be imaginary or real.

Plot The sequence of events in a story is called the **plot.** The plot is the writer's blueprint for what happens, when it happens, and to whom it happens. One event causes another, which causes another, and so on until the end of the story.

Generally, plots are built around a **conflict**—a problem or struggle between two or more opposing forces. Conflicts can range from a life-or-death struggle to a disagreement between friends.

While the development of each plot is different, traditional works of fiction generally follow a pattern that includes the following stages:

- **Exposition** Exposition sets the stage for the story. Characters are introduced, the setting is described, and the conflict begins to unfold.
- **Complications** As the story continues, the plot gets more complex. While the characters struggle to find solutions to the conflict, suspense and a feeling of excitement and energy build.
- **Climax** The climax is the highest point of interest or suspense in the story. It is the turning point when the action reaches a peak and the outcome of the conflict is decided. The climax may occur because of a decision the characters reach or because of a discovery or an event that changes the situation. The climax usually results in a change in the characters or a solution to the problem.
- **Resolution** The resolution occurs at the conclusion of the story. Loose ends are tied up and the story ends.

Theme The **theme** of a story is the main message the writer wishes to share with the reader. This message might be a lesson about life or a belief about people and their actions. Most themes are not stated directly. They are like hidden messages that the reader must decode. You will find, however, as you discuss literature, that different readers discover different themes in the same selection. The following suggestions will help you unlock the theme.

• Review what happened to the main character. Did he or she change during the story? What did he or she learn about life?

• Skim the selection for key phrases and sentences—statements that move beyond the action of the story to say something important about life or people.

• Think about the title of the selection. Does it have a special meaning that could lead you to the main idea of the piece?

Strategies for Reading Fiction

To really "get inside" a story, try the following strategies.

1. **Preview** a story before you read it by looking at the title and the pictures, or even skimming through the pages, reading some words here and there.

2. Try to **visualize** the setting and the characters. Can you picture a similar place in your mind? Can you "see" the action and the characters?

3. As you read, **make connections.** Do any of the characters have the same thoughts or experiences that you have had? Does the story remind you of an event or person you've heard of or read about?

4. While you read, **question** events, characters, and ideas. "Why is the door unlocked?" "Why is she so rude?" Asking good questions is at the heart of good reading.

5. During your reading, stop occasionally and **predict** what might happen next and how the story will end.

6. As you read, **build** on what you're learning about the characters and events in the story. Let your thoughts change and grow as you learn more.

7. Continually **evaluate** the story as you read. Think about your feelings toward the characters and their actions. Also consider how well the author is telling his or her story.

When you have finished reading, discuss the story with someone else.

Remember, a story never tells you everything. It leaves room for you to build your own ideas. When you read, you are left with first impressions, but you need to be able to elaborate and explain them based on the story, your own experiences, and other stories you have read.

Fiction

Tuesday of the Other June

NORMA FOX MAZER

Examine What You Know

Have you ever had to deal with a bully? What did you do or say to defend yourself? Have you ever been a bully? What were the circumstances? What bullies have you read about in books or seen in the movies or on television? With your classmates complete a word web similar to the one below.

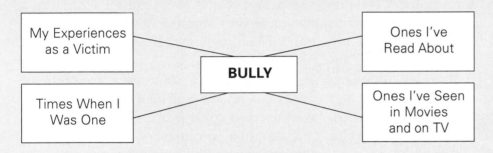

My Experiences as a Victim		Ones I've Read About
BULLY	
Times When I Was One		Ones I've Seen in Movies and on TV

Expand Your Knowledge

Realistic fiction, such as "Tuesday of the Other June," is fiction that shows you the ups and downs of everyday life. In this story you will read about a girl's problem in dealing with a bully—a problem that almost everyone faces at one time or another. Though fiction may not provide solutions to the problems in your life, it can give you a sense that you are not alone, that other people have had experiences similar to yours. Reading fiction can help you gain an understanding of your own feelings as well as those of other people.

Write Before You Read

Write about a time when you either faced the problem of how to deal with a bully or a time when you were a bully yourself, perhaps to a younger brother or sister. Be sure to include your feelings and thoughts as well as what you did or wished you had done.

■ *Author biography on Extend page*

Tuesday of the Other June

NORMA FOX MAZER

Be good, be good, be good, be good, my Junie," my mother sang as she combed my hair; a song, a story, a croon, a plea. "It's just you and me, two women alone in the world, June darling of my heart; we have enough troubles getting by, we surely don't need a single one more, so you keep your sweet self out of fighting and all that bad stuff. People can be little-hearted, but turn the other cheek, smile at the world, and the world'll surely smile back."

We stood in front of the mirror as she combed my hair, combed and brushed and smoothed. Her head came just above mine; she said when I grew another inch, she'd stand on a stool to brush my hair. "I'm not giving up this pleasure!" And she laughed her long honey laugh.

My mother was April, my grandmother had been May, I was June. "And someday," said my mother, "you'll have a daughter of your own. What will you name her?"

"January!" I'd yell when I was little. "February! No, November!" My mother laughed her honey laugh. She had little emerald eyes that warmed me like the sun.

Every day when I went to school, she went to work. "Sometimes I stop what I'm doing," she said, "lay down my tools, and stop everything, because all I can think about is you. Wondering what you're doing and if you need me. Now, Junie, if anyone ever bothers you—"

"—I walk away, run away, come on home as fast as my feet will take me," I recited.

"Yes. You come to me. You just bring me your trouble, because I'm here on this earth to love you and take care of you."

I was safe with her. Still, sometimes I woke up at night and heard footsteps slowly creeping up the stairs. It wasn't my mother, she was asleep in the bed across the room, so it was robbers, thieves, and murderers, creeping slowly . . . slowly . . . slowly toward my bed.

I stuffed my hand into my mouth. If I screamed and woke her, she'd be tired at work tomorrow. The robbers and thieves filled the warm darkness and slipped across the floor more quietly than cats. Rigid under the covers, I stared at the shifting dark and bit my knuckles and never knew when I fell asleep again.

Words to Know and Use

emerald (em′ ər əld) *adj.* bright green
rigid (rij′ id) *adj.* stiff; not moving

18

In the morning we sang in the kitchen. "Bill Grogan's GOAT! Was feelin' FINE! Ate three red shirts, right off the LINE!" I made sandwiches for our lunches, she made pancakes for breakfast, but all she ate was one pancake and a cup of coffee. "Gotta fly, can't be late."

I wanted to be rich and take care of her. She worked too hard; her pretty hair had gray in it that she joked about. "Someday," I said, "I'll buy you a real house, and you'll never work in a pot factory again."

"Such delicious plans," she said. She checked the windows to see if they were locked. "Do you have your key?"

I lifted it from the chain around my neck.

"And you'll come right home from school and—"

"—I won't light fires or let strangers into the house, and I won't tell anyone on the phone that I'm here alone," I finished for her.

"I know, I'm just your old worrywart mother." She kissed me twice, once on each cheek. "But you are my June, my only June, the only June."

She was wrong; there was another June. I met her when we stood next to each other at the edge of the pool the first day of swimming class in the Community Center.

"What's your name?" She had a deep growly voice.

"June. What's yours?"

She stared at me. "June."

"We have the same name."

"No we don't. June is *my* name, and I don't give you permission to use it. Your name is Fish Eyes." She pinched me hard. "Got it, Fish Eyes?"

THE CASE FOR MORE SCHOOL DAYS   C. F. Payne
First appeared in *The Atlantic Monthly*.

*J*une is my name, and I don't give you permission to use it.

The next Tuesday, the Other June again stood next to me at the edge of the pool. "What's your name?"

"June."

"Wrong. Your—name—is—Fish—Eyes."

"June."

"Fish Eyes, you are really stupid." She shoved me into the pool.

The swimming teacher looked up, frowning, from her chart. "No one in the water yet."

Later, in the locker room, I dressed quickly and wrapped my wet suit in the towel. The Other June pulled on her jeans. "You guys see that bathing suit Fish Eyes was wearing? Her mother found it in a trash can."

"She did not!"

The Other June grabbed my fingers and twisted. "Where'd she find your bathing suit?"

"She bought it, let me go."

"Poor little stupid Fish Eyes is crying. Oh, boo hoo hoo, poor little Fish Eyes."

After that, everyone called me Fish Eyes. And every Tuesday, wherever I was, there was also the Other June—at the edge of the pool, in the pool, in the locker room. In the water, she swam alongside me, blowing and huffing, knocking into me. In the locker room, she stepped on my feet, pinched my arms, hid my blouse, and knotted my braids together. She had large square teeth; she was shorter than I was, but heavier, with bigger bones and square hands. If I met her outside on the street, carrying her bathing suit and towel, she'd walk toward me, smiling a square, friendly smile. "Oh well, if it isn't Fish Eyes." Then she'd punch me, *blam!* her whole solid weight hitting me.

I didn't know what to do about her. She was training me like a dog. After a few weeks of this, she only had to look at me, only had to growl, "I'm going to get you, Fish Eyes," for my heart to <u>slink</u> like a whipped dog down into my stomach. My arms were covered with bruises. When my mother noticed, I made up a story about tripping on the sidewalk.

My weeks were no longer Tuesday, Wed-nesday, Thursday, and so on. Tuesday was Awfulday. Wednesday was Badday. (The Tuesday bad feelings were still there.) Thursday was Betterday, and Friday was Safeday. Saturday was Goodday, but Sunday was Toosoonday, and Monday—Monday was nothing but the day before Awfulday.

Tuesday was Awfulday. Wednesday was Badday.

I tried to slow down time. Especially on the weekends, I stayed close by my mother, doing everything with her, shopping, cooking, cleaning, going to the laundromat. "Aw, sweetie, go play with your friends."

"No, I'd rather be with you." I wouldn't look at the clock or listen to the radio (they were always telling you the date and the time). I did special magic things to keep the day from going away, rapping my knuckles six times on the bathroom door six times a day and never, ever touching the chipped place on my bureau. But always I woke up to the day before Tuesday, and always, no matter how many times I circled the worn spot in the living-room rug or counted twenty-five cracks in the ceiling, Monday disappeared and once again it was Tuesday.

The Other June got bored with calling me Fish Eyes. Buffalo Brain came next, but as soon as everyone knew that, she renamed me Turkey Nose.

Now at night it wasn't robbers creeping up the stairs, but the Other June, coming to torment me. When I finally fell asleep, I

Words to Know and Use | **slink** (slĭnk) *v.* to creep along quietly dreamed of kicking her, punching, biting, pinching. In the morning I remembered my dreams and felt brave and strong. And then I remembered all the things my mother had taught me and told me.

Be good, be good, be good; it's just us two women alone in the world. . . Oh, but if it weren't, if my father wasn't long gone, if we'd had someone else to fall back on, if my mother's mother and daddy weren't dead all these years, if my father's daddy wanted to know us instead of being glad to forget us— oh, then I would have punched the Other June with a frisky heart, I would have grabbed her arm at poolside and bitten her like the dog she had made of me.

One night, when my mother came home from work, she said, "Junie, listen to this. We're moving!"

Alaska, I thought. Florida. Arizona. Someplace far away and wonderful, someplace without the Other June.

"Wait till you hear this deal. We are going to be caretakers, trouble-shooters for an eight-family apartment building. Fifty-six Blue Hill Street. Not janitors; we don't do any of the heavy work. April and June, Trouble-shooters, Incorporated. If a tenant has a complaint or a problem, she comes to us and we either take care of it or call the janitor for service. And for that little bit of work, we get to live rent free!" She swept me around in a dance. "Okay? You like it? I do!"

So. Not anywhere else, really. All the same, maybe too far to go to swimming class? "Can we move right away? Today?"

"Gimme a break, sweetie. We've got to pack, do a thousand things. I've got to line up someone with a truck to help us. Six weeks, Saturday the fifteenth." She circled it on the calendar. It was the Saturday after the last day of swimming class.

Soon, we had boxes lying everywhere, filled with clothes and towels and glasses wrapped in newspaper. Bit by bit, we cleared the rooms, leaving only what we needed right now. The dining-room table staggered on a bunched-up rug, our bureaus inched toward the front door like patient cows. On the calendar in the kitchen, my mother marked off the days until we moved, but the only days I thought about were Tuesdays— Awfuldays. Nothing else was real except the too fast passing of time, moving toward each Tuesday . . . away from Tuesday . . . toward Tuesday. . . .

And it seemed to me that this would go on forever, that Tuesdays would come forever and I would be forever trapped by the side of the pool, the Other June whispering *Buffalo Brain Fish Eyes Turkey Nose* into my ear, while she ground her elbow into my side and smiled her square smile at the swimming teacher.

And then it ended. It was the last day of swimming class. The last Tuesday. We had all passed our tests, and, as if in celebration, the Other June only pinched me twice. "And now," our swimming teacher said, "all of you are ready for the Advanced Class, which starts in just one month. I have a sign-up slip here. Please put your name down before you leave." Everyone but me crowded around. I went to the locker room

Words to Know and Use | **stagger** (stag' er) *v.* to stand or move unsteadily

21

Illustration by Will Williams.

and pulled on my clothes as fast as possible. The Other June burst through the door just as I was leaving. "Goodbye," I yelled, "good riddance to bad trash!" Before she could pinch me again, I ran past her and then ran all the way home, singing, "Goodbye. . . goodbye . . . goodbye, good riddance to bad trash!"

Later, my mother carefully untied the blue ribbon around my swimming class diploma. "Look at this! Well, isn't this wonderful! You are on your way, you might turn into an Olympic swimmer, you never know what life will bring."

"I don't want to take more lessons."

"Oh, sweetie, it's great to be a good swimmer." But then, looking into my face, she said, "No, no, no, don't worry, you don't have to."

The next morning, I woke up hungry for the first time in weeks. No more swimming class. No more Baddays and Awfuldays. No more Tuesdays of the Other June. In the kitchen, I made hot cocoa to go with my mother's corn muffins. "It's Wednesday, Mom," I said, stirring the cocoa. "My favorite day."

"Since when?"

"Since this morning." I turned on the radio so I could hear the announcer tell the time, the temperature, and the day.

Thursday for breakfast I made cinnamon toast, Friday my mother made pancakes, and on Saturday, before we moved, we ate the last slices of bread and cleaned out the peanut butter jar.

"Some breakfast," Tilly said. "Hello, you must be June." She shook my hand. She was a friend of my mother's from work; she wore big hoop earrings, sandals, and a skirt as dazzling as a rainbow. She came in a truck with John to help us move our things.

John shouted cheerfully at me, "So you're moving." An enormous man with a face covered with little brown bumps. Was he afraid his voice wouldn't travel the distance from his mouth to my ear? "You looking at my moles?" he shouted, and he heaved our big green flowered chair down the stairs. "Don't worry, they don't bite. Ha, ha, ha!" Behind him came my mother and Tilly balancing a bureau between them, and behind them I carried a lamp and the round, flowered Mexican tray that was my mother's favorite. She had found it at a garage sale and said it was as close to foreign travel as we would ever get.

The night before, we had loaded our car, stuffing in bags and boxes until there was barely room for the two of us. But it was only when we were in the car, when we drove past Abdo's Grocery, where they always gave us credit, when I turned for a last look at our street—it was only then that I understood we were truly going to live somewhere else, in another apartment, in another place mysteriously called Blue Hill Street.

Tilly's truck followed our car.

"Oh, I'm so excited," my mother said. She laughed. "You'd think we were going across the country."

Our old car wheezed up a long, steep hill. Blue Hill Street. I looked from one side to the other, trying to see everything.

My mother drove over the crest of the hill. "And now—ta da!—our new home."

"Which house? Which one?" I looked out the window and what I saw was the Other June. She was sprawled on the stoop of a pink house, lounging back on her elbows, legs outspread, her jaws working on a wad of gum. I slid down into the seat, but it was too late. I was sure she had seen me.

My mother turned into a driveway next to a big white building with a tiny porch. She leaned on the steering wheel. "See that window there, that's our living-room window . . . and that one over there, that's your bedroom. . . . "

We went into the house, down a dim, cool hall. In our new apartment, the wooden floors clicked under our shoes, and my mother showed me everything. Her voice echoed in the empty rooms. I followed her around in a daze. Had I imagined seeing the Other June? Maybe I'd seen another girl who looked like her. A double. That could happen.

"Ho yo, where do you want this chair?" John appeared in the doorway. We brought in boxes and bags and beds and stopped only to eat pizza and drink orange juice from the carton.

"June's so quiet, do you think she'll adjust all right?" I heard Tilly say to my mother.

"Oh, definitely. She'll make a wonderful adjustment. She's just getting used to things."

Words to Know and Use

wheeze (hwēz) *v.* to make a whistling, breathy sound
crest (krest) *n.* the highest point; top

But I thought that if the Other June lived on the same street as I did, I would never get used to things.

That night I slept in my own bed, with my own pillow and blanket, but with floors that creaked in strange voices and walls with cracks I didn't recognize. I didn't feel either happy or unhappy. It was as if I were waiting for something.

Monday, when the principal of Blue Hill Street School left me in Mr. Morrisey's classroom, I knew what I'd been waiting for. In that room full of strange kids, there was one person I knew. She smiled her square smile, raised her hand, and said, "She can sit next to me, Mr. Morrisey."

"Very nice of you, June M. OK, June T., take your seat. I'll try not to get you two Junes mixed up."

"Good riddance to bad trash," she mocked.

I sat down next to her. She pinched my arm. "Good riddance to bad trash," she mocked.

I was back in the Tuesday swimming class, only now it was worse, because every day would be Awfulday. The pinching had already started. Soon, I knew, on the playground and in the halls, kids would pass me, grinning. "Hiya, Fish Eyes."

The Other June followed me around during recess that day, droning in my ear, "You are my slave, you must do everything I say,

I am your master, say it, say, 'Yes, master, you are my master.'"

I pressed my lips together, clapped my hands over my ears, but without hope. Wasn't it only a matter of time before I said the hateful words?

"How was school?" my mother said that night.

"OK."

She put a pile of towels in a bureau drawer. "Try not to be sad about missing your old friends, sweetie; there'll be new ones."

The next morning, the Other June was waiting for me when I left the house. "Did your mother get you that blouse in the garbage dump?" She butted me, shoving me against a tree. "Don't you speak anymore, Fish Eyes?" Grabbing my chin in her hands, she pried open my mouth. "Oh, ha ha, I thought you lost your tongue."

We went on to school. I sank down into my seat, my head on my arms. "June T., are you all right?" Mr. Morrisey asked. I nodded. My head was almost too heavy to lift.

The Other June went to the pencil sharpener. Round and round she whirled the handle. Walking back, looking at me, she held the three sharp pencils like three little knives.

Someone knocked on the door. Mr. Morrisey went out into the hall. Paper planes burst into the air, flying from desk to desk. Someone turned on a transistor radio. And the Other June, coming closer, smiled and licked her lips like a cat sleepily preparing to gulp down a mouse.

I remembered my dream of kicking her, punching, biting her like a dog.

Words to Know and Use

mock (mäk) *v.* to make fun of; jeer
drone (drōn) *v.* to talk on and on in a low, dull way

Then my mother spoke quickly in my ear: *Turn the other cheek, my Junie; smile at the world, and the world'll surely smile back.*

But I had turned the other cheek and it was slapped. I had smiled and the world hadn't smiled back. I couldn't run home as fast as my feet would take me. I had to stay in school—and in school there was the Other June. Every morning, there would be the Other June, and every afternoon, and every day, all day, there would be the Other June.

She frisked down the aisle, stabbing the pencils in the air toward me. A boy stood up on his desk and bowed. "My fans," he said, "I greet you." My arm twitched and throbbed, as if the Other June's pencils had already poked through the skin. She came closer, smiling her Tuesday smile.

"No," I whispered, "*no*." The word took wings and flew me to my feet, in front of the Other June. "*Noooooo*." It flew out of my mouth into her surprised face.

The boy on the desk turned toward us. "You said something, my devoted fans?"

"No," I said to the Other June. "Oh, no! No. No. No. No more." I pushed away the hand that held the pencils.

The Other June's eyes opened, popped wide like the eyes of somebody in a cartoon.

It made me laugh. The boy on the desk laughed, and then the other kids were laughing, too.

"No," I said again, because it felt so good to say it. "No, no, no, no." I leaned toward the Other June, put my finger against her chest. Her cheeks turned red, she squawked something—it sounded like "Eeeraaghyou!"—and she stepped back. She stepped away from me.

The door banged, the airplanes disappeared, and Mr. Morrisey walked to his desk. "OK. OK. Let's get back to work. Kevin Clark, how about it?" Kevin jumped off the desk, and Mr. Morrisey picked up a piece of chalk. "All right, class—" He stopped and looked at me and the Other June. "You two Junes, what's going on there?"

I tried it again. My finger against her chest. Then the words. "No—more." And she stepped back another step. I sat down at my desk.

"June M.," Mr. Morrisey said.

She turned around, staring at him with that big-eyed cartoon look. After a moment she sat down at her desk with a loud slapping sound.

Even Mr. Morrisey laughed.

And sitting at my desk, twirling my braids, I knew this was the last Tuesday of the Other June. ❧

Responding to Reading

First Impressions

1. How did you react to June T.'s actions at the end of the story? Jot down your ideas and share them with the class.

Second Thoughts

2. At the end of the story, June T. changes her behavior. In your opinion, what causes her to do this?

3. Why do you think June doesn't fight back physically when the other June acts like a bully?

   Think about
   - the concerns and advice June's mother shares
   - the daily attacks on June's self-confidence

4. Why do you think June T. doesn't tell anyone about her problem?

5. What kind of person do you think the other June is? Use examples from the story to explain your ideas.

Broader Connections

6. June's mother tells her daughter to "turn the other cheek." Discuss whether or not this is practical advice in today's world.

Literary Concepts: Plot and Conflict

To create a story that readers can understand and enjoy, a writer connects the events carefully. The **plot** consists of the actions or events that make up a story. The plot is the writer's plan for what happens, when it happens, and to whom it happens.

The plot usually centers around a problem or **conflict** and around the actions a character takes to solve the conflict. The conflict usually becomes clear early in the story. As the story develops, the reader starts to wonder what will happen and how the characters will handle the conflict. In "Tuesday of the Other June," June T. is the character with a conflict to solve. What is the conflict?

Writing Options

1. Imagine that June wants outside help for her problem. Write a **letter** June would write to "Dear Abby."

2. "We have the same name," June T. says when meeting the other June. Are there other similarities or differences? Make a compare-and-contrast diagram of the two characters. Draw two circles that overlap. Write details about June T. in the far left side of the left circle. Write details about June M. in the far right side of the right circle. Write the things the two Junes have in common in the space where the circles overlap. Use this diagram to write a **comparison** of the two Junes.

3. At the end of the story, June says, "It was the last Tuesday of the Other June." Do you think she has solved her problem? Write a **prediction** that describes how you think the two Junes will act toward each other a month after the story ends.

4. Write a **diary entry** about a time you or someone you know has had to deal with a bully. Be sure to express your feelings about what happened and what you learned.

Vocabulary Practice

Exercise A On your paper, write the word from the list that matches the meaning of the boldfaced word or phrase.

1. June lay **unmoving** in her bed, fearful of the robbers she imagined were present in the dark.

2. June's mother has eyes that are **bright green** in color.

3. June would try to **creep quietly** past the other June because she was afraid of getting hurt.

4. The old car was so full that it seemed to **gasp for breath** as it went up the hill.

5. To bother June, the other June would **talk on and on in a low, dull way.**

Words to Know and Use

crest
drone
emerald
mock
rigid
slink
stagger
wheeze

Exercise B On your paper, write the letter of the word that doesn't match the meaning of the other words in the set.

1. (a) valley (b) crest (c) peak (d) top

2. (a) stiff (b) rough (c) unmoving (d) rigid

3. (a) sway (b) wobble (c) fall (d) stagger

4. (a) praise (b) admire (c) mock (d) applaud

5. (a) wheeze (b) whistle (c) smell (d) breathe

Options for Learning

1 • Mirror Image Using information from the selection, draw portraits of the two Junes, or find magazine photographs of people who resemble the characters.

2 • A Problem-Solver's Guide With your classmates, brainstorm a list of choices June had in dealing with a bully. Discuss the pros and cons of each solution. Then create a class booklet of techniques that could be used to resolve conflicts. If possible, place the booklet in the school library.

3 • Blue Hill Street Blues With some classmates, create a skit of June's first two days at Blue Hill Street School. If possible, videotape your skit and invite the rest of the class to review it.

4 • Stay Tuned to June Suppose that this story was to become a TV series. With a small group of classmates, develop a plot summary for the next episode. Compare your plot summary with those created by other groups.

FACT FINDER VOCABULARY

For whom is the month of June named?

Norma Fox Mazer
1931-

Norma Fox Mazer believes stories are a way to understand the world and the people in it. She says that readers of fiction "will find a world where people face troubles but act to help themselves."

Mazer's interest in writing started in high school, where she was editor of her school paper and a correspondent for her town's newspaper. After a year at college, she married novelist Harry Mazer. For ten years, she and her husband struggled to write while raising their four children. Today she is a widely recognized and prize-winning writer of fiction for young adults.

Mazer lives in New York but spends the summers in Canada, where she does without electricity, telephones, newspapers, radios, or indoor plumbing. About her writing, Mazer says, "I seem to deal in the ordinary, the everyday, the real. I should like in my writing to give meaning and emotion to ordinary moments. In my books and stories I want people to eat chocolate pudding, break a dish, yawn, look in a store window, wear socks with holes in them." Readers can encounter many of Mazer's true-to-life characters in *Dear Bill, Remember Me? and Other Stories; Taking Terri Mueller;* and *After the Rain,* a Newbery Honor Book.

Fiction

Cricket in the Road

MICHAEL ANTHONY

Examine What You Know

The young Trinidadian boy in this story becomes upset with his friends at the start of a cricket game. Recall a disagreement you had with a friend. What caused it and what steps were taken to settle it? Describe your experience in your journal or on a sheet of paper. As you read, compare your experiences to those of the characters in the story.

Expand Your Knowledge

The **setting** of this story is the village of Mayaro on the island of Trinidad. Trinidad is one of two islands that form the country called Trinidad and Tobago. Trinidad lies in the Caribbean Sea, seven miles east of Venezuela. The climate is hot and humid, and the rainy season lasts from late May until November. Trinidad and Tobago was a colony of Great Britain until 1962 and still has many British customs. Cricket, a game similar to baseball, is popular in both countries.

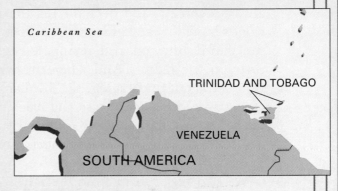

Enrich Your Reading

Dialect   Although English is Trinidad and Tobago's official language, many people speak Trinidad English, a form of English that has French and Spanish influences. When you read this story, you will notice that the author uses dialect in his writing. Dialect means the speech patterns of a certain group or region. By using dialect, the writer lets you "hear" how the disagreement between the cricket players would actually sound. Look at these examples.

Trinidad English	Standard U.S. English
Who second bat?	*Who bats second?*
What you want?	*What do you want?*
He throw them away.	*He threw them away.*

■ *Author biography on Extend page*

Cricket in the Road

MICHAEL ANTHONY

In the rainy season we got few chances to play cricket in the road. For whenever we were at the game, the rains came down, chasing us into the yard again. That was the way it was in Mayaro in the rainy season. The skies were always overcast, and over the sea the rain clouds hung low and gray and scowling, and the winds blew in and whipped angrily through the palms. And when the winds were strongest and raging, the low-hanging clouds would become dense and black, and the sea would roar, and the torrents of rain would come sweeping with all their tumult upon us.

We had just run in from the rain. Amy and Vern from next door were in good spirits and laughing, for oddly enough they seemed to enjoy the downpour as much as playing cricket in the road. Amy was in our yard, giggling and pretending to drink the falling rain, with her face all wet and her clothes drenched, and Vern, who was sheltering under the eaves,[1] excitedly jumped out to join her. "Rain, rain, go to Spain," they shouted. And presently their mother, who must have heard the noise and knew, appeared from next door, and Vern and Amy vanished through the hedge.

I stood there, depressed about the rain, and then I put Vern's bat and ball underneath the house and went indoors. "Stupes!" I said to myself. I had been batting when the rains came down. It was only when *I* was batting that the rains came down! I wiped my feet so I wouldn't soil the sheets and went up on the bed. I was sitting, sad, and wishing that the rain would really go away—go to Spain, as Vern said—when my heart seemed to jump out of me. A deafening peal of thunder struck across the sky.

Quickly I closed the window. The rain hammered awfully on the rooftop, and I kept tense for the thunder which I knew would break again and for the unearthly flashes of lightning.

Secretly I was afraid of the violent weather. I was afraid of the rain, and of the thunder and the lightning that came with them, and of the sea beating against the headlands,[2] and of the storm winds, and of everything being so deathlike when the

---

1. **eaves** (ēvz): roof edges that hang over the walls of a building.
2. **headlands:** land that juts out into the water.

Words to Know and Use

tumult (tōo′ mult) *n.* noisy uproar
peal (pēl) *n.* a long-lasting, loud sound

SCHOOLBOYS Frané Lessac.

rains were gone. I started[3] again at another flash of lightning, and before I had recovered from this, yet another terrifying peal of thunder hit the air. I screamed. I heard my mother running into the room. Thunder struck again, and I dashed under the bed.

question   Why does the narrator resent the rain?

"Selo! Selo! First bat!" Vern shouted from the road. The rains had ceased and the sun had come out, but I was not quite recovered yet. I brought myself reluctantly to look out from the front door, and there was Vern, grinning and impatient and beckoning to me.

"First bat," he said. And as if noting my indifference, he looked toward Amy, who was just coming out to play. "Who second bat?" he said.

"Me!" I said.

"Me!" shouted Amy almost at the same time.

"Amy second bat," Vern said.

"No, I said 'Me' first," I protested.

Vern grew impatient while Amy and I argued. Then an idea seemed to strike him. He took out a penny from his pocket. "Toss for it," he said. "What you want?"

"Heads," I called.

"Tail," cried Amy. "Tail bound to come!"[4]

The coin went up in the air, fell down and overturned, showing tail.

"I'm *not* playing!" I cried, stung. And as that did not seem to disturb enough, I ran toward where I had put Vern's bat and ball and disappeared with them behind our

house. Then I flung them with all my strength into the bushes.

When I came back to the front of the house, Vern was standing there dumbfounded. "Selo, where's the bat and ball?" he said.

I was fuming. "I don't know about *any* bat and ball!"

"Tell on him," Amy cried. "He throw them away."

Vern's mouth twisted into a forced smile. "What's an old bat and ball," he said.

But as he walked out of the yard, I saw tears glinting from the corners of his eyes.

Describe the friendship up to this point.   *review*

For the rest of that rainy season, we never played cricket in the road again. Sometimes the rains ceased and the sun came out brightly, and I heard the voices of Amy and Vern on the other side of the fence. At such times I would go out into the road and whistle to myself, hoping they would hear me and come out, but they never did, and I knew they were still very angry and would never forgive me.

And so the rainy season went on. And it was as fearful as ever, with the thunder and lightning and waves roaring in the bay, and the strong winds. But the people who talked

---

3. **started:** jumped suddenly after being surprised.
4. **Toss for it. . . . Tail bound to come:** refers to the practice in games of flipping a coin and having players call heads or tails to determine who starts or as in this story, who bats second.

Words to Know and Use | **indifference** (in dif′ ər əns) *n.* lack of interest
dumbfounded (dum′ found′ əd) *adj.* made speechless by shocking; astonish
fume (fyo͞om) *v.* to show anger

of all this said that was the way Mayaro was, and they laughed about it. And sometimes when through the rain and even thunder I heard Vern's voice on the other side of the fence shouting "Rain, rain, go to Spain," it puzzled me how it could be so. For often I had made up my mind I would be brave, but when the thunder cracked, I always dashed under the bed.

It was the beginning of the new year when I saw Vern and Amy again. The rainy season was, happily, long past, and the day was hot and bright, and as I walked toward home, I saw that I was walking toward Vern and Amy just about to start cricket in the road. My heart thumped violently. They looked strange and new, as if they had gone away, far, and did not want to come back anymore. They did not notice me until I came up quite near, and then I saw Amy start, her face all lit up.

"Vern—" she cried, "Vern look—look Selo!"

Embarrassed, I looked at the ground and at the trees, and at the orange sky, and I was so happy I did not know what to say. Vern stared at me, a strange grin on his face. He was ripping the cellophane paper off a brand new bat.

"Selo, here—*you* first bat," he said gleefully.

And I cried as though it were raining and I was afraid. ❧

I N S I G H T

The Quarrel
ELEANOR FARJEON

I quarreled with my brother,
I don't know what about,
One thing led to another
And somehow we fell out.
The start of it was slight,
The end of it was strong,
He said he was right,
I knew he was wrong!

We hated one another.
The afternoon turned black.
Then suddenly my brother
Thumped me on the back,
And said, "Oh, come along!
We can't go on all night—
I was in the wrong."
So he was in the right.

LES ENFANTS (THE CHILDREN)   1937
Balthus   Musée Louvre, Paris.

Responding to Reading

First Impressions

1. Why do you think Selo cries and is afraid at the end of the story? Write down your thoughts in your journal.

Second Thoughts

2. In what ways do you think Selo and Vern are alike and different?

   Think about
   - their actions during the downpour
   - the way they determine the batting order
   - their reactions to seeing each other after the rainy season

3. Why do you think Selo hides the ball and bat?

4. In a way, both Selo and Vern treat one another badly. Discuss how.

5. If Vern had not reached out to Selo, what do you suppose would have happened to their relationship?

6. Selo, Vern, and Amy have different reactions to the rainy season. How do you think these feelings affect their game of cricket?

Broader Connections

7. What do you think is the fairest and fastest way to settle a disagreement with friends? Support your opinion with ideas from "Cricket in the Road" and "The Quarrel" as well as the experience you wrote about before reading.

Literary Concept: Setting

The **setting,** or time and place in which a story occurs, plays an important role in this story. As you discussed in question six, the narrator often refers to the setting, describing various sights and sounds in detail. Skim the story and make a list of details about the setting. In what ways does the setting influence how the characters feel and act?

Writing Options

1. Write a **dialogue,** or conversation, in which Selo, Vern, and Amy talk about their disagreement, the reasons for it, and the ways to avoid future problems.

2. Would you want Selo, Vern, Amy, or either of the Junes in "Tuesday of the Other June" as friends? Make a list of the qualities you feel are needed in a good friend. Choose one of the characters and write your **opinion** on why you would not want this person for a friend. Use your list to help you decide.

3. An **epilogue** is an addition to the ending of a story. Write an epilogue in which Vern and Selo have another disagreement.

4. Selo's need for Vern and Amy's forgiveness builds throughout the story. Write a **journal entry** about a time when you forgave or were forgiven by someone important to you.

Vocabulary Practice

Exercise On your paper, write the letter of the sentence that best describes the meaning of the boldfaced word.

1. **tumult**
   a. The acrobats performed amazing leaps.
   b. Selo was overjoyed when the rain stopped.
   c. Due to the noisy uproar of the storm, no one was able to hear.

2. **peal**
   a. The banana skin is on top of the compost heap.
   b. The sound of the pipes could be heard even after the organist stopped playing.
   c. The boy asked his mother for suggestions.

3. **indifference**
   a. The boy's lack of interest in school worried his father.
   b. The two boys looked very much alike.
   c. The suddenness of the rain annoyed Selo.

4. **dumbfounded**
   a. Her information is not based on facts.
   b. Selo's behavior left Vern speechless.
   c. Anita's stories amused her listeners.

5. **fume**
   a. The tourist enjoyed the island's beauty.
   b. The waves crashed against the shore.
   c. The boat's delay will cause the passengers to complain angrily.

Options for Learning

1 • Travel to Trinidad By yourself or in a small group, design and write a travel brochure advertising the island. Use details from the story and do additional research to provide information about tourist attractions and the island's history. Include pictures of Trinidad, or your own drawings, and use persuasive writing to make your readers want to visit Trinidad.

2 • Cricket Anyone? Research the game of cricket and write the directions for playing it. Be sure to describe the object of the game, the playing positions, and the equipment, as well as the rules and etiquette, or manners, required to play it. Present the information on a poster or in an oral report to the class.

3 • Stormy Weather Suppose Selo asks his mother or father how he should deal with his fears about violent weather. With a partner, improvise a conversation between the characters.

4 • "Cricket" Lyrics Imagine that "Cricket in the Road" has been made into a television special. Create a theme song to introduce viewers to the characters, the setting, or the conflict. You may want to combine the lyrics with the music of a familiar song.

FACT FINDER MUSIC

What famous type of folk music originated in Trinidad?

Michael Anthony
1932-

Michael Anthony writes tales about life on the island of Trinidad. His stories offer readers a taste of Caribbean life and the chance to consider the more important things in life.

Born in Mayaro, Trinidad and Tobago, Anthony started work at the age of fifteen in an iron foundry. Eight years later, he went to England, where he held a variety of factory jobs and eventually became a journalist. From England he went to Brazil. After a two-year stay in Brazil, he and his wife and four children returned to Trinidad to live.

The book of short stories that includes the selection you have just read is also called *Cricket in the Road*. Michael Anthony has also published several novels and poems. The author says, "I feel very strongly about the brotherhood of mankind. . . . One of my main hopes is that human beings will find a way to live together without friction." He says he is an optimist who would like to see all the nations of the world join together to become one strong nation.

Fiction

The White Umbrella

GISH JEN

Examine What You Know

In small groups, discuss the meaning of the expression "keeping up appearances." Jot down examples of when, why, and how people might try to keep up appearances. Share your observations with the class.

Expand Your Knowledge

The twelve-year-old narrator of "The White Umbrella" is embarrassed that her mother has to work. At the time the story takes place, few mothers were working outside the home. Look over the chart to discover how the presence of mothers in the United States labor force has changed since 1965.

	Mothers Participating in Labor Force (figures in percentages)		
Year	with children under age 18	with children ages 6 to 17	with children under age 6[1]
1965	35.0%	45.7%	25.3%
1975	47.4	54.8	38.9
1985	62.1	69.9	53.5
1990	66.7	74.7	58.2

1. May also have older children.

(Source: Department of Labor, Bureau of Labor Statistics)

Enrich Your Reading

Making Inferences When you develop your own ideas about what you are reading, you are making an **inference.** One way you infer is by combining the information the writer provides with what you know from your own experience. In this story, for example, Miss Crosman, the piano teacher, offers the girls food, a ride home, and dry towels. From this information you can infer that Miss Crosman is a concerned and warm-hearted person. As you read, look for words or actions that will help you make inferences about the personality of the narrator—a character concerned with keeping up appearances.

■ *Author biography on Extend page*

The *White Umbrella*

GISH JEN

When I was twelve, my mother went to work without telling me or my little sister.

"Not that we need the second income." The lilt of her accent drifted from the kitchen up to the top of the stairs, where Mona and I were listening.

"No," said my father, in a barely <u>audible</u> voice. "Not like the Lee family."

The Lees were the only other Chinese family in town. I remembered how sorry my parents had felt for Mrs. Lee when she started waitressing downtown the year before; and so when my mother began coming home late, I didn't say anything and tried to keep Mona from saying anything either.

"But why shouldn't I?" she argued. "Lots of people's mothers work."

"Those are American people," I said.

"So what do you think we are? I can do the pledge of allegiance with my eyes closed."

Nevertheless, she tried to be <u>discreet</u>; and if my mother wasn't home by 5:30, we would start cooking by ourselves, to make sure dinner would be on time. Mona would wash the vegetables and put on the rice; I would chop.

For weeks we wondered what kind of work she was doing. I imagined that she was selling perfume, testing dessert recipes for the local newspaper. Or maybe she was working for the florist. Now that she had learned to drive, she might be delivering boxes of roses to people.

"I don't think so," said Mona as we walked to our piano lesson after school. "She would've hit something by now."

A gust of wind littered the street with leaves.

"Maybe we better hurry up," she went on, looking at the sky. "It's going to pour."

"But we're too early." Her lesson didn't begin until 4:00, mine until 4:30, so we usually tried to walk as slowly as we could. "And anyway, those aren't the kind of clouds that rain. Those are cumulus clouds."[1]

We arrived out of breath and wet.

"Oh, you poor, poor dears," said old Miss Crosman. "Why don't you call me the next time it's like this out? If your mother won't drive you, I can come pick you up."

"No, that's OK," I answered. Mona wrung her hair out on Miss Crosman's rug.

---

1. **cumulus clouds** (kyo͞o′ myo͞o ləs): bright clouds with flat bottoms and fluffy, rounded tops.

| *Words to Know and Use* | **audible** (ô′ də bəl) *adj.* able to be heard
discreet (di skrēt′) *adj.* careful about what one says or does |

"We just couldn't get the roof of our car to close, is all. We took it to the beach last summer and got sand in the mechanism." I pronounced this last word carefully, as if the credibility[2] of my lie depended on its middle syllable. "It's never been the same." I thought for a second. "It's a convertible."

"Well, then, make yourselves at home." She exchanged looks with Eugenie Roberts, whose lesson we were interrupting. Eugenie smiled good-naturedly. "The towels are in the closet across from the bathroom."

Huddling at the end of Miss Crosman's nine-foot leatherette couch, Mona and I watched Eugenie play. She was a grade ahead of me and, according to school rumor, had a boyfriend in high school. I believed it. She had auburn hair, blue eyes, and, I noted with a particular pang, a pure white folding umbrella.

"I can't see," whispered Mona.

"So clean your glasses."

"My glasses *are* clean. You're in the way."

I looked at her. "They look dirty to me."

"That's because *your* glasses are dirty."

Eugenie came bouncing to the end of her piece.

"Oh! Just stupendous!" Miss Crosman hugged her, then looked up as Eugenie's mother walked in. "Stupendous!" she said again. "Oh! Mrs. Roberts! Your daughter has a gift, a real gift. It's an honor to teach her."

Mrs. Roberts, radiant with pride, swept her daughter out of the room as if she were royalty, born to the piano bench. Watching the way Eugenie carried herself, I sat up and concentrated so hard on sucking in my stomach that I did not realize until the Robertses were gone that Eugenie had left her umbrella. As Mona began to play, I jumped up and ran to the window, meaning to call to them—only to see their brake lights flash, then fade, at the stop sign at the corner. As if to allow them passage, the rain had let up; a quivering sun lit their way.

The umbrella glowed like a scepter[3] on the blue carpet while Mona, slumping over the keyboard, managed to eke out[4] a fair rendition of a cat fight. At the end of the piece, Miss Crosman asked her to stand up.

"Stay right there," she said, then came back a minute later with a towel to cover the bench. "You must be cold," she continued. "Shall I call your mother and have her bring over some dry clothes?"

"No," answered Mona. "She won't come because she . . ."

"She's too busy," I broke in from the back of the room.

"I see." Miss Crosman sighed and shook her head a little. "Your glasses are filthy, honey," she said to Mona. "Shall I clean them for you?"

Sisterly embarrassment seized me. Why hadn't Mona wiped her lenses when I told her to? As she resumed abuse of the piano, I stared at the umbrella. I wanted to open it, twirl it around by its slender silver handle; I

---

2. **credibility:** believability.

3. **scepter** (sep′ tər): the rod or baton a ruler holds as a sign of authority.

4. **eke out:** to struggle through.

39

wanted to dangle it from my wrist on the way to school the way the other girls did. I wondered what Miss Crosman would say if I offered to bring it to Eugenie at school tomorrow. She would be impressed with my consideration for others; Eugenie would be pleased to have it back; and I would have possession of the umbrella for an entire night. I looked at it again, toying with the idea of asking for one for Christmas. I knew, however, how my mother would react.

"Things," she would say. "What's the matter with a raincoat? All you want is things, just like an American."

Sitting down for my lesson, I was careful to keep the towel under me and sit up straight.

All you want is things, just like an American.

"I'll bet you can't see a thing either," said Miss Crosman, reaching for my glasses. "And you can relax, you poor dear. This isn't a boot camp."[5]

When Miss Crosman finally allowed me to start playing, I played extra well, as well as I possibly could. See, I told her with my fingers. You don't have to feel sorry for me.

"That was wonderful," said Miss Crosman. "Oh! Just wonderful."

An entire constellation rose in my heart.

"And guess what," I announced proudly. "I have a surprise for you."

Then I played a second piece for her, a much more difficult one that she had not assigned.

"Oh! That was stupendous," she said without hugging me. "Stupendous! You are

GIRL AT PIANO   1966   Will Barnet
© Will Barnet/VAGA, New York.

a genius, young lady. If your mother had started you younger, you'd be playing like Eugenie Roberts by now!"

I looked at the keyboard, wishing that I had still a third, even more difficult piece to

---

5. **boot camp:** a military base where new members of the armed forces receive basic training.

play for her. I wanted to tell her that I was the school spelling bee champion, that I wasn't ticklish, that I could do karate.

"My mother is a concert pianist," I said.

She looked at me for a long moment, then finally, without saying anything, hugged me. I didn't say anything about bringing the umbrella to Eugenie at school.

The steps were dry when Mona and I sat down to wait for my mother.

"Do you want to wait inside?" Miss Crosman looked anxiously at the sky.

"No," I said. "Our mother will be here any minute."

"In a while," said Mona.

"Any minute," I said again, even though my mother had been at least twenty minutes late every week since she started working.

According to the church clock across the street, we had been waiting twenty-five minutes when Miss Crosman came out again.

"Shall I give you ladies a ride home?"

"No," I said. "Our mother is coming any minute."

"Shall I at least give her a call and remind her you're here? Maybe she forgot about you."

"I don't think she *forgot*," said Mona.

"Shall I give her a call anyway? Just to be safe?"

"I bet she already left," I said. "How could she forget about us?"

Miss Crosman went in to call.

"There's no answer," she said, coming back out.

"See, she's on her way," I said.

"Are you sure you wouldn't like to come in?"

"No," said Mona.

"Yes," I said. I pointed at my sister. "She meant yes too. She meant no, she wouldn't like to go in."

Miss Crosman looked at her watch. "It's 5:30 now, ladies. My pot roast will be coming out in fifteen minutes. Maybe you'd like to come in and have some then?"

"My mother's almost here," I said. "She's on her way."

We watched and watched the street. I tried to imagine what my mother was doing; I tried to imagine her writing messages in the sky, even though I knew she was afraid of planes. I watched as the branches of Miss Crosman's big willow tree started to sway; they had all been trimmed to exactly the same height off the ground, so that they looked beautiful, like hair in the wind.

It started to rain.

"Miss Crosman is coming out again," said Mona.

"Don't let her talk you into going inside," I whispered.

"Why not?"

"Because that would mean Mom isn't really coming any minute."

"But she isn't," said Mona. "She's *working*."

"Shhh! Miss Crosman is going to hear you."

"She's working! She's working! She's working!"

I put my hand over her mouth, but she licked it, and so I was wiping my hand on my wet dress when the front door opened.

"We're getting even *wetter*," said Mona right away. "Wetter and wetter."

"Shall we all go in?" Miss Crosman pulled Mona to her feet. "Before you young ladies catch pneumonia? You've been out here an hour already."

"We're *freezing*." Mona looked up at Miss

RAIN, LOS ANGELES   1983   William Clutz
Collection of Janice C. Oresman.

the door. "Shall we get you inside first?"

"See you in the hospital," said Mona as she went in. "See you in the hospital with *pneumonia*."

I stared out into the empty street. The rain was pricking me all over; I was cold; I wanted to go inside. I wanted to be able to let myself go inside. If Miss Crosman came out again, I decided, I would go in.

She came out with a blanket and the white umbrella.

I could not believe that I was actually holding the umbrella, opening it.

I could not believe that I was actually holding the umbrella, opening it. It sprang up by itself as if it were alive, as if that were what it wanted to do—as if it belonged in my hands, above my head. I stared up at the network of silver spokes, then spun the umbrella around and around and around. It was so clean and white that it seemed to glow, to <u>illuminate</u> everything around it. "It's beautiful," I said.

Miss Crosman sat down next to me, on one end of the blanket. I moved the umbrella over so that it covered that too. I could feel the rain on my left shoulder and shivered. She put her arm around me.

"You poor, poor dear."

Crosman. "Do you have any hot chocolate? We're going to catch *pneumonia*."

"I'm not going in," I said. "My mother's coming any minute."

"Come on," said Mona. "Use your *noggin*."[6]

"Any minute."

"Come on, Mona," Miss Crosman opened

---

6. **noggin:** head.

Words
to Know
and Use

illuminate (i lōō′ mə nāt′) *v.* to light up

42

I knew that I was in store for another bolt of sympathy and braced myself by staring up into the umbrella.

"You know, I very much wanted to have children when I was younger," she continued.

"You did?"

She stared at me a minute. Her face looked dry and crusty, like day-old frosting.

"I did. But then I never got married."

I twirled the umbrella around again.

"This is the most beautiful umbrella I have ever seen," I said. "Ever, in my whole life."

"Do you have an umbrella?"

"No. But my mother's going to get me one just like this for Christmas."

"Is she? I tell you what. You don't have to wait until Christmas. You can have this one."

"But this one belongs to Eugenie Roberts," I protested. "I have to give it back to her tomorrow in school."

"Who told you it belongs to Eugenie? It's not Eugenie's. It's mine. And now I'm giving it to you, so it's yours."

"It is?"

She hugged me tighter. "That's right. It's all yours."

"It's mine?" I didn't know what to say. "Mine?" Suddenly I was jumping up and down in the rain. "It's beautiful! Oh! It's beautiful!" I laughed.

Miss Crosman laughed too, even though she was getting all wet.

"Thank you, Miss Crosman. Thank you very much. Thanks a zillion. It's beautiful. It's *stupendous!*"

"You're quite welcome," she said.

"Thank you," I said again, but that didn't seem like enough. Suddenly I knew just what she wanted to hear. "I wish you were my mother."

Right away I felt bad.

"You shouldn't say that," she said, but her face was opening into a huge smile as the lights of my mother's car cautiously turned the corner. I quickly collapsed the umbrella and put it up my skirt, holding onto it from the outside, through the material.

"Mona!" I shouted into the house. "Mona! Hurry up! Mom's here! I told you she was coming!"

Then I ran away from Miss Crosman, down to the curb. Mona came tearing up to my side as my mother neared the house. We both backed up a few feet, so that in case she went onto the curb, she wouldn't run us over.

"But why didn't you go inside with Mona?" my mother asked on the way home. She had taken off her own coat to put over me and had the heat on high.

"She wasn't using her noggin," said Mona, next to me in the back seat.

"I should call next time," said my mother. "I just don't like to say where I am."

That was when she finally told us that she was working as a checkout clerk in the A&P. She was supposed to be on the day shift, but the other employees were unreliable, and her boss had promised her a promotion if she would stay until the evening shift filled in.

For a moment no one said anything. Even Mona seemed to find the revelation disappointing.

"A promotion already!" she said, finally.

I listened to the windshield wipers.

"You're so quiet." My mother looked at me in the rear-view mirror. "What's the matter?"

"I wish you would quit," I said after a moment.

She sighed. "The Chinese have a saying: one beam cannot hold the roof up."

"But Eugenic Roberts's father supports their family."

She sighed once more. "Eugenie Roberts's father is Eugenie Roberts's father," she said.

As we entered the downtown area, Mona started leaning hard against me every time the car turned right, trying to push me over. Remembering what I had said to Miss Crosman, I tried to maneuver the umbrella under my leg so she wouldn't feel it.

"What's under your skirt?" Mona wanted to know as we came to a traffic light. My mother, watching us in the rear-view mirror again, rolled slowly to a stop.

"What's the matter?" she asked.

"There's something under her skirt," said Mona, pulling at me. "Under her skirt."

Meanwhile, a man crossing the street started to yell at us. "Who do you think you are, lady?" he said. "You're blocking the whole crosswalk."

We all froze. Other people walking by stopped to watch.

"Didn't you hear me?" he went on, starting to thump on the hood with his fist. "Don't you speak English?"

My mother began to back up, but the car behind us honked. Luckily, the light turned green right after that. She sighed in relief.

"What were you saying, Mona?" she asked.

We wouldn't have hit the car behind us that hard if he hadn't been moving too; but as it was, our car bucked violently, throwing us all first back and then forward.

"Uh oh," said Mona when we stopped. "*Another* accident."

I was relieved to have attention <u>diverted</u> from the umbrella. Then I noticed my mother's head, tilted back onto the seat. Her eyes were closed.

"Mom!" I screamed. "Mom! Wake up!"

She opened her eyes. "Please don't yell," she said. "Enough people are going to yell already."

"I thought you were dead," I said, starting to cry. "I thought you were dead."

She turned around, looked at me intently, then put her hand to my forehead.

"Sick," she <u>confirmed</u>. "Some kind of sick is giving you crazy ideas."

As the man from the car behind us started tapping on the window, I moved the umbrella away from my leg. Then Mona and my mother were getting out of the car. I got out after them; and while everyone else was inspecting the damage we'd done, I threw the umbrella down a sewer. ❧

*R*esponding to Reading

First Impressions

1. How did you feel at the end of the story? Jot down your thoughts in your journal or on a sheet of paper.

Second Thoughts

2. Why do you think the narrator throws the umbrella down a sewer? Be ready to explain your opinion.

3. Why do you think the narrator wanted the white umbrella?

   Think about
   - her attitude toward Eugenie Roberts
   - the way she describes the umbrella
   - what the umbrella might represent to her

4. The narrator lies about her family owning a convertible, her mother being a concert pianist, and other matters. Why do you think she does this?

5. What kind of person do you think the mother is? Explain, using examples from the story and your own experiences.

Broader Connections

6. The main **character** in this story is very concerned about her own and other people's possessions. How much can you tell about people from the things they own?

*L*iterary Concept: Character

Characters are the people or animals that take part in the action of the story. A writer can develop a character by explaining the character's thoughts, words, and actions. The writer can also give a physical description of the character and have the character talk to other characters. You get to know the narrator, for example, through the lies she tells her piano teacher, the thoughts she has about her mother working, and what she does with the white umbrella at the end. Find examples to show how the writer develops the main character's sister, Mona.

Concept Review: Setting Remember that the setting, or time and place in which a story occurs, can play an important role in a story. What role does the setting play in this story?

Writing Options

1. It is interesting to see how different a story can be when seen from another character's perspective. With a classmate write the **story** through the eyes of one of the following: the mother, Mona, the piano teacher, or the father.

2. Do you think the narrator would have felt or acted differently if her mother had openly discussed her decision to work? In a journal or on a piece of paper, express your **opinion** about how much parents should discuss family decisions with their children. Use examples from the story to support your opinion.

3. How do you think the narrator feels about her mother at the end of the story? Write the message the narrator would want to express to her mother on a Mother's Day **card.** Include comments that relate directly to the events in this story.

4. In your **journal,** write about a time when some event, such as the car accident in this story, forced you to rethink what is really important to you. Include the thoughts and feelings you had before and after the mind-changing event.

Vocabulary Practice

Exercise A Decide whether the boldfaced word is used correctly. On your paper, write *Correct* or *Incorrect.*

1. A **discreet** person embarrasses people by speaking rudely.

2. An **audible** voice can be heard clearly.

3. If your mother is able to **maneuver** her way through traffic, she will stay stuck in one place.

4. A student who **diverts** the attention of the class is helpful to the teacher.

5. A good **rendition** of a song will bring applause from the audience.

Words to Know and Use

audible
confirm
discreet
divert
illuminate
maneuver
rendition
resume
revelation
stupendous

Exercise B Decide if the following pairs of words are synonyms (the same) or antonyms (opposite). On your own paper, write *Synonym* or *Antonym.*

1. confirm—disprove

2. illuminate—brighten

3. revelation—secret

4. stupendous—astonishing

5. resume—stop

Options for Learning

1 • On Stage With classmates plan a story theater presentation of a scene from "The White Umbrella." Pick a narrator to read the scene as classmates pantomime the actions of the characters.

2 • Musical Notes If you play the piano, find a composition that you think fits the mood of "The White Umbrella." Play your selection for the class. If several people select piano pieces to play, ask the class to decide which piece captures the flavor of the story best.

3 • Moms Survey Survey the class to find out the number of mothers who work outside the home. Then find out how many of the working mothers have children under six years of age and how many have children ages six to seventeen. Remember that some mothers will fit in both categories. Convert your numbers to percentages and compare the results to the numbers on the chart on page 37. Report your findings to the class.

FACT FINDER SCIENCE

Name the terms used to describe the most common cloud types.

Gish Jen
1956-

The daughter of immigrant Chinese parents, Gish Jen grew up in Yonkers and Scarsdale, two cities just north of New York City. She remembers her family feeling the need to fit in—to be absorbed into the main culture. "We were almost the only Asian-American family in town," she recalls. "In Yonkers, people threw things at us and called us names. We thought it was normal— it was only much later that I realized it had been hard." Jen says the experience did not cause her to have an unhappy childhood, and she refuses to give it any special attention. In fact, much of her writing contains a great deal of humor.

Jen's first name is really Lillian. She adopted the name Gish—as in the famous silent picture actress Lillian Gish—just for fun in high school. "It was part of becoming a writer," she says, "not becoming the person I was supposed to be." After Jen graduated from college, she went to China to teach English and then enrolled in the famous Iowa Writer's Program at the University of Iowa, where she wrote "The White Umbrella."

About her writing Jen says, "The biggest influence on my work has come from Jewish-American writers. It's partly Scarsdale, and partly the sympathy I see between the Jewish and Chinese cultures. If there is one thing I hope readers come away with, it's to see Asian Americans as 'us' rather than 'other.'"

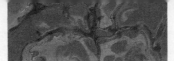

Elements of
NONFICTION

While some readers enjoy getting lost in the imaginary world of fiction, others prefer the authenticity of stories from real life. **Nonfiction** is writing about real people, places, and events.

There are two broad categories of nonfiction. One category, called **informative nonfiction,** is mainly written to provide factual information. Nonfiction of this type includes science and history texts, informational books, encyclopedias, pamphlets, and most of the articles in magazines and newspapers. The main purpose of this material is to inform.

The other category of nonfiction is called **literary nonfiction** because it is written to be read and experienced in much the same way you experience fiction. However, literary nonfiction differs from fiction in that real people take the place of fictional characters, and the settings and plots are not imagined but are actual places and true events.

The following are the types of literary nonfiction you will read in this book.

*U*nderstanding Nonfiction

Autobiography   An **autobiography** is the true story of a person's life, told by that person. It is almost always written using the first-person point of view. In this book you will read excerpts from several autobiographies.

An autobiography is usually book length because it covers a long period of the writer's life. However, there are shorter types of autobiographical writing such as **journals, diaries,** and **memoirs.**

Biography   A **biography** is the true story of a person's life, told by someone else. The writer, or **biographer,** interviews the subject if possible and also researches the person's life by reading letters, books, diaries, and any other information he or she can find. A short biography of African-American inventor, Elijah McCoy, is included in this book. As you will see, biographies and autobiographies often seem like fiction because they contain many of the same elements such as character, setting, and plot.

Essay   An **essay** is a short piece of nonfiction writing that deals with one subject. Essays are often found in newspapers and magazines. The writer might share an opinion, try to entertain or persuade the reader, or simply describe an incident that has special significance. These essays that explain how the author feels about a subject are called **informal,** or **personal, essays.** In this book, the selection "Love and the Cabbie" is an example of an informal essay. **Formal essays** are serious and scholarly and are rarely found in literature textbooks.

Strategies for Reading Nonfiction

Nonfiction can be read as a piece of literature or as a source of information. The nonfiction you will read in this book has been included because of its literary quality. As you read, try to step into and enjoy the true stories and opinions the authors have to share.

Use the following strategies when you read nonfiction.

1. **Preview** a selection before you read. Look at the title, pictures, diagrams, subtitles, and any terms in boldface or italic type. All of these will give you an idea of what the selection is about.

2. **Figure out the organization.** If the work is a biography or autobiography, the organization is probably chronological, that is, in the order that events happen. Other selections may be arranged around ideas the author wants to discuss.

3. **Separate facts and opinions. Facts** are statements that can be proved, such as "There are several autobiographies in this book." **Opinions** are statements that cannot be proved. They simply express the writer's beliefs, such as "the excerpt from *Sweet Summer* is the best autobiography in this book." Writers sometimes present opinions as if they were facts. Be sure you can tell the difference.

4. **Question** as you read. Why did things happen the way they did? How did people feel? What is the writer's opinion? Do you share the writer's opinion, or do you have different ideas on the subject?

5. During your reading, stop now and then and try to **predict** what will come next. Sometimes you will be surprised by what happens or by what the author has to say about an issue.

6. As you read, **build** on your understanding. Add new information to what you have already learned and see if your ideas and opinions change.

7. Continually **evaluate** what you read. Evaluation should be an ongoing process, not just something that is done when you have finished reading. Remember that evaluation means more than saying a selection is good or bad. Form opinions about people, events, and ideas that are presented. Decide whether or not you like the way the piece was written.

Finally, it is important to recognize that your understanding of a selection does not end when you stop reading. As you think more about what you have read and discuss it with others, you will find that your understanding continues to grow.

Nonfiction *from* **Woodsong**

GARY PAULSEN

*E*xamine What You Know

The selection you are about to read was written by someone who lives in the wilderness. Wild animals, such as bears, are part of this writer's everyday experience. In small groups, discuss what you know about animals in the wild. Make a web like the one below. Use the suggested topics in the smaller circles as discussion starters.

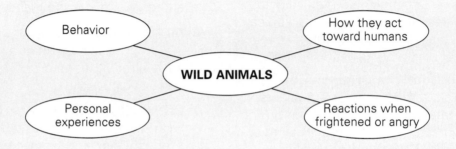

Behavior

How they act toward humans

WILD ANIMALS

Personal experiences

Reactions when frightened or angry

*E*xpand Your Knowledge

This selection is from *Woodsong,* Gary Paulsen's account of his experiences in the wilderness areas of Minnesota and Alaska. The book is an **autobiography,** but it does not cover all aspects of the writer's life. Instead, Paulsen focuses on his wilderness experiences and the lessons he learned from these experiences. Much of the book is an account of how Paulsen prepares his dogs and himself for the Iditarod, the grueling 1,180-mile dogsled race across the Alaskan tundra.

*W*rite Before You Read

■ *Author biography on Extend page*

In your journal or on a piece of paper, describe a time when you learned an important lesson from an animal. The lesson can be about fear or friendship or anything else you choose. After you have read the selection, compare your experience to the one described by the author.

from *Woodsong*

GARY PAULSEN

In Woodsong *Gary Paulsen describes his life as a trapper in the woods of northern Minnesota. He lived with his wife, Ruth, and his son, James, in a small cabin that did not have plumbing or electricity. At the time, the author was not writing stories but simply learning the ways of the woods. This episode describes one of the lessons he learned.*

We have bear trouble. Because we feed processed meat to the dogs, there is always the smell of meat over the kennel. In the summer it can be a bit high[1] because the dogs like to "save" their food sometimes for a day or two or four—burying it to dig up later. We live on the edge of wilderness, and consequently the meat smell brings any number of visitors from the woods.

Skunks abound, and foxes and coyotes and wolves and weasels—all predators. We once had an eagle live over the kennel for more than a week, scavenging from the dogs, and a crazy group of ravens has pretty much taken over the puppy pen. Ravens are protected by the state, and they seem to know it. When I walk toward the puppy pen with the buckets of meat, it's a tossup to see who gets it—the pups or the birds. They have actually pecked the puppies away from the food pans until they have gone through and taken what they want.

Spring, when the bears come, is the worst. They have been in hibernation through the winter, and they are hungry beyond caution. The meat smell draws them like flies, and we frequently have two or three around the kennel at the same time. Typically they do not bother us much—although my wife had a bear chase her from the garden to the house one morning—but they do bother the dogs.

They are so big and strong that the dogs fear them, and the bears trade on this fear to get their food. It's common to see them scare a dog into his house and take his food. Twice we have had dogs killed by rough bear swats that broke their necks—and the bears took their food.

---

1. **it can be a bit high:** the smell can be somewhat strong.

Words to Know and Use

predator (pred′ ə tər) *n.* an animal that kills other animals for food
scavenge (skav′ inj) *v.* to take things left by others

51

We have evolved[2] an uneasy peace with them, but there is the problem of familiarity. The first time you see a bear in the kennel it is a novelty, but when the same ones are there day after day, you wind up naming some of them (old Notch-Ear, Billy-Jo, etc.). There gets to be a too relaxed attitude. We started to treat them like pets.

A major mistake.

We called him Scarhead, and now and again we would joke about him.

There was a large male around the kennel for a week or so. He had a white streak across his head, which I guessed was a wound scar from some hunter—bear hunting is allowed here. He wasn't all that bad, so we didn't mind him. He would frighten the dogs and take their hidden stashes now and then, but he didn't harm them and we became accustomed to him hanging around. We called him Scarhead, and now and again we would joke about him as if he were one of the yard animals.

At this time we had three cats, forty-two dogs, fifteen or twenty chickens, eight ducks, nineteen large white geese, a few banty hens—one called Hawk—ten fryers which we'd raised from chicks and couldn't (as my wife put it) "snuff and eat," and six woods-wise goats.

The bears, strangely, didn't bother any of the yard animals. There must have been a rule, or some order to the way they lived, because they would hit the kennel and steal from the dogs but leave the chickens and goats and other yard stock completely alone—although you would have had a hard time convincing the goats of this fact. The goats spent a great deal of time with their back hair up, whuffing and blowing snot at the bears—and at the dogs who would *gladly* have eaten them. The goats never really believed in the truce.

There is not a dump or landfill to take our trash to, and so we separate it—organic, inorganic[3]—and deal with it ourselves. We burn the paper in a screened enclosure, and it is fairly efficient; but it's impossible to get all the food particles off wrapping paper, so when it's burned, the food particles burn with it.

And give off a burnt food smell.

And nothing draws bears like burning food. It must be that they have learned to understand human dumps—where they spend a great deal of time foraging. And they learn amazingly fast. In Alaska, for instance, the bears already know that the sound of a moose hunter's gun means there will be a fresh gut pile when the hunter cleans the moose. They come at a run when they hear the shot. It's often a close race to see if the hunter will get to the moose before the bears take it away. . . .

---

2. **evolved:** brought about by a series of slow changes.
3. **organic:** made of plant or animal material; **inorganic:** made of things that have never been alive.

Words to Know and Use | **novelty** (näv′ əl tē) *n.* something new or different

Because we're on the south edge of the wilderness area, we try to wait until there is a northerly breeze before we burn so the food smell will carry south, but it doesn't always help. Sometimes bears, wolves, and other predators are already south, working the sheep farms down where it is more settled—they take a terrible toll[4] of sheep—and we catch them on the way back through.

That's what happened one July morning.

Scarhead had been gone for two or three days and the breeze was right, so I went to burn the trash. I fired it off and went back into the house for a moment—not more than two minutes. When I came back out, Scarhead was in the burn area. His tracks (directly through the tomatoes in the garden) showed he'd come from the south.

He was having a grand time. The fire didn't bother him. He was trying to reach a paw in around the edges of flame to get at whatever smelled so good. He had torn things apart quite a bit—ripped one side off the burn enclosure—and I was having a bad day and it made me mad.

I was standing across the burning fire from him, and without thinking—because I was so used to him—I picked up a stick, threw it at him, and yelled, "Get out of here."

I have made many mistakes in my life, and will probably make many more, but I hope never to throw a stick at a bear again.

In one rolling motion—the muscles seemed to move within the skin so fast that I

---

4. **take a terrible toll:** cause the death of many.

couldn't take half a breath—he turned and came for me. Close. I could smell his breath and see the red around the sides of his eyes. Close on me he stopped and raised on his back legs and hung over me, his forelegs and paws hanging down, weaving back and forth gently as he took his time and decided whether or not to tear my head off.

I could not move, would not have time to react. I knew I had nothing to say about it. One blow would break my neck. Whether I lived or died depended on him, on his thinking, on his ideas about me—whether I was worth the bother or not.

Whether I lived or died depended on him.

I did not think then.

Looking back on it, I don't remember having one coherent[5] thought when it was happening. All I knew was terrible menace. His eyes looked very small as he studied me. He looked down on me for what seemed hours. I did not move, did not breathe, did not think or do anything.

And he lowered.

Perhaps I was not worth the trouble. He lowered slowly and turned back to the trash, and I walked backward halfway to the house and then ran—anger growing now—and took the rifle from the gun rack by the door and came back out.

He was still there, rummaging through the trash. I worked the bolt and fed a cartridge in and aimed at the place where you kill bears and began to squeeze. In raw anger, I began to take up the four pounds of pull necessary to send death into him.

And stopped.

Kill him for what?

That thought crept in.

Kill him for what?

For not killing me? For letting me know it is wrong to throw sticks at four-hundred-pound bears? For not hurting me, for not killing me, I should kill him? I lowered the rifle and ejected the shell and put the gun away. I hope Scarhead is still alive. For what he taught me, I hope he lives long and is very happy, because I learned then—looking up at him while he made up his mind whether or not to end me—that when it is all boiled down, I am nothing more and nothing less than any other animal in the woods. ❧

---

5. **coherent:** clear, logical.

Words to Know and Use

menace (men' əs) *n.* threat; danger
rummage (rum' ij) *v.* to sort or search through

Responding to Reading

First Impressions

1. Write three words that describe your reaction to this selection. Then compare your words with those of your classmates.

Second Thoughts

2. What kind of person is Paulsen? Describe what you learned about him in this selection.

Think about
- his observations about the animals around the kennel
- his feelings and actions toward the bear
- his comments about himself and the lesson he learned

3. What do you think it would be like to live where Paulsen lived?

4. Why does Paulsen decide not to shoot the bear? Describe, in your own words, why he comes to the conclusions he does.

Broader Connections

5. In urban (city) and rural (country) areas, animals such as deer, skunks, woodchucks, rats, and pigeons may cause problems for the people who live there. Discuss the problems caused by unwanted wildlife that you have heard about or experienced. What might be done to solve these problems?

Literary Concept: Author's Purpose

Authors write for four main purposes: to entertain, to inform, to express opinions, and to persuade. A writer may combine two or three purposes in one piece, but one purpose is usually the most important. What purposes do you think Gary Paulsen had in mind when he wrote this selection? Which of these purposes do you think was most important to him and why?

Writing Options

1. Create a chart to show how the author's attitude toward the bear (and wild animals in general) changes. In the first column, list his attitudes before he decides not to shoot. In the second column, list his attitudes at the end of the selection. Use your chart to write a brief **comparison-and-contrast essay.**

2. Rewrite the trash-burning **scene** from the bear's point of view. Use details from the story and your own imagination to describe what Scarhead thinks and feels as he picks through the garbage, has a stick thrown at him, and goes after the narrator "in one rolling motion."

3. Paulsen ends his story by saying, "I am nothing more and nothing less than any other animal in the woods." In a brief **essay,** discuss how you feel about this statement.

4. Review the word web on wild animals that you made earlier. Then, in a **journal entry,** describe your personal reaction to the selection. How do your attitudes toward nature and wildlife compare with Gary Paulsen's? Did the selection change your mind in any way? Explain.

Vocabulary Practice

Exercise   On your paper, write the letter of the phrase that best completes each sentence below.

1. A **predator** usually eats (a) grass and fruits (b) vegetables (c) other animals.

2. You would most likely find bears trying to **scavenge** in (a) a garbage pile (b) a stream (c) a cave.

3. An animal that is a **menace** to humans is (a) dangerous (b) harmless (c) helpful.

4. A polar bear would be a **novelty** in (a) Alaska (b) a zoo (c) Africa.

5. If a bear were to **rummage** through your campsite, it would (a) cause a mess (b) only circle your campfire (c) leave no trace of its presence.

Words to Know and Use

menace
novelty
predator
rummage
scavenge

Options for Learning

1 • The Bear Facts Skim the selection and list all the details Gary Paulsen includes about bears. Then do research to find out more about the biological family called *Ursidae*. Does Scarhead demonstrate typical bear behavior? Is Paulsen's portrayal accurate? Present an oral report explaining your findings.

2 • Dogsledding Create a poster or a bulletin board display on the subject of dogsled racing. Include a section on the history of this sport, as well as pictures or drawings of modern sleds and sled dogs. List the types of dogs most commonly used in this sport. You might also include a world map with labels to show where some of the most famous dogsled races, such as the Iditarod, are held.

3 • Woodsong Interested in the outdoors, dogs, and dogsledding? You'll enjoy *Woodsong,* a short book. Read it and prepare an oral book report.

4 • Stage a Debate The needs of civilization are often at odds with nature. Do people have the right to destroy wildlife or use wildlife habitats to serve their needs and interests? Choose an environmental issue, such as the preservation of endangered species, to research and debate. Use the *Readers' Guide to Periodical Literature* to find articles.

FACT FINDER GEOGRAPHY

What kinds of bears live in the wilderness of Minnesota?

Gary Paulsen
1939-

Besides being a writer, Paulsen has been a soldier, animal trapper, and rancher. As a trapper for the state of Minnesota, Paulsen was given four sled dogs to help him with his work. The time spent with the dogs convinced him that he could no longer kill animals. He quit trapping and began training for the seventeen-day Iditarod dogsled race. His experiences motivated him to write *Woodsong* and the novels *Dogsong* and *Hatchet,* Newbery Honor Books.

As a young boy, Paulsen's family moved constantly because his father was an army officer. "School was a nightmare because I was unbelievably shy, and terrible at sports," he recalls.

Paulsen was introduced to books by a friendly librarian who gave him his first library card. "She didn't care if I looked right, wore the right clothes, dated the right girls, was popular at sports—none of those prejudices existed in the public library." Paulsen read everything "as though I had been dying of thirst and the librarian had handed me a five-gallon bucket of water. I drank and drank." As a writer, he has satisfied both young and adult readers, publishing more than forty books, two hundred articles, and two plays.

WRITER'S WORKSHOP

PERSONAL WRITING

USE PERSONAL WRITING FOR

journals
logs
notes
letters
diaries
autobiographies

June. Selo. Mona's sister. Before reading the stories in this subunit, you didn't know these characters. What about now? The characters' personal experiences helped them—and you—"see the light."

In this workshop you will write a **friendly letter** to your teacher to help him or her "see the light" about you. Remember, a friendly letter is like a great one-way chat. Keep it lively and interesting! At the same time, don't forget that your letter is a school assignment. Think it through carefully and polish your words.

> Here is one writer's PASSkey to this assignment.

GUIDED ASSIGNMENT: A LETTER ABOUT ME

Write a letter to your teacher. Include a personal experience that shows something special about you.

P URPOSE: To introduce myself

A UDIENCE: My teacher

S UBJECT: Me

S TRUCTURE: A friendly letter

STUDENT MODEL

Look at the form of Adam's letter. It has
a **heading,**
a **salutation,**
a **body,**
a **closing,**
and a **signature.**

The writer begins with a brief description of himself, then tells about his experience, using **chronological order.**

```
                                    756 Elm Street
                        Heading     Clayton, Ohio 45315
                                    September 26, 19--
        Salutation
        Dear Ms. Klimsky,

                            Body
          My name is Adam Lark, and I sit on the left
        side of the class, near the door. I wear
        glasses and an Oakland A's jacket, and my hair
        is light brown. That is, it's usually light
        brown. Once my hair was a different color for
        a while, and it taught me something about
        myself. I think one of my special qualities is
        that I don't get embarrassed very easily.
        Here's how I found this out.
```

Last fall my sister Miki and I were looking for something to do. We found some styling gel, and Miki put it in her hair so that her hair stuck out like porcupine spines. Her hair looked so funny that I wanted to do it too. The can of styling gel ran out, so we took another one down from the cabinet. I put that other stuff in my hair so that it stuck out, and it was so funny Miki couldn't stop laughing.

However, I was in for a surprise. When I washed the stuff out, my hair was so dark that it was almost blue! I looked like a cartoon! When my mom came home, the first thing she said was, "What did you DO?" I told her I had only put on some styling gel. She got the can out of the cabinet and told me it was some kind of hair dye, not styling gel!

Of course I had to go to school the next day, and I knew everybody would laugh. I remembered my friend Jim, who once got a bad haircut and stayed home from school for a week because he was so embarrassed. For some reason my blue hair didn't bother me too much. It was funny, not terrible--and now I know what to do for Halloween.

Closing	Sincerely,
Signature	*Adam Lark*

The paragraphs help divide the story into its important parts.

Adam's final paragraph describes what he learned about himself.

Adam uses a **dash (––)** to show a pause in his thinking.

Prewrite and Explore

1 **Pinpoint your personality**   Think about a personal trait that you want your teacher to know about. Are you persistent? Daring? Funny? List words that describe your personality. Then choose the trait that really nails down who you are.

2 **Demonstrate your trait**   Now you need to think of an experience that demonstrates the trait you chose. What has happened or what have you done that shows you to be daring or shy or friendly? If you can't think of an experience, try the following idea.

WRITER'S CHOICE

If it's easier for you, reverse the order of steps 1 and 2 on page 59. Take the house tour first. Do your memories suggest a personality trait to write about?

▶ **Take a House Tour**   Wander around your house, looking for objects that trigger memories. Does the gerbil cage in your closet bring to mind the night you left the cage open? Does the skateboard in the basement remind you of an accident you had? Choose a memory that sheds light on some part of your personality. Adam's tour led him to the bottle of hair dye in the medicine cabinet.

GATHERING INFORMATION

Now you can zero in on the memory you've chosen. Before you start, brainstorm a list of details about the experience. Adam chose to write about the time he accidentally dyed his hair. To jog his memory, he listed the details below. Notice that Adam chose not to use all these details in his final draft.

STUDENT MODEL ▶

```
The Time I Dyed My Hair

--boring day

--Miki wanted to spike her hair

--looked like a porcupine—really funny

--weird smell

--thought about spiking the dog

--Mom came home tired

--bathroom a mess

--hair grew out a little at a time

--Jim's haircut in fourth grade

--couldn't find camera to take a picture
```

3 **Use vivid details**   Saying what kind of person you are is one thing. Showing it is even better. For example, the narrator of "Cricket in the Road" says he is afraid of storms. Then he gives this description:

LITERARY MODEL

from "Cricket in the Road" by Michael Anthony

▶   I started again at another flash of lightning, and before I had recovered from this, yet another terrifying peal of thunder hit the air. I screamed. . . . Thunder struck again and I dashed under the bed.

In your letter use vivid details like these to describe your experience. Then both your words *and* your personality will come alive.

Draft and Discover

1 **Organize your ideas**   As you write, organize your ideas clearly. You are retelling a personal experience, so chronological order will probably work best. In **chronological order,** events are arranged in the order in which they happened. End your letter by describing the result of your experience.

2 **Make the sequence clear**   When you use chronological order, the sequence of events should be clear. Use **time words** such as *first, later, once,* and *every summer.* Read the excerpt below. Notice how the underlined words move the story along.

> <u>As</u> the man from the car behind us started tapping on the window, I moved the umbrella away from my leg. <u>Then</u> Mona and my mother were getting out of the car. I got out after them; and <u>while</u> everyone else was inspecting the damage we'd done, I threw the umbrella down a sewer.

◀ LITERARY MODEL
. . . .
from "The White Umbrella" by Gish Jen

Revise Your Writing

1 **Elaborate on your experience**   Add details that make your experience clearer and more interesting. Think of yourself as a word mechanic. A few new parts will make your letter a "smoother road." Note how Adam improved this sentence by adding details.

Before   We found some styling gel, and Miki put it in her hair.

After   We found some styling gel, and Miki put it in her hair so that her hair stuck out like porcupine spines.

2 **Use a peer reader**   Look over your draft. Then ask a classmate to review it. Use the following questions to help you revise and improve your draft.

Revision Questions	
For You	For a Peer Reader
1. How clear is the order of events?	1. How could I tell about my experience more thoroughly?
2. Can I add any other interesting details?	2. How would you describe me on the basis of my letter? Did I make my personality clear?

Proofread

Reread your draft, looking for errors in grammar, punctuation, spelling, and capitalization. Pay special attention to possessive nouns. Make sure you used correct letter form. Your letter should have a heading, a salutation, a body, a closing, and a signature.

THE EDITOR'S EYE: POSSESSIVE NOUNS

When you use a possessive noun, make sure you put the apostrophe in the right place.

A **possessive noun** shows who or what owns something. To form the possessive of any singular noun, add an apostrophe and an *s*.

Singular my *sister's* hair   the *duchess's* pearls
           the *man's* suit

There are two rules for making a plural noun possessive:
(1) If the plural noun ends in *s*, simply add an apostrophe.
(2) If the noun does not end in *s*, add an apostrophe and an *s*.

Plural   my *sisters'* hair   the *duchesses'* pearls
           the *men's* suits

NEED MORE HELP?
See the Language Workshop that follows (pages 63-65) and Section 4 in the Language Handbook.

COMPUTER TIP
Make an extra copy of your letter and start a personal-letters file. Keep your letters in chronological order. You'll enjoy reading them later.

Publish and Present

Here is a suggestion for sharing your work with others.

Mixed Messages   First, of course, you will share your letter with your teacher. If time permits, you might ask him or her to read some of the letters aloud and see if the class can guess the authors. **Important:** If you do *not* want your letter read, draw a star in the upper right-hand corner.

Reflect on Your Writing

Answer the following questions. Place the answers and a copy of your letter in your writing portfolio.

FOR YOUR PORTFOLIO ▶

1. Does your letter convey the unique person you are?
2. Did you learn something new about yourself in writing your letter?

LANGUAGE WORKSHOP

USING PLURAL AND POSSESSIVE NOUNS CORRECTLY

> A **singular noun** names one person, place, thing, or idea.
> A **plural noun** names more than one person, place, thing, or idea.
> A **possessive noun** shows who or what owns something.

Plural Nouns

Some nouns name just one person, place, thing, or idea. *Skunk,* for example, names one thing. It is a **singular noun.** Nouns that name more than one thing are **plural nouns.** Notice the plural nouns in the following sentence.

> *Skunks* abound, and *foxes* and *coyotes* and *wolves* and *weasels*—all *predators.*

◄ **LITERARY MODEL** · · · · · · · · · · ·
from *Woodsong,* by Gary Paulsen

Follow these rules to form the plurals of nouns.

1. To form the plurals of most nouns, simply add *-s.*
   mirror*s*   hedge*s*   bear*s*   umbrella*s*

2. When a noun ends in *s, sh, ch, x,* or *z,* add *-es.*
   glass*es*   dish*es*   batch*es*   fox*es*   buzz*es*

SPELLING TIP · · · · · · · · · · ·
Not sure how to form the plural of a noun? Look up the noun in a dictionary. If the plural form is not listed, just add *-s* or *-es* to the word.

3. When a noun ends in *o,* add *-s.*
   studio*s*   photo*s*   radio*s*   Eskimo*s*
   Exceptions: For the following nouns ending in *o,* add *-es.*
   hero*es*   tomato*es*   echo*es*   potato*es*

4. When a noun ends in *y* with a consonant before it, change the *y* to *i* and add *-es.*
   baby—bab*ies*   country—countr*ies*   sky—sk*ies*

◄ **REMINDER** · · · · · · · · · · ·
a, e, i, o, and *u,* and sometimes *y* are **vowels.** All the other letters are **consonants.**

5. For most nouns ending in *f* or *fe,* add *-s.* For some of these nouns, however, change the *f* to *v* and add *-es.*
   belief—belief*s*   safe—safe*s*   wolf—wol*ves*
   roof—roof*s*   leaf—lea*ves*   thief—thie*ves*

6. For some nouns, the singular and plural forms are the same.
   scissors   deer   moose   sheep   news

7. Some nouns have special plural forms.
   child—children   goose—geese   ox—oxen

TWO FOR ONE

Some nouns have more than one correct plural form. For example, a lot of *eels* can also be a lot of *eel*. Several *cactuses* can be several *cacti*. So before you say "There's no such word as *hippopotami,*" look up the plural forms of *hippopotamus.*

Exercise 1 **Concept Check** Write the plural form of each italicized noun.

1. For my music recital I played two *waltz.*
2. My *number* were both *solo.*
3. I had *butterfly* in my stomach, and my *knee* felt weak.
4. As the *man* and *woman* filled the room, I sat down at one of the *piano.*
5. I had to play from memory, but *copy* of the music lay on the piano.
6. Taking several deep *breath,* I began.
7. I let my *finger* leap and run over the *key* like *deer.*
8. I kept my *eye* straight ahead on a tree with gorgeous fall *leaf* outside the window.
9. When I was done, the *echo* of applause rang in my ears.
10. Afterwards, all of us drank tall *glass* of lemonade and gobbled down several *loaf* of banana bread.

Possessive Nouns

Possessive nouns show ownership or belonging.

> the *boy's* bat (The boy owns the bat.)
> the *bear's* paw (The paw belongs to the bear.)

SPELLING TIP

Although a little thing, an apostrophe can make a huge difference. For example, a *boy's* room is a room that belongs to one boy. A *boys'* room is a room that is shared by two or more boys.

▶ To form the possessive of a singular noun, add an apostrophe (') and an *s* to the noun. Do this even if the noun ends in *s.*

Singular Noun	Possessive Form
girl	girl's
Carlos	Carlos's

To form the possessive of a plural noun that ends in *s,* simply add an apostrophe to the end of the word.

Plural Noun	Possessive Form
girls	girls'
coyotes	coyotes'

To form the possessive of a plural noun that does not end in *s,* add an apostrophe and an *s.*

Plural Noun	Possessive Form
children	children's
geese	geese's

Exercise 2   Concept Check   Write the possessive form of each italicized noun.

1. My friend *Ross* favorite sport is cricket.
2. Ross comes from England, and cricket is one of *England* most popular games.
3. The game of cricket is played with a bat and a ball; the two *teams* players compete to score runs.
4. The *bat* shape is like a paddle's.
5. A cricket *field* size is about 450 feet by 500 feet.
6. Both *teams* players act as both batsmen and fielders.
7. Hitting the ball and running are *batsmen* duties.
8. In each team's time at bat, the *players* batting order stays fixed.
9. A cricket *game* length can vary from hours to days.
10. Watching a cricket tournament often tests *people* patience.

Exercise 3   Revision Skill   With a small group of classmates, identify all the nouns in the following paragraph. Then rewrite the paragraph by yourself. Correct errors in the use of plural and possessive nouns.

> The two bears eyes glowed like lanternes in the bushs. Leafs rustled as the bears edged closer to the campfire. Pablo glanced up at his catch of salmons hanging from a tree. While he was fishing, the rivers' current had nearly swept him and his catch away twice. Was Pablos hard work for nothing? With a sigh Pablo reached for one of his knifes. "Only fools and heros fight grizzlys," he muttered, cutting down the fish and tossing them in the hungry creatures's direction.

Exercise 4   Revising Your Writing   Look over the friendly letter that you wrote to your teacher for the Writer's Workshop on page 58. Lightly underline all the plural and possessive nouns that you used. Correct any mistakes that you find.

LANGUAGE HANDBOOK
For review and practice: Section 4, Using Nouns.

SPEAKING AND LISTENING
WORKSHOP

WORKING WITH PEERS

Have you ever been part of a sports team? If so, you know that working together is the best way to win. Teamwork can also make you a winner in school. Many assignments in this book will ask you to work in groups or pairs. The guidelines below will help you be a great "team player."

1. **Be a good listener.** Listen carefully to what each group member says. Don't daydream or let your attention wander. Listen for important ideas and details. Remember, listening is a two-way street. When your turn to speak or read your writing comes around, you will want others to listen closely.

2. **Contribute to the group.** Join in discussions and share your ideas. Take chances! Share what's on your mind, even if you don't have your idea completely thought through. Nothing causes more tension in a group than one or two members who don't participate.

3. **Have respect for others.** Be sensitive and thoughtful toward others. Do not rudely dismiss others' ideas. Saying "I don't agree with that" is quite different from saying "You're wrong." Avoid sarcasm. Aim for an atmosphere in which everyone feels comfortable.

4. **Offer useful suggestions.** Be positive and helpful when you discuss a classmate's work. There are lots of ways to do this. For example, tell your classmate what you like best about his or her work before you say what you like least. Ask questions such as "What idea are you trying to get across?" instead of saying "This part is stupid and doesn't make sense."

Exercise   Working in a small group, create a story about a character who is trapped in a dark, dangerous place. As a group, brainstorm specific details about the setting and the character. Then decide which of your details will work best.

Select one student to record the story. Have one person begin telling the story by making up the first five or six sentences. Then have each member add five or six more sentences until the story is complete. Make sure each member of the group has at least one turn.

GROUP EVALUATION
Name two things your group did well. Then name one thing your group needs to improve.

After your story is recorded, look it over as a group. If you see any problems with the story, work together to fix them. Then share your story with the rest of the class, either by reading it aloud or by making copies to pass out. As a class discuss your reactions to the stories. During your discussion, use the speaking and listening skills you have learned.

$\mathscr{F}$ROM MY POINT OF VIEW

Do you and a friend ever form different opinions of a situation? You might differ because each of you sees the situation from his or her own perspective, or point of view. Take rain, for example. A farmer might welcome it because his fields are dry, but a camper might dread it because it could ruin his or her camping trip.

Everyone has a special way of seeing the world. It grows out of personal experiences, books, family relationships, and even school. In fact, your point of view is affected by almost everything you do, and it is always changing and growing.

In this subunit you will discover a different point of view in each selection. Put yourself into the action and see if you would react in the way the characters do.

Fiction

*E*leven

SANDRA CISNEROS (sis' ner' ōs)

*E*xamine What You Know

This story is told from the point of view of a girl on her eleventh birthday. In your journal, write how you feel about being the age you are. Are there times when you feel younger or older? If you could be another age, what would it be? Why?

*E*xpand Your Knowledge

When she was interviewed about this piece, the writer Sandra Cisneros said she sometimes feels eleven years old inside, even as an adult. "When I think how I see myself, I would have to be at age eleven. I know I'm thirty-two on the outside, but inside I'm eleven. I'm the girl in the picture with skinny arms and a crumpled shirt and crooked hair. I didn't like school because all they saw was the outside me." She remembers being shy and afraid in school: "I never opened my mouth except when the teacher called on me, the first time I'd speak all day."

LIZZIE AND BRUNO
1970 Fairfield Porter

*E*nrich Your Reading

Descriptive Language   As you read the story, pay attention to the way Rachel describes her thoughts. Notice how she uses images such as "the way you grow old is kind of like an onion." This helps you understand how Rachel feels about getting older. After you finish reading, record other descriptions from the story on a chart like the one started below. In the first column, write the descriptive image; in the second column, write what the description tells you about Rachel.

Image	What It Tells You About Rachel
Growing old is like an onion.	Tells how she feels about getting older She has a good imagination and an interesting way of seeing things.

■ *Author biography in Reader's Handbook*

Eleven

SANDRA CISNEROS

What they don't understand about birthdays and what they never tell you is that when you're eleven, you're also ten, and nine, and eight, and seven, and six, and five, and four, and three, and two, and one. And when you wake up on your eleventh birthday, you expect to feel eleven, but you don't. You open your eyes and everything's just like yesterday, only it's today. And you don't feel eleven at all. You feel like you're still ten. And you are—underneath the year that makes you eleven.

Like some days you might say something stupid, and that's the part of you that's still ten. Or maybe some days you might need to sit on your mama's lap because you're scared, and that's the part of you that's five. And maybe one day when you're all grown up, maybe you will need to cry like if you're three, and that's OK. That's what I tell Mama when she's sad and needs to cry. Maybe she's feeling three.

Because the way you grow old is kind of like an onion or like the rings inside a tree trunk or like my little wooden dolls that fit one inside the other, each year inside the next one. That's how being eleven years old is.

You don't feel eleven. Not right away. It takes a few days, weeks even, sometimes even months before you say Eleven when they ask you. And you don't feel smart eleven, not until you're almost twelve. That's the way it is.

Only today I wish I didn't have only eleven years rattling inside me like pennies in a tin Band-Aid box. Today I wish I was one hundred and two instead of eleven because if I was one hundred and two, I'd have known what to say when Mrs. Price put the red sweater on my desk. I would've known how to tell her it wasn't mine instead of just sitting there with that look on my face and nothing coming out of my mouth.

"Whose is this?" Mrs. Price says, and she holds the red sweater up in the air for all the class to see. "Whose? It's been sitting in the coatroom for a month."

"Not mine," says everybody. "Not me."

"It has to belong to somebody," Mrs. Price keeps saying, but nobody can remember. It's an ugly

sweater with red plastic buttons and a collar and sleeves all stretched out like you could use it for a jump rope. It's maybe a thousand years old, and even if it belonged to me, I wouldn't say so.

Maybe because I'm skinny, maybe because she doesn't like me, that stupid Sylvia Saldívar says, "I think it belongs to Rachel." An ugly sweater like that, all raggedy and old, but Mrs. Price believes her. Mrs. Price takes the sweater and puts it right on my desk, but when I open my mouth, nothing comes out.

"That's not, I don't, you're not . . . Not mine," I finally say in a little voice that was maybe me when I was four.

"Of course it's yours," Mrs. Price says. "I remember you wearing it once." Because she's older and the teacher, she's right and I'm not.

Not mine, not mine, not mine, but Mrs. Price is already turning to page thirty-two, and math problem number four. I don't know why, but all of a sudden I'm feeling sick inside, like the part of me that's three wants to come out of my eyes, only I squeeze them shut tight and bite down on my teeth real hard and try to remember today I am eleven, eleven. Mama is making a cake for me for tonight, and when Papa comes home, everybody will sing Happy birthday, happy birthday to you.

But when the sick feeling goes away and I open my eyes, the red sweater's still sitting there like a big red mountain. I move the red sweater to the corner of my desk with my ruler. I move my pencil and books and eraser as far from it as possible. I even move my chair a little to the right. Not mine, not mine, not mine.

In my head I'm thinking how long till lunchtime, how long till I can take the red sweater and throw it over the schoolyard fence, or leave it hanging on a parking meter, or bunch it up into a little ball and toss it in the alley. Except when math period ends, Mrs. Price says loud and in front of everybody, "Now, Rachel, that's enough," because she sees I've shoved the red sweater to the tippy-tip corner of my desk and it's hanging all over the edge like a waterfall, but I don't care.

"Rachel," Mrs. Price says. She says it like she's getting mad. "You put that sweater on right now and no more nonsense."

"But it's not—"

"Now!" Mrs. Price says.

This is when I wish I wasn't eleven, because all the years inside of me—ten, nine, eight, seven, six, five, four, three, two, and one—are pushing at the back of my eyes when I put one arm through one sleeve of the sweater that smells like cottage cheese, and then the other arm through the other and stand there with my arms apart like if the sweater hurts me and it does, all itchy and full of germs that aren't even mine.

I wish I was invisible, but I'm not.

That's when everything I've been holding in since this morning, since when Mrs. Price put the sweater on my desk, finally lets go, and all of a sudden I'm crying in front of everybody. I wish I was invisible, but I'm not. I'm eleven and it's my birthday today and I'm crying like I'm three in front of everybody. I put my head down on the desk and bury my face in my stupid clown-sweater arms. My face all hot and spit coming out of my mouth because I can't stop the little animal noises from coming out of me, until there aren't any more tears left in my eyes, and it's just my body shaking like when you have the hiccups, and my whole head hurts like when you drink milk too fast.

But the worst part is right before the bell rings for lunch. That stupid Phyllis Lopez, who is even dumber than Sylvia Saldívar, says she remembers the red sweater is hers! I take it off right away and give it to her, only Mrs. Price pretends like everything's OK.

Today I'm eleven. There's a cake Mama's making for tonight, and when Papa comes home from work, we'll eat it. There'll be candles and presents, and everybody will sing Happy birthday, happy birthday to you, Rachel, only it's too late.

I'm eleven today. I'm eleven, ten, nine, eight, seven, six, five, four, three, two, and one, but I wish I was one hundred and two. I wish I was anything but eleven, because I want today to be far away already, far away like a runaway balloon, like a tiny *o* in the sky, so tiny-tiny you have to close your eyes to see it. ❧

*R*esponding to Reading

First Impressions

1. How did you feel about Rachel when you finished the story? Jot down your response in your journal or on a piece of paper.

Second Thoughts

2. Rachel reacts strongly when Mrs. Price insists that the sweater is Rachel's. Explain whether or not Rachel has good reasons to feel the way she does.

   Think about
   - Mrs. Price's attitude and behavior toward Rachel
   - Rachel's thoughts about being eleven but feeling younger
   - the notes you made about Rachel

3. Is Mrs. Price acting unfairly to Rachel, or is she simply making a mistake?

4. What does the fact that it is Rachel's birthday have to do with the way she feels?

*L*iterary Concept: Point of View

Point of view refers to the way a writer tells a story. A story may be told from a first-person point of view or from a third-person point of view. In a story told from a **first-person point of view,** the narrator is a character in the story. He or she uses pronouns such as *I, me,* and *we.* When a story is told from a **third-person point of view,** the narrator is not a character in the story and uses pronouns such as *he, she,* and *they.* Rachel, the narrator of this story, has her own particular first-person point of view. How would the story be different if it were narrated by another character?

*W*riting Options

1. Using the descriptive images in the story as well as your own feelings and experiences, write a **poem** about becoming or being eleven years old.

2. Write a birthday **letter** to Rachel, including a message that might make her feel better.

Fiction

*A*aron's *G*ift
MYRON LEVOY

*E*xamine What You Know

In your journal, write about the best gift you ever gave or received. What made this gift so special?

*E*xpand Your Knowledge

In this story, one character's ideas about gifts are strongly influenced by her childhood in a Jewish village in the Ukraine. Ukraine is now an independent country in the southwestern part of the former Soviet Union. During the late nineteenth century, however, Ukraine was part of the Russian Empire. The brutal leader of the Russian Empire was Czar Alexander the Third. At that time, Jews in the Ukraine lived in constant fear of the Cossacks—soldiers loyal to the czar. These soldiers frequently attacked the Jewish communities in raids called pogroms. While Alexander the Third was czar, thousands of Jews left the Ukraine and came to the United States.

*E*nrich Your Reading

Predicting   When you read a story, guessing what will happen next keeps you involved in the action. The title of this story, for example, encourages you to predict what Aaron's gift will be. As you read the story, you will find a question that asks you to predict what the main character will do next. Look for other points where you might predict what will happen. Jot down your predictions, then read on to see where the action takes you.

■ *Author biography on Extend page*

Aaron's Gift

MYRON LEVOY

Aaron Kandel had come to Tompkins Square Park to roller skate, for the streets near Second Avenue were always too crowded with children and peddlers and old ladies and baby buggies. Though few children had bicycles in those days, almost every child owned a pair of roller skates. And Aaron was, it must be said, a Class A, triple-fantastic roller skater.

Aaron skated back and forth on the wide walkway of the park, pretending he was an aviator in an air race zooming around pylons,[1] which were actually two lampposts. During his third lap around the racecourse, he noticed a pigeon on the grass, behaving very strangely. Aaron skated to the line of benches, then climbed over onto the lawn.

The pigeon was trying to fly, but all it could manage was to flutter and turn round and round in a large circle, as if it were performing a <u>frenzied</u> dance. The left wing was only half open and was beating in a clumsy, jerking fashion; it was clearly broken.

Luckily, Aaron hadn't eaten the cookies he'd stuffed into his pocket before he'd gone clacking down the three flights of stairs from his apartment, his skates already on. He broke a cookie into small crumbs and tossed some toward the pigeon. "Here pidge, here

pidge," he called. The pigeon spotted the cookie crumbs and, after a moment, stopped <u>thrashing</u> about. It folded its wings as best it could, but the broken wing still stuck half out. Then it strutted over to the crumbs, its head bobbing forth-back, forth-back, as if it were marching a little in front of the rest of the body—perfectly normal, except for that half-open wing, which seemed to make the bird stagger sideways every so often.

The pigeon began eating the crumbs as Aaron quickly unbuttoned his shirt and pulled it off. Very slowly, he edged toward the bird, making little kissing sounds like the ones he heard his grandmother make when she fed the sparrows on the back fire escape.

Then suddenly Aaron plunged. The shirt, in both hands, came down like a torn parachute. The pigeon beat its wings, but Aaron held the shirt to the ground, and the bird couldn't escape. Aaron felt under the shirt, gently, and gently took hold of the wounded pigeon.

"Yes, yes, pidge," he said, very softly. "There's a good boy. Good pigeon, good."

---

1. **pylons** (pī′ länz′): towers used as turning points for airplanes in a race.

Words to Know and Use | **frenzied** (fren′ zēd) *adj.* wild; frantic **frenzy** *n.*
thrash (thrash) *v.* to move wildly

 **predict** What will Aaron do with the pigeon?

The pigeon struggled in his hands, but little by little Aaron managed to soothe it. "Good boy, pidge. That's your new name. Pidge. I'm gonna take you home, Pidge. Yes, yes, ssh. Good boy. I'm gonna fix you up. Easy, Pidge, easy does it. Easy, boy."

Aaron squeezed through an opening between the row of benches and skated slowly out of the park while holding the pigeon carefully with both hands as if it were one of his mother's rare, precious cups from the old country. How fast the pigeon's heart was beating! Was he afraid? Or did all pigeons' hearts beat fast?

It was fortunate that Aaron was an excellent skater, for he had to skate six blocks to his apartment, over broken pavement and sudden gratings and curbs and cobblestones. But when he reached home, he asked Noreen Callahan, who was playing on the stoop, to take off his skates for him. He would not chance going up three flights on roller skates this time.

"Is he sick?" asked Noreen.

"Broken wing," said Aaron. "I'm gonna fix him up and make him into a carrier pigeon[2] or something."

"Can I watch?" asked Noreen.

"Watch what?"

"The operation. I'm gonna be a nurse when I grow up."

"OK," said Aaron. "You can even help. You can help hold him while I fix him up."

Aaron wasn't quite certain what his

EARLY EVENING, NEW YORK   1954   Jane Freilicher
Private collection   Courtesy, Fischbach Gallery   New York.

mother would say about his new-found pet, but he was pretty sure he knew what his grandmother would think. His grandmother had lived with them ever since his grandfather had died three years ago. And she fed

---

2. carrier pigeon: a pigeon trained to deliver messages and then return home.

the sparrows and jays and crows and robins on the back fire escape with every spare crumb she could find. In fact, Aaron noticed that she sometimes created crumbs where they didn't exist by squeezing and tearing pieces of her breakfast roll when his mother wasn't looking.

Aaron didn't really understand his grandmother, for he often saw her by the window having long conversations with the birds, telling them about her days as a little girl in the Ukraine. And once he saw her take her mirror from her handbag and hold it out toward the birds. She told Aaron that she wanted them to see how beautiful they were. Very strange. But Aaron did know that she would love Pidge, because she loved everything.

To his surprise, his mother said he could keep the pigeon, temporarily, because it was sick, and we were all strangers in the land of Egypt,[3] and it might not be bad for Aaron to have a pet. Temporarily.

The wing was surprisingly easy to fix, for the break showed clearly and Pidge was remarkably patient and still, as if he knew he was being helped. Or perhaps he was just exhausted from all the thrashing about he had done. Two Popsicle sticks served as splints, and strips from an old undershirt were used to tie them in place. Another strip held the wing to the bird's body.

Aaron's father arrived home and stared at the pigeon. Aaron waited for the expected storm. But instead, Mr. Kandel asked, "Who did this?"

"Me," said Aaron. "And Noreen Callahan."

"Sophie!" he called to his wife. "Did you see this! Ten years old and it's better than Dr. Belasco could do. He's a genius!"

As the days passed, Aaron began training Pidge to be a carrier pigeon. He tied a little cardboard tube to Pidge's left leg and stuck tiny rolled-up sheets of paper with secret messages into it: THE ENEMY IS ATTACKING AT DAWN. Or: THE GUNS ARE HIDDEN IN THE TRUNK OF THE CAR. Or: VINCENT DeMARCO IS A BRITISH SPY. Then Aaron would set Pidge down at one end of the living room and put some popcorn at the other end. And Pidge would waddle slowly across the room, cooing softly, while the ends of his bandages trailed along the floor.

At the other end of the room, one of Aaron's friends would take out the message, stick a new one in, turn Pidge around, and aim him at the popcorn that Aaron put down on his side of the room.

And Pidge grew fat and contented on all the popcorn and crumbs and corn and crackers and Aaron's grandmother's breakfast rolls.

Aaron had told all the children about Pidge, but he only let his very best friends come up and play carrier pigeon with him. But telling everyone had been a mistake. A group of older boys from down the block had a club—Aaron's mother called it a gang—and Aaron had longed to join as he had never longed for anything else. To be with them and share their secrets, the secrets of older boys. To be able to enter their clubhouse shack on the empty lot on the next street. To know the password and swear the secret oath. To belong.

---

3. **we were all strangers . . . Egypt:** refers to the Hebrews who, as told in the Bible, moved to Egypt to avoid death from hunger but were treated harshly there until they left.

About a month after Aaron had brought the pigeon home, Carl, the gang leader, walked over to Aaron in the street and told him he could be a member if he'd bring the pigeon down to be the club mascot. Aaron couldn't believe it; he immediately raced home to get Pidge. But his mother told Aaron to stay away from those boys, or else. And Aaron, miserable, argued with his mother and pleaded and cried and coaxed. It was no use. Not with those boys. No.

Aaron's mother tried to change the subject. She told him that it would soon be his grandmother's sixtieth birthday, a very special birthday indeed, and all the family from Brooklyn and the East Side would be coming to their apartment for a dinner and celebration. Would Aaron try to build something or make something for Grandma? A present made with his own hands would be nice. A decorated box for her hairpins or a crayon picture for her room or anything he liked.

In a flash Aaron knew what to give her: Pidge! Pidge would be her present! Pidge with his wing healed, who might be able to carry messages for her to the doctor or his Aunt Rachel or other people his grandmother seemed to go to a lot. It would be a surprise for everyone. And Pidge would make up for what had happened to Grandma when she'd been a little girl in the Ukraine, wherever that was.

Often, in the evening, Aaron's grandmother would talk about the old days long ago in the Ukraine, in the same way that she talked to the birds on the back fire escape. She had lived in a village near a place called Kishinev[4] with hundreds of other poor peasant families like her own. Things hadn't been too bad under someone called Czar Alexander the Second,[5] whom Aaron always pictured as a tall, handsome man in a gold uniform. But Alexander the Second was assassinated, and Alexander the Third,[6] whom Aaron pictured as an ugly man in a black cape, became the czar. And the Jewish people of the Ukraine had no peace anymore.

One day, a thundering of horses was heard coming toward the village from the direction of Kishinev. "The Cossacks![7] The Cossacks!" someone had shouted. The czar's horsemen! Quickly, quickly, everyone in Aaron's grandmother's family had climbed down to the cellar through a little trapdoor hidden under a mat in the big central room of their shack. But his grandmother's pet goat, whom she'd loved as much as Aaron loved Pidge and more, had to be left above, because if it had made a sound in the cellar, they would never have lived to see the next morning. They all hid under the wood in the woodbin and waited, hardly breathing.

Suddenly, from above, they heard shouts and calls and screams at a distance. And then the noise was in their house. Boots pounding on the floor, and everything breaking and crashing overhead. The smell of smoke and the shouts of a dozen men.

The terror went on for an hour, and then the sound of horses' hooves faded into the distance. They waited another hour to make

---

4. **Kishinev** (kish' ə nev')
5. **Czar Alexander the Second:** 1818–81; czar of Russia 1855–81.
6. **Alexander the Third:** 1845–94; czar of Russia 1881–94.
7. **Cossacks:** troops on horseback that served the Russian czars.

sure, and then the father went up out of the cellar and the rest of the family followed. The door to the house had been torn from its hinges, and every piece of furniture was broken. Every window, every dish, every stitch of clothing was totally destroyed, and one wall had been completely bashed in. And on the floor was the goat, lying quietly. Aaron's grandmother, who was just a little girl of eight at the time, had wept over the goat all day and all night and could not be <u>consoled</u>.

But they had been lucky. For other houses had been burned to the ground. And everywhere, not goats alone, nor sheep, but men and women and children lay quietly on the ground. The word for this sort of massacre, Aaron had learned, was *pogrom*.[8] It had been a pogrom. And the men on the horses were Cossacks. Hated word. Cossacks.

review | **What had happened to Aaron's grandmother?**

And so Pidge would replace that goat of long ago. A pigeon on Second Avenue, where no one needed trapdoors or secret escape passages or woodpiles to hide under. A pigeon for his grandmother's sixtieth birthday. *Oh wing, heal quickly so my grandmother can send you flying to everywhere she wants!*

But a few days later, Aaron met Carl in the street again. And Carl told Aaron that there was going to be a meeting that afternoon in which a map was going to be drawn up to show where a secret treasure lay buried on the empty lot. "Bring the pigeon and you can come into the shack. We got a badge for you. A new kinda membership badge with a secret code on the back."

Aaron ran home, his heart pounding almost as fast as the pigeon's. He took Pidge in his hands and carried him out the door while his mother was busy in the kitchen making stuffed cabbage, his father's favorite dish. And by the time he reached the street, Aaron had decided to take the bandages off. Pidge would look like a real pigeon again, and none of the older boys would laugh or call him a bundle of rags.

Gently, gently he removed the bandages and the splints and put them in his pocket in case he should need them again. But Pidge seemed to hold his wing properly in place.

When he reached the empty lot, Aaron walked up to the shack, then hesitated. Four bigger boys were there. After a moment, Carl came out and commanded Aaron to hand Pidge over.

"Be careful," said Aaron. "I just took the bandages off."

"Oh sure, don't worry," said Carl. By now Pidge was used to people holding him, and he remained calm in Carl's hands.

"OK," said Carl. "Give him the badge." And one of the older boys handed Aaron his badge with the code on the back. "Now light the fire," said Carl.

"What . . . what fire?" asked Aaron.

"The fire. You'll see," Carl answered.

"You didn't say nothing about a fire," said Aaron. "You didn't say nothing to—"

---

8. *pogrom* (pō grăm′) a Russian word that refers to organized cruelty toward a large group of people, often Jews.

Words to Know and Use | **console** (kən sōl′) *v.* to cheer up; comfort

FREEFLIGHT 1989
Robert Vickrey
Courtesy, Kennedy Galleries,
New York.

"Hey!" said Carl. "I'm the leader here. And you don't talk unless I tell you that you have p'mission. Light the fire, Al."

The boy named Al went out to the side of the shack, where some wood and cardboard and old newspapers had been piled into a huge mound. He struck a match and held it to the newspapers.

"OK," said Carl. "Let's get 'er good and hot. Blow on it. Everybody blow."

Aaron's eyes stung from the smoke, but he blew alongside the others, going from side to side as the smoke shifted toward them and away.

"Let's fan it," said Al.

In a few minutes, the fire was crackling and glowing with a bright yellow-orange flame.

"Get me the rope," said Carl.

One of the boys brought Carl some cord and Carl, without a word, wound it twice around the pigeon, so that its wings were tight against its body.

"What . . . what are you doing!" shouted Aaron. "You're hurting his wing!"

"Don't worry about his wing," said Carl. "We're gonna throw him into the fire. And when we do, we're gonna swear an oath of loyalty to—"

"No! No!" shouted Aaron, moving toward Carl.

"Grab him!" called Carl. "Don't let him get the pigeon!"

But Aaron had leaped right across the fire at Carl, taking him completely by surprise. He threw Carl back against the shack and hit out at his face with both fists. Carl slid down to the ground, and the pigeon rolled out of his hands. Aaron scooped up the pigeon and ran, pretending he was on roller skates so that he would go faster and faster. And as he ran across the lot he pulled the cord off Pidge and tried to find a place, any place, to hide him. But the boys were on top of him, and the pigeon slipped from Aaron's hands.

"Get him!" shouted Carl.

Aaron thought of the worst, the most horrible thing he could shout at the boys. "Cossacks!" he screamed. "You're all Cossacks!"

Two boys held Aaron back while the others tried to catch the pigeon. Pidge fluttered along the ground just out of reach, skittering one way and then the other. Then the boys came at him from two directions. But suddenly Pidge beat his wings in rhythm, and rose up, up, over the roof of the nearest <u>tenement</u>, up over Second Avenue toward the park.

With the pigeon gone, the boys turned toward Aaron and tackled him to the ground and punched him and tore his clothes and punched him some more. Aaron twisted and turned and kicked and punched back, shouting "Cossacks! Cossacks!" And somehow the word gave him the strength to tear away from them.

When Aaron reached home, he tried to go past the kitchen quickly so his mother wouldn't see his bloody face and torn clothing. But it was no use; his father was home from work early that night and was seated in the living room. In a moment Aaron was surrounded by his mother, father, and grandmother, and in another moment he had told them everything that had happened, the words tumbling out between his broken sobs. Told them of the present he had planned, of the pigeon for a goat, of the gang, of the badge with the secret code on the back, of the shack, and the fire, and the pigeon's flight over the tenement roof.

And Aaron's grandmother kissed him and thanked him for his present, which was even better than the pigeon.

"What present?" asked Aaron, trying to stop the series of sobs.

And his grandmother opened her pocketbook and handed Aaron her mirror and asked him to look. But all Aaron saw was his dirty, bruised face and his torn shirt.

Aaron thought he understood, and then, again, he thought he didn't. How could she be so happy when there really was no present? And why pretend that there was?

Later that night, just before he fell asleep, Aaron tried to imagine what his grandmother might have done with the pigeon. She would have fed it, and she certainly would have talked to it, as she did to all the birds, and . . . and then she would have let it go free. Yes, of course. Pidge's flight to freedom must have been the gift that had made his grandmother so happy. Her goat has escaped from the Cossacks at last, Aaron thought, half dreaming. And he fell asleep with a smile. ❧

Words to Know and Use | **tenement** (ten′ ə mənt) *n.* an apartment building in a run-down, crowded city area

INSIGHT

Street Corner Flight

NORMA LANDA FLORES

From this side . . .
    of their concrete barrio[1]
        two small boys hold
            fat white pigeons
trapped in their trembling hands.

Then,
    gently,
        not disturbing
            their powers of flight,
                release them
into the air.

They were free
    to glide above
        rushing traffic,
            soar beyond
            labyrinths[2] of
food stamps . . . loneliness . . . and want.

They were free
    to fly
        toward the other side . . .
a world away.

---

1. barrio (bär′ ē ō): a city neighborhood where many
Spanish-speaking people live.
2. labyrinths (lab′ ə rinths′): mazes.

*R*esponding to Reading

First Impressions

1. Draw a picture of the one scene, object, or character that stands out most from your reading of the story.

Second Thoughts

2. From your point of view, what kind of person is Aaron? Describe his **character** and values.

   Think about
   - his feelings about the gang
   - his behavior toward Pidge
   - his relationship with his family and his friend Noreen

3. What do you think is Aaron's gift to his grandmother?

4. Compare Aaron's gift with the gift you wrote about in Examine What You Know on page 73. How is Aaron's gift similar to or different from the gift you wrote about?

Broader Connections

5. Aaron wants to belong to a club that his mother calls a gang. What is the difference between a club and a gang? How is the gang in the story similar to and different from gangs today?

*L*iterary Concept: Theme

A **theme** is an author's message about life or people An author rarely states the theme directly. Instead, the reader must infer, or figure out, the theme after carefully reading the selection. For example, one theme of the story "Eleven," by Sandra Cisneros, could be explained this way: People sometimes feel like little children, even when they get older. What do you think the theme is in "Aaron's Gift"? What is this story's message about life or people?

Concept Review: Plot As you may recall, **plot** is the sequence of events in a story. In several brief sentences or a simple outline, summarize the plot of "Aaron's Gift."

Writing Options

1. Write a **prediction** of how Aaron's life might be affected by the events in the story. You may choose to focus on short-term effects, such as whether Aaron will have further problems with the gang, or on long-term effects, such as the kind of person Aaron will become as an adult.

2. Imagine Aaron has to decide what to give his grandmother for her next birthday. Write an **explanation** of what he might choose and why.

3. "Aaron's Gift" is told from a third-person point of view. Pretend you are Aaron's grandmother, and write a **diary entry** for the day Pidge flies away, using a first-person point of view. Describe how you feel about your grandson's actions and what Pidge's freedom means to you.

4. Imagine that you observed the events that take place during the climax of the story. Write an **eye-witness account** for a newspaper.

Vocabulary Practice

Exercise   On your paper, write the word from the list that best completes each sentence below.

1. Pidge began to __?__ his wings in an attempt to fly, but all he could do was flutter on the ground.

2. Noreen Callahan helped Aaron take off his skates on the __?__ in front of their apartment building.

3. Aaron's family lived in an apartment building, or __?__.

4. Angered by the thought of the Cossacks, Aaron defended himself in a __?__ manner against the boys.

5. Aaron's grandmother was able to __?__ him by telling him that helping Pidge escape was more important than giving Pidge to her.

> *Words to Know and Use*
>
> ---
>
> **console**
> **frenzied**
> **stoop**
> **tenement**
> **thrash**

Options for Learning

1 • Oral History Aaron's grandmother tells him stories, or an oral history, of her past. Ask an older relative or a family friend to share an important story from his or her past. Tape-record this oral history. Also, gather some information about the storyteller, such as name, age, and birthplace. Ask the person you interview why he or she remembers this particular story, and what lesson the story teaches. Share highlights of your recording and your observations with the class.

2 • Comic Book Illustrate four scenes from the story in comic-book style. Draw each scene in a square border, and use actual quotations from the story for the characters' words. Include as many visual details from the story as you can.

3 • Pigeons—Pets or Pests? With a group of classmates, research the subject of pigeons. Discover how many kinds there are, where they live, what their habits are, and what their place in the environment is. Stage a debate for the class on whether or not the number of pigeons should be controlled in some manner. Discuss both the value of pigeons and the problems they cause.

4 • Friends of Animals Find information on careers involving animals and prepare a chart and an oral report on this subject. Consult library sources such as *The Dictionary of Occupational Titles.*

FACT FINDER GEOGRAPHY
What is the capital of Ukraine?

Myron Levoy

Myron Levoy was born in New York City and worked as a chemical engineer before becoming a professional writer. He writes poetry, plays, and short stories. In describing his work, he says, "My continuing concern has been for the 'outsider,' the loner." In *Alan and Naomi*, Levoy writes about a Jewish boy facing anti-Semitism who befriends a deeply troubled refugee girl. In another novel, *A Shadow Like a Leopard*, Levoy depicts a boy from the ghetto who is torn between two worlds—he carries a knife but also writes poetry. Each of these people, says Levoy, must grow and struggle to discover who he or she is.

Levoy has won many national and international awards for his work. His book *A Shadow Like a Leopard* was named one of the best books for young adults by the American Library Association, and his book *The Witch of Fourth Street and Other Stories* (from which this story is taken) was named a *Book World* honor book.

Nonfiction

from *How It Feels When Parents Divorce*

JILL KREMENTZ

Examine What You Know

Divorce is a subject that most people have strong feelings about. Brainstorm some ways in which divorce can affect members of a family. Then list your ideas on a web like the one below. You might include effects on housing, transportation, finances, vacations, holidays, feelings, problems, responsibilities, and any others you think are important.

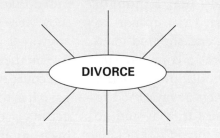

Expand Your Knowledge

In 1989, according to the U.S. Census Bureau, 27 percent of all children were not living in homes with both a mother and a father present. Many of these were children of divorce. Jill Krementz, a well-known photographer and author, decided that the feelings and stories of these children should be told. For her book *How It Feels When Parents Divorce*, Krementz interviewed nineteen young people from different backgrounds about their parents' divorces. The subjects used their real names, agreed to be photographed, and spoke honestly about the divorces. This interview is with fourteen-year-old Meredith, whose parents divorced when she was ten.

Write Before You Read

In your journal, write about a difficult time in your life, such as a divorce in the family, or your observations about someone else's difficult experience. What were some of the things that helped you or the person you are describing get through the experience?

■ *Author biography in Reader's Handbook*

from *How It Feels When Parents Divorce*

JILL KREMENTZ

I was nine when my parents separated, and it was a total shock to me. In fact, when my father and older sister told me, I thought they were joking. I ran upstairs to ask my mother, and she told me it was true. The reason it was a complete surprise is because my parents never really argued, or if they did, they always tried to hide it from us. Sometimes they would go into the kitchen and close the door. Looking back, I suppose I knew there were problems, but I never wanted to admit it. If once in a while I actually heard them arguing, I'd say to myself, "Boy, I wonder what would happen if they got separated?" But I would always know that was never going to happen to *my* parents.

I don't remember when my father actually moved out, because sometimes he was there and sometimes he wasn't. It was like he was always moving his things around, and I never really knew if he was in the house or not. One day he would be there and spend the night, and the next day he would be gone. It was very disruptive,[1] and I didn't realize until a few years later that he had moved back with us a few times, hoping to work things out.

They finally got divorced about a year later, when I was ten. My mother wasn't going to tell me, because she was trying to prove that life would be the same as when they were only separated, but I found out, anyway. I was home by myself one day, and my mother's lawyer called to say they'd set the court date. So when Mom came home, I gave her the message and asked if they were getting a divorce, and she said yes. I had been hoping they would get back together, so the news made me sad. Even now I still hope they'll get back together; but I realize it will never happen, and I've learned to live with it.

My two sisters and I live with my mother, and we go on seeing our father often, though not on a regular basis. Even when my parents were still married, we didn't see him that much, because he's a police officer and he worked nights a lot. I would get up in the morning and kiss him goodbye while he was still asleep. Then I'd go to school. By the time I came home, he'd be gone to work, and when he came home, I'd be

---

1. disruptive: upsetting to the normal routine

asleep. So the divorce didn't really affect my life in terms of not seeing my Dad. But it really affected me emotionally. I just felt bad all the time. I used to cry a lot, and when I wasn't crying, I would feel like crying. Even some of my teachers noticed I was depressed—it was just a terrible time in my life. My older sister seemed to deal with it better than I did, and my younger sister didn't deal with it at all—until just last year, when she started getting stomachaches all the time. Even though my sisters and I didn't talk much about our feelings, I know I would have felt more alone and lonely if I was an only child. In the beginning we all comforted each other. But the only thing that really helped me was time.

The divorce has brought me much closer to my mother because when I was going through the worst of it—all those times when I was crying—I talked to her a lot. My relationship with my parents has changed because now my mother does all the disciplining and sometimes she resents it—especially when we tell her how much fun we have with Dad. It's as if it's all fun and games with him because we're with him so little that there's not much we can do in those few hours to get ourselves in trouble.

I would like to see my father more than I do. In the beginning he saw me a lot, but now there are weeks when I don't see him at all or even talk to him. I think that when parents do get divorced, whichever parent doesn't get custody should try to see his or her kids as much as possible. And I think that when people get divorced, they shouldn't say bad things about each other to their kids. For example, my mother will say something like "Well, you'd better call your father this week and remind him to pick you up," as if he would forget if we didn't remind him. Those are the kind of remarks I resent. My father does it too, and I wish they both would stop.

I know that I'll get married someday. But I also know that I can't say for sure that I'm never going to get divorced. That's because my mother used to tell me that when she got married, she thought that *she* wasn't going to get divorced. All I know for sure is that I'm going to try my best. Growing up with divorced parents might make me think twice. I mean, if somebody proposed to me, I might wait until I was older so I could feel more sure that the marriage would work. My parents were only twenty, and maybe things would have worked out better if they had waited a few more years. ❧

Left, Meredith with her mother and sisters; *right,* Meredith with her father.

Responding to Reading

First Impressions

1. What is your reaction to this selection? Share your thoughts with your classmates.

Second Thoughts

2. What can you infer about Meredith from the interview?

   Think about
   - her statements and feelings
   - her relationships with her parents and with her sisters
   - the photographs of Meredith and her family

3. Describe the ways in which Meredith's relationship with her parents changed. Why do you think those changes occurred?

4. Why do you think Meredith's **point of view** was different from her sisters' points of view?

Broader Connections

5. Meredith thinks that getting married too young may cause problems later on in a marriage. How old do you think people should be before they get married? Why?

Writing Options

1. Write a **letter** with suggestions that Meredith might make to help other children cope with divorce.

2. Meredith says that the only thing that helped her was time. Similarly, Rachel in "Eleven" hopes that time will help her forget and describes wanting her experience to be "far away like a runaway balloon." Describe an **incident** from your own experience or other stories you have read in which time helped heal a wound.

3. Imagine that you have been asked to do a follow-up interview with Meredith when she is twenty-five years old. Write an imaginary **interview,** including the questions you would ask her and her answers. What is she like? Is she married?

Elements of
POETRY

Poetry is the most compact form of literature. A poem packs all kinds of ideas, feelings, and sounds into a few carefully chosen words. The look, sound, and language of poetry all work together to create a total effect.

Understanding Poetry

Form The way a poem looks—or its arrangement on the page—is **form.** Poetry is written in **lines,** which may or may not be sentences. Sometimes the lines are separated into groups called **stanzas.** Remember that poets choose the arrangements of words and lines deliberately. The form of a poem can add to its meaning.

Sound Poems are meant to be read aloud. Therefore, poets choose and arrange words to create the sounds they want the listener to hear. There are many techniques that poets can use to achieve different sounds. Three of these are described below.

• **Rhyme** When words end with the same sounds, the words rhyme. Poems often contain rhyming words at the ends of the lines. Read these lines from "Life Doesn't Frighten Me" on page 360:

> Shadows on the wall
> Noises down the hall
> Life doesn't frighten me at all

• **Rhythm** The rhythm is sometimes called the "beat" of the poem. It is the pattern of stressed (´) and unstressed (˘) syllables, or those word parts that are read with more and less emphasis, in a line of poetry. Listen for the rhythm in these lines from "The Walrus and the Carpenter" on page 92.

> ˘ ´ ˘ ´ ˘ ´ ˘ ´
> The sea was wet as wet could be
>
> ˘ ´ ˘ ´ ˘ ´
> The sands were dry as dry.

Poems that do not have a regular rhythm and sound more like conversation are called **free verse.** "Petals" on page 403 is written in free verse.

• **Repetition** Poets often choose to repeat sounds, words, phrases, or whole lines in a poem. Repetition helps the poet emphasize an idea or create a certain feeling.

Imagery Imagery involves words and phrases that appeal to the five senses. Poets use imagery to create a picture in the reader's mind, or to remind the reader of a familiar sensation. An example of imagery is contained in the opening lines of the poem "Street Corner Flight" on page 81:

> From this side . . .
> of their concrete barrio
> two small boys hold
> fat white pigeons
> trapped in their trembling hands.

Figurative Language Poets use figurative language when they choose words and phrases that help the reader to see ordinary things in new ways. These special descriptions are called **figures of speech.** Three figures of speech are explained on the next page.

- **Simile**   A comparison that uses the words *like, as, than,* or *resembles* is called a simile. This simile from "Mama Is a Sunrise" on page 449 compares Mama's warmth to the comfort of a breakfast of grits and gravy.

> When she comes sweet-talking
>   in the room,
> she warms us
> like grits and gravy,
> and we rise up shining.

- **Metaphor**   A comparison that does *not* use the words *like, as, than,* or *resembles* is called a metaphor. The title "Mama Is a Sunrise" is a metaphor. The poem compares Mama's warmth and sparkle to a sunrise.

- **Personification**   When a poet describes an animal or object as if it were human or had human qualities, he or she is using personification. In "Southbound on the Freeway" on page 164, cars are described from the perspective of a being from outer space who thinks cars are live creatures:

> They have four eyes.
> The two in back are red.

Theme   All the poetic elements you have read about help the poet establish the theme. Just as in fiction, the message about life that the poem conveys is the poem's theme.

*S*trategies for Reading Poetry

1. **Preview the poem.** Notice the poem's form: its shape, its length, the length of the lines, and whether or not it has stanzas.

2. **Read the poem aloud.** Pause at the ends of complete thoughts, not necessarily at the ends of lines. Look for end punctuation to help you find the end of a complete thought. As you read, see if there is rhyme and listen for rhythm as well as the overall sound of the words in the poem.

3. **Visualize the images.** In your mind's eye, picture the images and comparisons the poem makes. Do the images remind you of feelings or experiences you have had?

4. **Think about the words and phrases.** Allow yourself to wonder about any phrases or words that seem to stand out. Think about what that choice of words adds to the poem.

5. **Try to figure out the theme.** Ask yourself, What's the point of the poem? What message is the poet trying to send or help you create?

6. **Let your understanding grow.** When you finish reading, you are left with first impressions of the poem. Over time, you will add to your understanding based on the poem, your discussions in class, and other poetry you read.

7. **Allow yourself to enjoy poetry.** You may connect with a particular poem because it expresses feelings that you have felt or shows you the world through different eyes.

Poetry

The Walrus and the Carpenter

LEWIS CARROLL

Examine What You Know

Have you ever been tricked into doing something? How were you tricked? In your journal, write about this experience. In this poem, watch for who gets tricked and what happens as a result.

Expand Your Knowledge

Lewis Carroll was the author of the famous fantasy *Alice's Adventures in Wonderland* and its sequel *Through the Looking Glass.* "The Walrus and the Carpenter" is from *Through the Looking Glass,* a book in which everything seems backwards or absurd. For example, Alice must walk away from a place in order to reach it and must run fast in order to remain where she is.

Carroll enjoyed tricks and puns and nonsense. He wrote the Alice tales to amuse a ten-year-old friend named Alice Liddell. In Carroll's day, English schoolchildren, such as Alice, were often made to memorize long, boring poems that taught lessons. Carroll made fun of this by writing poems such as "The Walrus and the Carpenter."

Enrich Your Reading

Reading Narrative Poetry   Narrative poetry is poetry that tells a story, even if it is the story of a trick that could never happen. Like a story, a narrative poem contains the elements of fiction, such as character, setting, plot, and dialogue. It also contains many of the elements of poetry described on pages 89–90. "The Walrus and the Carpenter" is a narrative poem. Read the poem as you would a story, stopping not at the end of each line, but at the punctuation that shows the end of each sentence.

■ *Author biography on Extend page*

The *Walrus and the Carpenter*

LEWIS CARROLL

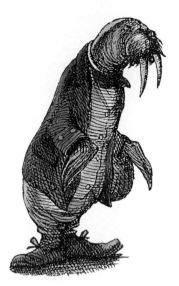

The sun was shining on the sea,
    Shining with all his might:
He did his very best to make
    The billows[1] smooth and bright—
5 And this was odd, because it was
    The middle of the night.

The moon was shining sulkily,[2]
    Because she thought the sun
Had got no business to be there
10   After the day was done—
"It's very rude of him," she said,
    "To come and spoil the fun!"

The sea was wet as wet could be,
    The sands were dry as dry.
15 You could not see a cloud, because
    No cloud was in the sky:
No birds were flying overhead—
    There were no birds to fly.

---

1. billows: large waves.
2. sulkily: in a moody, pouting way.

The Walrus and the Carpenter
20   Were walking close at hand;
They wept like anything to see
    Such quantities of sand:
"If this were only cleared away,"
    They said, "it *would* be grand!"

25   "If seven maids with seven mops
    Swept it for half a year,
Do you suppose," the Walrus said,
    "That they could get it clear?"
"I doubt it," said the Carpenter,
30   And shed a bitter tear.

"O Oysters, come and walk with us!"
    The Walrus did beseech.[3]
"A pleasant walk, a pleasant talk,
    Along the briny[4] beach:
35   We cannot do with more than four,
    To give a hand to each."

The eldest Oyster looked at him
    But never a word he said:
The eldest Oyster winked his eye,
40   And shook his heavy head—
Meaning to say he did not choose
    To leave the oyster-bed.

But four young Oysters hurried up,
    All eager for the treat:
45   Their coats were brushed, their faces washed,
    Their shoes were clean and neat—
And this was odd, because, you know,
    They hadn't any feet.

---

3. **beseech:** ask earnestly; beg.
4. **briny:** very salty.

Four other Oysters followed them,
50   And yet another four:
And thick and fast they came at last,
        And more, and more, and more—
All hopping through the frothy waves,
        And scrambling to the shore.

55 The Walrus and the Carpenter
        Walked on a mile or so,
And then they rested on a rock
        Conveniently low:
And all the little Oysters stood
60   And waited in a row.

"The time has come," the Walrus said,
        "To talk of many things:
Of shoes—and ships—and sealing-wax—
        Of cabbages—and kings—
65 And why the sea is boiling hot—
        And whether pigs have wings."

"But wait a bit," the Oysters cried,
        "Before we have our chat;
For some of us are out of breath,
70   And all of us are fat!"
"No hurry!" said the Carpenter.
        They thanked him much for that.

"A loaf of bread," the Walrus said,
        "Is what we chiefly need:
75 Pepper and vinegar besides
        Are very good indeed—
Now, if you're ready, Oysters dear,
        We can begin to feed."

"But not on us!" the Oysters cried,
80   Turning a little blue.
"After such kindness, that would be
        A dismal⁵ thing to do!"
"The night is fine," the Walrus said.
        "Do you admire the view?"

---

5. dismal: dreadful; terrible.

85   "It was so kind of you to come!
      And you arc very nice!"
  The Carpenter said nothing but
      "Cut us another slice.
  I wish you were not quite so deaf—
90   I've had to ask you twice!"

  "It seems a shame," the Walrus said,
      "To play them such a trick,
  After we've brought them out so far,
      And made them trot so quick!"
95   The Carpenter said nothing but
      "The butter's spread too thick!"

  "I weep for you," the Walrus said:
      "I deeply sympathize."
  With sobs and tears he sorted out
100   Those of the largest size,
  Holding his pocket-handkerchief
      Before his streaming eyes.

  "O Oysters," said the Carpenter,
      "You've had a pleasant run!
105 Shall we be trotting home again?"
      But answer came there none—
  And this was scarcely odd, because
      They'd eaten every one.

E X P L A I N

Responding to Reading

First Impressions

1. What was your reaction to this poem?

Second Thoughts

2. Many people think this is a humorous and playful poem. Do you agree?

   Think about
   - the description of the **setting** and the **characters**
   - the choice of words, the images, and the actions

3. The eldest Oyster refuses the Walrus's invitation, but the younger Oysters accept. What do you think this says about Carroll's attitude toward old age and youth? Do you agree with his **point of view?**

Literary Concepts: Rhyme and Rhythm

Rhyme occurs when the same sound is repeated at the ends of words. Read the rhyming lines below from Henry Wadsworth Longfellow's poem "Paul Revere's Ride."

> Listen, my children, and you shall *hear*
> Of the midnight ride of Paul Re*vere*,

Rhythm is the pattern of strong beats you hear when you read a poem aloud. Some poems have an even, regular beat that gives the poem a musical sound. In other poems, rhythm sounds more like normal conversation. How do the rhyme and rhythm in "The Walrus and the Carpenter" add to your enjoyment of the poem?

Writing Options

1. How might the ghosts of the Oysters seek revenge for the trick that was played on them? Change the **ending** by adding one or more stanzas to the poem.

2. Make a **sensory image chart** with the five senses as headings. Under each heading, list appropriate images from the poem (for instance, "The sun was shining" can be listed under "Sight"). Which of the senses is not referred to in the poem?

Options for Learning

1 • Seaside Scene With a small group of classmates, create a diorama based on this poem. (A diorama is a miniature three-dimensional scene.) Use materials such as sand, shells, blue paper, and glass to represent the seashore, and pictures or models of a walrus and a carpenter, the oysters, and anything else from the poem that you would like to depict. Choose a line or two from the poem to serve as a title for the diorama.

2 • Oral Reading In a group, prepare an oral reading of this poem. Decide on the proper tone of voice for the narrator and for each of the characters. Emphasize the rhyme and rhythm of the poem and observe all punctuation marks.

3 • Illustrator Wanted Lewis Carroll chose Sir John Tenniel, one of the most famous illustrators of the last century, to draw the pictures for his books. The illustrations on pages 92, 93, and 95 were done by Tenniel. Imagine that you have been asked to illustrate a new edition of "The Walrus and the Carpenter." Draw or paint a scene from the poem in a modern style. Think about how to make your drawing reveal the setting, the traits of the characters, and the humor of the poem.

FACT FINDER SCIENCE

To what major division of the animal kingdom do oysters belong?

Lewis Carroll
1832-1898

"Lewis Carroll" was the pen name of Charles Lutwidge Dodgson, an English mathematician. The eldest son in a family of thirteen, Dodgson was a creative child who made pets of snails and worms and invented games for his brothers and sisters. Although brilliant, Carroll was shy and stammered in the company of adults. In the presence of children, however, he became a witty, affectionate storyteller.

Carroll would send children letters barely the size of a postage stamp or ones written in reverse to be read with a mirror. He might begin a letter with "CLD (his initials), Uncle loving your," and end it with "Nelly dear my." In one of his letters he wrote what some say is the core of his belief: "One of the deep secrets of Life . . . is that all that is really worth the doing, is what we do for others."

Some say Carroll never grew up. Perhaps he didn't. Upon his death at the age of sixty-five, the doctor attending him told his sisters, "How wonderfully young your brother looks!"

Poetry  **Fog**

CARL SANDBURG

Three Haiku

ISSA

Examine What You Know

Choose an object in the room and try to observe it as though you were seeing it for the first time. On a piece of paper, write the name of the object and five words that describe what it looks like or how it makes you feel.

Expand Your Knowledge

"Fog" by Carl Sandburg shows the reader a single image and uses very few words to describe that image. The other three poems are written in a form called **haiku.** This form, developed over many centuries in Japan, is made up of three lines and usually contains only seventeen syllables. Traditional haiku has five syllables in the first line, seven in the second, and five in the third. In haiku, the poet describes a single small moment, feeling, or thing. With only a few carefully chosen words, the poet captures that moment or image for the reader.

Enrich Your Reading

■ *Author biographies on Extend page*

Word Choice   Word choice is the writer's selection of the best words for expressing thoughts, feelings, and images. Word choice is especially important to poets because they use so few words. Each word counts, and each word changes the meaning and feeling of a poem. As you read these poems, try to visualize, or form a mental picture of, the image in the poem. Reread each poem a few times to experience the feeling or emotion created by the image.

Fog

CARL SANDBURG

The fog comes
on little cat feet.

It sits looking
over harbor and city
on silent haunches[1]
and then moves on.

5

---

1. haunches: the upper parts
of the legs and buttocks on
which an animal sits.

© Ron Watts / Westlight.

---

*R*esponding to Reading

First Impressions of "Fog"

1. How did the poet's description of fog make you feel?

Second Thoughts on "Fog"

2. Do you think the poet's comparison of the fog to a cat is a good one? Why or why not?

Think about
- the appearances, sounds, and actions of fog and cats
- the way you feel about these two subjects

Three Haiku

ISSA

Children
Sitting cheerfully
Around the fire—
The only treasure of the house.

The flying butterfly:
I feel myself
A creature of dust.

Even among insects, in this world,
Some are good at singing,
Some bad.

FLOWERS AND INSECTS (detail)   Seventeenth century   Qing dynasty, Kangxi period (1622–1722)   Chai Zhengyi and Chai Jingyi
Handscroll, ink and color on paper   27.9 x 430.6 cm. © 1992 The Art Institute of Chicago, S.M. Nickerson Fund, 1954. 104, view #2.

Responding to Reading

First Impressions of the Haiku

1. Which image in these poems did you like the most? Why?

Second Thoughts on the Haiku

2. What do these poems tell you about the poet?

3. Haiku poets often use an image of a simple thing to suggest a **theme,** or truth, about the world. Choose one of the poems and explain the message it conveys to you. Compare your response with your classmates'.

Comparing the Poems

4. Compare and contrast "Fog" with the haiku. How is the language different in the two types of poems? How is it similar?

Literary Concept: Imagery

Imagery refers to the use of words that appeal to the senses of sight, hearing, touch, taste, and smell. Most poetic images appeal to the sense of sight. They help the reader "see" something in his or her mind. For example, the imagery in the first haiku is of children sitting around a fire. What kind of imagery can you find in "Fog"? Use the sensory image chart you began for the writing option on page 96. Add images for the haiku and "Fog."

Writing Options

1. Write a **haiku** about the object you described in Examine What You Know on page 98. Refer to the Expand Your Knowledge section on the same page for specific information on haiku.

2. You have read three different types of poems in this subunit: narrative, the unrhymed modern poem "Fog," and haiku. Write a brief **essay,** explaining which type you prefer and why. (Remember that your ideas may change later.)

*O*ptions for Learning

1 • **Illustrate** How do you visualize Sandburg's fog or the haiku images? Draw or paint a picture to illustrate one of the poems.

2 • **Fog** Write a scientific description or explanation of fog that could be used as part of a science report on weather. Include illustrations.

*C*arl Sandburg 1878-1967

Carl Sandburg, a son of Swedish immigrants, grew up in Galesburg, Illinois. Before settling into a career as a writer, Sandburg held many different jobs. He delivered milk, sold newspapers, and worked as a fireman and as a truck driver.

At the age of thirty-four he began working as a reporter, first in Milwaukee and later in Chicago. He was considered a top-notch reporter, but it was his poetry and historical works that brought him fame. In fact, Sandburg's biography of Abraham Lincoln is considered a classic. He won two Pulitzer Prizes—for history in 1940 and for poetry in 1951.

Sandburg wrote about the hopes and sufferings of the common people he knew well. With his guitar in hand, Sandburg frequently gave performances of folk songs and read his poetry to audiences across the United States.

*I*ssa 1763-1827

Yataro Kobayashi, who took the pen name Issa (meaning "cup of tea"), was one of the greatest haiku poets of Japan. Unfortunately, Issa's life was full of poverty, illness, and tragedy. His mother died when he was three. His father remarried when he was eight, and his stepmother was so unkind to him that he left home for Edo (now Tokyo) at the age of thirteen to find work. There he studied haiku and decided to live as a poet. In 1814 he married a woman named Kiku and they had five children, all of whom died as infants. Kiku herself died in 1823.

The poverty and traumas of Issa's life helped him understand the struggles of the weak and led him to feel tenderness and compassion toward all things. Even the smallest insect was important to Issa. He remains Japan's most deeply loved poet.

WRITER'S WORKSHOP

PERSONAL WRITING

Listen to these opinions: "I wish I was anything but eleven," says the narrator in the short story "Eleven." "I think that when people get divorced they shouldn't say bad things about each other to their kids," says Meredith, in the excerpt from *How It Feels When Parents Divorce.* Each girl speaks in a clear, strong voice. Each has her own special viewpoint.

You too have your own voice and point of view. Through personal writing you can tell others how you think and feel. In this workshop you will write about something very personal—your tastes in reading. What books or magazines excite you? What kind of reading makes you yawn? Now is your chance to think and write about the kinds of reading you like and dislike.

USE PERSONAL
WRITING FOR

journals
logs
notes
letters
diaries
autobiographies

GUIDED ASSIGNMENT: REFLECTIONS ON READING

Write an informal essay about your reading tastes. Describe what you like and don't like to read and explain your reasons.

Here is one writer's PASSkey to this assignment.

PURPOSE: To describe my reading tastes

AUDIENCE: My teacher and classmates

SUBJECT: My reading tastes

STRUCTURE: An informal essay

STUDENT MODEL

◄ Before you write, read how one student responded to the assignment.

◄ A comparison conveys the writer's excitement about sci-fi.

```
          Reading That's Out of This World

                  by Curtis Baker

    Reading science fiction is the best--it's
like steering a spaceship through the stars.
From the time I began to read, I was
interested in any book that had a spaceship on
the cover. Space Ship Under the Apple Tree was
one of the first science fiction books I
remember reading, but soon afterward I
```

discovered <u>Matthew Looney and the Space Pirates</u> and <u>Matthew Looney's Voyage to Earth,</u> and I've probably read all of the Norby books that Isaac Asimov ever wrote.

Last year my friend Kevin lent me <u>Enterprise: The First Adventure</u>, and by now I've read five <u>Star Trek</u> books. Some people like to read about new characters in every book, but I'd rather see the same characters in different adventures. I feel like I really know these guys, and I want to find out what happens to them next.

In June, Dad took me to a <u>Star Trek</u> convention. He and I were surrounded by six hundred people talking about time warps, starships, and interstellar travel. It was great, and I found out that science fiction is definitely not just for kids.

I also like reading about science, especially space travel. <u>Odyssey</u> magazine has good articles about the space shuttle. One writer described what a mission to Mars might be like. The writing was very realistic, and it made me wish I could travel to Mars someday.

If I visit Mars, though, I won't bring any animal stories. I'm not sure why I don't like stories about dogs or cats or horses because I really like animals, but these stories bore me. They just don't seem very exciting. Give me science fiction any day. That's what I'll be reading on Mars.

▶ Notice that the writer explains why he likes the writing in the *Star Trek* series.

▶ Curtis describes an experience that sparked even more enthusiasm for science fiction.

▶ Curtis states a second preference and gives a reason.

▶ Notice how the writer ends by contrasting what he doesn't like with what he likes.

WRITER'S CHOICE

If the books in your room don't give you a clue, think about what part of the library interests you most. Do you head for the bookshelves that hold novels? the racks of paperback mysteries? the magazines about cars or computers?

Prewrite and Explore

1 Target your tastes Think about what you like—and don't like—to read. Do you enjoy mysteries, biographies, fantasy stories, westerns, humor, magazine articles about movie stars? What school reading assignments have excited or bored you? You might want to fill in word webs like the ones on the next page.

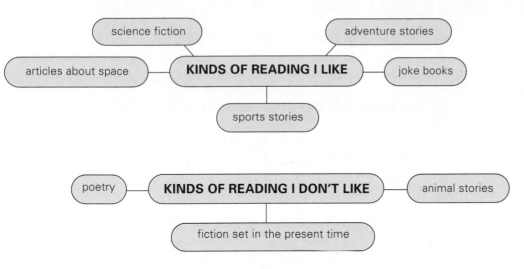

THE LITERATURE
CONNECTION
. . . .
Glance over the
selections in this
subunit or unit. Which
selections did you like?
Which did you dislike?
Your feelings about
these selections might
help you understand
your reading tastes.
You could use poems
or stories from this
subunit as examples
in your essay.

2 **Give your reasons**   Think of possible reasons for your likes and dislikes. Did your love of horses get you interested in animal stories? Did visiting Washington, D.C., with your family get you interested in history? Did a friend's reading interest rub off on you? Telling how you got interested in a particular type of reading will make your essay more interesting.

GATHERING INFORMATION

Examine your word webs and choose the types of reading you feel strongest about. List these in a column as shown below. In a second column list the reasons why you like or dislike a particular kind of writing. Look at Curtis's notes below.

My Likes/Dislikes	Reasons
Science fiction	exciting like the characters learn about future inventions
Sports stories	action-packed real people and events
Animal stories	boring not enough action

◀ STUDENT MODEL
. . . .

Draft and Discover

1 Shape your draft Begin writing about your ideas. To help you get organized, use your prewriting notes as a guide. Each opinion—and your reasons for it—could become a separate paragraph.

2 Give your opinions zing As you put your opinions on paper, use vivid words and images to make your writing sparkle. The narrator in "Eleven" doesn't simply say, "The sweater is ugly." Instead, she uses description to show how much she *loathes* the sweater.

LITERARY MODEL
from "Eleven" by
Sandra Cisneros

▶ It's an ugly sweater with red plastic buttons and a collar and sleeves all stretched out like you could use it for a jump rope. It's maybe a thousand years old, and even if it belonged to me, I wouldn't say so.

Revise Your Writing

1 Include examples As you read your draft, make sure you have supported your opinions with examples. Did you give specific details about what you like to read? Now is the time to add examples of books, magazines, articles, and stories that reflect your tastes. These examples will make your essay clearer and more interesting.

Before I also like reading about science.

After I also like reading about science, especially space travel. <u>Odyssey</u> magazine has good articles about the space shuttle.

2 Use a peer reader Review your draft. Then ask a peer reader to read it and respond. Use the following questions.

COMPUTER TIP
Describe your reading likes and dislikes in separate paragraphs. Reverse your paragraphs to see if your essay sounds better if you start with what you don't like and build up to what you like.

Revision Questions	
For You	**For a Peer Reader**
1. Do I explain why I like and don't like certain kinds of writing?	1. What part of this essay did you enjoy most?
2. Have I expressed my point of view in an interesting way?	2. Did I organize my essay clearly enough?
3. Where could I add more examples and details?	3. Can you tell what my main reading likes and dislikes are?

Proofread

Check your work for errors in grammar, spelling, punctuation, and capitalization. Pay special attention to the following point.

◀ NEED MORE HELP? ....

See the Language Workshop that follows (pages 108–110) and Section 5 in the Language Handbook.

THE EDITOR'S EYE: USING PRONOUNS CORRECTLY

Do not confuse subject pronouns with object pronouns when you write.

Subject pronouns (*I, you, he, she, it, we, they*) should be used as the subjects of verbs. Object pronouns (*me, you, him, her, it, us, them*) should be used as the objects of verbs or prepositions.

Incorrect *Him* and *me* were surrounded by six hundred people talking about time warps, starships, and interstellar travel.

Correct *He* and *I* were surrounded by six hundred people talking about time warps, starships, and interstellar travel.

◀ STUDENT MODEL ....

Publish and Present

Compare your views on reading with those expressed in classmates' essays. With other students who share your reading tastes, form a small group to discuss your current reading. You may want to use information from the class's essays to compile a reading list of favorite books.

After you have shared your essay, be sure to put it in your writing portfolio. At the end of the year, you can look back at your essay to see whether your reading tastes have changed and, if they have, in what ways.

Reflect on Your Writing

Write answers to the questions below. Include your answers with your essay when you put it in your writing portfolio.

◀ FOR YOUR PORTFOLIO ....

1. Did you have a hard time deciding what your reading tastes are? Why or why not?
2. What is the strongest part of your essay? Why?

LANGUAGE
· · WORKSHOP · ·

PRONOUN PROBLEMS

> **Personal pronouns** have three forms: subject, object, and possessive.

Personal Pronouns

In your personal essays, as with most writing, you'll use pronouns often. You need to be aware of common pronoun problems. Learning to avoid these problems is like steering a bicycle around potholes. Look at this excerpt from *How It Feels When Parents Divorce.* The narrator manages to steer her way around many possible pronoun problems.

LITERARY MODEL

from *How It Feels When Parents Divorce* by Jill Krementz

> My two sisters and I live with my mother and we go on seeing our father often, though not on a regular basis. Even when my parents were still married we didn't see him that much, because he's a police officer and he worked nights a lot.

Each of the personal pronouns has a subject form, an object form, and a possessive form. The form that a personal pronoun takes depends on how the pronoun is used. Study the following chart.

SPELLING TIP

Notice that possessive pronouns are spelled without apostrophes: *hers, its, ours, yours, theirs.*

Forms of Personal Pronouns

	Subject	Object	Possessive
Singular	I	me	my, mine
	you	you	your, yours
	she, he, it	her, him, it	her, hers, his, its
Plural	we	us	our, ours
	you	you	your, yours
	they	them	their, theirs

Exercise 1   Concept Check   Copy the personal pronouns that you find in each sentence. Above each, write *S, O,* or *P,* for subject form, object form, or possessive form.

1. Rachel didn't feel eleven on her birthday.
2. Parts of her still felt like she was ten.
3. Her birthday started off badly.
4. Her teacher tried to find the owner of an ugly red sweater.
5. "Not mine," said Rachel, when Mrs. Price asked.
6. "I remember you wearing it once," Mrs. Price said.
7. Rachel was upset, but she tried to stay calm.
8. Soon she was crying in front of her whole class.
9. Phyllis suddenly remembered the sweater was hers.
10. It might be too late to have a good day, thinks Rachel.

Using the Subject Form

You use the subject form for a personal pronoun that is the subject of a sentence. You also use the subject form for a **predicate pronoun**—a pronoun that follows a linking verb and renames, or refers to, the subject. Study the following examples.

Subject	**Predicate Pronoun**
He was a hero.	The hero was he.
Maria and I made the calls.	The callers were Maria and I.
Neither she nor I won.	The winners were neither she nor I.

COMMON LINKING VERBS

am	was
are	were
is	will be
seem	become
look	feel
appear	taste
has been	
have been	
had been	

Subject and predicate pronouns can be **compound**. One type of compound pronoun consists of two pronouns joined by *and, or,* or *nor.* Another type consists of a noun and a pronoun. In these cases, choosing the correct pronoun form can be confusing. However, as in the second and third examples above, the subject form is correct.

Using the Object Form

The examples below show the three uses of object pronouns.

Direct Object	Aaron met them.
Indirect Object	He gave them Pidge.
Object of Preposition	The gang ran after him.

You use the object form when the pronoun is a **direct object** or an **indirect object**—when the pronoun receives the action of a verb. You also use the object form when the pronoun is the **object of a preposition**—when it is part of a prepositional phrase.

Problems with object pronouns are most likely to occur when the object pronoun is part of a compound. Just remember—if the pronoun is used as an object, you must use the object form.

Direct Object	Mother called Aaron and <u>her</u>.
Indirect Object	Carl gave <u>him</u> and <u>me</u> the badges.
Object of Preposition	The fire danced between <u>him</u> and <u>them</u>.

Exercise 2   Concept Check   For each sentence, choose the correct subject or object pronoun.

1. Our English teacher taught (we, us) about Carl Sandburg.
2. The reader that she chose was (I, me).
3. (She and I, Her and me) talked about his poetry.
4. Sandburg's biography of Lincoln made (he, him) a success.
5. Sandburg didn't always do what was expected of (he, him).
6. The story of Sandburg's life amazed (Mark and I, Mark and me).
7. It was (he, him) who discovered that Sandburg was a hobo for a time.
8. (He and I, Him and me) checked out a biography of Sandburg.
9. We went to the library to find more information for (he and I, him and me).
10. Just between (you and I, you and me), I enjoy poetry.

Exercise 3   Revision Skill   Rewrite the paragraph below, correcting errors in subject and object pronoun use.

Last summer, Saul, Gabe, and me decided to start a messenger service. Without cars, how would us deliver messages? Gabe had an idea. "I know who our messengers will be," he told Saul and I. Gabe pointed to a flock of pigeons bobbing their heads at he and us. "Us and them will be partners," he said, "but you and me will collect the money." Gabe has good ideas. For now our leader is him.

Exercise 4   Revising Your Writing   Review the personal essay you wrote for the Writer's Workshop on page 103 and lightly underline each personal pronoun you used. Correct any errors in the pronoun forms that you find.

VOCABULARY
WORKSHOP

USING A THESAURUS

When you write, choosing the right words can be like seasoning a pot of soup. You can settle for salt and pepper, or you can add a variety of spices. Writers find that a thesaurus is a helpful reference for adding flavor to their writing. A **thesaurus** is a book of synonyms and antonyms. **Synonyms** are words with similar meanings. **Antonyms** are words with opposite meanings. A thesaurus can help you replace dull, general words with specific, precise words. Read this sentence.

The pigeon *walked* across the sidewalk.

The word *walked* is a very general word that means "to move about on foot." If you wanted to replace *walked* with a more specific verb, the thesaurus would be helpful. Under the word *walk,* for example, you might find *stroll, strut, tramp,* and *trudge.* Though these words are similar, each has a slightly different meaning. The context determines which synonym to use.

If you wanted to find a word that means *not shy* or *not afraid* or *not happy,* you could also use a thesaurus. Antonyms are listed at the end of many entries.

Exercise 1   Look up each italicized word in a thesaurus. Rewrite the sentence, using a suitable synonym.

1. Curtis asked about the *new* notebook computer.
2. He *liked* technology and wanted to stay up-to-date.
3. The salesperson gave *good* answers to his many questions.
4. A *group* of customers gathered to overhear the conversation.
5. "I'll be back next week," Curtis *said* as he left the store.

Exercise 2   Use a thesaurus to find two synonyms for each word below. Write a sentence for each synonym. Underline the synonym.

1. interesting
2. funny
3. awful
4. see
5. laugh

ANOTHER WORD, PLEASE!

Some adjectives get overworked. They need a rest. Whenever possible, replace the following words with more precise synonyms:

good	pretty
wonderful	interesting
bad	big
exciting	nice
fun	small
awful	ugly

Reading on Your Own

Suggested Novels for Unit One

The novels introduced on these pages allow you to explore the unit theme, "With Open Eyes," in more depth and in different ways.

SHILOH

PHYLLIS REYNOLDS NAYLOR ©1991

What would you do if you found a lost dog that you suspected had been mistreated by its owner? What if you discovered the identity of the dog's owner and had proof that the dog had been beaten? Would you return the dog to its owner, or would you try to hide the dog to protect it? This is the problem that eleven-year-old Marty faces in the novel, *Shiloh*. Though Marty is sure that cruelty to animals is wrong, he learns that things are not always as simple as they first appear. As you read this book, think about . . .

- what kind of a person the dog's owner is and what made him that way

- what Marty decides to do about the dog he has found

- how Marty figures out what is right and wrong in a complicated situation

- how you might have responded in a similar situation

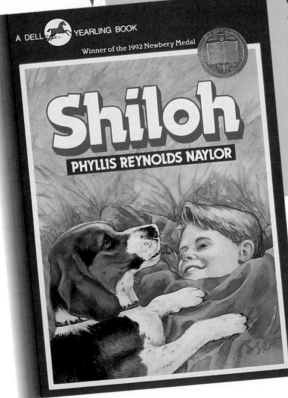

A DELL YEARLING BOOK

Winner of the 1992 Newbery Medal

Shiloh

PHYLLIS REYNOLDS NAYLOR

TUCK EVERLASTING
NATALIE BABBITT ©1975

Imagine that you have been given the chance to live forever. Would you take that chance, or would you choose to live and die with all the other people you know and love? This is the situation that ten-year-old Winnie Foster finds herself in after meeting the Tuck family in *Tuck Everlasting*. As you read the story, think about how you might feel if you were in Winnie's place and how you might respond to these questions.

- What advice would you give Winnie?

- Is eternal life on earth a blessing or a curse?

- Does Winnie make the right decision?

HAWK, I'M YOUR BROTHER
BYRD BAYLOR ©1976

Have you ever had a dream that was so important to you that it influenced your whole life? Rudy Soto, the Native American boy in *Hawk, I'm Your Brother*, dreams of flying through the air like a hawk. He is determined to make his dream a reality. Think about the title of this book. What could the author mean when she infers that Rudy is the brother to a hawk? As you read, think about . . .

- how Rudy and the hawk are similar

- how Rudy and the hawk are brothers

- whether Rudy accomplishes his dream

Other Recommended Books

Dear Mr. Henshaw by Beverly Cleary (©1983). This contemporary novel, written in the form of diary entries, describes a young boy's struggle to cope with and understand his parents' divorce.

A Girl from Yamhill: A Memoir by Beverly Cleary (©1988). This autobiographical account of Cleary's childhood experiences will interest students who want to learn more about one of their favorite authors.

One at a Time by David McCord (©1986). One of the best-known U.S. poets for young people shares his poems and describes how to write various forms of poetry.

Going Home by Nicholasa Mohr (©1986). In this novel, an American girl of Puerto Rican ancestry visits her parents' homeland where she must face and overcome the fact that she is not accepted by some of the Puerto Rican girls.

113

RISING TO THE CHALLENGE

You must do the thing

you think you cannot do.

Eleanor Roosevelt

PROMISES TO KEEP

Promises are easy to make and, like secrets, hard to keep. What kinds of promises have you made recently? You might have promised a parent that you would clean your room when you got home, or you might have promised a friend not to tell his or her secret. You also might have made a promise to yourself to practice for your music lesson, to stop nagging your younger brother, to improve your batting average, or not to bite your nails.

Keeping a promise can be difficult under any circumstances. As you read the following selections, notice what spoken and unspoken promises are made and how they are kept.

Fiction

Nadia the Willful

SUE ALEXANDER

Examine What You Know

Think about the title of this story. What does the title suggest the story will be about? What does it mean to say that someone is willful? Complete a web like the one below.

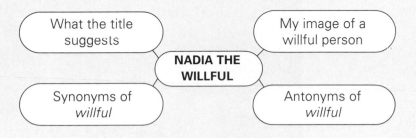

What the title suggests

My image of a willful person

NADIA THE WILLFUL

Synonyms of *willful*

Antonyms of *willful*

Expand Your Knowledge

Nadia the Willful, the main character in this story, is a young Bedouin girl. The Bedouins are Arab people of the Sahara and the desert lands of the Middle East. The leader of a Bedouin tribe or clan is called a sheik. Bedouins live as nomads, or wanderers, searching the desert for oases, places with water and pasture, where they can settle with their goats, sheep, camels, and horses. When an oasis dries up, the group moves on. Life in the desert is harsh and dangerous. Food is scarce, and temperatures can reach 130°F. Blinding sandstorms are common.

Write Before You Read

In your journal or on a sheet of paper, write about a person that you would describe as willful. How does this person speak and act? How does she or he get along with other people? If possible, give examples of words or actions that show this person's willfulness. As you read, compare Nadia with the person you wrote about.

■ *Author biography on Extend page*

Nadia the Willful

SUE ALEXANDER

In the land of the drifting sands where the Bedouins[1] move their tents to follow the fertile grasses, there lived a girl whose stubbornness and flashing temper caused her to be known throughout the desert as Nadia the Willful.

Nadia's father, the sheik[2] Tarik, whose kindness and graciousness caused his name to be praised in every tent, did not know what to do with his willful daughter.

Only Hamed, the eldest of Nadia's six brothers and Tarik's favorite son, could calm Nadia's temper when it flashed. "Oh, angry one," he would say, "shall we see how long you can stay that way?" And he would laugh and tease and pull at her dark hair until she laughed back. Then she would follow Hamed wherever he led.

One day before dawn, Hamed mounted his father's great white stallion and rode to the west to seek new grazing ground for the sheep. Nadia stood with her father at the edge of the oasis and watched him go.

Hamed did not return.

Nadia rode behind her father as he traveled across the desert from oasis to oasis, seeking Hamed.

Shepherds told them of seeing a great white stallion fleeing before the pillars of wind that stirred the sand. And they said that the horse carried no rider.

Passing merchants, their camels laden

A BEDOUIN ARAB   John Singer Sargent   Private collection.

---

1. **Bedouins** (bed′ oo inz′): Arab tribes that wander the deserts of Africa and the Middle East.
2. **sheik** (shāk): the chief of an Arab tribe or family.

with spices and sweets for the <u>bazaar</u>, told of the emptiness of the desert they had crossed.

Tribesmen, strangers, everyone whom Tarik asked, sighed and gazed into the desert, saying, "Such is the will of Allah."[3]

At last Tarik knew in his heart that his favorite son, Hamed, had been claimed, as other Bedouins before him, by the drifting sands. And he told Nadia what he knew—that Hamed was dead.

Nadia screamed and wept and stamped the sand, crying, "Not even Allah will take Hamed from me!" until her father could bear no more and sternly bade her to silence.

Nadia's grief knew no bounds. She walked blindly through the oasis neither seeing nor hearing those who would console her. And Tarik was silent. For days he sat inside his tent, speaking not at all and barely tasting the meals set before him.

"*From this day forward,*" *he said, "let no one utter Hamed's name.*"

Then, on the seventh day, Tarik came out of his tent. He called all his people to him, and when they were assembled, he spoke. "From this day forward," he said, "let no one utter Hamed's name. Punishment shall be swift for those who would remind me of what I have lost."

Hamed's mother wept at the <u>decree</u>. The people of the <u>clan</u> looked at one another uneasily. All could see the hardness that had settled on the sheik's face and the coldness in his eyes, and so they said nothing. But they obeyed.

Nadia, too, did as her father decreed, though each day held something to remind her of Hamed. As she passed her brothers at play, she remembered games Hamed had taught her. As she walked by the women weaving patches for the tents and heard them talking and laughing, she remembered tales Hamed had told her and how they had made her laugh. And as she watched the shepherds with their flock, she remembered the little black lamb Hamed had loved.

Each memory brought Hamed's name to Nadia's lips, but she stilled the sound. And each time that she did so, her unhappiness grew until, finally, she could no longer contain it. She wept and raged at anyone and anything that crossed her path. Soon everyone at the oasis fled at her approach. And she was more lonely than she had ever been before.

One day, as Nadia passed the place where her brothers were playing, she stopped to watch them. They were playing one of the games that Hamed had taught her. But they were playing it wrong.

Without thinking, Nadia called out to them. "That is not the way! Hamed said that first you jump this way and then you jump back!"

---

3. **Allah** (al′ ə): the name for God in the Islamic religion.

Her brothers stopped their game and looked around in fear. Had Tarik heard Nadia say Hamed's name? But the sheik was nowhere to be seen.

"Teach us, Nadia, as our brother taught you," said her smallest brother.

And so she did. Then she told them of other games and how Hamed had taught her to play them. And as she spoke of Hamed, she felt an easing of the hurt within her.

So she went on speaking of him.

She went to where the women sat at their loom and spoke of Hamed. She told them tales that Hamed had told her. And she told how he had made her laugh as he was telling them.

At first the women were afraid to listen to the willful girl and covered their ears, but after a time, they listened and laughed with her.

"Remember your father's promise of punishment!" Nadia's mother warned when she heard Nadia speaking of Hamed. "Cease, I implore you!"

Nadia knew that her mother had reason to be afraid, for Tarik, in his grief and bitterness, had grown quick-tempered and sharp of tongue. But she did not know how to tell her mother that speaking of Hamed eased the pain she felt, and so she said only, "I will speak of my brother! I will!" And she ran away from the sound of her mother's voice.

She went to where the shepherds tended the flock and spoke of Hamed. The shepherds ran from her in fear and hid behind the sheep. But Nadia went on speaking. She told of Hamed's love for the little black lamb and how he had taught it to leap at his whistle. Soon the shepherds left off their hiding and came to listen. Then they told their own stories of Hamed and the little black lamb.

The more Nadia spoke of Hamed, the clearer his face became in her mind. She could see his smile and the light in his eyes. She could hear his voice. And the clearer Hamed's voice and face became, the less Nadia hurt inside and the less her temper flashed. At last, she was filled with peace.

But her mother was still afraid for her willful daughter. Again and again she sought to quiet Nadia so that Tarik's bitterness would not be turned against her. And again and again Nadia tossed her head and went on speaking of Hamed.

Soon, all who listened could see Hamed's face clearly before them.

One day, the youngest shepherd came to Nadia's tent calling, "Come, Nadia! See Hamed's black lamb; it has grown so big and strong!"

But it was not Nadia who came out of the tent.

It was Tarik.

On the sheik's face was a look more fierce than that of a desert hawk, and when he spoke, his words were as sharp as a scimitar.[4]

"I have forbidden my son's name to be said. And I promised punishment to whoever disobeyed my command. So shall it be. Before the sun sets and the moon casts its first shadow on the sand, you will be gone from this oasis—never to return."

"No!" cried Nadia, hearing her father's words.

---

4. **scimitar** (sim′ ə tər): a curved sword.

"I have spoken!" roared the sheik. "It shall be done!"

Trembling, the shepherd went to gather his possessions.

And the rest of the clan looked at one another uneasily and muttered among themselves.

In the hours that followed, fear of being <u>banished</u> to the desert made everyone turn away from Nadia as she tried to tell them of Hamed and the things he had done and said.

And the less she was listened to, the less she was able to recall Hamed's face and voice. And the less she recalled, the more her temper raged within her, destroying the peace she had found.

By evening, she could stand it no longer. She went to where her father sat, staring into the desert, and stood before him.

"You will not rob me of my brother Hamed!" she cried.

"You will not rob me of my brother Hamed!" she cried, stamping her foot. "I will not let you!"

Tarik looked at her, his eyes colder than the desert night.

But before he could utter a word, Nadia spoke again. "Can you recall Hamed's face? Can you still hear his voice?"

Tarik started in surprise, and his answer seemed to come unbidden to his lips. "No, I cannot! Day after day I have sat in this spot

BEDOUIN CAMP FIRES   about 1911   Henry Bacon
Worcester Art Museum   Worcester, Massachusetts.

where I last saw Hamed, trying to remember the look, the sound, the happiness that was my beloved son—but I cannot."

And he wept.

Nadia's tone became gentle. "There is a way, honored father," she said. "Listen."

And she began to speak of Hamed. She told of walks she and Hamed had taken and of talks they had had. She told how he had taught her games, told her tales, and calmed her when she was angry. She told many things that she remembered, some happy and some sad.

And when she was done with the telling, she said gently, "Can you not recall him now, Father? Can you not see his face? Can you not hear his voice?"

Tarik nodded through his tears, and for the first time since Hamed had been gone, he smiled.

Words to Know and Use | **banish** (ban′ ish) *v.* to send away

121

BEDOUIN CAMP   1905-1906   John Singer Sargent   The Brooklyn Museum   Purchased by Special Subscription.

"Now you see," Nadia said, her tone more gentle than the softest of the desert breezes, "there is a way that Hamed can be with us still."

The sheik pondered what Nadia had said. After a long time, he spoke, and the sharpness was gone from his voice.

"Tell my people to come before me, Nadia," he said. "I have something to say to them."

When all were assembled, Tarik said, "From this day forward, let my daughter Nadia be known not as Willful but as Wise. And let her name be praised in every tent, for she has given me back my beloved son."

And so it was. The shepherd returned to his flock, kindness and graciousness returned to the oasis, and Nadia's name was praised in every tent. And Hamed lived again—in the hearts of all who remembered him. 🙰

Words to Know and Use | **ponder** (pän′ dər) *v.* to think carefully about

Responding to Reading

First Impressions

1. What were your thoughts about Nadia as you finished reading? Write about her in your journal or on a sheet of paper.

Second Thoughts

2. Think about your word web and journal entry on the word *willful* on page 117. In your opinion does Nadia deserve to be called willful?

3. Nadia's father promises to punish anyone who speaks Hamed's name. Why do you think Nadia is able to change her father's mind?

   Think about
   - the **characterization** of Nadia
   - the effect of grief on her father

4. What other actions could Nadia have taken to change Tarik's mind?

Broader Connections

5. Nadia and Tarik have different ways of dealing with death. Do their actions bring to mind any feelings about or experiences of grief and death you have had or read about?

Literary Concept: Conflict

A **conflict** is a struggle between opposing forces. There are two main kinds of conflicts in stories: external and internal. A struggle between a character and an outside force, such as another character or nature, is an **external conflict.** A struggle within a character's mind, such as deciding between right and wrong, is an **internal conflict.** For example, in the story "Tuesday of the Other June," on page 17, June has an external conflict with a bully. June's internal conflict is deciding the best way to handle the problem. Describe Nadia's external and internal conflicts.

Writing Options

1. If you have read the excerpt from *How It Feels When Parents Divorce* on page 85, compare Meredith's feelings about the breakup of her family with Nadia's feelings about her brother's death and its effects on her family and clan. Using examples from these selections and from your own experience, write an **opinion essay** telling whether it is more difficult for a family to recover from a death or from a divorce.

2. Compose a **narrative poem** that tells the events of this story. (To review narrative poetry, see page 91.)

3. Prepare a **character sketch** that will help an actor in a film version of "Nadia the Willful" understand the character of Nadia's father, Tarik.

4. For the film version described above, write a **memo** from the scene designer to the director. Describe the setting that you want to create. Use details from the story in your memo.

Vocabulary Practice

Exercise   On your paper, write the word from the list that best completes each sentence.

One morning the Bedouin sheik came out of his tent in a rage. He called together the people of his (1) . "My golden scimitar, the sword of my father, has been stolen!" he shouted. Then he proclaimed this (2) : "I will (3) from my presence forever the one who has stolen my scimitar." A young woman stood apart from the others and began to (4) what had happened. She remembered that two nights before, strangers had stopped at the oasis. They were seeking water and directions to the (5) , where they could purchase spices and other supplies. As they left, the woman had noticed an oddly shaped bundle on one of their camels. Suddenly she knew what had happened to the sheik's scimitar.

Words to Know and Use

banish
bazaar
clan
decree
ponder

*O*ptions for Learning

1 • **Nomads**   Research the life of the Bedouins. What is their history? Why do they live in the desert? What do they wear and eat? What are their customs and religious beliefs? What languages do they speak? How are the clans formed? Prepare an oral report for your class. Illustrate your report with pictures and maps.

2 • **Desert Storm**   Reread the scene that begins with Nadia's standing up to her father and saying that she will not let him rob her of her brother Hamed's memory. Working with a partner, create a script based on the scene and act it out in front of the class. Use gestures and tones of voice to show the characters' thoughts and feelings.

3 • **Desert Diorama**   Cut a small square opening in the front of a shoebox. Using sand, sandpaper, paint, and other materials, create the setting of this story inside the shoebox. Then make paper figures of the characters and their animals to position within the scene. View the scene from the top or through the square opening.

4 • **Portrait Artist**   Paint a realistic portrait of Nadia as you imagine her. Use details from the story and information about Bedouin features and clothing to capture her appearance.

FACT FINDER SOCIAL STUDIES

Approximately how many Bedouins live in Africa and the Middle East today?

*S*ue Alexander
1933–

At the age of eight, Sue Alexander began writing stories for her friends. She says, "At that time I was small for my age (I still am) and very clumsy. So clumsy, in fact, that none of my classmates wanted me on their teams at recess time." One day Alexander spent recess telling a made-up story to someone else who wasn't playing. Before her story was finished, all the rest of the class had come to listen. This incident sparked a love of storytelling for Alexander.

Alexander says she wouldn't trade writing for any other profession because writing satisfies her sense of fun and her need to share. Her fantasy stories all begin the same way—with how she feels about something. She writes for young people because she likes to excite their imaginations.

Alexander's short stories have been published in *My Weekly Reader* and other magazines for younger readers. *Nadia the Willful* is a book that won many honors, including one from the American Library Association in 1983. Other books by Sue Alexander include *World Famous Muriel* and *Witch, Goblin, and Sometimes Ghost.*

Fiction

A *Secret* for *Two*

QUENTIN REYNOLDS

*E*xamine What You Know

Even though animals can't talk, people often have important relationships with them. What benefits do people receive from friendships with animals? How is it possible for animals and people to communicate when they don't share a common language? In small groups discuss these questions and jot down several responses to share with your classmates.

*E*xpand Your Knowledge

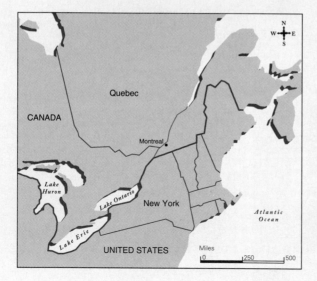

The **setting** of this story is Montreal, Canada, during the early part of the twentieth century. The city of Montreal is located in an eastern province of Canada called Quebec. Montreal is one of the largest cities in Canada. The main language of Montreal, and of Quebec, is French because many of Quebec's citizens emigrated from France. At the time of this story, milk was delivered to people each day by milkmen who relied on horses to draw their wagons through the cobbled streets.

*E*nrich Your Reading

Foreign Expressions   The milkman in this story speaks to his horse in French. As you read, notice how the writer's use of French helps the writer to portray Pierre, the main character. French words and expressions also help the reader experience the Montreal setting more realistically. It is not necessary to understand French to enjoy the story, but translations of all French words and phrases in the story can be found in the footnotes.

■ *Author biography in Reader's Handbook*

A Secret for Two

QUENTIN REYNOLDS

Montreal is a very large city, but like all cities, it has some very small streets. Streets, for instance, like Prince Edward Street, which is only four blocks long, ending in a cul-de-sac.[1] No one knew Prince Edward Street as well as did Pierre Dupin, for Pierre had delivered milk to the families on the street for thirty years now.

During the past fifteen years the horse which drew the milk wagon used by Pierre was a large white horse named Joseph. In Montreal, especially in that part of Montreal which is very French, the animals, like children, are often given the names of saints. When the big white horse first came to the Provincale Milk Company, he didn't have a name. They told Pierre that he could use the white horse henceforth. Pierre stroked the softness of the horse's neck, he stroked the sheen of its splendid belly, and he looked into the eyes of the horse.

"This is a kind horse, a gentle and a faithful horse," Pierre said, "and I can see a beautiful spirit shining out of the eyes of the horse. I will name him after good St. Joseph, who was also kind and gentle and faithful and a beautiful spirit."

Within a year Joseph knew the milk route as well as Pierre. Pierre used to boast that he didn't need reins—he never touched them. Each morning Pierre arrived at the stables of the Provincale Milk Company at five o'clock. The wagon would be loaded, and Joseph hitched to it. Pierre would call *"Bonjour, vieil ami"*[2] as he climbed into his seat, and Joseph would turn his head, and the other drivers would smile and say that the horse would smile at Pierre. Then Jacques, the foreman, would say, "All right, Pierre, go on," and Pierre would call softly to Joseph, *"Avance, mon ami,"*[3] and this splendid combination would stalk proudly down the street.

The wagon, without any direction from Pierre, would roll three blocks down St. Catherine Street, then turn right two blocks along Roslyn Avenue, then left, for that was Prince Edward Street. The horse would stop at the first house, allow Pierre perhaps thirty seconds to get down from his seat and put a bottle of milk at the front door, and would then go on, skipping two houses and stopping at the third. So down the length of the

---

1. **cul-de-sac** (kul′ də sak′): a dead-end street.
2. ***Bonjour, vieil ami*** (bōn zhōōr′ vye ä mē′) *French:* Good morning, old friend.
3. ***Avance, mon ami*** (ä väns′ mōn ä mē′) *French:* Go ahead, my friend.

street. Then Joseph, still without any direction from Pierre, would turn around and come back along the other side. Yes, Joseph was a smart horse.

 **What kind of relationship do Pierre and Joseph have?**

Pierre would boast at the stable of Joseph's skill. "I never touch the reins. He knows just where to stop. Why, a blind man could handle my route with Joseph pulling the wagon."

So it went on for years—always the same. Pierre and Joseph both grew old together, but gradually, not suddenly. Pierre's huge walrus mustache was pure white now, and Joseph didn't lift his knees so high or raise his head quite as much. Jacques, the foreman of the stables, never noticed that they were both getting old until Pierre appeared one morning carrying a heavy walking stick.

"Hey, Pierre," Jacques laughed. "Maybe you got the gout,[4] hey?"

"*Mais oui,*[5] Jacques," Pierre said a bit uncertainly. "One grows old. One's legs get tired."

"You should teach that horse to carry the milk to the front door for you," Jacques told him. "He does everything else."

He knew every one of the forty families he served on Prince Edward Street. The cooks knew that Pierre could neither read nor write, so instead of following the usual custom of leaving a note in an empty bottle if an additional quart of milk was needed, they would sing out when they heard the rumble of his wagon wheels over the cobbled street, "Bring an extra quart this morning, Pierre."

"So you have company for dinner tonight," he would call back gaily.

Pierre had a remarkable memory. When he arrived at the stable, he'd always remember to tell Jacques, "The Paquins took an extra quart this morning; the Lemoines bought a pint of cream."

Jacques would note these things in a little book he always carried. Most of the drivers had to make out the weekly bills and collect the money, but Jacques, liking Pierre, had always excused him from this task. All Pierre had to do was to arrive at five in the morning, walk to his wagon, which was always in the same spot at the curb, and deliver his milk. He returned some two hours later, got down stiffly from his seat, called a cheery "*Au 'voir*"[6] to Jacques, and then limped slowly down the street.

You know, I think those two share a secret.

One morning the president of the Provincale Milk Company came to inspect the early morning deliveries. Jacques pointed Pierre out to him and said: "Watch how he talks to that horse. See how the horse listens and how he turns his head toward Pierre? See the look in that horse's eyes? You know, I think those two share a secret. I have often noticed it. It is as though they both sometimes chuckle at us as they go off

---

4. **gout** (gout): a disease in the joints of the feet and hands.
5. ***Mais oui*** (mā wē) *French:* But yes.
6. ***Au 'voir*** (ō vwär') *French:* short for *au revoir,* meaning "goodbye."

WINTER STREET WITH HORSES
AND SLEIGHS   about 1896
J. W. Morrice
The Art Gallery of Ontario, Toronto
Gift of J. S. McLean Canadian Fund.

on their route. Pierre is a good man, Monsieur[7] President, but he gets old. Would it be too bold of me to suggest that he be retired and be given perhaps a small pension?" he added anxiously.

"But of course," the president laughed. "I know his record. He has been on this route now for thirty years, and never once has there been a complaint. Tell him it is time he rested. His salary will go on just the same."

But Pierre refused to retire. He was panic-stricken at the thought of not driving Joseph every day. "We are two old men," he said to Jacques. "Let us wear out together. When Joseph is ready to retire—then I, too, will quit."

Which of the partners will "wear out" first?

Jacques, who was a kind man, understood. There was something about Pierre

---

7. **Monsieur** (mə syö′) *French:* Mister.

A SECRET FOR TWO   129

and Joseph which made a man smile tenderly. It was as though each drew some hidden strength from the other. When Pierre was sitting in his seat and when Joseph was hitched to the wagon, neither seemed old. But when they finished their work, then Pierre would limp down the street slowly, seeming very old indeed, and the horse's head would drop, and he would walk very wearily to his stall.

Then one morning Jacques had dreadful news for Pierre when he arrived. It was a cold morning and still pitch-dark. The air was like iced wine that morning, and the snow which had fallen during the night glistened like a million diamonds piled together.

Jacques said, "Pierre, your horse, Joseph, did not wake up this morning. He was very old. Pierre, he was twenty-five, and that is like being seventy-five for a man."

"Yes," Pierre said slowly. "Yes. I am seventy-five. And I cannot see Joseph again."

"Of course you can," Jacques soothed. "He is over in his stall, looking very peaceful. Go over and see him."

Pierre took one step forward then turned. "No . . . no . . . you don't understand, Jacques."

Jacques clapped him on the shoulder. "We'll find another horse just as good as Joseph. Why, in a month you'll teach him to know your route as well as Joseph did. We'll . . ."

The look in Pierre's eyes stopped him. For years Pierre had worn a heavy cap, the peak of which came low over his eyes, keeping the bitter morning wind out of them. Now Jacques looked into Pierre's eyes, and

he saw something which startled him. He saw a dead, lifeless look in them. The eyes were mirroring the grief that was in Pierre's heart and his soul. It was as though his heart and soul had died.

"Take today off, Pierre," Jacques said, but already Pierre was hobbling off down the street, and had one been near, one would have seen tears streaming down his cheeks and have heard half-smothered sobs. Pierre walked to the corner and stepped into the street. There was a warning yell from the driver of a huge truck that was coming fast, and there was the scream of brakes, but Pierre apparently heard neither.

Five minutes later an ambulance driver said, "He's dead. Was killed instantly."

Jacques and several of the milk-wagon drivers had arrived, and they looked down at the still figure.

"I couldn't help it," the driver of the truck protested. "He walked right into my truck. He never saw it, I guess. Why, he walked into it as though he were blind."

The ambulance doctor bent down. "Blind? Of course the man was blind. See those cataracts?[8] This man has been blind for five years." He turned to Jacques. "You say he worked for you? Didn't you know he was blind?"

"No . . . no . . ." Jacques said softly. "None of us knew. Only one knew—a friend of his named Joseph. . . . It was a secret, I think, just between those two." ❧

---

8. **cataracts:** cloudy patches in the eyes.

E X P L A I N

Responding to Reading

First Impressions

1. How did you react when you learned the secret? Write about your reaction in your journal or on a piece of paper.

Second Thoughts

2. How would you describe Pierre and Joseph's friendship?

Think about
- what they do for each other
- what they have in common

3. What can you tell about Pierre's **character** from his actions in the story?

4. How do you think the title of this subunit, "Promises to Keep," relates to the story of Pierre and Joseph?

Broader Connections

5. Think about the story you have just read and the discussion about animals you had before reading it. Discuss ways that animals are being used or could be used to help disabled people.

Literary Concept: Foreshadowing

Foreshadowing is a writer's use of hints or clues to indicate something that will occur later in the plot. For example, the title "A Secret for Two" foreshadows the discovery of the secret that Pierre and Joseph share. Find another example of foreshadowing in the story.

Writing Options

1. What do you think Jacques, Pierre's boss, would say to his wife on the evening of Pierre's death? Write the **dialogue** they might have about Pierre.

2. Consider the theme of this story. What is the author's message or comment about life? Explain your answer in an **essay.**

Poetry

The Cremation of Sam McGee

ROBERT SERVICE

Examine What You Know

Promises are easy to make and sometimes hard to keep. In your journal, list six promises that you have made in the last year or two. Number the promises from one to six, with number one being the promise that was easiest to keep and number six being the promise that was most difficult to keep. Then explain why keeping promise number six was so hard.

Expand Your Knowledge

For the narrator of this poem, keeping a promise becomes especially difficult because of his surroundings. He is a gold miner in the frozen Yukon Territory, the **setting** of this poem. The Yukon Territory is located in the northwestern corner of Canada, east of Alaska. On the north the Arctic Ocean borders the Yukon. This area is known for its long, dark, cold winters. In the late 1800s many people risked their lives in the cold Yukon, searching for gold near the Klondike River.

Enrich Your Reading

Mood   The feeling that the writer wants the reader to get from a work of literature is called **mood.** Words are carefully chosen to create this special feeling. For example, in the first stanza of this poem, the words *strange, secret tales,* and *queer sights* set an eerie mood. As you read, see if the mood changes.

■ *Author biography on Extend page*

The Cremation of Sam McGee

ROBERT SERVICE

There are strange things done in the midnight sun
  By the men who moil[1] for gold;
The Arctic trails have their secret tales
  That would make your blood run cold;
5 *The Northern Lights have seen queer sights,*
  But the queerest they ever did see
Was that night on the marge[2] of Lake Lebarge
  I cremated Sam McGee.

Now Sam McGee was from Tennessee,
10   where the cotton blooms and blows.
Why he left his home in the South to roam
    'round the Pole, God only knows.
He was always cold, but the land of gold
    seemed to hold him like a spell;
15 Though he'd often say in his homely way
    that he'd "sooner live in Hell."

On a Christmas Day we were mushing[3] our way
    over the Dawson trail.[4]
Talk of your cold! through the parka's fold
20   it stabbed like a driven nail.
If our eyes we'd close, then the lashes froze
    till sometimes we couldn't see,
It wasn't much fun, but the only one
    to whimper was Sam McGee.

---

1. **moil:** work very hard.
2. **marge:** edge.
3. **mushing:** traveling with a dog sled.
4. **Dawson trail:** route in the Yukon Territory of Canada.

25 And that very night, as we lay packed tight
        in our robes beneath the snow,
    And the dogs were fed, and the stars o'erhead
        were dancing heel and toe,
    He turned to me, and "Cap," says he,
30   "I'll cash in this trip, I guess;
    And if I do, I'm asking that you
        won't refuse my last request."

    Well, he seemed so low that I couldn't say no;
        then he says with a sort of moan,
35 "It's the cursed cold, and it's got right hold
        till I'm chilled clean through to the bone.
    Yet 'taint being dead—it's my awful dread
        of the icy grave that pains;
    So I want you to swear that, foul or fair,
40   you'll cremate my last remains."

WINTER NIGHT IN RONDANE
1914   Harald Sohlberg
Nasjongalleriet   Oslo, Norway
Photo J. Lathion © 1992 NG.

A pal's last need is a thing to heed,
 so I swore I would not fail;
And we started on at the streak of dawn;
 but God! he looked ghastly pale.
45 He crouched on the sleigh, and he raved all day
 of his home in Tennessee;
And before nightfall a corpse was all
 that was left of Sam McGee.

There wasn't a breath in that land of death,
50 and I hurried, horror-driven,
With a corpse half hid that I couldn't get rid,
 because of a promise given;
It was lashed to the sleigh, and it seemed to say:
 "You may tax your brawn and brains,
55 But you promised true, and it's up to you
 to cremate these last remains."

Now a promise made is a debt unpaid,
 and the trail has its own stern code.
In the days to come, though my lips were dumb,
60 in my heart how I cursed that load!
In the long, long night, by the lone firelight,
 while the huskies, round in a ring,
Howled out their woes to the homeless snows—
 Oh God, how I loathed the thing!

65 And every day that quiet clay
 seemed to heavy and heavier grow;
And on I went, though the dogs were spent
 and the grub was getting low.
The trail was bad, and I felt half mad,
70 but I swore I would not give in;
And I'd often sing to the hateful thing,
 and it hearkened with a grin.

Till I came to the marge of Lake Lebarge,
    and a derelict[5] there lay;
75 It was jammed in the ice, but I saw in a trice
    it was called the *Alice May*.
And I looked at it, and I thought a bit,
    and I looked at my frozen chum;
Then "Here," said I, with a sudden cry,
80   "is my cre-ma-tor-eum!"

Some planks I tore from the cabin floor,
    and I lit the boiler fire;
Some coal I found that was lying around,
    and I heaped the fuel higher;
85 The flames just soared, and the furnace roared—
    such a blaze you seldom see,
And I burrowed a hole in the glowing coal,
    and I stuffed in Sam McGee.

Then I made a hike, for I didn't like
90   to hear him sizzle so;
And the heavens scowled, and the huskies howled,
    and the wind began to blow.
It was icy cold, but the hot sweat rolled
    down my cheeks, and I don't know why;
95 And the greasy smoke in an inky cloak
    went streaking down the sky.

I do not know how long in the snow
    I wrestled with grisly fear;
But the stars came out and they danced about
100   ere[6] again I ventured near;
I was sick with dread, but I bravely said,
    "I'll just take a peep inside.
I guess he's cooked, and it's time I looked."
    Then the door I opened wide.

---

5. **derelict:** an abandoned ship.
6. **ere** (er): before.

Illustration by Frank Street.   Courtesy, Illustration House, Inc., New York.

105 And there sat Sam, looking cool and calm,
     in the heart of the furnace roar;
And he wore a smile you could see a mile,
     and he said, "Please close that door.
It's fine in here, but I greatly fear
110   you'll let in the cold and storm—
Since I left Plumtree, down in Tennessee,
     it's the first time I've been warm."

There are strange things done in the midnight sun
    By the men who moil for gold;
115 *The Arctic trails have their secret tales*
    That would make your blood run cold;
The Northern Lights have seen queer sights,
    But the queerest they ever did see
Was that night on the marge of Lake Lebarge
120   *I cremated Sam McGee.*

Responding to Reading

First Impressions

1. Write the images from the poem that stand out in your mind.

Second Thoughts

2. What did you enjoy most about this poem?

   Think about
   - the **characters** and the **setting**
   - the images and descriptions

3. What words would you use to describe Cap, the narrator of this poem? Use examples to support your answer.

4. The words in the first and last stanzas of the poem are the same. Do you think the **mood** created by these stanzas is the same or different? Explain.

Literary Concepts: End Rhyme and Internal Rhyme

Rhyme that occurs at the ends of lines is called **end rhyme.** Rhyme used within a line is called **internal rhyme.** The following lines show both internal and end rhyme.

There are strange things *done* in the midnight *sun*
  By the men who moil for *gold;*
The Arctic *trails* have their secret *tales*
  That would make your blood run *cold;*

Find another example of end rhyme and of internal rhyme in the poem.

Concept Review: Rhythm As you know, a poem's "beat" is called its rhythm. Why do you think the poet created such a steady rhythm for this poem?

Writing Options

1. "The Cremation of Sam McGee" and "The Walrus and the Carpenter" on page 91 are both humorous narrative poems. Compare the two poems in a **review column** for a school poetry magazine.

2. Convert "The Cremation of Sam McGee" to the style of a **rap song.** Perform the new version for your class.

Options for Learning

1 • **Catch Gold Fever!** Research the Klondike gold rush of the late 1800s. Who were the miners who poured into the Yukon in hopes of striking it rich? Where did they come from? What tools did they use? How long did they stay to search for gold? How did they get around in the snow? Prepare an oral report for your class. Illustrate your report with pictures and maps.

2 • **Illustrate the Poem** Reread the poem and jot down details and descriptions that paint vivid pictures in your mind. Then choose a scene from the poem to draw or paint. Bring out the eerie or humorous mood of the scene.

3 • **Tell a Whopper** As a class decide on a setting and characters for a story. Ask one person to serve as a timekeeper. Select a group of six or seven classmates to take turns making up the story. Choose one person to begin the storytelling. After a minute the timekeeper should tell the next person in the storytelling group to continue the story. Begin with ordinary, believable details but feel free to add details that are amazing or fantastic. If several groups tell stories, you may want to vote on which tale was the most entertaining.

FACT FINDER GEOGRAPHY

What is the average winter temperature in the Yukon Territory?

Robert Service
1874–1958

Robert Service said that "The Cremation of Sam McGee" was "the result of an accident." He explained that he was at a party when a miner told a far-fetched story of a man who cremated his friend. Service left the party and immediately started writing the poem in his mind. When he woke up the next day, he wrote it all down from memory, and it quickly became a big success. In fact, many people who have studied this poem have enjoyed it so much that they have memorized stanzas or even the entire poem.

Service was born in England and moved to the Yukon when he was in his twenties. He worked as a bank teller but wrote poems about the miners and the lumberjacks of Canada. When he became a popular writer, he quit his job at the bank and wrote full time. In addition to "The Cremation of Sam McGee," Service wrote another famous narrative poem, "The Shooting of Dan McGrew."

When Service was in his thirties, he moved to Europe and continued to write poems and novels. He also served as an ambulance driver during World War I. He lived for many years far from the Yukon, in Paris, where he died in 1958.

Nonfiction

The Real McCoy

JIM HASKINS

Examine What You Know

Have you ever thought about inventing something? Look around the room at all the things that were invented to meet a need or solve a problem. On your paper, create a chart like the one started below. In the left-hand column, write down the names of three inventions. In the right-hand column, list the need or problem that might have inspired someone to invent each item.

INVENTION (Solution)	NEED (Problem)
1. Pencil-sharpener	1. Had to sharpen pencils with a knife

Expand Your Knowledge

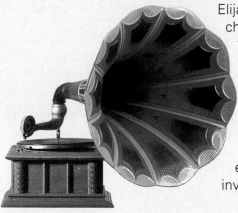

An early phonograph.

Elijah McCoy lived during a time when inventions were changing this country very rapidly. Between 1865 and 1900 people were introduced to many things they had never seen before: light bulbs, telephones, phonographs, and even zippers. The first automobiles had been built, but they needed improvements; and there were still no such things as airplanes, televisions, or frozen foods. During McCoy's lifetime, challenges could be found everywhere—challenges to create new useful inventions and challenges to improve older ones.

Enrich Your Reading

Setting Purposes for Reading The title of a selection is your first clue about a selection's contents. Before you read, think about the title of this selection. What do you think it means to say that something is "the real McCoy"?

■ *Author biography on Extend page*

The Real McCoy

JIM HASKINS

Elijah McCoy's name has become synonymous with the ideas of perfection and quality. When we say that something is "the real McCoy," we are remembering Elijah McCoy whether we are aware of it or not.

Elijah McCoy (1843–1929) was born on May 2, 1843, in Colchester, Ontario, Canada, the son of two runaway slaves, fugitives who had escaped from Kentucky by way of the Underground Railroad.[1] After the Civil War, Elijah and his parents returned to the United States, settling down near Ypsilanti,[2] Michigan. There Elijah attended school and worked in a machine shop.

McCoy, even as a boy, was fascinated with machines and tools. He was fortunate to have been born into an era that suited him perfectly, a time when newer and better machines were being invented—the age of the machine. Following the footsteps of steam was that new energy source, electricity, which opened up even more opportunities for the inventive mind.

McCoy's interest only deepened with the emergence of each new device. He decided to go to Edinburgh, Scotland, where the bias against his color was not so evident, and

ELIJAH McCOY ©1937 The Associated Publishers Inc., and Schomburg Collection New York Public Library Astor, Lenox, and Tilden Foundations.

serve an apprenticeship in mechanical engineering. After finishing his apprenticeship, McCoy returned to the United States a mechanical engineer, eager to put his skills to work. But companies at that time were reluctant to hire a black man to fill such a highly skilled position. Prejudice was strong, and the myth that blacks were intellectually

---

1. **Underground Railroad:** a system used before the U.S. Civil War to help runaway Southern slaves escape to the North.
2. **Ypsilanti** (ip′ sə lan′ tē).

141

inferior to whites persisted. Companies felt that McCoy could not possibly be as skilled as he claimed to be, and even if he were, the white workers he might have to supervise would never take orders from a black man. The only job he was able to find was as a fireman on the Michigan Central Railroad.

The job of fireman was hardly one that required the sophisticated skills McCoy had obtained. His duties consisted of fueling the firebox of the engine to "keep the steam up" and oiling the engine. The way train and other types of engines were built meant that it was necessary to stop the train periodically–or to shut down whatever engine was being used–so the moving parts could be lubricated. If the engines were not oiled, the parts would wear out quickly or friction would cause the parts to heat up, causing fires. Hand-lubricating engines was an inefficient but necessary procedure.

Many men or women, when faced with a repetitive, essentially mindless task, might sink into an unthinking lethargy,[3] doing only that which is required of them and no more, but this was not true of Elijah McCoy. He did his job–oiling the engines–but that job led him to become interested in the problems of lubricating any kind of machinery that was in motion. For two years he worked on the problem on his own time in his own homemade machine shop. His initial idea was to manufacture the machines with canals cut into them, with connecting devices between their various parts to distribute the oil throughout the machines while they were running. He wanted to make lubrication automatic.

Finally McCoy came up with what he called "the lubricating cup," or "drip cup." The lubricating cup was a small container filled with oil, with a stopcock to regulate the flow of oil into the parts of a moving machine. The lubricating or drip cup seemed an obvious invention, yet no one had thought of it before McCoy; it has since been described as the "key device in perfecting the overall lubrication system used in large industry today." With a drip cup installed, it was no longer necessary to shut down a

Left, a lubricator for locomotives invented by Elijah McCoy.

---

3. **lethargy** (leth' ər jē): lack of energy or activity.

machine in order to oil it, thus saving both time and money. McCoy received his patent for it on July 12, 1872.

The drip cup could be used on machinery of all types, and it was quickly adopted by machine manufacturers everywhere. Of course, there were imitators, but their devices were not as effective or efficient as McCoy's. It soon became standard practice for an equipment buyer to inquire if the machine contained "the real McCoy." So commonly was this expression used that it soon spread outside the machine industry and came to have the general meaning of "the real thing," of perfection. Nowadays if someone states they want "the real McCoy," it is taken to mean that they want the genuine article, the best, not a shoddy imitation. In 1872, of course, Elijah McCoy could not foresee that his name would soon become associated with the idea of perfection. All he knew was that the thing worked and worked well on machinery of all types.

The lubrication of machinery fascinated McCoy, and he continued to work in that area. In 1892 he invented and patented a number of devices for lubricating locomotive engines. These inventions were used in all western railroads and on steamers plying the Great Lakes. Eventually McCoy would invent a total of twenty-three lubricators for different kinds of equipment, and in 1920 he applied his system to air brakes on vehicles.

Elijah McCoy was awarded over fifty-seven patents.

During his lifetime, Elijah McCoy was awarded over fifty-seven patents and became known as one of the most prolific black inventors of the nineteenth century. In addition to his patents on various kinds of lubricating systems, he also received patents for such "homey" objects as an ironing table (a forerunner of today's ironing board), a lawn sprinkler, a steam dome, and a dope cup (a cup for administering medicine). He eventually founded the Elijah McCoy Manufacturing Company in Detroit, Michigan, to develop and sell his inventions.

Until his death in 1929, McCoy continued working and inventing, sometimes patenting two or three new devices a year. Today, although many may not know who he was or what he did, his name remains to remind us of the idea of quality, and the steady, ceaseless roar of machinery is a paean[4] to his inventiveness. ❧

---

4. **paean** (pē′ ən): a song of praise.

Words to Know and Use | **shoddy** (shäd′ ē) *adj.* poorly made
ceaseless (sēs′ lis) *adj.* constant; never ending

Another Mountain

ABIODUN OYEWOLE

Sometimes there's a mountain
that I must climb
even after I've climbed one already
But my legs are tired now
and my arms need a rest
my mind is too weary right now
But I must climb before the storm comes
before the earth rocks
and an avalanche of clouds buries me
and smothers my soul
And so I prepare myself for another climb
Another Mountain
and I tell myself it is nothing
it is just some more dirt and stone
and every now and then I should reach
another plateau and enjoy the view
of the trees and the flowers below
And I am young enough to climb
and strong enough to make it to any top
You see the wind has warned me
about settling too long
about peace without struggle
The wind has warned me
and taught me how to fly
But my wings only work
After I've climbed a mountain

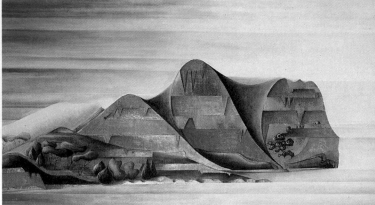

LES ROCHES DE CASSIS   1990   Susanne Schuenke
Private collection   Courtesy of the artist.

Responding to Reading

First Impressions

1. In your journal, make a note on what impressed you most about McCoy's life.

Second Thoughts

2. What kind of person was Elijah McCoy?

Think about
- his education
- how he handled his job as a fireman
- the time it took him to create the lubricating cup
- the variety of his inventions

3. If Elijah McCoy were alive today, do you think he would be more successful or less successful than he actually was? Give reasons for your opinion.

Broader Connections

4. What other inventors and inventions have you heard or read about? How are the stories of these similar to or different from what you learned about Elijah McCoy?

Literary Concept: Biography

A **biography** is a true account of a person's life written by another person. The writer looks at all the information that is available about the person and chooses which facts and which parts of the person's life to include in the biography.

Concept Review: Author's Purpose Remember that authors write to entertain, to inform, to express opinions, and to persuade. What purpose or purposes do you think the author might have had for writing "The Real McCoy"?

*W*riting Options

1. Write the **dialogue** you might have with Elijah McCoy if you were to interview him for a magazine. Ask him specific questions about his life and inventions and base his answers on what you have read.

2. If you have not already done so, read the Insight poem "Another Mountain" on page 144. Think about the theme, or message, of the poem. Then write a short **essay** that explains how you think the poem relates to Elijah McCoy.

3. Consider the chart you made on page 140, listing inventions and the needs that inspired them. Then think of a need that hasn't been met or a problem that could use a solution. Write a **proposal** for a new invention that would meet the need. First describe the need, then explain how your invention would meet it.

4. Summarize the information in this selection. Use your summary to write an **encyclopedia entry** about Elijah McCoy.

*V*ocabulary Practice

Exercise   On your paper, write the vocabulary word that best completes each sentence.

1. McCoy's parents escaped to Canada because a runaway, or _?_ , slave was considered property and, by law, could be returned to his or her master if caught.

2. McCoy served an _?_ in mechanical engineering, studying and training under experts in the field.

3. The prejudice, or _?_ , against people of African descent was less noticeable in Scotland than in the United States.

4. Companies at the time doubted that an African American could have the _?_ skills needed to be an engineer.

5. With no one to hire him, McCoy took an _?_ boring job on the railroad and made it interesting.

6. Engines in those days had to be stopped and oiled _?_ so that the moving parts would not overheat.

7. For two years McCoy continued to _?_ in his efforts to invent a way to oil a machine while it was running.

8. His determination and _?_ effort on his own time paid off with his patented invention of the drip cup.

9. Soon others were creating _?_ imitations of the drip cup that were not as good as the original.

10. To be sure they got McCoy's drip cup, people asked for "the real McCoy," and soon his name became _?_ with the "real thing."

Words to Know and Use

———

apprenticeship
bias
ceaseless
essentially
fugitive
periodically
persist
shoddy
sophisticated
synonymous

Options for Learning

1 • Draw a Familiar Invention A technical drawing is a detailed and carefully drawn picture of an object. Choose a simple invention, such as a can opener or a tire pump, and make a technical drawing of it. Be sure your drawing includes all the important details. Label each essential part.

2 • Patent Process A patent is an official document that states who owns the rights to a particular invention. A patent protects an invention so that only the inventor can sell it for a certain period of time. Research the steps an inventor must go through to get a patent. Write a report on the process, or give an oral report to your class.

3 • Advertising Design a newspaper advertisement for one of McCoy's inventions. Think about the uses of the product, how it affects people's lives, and other reasons to persuade readers to order the product. Include a picture.

4 • The Real McCoy The English language has many expressions like "the real McCoy" that have interesting histories. With your classmates brainstorm a list of five or six phrases and then research their origins. Create an illustrated booklet that gives the stories behind these phrases.

FACT FINDER SOCIAL STUDIES

Who were the inventors of the cotton gin and the electric light bulb?

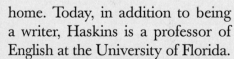

Jim Haskins
1941–

Jim Haskins has written more than eighty books. Every one of those books is nonfiction because Haskins has always liked true stories better than made-up ones. He says, "It seems to me that the more you know about the real world the better off you are."

Haskins learned to read early in his childhood, but he was not allowed to take advantage of the public library in his town because it was off-limits to African Americans. So instead of going to the library, he read through the encyclopedia his family had at home. Today, in addition to being a writer, Haskins is a professor of English at the University of Florida.

Most of Haskins's books are about African-American subjects because, he says, "I remember being a child and not having many books about black people to read. I want children today, black and white, to be able to find books about black people and black history in case they want to read them." Haskins has written biographies of African Americans important in history and politics, such as Shirley Chisholm and Barbara Jordan, as well as books on Magic Johnson and Stevie Wonder.

WRITER'S WORKSHOP

DESCRIPTIVE WRITING

USE DESCRIPTIVE WRITING FOR

notes
descriptive essays
character sketches
biographies
autobiographies

What power words have! In "Nadia the Willful," Nadia uses words to keep alive the memory of her brother. Keeping a promise leads to an unforgettable encounter in "The Cremation of Sam McGee." Now it's your turn to make a person memorable.

In this workshop you will use descriptive writing to create a **biographical sketch** of someone you know—someone who has made a strong, lasting impression on you. In a sense, you will be making a word picture or sketch of that person. Like a biography, the sketch will reveal a part of his or her life, from a point of view that is strictly your own.

Here is one writer's PASSkey to this assignment.

GUIDED ASSIGNMENT: "YOU ARE THERE" BIOGRAPHY

Write a biographical sketch describing someone you know. The sketch should also tell why you chose your subject and how you feel about this person.

PURPOSE: To describe a person I know

AUDIENCE: My teacher and classmates

SUBJECT: Someone I know well

STRUCTURE: Biographical sketch

STUDENT MODEL

Before you write, read how one student responded to the assignment.

▶ Lori begins with an attention-grabbing scene. She explains why she chose her subject.

▶ Describing the subject in action makes him seem to come alive.

> ### Silver Blades on Ice
>
> #### by Lori Melendez
>
> "Don't worry--I won't let you fall!" Mr. Eastman promised. He reached out his hands as I wobbled out on the slippery ice for the very first time. His warm, steady hands wrapped around my cold, nervous ones. I knew right then that Mr. Eastman could make me a figure skater.
>
> When I think of Mr. Eastman, I see the flash of silver blades as he glides around the rink. His brown eyes twinkle from beneath his red wool cap. His legs are so long that he looks

like an ostrich on skates. When he shows me
how to do a jump, though, Mr. Eastman is as
graceful as a flamingo. He soars up into the
air and always lands perfectly.

   When I began learning to make jumps, I was
pretty clumsy at landing. Mr. Eastman would
say nice things to me anyway. "You're getting
there!" he would say. "Just see yourself
landing perfectly in your mind." He would
encourage me with smiles as I tried a jump
over and over. I listened to his kind words
and advice, and my landings got much better.

   It's been two years since Mr. Eastman first
helped me onto the skating rink. He has taught
me skating moves I thought I could never do,
like axels, camel spins, and spirals. The most
amazing thing about Mr. Eastman is his
kindness. He spends all his time on ice and
yet his heart is as warm as the sun.

Similes—comparisons that use *like, as, than* or *resembles*—sharpen the writer's descriptions.

Note how this paragraph focuses on Mr. Eastman's personality traits.

Lori shares an event that shows her teacher's kindness.

Lori sums up her feelings about her subject.

Prewrite and Explore

1 **Pick a person**   First you will need to choose a subject. Your best choice is the person who first comes to mind, since he or she probably made a strong impression. If you need help finding a subject, try the following strategies. Leaf through a family photo album or a school yearbook. Think of a sport or a hobby in which you participate. Lori thought about her favorite sport. That led her to write about her figure-skating teacher.

NO LIMITS
Don't hesitate to choose a person who is no longer alive. Your subject may be anyone who has helped or inspired you.

OBSERVATION
If your subject is close at hand, take the opportunity to observe him or her without revealing your purpose. Make mental notes of that person's appearance and behavior.

GATHERING INFORMATION

Now you are ready to collect details about your subject. Using a chart like the one on the next page will help. Before you fill in the chart, close your eyes and form a mental picture of your subject. Describe the person. Does she or he have a special way of speaking? gesturing? dressing? behaving? What personality traits stand out? Look at the chart Lori used to organize her thoughts.

STUDENT MODEL

Notice that Lori's details start from the top. Going from head to toe is the most natural way to picture someone.

Physical Traits	Personality Traits
red wool cap	warm-hearted
twinkly brown eyes	encouraging words
long legs	full of energy
flashing blades	thoughtful
never stops moving	sensitive
incredible jumper	patient

2 **Make your subject active**   Showing your subject in action will help to bring that person to life in your writing. What did he or she do to make a strong impression? Think of at least one outstanding, meaningful event connected with your subject. For example, Lori focused on times when Mr. Eastman helped her—her first steps on the ice and her first jumps.

3 **Include yourself**   As a firsthand biographer, you are painting a word picture of your subject, but don't leave yourself out of the picture! Your readers have questions such as the following: What experiences did you and this person share? Why is this person important to you? How do you feel about him or her? Jot down your answers.

Draft and Discover

WRITER'S CHOICE

Need a strong opening? Begin with interesting dialogue. Have your subject say something forceful, touching, or funny. That way he or she will seem active and real.

1 **Grab your readers' attention**   Start your draft with an attention-getting paragraph to pull in readers. You might try using a vivid scene or a startling description. Look at these lines from the first stanza of "The Cremation of Sam McGee." Notice how the description stirs your curiosity.

> The Northern Lights have seen queer sights,
>   But the queerest they ever did see
> Was that night on the marge of Lake Lebarge
>   I cremated Sam McGee.

2 **Focus your paragraphs**   As you draft, remember that each paragraph should describe only one aspect of your subject. For example, Lori describes Mr. Eastman's physical traits in her second paragraph. Her third paragraph describes his personality traits. In her final paragraph, Lori details her feelings about Mr. Eastman.

Revise Your Writing

1 **Paint a word picture**   Now that you have a first draft, study it as if you were an artist examining a portrait. Can you "see" the person clearly? Are any important details missing? Look for descriptions that seem flat or lifeless. Flesh them out with fresh, colorful details. Notice how Mr. Eastman seems more vivid after Lori expands her description by using a quotation.

COMPUTER TIP
Computers make inserting and deleting details easy and painless. Feel free to play with your sentences. Add and subtract details until you are satisfied.

Before   Mr. Eastman would say nice things to me anyway.

After   Mr. Eastman would say nice things to me anyway. "You're getting there!" he would say.

To help sharpen your descriptions, you might also try the following idea.

2 **Make comparisons**   Using similes and metaphors is a good way to create word pictures for your readers. In your writing, try to use strong comparisons like the ones below.

On the sheik's face was a look more fierce than that of a desert hawk, and when he spoke, his words were as sharp as a scimitar.

"Now you see," Nadia said, her tone more gentle than the softest of the desert breezes.

LITERARY MODELS
from "Nadia the Willful" by Sue Alexander

3 **Use a peer reader**   Look over your draft, then share it with a classmate. Use these questions to guide your revision.

Revision Questions

For You	For a Peer Reader
1. Did I create a clear picture of my subject?	1. What else would you like to know?
2. Does this person seem active and alive?	2. Do you understand how I feel about my subject?
3. Did I explain why he or she is important to me?	3. Which details did you like best?

Proofread

When you have finished revising your sketch, read it closely. Look for mistakes in grammar, punctuation, spelling, and capitalization. Did you include any dialogue? Check Section 10 of the Language Handbook to make sure you used quotation marks correctly.

NEED MORE HELP?

See the Language Workshop that follows (pages 153–155) and Section 2 in the Language Handbook.

THE EDITOR'S EYE: CORRECTING SENTENCE FRAGMENTS

Watch out for sentence fragments in your writing. Make sure each sentence tells a complete thought.

A **sentence fragment** is a group of words that does not express a complete idea. To correct a fragment, add the missing information.

Incorrect	The most amazing thing about Mr. Eastman.
Correct	The most amazing thing about Mr. Eastman is his kindness.

Publish and Present

Here is a suggestion for sharing your work with others.

Picture This   Exchange papers with a classmate. Draw a picture of the person described in that student's sketch. As a class, make a "portrait gallery" that displays your biographical sketches and the pictures that go with them. If you have a photograph of the actual person, you might want to display it with the biographical sketch and the drawing your classmate has made.

Reflect on Your Writing

Answer the following questions. Attach your answers to your sketch, then place it in your writing portfolio.

FOR YOUR PORTFOLIO ▶

1. Do you know more about your subject now than you did before writing your sketch?
2. Compare descriptive writing to the personal writing you did in Unit One. Which do you find easier? Why?

LANGUAGE WORKSHOP

CORRECTING FRAGMENTS AND RUN-ONS

> A **sentence fragment** is a group of words that is only part of a sentence. A fragment does not have a subject, a verb, or both.
>
> A **run-on sentence** is two or more sentences written incorrectly as one. To correct a run-on, separate it into two or more sentences.

Sentence Fragments

A group of words. Confusing and difficult to read. In the middle of a paragraph. Are missing something.

If you had trouble understanding the sentences above, that's because they are not really sentences. They are **sentence fragments**—sentences that do not have a subject, a verb, or both. Fragments like these leave readers wondering what happened or what the sentence is about.

To avoid confusing your readers, watch out for sentence fragments in your writing. Remember that a sentence fragment may be missing a subject, a verb, or both. If you find a fragment, add words to make it a complete sentence. Look at the examples below.

◀ REMINDER
The subject and the verb are the main parts of a sentence. The **subject** tells *whom* or *what* the sentence is about. The **verb** tells what the subject *does* or *did.* The sentence below is divided into these two parts.

Subject   **Verb**
The wind   howled.

Fragment   Made an important promise to his best friend. (The subject is missing. Readers will wonder *who* made a promise.)

Sentence   Cap made an important promise to his best friend.

Fragment   Cap, with a feeling of dread and a heavy heart. (Here the verb is missing, leaving readers wondering *what* Cap did.)

Sentence   Cap, with a feeling of dread and a heavy heart, cremated Sam McGee.

Fragment   On the marge of Lake Lebarge. (Both subject and verb are missing in this fragment.)

Sentence   Cap cremated Sam on the marge of Lake Lebarge.

BREAKING THE RULES

In two instances fragments may be used.

1. Personal writing such as the following:
- class notes
- journal writing
- first drafts

2. Dialogue

People don't always talk in complete sentences, so when you write dialogue, feel free to use fragments.

Exercise 1   Concept Check   Label each group of words *Sentence* or *Fragment*. Then add words to make each fragment a sentence.

1. A grizzled gold miner and his mule.
2. Searched for gold in the Yukon Territory.
3. A mysterious stranger appeared one day.
4. Led the miner to a cave.
5. A vein of gold.
6. The miner promised to keep the discovery secret.
7. Went into town to buy supplies.
8. Closely listened to his foolish bragging.
9. A band of greedy miners.
10. They looked for the gold-filled cave.
11. He was gone.
12. The legend of the Gold Cave.

Run-on Sentences

QUITE THE OPPOSITE

A run-on sentence is the opposite of a fragment. Instead of having too little information, a run-on has too much information in it.

▶   When you write, you have many thoughts to express. If you were to put all these thoughts into a single sentence, you would end up with a **run-on sentence.** Sometimes, no end mark is placed at the end of the first thought. At other times, a comma is incorrectly used. Read these examples.

Run-on   The sheik sat in his tent he barely tasted his meals.

Correct   The sheik sat in his tent. He barely tasted his meals.

Run-on   The messenger came, he delivered his message.

Correct   The messenger came. He delivered his message.

Remember to end each sentence with a period, a question mark, or an exclamation point. Start new sentences with capital letters.

USE YOUR EARS

Not sure how to fix a run-on sentence? Read it aloud. At the end of a complete thought, you will naturally pause. The end punctuation belongs at the point where you pause.

▶ **Exercise 2   Concept Check**   Correct the following run-ons by dividing them into separate sentences.

1. Kasha was the daughter of a poor carpet maker she was brave and adventurous.
2. Kasha dreamed of distant places, the desert beckoned to her.
3. She wanted to see the world her father had other plans for her, though.

4. Her father reminded Kasha that she had promised to help him with his business she didn't want to remember.

5. One day she ran off and joined a camel caravan it carried her across the desert.

6. Kasha traveled far and wide, she visited foreign lands.

7. How could Kasha forget her promise she never did.

8. During her travels Kasha sold her father's carpets people loved his beautiful designs.

9. Kasha returned home she gave her father the money she had earned.

10. How proud the carpet maker was of his daughter thanks to Kasha his business prospered.

Exercise 3   Revision Skill   Rewrite the following paragraph. Correct any fragments and run-ons that you find.

In 1893, an American named Whitcomb L. Judson. Invented the first zipper. It had two thin metal chains there was a slider that could be pulled up and down the chains. Was meant to replace laces, buttons, and hooks on shoes. People were not very interested in this early zipper, sales of the "hookless fastener" were slow at first. By 1915, however, public interest in the zipper had increased, the zipper was a success.

Exercise 4   Revising Your Writing   Skim through the biographical essay that you wrote for the Writer's Workshop on page 148. Look for sentence fragments and run-ons. Correct any mistakes that you find.

LANGUAGE HANDBOOK
. . . .
For review and practice: Section 2, Understanding Sentences.

VOCABULARY
WORKSHOP

CONTEXT CLUES

You may not realize it, but you are a detective. You have been using your sleuthing skills ever since you began reading. Each time you read, you use context clues to detect the meanings of words you don't know. **Context clues** are the words and sentences that surround an unfamiliar word.

A writer may define an unfamiliar word or restate it in a different way. Look at these examples.

> Elijah McCoy was *ingenious;* that is, he was clever at finding new solutions to common problems. (definition)

> McCoy invented a way to *lubricate,* or apply oil to, working machinery. (restatement)

An example in a sentence may also help to explain an unfamiliar word. What does *bias* mean in the following sentence?

> *Bias,* such as not wanting an African American to fill a highly skilled position, created additional challenges for McCoy. (example)

The context tells you that *bias* is a prejudice that may result in a person being treated unfairly.

Exercise Write your definition for each italicized word. Use context clues to help you decide on each word's meaning.

1. Inventors work for *incentives* like fame and fortune.
2. Elijah McCoy was a natural *troubleshooter;* he loved to solve difficult problems.
3. *Tenacity,* also known as persistence, was one of McCoy's strongest character traits.
4. *Innovations,* such as the ironing table and a lawn sprinkler, seemed to flow from McCoy's mind.
5. In his earlier years Elijah McCoy served as an *apprentice,* or unpaid assistant, to a mechanical engineer.
6. His inventions were widely *lauded;* that is, people eventually recognized his talents.
7. The lubricating cup was *pivotal,* or crucial, in making machines efficient.
8. "The Real McCoy" means something is *authentic,* or in other words, genuine.

SIGNALS

The following words signal that a writer is giving a context clue.

Definition or Restatement

also known as
in other words
that is
which is
or
also called

Example

and other
especially
for example
for instance
like
such as

How many times have you been surprised when something happened that you did not expect? Perhaps a day that started out to be terrible turned out to be terrific, or a wonderful day ended up in disaster. Perhaps you found a twenty-dollar bill on the street or discovered that you had lost the money you were planning to spend on something special. Life is full of surprises and unexpected twists and turns.

Whatever happens, the most important thing may be "rising to the challenge," the theme of Unit Two. In this sub-unit you will meet characters who are faced with unexpected challenges and will see their unique responses.

Fiction

Playing for Keeps

JACK C. HALDEMAN II

Examine What You Know

Think about stories you have read or movies you have seen in which aliens from outer space come to Earth. Use what you know to add to a web like the one below.

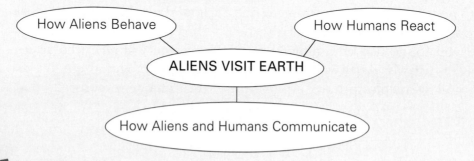

How Aliens Behave

How Humans React

ALIENS VISIT EARTH

How Aliens and Humans Communicate

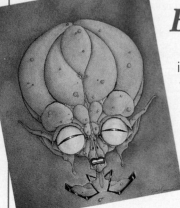

Expand Your Knowledge

Science fiction is a type of fiction that is based on real or imaginary scientific ideas. Many science fiction stories feature visits to Earth by aliens. One famous example of science fiction is *The War of the Worlds,* by H. G. Wells, published in 1898. When the story was broadcast as a radio play in 1938, it terrified many listeners. They believed that creatures from Mars had actually landed in New Jersey. The idea of meeting an alien still fascinates many people. In recent times, *E.T.* and the *Star Trek* and *Star Wars* movies have thrilled audiences with aliens, some likeable and some dangerous.

Enrich Your Reading

Context Clues   In a description of an alien attack, the author of this story uses the word *vaporizing.* In the next sentence he describes aircraft that "vanished in white-hot explosions." This phrase is a **context clue** that can help you understand what *vaporizing* means— "changing into a cloud of mist or smoke." When you read an unfamiliar word in this or any other story, look at surrounding words or sentences for clues to its meaning.

■ *Author biography in Reader's Handbook*

Playing for Keeps

JACK C. HALDEMAN II

Johnny Russell was playing in his back yard when the aliens landed. He was Tarzan in a land of giant ferns while they invaded Philadelphia, but had shifted over to Superman before Baltimore fell. Johnny was eight years old and easily bored. By the time his mother called him in for dinner, the aliens were all over Washington, D.C. Things were a mess. Ugly green monsters were everywhere. Lots of people were real upset, especially Johnny. They were having spinach for dinner.

Johnny hated spinach more than anything else in the world, except maybe Brussels sprouts and creamed corn.

He made such a fuss at the table, trying to slip the dog his spinach, that his parents sent him to bed early. That was too bad, because there was a lot of neat stuff on television that night. Eight years old is just the right age for appreciating a good monster or two. Johnny slept through it all, dreaming that he was flying his treehouse over the ocean in search of lost continents.

His parents, on the other hand, were totally immersed in aliens of the real sort. There was no escaping them. Even the twenty-four-hour sports network was full of monsters. Specials followed specials all night long. Bert and Sara stayed glued to the tube, afraid they might miss something. It was an exciting time to watch television, even better than the time the dam burst at Fort Mudge. A good crisis brought out the best in the electronics media, no doubt about that.

They watched the national news for a while and then switched over to the local news. They even tuned in PBS and watched a panel of distinguished professors pointing sticks at an alien's picture. It was exciting. Sara made popcorn, and Bert put another six-pack in the fridge.

Things were a mess. Ugly green monsters were everywhere.

"Don't you think we ought to wake up Johnny?" asked Sara, salting the popcorn.

"No," he said. "We've got to teach him not to play with his food. A parent has certain obligations, you know." Bert had always been the strict one.

"But isn't that a little severe?" asked Sara. "After all, he's very fond of hideous beasts."

"No," said Bert. "Remember what he did with the Brussels sprouts?"

Sara turned pale. "I thought I'd never get it all out. The air conditioning hasn't worked right since."

"And the creamed corn?"

Sara shuddered at the memory of the bomb squad marching through their living room in knee-deep water. "You're right," she said, passing him the popcorn.

 **question** Why are Johnny's parents eating popcorn if the aliens have landed?

They settled back and watched the early news, the special news, the update news, the fast-break news, the late news, and the late-late news. In between, they watched the news in brief and the news in detail. They were saturated with news and popcorn, and all they got out of it was indigestion and no news at all. Nobody knew much of anything about the aliens except they were crawling all over the place and were meaner than junkyard dogs.

Their silver, cigar-shaped spaceships had simply appeared out of nowhere with a shimmering colorful splash of glitter not unlike the special effects of a once-popular TV show still in reruns. It was horrible. People fled in panic, especially when the monsters started coming out of the space-ships.

The aliens stood about eight feet tall with thick, stocky bodies. Their four arms had too many elbows and not enough fingers. Folds of wrinkled green skin covered their neckless heads, and their three unblinking eyes held what could only be interpreted as malice and contempt for the entire human race.

At first it was hoped that they might be a congenial star-roving race of beings, eager as puppy dogs to give mankind all sorts of marvelous inventions. These hopes were quickly dashed. The aliens seemed far more interested in vaporizing people. Helicopters and airplanes that approached the hovering ships vanished in white-hot explosions. People who were foolish enough to make threatening gestures or stray too close went up in smoke. It made for good television footage but did little to aid any kind of mutual understanding.

Mutual understanding, as a matter of fact, didn't seem to be the aliens' strong suit.[1] They just didn't appear to be interested. Some of the best minds on Earth had attempted to establish communication with the aliens. Some of the best minds on Earth had been vaporized, too. The aliens were obviously intelligent, but they didn't have much to say.

Bert and Sara were about ready to turn in, having watched the instant replay of the destruction of Washington for the fourth or fifth time. It was impressive but not really all that great. The Japanese had done it better in that movie about the radioactive frog. Sara washed the popcorn bowls.

"I'll bet Johnny will be excited when he wakes up," she said. "Channel Four said they've even seen a couple aliens right here in town. Imagine that."

---

1. **strong suit:** greatest talent; area of excellence.

Words to Know and Use | **stocky** (stäk′ ē) *adj.* built solidly; sturdy
malice (mal′ is) *n.* a desire to cause harm; ill will
congenial (kən jēn′ yəl) *adj.* friendly

"I don't think we ought to tell the boy about them," said Bert. "At least not yet."

"For goodness sakes, honey. Why not?"

"The child has an active enough imagination as it is. There's no sense in getting him all riled up. Remember the time he thought he saw that UFO down by the river?"

Sara nearly dropped the bowl she was drying. That had been a near thing. Johnny had pulled every fire alarm in town, and only their friendship with the judge had kept their names out of the paper.

What does a kid know about monsters?

"Besides," said Bert, "what does a kid know about monsters? He's only eight years old."

Sara nodded. He was right, as always.

But Johnny wasn't completely fooled. When little Freddy Nabors didn't show up by twelve o'clock, he knew something was wrong. He and Freddy *always* messed around together on Saturday afternoon. Sometimes they went on dangerous secret missions, but usually they just played. By twelve-fifteen Johnny had decided a <u>plague</u> must have killed all the kids on Earth but him, so he went out into the back yard to play.

He wasn't allowed to go out behind the garage, so naturally it was his favorite place. It was full of old lumber and rusty nails. Lumber was more fun to play with than almost anything. Sometimes he built boats out of the scraps, and sometimes spaceships. Today he built a Grand Prix car. It was low

and sleek, faster than a bat. He pretended it was orange with black trim. Since he couldn't find any wheels, he used cinder blocks for racing tires.

Diving into the hairpin turn,[2] he had just passed Fangio and was gaining on Andretti[3] when he saw the monster. Johnny was not impressed. He'd seen better ones on television. Sticking his tongue out between his lips and making a rude noise, he downshifted with a raspberry and pulled to the side of the road. After taking off his imaginary helmet and racing gloves, he got out of his fabricated car and stared at the alien. The alien stared back. Three eyes to two, the alien had an edge; but Johnny never flinched. The Lone Ranger wouldn't have backed down, and neither would he.

In the distance Johnny could see one of their spaceships hovering over the river. It looked just like the one he'd seen before. He knew better than to head for the fire alarms this time, though. His father would tan his hide.

The alien grunted and pointed at his ship and then to himself. Johnny stood as firm as Wyatt Earp,[4] his jaw set like Montgomery Clift's, playing for keeps, his body held with the stern pride of John Wayne. He didn't nod; he didn't blink. He stared at the monster with Paul Newman's [5] baby-blue eyes,

---

2. **hairpin turn:** a U-shaped curve in a road.

3. **Fangio . . . Andretti** (fän′ jē ō, an dret′ ē): Juan Manuel Fangio and Mario Andretti, famous racing-car drivers.

4. **Wyatt Earp:** law officer of the American West, 1848–1929.

5. **Montgomery Clift . . . John Wayne . . . Paul Newman:** movie actors who have portrayed Western heroes.

Words to Know and Use | **plague** (plāg) *n.* a deadly disease that spreads widely

GLASSIES (MARBLES XIV) 1985 Charles Bell Courtesy, Louis K. Meisel Gallery New York.

hard as ice. He wished he'd worn long pants, though. Shorts just didn't cut it when you were staring down a monster.

The alien started waving all its arms in the air, grunting like crazy. Johnny was frightened, but he didn't give an inch. He could have been Gary Cooper standing alone in the middle of a dusty street facing an angry mob with only the badge on his chest and the goodness in his heart to protect him. Johnny could almost hear the people scurrying for cover. The helmet and racing gloves were useless. He should have had his six-shooter.

The alien kicked at the dust, smoothing out an area between them. He bent over, and Johnny hunkered down to join him. At least now he knew what to expect. They were about to talk, or *palaver*, as Slim Pickens[6] would say.

The alien picked up a stick and drew a large circle in the dirt. From a fold in his <u>tunic</u> he removed a small golden globe, which he placed precisely in the center. He pointed to the sun and then to the globe. Johnny nodded, his face as deadpan as if he were trying to fill an inside straight.[7]

The monster drew three concentric circles around the golden globe and placed another globe on the third circle. It was smaller than the first and covered with blue and white swirls. He patted the dirt, waved his arms in

---

6. **Gary Cooper . . . Slim Pickens:** movie actors who have portrayed Western heroes.

7. **deadpan . . . inside straight:** without expression as though trying to bluff poker opponents.

Words to Know and Use | **tunic** (tōo' nik) *n.* a loose, knee-length garment like that worn in ancient Greece and Rome

circles all around them, and pointed to the globe. Johnny bit his lip. This was getting complicated.

The alien continued drawing circles in the dust and setting down the small globes. When he had finished, nine of them surrounded the larger yellow one. With a <u>flourish</u> he took one more from his tunic. This one was special; it was silver and seemed to glow with a light from within. He set it outside the farthest circle and pointed first to himself, then to the spaceship, and finally to the silver sphere.

What is the alien trying to communicate?

Slowly he began rolling the sphere into the ring of circles. As he passed the outermost globe, he snarled and crushed it into the dirt beneath one of his massive thumbs. He continued rolling the silver sphere toward the center, snarling and crushing as he demolished each of the small globes. When he reached the third globe from the center, his lips drew back in a hideous sneer and he rose to his full height, towering over the crouching boy. The alien <u>gloated</u>, roaring with bone-chilling laughter as he crushed the small blue globe under his foot, grinding it into the dirt with a <u>vengeance</u>.

This, at last, was something Johnny could understand. It was a challenge. Without rising, he reached around to his back pocket. It was still there, as he knew it would be. He'd won it from Freddy Nabors two years ago, and he never went anywhere without it. It was his talisman, his good luck piece. It was

also his weapon and had never let him down. He gritted his teeth and took it reassuringly in his hand. It was blue with milky white bands, a perfect agate.[8]

He dropped and took quick aim, <u>oblivious</u> to the ranting and raving of the alien. He'd been under pressure before. This was nothing new. With a flick of his thumb, the aggie sailed across the dust, crashing into the silver ball, sending it careening out of orbit into the yellow one. They both flew outside the circle.

He stood—as a man would stand after battle—and retrieved all the marbles. He held them high above his head.

"Keepsies,"[9] he said and slipped them into his pocket.

The alien backed away in horror, babbling wildly. With a shimmer and a pop, he disappeared. An instant later the spaceship vanished in a similar fashion, as did all the spaceships and all the aliens all over the world.

Johnny climbed back into his Grand Prix car and accelerated through the gears. He was nearly a lap behind by now and would have to do some fancy driving to catch up. Besides, his mother was fixing creamed corn tonight, and the boy who had saved the world had important things on his mind.

As he took the checkered flag, he wondered how Conan would have handled creamed corn. ✌

---

8. agate (ag′ it): a marble made of a semiprecious stone.
9. keepsies: a slang term referring to one's winnings in a game of marbles.

Southbound on the Freeway

MAY SWENSON

A tourist came in from Orbitville,
parked in the air, and said:

The creatures of this star
are made of metal and glass.

Through the transparent parts
you can see their guts.

Their feet are round and roll
on diagrams or long

measuring tapes, dark
with white lines.

They have four eyes.
The two in back are red.

Sometimes you can see a five-eyed
one, with a red eye turning

on the top of his head.
He must be special—

the others respect him
and go slow

when he passes, winding
among them from behind.

They all hiss as they glide,
like inches, down the marked

tapes. Those soft shapes,
shadowy inside

the hard bodies—are they
their guts or their brains?

HIGHWAYS 1 1976 Ingo Swann American Oil on canvas
National Air and Space Museum, Smithsonian Institution, Washington, D.C.
Gift of the artist.

Responding to Reading

First Impressions

1. What were your reactions as you read this story? Jot down your reactions in your journal or on a sheet of paper.

Second Thoughts

2. Johnny's parents mention that their son once tried to warn the town about a UFO. Why do you think no one believed Johnny?

3. Look back at the web you made in Examine What You Know on page 158. How do the reactions of Johnny's parents to the alien invasion compare to the reactions you listed? Why aren't they more frightened?

4. What do you think happens to the aliens and their spaceships?

5. Why do you think Johnny is able to save the world when attempts by adults fail?

> **Think about**
> • the comments Johnny's parents make about him
> • his interest in TV and movie heroes
> • the way he observes the alien

6. Johnny now owns the alien's glowing silver marble. What unexpected thing might happen if he plays with it again?

Broader Connections

7. In this story constant TV watching has made people unable to tell the difference between entertainment and a crisis. Does television have this effect in real life? Explain why or why not.

Literary Concept: Humor

Writers sometimes add **humor** to a story by treating a serious idea as if it were unimportant. Describing a minor problem right after describing a major one can create a mood of comedy. For example, the alien attack on Earth is described as a crisis. The writer, however, makes the ordinary fact that Johnny hates certain vegetables seem just as serious. Give another example of a serious thing that is treated in a humorous way in the story.

Writing Options

1. The aliens all disappear from Earth at the end of the "battle." Write a **memo** that the defeated alien might transmit to his home planet about what has happened.

2. Johnny's parents were tuned in to TV news reports for hours. Write a **news bulletin** about the aliens' mysterious disappearance, one that might interrupt the television coverage of the ongoing crisis.

3. The alien invaders are described as monsters in the story. Find other details and make an observation chart about the alien Johnny faces. Record such information as the alien's physical appearance, clothing, temperament, and level of intelligence and anything else that you might glean from the story. Use this information to write a **character sketch** of the alien.

4. Review the alien's actions as he draws circles, then sets down marbles and crushes them. Take the alien's point of view and write a **monologue,** a speech by one actor, in which he explains what he is doing and what his actions represent.

5. Read the Insight poem on page 164. Think about the way the alien in the poem views an ordinary highway scene on Earth. Choose a scene from "Playing for Keeps" and write your own humorous **poem,** using the alien's point of view.

Vocabulary Practice

Exercise   On your paper, write the word from the list that best completes each sentence. Each word is used only once.

We were hoping the short, (1) aliens would be talkative and (2) so that we could learn to communicate and share ideas. Instead, the aliens brought germs from their planet that caused a (3) . They seemed to (4) over the hardships they had caused and the headlines they were creating. Dressed in a long, flowing (5) , one alien showed his (6) toward the human race by waving with a (7) the warning notice from the U.S. Health Department. The (8) , both print and electronic, recorded every stage of the crisis. The aliens were so interested in being the center of attention that they were (9) to our plans to destroy their leaders. Now we wait to see whether these aliens believe in (10) , whether they will seek an eye for an eye or leave us in peace.

Fiction

The Secret of the Wall

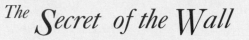

ELIZABETH BORTON DE TREVIÑO (dã tre vē' nyô)

Examine What You Know

What are the most important qualities a friend should have? In your journal, list the qualities that you value most in a friend. Number them in order of importance to you.

Expand Your Knowledge

The narrator and his two friends live in Guanajuato (gwä' nä hwä' tô), a city in the rugged central highlands of Mexico. At one time, the mining of silver brought wealth to Guanajuato, but in 1821 troubled times began. Mexico had freed itself from Spanish control, but wars and revolutions shook the country for another hundred years. The desperate citizens of Mexico hid silver and other valuables from the bands of raiding soldiers and revolutionaries who battled back and forth across the country, trying to gain control.

Enrich Your Reading

Examining Characters As you read this story, think about the appearance, values, and actions of the narrator (Carlos) and his two friends. Copy the chart below in your journal. To help you understand these characters, review the story when you have finished reading it. Then fill in the columns under each heading.

	APPEARANCE	VALUES	ACTIONS
Carlos			
Serafin			
Martin			

■ *Author biography on Extend page*

The Secret of the Wall

ELIZABETH BORTON DE TREVIÑO

On a day in September, I walked down to Cantaranas Plaza and past it, along the narrow cobblestone street, and there was the great *zaguán*, the entrance to the *secundaria*,[1] our high school. Beyond I could see the broad, white ascending steps of the university, where I would go one day.

The streets of Guanajuato smell of dried chilies, of jasmine and carnations in pots behind the iron-barred windows, of hot baked bread, and of burro droppings. It is my town in central Mexico, a romantic old town that has lived days of wealth and luxury, because of the rich silver mines nearby, and days of poverty, because of the turmoil of revolutions and social change. Heroism has been here, in these little winding alleys and broad, fountain-centered plazas. Faith is here, in our many beautiful churches, soaring into the sky. Many artists have lived here and loved Guanajuato and painted it. My family has lived here since the days of my great-grandfather, and I always knew the legends of some of the streets, of many of the old houses, and the stories of ghosts and hauntings, some violent, some tender.

School smelled like schools everywhere, of chalk dust and disinfectant soap and boys. I found my classroom and a seat on the aisle where I could rest my leg by extending it out along my desk. Three years ago I had had polio.[2] It left me weak in the back and in one leg; I still have to take special exercises and wear a brace for some hours every day. But Dr. Del Valle, who took care of me when I was sick, had said at last that I could walk to and from school every day and that I would be getting stronger all the time. Yet I knew that I would not be able to take part in the games or play out in the court during recess. All the boys were younger than I, but almost all were taller and broader, too. The only one I knew was Serafin, Dr. Del Valle's youngest boy. He stood half a head taller than any of the others and was handsome and strong. I thought, Serafin will surely captain one of the ball teams—soccer or basketball or baseball—and he will be president of the class.

But I was wrong. When the first recess for games came, I went to sit under the arcades[3] and watch, and I saw the shouting

---

1. *zaguán* . . . *secundaria* (sä gwän′, se kōͺn dä′ ryä) *Spanish.*

2. polio: short for *poliomyelitis,* a disease that often results in muscle weakness and crippling.

3. arcades: covered passageways.

Words to Know and Use | **turmoil** (tɐr′ moil′) *n.* a state of confusion; commotion

GROUP OF HOUSES IN SANTA TERESA   Gustavo dall'Ara   Agnaldo de Oliveira Collection   São Paulo, Brazil.

boys choose up sides. The games professor passed out mitts and bats and balls. Serafín was a swift runner, but he didn't try very hard. He seemed uninterested, and when one of the other boys jostled him, he dropped out. "Coward!" they called after him, but he just shrugged his shoulders. He came over and sat down by me, looking very <u>sullen</u>.

"It's a silly game anyhow," he said.

"I wish I could play!" I burst out.

"Why?" he asked. "You don't get anything out of it. It's just exercise. Getting knocked about and hurt sometimes. Foolishness. I play a much better game, by myself, every day."

"You do? What game?"

"I may tell you someday." Then he got up and sauntered off. He walked down one of the corridors slowly, looking at his feet, and then he stooped to pick up something and put it in his pocket. I turned my eyes back to the noisy fun in the school patio. I had hopes of distinguishing myself in another way. My father is a fine chess player, and groups of the best players in our town meet at our house on Saturday evenings. During the years of my illness, Papacito[4] had taught me how to play and had bought me a small

---

4. **Papacito** (pä pä sē′ tô) *Spanish*: dear papa.

Words to Know and Use | **sullen** (sul′ ən) *adj.* sad and grumpy; sulky

169

chess set that was portable and on which the pieces could be fixed so that a game might go on from where it had been left off days before. There were no gentlemen in Papacito's chess circle who were unwilling to sit down to a game with me, and once I had even beaten Don Mario, the postman, who often came. He was Guanajuato's champion.

Limping home after that first day in class, I tried to place Serafin in my chess game. A knight? Perhaps. Not a bishop or a tower. And, of course, not a pawn. He was too independent for that.

As I passed Cantaranas Plaza, I saw several country fellows with their weary burros taking water at the fountain, and I sat there a moment, on the lip of the fountain, dipping my hand in the water and talking with them. As they went away, single file, down the street toward the country, the dusty peons,[5] who worked on buildings in the city, came tramping along. They smelled of sweat and of chili, and though they were so tired that they could scarcely lift their feet, they laughed and joked with each other. Many were boys not much older than I. I felt sorry that they could not be in school, but I knew that most of them worked to help support families.

Tía[6] Lola had made my favorite *polvorones*[7] for supper, to celebrate my first day back at school. Tía Lola is Papacito's sister, who came to live with us after my mother's death. When we had finished supper that night, we sat and talked for half an hour

before Papacito went into his library to work and study.

As the days went by, I became more interested in all my classes. I often took my chessboard to school, and while the others were at games, Professor Morado sometimes played with me. The boys were pleasant, but careless with me; they thought me a cripple, because I had to wear my brace some days. Only one sought me out. Serafin. I took this <u>philosophically</u>, for I had observed him, and he, who could have done so, did not try to make friends. When the boys shoved him in the halls or pushed at him, he backed away and seemed to be afraid of them. I suppose he thought that I, so obviously outside the circle of the other boys in class, would be grateful for his company. And, in a way, that was true.

He began walking home with me afternoons, sometimes chatting, sometimes morosely[8] making no comment on anything I said. He often leaned down to pick up a button, or a bit of cord, or a pin.

"That's my game," he told me suddenly one day. "Finders keepers!"

"How silly! You can't often find anything worthwhile."

"Oh, but you're wrong! I often do! I must have one hundred pesos'[9] worth of

---

5. **peons** (pē′ ənz): unskilled laborers.

6. **Tía** (tē′ ä): *Spanish:* aunt.

7. *polvorones* (pôl vô rô′ nes) *Spanish:* cinnamon cookies.

8. **morosely:** in a gloomy, sullen way.

9. **pesos** (pā′ sōz): Mexican money.

Words to Know and Use | **philosophically** (fil′ ō säf′ ik lē) *adv.* in a calm and sensible way

stuff piled up at home that I found this way. Besides, just now we were only wandering along. But sometimes I pick out somebody and follow them.

"You'd be surprised how often they put down a package and forget it, or leave their umbrella, or even drop money!"

"But . . . but . . . ." I stuttered, "if you see them drop something, you ought to give it back!"

*F*inders keepers.
That's the game.

"No," he answered stubbornly. "Finders keepers. That's the game."

"But what do your parents think about this? Tía Lola would never let me keep anything I found if it were valuable. Or my father either. I'd have to find out who it belonged to and give it back, or give it to the poor."

"Ah, my father and mother don't even know about my game, and I shan't tell them," he responded. "Papá is always out, all hours of the day or night on his calls, and Mámacita is usually in bed with a headache. They don't care what I do."

I was troubled about all this, but I did not talk it over with my father or Tía Lola for a very selfish reason: I had no other friend, and I did not want to be deprived of Serafin, unsatisfactory and worrisome though he was. I knew he was cowardly, secretive, and selfish, but he was a companion. So I kept silent, though I never did go to his house. He sometimes came to mine, but only to talk or play with my dog in the patio.

I was not very lonely. I often went to Cantaranas fountain and took my chessboard. I could work out problems in chess there and watch the people passing by.

I was doing this about five o'clock of a November day when dusk was beginning to let down veils of darkness over the town. I had just closed my chessboard and was about to start home when a workman came toward me from one of the streets that led down into town. From his plaster-covered shoes and the sacking that he still wore over his shoulders, and his dusty shirt and trousers, I could tell he was probably working on one of the new buildings that were going up near the entrance of the city.

He was about nineteen, I thought. He smiled at me shyly.

"I have seen you going to high school early in the morning," he said.

He paused and shuffled his feet. "And I have seen you sitting here in the afternoons, studying."

"That's right."

"My name is Martin Gonzales," he said suddenly, after a long pause. "I am going to ask you to do me a favor."

"Gladly, if I can." I thought he might ask for a peso.

"I want you to write a letter for me."

"But I have no paper and envelope."

"Bring them tomorrow and write a letter, please. I will pay you the fee."

That night at supper I said, "Papacito, I am going to be an evangelist."

All the men who sit at their typewriters in the big main square downtown are called, by the country people, *evangelists*, after St. John the Evangelist, I suppose. These men keep a few legal forms in their pockets and write collection letters and the like. Quite a few are busy writing personal letters for the people who cannot read or write.

"But you have no typewriter!" cried Tía Lola, serving me a big dish of *chongos,*[10] my favorite dessert.

"I will only do this one letter. It is for a nice fellow, a laborer. I suppose he is <u>illiterate</u>."

Papacito sighed. "We have too many of them," he said. "Mexico needs more schools, more teachers. We have made some progress, but not enough."

The next day Serafin wanted me to go with him rambling through the town, playing that game of finders keepers. But I told him about the letter I was to do. He made a face and would not come with me. But he said, "A workman on buildings? Maybe he will know where they plan to knock down some old places. Ask him."

I waited for Martin and wrote his letter for him. It was a note to a girl in another town. He was ashamed for her to know that he could not write, and if he had gone to one of the evangelists down in the main square, she would have suspected, knowing very well that he had no typewriter.

I accepted the payment he offered me, so as not to wound his pride and so as to leave the door open for him should he want me to do other letters for him. Like my father, I felt very sad that this big, nice man could not read or write.

He put the letter away carefully inside his dirty shirt and turned his bright eyes toward my chessboard. I asked if he knew the game, but he shook his head. Idly I explained the moves and the names of the pieces.

Then began a curious friendship. Martin passed by the fountain every afternoon, sometimes bringing with him another big, shy workman who wanted a letter. I began to develop a small but regular business, and I looked forward to that hour in Cantaranas Plaza. It comforted me to think I was doing something useful, and I began to plan on teaching them to read a little when vacations came.

Serafin was <u>scornful</u> and did not often drop by anymore. "How stupid!" he said. "Writing silly letters for oafs."

"Martin is no oaf! I am teaching him chess, and he will be a good player!"

"I don't believe it!"

"Stay and watch then! Here he comes now."

Martin came hurrying along. I presented them, and Serafin had the grace to take Martin's calloused hand after it had been dusted against his trousers and deferentially[11] offered.

I had the pieces set up on my little board. Martin drew the white, so he had first move. He made an opening gambit[12] I had never before seen used. I did not know the defense, and he soundly beat me. Serafin's eyes were starting from his head, for like most of us boys in Guanajuato, he knew something of the game.

"*Caray,*[13] you stopped me in my tracks,

---

10. *chongos* (chôn′ gôs) *Spanish:* a custard made with eggs and milk.
11. **deferentially:** very respectfully.
12. **gambit:** a move in chess in which one gives up a piece to gain an advantage.
13. *Caray* (kä räy′) *Spanish:* an exclamation of surprise.

Words to Know and Use | **illiterate** (il lit′ ər it) *adj.* not able to read or write
scornful (skôrn′ fəl) *adj.* full of disgust

A QUIET READ
Francisco Sant'Olalla
Agnaldo de Oliveira Collection
Rio de Janeiro, Brazil.

Martin!" I cried. "Who showed you that gambit?"

"I made it up," he told me, pleased. "I thought about the chessboard all day, as I was working. I could see it in front of my eyes, and every piece, and so I played a game with myself, in imagination, and it seemed to me that the opening I used just now was a good one."

Martin arrived on Saturday evening in clean, freshly ironed cotton work clothes. Like all our country people, he has perfect manners, and, of course, so has my father and so have his friends. They made Martin welcome, and my father sat down to play his first game with him. To my amazement, he defeated my father in the first game, and the second one was a real struggle, finally ending in stalemate. My father was perfectly delighted, and all the others crowded round to congratulate Martin.

"Young man, you are a chess genius, I think!" cried Don Mario, the postman. "You must join us every Saturday! Keep our game keen!"

After he had left, my father and his friends talked excitedly about Martin. They had in mind to train and polish him, and enter him in the state championship chess games in the spring.

The next day there was a piece in the paper about a treasure having been found by workmen when tearing down an old house in Celaya. Under the flagstones of the patio they came upon a strongbox filled with silver coins. My father read the item aloud.

"Too bad we live in a house built by my grandfather," chuckled Papacito, "and that I know he happened to die land-poor. And my father was a believer in banks."

"My friend Luisa, in Guadalajara,[14] had a friend who found a buried treasure in the kitchen of the house they bought," contributed Tía Lola.

"Well, it happens often, and it is reasonable," explained Papacito. "Mexico has gone through violent times, and insurgent[15] and revolutionary armies have swept in and out of so many towns that the people often buried or hid their valuables so as not to have to surrender them. And then, of course, sometimes they couldn't get back to retrieve them. Or they died, and nobody ever knew what had happened to their money."

I was thinking this over as I walked to school, and in the first recess Serafin sought me out, full of excitement.

"Did you read about the treasure in Celaya?" he asked me, breathless. "Let's go treasure hunting here! There must be quantities of old houses where people have buried money!"

"*Did you read about the treasure in Celaya?" he asked me, breathless.*

"Well, yes. My father said there was every likelihood. But how? Which houses? And how would you start? Nobody would even let you begin!"

"Why couldn't Martin tell us where? He works with a wrecking crew, knocking down old houses, doesn't he? He could sneak us into one some night!"

"Tía Lola wouldn't let me go."

"Don't tell her!" counseled Serafin impatiently.

"Well . . ."

It is one of the joys in our town to go out in the dusk or in the evening, wandering through the narrow little alleys and streets, singing and serenading the young ladies behind their barred windows. I had never done this, because of my leg, but I was really strong enough to start out soon.

It was the deceit that unnerved me. But the call of adventure was strong, and, I'll confess it, I longed to go treasure hunting. I resolved to speak to Martin.

I had my chance when he stopped by

---

14. **Guadalajara** (gwä′ d'l ə här′ ə).
15. **insurgent:** rebelling against a government.

Cantaranas Plaza after work. I was waiting for him.

"We began to tear down the old house of the Lost Grandfather today," he told me. "The workmen are not happy about it. They say it is haunted."

"Yes? Tell me about it?"

"The Lost Grandfather groans and howls there on windy nights; people have heard him. He was an old gentleman who simply disappeared during the Revolution."

"Strange. Aren't you afraid to work there, Martin?"

"I? No. I am only a simple, uneducated fellow. But I do not believe in ghosts," he told me scornfully.

Serafin was eager to go out that very night, but he decided that he had better reconnoiter[16] first. But the next day at recess, he told me, in whispers, that the situation was perfect. There was a watchman, but he was very old and deaf and did not know anything about the ghost.

"His daughter brings him his supper at about nine o'clock, and he eats it, and then he goes to sleep on some sacks in the back. To try him out, I even pounded on the gate and struck the rocks of the patio with a small steel bar I have. The old fool did not hear a sound. We'll go tonight!"

I was scared, but terribly eager to go just the same. Little prickles of excitement ran up and down my spine all day.

Just at dusk, Serafin came by for me. He had a long, paper-wrapped parcel under his arm. "An iron bar with a pointed tip," he said, "and a candle."

As we left, I had a bad time with Tuerto, my little white dog with the black spot around one eye. Tuerto whined and begged to come with us, and he got out twice and

had to be brought back in and scolded before he would not try to follow me. I believe he smelled my excitement.

As we came near the haunted house, we saw the watchman's daughter just arriving.

"Good! She's early!" hissed Serafin. She left the big *zaguán* slightly ajar as she went in, and, pulled and pushed by Serafin, I followed. We were inside!

We had to wait a long time, pressed up hard against the wall where we would not be seen, while the old watchman and his daughter talked a long time over some family problem. A little wind began to rise, and I shivered with nerves and with cold.

At last she left, calling *adios*, and the old man made the sign of the cross behind her as the *zaguán* clanged to. Then he shuffled off to somewhere in the back.

"Come in now," said Serafin. "He eats and rests way back there, where they have begun taking out the rear walls. I want to try inside, around the fireplace. That's where lots of treasures have been buried."

We went cautiously into the big central hall of the house. It was quite dark and very mysterious. A little light drifted in from the street, but the shadows were deep, and there were strange noises, little scurryings and rattlings. Our eyes grew used to the dark. Soon we made out the fireplace. From it stretched out two walls, at the far ends of which there were doors into other rooms.

"Let's sound those walls," suggested Serafin. "You go along there, and I'll go here. See if they sound hollow to you. Like this."

---

16. **reconnoiter** (rek′ ə noit′ ər): to scout or explore.

And he went along, giving a smart rap on the plaster. I dutifully did as I was told, almost forgetting the watchman, but the walls sounded the same along their length to me.

"We might as well open up anyhow and see how solid they are," whispered Serafin, and he went at a place in the wall not far from the chimney. I was terrified. It seemed to me that the clanging and banging would bring not only the watchman, but even people from the street, in upon us. However, Serafin labored away, to no avail.

"I'll try over here," he panted, and again he dug at the wall, but there seemed to be nothing but firmly set bricks inside.

"Here. You try." He gave me his improvised pick, and I went at a place on the other side of the fireplace. At first the plaster gave way easily. Then I came upon the same hard bricks. But as I struck and pried at them, one of them crumbled away, and another, and I put my hand in. There was an opening!

Serafin almost shouted in his joy. "I'll open it up more, and then you get inside and see what's there!" He worked away very fast and soon had a hole in the hollow wall through which I could just squeeze my shoulders.

"Get in!" he urged, and pushed me.

"It's terribly dark," I said. "Give me the candle."

He passed it in to me, and I lighted it. I stood inside the wall, in a very narrow passage. The air was still and dead, and the candle flickered along the wall.

And then suddenly there was a deep, mournful groan. I started and dropped the candle. As I struck against the wall, plaster and bricks rained down, and I found myself cut off. I tried to scratch and scrabble my way out, but in the dark I had no way of knowing whether I would be able to get free again.

"Serafin!" I called with all my might, but there was no answer. Only, at my shout, more plaster and bricks fell.

I was scared to death. I stood there and cried, until I realized that I would have to be sensible and think.

EL GLOTÓN (The Glutton) 1958 Alberto Gironella
Art Museum of the Americas, Organization of the American States
Washington, D.C.

I cannot pretend that I was able to do this immediately. I suffered from a confusion of feelings. I thought I might be buried alive; I feared our being caught in that house where we had no permission to be; I was frightened of the dark and of the sounds. But eventually I was able to control myself.

I was not scared by the groan. I did not believe in ghosts, and I knew there must be some natural explanation. I felt sure Serafin would go at once and bring help. And after a bit, I realized I would not smother, for there was a thin breath of air, from somewhere in the wall, that moved along my cheek.

It came to me, at last, that I might find some opening in the wall, and cautiously I started exploring. Luckily I had some matches in my pocket, and though I scrabbled around trying to find the candle, I could not. So I lit a match, and in that light went along, feeling the sides of the hollow wall close against me, until the match burned down to my fingers and I was in darkness again. In this way I passed around a bend in the wall, where it curved out around the fireplace I thought, and emerged into the wall beyond, which was also hollow. But there, as I lit a third match, I saw, suddenly illuminated, a skeleton fully dressed in the clothes of last century and sitting on a low bench. It was wedged between the walls, and on its knees was a box. It was a terrible figure, but even in that first moment of shock and <u>revulsion</u>, I felt pity. What had been a man must have had himself walled in here with his treasure . . . and no one had ever come back to free him. Was it the Lost Grandfather?

I said a prayer for the soul of that pitiful skeleton man and then tried to maneuver myself around in the wall and feel my way back whence I had come. I decided to save my matches, and when I felt the fallen rubble, I lay down, very gingerly, to wait for rescue, saying my prayers all the while.

I said a prayer for the soul of that pitiful skeleton man.

I may have dozed, from fear and hunger and cold, for I awoke startled to hear a dog yelping. It was my Tuerto! And, as I came to myself and realized where I was, I heard scratching and striking along the wall. I hurried back, in case some more bricks should tumble down; but before long there was an opening, the rubble was being pulled away, and there was Martin, looking in, with his face all pale and drawn.

"Thank God! He's all right!" he called.

And I heard Tía Lola and my father echo, "Thank God!"

He pulled me out, and Tuerto leaped upon me and almost smothered me with doggy kisses. Then I was enclosed in my aunt's arms, and I felt my father's hand on my hair.

I can't remember much more of what happened until they got me home and to bed and Tía Lola gave me a drink of hot lemonade.

Serafin had abandoned me. They did not

know he had even been with me until I told them.

Martin had happened to come back to our house that evening to tell my father he could not come to play chess on Saturday; and as Tía Lola opened the *zaguán* to him, Tuerto had shot out and into the street.

Tía Lola had been crying. She was worried, for it was after eight and I had not come home. Martin said to her, "Look, the little dog is trailing him! I'll follow and bring back Carlitos."

My loyal Tuerto led Martin straight into the haunted house and to the wall. Martin had called and called, but I had been asleep and did not hear. Anyhow, he rushed back to bring my father and Tía Lola, and also a pick. And so they had found me.

In bed, safe and warm, I remembered the poor skeleton. "There is a dead man in the walls," I told them, "holding a treasure on his lap. Please go back and get it, Martin!"

"Shall I?" Martin looked at my father.

"We'll go," said my father, and they left me to Tía Lola.

I tried to stay awake until they came back, but excitement and fright had taken their toll and I fell deeply asleep. I did not know until the next morning that Martin and I had a fortune between us. The skeleton was extracted from the wall and given decent burial, and my father looked up in the old records of the city, and of taxpayers on the old houses, to find out his probable identity. Then he had searched for relatives, but there seemed to be none. So, after my father

paid the taxes on the treasure, it remained for us. Finders keepers.

It was not so very much, after all. The box had held silver coins and some jewels, but these were not of much intrinsic value anymore. Still, something like twenty thousand pesos remained to be divided between Martin and me.

"What will you do with your part?" I asked Martin a few days later.

"I will take care of my mother and my little brothers, and I shall go to school," he cried.

But in the Saturday evening chess circle, my father and his friends decided among them they would teach Martin to read and write, and coach him until he could pass examinations and then go on to evening classes. Meanwhile, he was going to be their champion in chess tournaments, and he could make some money giving exhibition games.

"What will you do with your part of the treasure?" Don Mario asked me. They were all eating *enchiladas*[17] and drinking coffee after their game. Before I could answer, there was a <u>clamor</u> at our *zaguán*. And the big knocker sounded several times. Tía Lola ushered in Dr. Del Valle and Serafin.

Dr. Del Valle gave Serafin a push into the center of the room. "Begin," he ordered his son.

"I am sorry," stammered Serafin.

Dr. Del Valle was trembling with emotion. "I never thought I would see the day when I

---

17. *enchiladas* (en′ chē lä′ däs) *Spanish:* rolled tortillas with a meat filling, served with chili sauce.

Words to Know and Use | **clamor** (klam′ ər) *n.* a loud noise; uproar

would feel so ashamed of my son," he told my father. "He has just now confessed to me that he induced Carlos to go with him to that house, to break into the walls and look for treasure, and that when the wall caved in, he ran home and left Carlos there, perhaps to die!"

Serafin stood with drooping head, and two tears slid down his cheeks. "I am sorry," he whispered again.

"We knew," said my father. "We realized that Serafin must have been paralyzed with fear. That is why I did not speak of it to you. He is forgiven. Isn't he, Carlos?"

"Of course," I answered at once.

I couldn't hate Serafin.

For what else could I say? I knew what it was to be scared senseless, almost to panic. I couldn't hate Serafin, even though Tía Lola did. I was even, in a way, sorry for him. For I knew that he would never be anything in the Great Chess Game but a simple pawn, like me. Martin would end as a knight.

"I suppose by rights," I said to Serafin, not being above heaping some coals of fire on his head, "at least part of the treasure should be yours. You started looking in the wall where it was found."

He glanced hopefully at me as I went on. "So I trust you will agree with me about what to do with it. I want to give it for a classroom in one of the new schools being built down by the highway. We could name that room." He was disappointed, I could see. But he was trapped. Or, as Tía Lola said later, he made a virtue of necessity.[18]

"Whatever you say, Carlos," he answered meekly.

"Why don't we name it for the Lost Grandfather?" I cried.

And so it will be. My father turned over the money to the education department, and a plaque will be affixed to one of the rooms, saying, "This room was built with funds left by the Lost Grandfather." The president of Mexico is coming to inaugurate[19] the school, and several others, and Serafin and I and all our relatives, and Martin, and the whole class at school and Professor Morado, and many others, will be there. All Guanajuato will be in gala dress. The day will be a great *fiesta*.

Olé, poor Lost Grandfather. Your treasure will be of good use at last. 🙦

---

18. made a virtue of necessity: appeared to choose to do something that he actually was forced to do.

19. inaugurate: to open officially with a formal ceremony.

Responding to Reading

First Impressions

1. Which character do you have the strongest feelings about? Describe your reaction in your journal or on a sheet of paper.

Second Thoughts

2. What do you think of the way Carlos treats Serafin at the end?

3. What kind of person is Martin Gonzales?

   Think about
   - his first meeting with Carlos
   - his interest in chess
   - his plans for his share of the treasure

4. Review the list you made in Examine What You Know on page 167. Compare Carlos, Martin, and Serafin in terms of the qualities of friendship that you find most important.

5. Do you think that if the wall had not caved in on Carlos, he would have continued his friendship with Serafin? Explain your answer.

Broader Connections

6. Carlos and Serafin have different opinions about what should be done with something of value found in the street. Do you believe in the rules of "finders keepers"? Explain why or why not.

Literary Concept: Characterization

The way a writer creates and develops a character's personality is called **characterization.** A writer can make a character come alive through direct description of the character, through the character's words and actions, and through the words and actions of other characters. Martin, for example, is described as wearing "clean, freshly ironed cotton work clothes." This might tell you that Martin is a working person who cares about his appearance. Find other examples of ways in which de Treviño shows us Martin's or Serafin's character. To help you find examples, use the Examining Characters chart on page 167 that you completed after reading the story.

Concept Review: Setting As you know, the setting is the time and place of a story. What different settings does de Treviño use in this story and why?

Writing Options

1. Compare what Carlos learns about choosing friends with what Aaron learns in "Aaron's Gift" on page 73. Write a **dialogue** between the two characters.

2. Consider how the characters will have changed in ten years. Conduct an imaginary **interview** with Martin or Serafin. Write questions you would ask them, such as whether the events in this story changed their lives and what they are doing now. Leave space to write the answers that they might give.

3. Imagine that you are present at the ceremony at which Martin and Serafin turn over the treasure to the education department. Write a short **speech** for either Martin or Serafin, explaining the decision to donate the treasure to the new school.

4. Legends are stories that are passed down through many generations and are thought to have a historic basis. Write a **legend** about what happened to the poor Lost Grandfather. Weave details from the story into your tale.

Vocabulary Practice

Exercise A Write the word from the list that is most clearly related to the situation in each description.

1. The once peaceful town was now swept into a state of confusion. The citizens soon learned to expect the unexpected.

2. Within days the streets were filled with the sounds of braying donkeys, fleeing people, and ringing church bells.

3. The rich mine owner reacted sensibly. He took all the confusion in stride.

4. The peasants, unfortunately, were not able to read the letters of warning posted in the town.

5. When an innocent shopkeeper was shot the next morning, the people were shocked and horrified.

Words to Know and Use

clamor
illiterate
philosophically
revulsion
scornful
sullen
turmoil

Exercise B Decide if the following pairs of words are synonyms or antonyms. On your paper, write *S* for *synonyms* and *A* for *antonyms.*

1. philosophically—reasonably
2. sullen—cheerful
3. clamor—uproar
4. revulsion—attraction
5. scornful—respectful

*O*ptions for Learning

1 • Mexican Fiesta   Celebrate the new school in Guanajuato with a Mexican fiesta. With your classmates prepare some of the foods mentioned in the story. Play Mexican music to create the feeling of a fiesta. Display a Mexican flag, a map of Mexico, travel posters, and any Mexican coins, artwork, and crafts that you or your classmates may be able to bring.

2 • Checkmate   Learn the basic rules of chess and introduce them to your class. Bring a chessboard and chess pieces to class. Discuss the reasons why the characters in the selection are amazed at Martin's abilities and why he is compared to a knight, while Serafin is compared to a pawn.

3 • Glorious Guanajuato   Carlos says that many artists have lived in and painted Guanajuato. Using details from the story and any information you can find about Guanajuato or similar Mexican towns, draw or paint a scene from the story.

4 • Treasure Hunt   Design a treasure hunt game that covers the entire country of Mexico. Research the history of Mexico and study a map of the country. Using clues about geography or history, lead treasure hunters from place to place on a map of Mexico. The winner is the first to discover the location of the buried treasure.

FACT FINDER SOCIAL STUDIES

What Mexican president decreed in 1944 that every Mexican who could read and write must teach another to do so?

*E*lizabeth Borton de Treviño
1904-

As a child in California, Elizabeth Borton de Treviño was delighted by the sounds of the piano, the violin, and the Spanish language. These interests remained with her, leading her to study the literature, language, and history of Spain at Stanford University.

Her knowledge of music and Spanish helped de Treviño win her first job as a reporter for the *Boston Herald*. After working as a music reviewer, she was asked to use her Spanish to interview a dancer and musi-

cian from Spain. From that point, her working opportunities improved. Traveling to Mexico on a newspaper assignment, she met Luis Treviño Gomez, who became her husband. Mexico became her adopted country, and she has lived there since 1935.

De Treviño once said, "I generally get story ideas from some true event or moment in history that fires my imagination." *I, Juan de Pareja* is her most famous novel. This story of a slave who worked with the real-life painter Diego Velazquez earned de Treviño the Newbery Medal in 1966.

Poetry

Unfolding Bud
NAOSHI KORIYAMA
(nä ō′ shē kō′ re yä′ mä)

The Secret
DENISE LEVERTOV

Examine What You Know

What are the qualities you like or do not like in poetry? On your paper, copy the chart below. Then place an *X* on each line to show where your opinion lies. For example, if you like poems that rhyme, mark an *X* close to the word *Rhyme.* When you have completed the chart, write a few sentences that tell what you like best or least about poetry.

Rhyme———————————	No Rhyme
Humorous———————————	Serious
Long———————————	Short
Obvious Meaning———————————	Hidden Meaning
Tells a Story———————————	Paints a Picture
Uses Imagery———————————	Does Not Use Imagery

Expand Your Knowledge

Form refers to how a poem looks on the page. The way the words and lines are arranged is the form of the poem. Words can be arranged in lines, which may or may not be sentences. In poetry, a group of lines with space between them is called a **stanza.** A stanza is like a paragraph in other types of writing. Often each stanza introduces a new thought or image.

Write Before You Read

Imagine that a famous poet has been invited to your school and you have been selected to interview him or her. In your journal, make a list of the questions you would ask about what a poet does and why a person might become a poet.

■ *Author biographies on Extend page*

Unfolding Bud

NAOSHI KORIYAMA

WHITE LILY IN BLUE WATER   1978   Joseph Raffael
Courtesy, Nancy Hoffman Gallery   New York.

One is amazed
By a water-lily bud
Unfolding
With each passing day,
5 Taking on a richer color
And new dimensions.

One is not amazed,
At a first glance,
By a poem,
10 Which is as tight-closed
As a tiny bud.

Yet one is surprised
To see the poem
Gradually unfolding,
15 Revealing its rich inner self,
As one reads it
Again
And over again.

*R*esponding to Reading

First Impressions of "Unfolding Bud"

1. In your journal, record the details from the poem that you remember most.

Second Thoughts on "Unfolding Bud"

2. Why do you think the speaker finds the unfolding bud amazing?

3. The poem compares the unfolding of a poem to the unfolding of a water-lily bud. Is this a good comparison? Explain why or why not.

4. Suppose this poem were about understanding rock music instead of understanding poetry. What images might be used to describe rock music?

The Secret

DENISE LEVERTOV

Two girls discover
the secret of life
in a sudden line of
poetry.

5 I who don't know the
secret wrote
the line. They
told me

(through a third person)
10 they had found it
but not what it was
not even

what line it was. No doubt
by now, more than a week
15 later, they have forgotten
the secret,

the line, the name of
the poem. I love them
for finding what
20 I can't find,

and for loving me
for the line I wrote,
and for forgetting it
so that

25 a thousand times, till death
finds them, they may
discover it again, in other
lines

in other
30 happenings. And for
wanting to know it,
for

assuming there is
such a secret, yes,
35 for that
most of all.

Responding to Reading

First Impressions of "The Secret"

1. What are your impressions of the girls in this poem? Describe your impressions in your journal or on a sheet of paper.

Second Thoughts on "The Secret"

2. What kind of secret do you think this poem is about?

3. How could the secret be discovered "in other lines" and "in other happenings"?

Comparing the Poems

4. Each poem focuses on finding the meaning of poetry. Are the authors' ideas the same or different? Explain.

5. Compare and contrast the **forms** of "Unfolding Bud" and "The Secret."
   Think about
   • the number of **stanzas** and the number of lines in each stanza
   • the use of capitalization and punctuation

6. What advice do you think each poet might give about how to appreciate and enjoy poetry?

Literary Concept: Speaker

In a poem the **speaker** is the voice that talks to the reader. The speaker in a poem is like the narrator in a story. Often the speaker expresses the poet's own thoughts. Sometimes, however, the speaker of a poem is not the poet but a person or creature that the poet invents. In such cases the poem expresses the thoughts of someone other than the poet. Whose thoughts do you think the speaker is expressing in "The Secret"? Explain your answer.

Writing Options

1. Review what you wrote about poetry in Examine What You Know on page 183. Write an **essay** that explains which poem comes closest to the kind of poetry you like.

2. Write a **letter** from the author of "Unfolding Bud" to the author of the haiku on page 100. Explain why Koriyama might enjoy Issa's poetry.

Options for Learning

1 • **Poetry Sampler** Imagine that "Unfolding Bud" and "The Secret" are to be published in a new anthology called *Expect the Unexpected*. With a partner, design a book jacket for the anthology. Create art for the cover, and on the inside flap of the book jacket, describe the kinds of poetry included in this collection.

2 • **Dance the Poem** Create a dance interpretation of one of these poems. Choose music to accompany your dance and let your movements convey the mood, or feeling, of the poem.

Naoshi Koriyama 1926–

Although the native language of Naoshi Koriyama is Japanese, he set himself the challenge of creating his poetry in English.

Koriyama was born on Kikai Island in Japan. He attended colleges in his own country and also received a degree from the New York State College for Teachers in Albany, New York.

Koriyama is a professor of English literature in Japan. His poems appear in poetry collections, textbooks, and magazines.

Denise Levertov 1923–

The simple language and images of Denise Levertov's poetry have been called "thoroughly American." Levertov, however, was raised in a suburb of London, England, and educated by her mother at home. When she was twelve years old, she sent several of her poems to the famous poet T. S. Eliot. The positive comments in Eliot's two-page reply helped to boost Levertov's opinion of herself as a poet. She went on to publish her first poem when she was seventeen.

During World War II, Levertov served Britain as a nurse. In 1948, three years after the war ended, she moved to the United States with her American husband. In addition to writing, Levertov often teaches English at universities and actively supports many social and political causes, some of which she has written poetry about. Says Levertov: "I still hope for change and believe work and prayer can produce results. I have a button that says Picket and Pray."

Elements of
DRAMA

A **drama** is a story that is meant to be acted out for an audience. In a drama, or **play,** the plot is told through the words and actions of the characters. A drama can take place on stage, before a radio microphone, or before a TV or movie camera.

All dramas have three elements that are similar to the elements of fiction. These elements are character, plot, and setting. Unlike fiction, however, drama is written in a special form called a **script.** The script contains the words, or lines, that each character says as well as the type of information described below.

Understanding Drama

Cast of Characters   The script begins with a list, or cast, of characters in the play. Sometimes, the list includes brief descriptions of the characters.

Dialogue   Most of the script consists of the dialogue for the play. **Dialogue** is the term for conversation between the characters. Through the dialogue you get to know both the characters and the plot of the drama. Take a look at the following example from *A Christmas Carol.*

> **Scrooge.** Who are you?
>
> **Marley.** Ask who I was.
>
> **Scrooge.** Who were you?
>
> **Marley.** In life, I was your partner, Jacob Marley.

Stage Directions   The script also includes **stage directions.** These are the instructions for the actors, the director, and the stage crew. Stage directions are printed in italics in this book so that you will not confuse the stage directions with the dialogue. Sometimes the stage directions are also enclosed in parentheses. The stage directions also describe the objects—called **props**—that actors need during the play.

In addition, stage directions describe the **scenery** for the play. Scenery is the painted screens, backdrops, and other materials that help a stage look like a city street or a tropical jungle. Scenery creates the setting for a drama. For example, the scenery for *A Christmas Carol* gives the audience the feeling that they are looking back in time at an English businessman's office. In the following example, you can see how the stage directions tell the actor what to do as well as describe the props and scenery.

> **Cratchit** *comes in. He takes some coal from the mound and puts it into a small bucket; as he carries it to a small corner of the stage, the stage area is transformed from street to office.*

Scenes and Acts   Fiction or nonfiction books are usually divided into chapters. Plays, however, are divided into **scenes** and **acts.** Each time the setting or the time of the play changes, a new scene appears. In longer plays, the scenes are grouped into larger units called acts.

*S*trategies for Reading Drama

Drama is meant to be performed or read aloud, but since plays are written, you can also read them on your own. The following strategies will help increase your enjoyment, whether you perform a play with friends, read it aloud in class, or read it by yourself.

1. **Read the play silently.** Before you perform a play or read it aloud with others, read it to yourself. This way, you will understand the entire plot and get to know the characters ahead of time.

2. **Figure out what is happening.** Don't expect to understand everything about the play right away. When you read a book or watch a movie, you don't immediately understand what is going on. The same is true for drama.

3. **Read the stage directions carefully.** When you watch a drama on stage, you actually see the action and the scenery. When you read a drama, however, you have to use your imagination. The stage directions tell you where and when each scene is happening and help you understand more about the characters and the plot. If you skip over the stage directions, you miss out on much of the play.

4. **Get to know the characters.** In fiction, the author can describe a character and his or her personality in great detail. In a play, the characters' own words and actions tell you what the characters are like. Read the dialogue carefully, as well as the stage directions that accompany it. In addition, try to discover the feelings behind the words.

5. **Keep track of the plot.** The plot in a play centers around a main conflict that the characters try to resolve. When you read or watch a play, look for the conflict and get involved in the story. Notice how the characters try to work out the conflict or solve their problems.

6. **Read the play aloud with others.** People of all ages and in all countries have been performing and reading plays for centuries. When you read the part of a character, you become an actor. Let yourself get into the part. For a brief while, become that character. React to what other characters say and do to you. Remember to be ready with your character's lines of dialogue and read only the words your character says. Pay attention to the stage directions so that you know how to read your lines and what to do next, but don't read these italicized instructions aloud.

Perhaps everyone wonders at times what it would be like to be someone else. Drama gives you that opportunity. When you are a character in a play, you have a chance to step into someone else's feelings and experience something new.

Drama

A *Shipment*
of *Mute Fate*

LES CRUTCHFIELD
Based on a story by MARTIN STORM

Examine What You Know

In your journal, describe a time when you felt fear or terror over something in nature that you could not control. Describe both the situation and your responses.

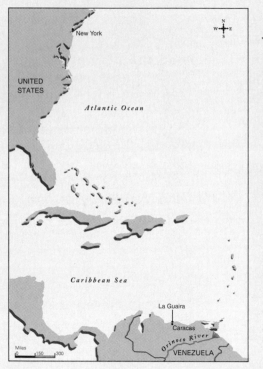

Expand Your Knowledge

Most of this suspenseful play is set aboard a ship that is sailing from Venezuela to New York City. Understanding some of the technical terms in this play will help you enjoy it more. A ship's *captain* leads the *crew.* Various *mates* (officers) help keep order and *navigate* (steer) from the *bridge,* the control room of the ship. A chief *steward* (a ship's officer in charge of supplies) directs assistants in the *galley,* or kitchen. Everyone sleeps in *bunks* or *berths* (beds). The word *port* refers to the side of the ship that is on the left as you face the *bow,* or front.

Enrich Your Reading

Radio Plays and Sound Effects   Sound effects help create the setting and atmosphere of a radio play. Because the audience cannot see the action, they have to imagine it. Sound effects are part of the stage directions. They are italicized and placed inside parentheses throughout this play. When you come to a stage direction describing sound effects, pause. Create the sound in your mind before reading on.

■ *Author biography on Extend page*

A *Shipment of Mute Fate*

LES CRUTCHFIELD
Based on a story by MARTIN STORM

CHARACTERS

Chris Warner, a young zoologist

Mrs. Willis, stewardess

Captain Wood, captain of the *Chancay*

Sanchez, native guide

Mr. Bowman, chief steward

Other Crew Members and Passengers

Chris *(narrating).* I stopped on the wharf at La Guaira[1] and looked up the gangplank[2] toward the liner *Chancay*—standing there quietly at her moorings.[3] The day was warm under a bright Venezuela sun—and the harbor beyond the ship lay drowsy and silent. But all at once in the midst of those peaceful surroundings, a cold chill gripped me, and I shivered with sudden dread—dread of the thing I was doing, and was about to do! *(Pause. Music comes up and dissolves slowly.)* But too much had happened to turn back now. I'd gone too far to stop. *(Sound: Wooden box set on wooden wharf, boat whistles, etc.)*

I set the box down on the edge of the wharf, placed it carefully so as to be in plain sight—and within gunshot—of the captain's bridge. *(Sound: Steps on gangplank; fade.)*

Then I turned and started up the gangplank. I knew what I was going to do—but I couldn't forget that a certain pair of beady eyes was watching every move I made. Eyes that never blinked and never closed—just watched . . . and waited!

Sound (shipboard commotion)

Willis *(coming in).* Oh! You startled me, sir! I didn't hear—why . . . *(with relief)* why, it's Mr. Warner!

Chris. Hello, Mother Willis. How's the best-looking stewardess on the seven seas?

---

1. **La Guaira** (lə gwī′ rə).
2. **gangplank:** a ramp used to board or leave a ship docked at a pier.
3. **moorings:** a place where a ship is docked.

Willis *(a bit evasive)*. Why, I'm . . . I'm fine, Mr. Warner. *(hurriedly)* Nice to see you again.

Chris *(joshing)*. Wait a minute! That's a fine greeting after two months.

Willis. Well—it's just that I'm so . . . so busy just now.

Chris. I don't believe a word of it—sailing day's tomorrow. And on the trip down from New York—you said I was your favorite passenger.

Willis. But—

Chris. Here—what's that you're carrying in your apron?

Willis *(obviously nervous)*. Oh, it's nothing. Just . . . supplies.

Chris. Supplies? Let's have a look.

Willis. No! Please!

Chris. Why—it's a cat!

Willis *(almost in tears)*. It's Clara, Mr. Warner. Mr. Bowman said I had to leave her ashore—and I just couldn't!

Chris. Who's Mr. Bowman?

Willis. The new chief steward. Clara's been aboard with me for two years—and I just can't leave her here in a foreign country. Especially with her condition so delicate and all!

Chris. Yes *(ahem)*, I see! I see what you mean. Well, I hope you get away with it.

Willis. You . . . you won't tell anyone?

Chris. Not a soul. As a matter of fact, if I don't get my way with the Captain, you and I may both end up smuggling!

Music (brief transition, dissolves)

Captain *(fades in)*. Most happy to have had you aboard on the trip down two months ago, Christopher, and I'm very glad you're coming along with us on the run back to New York.

Chris. Thanks, Captain Wood. There is one thing, though. I'm having a little trouble with the customs men here, and I wondered if you—

Captain. I can't do it, Christopher. I cabled[4] your father this morning—told him I'd have done it for you if I possibly could. He sent a request from New York, you know.

Chris. Yes, I thought he would . . . I . . . wired him from upriver last week.

Captain. I hated to refuse—but it's out of the question.

Chris. Captain Wood, I'm afraid I don't follow you.

Captain. Responsibility to the passengers, son. We'll have women and children aboard—and on a liner, the safety of the passengers comes ahead of anything else.

Chris. But with proper precautions!

Captain. Something might happen. I don't know what—but something might.

Chris. You've carried worse things!

Captain. There isn't anything worse—and any skipper afloat'll bear me out. No, son—I simply can't take the chance, and that's final!

---

4. **cabled:** sent a telegraph message by undersea cable.

Words to Know and Use | **evasive** (ē vā′ siv) *adj.* not straightforward
transition (tran zish′ ən) *n.* a passage from one activity to another
customs (kus′ təmz) *adj.* collecting duties or taxes on imported goods

Music (hit and out)

Chris *(narrating)*. Final! It wasn't final if I could do anything about it. I hadn't come down here to spend two months in that stinking back country and then be stopped on the edge of the wharf! Two months of it—heat, rain, insects, malaria—I'd gone clear into the headwaters of the Orinoco.[5] *(fading from mike)* Traveled through country where every step along the jungle trail might be the last one. . . .

Music (Swells and dissolves. Sound of men on a trail.)

Chris. Oh . . . Sanchez!

Sanchez *(coming toward mike)*. *Sí*, Señor Warner.

Chris. Better start looking for a place to camp. Be dark in a little while.

Sanchez. *Sí*, Señor—very soon we turn to river, camp on rocks by water. This very bad country.

Chris. This very bad country! You've been saying that for ten days now. Very bad country.

Sanchez. *Sí*, Señor Warner—this very bad country.

Chris. Oh, skip it. For all the luck we've had so far, it might as well be Central Park.[6]

Sanchez. Central Park? I no understand.

Chris. Never mind. If we don't—

(Excited cries of "Bushmaster!" Sounds of scrambling.)

Chris. Here—what's the matter? Quiet now! Sanchez—what's wrong?

Sanchez. There in the path! See? Bushmaster!

ECHAR LUZ SOBRE MIS RAICES   (Cast Light upon My Roots)
Orlando Gabino Leyba   Courtesy of the artist.

Music (loud, then fades)

Chris *(narrating)*. Bushmaster! The deadliest snake in the world! Bushmaster—its Latin name was *Lachesis mutus*—Mute Fate! It lay there in the center of the path—an eight-foot length of silent death—coiled loosely in an undulant[7] loop, ready to strike violently at the least movement.

---

5. **Orinoco** (ôr′ ə nō′ kō): a long river in Venezuela.
6. **Central Park:** a large park in New York City.
7. **undulant** (un′ dyo͞o lənt): wavy.

Here was the one snake that would go after any animal that walked—or any man. It lay there and watched us—not moving—not afraid—ready for anything. . . . The splotch of its colors stood out like some horribly gaudy floor mat—lying there on the brown background of the jungle—waiting for someone to step on it. Here was what I'd come two thousand miles for . . . a bushmaster!

Sound (pistol shot) Music (up and out sharply as . . .)

Chris. Sanchez! . . . I didn't want that snake killed!

Sanchez. He no killed, Señor—he gone. Bushmaster very smart, very quick—see bullet in time to dodge.

Chris. Anyway, he's gone! And the only one we've seen in five weeks!

Sanchez. Oh, we find other. This very bad country.

Chris. Well, lay off that gun the next time. Don't shoot—do you understand?

Sanchez. Why you say no shoot? You want bushmaster.

Chris. Sure—but I want it alive!

Sanchez. Señor Warner—you tell me you want bushmaster, but you no say "alive"!

Chris. You're getting two hundred dollars for it.

Sanchez. For dead man—what is two hundred dollars? Tomorrow we go back to Caracas.[8]

Chris *(going away from mike)*. Sanchez—I'll give you a thousand dollars! *(Music swells, then fades; Chris narrates.)* It cost me fifteen hundred—but three days later,

Sanchez brought me the snake in a rubber bag. He was shaking so hard I thought for a moment the thing had struck him. . . .

Sanchez *(excitedly)*. One thing you make sure, Señor Warner. No turn him loose in Venezuela. Because he know I the one who catch him—and he know where I live!

Chris. All right, Sanchez—I'll keep an eye on him.

Sanchez. He know you pay me to catch him. All the time he watch and wait. You no forget that, Señor Warner—because *he* no forget . . . not ever!

Music (loud, then under voice)

Chris *(narrating)*. Well, after going through all that trouble and danger—I wasn't going to let a pigheaded ship captain stop me at the last minute! At least not as long as the cables were still in operation between La Guaira and New York. . . .

Music (swells for transition, then cuts as door closes and steps come in)

Chris *(coming in)*. Morning, Captain Wood. The boy at the hotel said you wanted to see me.

Captain. That's right, Christopher. Uh . . . Sit down. *(sound of chair)* Seems you weren't willing to let matters stand the way we left them yesterday.

Chris. Sorry to go over your head, Captain Wood—but I had to. The museum sent me all the way down here for it, and I'm not going to be stopped by red tape.

---

8. **Caracas** (kə räk′ əs).

This'll be the *only* live bushmaster ever brought to the United States.

Captain. If I had my way . . . but orders are orders. Got a cable from the head office this morning. All right. Suppose we talk about precautions.

Chris. I'll handle it any way you say.

Captain. It's got to have a stronger box. That crate's too flimsy.

Chris. It's stronger than it looks—and that wire screen on top'd hold a wildcat. But anyway, I bought a heavy sea chest this morning. We'll put the crate inside of it.

Captain. Sounds all right. Got a lock on it?

Chris. Heavy padlock. It's fixed so the lid can be propped open a crack without unlocking it. The snake's got to have air.

Captain. But in dirty weather, that lid stays shut. I'll take no chances.

Chris. Fair enough.

Captain. We'll keep the thing in my inside cabin, where I sleep. Can't have it in the baggage room. And nobody on board's to know about it.

Chris. Whatever you say, Captain. But we won't have any trouble. After all, it's only a snake—it doesn't have any magical powers.

Captain. I saw a bushmaster in the zoo at Caracas once. Had it in a glass cage with double walls. It'd never move—just lie there and look at you as long as you were in sight. Gave a man the creeps!

Chris. I didn't know they had a bushmaster at the Caracas Zoo.

Captain. They don't *now*. Found the glass broken one morning, and the snake gone. The night watchman was dead. They never found out what happened.

Chris. Well . . . the watchman must've broken the glass by accident.

Captain. The way they figured it—the glass was broken from the inside! *(pause)* We . . . sail in four hours.

Music (transition . . . to sound of the open sea . . . music background)

Chris *(narrating)*. Into the Caribbean—with perfect weather and a sea as smooth as an inland lake. The barometer dropped a little on the third day—but cleared up overnight and left nothing worse than a heavy swell.[9] But in spite of the calm seas and pleasant weather, I was becoming possessed with an <u>ominous</u> anxiety. I was developing an obsessive fear of that snake! I stayed clear of the passengers pretty much—got the habit of dropping into Captain Wood's quarters several times a day. . . . *(Sound: Door opens and closes. Steps.)*

He kept the heavy box underneath his berth. I'd approach it quietly and shine my flashlight through the open crack. *(Pause. Sound of two or three steps and stop.)*

Never once could I catch that eight-foot devil asleep, or even excited. He'd be lying there half-coiled, his head raised a little, staring out of those beady black

---

9. **swell:** a large wave.

Words to Know and Use | **ominous** (äm′ ə nəs) *adj.* threatening harm or evil

195

eyes—waiting. He'd still be like that when I'd turn away to leave. *(slow steps)*

Maybe that's what bothered me—that horrible and constant watchful waiting. *(Sound: Door opens.)* What in the name of heaven was he *waiting* for?

Sound (door closes)

Willis *(fading in)*. Well—hello there, Mr. Warner!

Chris. Oh . . . how are you, Mother Willis?

Willis. My, but you and the Captain spend an awful lot of time around this cabin. I'm beginning to think the two of you must have some guilty secret!

Chris. Oh, no, nothing like that, Mother Willis. I don't know about Captain Wood—but I . . . I certainly don't have any guilty secret!

Music (transition) Sound (open foredeck of liner bucking a swell)

Chris. Well! She's running quite a swell out there, Mr. Bowman!

Bowman. Yeah—it's a little heavy, all right, Mr. Warner. Guess a storm passed through to the west of us yesterday when the glass dropped.

Chris. Think it missed us, then, huh?

Bowman. Yeah—that's what the mate figures. Sure stirred up some water, though.

Chris *(laughs)*. This'll put half the passengers in their bunks.

Illustration by Vivienne Flesher.

Bowman. Make it great for my department. Two thirds of 'em will want a steward to hold their heads!

Chris. They'll keep Mother Willis so busy she'll–Hey! Look at that wave!

Bowman. Huh? . . . Great Jehoshaphat! We're taking it on the port bow! Hang on!

Sound (wave crashes across the foredeck . . . seems to shake the whole ship . . . and subsides)

Chris. Whew! Not another wave that size in sight. That was a freak if there ever was one.

Bowman. You see 'em like that sometimes– even in a calm sea. *(pause)* Gotta get topside, Mr. Warner. Wave really smashed into the officers' deck. Probably did some damage. . . .

Chris. Yeah, I suppose . . . *What did you say?*

Bowman. Wheel companionway was open on the port side–bridge cabins musta taken a pretty bad smashing. They're right below the–Say, is something wrong, Mr. Warner?

Chris. No. No–nothing at all, Mr. Bowman. At least . . . I hope not!

Music (attacks and holds under voice)

Chris *(narrating).* Of course, I knew it was only one chance in a thousand–but the chances against that freak wave were one in a thousand, too! I stumbled up the companionway and along the passage to the Captain's cabin.

Music . . . Sound (door opening)

Willis *(surprised, affably).* Oh . . . come on in, Mr. Warner.

Chris. Mother Willis!

Willis. My, isn't this cabin a mess? I'd better get some of these things out to dry.

Chris. Yeah. Well, I just wanted to check– Where's that box that was under the Captain's bunk?

Willis. Oh, that! I just shoved it out on deck.

Chris. What!

Willis. The desk over there slid into it. It was all smashed.

Chris. But the small box inside of it! What happened to it?

Willis. Oh, they were both splintered, Mr. Warner–broken wide open.

Chris. Oh, no!

Willis. Why, Mr. Warner–you're as white as a sheet!

Chris. Mother Willis–will you go find Captain Wood? Tell him to . . . come down here immediately.

Willis. Well . . . of course, Mr. Warner. *(going)* I'll go tell him right away.

Sound (door closing). Sounds as cued under the following:

Chris *(narrating).* I pulled open the top drawer of the bureau beside me *(drawer opening)* and took out the Captain's flashlight and a loaded pistol *(drawer closing).* Mother Willis had left a mop standing by the door. I put my foot on the head of it and snapped off the handle *(snap of handle).* Every move I made turned into slow motion. I could hear my own heart beating. Slowly I started to search the cabin. *(Music: suspense motif)*

<u>Sodden</u> heaps of clothing were scattered around on the wet, black floor. I punched at them one at a time—holding the gun cocked—the flashlight pointing along the stick. Nothing. I worked around the room—throwing the light into the dark corners, back of the desk, under the bunk. And wherever I turned, I could feel those cold, unblinking eyes at my back—watching and waiting. *(pause)* Using the stick, I pushed open the closet door and threw the light inside. Carefully I poked at the boxes and junk on the floor. *(pause)* The snake was not in the closet. Inch by inch, I covered the entire cabin—and then at last I realized the horrible truth.

Sound (door opening) Music (up and clip off)

Captain. Mother Willis just told me, Christopher. *(door closes)* So it's happened!

Chris. That's right, Captain. It's happened.

Captain. I see you found the gun. We'd better start searching the cabin.

Chris. Captain Wood, I . . . just finished searching it.

Captain. Then . . . ! *(pause)* Women, kids—and that thing loose on board. A thousand places for it to hide. Heaven help us!

Music (establish theme for the "search")

Captain *(fades in)*. There's no use starting to blame anybody now, gentlemen. I didn't call you officers in here to pass judgment. The thing's done—and that's that.

Mate. You're right there, Captain.

Captain. What we *have* got to do is decide how to handle it.

Bowman. It'd be easier if we didn't have to tell the passengers and crew, sir. I've seen panics aboard ship before!

Captain. Yes, I agree with you, Mr. Bowman—but I don't quite see how we can avoid it.

Mate. They gotta right to know! As long as that snake's loose, everybody on board's in the same danger—and they all oughta know about it!

Chris. Captain Wood—that thing is eight feet long. It can't simply crawl into a crack. Why don't we make a quick search of the whole ship before we spread any alarm?

Captain. Yes, I've thought of that, Christopher.

Bowman. As far as I can see, the only place it *couldn't* be is in the boilers or on top of the galley stove.

Mate. It might've crawled overboard.

Captain. We can't count on that. We've got to assume it's on the ship somewhere.

Mate. Yeah, and that could be anywhere. In a coil of rope—or in a pile of clothes.

Bowman. Yes, or under some woman's berth—or a baby's crib.

Mate. Or even in—

Chris. You've already said it! That bushmaster could be anywhere. We've got to do something, and do it fast!

Captain. All right. I think the best idea's to make a quick search first. You agree to that?

Words to Know and Use | **sodden** (säd′ ′n) *adj.* thoroughly wet

(Cast ad-libs assent.[10])

Captain. Then if we don't find it—we'll have to warn the passengers.

Chris. We've *got* to find it!

Music (up and sustained under voice)

Chris *(narrating)*. Alone in the dim baggage room, I went through the same movements as I had earlier in the Captain's cabin—gun in one hand, flashlight in the other, poking into every dark corner, behind every trunk and box. Since there was no one in the baggage room, I could keep the gun cocked and ready. The rest of those poor devils were having to do the same thing—barehanded! All over the ship the search went on.

Music (up and cut off)

Woman *(fade in)*. Here, now, Steward! What on earth are you doing, rummaging through my cabin?

Bowman. Just checking up, ma'am!

Woman. Well, I'm sure there's nothing in here that has to be checked.

Bowman. Sorry, ma'am—Captain's orders. It'll only take a few minutes.

Woman. Well, I never heard of such a thing! A passenger simply doesn't have any privacy at all! *(fading back into music)* I've traveled on a lot of different lines, but I've certainly never heard of anything so completely highhanded before . . . !

Music (up and under voices)

Mate. Sorry, sir. Wonder if you'd mind moving over to the other rail? I'd like to look through these lockers.

Man. Sure—go ahead. What's the matter . . . you lost something?

Mate. No. No—just looking things over.

Man. Nothing in there but life preservers.

Mate. Yeah—that's right.

Man. You must be getting ready to sink the boat. *(laughs)* Gonna collect the insurance, eh? *(fading)* Gonna send us all to the bottom! *(laughs)*

Music (up and out)

Chris *(narrating)*. But not one of us could find that deadly shape—coiled in some dark corner or outstretched along a window seat. Not one of us caught a glimpse of that horrid head, with its beady black, watchful eyes. *(fades)* It was nearly dark when we met together again in the chart room.

Captain *(fades in)*. Well, gentlemen—there's no other way. We've risked all the time we can. We must warn the passengers!

Mate. How'll we do it, Captain? Call 'em all together in the lounge?

Captain. No. If we did anything like that, we'd be asking for a panic.

Bowman. We'll get one—whether we ask for it or not!

Captain. Pick a few men and go through the cabin decks. Tell 'em individually—*inside their cabins.* Watch for any that act like they might cause trouble—and we'll keep an eye on 'em. Handle the crew the same way.

(Officers ad-lib agreement. Sounds of steps, chairs.)

Captain *(up a bit)*. As soon as you're finished—arm all the deck officers and start searching again. Our only chance of preventing a panic is to find that snake!

---

10. **ad-libs assent:** shows agreement in any way they please.

Music (sets growing tension, sustains it under voice)

Chris *(narrating)*. The slow nightmare that followed grew worse by the hour. None of us slept. All the ship's officers not on duty kept on with that endless search. Passengers locked themselves in their cabins or huddled together in the lounges—knowing all the time that no spot on board could be called safe. Fear was a heavy fog in the lungs of all of us—and every light on the vessel burned throughout the night. Morning came and brought no relief. Terror and tension mounted by the hour.

Music (swells, fades) Sound (woman sobbing)

Willis. There now, Mrs. Crane. Go back to your cabin. The horrid thing's probably crawled overboard by now.

Woman. You're just saying that! You're paid to say it! You don't *know!* Nobody does!

Willis. Now, now. Everything's going to be all right.

Woman. If we could only get off the ship, they could fumigate it. Yes! That's what we've got to do! *(fading from mike)* We've got to get off the ship!

Willis *(calling excitedly)*. Mr. Bowman—she's going to jump.

Bowman *(in distance)*. No you don't, lady.

Woman *(distance)*. Let me go! *(sobbing)*

Captain *(coming in)*. Nice work, Mr. Bowman. Get her down to her cabin. And whatever you do—don't turn her loose!

Music (up and under)

Man *(fading in)*. You never know when it might strike you. You can't put on a coat or move a chair without risking your life. Something's gotta be done. It might be right here in this lounge!

Sound (stir of fearful crowd)

Mate *(coming in)*. All right, mister—better quiet down and take it easy.

Man. Take it easy, huh? You're a great officer! Why don't you *do* something about it? That thing might be crawling around here right under our feet. . . .

Sound (rise of frightened voices)

Mate. I said shut up! Are you trying to start a riot?

Man. I gotta right to talk! I don't want to die! Nobody's gonna tell me what—

Sound (sock in jaw—body falling) Music (up and back under)

Chris *(narrating)*. The second night passed and morning came around again—a gray and rainy day that dragged by, and then night came down again—third night of the terror. Again every light burned, and the whole ship seethed in the throes of incipient panic.[11] Faced by a horror they'd never met on the sea before, crew and officers alike were on the verge of revolt.

---

11. **seethed in the throes . . . panic:** struggled with the beginnings of overpowering fear.

Words to Know and Use | **fumigate** (fyo͞o′ mə gāt′) *v.* to use smoke or gas to destroy pests

Passengers sat huddled in a trancelike stupor, ready to scream at the slightest unknown sound.

Music (dissolves slowly)

Chris. At seven bells,[12] I made my way forward to the chart room and found Captain Wood bent over a desk.

Sound (door closing, steps)

Captain *(wearily)*. Oh...hello, Christopher. Come on in and sit down.

Chris *(on edge)*. It's got to be *somewhere*, Captain Wood! It's got to be!

Captain. I don't know. You could search this ship for six months and never touch all the hiding places aboard. If we can only hold out for two more days—we'll be in port.

Chris. What's your home office say?

Captain. Here's the latest wireless from 'em. "Keep calm—and keep coming." Huh! What else *can* we do? How is it below?

Chris. Pretty bad. Anything could happen.

Captain. Yeah, that's why I took the guns away from the men. One pistol shot, and we'd have a riot on our hands.

Chris. The whole thing's my fault, Captain Wood! That's what I can't forget!

Captain. Take it easy, son.

Chris. If there was only some way I could pay for it myself. Alone!

Captain. No—I know how you feel. But it's no more your fault than mine, or the man who asked you to bring that snake back . . . alive. Nobody planned this. You'd better try to get a little sleep.

Chris. Sleep!

Captain. Mr. Bowman made some coffee down in the steward's galley a while ago. Better go on down and get yourself a cup—then rest for a couple hours.

Chris. Rest—I can't rest!

Captain. Christopher—it's not going to help anything if you stumble through a hatch[13] half-asleep—and break your neck. Go on and get some coffee. One way or another we've got to hold out for two more days.

Music (transition and dissolves) Sound (door closing and steps under . . . other sounds as cued)

Chris *(narrating)*. The light was on in the steward's galley—and the coffeepot was standing on the stove. *(steps stop)* It was still warm, so I didn't bother to heat it. *(pouring)* I poured out a cup . . . *(steps),* carried it over, and set it on the porcelain table top in the center of the room. I started to light a cigarette. The door of the pan cupboard beneath the sink was standing slightly ajar, and I happened to glance toward it. I dropped the cigarette and moved slowly backward. I'd found the bushmaster!

---

12. **seven bells:** the ringing of a ship's bell to announce the beginning of the seventh half-hour of a four-hour watch.

13. **hatch:** an opening in a ship's deck.

Words to Know and Use | **stupor** (stōō′ pər) *n.* a state of mental dullness; a daze

Music (loud, then continues softly, movement slow and tense)

Chris. As I moved, the snake slid out of the cupboard in a single sinuous slide—and drew back into a loose coil on the galley floor—never taking his eyes off me. I backed slowly away—waiting any moment for that deadly, slithering strike. How had he known it was me? He'd stayed quiet when Bowman was here. How had he picked the first time in five days that I was without a gun? My hands touched the wall behind me, and I stopped, in terror. . . . The call button and door were on the far side of the room. I'd backed into a dead end! I stared at the snake in fascination—expecting any moment the ripping slash of those poisoned fangs. The <u>lethal</u> coils tightened a little—then were still again. *Homo sapiens versus Lachesis mutus*—a man against mute fate. And all the odds were on . . . fate. I knew then that I was going to die!

Music (long chord and clip off)

Chris. I could feel the sweat run down between the wall and the palms of my hands pressing against it. My skin crawled and twitched, and the pit of my stomach was cold as ice. There was no sound but the rush of blood in my ears. The snake shifted again—drawing into a tighter coil—always tighter. Why didn't the devil get it over with? Then . . . for an instant his head veered away. Something moved by the stove. I didn't dare turn to look at it. Slowly it moved out into my line of vision. It was a cat! The scrawny cat that Mother Willis sneaked aboard in La Guaira!

Cat. *(a low, threatening growl)*

Chris. Its back was arched, and every hair stood on end. It moved stiff-legged now, walking in a half-circle around the snake. The bushmaster moved slowly and kept watching the cat. He tightened—he was going to strike at any second.

Sound (thud of striking snake, and scrape as it recovers)

Cat. *(snarl and spit . . . then back to the low growl)*

Chris. He struck and missed—the cat was barely out of reach. Now she was walking back and forth again. She was asking to die.

Sound (thud and recovery)

Cat. *(snarl, spit, and back to growl)*

Chris. Missed again—by a fraction of an inch. He was striking now without even going to a full coil!

Sound (thud and recovery)

Cat. *(snarl, spit, growl)*

Chris. Missed! Again and again—always missing by the barest <u>margin</u>. Each time the cat danced barely out of reach—and each time she <u>countered</u> with one precise spat of a dainty paw—bracing her skinny frame on three stiff legs. And then suddenly I realized what she was doing!

Sound (thud and recovery)

Words to Know and Use

lethal (lē′ thəl) *adj.* deadly
margin (mär′ jən) *n.* an amount to spare
counter (koun′ ər) *v.* to respond to another's action

WINTER: CAT ON A CUSHION
Théophile-Alexandre Steinlen
The Metropolitan Museum of Art New York
Gift of Henry J. Plantin, 1950.

Cat. *(snarl, spit, growl)*

Chris. The bushmaster was tiring—and one strike was just an instant slow. But in that split second, sharp claws raked across the evil head and ripped out both the lidless eyes. The cat had deliberately blinded the snake!

Sound (repeated thuds of struggle)

Cat. *(snarling, spitting)*

Chris. He didn't bother to coil now but slid after her in a fury—striking wildly but always missing. And every strike was a little slower than the last one. Until finally—

Sound (The thuds change to the frantic scraping of a heavy snake.)

Chris. As the snake's neck stretched out at the end of a strike, the cat made one leap and sank her razor-sharp teeth just back of the ugly head—sank 'em until they crunched bone with tooth and claw. She clung as the monstrous snake flailed and lashed on the floor . . . striving to get those hideous coils around her, trying to break her hold, to shake off the slow and certain paralyzing death . . . *(sound of cat out)* that gradually crept over him and at last stilled his struggles forever!

Pause. Music.

Chris. I took a deep breath—the first in minutes—the cat lay on her side on the floor, panting—resting from the fight just over. She had a right to rest. That mangy, brave, beautiful alley cat had just saved my life—and maybe others as well. But as I turned toward the stove—I suddenly became very humble. There were three reasons why that cat had fought and killed the world's deadliest snake. And those three reasons came tottering out from under the stove on shaky little legs—three kittens with their eyes bright with wonder and their tails stiff as pokers. Up on the decks, hundreds of passengers would sigh with relief at the news that the days and nights of terror were ended. They could wait a little longer. *(pause)* I pulled open the doors of the cabinet and found a can of milk. Then I dropped down on my knees . . . on the floor of the galley. ❧

*R*esponding to Reading

First Impressions

1. What would be the first thing you would say to a friend about this radio play? Write your comment in your journal or on a sheet of paper.

Second Thoughts

2. Do you think Chris Warner should have brought the bushmaster aboard the ship? Why or why not?

   Think about
   - the early descriptions of the bushmaster
   - the **theme** of this subunit, "Expect the Unexpected"
   - the presence of other passengers

3. What kind of person do you think Chris is?

   Think about
   - his early **conflict** with the captain
   - his actions after the bushmaster gets loose
   - his final words

4. If Mother Willis's cat had not killed the bushmaster, what do you think might have happened?

Broader Connections

5. Zoologists today know that the bushmaster does not survive in captivity because it refuses to eat. Do you think wild animals should be caught and placed in zoos? Give reasons for your opinion.

*L*iterary Concept: Suspense

Suspense is a feeling of tension and excitement that makes a reader curious about the outcome of a story. A writer creates suspense by raising in the reader's mind questions about possible endings to the **conflict.** Les Crutchfield begins to build suspense in the play's first speech by having Chris tell us that he felt a "cold chill" and that he "shivered with sudden dread." Find another example of how the writer creates suspense in this play.

Concept Review: Conflict As you know, conflict is a struggle between opposing forces. The struggle between the cat and the snake is one example of conflict in the play. Name another.

Writing Options

1. Write a headline and the accompanying **news article** about the events in this drama. Begin by asking and answering *what, when, why, where,* and *how* questions. Give all the important details needed to understand what happened, but omit unnecessary information.

2. Pretend you are a passenger who was not warned about the bushmaster's presence. Write a **letter of complaint** to the ship's owner.

3. Think of the characters that you have read about in this book or in your other reading. Which character might have had the courage to search for the bushmaster? Explain your choice in an **essay.**

4. A captain often keeps a daily log of the ship's progress and of any important events. Write a captain's **log entry** for the day he learns that his orders have been overruled and the bushmaster will be on board.

Vocabulary Practice

Exercise Write the letter of the word or phrase that best completes each sentence below.

1. If the deck of a ship is **sodden,** it is (a) dirty (b) wet (c) rotten (d) made of wood.

2. A **customs** official makes sure that (a) transported animals are well treated (b) travelers know local habits (c) taxes on imports and exports are paid (d) passengers have tickets.

3. To **fumigate** a ship is to (a) disinfect it (b) burn it down (c) abandon it (d) search it thoroughly.

4. If the passengers were in a **stupor,** they would best be described as (a) scared (b) dazed (c) angry (d) uneducated.

5. A **lethal** grip is one that is (a) weak (b) friendly (c) lively (d) deadly.

6. One example of a **transition** is (a) exchanging money for a snake (b) moving from land to sea (c) telegraphing the home office (d) the engine of a ship.

7. An animal that tried to **counter** an attack would (a) strike back (b) jump away (c) fake death (d) hide.

8. An **evasive** answer is one that involves (a) confessing the truth (b) being polite (c) avoiding the truth (d) helping the questioner.

9. The **margin** between the snake and the cat is (a) their hatred for each other (b) their strength and power (c) the structure between them (d) the space between them.

10. An **ominous** feeling makes a person (a) curious (b) sick (c) confident (d) fearful.

> *Words to Know and Use*
>
> counter
> customs
> evasive
> fumigate
> lethal
> margin
> ominous
> sodden
> stupor
> transition

Options for Learning

1 • Just Listen With some of your classmates, produce *A Shipment of Mute Fate* as a radio play, complete with sound effects. Some students can read parts, and others can find creative ways to produce the sound effects. For instance, someone might imitate the sound of the pistol shot by bursting a balloon. Rehearse the play until you can convey the high level of suspense.

2 • Music That Chills With a group of your classmates, select background music for *A Shipment of Mute Fate*. Read the stage directions for clues to the kinds of music needed. Experiment with different types of music, such as classical, jazz, or popular music or a combination of these. Make your music reflect the atmosphere suggested in the play.

3 • Reptile Research Find out more about the bushmaster and other poisonous and nonpoisonous snakes. Make a chart that compares the different features of the most common snakes. Present the chart in an oral report.

4 • Improvise a Drama With a group of your classmates, create a suspenseful radio drama for the class. Look for ideas in the journal entries you made in Examine What You Know on page 190, or brainstorm for new ideas. Sketch out a plot, draw up a cast of characters, and rehearse the dialogue. Create sound effects and choose appropriate background music.

 FACT FINDER GEOGRAPHY

What countries and bodies of water border the Caribbean Sea?

Les Crutchfield
1916–1966

Les Crutchfield did not start out wanting to be a writer. He earned a college degree in engineering and became a specialist in rockets and explosives. During World War II, Crutchfield directed research programs on various secret rocket projects. He was the co-inventor of a rocket that helped heavily loaded airplanes take off.

It was only in the 1940s, when Crutchfield's wife took him to see a rehearsal for a radio show, that he became interested in script writing. In 1946 his first radio script was accepted and his writing career was launched. Over the next twenty years, Crutchfield created radio scripts for more than twenty adventure, mystery, and drama series.

In the 1950s Crutchfield started writing for a new entertainment sensation—television. He is probably best known as one of the main writers for *Gunsmoke,* a suspenseful series about law and order in the Old West. First broadcast as a radio program, *Gunsmoke* became one of the longest running shows in television history.

WRITER'S WORKSHOP

NARRATIVE WRITING

As you've learned in this subunit, life is full of unexpected adventures. Green aliens can land in a boy's back yard. A wall can reveal a dead man's secrets. A vengeful snake can cause terror aboard a ship. In an exciting story anything can happen anywhere, anytime.

What extraordinary adventure can you imagine happening? Now is your chance to tell about it. In this workshop, you will write an adventure story or a science fiction tale. As you work on this assignment, allow your imagination to run wild. Go ahead—let the unexpected happen!

USE NARRATIVE WRITING FOR
stories
ballads
plays
skits
biographies

GUIDED ASSIGNMENT: SCIENCE FICTION OR ADVENTURE STORY

Write a science fiction story or an adventure story in which the unexpected happens. Be as imaginative as you like.

Here is one writer's PASSkey to this assignment.

PURPOSE: To tell an imaginative story

AUDIENCE: My teacher and my classmates

SUBJECT: Science fiction or adventure

STRUCTURE: Short story

The Suit of Armor
by Rashad Freeman

The tour guide was talking about a painting, but Jackson wasn't listening. His class had been at the art museum all afternoon, and he was getting bored. Looking around, Jackson noticed an old suit of armor in another room. It looked interesting, so Jackson sneaked away from the group to get a closer look. He stuck his head up close to the metal helmet, and then he stepped back in total shock. Two bright eyes were blinking out at him!

"Be quiet, lad," rumbled a voice from deep inside the armor. "Ye will give away my secret."

"Who--who--who are you?" Jackson stammered.

STUDENT MODEL

◀ Before you write, read the beginning of one student's short story.

◀ The writer chooses to use a third-person point of view.

"I am the knight, Sir Purpleheart," the voice replied.

Jackson rubbed his eyes and wondered if he was dreaming.

"Aye," the knight said. "I have been stuck in this suit of armor for six hundred years. My neck is as stiff as a board. I have not eaten since 1394. Lad, I am miserable."

Jackson began to get over his shock. He even began to feel sorry for the knight. "Can I help?"

Sir Purpleheart's eyes looked craftily out at Jackson. "Why yes, lad, perhaps you can. Just touch my sword thrice, and I will be free of this dratted metal prison."

Jackson paused and looked over his shoulder. Nobody was around to tell him not to, so he reached out his hand and touched the sword-- one, two, three times. POOF! CLANK! Suddenly Jackson felt as if a tornado were sucking him inside the suit of armor. Before he could even say, "You tricked me!" he was stuck inside the armor. He couldn't move his arms or his legs or his head. He could only see through a narrow slit in the visor. Looking out, Jackson saw Sir Purpleheart pointing at him.

"Now it's your turn to stand still for six hundred years!" said the knight. He gave a nasty laugh and disappeared from view.

Prewrite and Explore

1 **Decide on a situation and characters** First, brainstorm about interesting situations and characters. Think of the theme of this subunit, "Expect the Unexpected." Skim through the newspaper or think of television dramas you have enjoyed. Let your imagination roam through all sorts of possibilities. Jot down your ideas for situations and characters, as Rashad did on the chart on the next page. Then choose the situation or the character that appeals to you most.

Situations	Characters
becoming invisible	aliens who invade playground
going on safari	dinosaur in park
traveling in time machine	ancient knight trapped in armor

2 **Create a setting** Choose a real setting or create an imaginary setting for your story. The story may be set in the past, the present, or the future. If you wish, limit your story to the events of a single day or part of a day. Then your narrative will be focused and easy to follow.

3 **Define the conflict and plot** In short stories there is usually one major conflict or problem. Set up a conflict for your characters early in the story. The plot should keep your readers wondering how your characters will resolve the conflict. Use the plot to show how your characters solve their problem or get out of trouble.

◀ STARTING POINTS
You can begin thinking about a story from the angle of characters, setting, or plot. Start with whichever element seems most interesting or most exciting to you, and build from there.

GATHERING INFORMATION

Do you have a rough idea of the characters, setting, conflict, and plot of your story? Once you have these basic ingredients, you can sketch out the main ideas for the beginning, middle, and conclusion of your story. Look at the outline that Rashad made for his story.

Beginning

Jackson visits art museum
discovers knight trapped in armor

Middle Events

Sir Purpleheart tricks Jackson into changing
    places
museum guard accidentally touches sword
    three times

Conclusion

guard replaces Jackson in armor
Jackson thinks of way to free guard
Sir Purpleheart never seen again

Draft and Discover

REMINDER
Chronological order is the order in which events actually happen.

1 **Use chronological order**   When you made your story map, you probably listed the events in chronological, or time, order. Use chronological order to organize your draft.

2 **Bring your story to life**   As you begin writing, remember that a good story is more than just a series of events. To give life to your story, pack it with vivid description, action, and dialogue. Notice how the excerpt below combines all of these elements.

LITERARY MODEL
from "The Secret of the Wall" by Elizabeth Borton de Treviño

"Good! She's early!" hissed Serafin. She left the big *zaguán* slightly ajar as she went in, and, pulled and pushed by Serafin, I followed. We were inside!

Revise Your Writing

LISTEN
Not sure if your dialogue sounds natural? Listen as a friend reads it aloud.

1 **Fine-tune your dialogue**   Look over the dialogue in your draft. Make sure the characters speak like real people—or maybe Martians or real crocodiles. Don't be afraid to use slang or sentence fragments. For example, look at the dialogue below.

LITERARY MODEL
from *A Shipment of Mute Fate* by Les Crutchfield

"Whew! Not another wave that size in sight. That was a freak if there ever was one."

2 **Check for story basics**   Does your story have a definite time, place, and plot? Are the characters clearly presented? Is the conflict obvious, and does the ending tie up loose ends? Check your draft for any weaknesses in setting, plot, and characters. Strengthen these elements by adding or subtracting details. Review your writing, then ask a classmate to read it. Use the questions below.

Revision Questions

For You	For a Peer Reader
1. Does the story have a clear beginning, middle, and end?	1. What else do you need to know about the characters or the setting?
2. Are the descriptions and action vivid enough?	2. Can you follow the plot?
3. Does the dialogue sound natural?	3. Which details did you like best?

Proofread

As with any class assignment, you need to check your story carefully for errors. Proofread it for punctuation, spelling, grammar, and other errors.

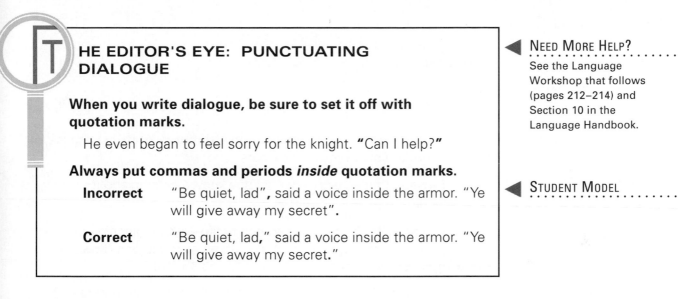

THE EDITOR'S EYE: PUNCTUATING DIALOGUE

When you write dialogue, be sure to set it off with quotation marks.

He even began to feel sorry for the knight. **"Can I help?"**

Always put commas and periods *inside* quotation marks.

Incorrect "Be quiet, lad**"**, said a voice inside the armor. "Ye will give away my secret**"**.

Correct "Be quiet, lad**,**" said a voice inside the armor. "Ye will give away my secret**.**"

◀ NEED MORE HELP?
See the Language Workshop that follows (pages 212–214) and Section 10 in the Language Handbook.

◀ STUDENT MODEL

Publish and Present

Story Circles In small groups read your stories to one another or arrange to read some of your stories to a class of younger students. If time permits, illustrate your story or find pictures that will help your readers visualize the characters or setting of your story.

COMPUTER TIP
Save your story on a disk. Then, if you want to turn your story into a series, you can add chapters to your original document.

Reflect on Your Writing

Briefly answer these questions. Keep your answers with your story as part of your writing portfolio.

◀ FOR YOUR PORTFOLIO

1. Did you enjoy the opportunity to write fiction? Why or why not?
2. Could you continue this story in a sequel?

LANGUAGE WORKSHOP

PUNCTUATING DIALOGUE

> When characters talk to one another, their conversation is called **dialogue.**

Dialogue is a way of showing action rather than just telling about it. A ho-hum explanation can come to life through dialogue. Look at the following sentence. It is an example of an **indirect quotation** because it does not give the speaker's exact words.

WATCH *THAT*!
The tip-off to an indirect quotation is often the word *that.*

▶ Bert said that an eight-year-old boy knows nothing about monsters.

Now see how Bert's character comes to life with the addition of dialogue. The words in quotation marks are an example of a **direct quotation** because they are the speaker's exact words.

LITERARY MODEL
from "Playing for Keeps" by Jack C. Haldeman II

▶ "Besides," said Bert, "what does a kid know about monsters? He's only eight years old."

There's more to dialogue than putting words in characters' mouths, however. The following rules will help you punctuate dialogue correctly. By learning these rules, you can confidently let your characters speak for themselves.

1. Use quotation marks to begin and end the words a person says. Capitalize the first word of a direct quotation.

LITERARY MODELS
from "The Secret of the Wall" by Elizabeth Borton de Treviño

▶ "**M**y name is Martin Gonzales," he said.

Carlos said, "**P**apacito, I am going to be an evangelist."

2. If a quotation is divided by words such as *he said,* enclose both parts of the quotation with quotation marks.

"It's terribly dark," I said. "Give me the candle."

TIP
Do commas and periods go inside or outside quotation marks? Use this memory device. Commas and periods are *too little* to go outside all by themselves!

3. Put commas and periods inside the quotation marks.

"I want you to write a letter for me**,**" Martin said.

Carlos answered, "But I have no paper and envelope**.**"

4. Put question marks or exclamation points *inside* quotation marks if they are part of the quotation.

"Serafin**!**" I called with all my might.

"What will you do with your part of the treasure**?**" Don Mario asked.

5. Put question marks or exclamation points *outside* the quotation marks if they are not part of the quotation.

How ashamed Serafin felt as he stammered "I am sorry"**!**

Did Carlos say "I forgive Serafin"**?**

6. Begin a new paragraph every time the speaker changes.

"But . . . but. . . . " I stuttered, "if you see them drop something, you ought to give it back!"

"No," he answered stubbornly. "Finders keepers. That's the game."

Exercise 1   Concept Check   Rewrite each of the following sentences. Add the necessary quotation marks.

1. Have you looked under the table? Mrs. Boyle asked.
2. Mr. Boyle grumbled, I'm busy eating breakfast.
3. But Dad, Chris exclaimed, my boa constrictor got loose!
4. Mr. Boyle asked, Are you pulling my leg?
5. My dear, Mrs. Boyle answered, we are perfectly serious.
6. And so am I, her husband said. Someone or something is squeezing my leg.
7. It's the boa! Jenny and Chris yelled.
8. Get the boa inside the cage! Mrs. Boyle cried.
9. Mission accomplished, Chris reported.
10. Please pass me the juice, said Mr. Boyle calmly.

Exercise 2   Revision Skill   On your paper, change the following indirect quotations to direct quotations. Use correct punctuation.

1. The radio announcer said Martians have landed in New Jersey.
2. A newscaster said that it was a national emergency.
3. A telephone operator said poisonous black smoke was pouring into Newark.

These sentences describe a radio play by Orson Welles that caused widespread panic in the United States when it was first broadcast on October 30, 1938. Listeners thought the drama was describing real events and that Martians had actually landed in New Jersey.

4. The announcer exclaimed the Martians had destroyed New Jersey.

5. A witness said the Martians were now invading New York.

6. People asked if it was the end of the world.

7. One mayor in the Midwest reported that citizens were fleeing their homes.

8. The radio announcer said to stay tuned for a station break.

9. The announcer explained the Martian landing was not real.

10. The station was broadcasting a play called *War of the Worlds,* the announcer said to everyone's relief.

Exercise 3   Looking at Style   With a partner, rewrite the passage below as a narrative without dialogue. Use indirect quotations if necessary. After you finish, evaluate your work. Which do you prefer— the original passage with dialogue or your own narrative without the dialogue? Compare and discuss results with a small group of your classmates.

LITERARY MODEL

From "Playing for Keeps" by Jack C. Haldeman II

▶

"I'll bet Johnny will be excited when he wakes up," she said. "Channel Four said they've even seen a couple aliens right here in town. Imagine that."

"I don't think we ought to tell the boy about them," said Bert. "At least not yet."

"For goodness sakes, honey. Why not?"

"The child has an active enough imagination as it is. There's no sense in getting him all riled up. Remember the time he thought he saw that UFO down by the river?"

LANGUAGE HANDBOOK

For review and practice: Section 10, Punctuation.

Exercise 4   Revising Your Writing   Look over the story that you wrote for the Writer's Workshop on page 207. Pencil a light check mark next to any dialogue. Using the rules you have learned for punctuating dialogue, correct any mistakes that you find.

SPEAKING AND LISTENING
WORKSHOP

ORAL READING

Imagine that you are broadcasting a radio play to millions of listeners. You cannot rely on costumes, sets, or visual action to show what is happening. How will you keep people tuned to your station?

Reading aloud in class or to younger children is not so different from putting on a radio play. In both cases, your voice must catch and hold the audience's attention. It must also convey a range of tones and emotions. Following the guidelines below will help you keep your audience tuned in.

1 **Speak clearly.** Practice pronouncing any difficult words before you read to an audience. As you speak, pronounce your words carefully and clearly. Don't mumble or let your words run together.

2 **Use the right volume.** Speak at a comfortable pitch. Let your voice rise and fall naturally. You should be loud enough to be heard, but not so loud that it sounds like you are shouting.

3 **Not too fast, not too slow.** Read at a moderate rate most of the time, but vary your pace according to the feelings and emotions of the character or the action you are describing. Pause between sentences and paragraphs. If you are feeling nervous, don't rush to get to the end. Instead, take a deep breath and slow down.

4 **Vary your voice.** Place extra stress on important words or phrases. Invent a slightly different voice for each character. Don't speak in a single, flat tone. Use your voice to express emotions and changing moods.

Exercise Use the story you wrote for the Writer's Workshop on page 207 as a script. Practice reading the story aloud. Concentrate on creating different voices for the characters. Also try using your voice to create suspense (you might try reading slightly faster or louder as the events build to a peak). When you feel your presentation is polished enough, read the story aloud to your class. Use the speaking guidelines that you have learned.

LISTEN AND LEARN

Start listening to the radio, or listen to the TV with your eyes closed. Pay attention to how speakers use volume, speed, and emotion to get their message across. Listen for voices that you particularly like. Use their best qualities in your own speaking.

A VOICE REHEARSAL

Try reading your story to a friend or family member before you read it to your class. Ask these questions: Do the characters sound different enough? Is my voice expressive? Am I speaking loudly and clearly enough?

Reading on Your Own

Suggested Novels for Unit Two

In the novels introduced on these pages, you can meet characters whose actions reflect the unit theme, "Rising to the Challenge."

THE LION, THE WITCH, AND THE WARDROBE
C. S. LEWIS ©1950

In this first in a series of seven fantasy novels, four children enter the magical kingdom of Narnia through the back of a closet in an old house. During their adventures in Narnia, the children meet talking animals, dwarfs, and giants; Aslan, the powerful and good lion; and the White Witch, whose icy spell keeps Narnia in endless winter. Soon all the characters are caught up in the battle for power between Aslan's forces of good and the White Witch's forces of evil. Years after the battle's surprising finale, the children return home, only to find that they have not been missed. On Earth only seconds have elapsed since the children disappeared. Read to discover . . .

- what it's like inside the kingdom of Narnia

- who these children are and how they change

- how the battle is fought and won

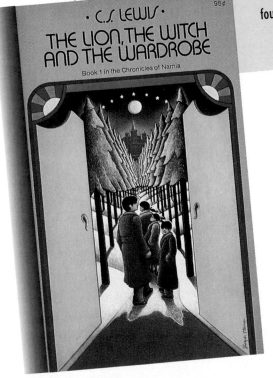

SHOEBAG
MARY JAMES ©1990

Shoebag is a happy young cockroach who one morning turns into a young boy. Adopted by the Biddle family and renamed Stuart Bagg, he becomes friends with the Biddle's seven-year-old daughter, Pretty Soft, the spoiled star of TV bathroom-tissue commercials. Stuart enrolls in the local elementary school and soon becomes a defender of the most unpopular kids in the school. In the midst of it all, he misses his life as a roach as well as his roach family. Read to find out . . .

• how a roach-turned-boy shows people how to be human beings

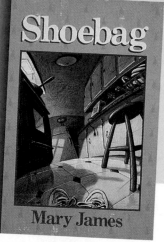

• how being a person changes Shoebag

• whether or not you agree with the decision he makes at the end of the book

ANTHONY BURNS: THE DEFEAT AND TRIUMPH OF A FUGITIVE SLAVE
VIRGINIA HAMILTON ©1988

In 1854 a Virginia-born slave named Anthony Burns escaped to freedom in Boston. Months later, Burns's former owner tracked Burns down and arrested him under the Fugitive Slave Law, a law that allowed slaveholders to reclaim slaves by showing proof of ownership. Thousands of people protested Burns's arrest and trial. Learn the outcome of this true but little-known incident in history. As you read, consider these questions:

• How far did those who opposed slavery go to fight it?

• How does a man who thinks he has found freedom deal with being recaptured?

• How might this trial have helped set the stage for the Civil War?

Other Recommended Books

The Secret Garden by Frances Hodgson Burnett (©1911, ©1962). In this classic novel, an orphan girl and a sickly boy learn to live and grow strong as they care for a long-abandoned garden.

The Great Little Madison by Jean Fritz (©1989). The fourth president of the United States comes to life in this biography. Share the problems and victories of James Madison—a person small in size but mighty in the role of making history.

The Spring of the Butterflies and Other Chinese Folktales by He Liyi (©1985). Collected from various parts of China, these folktales reveal the strengths and weaknesses of human nature.

East of the Sun & West of the Moon: A Play by Nancy Willard (©1989). Enjoy a classic story in a new way. Take a role in this play version of the Norwegian folktale about a girl who sets out to rescue the prince she loves.

FACE
TO
FACE

ring me all of your dreams,

You dreamers,

Bring me all of your

Heart melodies . . . .

Langston Hughes

THE COTTAGE HOME   1891
William H. Snape
Courtesy, Christopher Wood Gallery London.

219

$\mathscr{K}$EEPING FAITH

What do you think of when you hear someone say, "Keep the faith"? This expression is often used to encourage friends who are having a hard time or who are working for some cause that is important to them. While keeping faith can refer to faith in God, a higher power, or a set of principles, it can also mean holding on to the dreams that give life purpose.

In this group of selections, characters hold on to dreams of winning races, getting rich, and being released from the tyranny of slavery. In the play you will be reading, the main character's life is free of dreams until one Christmas Eve when his dreams come to life. In all of these selections, you will meet characters who come face to face with their dreams.

Fiction

Two Dreamers

GARY SOTO

Examine What You Know

The title of this story refers to a grandfather and his grandson. They are described as dreamers. How would you describe your own personality? Look at the four scales below. At which end of each scale do you think your personality falls? Jot down your answers in your journal or on a sheet of paper.

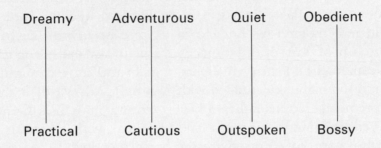

Dreamy	Adventurous	Quiet	Obedient
Practical	Cautious	Outspoken	Bossy

Expand Your Knowledge

In this story, the grandfather plans to make his dreams come true by buying and selling real estate, the land and buildings that make up pieces of property. The value of a piece of property depends on its location, size, and condition. A real-estate agent is a person who helps sell property. To buy a house, a person usually gets a mortgage, a loan agreement with a bank. The buyer must make a cash down payment, usually 10 or 20 percent of the price of the house. The rest of the money is paid in monthly payments over a period of years.

Enrich Your Reading

Reading Foreign Words   As you read the dialogue between the two dreamers, you will notice Spanish as well as English. When you come across a Spanish word or phrase, look for the pronunciation and the English translation in a footnote at the bottom of the page.

■ *Author biography in Reader's Handbook*

Two Dreamers

GARY SOTO

Hector's grandfather Luis Molina was born in the small town of Jalapa[1] but left Mexico to come to the United States when he was in his late twenties. Often, during quiet summer days, he sat in his back yard and remembered his hometown with its clip-clop of horse and donkey hooves, its cleanliness and dusty twilights, the crickets, and the night sky studded with stars. He also remembered his father, a barber who enjoyed listening to his radio, and his mother, who wore flower-print dresses and loved card games.

But that was many years ago, in the land of childhood. Now he lived in Fresno,[2] on a shady street with quiet homes. He had five children, more grandchildren than he had fingers and toes, and was a night watchman at Sun-Maid Raisin.

Luis's favorite grandson was Hector, who was like himself, dreamy and quiet. After work, Luis would sleep until noon, shower, and sit down to his *comida*.[3] Hector, who spent summers with his grandparents, would join Grandfather at the table and watch him eat plates of *frijoles*[4] with *guisado de carne*[5] smothered in chili.

Luis and Hector never said much at the table. It wasn't until his grandfather was finished and sitting in his favorite chair that Hector would begin asking him questions about the world, questions like, "What do Egyptians look like? Is the world really round like a ball? How come we eat chickens and they don't eat us?"

By the time Hector was nine, it was the grandfather who was asking the questions. He had become interested in real estate since he heard that by selling a house his son-in-law had made enough money to buy a brand-new car and put a brick fence around his yard. It impressed him that a young man like Genaro could buy one house, wait a month or two, sell it, and make enough to buy a car and build a brick fence.

After lunch the grandfather would beckon his grandson to come sit with him. *"Ven,*[6] Hector. Come. I want to talk to you. *Quiero hablar contigo."*[7]

They would sit near the window in silence until the grandfather would sigh and begin questioning his grandson. "How much do you think that house is worth? *Mucho dinero,*[8] no? A lot?"

---

1. **Jalapa** (hä lä′ pä): a town in Mexico.
2. **Fresno:** a city in central California.
3. *comida* (kô mē′ dä) *Spanish:* meal.
4. *frijoles* (frē hôl′ es) *Spanish:* beans.
5. *guisado de carne* (gē sä′ dô dā kär′ nä) *Spanish:* meat stew.
6. *Ven* (ven) *Spanish:* Come.
7. *Quiero hablar contigo* (kye′ rô ä blär′ kôn tē′ gō) *Spanish:* I want to talk to you.
8. *mucho dinero* (moo′ chô dē ne′ rô) *Spanish:* a lot of money.

"Grandfather, you asked me that question yesterday," Hector would say, craning his neck to look at the house. It was the yellow one whose porch light was kept on night and day.

"Yes, but that was yesterday. Yesterday I had five dollars in my pocket and now I have only three. Things change, *hijo*.[9] *Entiendes?*"[10]

Hector stared at the house a long time before making a wild guess. "Thirty thousand?"

"Do you really think so, my boy?" His grandfather would go dreamy with hope. If that house was worth thirty thousand, then his own house, which was better kept and recently painted, would be worth much more. And in Mexico, even thirty thousand dollars would buy a lot of houses. It was his hope that after he retired, he and his wife would return to Mexico, to Jalapa, where all the people would look on them with respect. Not one day would pass without the butcher or barber or pharmacist or ambitious children with dollar signs in their eyes waving to *"El Millonario."*[11]

One day after lunch his grandfather told Hector they were going to go see a house.

"What house?"

Hector's grandmother, who was wiping the table, scolded, *"Viejo, estás chiflado,*[12] you're crazy. Why do you want to buy a house when you already have one?"

The old man ignored her and went to the bathroom to splash cologne on his face and comb his hair. Gently prodding Hector in front of him, he left his house to see another house two blocks away.

Illustration by Denise Chapman Crawford / Repertoire.

Hector and his grandfather stopped in front of a pink house with a For Sale sign. The old man took a pencil and little note pad from his shirt pocket and asked Hector to write down the telephone number.

The grandfather paced off the length along the sidewalk and noted the cracks in the stucco.

---

9. *hijo* (ē′ hô) *Spanish:* son.
10. *Entiendes?* (en tyen′ des) *Spanish:* Do you understand?
11. *El Millonario* (el mē yô nä′ ryô) *Spanish:* The Millionaire.
12. *Viejo, estás chiflado* (vye′ hô es täs′ chē flä′ dô) *Spanish:* Old man, you're crazy.

"Está bonita, no?"[13] he asked Hector.

"I guess so."

"Claro que está bonita,[14] son. Of course it's pretty. And it's probably not so much money, *no crees?"*[15]

"I guess. If you think so."

"How much, do you think?"

"I don't know."

"Sure you do. *A ver, dime."*[16]

"Thirty thousand?"

"Thirty thousand? Do you think so?" His grandfather ran his hand slowly along the stubble of his jaw. Perhaps he could buy it. Perhaps he could put down eight thousand dollars, his life savings, and pay a little each month. He could repaint the house, put up a wrought-iron fence, and plant a lemon tree under the front window. He would also put in a redwood tree that would grow tall and dark so people driving on his street would see it and know Luis Salvador Molina lived in that beautiful house.

Later, while his grandmother was shopping at Hanoian's supermarket, his grandfather prodded Hector to pick up the phone and call the number. Hector, uncomfortable about talking to a grown-up, especially one who sold things, refused to get involved. He went out to the back yard to play fetch with Bon-Bon, his grandmother's poodle. His grandfather followed him into the yard and fiddled with his tomato plants. Finally, he walked over to Hector and said, "I'll give you two dollars."

Thinking it was a pretty good deal, Hector left the poodle sitting up on its hind legs and holding a slobbery tennis ball in his mouth. Hector followed his <u>anxious</u> grandfather inside the house.

"Son, just ask how much. *Es no problema,"*[17] his grandfather assured him. Hector dialed the number with a clumsy finger.

He held his breath as the phone on the other end began to ring. Then there was a click and a voice saying, "Sunny Days Realty." Before the person could ask, "May I help you," Hector, who felt faint and was having second thoughts about whether the phone call was worth two dollars, asked, "How much?"

"What?"

"How much money?" Hector repeated, cradling the phone nervously in both hands.

"Which property are you speaking of?" The lady seemed calm. Her voice was like the voice of his teacher, which scared Hector because she knew all the answers, more answers about the world than his grandfather, who knew a lot.

"It's a pink one on Orange Street."

"Please hold, and I'll look up that information."

Hector looked at his grandfather, who was combing his hair in the hallway mirror. "She's checking on the house."

After a minute, the woman came back. "That address is six forty-three South Orange, a charming little house. Two bedrooms, large yard, with appliances, and the

---

13. *Está bonita, no?* (es tä′ bô nē′ tä nô) *Spanish:* It's pretty, isn't it?

14. *Claro que está bonita* (klä′ rô kā es tä′ bô nē′ tä) *Spanish:* Of course, it's pretty.

15. *no crees?* (nô kre′ es) *Spanish:* don't you think so?

16. *A ver, dime* (ä ver dē′ mā) *Spanish:* What about it? Tell me.

17. *Es no problema* (es nô prô ble′ mä) *Spanish:* It's no problem.

Words to Know and Use | **anxious** (aŋk′ shəs) *adj.* worried

owners are willing to carry, with a substantial down payment.[18] The house also comes with—"

But Hector, his hands clenched tightly around the telephone, interrupted her and asked, "How much?"

There was a moment of silence. Then the woman said, "Forty-three thousand. The owners are anxious and perhaps may settle for less, maybe forty-one five."

"Wait a minute," he said to the woman. Hector looked up to his grandfather. "She says forty-three thousand."

His grandfather groaned, and his dream went out like a light bulb.

His grandfather groaned, and his dream went out like a light bulb. He put his comb in his back pocket.

"You said thirty thousand, Son."

"I didn't know—I was just guessing."

"But it's so much. *Es demasiado*."[19]

"Well, I didn't know."

"But you go to school and know about things."

Hector looked at the telephone in his hand. Why did he have to listen to his grandfather and call a person he didn't even know? He was conscious of his grandfather groaning at his side and of a woman's gnat-like voice coming from the telephone, asking, "Would you like to see the house? I can arrange it this afternoon, at two perhaps. And please, may I have your name?"

Hector placed the receiver to his ear and bluntly said, "It costs too much money."

"May I have your name?"

"I'm calling for my grandfather."

His grandfather put a finger before his mouth and let out a "Sshhhh." He didn't want to let her know who he was for fear that she would call him later and his wife would scold him for pretending to be a big shot like their son-in-law, Genaro. He took the receiver from Hector and hung up.

Hector didn't bother to ask for his two dollars. He went outside and played fetch with Bon-Bon until his grandmother came home, a bulky grocery bag in her arms. He carried it into the house for her and snuck a peek at his grandfather, who was playing solitaire on a TV tray near the window. He didn't seem disturbed. His face was long and cool, and his eyes were no longer filled with the excitement of money.

While his grandmother started dinner, Hector slouched on the couch reading a comic book until his grandfather whispered, "Hector, come here."

Hector looked over his comic book. His grandfather's eyes once again had that moist wildness of wealth and pink houses. He got up and said loudly, "What do you want, Grandpa?"

"Sshhhh," the old man said, pulling him close. "I want you to call and ask how come the stucco has cracks and why so much money."

"I don't want to," Hector said, trying to pull away from his grandfather's grip.

"Listen, I'll give you something very, very special. It'll be worth a lot of money, Son,

---

18. **willing to carry, with a substantial down payment:** willing to give credit, if a large amount of the purchase price is paid in advance.

19. *Es demasiado* (es de mä syä′ dô) *Spanish:* It is too much.

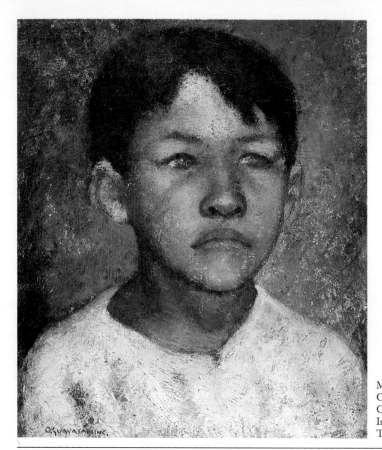

MY BROTHER   1942   Oswaldo Guayasamín Calero
Oil on wood 15⅞ x 12¾ inches
Collection, The Museum of Modern Art
Inter-American Fund, Photograph © 1992
The Museum of Modern Art   New York.

when you are old. Now it's only worth some money, but later it will be worth *mucho dinero*." He whistled and waved his hand. "Lots of money, my boy."

"I don't know, Grandfather. I'm scared."

"Yes, but, you know, you are going to be a rich man, Son."

"What are you going to give me?"

His grandfather rose, pulled his coin purse from his pants pocket, and took a thousand-dollar Confederate bill[20] from a secret fold in his purse. The bill was green, large, and had a picture of a soldier with a long beard.

Hector was impressed. He had seen his grandfather's collection of old bottles and photographs, but this was new. He bit his lower lip and said, "OK."

His grandfather tiptoed to the telephone and stretched the cord into the hallway, away from the kitchen. "Now, you call, and remember to ask how come the cracks, *¿y por qué cuesta tanto?,*[21] how come it costs so much?"

---

20. Confederate bill: a piece of paper money issued by the Confederate States of America at the time of the Civil War.

21. *¿y por qué cuesta tanto?* (ē pôr kā′ kwes′ tä tän′ tô) *Spanish:* and why does it cost so much?

Hector was beginning to sweat. His grandmother was in the next room, and if she caught them trying to be big-shot land barons, she would scold both of them. Grandfather would get the worst of it, of course. The <u>bickering</u> would never end between the two.

He dialed, waited two rings, and heard a man say, "Sunny Days Realty."

"I want to talk to the woman."

"Woman?" the salesman asked.

"The lady. I called her a while ago about the pink house."

Without another word, he put Hector on hold. Hector looked at his grandfather, who was watching out for his wife. "He put us on hold."

The phone clicked and the woman came on. "May I help you?"

"Yeah. I called you about the pink house, remember?"

"Yes. Why did you hang up?"

"My grandfather hung up, not me."

"Well, then, how can I be of help?" Her voice seemed to snap at Hector.

"My grandfather wants to know why the house has so many cracks and how come it's so expensive?"

"What?"

"My grandfather said he seen cracks."

Just then the grandmother's insistent voice rang out: *"Viejo, dónde andas?"*[22] I want you to open this bottle."

Terror filled their eyes. Grandfather hung up the phone as the woman was asking, in that faint gnat of a voice, "What in the world are you talking about?"

"Viejo, what are you doing?"

Hector wanted to hide inside the hall closet but knew it was stuffed with coats and the ironing board. Instead, he bent down and pretended to tie his shoe. His grandfather stared at the mirror and began combing his hair.

Grandmother came into the hallway with a jar of *nopales.*[23] She wrinkled her brow and asked, "What are you *locos*[24] doing?"

"Nada,"[25] they said in <u>unison</u>.

Y*ou two are up to something. Your faces are dirty with shame.*

"You two are up to something. Your faces are dirty with shame." She looked at the phone as if it were a thing she had never seen before and asked, "What is this doing here? You calling a girlfriend, *viejo?"*

"No, no, *viejita.*[26] I don't know how it got here." He shrugged his shoulders and whispered softly to Hector, "Four dollars." Then, in a loud voice, he said, "Do you know, *hijo?"*

Hector was glad to save his grandfather from a scolding that would go on for years. "Oh, I was calling my friend Alfonso about coming over to play."

She eyed both of them. *"Mentirosos!"*[27]

---

22. *Viejo, dónde andas?* (vye′ hô dôn′ dä än′ däs) *Spanish:* Old man, where are you going?

23. *nopales* (nô päl′ es) *Spanish:* prickly pears (the fruit of a kind of cactus) preserved for eating.

24. *locos* (lô′ kôs) *Spanish:* crazy people.

25. *Nada* (nä′ dä) *Spanish:* Nothing.

26. *viejita* (vye hē′ tä) *Spanish:* dear old woman.

27. *Mentirosos* (men tē rô′ sôs) *Spanish:* Liars.

Words to Know and Use	**bickering** (bik′ ər iŋ) *n.* quarreling; arguing **bicker** *v.* **unison** (yo͞on′ ə sən) *n.* a speaking of the same words at the same time

"*Es verdad, mi vida,*"[28] the grandfather said. "It's true. I heard him call his friend. He said, 'Alfonso, come over and play.'"

"Yeah, Grandma."

They argued, but the grandmother finally let them off the hook. They were glad to open the jar of *nopales* and delighted to go out, at the grandmother's suggestion, to mow the lawn before dinner.

Hector and his grandfather mowed with gusto, sweating up a dark storm in the folds of their armpits. They even went down on their knees to clip bunches of grass the mower had missed.

Hector was <u>reluctant</u> to ask his grandfather for the four dollars, but as he swept the driveway and sidewalk, he began to think that maybe his grandfather did owe him the money. He did call the lady, he argued with himself, not once but twice. It wasn't his fault the house cost too much money. As they were finishing up, Hector asked, "How about my four dollars?"

His grandfather, who was pushing the mower into the garage, pursed his lips and thought for a moment. "What is money to a young man like you?" he said finally. "You have no needs, do you?"

"I want my money!"

"What money?"

"You know what I mean. I'm going to tell Grandma."

"Son, I was just kidding." The last thing he wanted was his wife nagging him over dinner. He dug into his coin purse and brought out eight quarters.

"This is only two dollars," Hector complained.

"Yes, but you get the rest when I buy the pink house. You wait, Son, you'll be a rich man one of these days. One day it will all be yours."

Hector didn't say anything. He was glad to have the money and even gladder that his grandmother didn't scold them. After setting the sprinkler on the lawn, the two hardworking men went in for dinner. ❧

---

28. *Es verdad mi vida* (es ver däd′ mē vē′ dä) *Spanish:* It's true, my dearest.

Words to Know and Use | **reluctant** (ri luk′ tənt) *adj.* unwilling

EXPLAIN

Responding to Reading

First Impressions

1. How do you feel about Hector's relationship with his grandfather? Write down your thoughts in your journal or on a sheet of paper.

Second Thoughts

2. Why do you think Hector is Luis's favorite grandson?

3. Compare the grandfather and the grandmother in this story. Why do you think these two got married?

4. Do you think Luis Molina's dream of buying the pink house and becoming rich will ever come true?

Think about
- his age
- his job
- his interest in real estate
- his definition of rich

Writing Options

1. Write a real-estate **advertisement** that could renew Luis Molina's interest in the house on South Orange Street.

2. Write an **evaluation** of Luis, Hector, or the grandmother, using the personality scales in Examine What You Know on page 221.

3. Write a **character sketch** of Luis Molina from Hector's point of view. Include details from the story.

Vocabulary Practice

Exercise   On your paper, write the letter of the word that is most different in meaning from the other words in the set.

1. (a) unwilling   (b) eager   (c) hesitant   (d) reluctant

2. (a) unison   (b) division   (c) harmony   (d) agreement

3. (a) quarreling   (b) agreeing   (c) bickering   (d) arguing

4. (a) tense   (b) worried   (c) anxious   (d) curious

5. (a) cement   (b) plaster   (c) patio   (d) stucco

Words to Know and Use

**anxious
bickering
reluctant
stucco
unison**

Poetry

The *Sprinters*
LILLIAN MORRISON

Crystal Rowe
(Track Star)
MEL GLENN

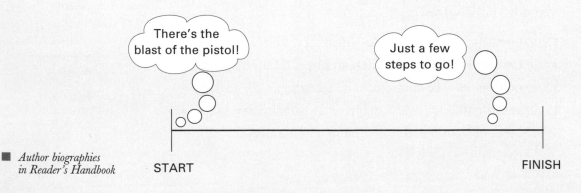

Examine What You Know

From ancient times people have run footraces. What are some of the reasons that people run races? Why do people enjoy watching races? Divide into small groups and discuss these questions. Share any experiences you have had that involve running or racing. Then read to see how the speakers in these two poems feel about why people race.

Expand Your Knowledge

Both of these poems about racing are written in **free verse.** A poem in free verse has no repeated rhyme pattern or steady rhythm. "Crystal Rowe (Track Star)" is also a **concrete poem.** In concrete poetry the poet arranges the words into a special shape or picture. The image helps reveal the poem's meaning. For example, a concrete poem about a cat might be written in the shape of a cat.

Write Before You Read

What do runners think about during a race? The graphic image below represents the time frame of a race. The thought balloons show what a runner might think about at the start and near the finish. In your journal or on a sheet of paper, draw a time line like the one below. Add at least four of your own thought balloons.

> There's the blast of the pistol!

> Just a few steps to go!

START   FINISH

■ *Author biographies in Reader's Handbook*

The *Sprinters*

LILLIAN MORRISON

The gun explodes them.
Pummeling,[1] pistoning[2] they fly
In time's face.
A go at the limit,
5 A terrible try
To smash the ticking glass,
Outpace the beat
That runs, that streaks away
Tireless, and faster than they.

10 Beside ourselves
(It is for us they run!)
We shout and pound the stands
For one to win
Loving him, whose hard
15 Grace-driven stride
Most mocks the clock
And almost breaks the bands
Which lock us in.

© Greg Shed/Stockworks.

---

1. pummeling (pum′ əl iŋ): beating or hitting repeatedly.
The sprinters' arms are moving like boxers' arms.
2. pistoning (pis′ tən iŋ): refers to the rapid motion of
the runners' legs, like the motion of pistons in an engine.

*R*esponding to Reading

First Impressions of "The Sprinters"

1. What sights and sounds do you remember most from the poem?
   Record them in your journal or on a sheet of paper.

Second Thoughts on "The Sprinters"

2. Why do you think people enjoy watching runners who "fly in time's
   face"?

3. The speaker says, "It is for us they run!" What do you think he or she
   means by this?

4. How do the speaker's feelings about this race compare with your
   feelings about races you have seen?

Crystal Rowe
(Track Star)

MEL GLENN

Allthegirlsarebunched
togetheratthestarting
_____line_____

But

When the gun goes off

I

J

U

M

P

out ahead and
never look back
and
HIT
the

__T__A__P__E__

a
WINNER!

*R*esponding to Reading

First Impressions of "Crystal Rowe (Track Star)"

1. What impressions did you have as you first read the poem? Describe them in your journal or on a sheet of paper.

Second Thoughts on "Crystal Rowe (Track Star)"

2. What effect does the poem's shape have on your enjoyment of it?

3. What if the poem had been written in **stanzas** instead of its unusual shape? How might this affect your enjoyment of it?

Comparing the Poems

4. Compare and contrast the **speakers** and the **forms** of the two poems.

5. Which of the poems do you think does a better job of capturing the feelings and images of a track competition? Use your own experiences and images from the poems to explain your answer.

Broader Connections

6. Why do people get excited about runners who break world records? Think about the poems, the Examine What You Know discussion on page 230, and your own experience before you answer.

*L*iterary Concept: Alliteration

Alliteration is the repetition of consonant sounds at the beginning of words. In "The Sprinters" the words "Pummeling, pistoning" and "terrible try" show alliteration. Find two other examples of alliteration in the poem and explain why the poet might have used this technique.

*W*riting Options

1. Look at the thought balloons in the time line you made for Write Before You Read on page 230. Express these thoughts and emotions in a **concrete poem.** Review "Crystal Rowe (Track Star)" for ideas on how to shape your poem.

2. Imagine you are a sportswriter. Describe Crystal Rowe's or the sprinters' race in a sports **column** for a newspaper.

Nonfiction

Ibrahima
from Now Is Your Time!
WALTER DEAN MYERS

*E*xamine What You Know

Imagine being kidnapped and taken to an unknown land far from your family and friends. The people of this place do not speak your language, nor do they think of you as a human being. You are their slave. In your journal, write down how you might feel and what you might try to do.

*E*xpand Your Knowledge

The imaginary scene described above was a reality for millions of Africans who were sold into slavery and brought to North, South, and Central America. Most of the Africans were taken from West Africa and the western coast of central Africa. They were brought by European slave traders to the New World, where they were cut off from all they had known. In the United States the practice of slavery began in the early 1600s and lasted until the end of the Civil War.

*E*nrich Your Reading

Setting Purposes for Reading Who were the Africans who became slaves? What culture and customs did they leave behind? On your own or with your classmates, record what you already know about this subject in a chart like the one below. In the middle column, list any questions you would like to find the answers to in the selection. After you read the selection, use the third column to list what you learned.

■ *Author biography on Extend page*

What I (We) Know	What I (We) Want to Learn	What I (We) Learned

Ibrahima

from Now Is Your Time!

WALTER DEAN MYERS

The Africans came from many countries and from many cultures. Like the Native Americans, they established their territories based on centuries of tradition. Most, but not all, of the Africans who were brought to the colonies[1] came from central and West Africa. Among them was a man named Abd al-Rahman Ibrahima.[2]

The European invaders, along with those Africans who cooperated with them, had made the times dangerous. African nations that had lived peacefully together for centuries now eyed each other warily. Slight insults led to major battles. Bands of outlaws roamed the countryside attacking the small villages, kidnapping those unfortunate enough to have wandered from the protection of their people. The stories that came from the coast were frightening. Those kidnapped were taken to the sea and sold to whites, put on boats, and taken across the sea. No one knew what happened then.

Abd al-Rahman Ibrahima was born in 1762 in Fouta Djallon,[3] a district of the present country of Guinea.[4] It is a beautiful land of green mountains rising majestically from grassy plains, a land rich with minerals, especially bauxite.

Ibrahima was a member of the powerful and influential Fula people and a son of one of their chieftains. The religion of Islam had swept across Africa centuries before, and the young Ibrahima was raised in the tradition of the Moslems.[5]

The Fula were taller and lighter in complexion than the other <u>inhabitants</u> of Africa's west coast; they had silky hair, which they often wore long. A pastoral[6] people, the Fula had a complex system of government, with the state divided into nine provinces and each province divided again into smaller districts. Each province had its chief and its subchiefs.

---

1. **colonies:** the original thirteen colonies in North America that became the United States of America.
2. **Abd al-Rahman Ibrahima** (əb do͞ol′ al räh män′ ib rä hēm′ ä).
3. **Fouta Djallon** (fo͞ot′ ə jə lōn′): a mountainous region of West Africa.
4. **Guinea** (gin′ ē): a small nation on the west coast of Africa.
5. **Islam . . . Moslems:** refers to the Arab conquests of territory in Africa, beginning in the seventh century. (A Moslem is a believer in the religion of Islam.)
6. **pastoral:** having a way of life based on raising livestock.

Words to Know and Use | **inhabitant** (in hab′ i tənt) *n.* a permanent resident

THE FIRST APPROACH TO TIMBUKTU   Nineteenth Century   Heinrich Barth   Historical Pictures/Stock Montage.

As the son of a chief, Ibrahima was expected to assume a role of political leadership when he came of age. He would also be expected to set a moral example and to be well versed in his religion. When he reached twelve, he was sent to Timbuktu[7] to study.

Under the Songhai dynasty leader Askia the Great, Timbuktu had become a center of learning and one of the largest cities in the Songhai Empire.[8] The young Ibrahima knew he was privileged to attend the best-known school in West Africa. Large and sophisticated, with wide, tree-lined streets, the city attracted scholars from Africa, Europe, and Asia. Islamic law, medicine, and mathematics were taught to the young men destined to become the leaders of their nations. It was a good place for a young man to be. The city was well guarded, too. It had to be, to prevent the chaos that, more and more, dominated African life nearer the coast.

Ibrahima learned first to recite from the Koran, the Moslem holy book, and then to read it in Arabic. From the Koran, it was felt, came all other knowledge. After Ibrahima had finished his studies in Timbuktu, he returned to Fouta Djallon to continue to prepare himself to be a chief.

What kind of person is Ibrahima?

evaluate

The Fula had little contact with whites, and what little contact they did have was filled with danger. So when, in 1781, a white man claiming to be a ship's surgeon stumbled into one of their villages, they were greatly surprised.

---

7. **Timbuktu** (tim′ buk tōō′): now known as Tombouctou, a city in the part of Africa now known as Mali.

8. **Songhai** (sôŋ′ hī) **Empire:** A West African empire that thrived in the 1400s and 1500s.

Words to Know and Use

dynasty (dī′ nəs tē) n. a series of rulers who are members of the same family
chaos (kā′ äs′) n. a state of total disorder

John Coates Cox hardly appeared to be a threat. A slight man, blind in one eye, he had been lost for days in the forested regions bordering the mountains. He had injured his leg, and it had become badly infected as he tried to find help. By the time he was found and brought to the Fula chiefs, he was more dead than alive.

Dr. Cox, an Irishman, told of being separated from a hunting party that had left from a ship on which he had sailed as ship's surgeon. The Fula chief decided that he would help Cox. He was taken into a hut, and a healer was assigned the task of curing his infected leg.

During the months Dr. Cox stayed with the Fula, he met Ibrahima, now a tall, brown-skinned youth who had reached manhood. His bearing reflected his status as the son of a major chief. Dr. Cox had learned some Fulani, the Fula language, and the two men spoke. Ibrahima was doubtless curious about the white man's world, and Dr. Cox was as impressed by Ibrahima's education as he had been by the kindness of his people.

When Dr. Cox was well enough to leave, he was provided with a guard; but before he left, he warned the Fula about the danger of venturing too near the ships that docked off the coast of Guinea. The white doctor knew that the ships were there to take captives.

Cox and Ibrahima embraced fondly and said their goodbyes, thinking they would never meet again.

Ibrahima married and became the father of several children. He was in his mid-twenties when he found himself leading the Fula cavalry[9] in their war with the Mandingo.[10]

The first battles went well, with the enemy retreating before the advancing Fula. The foot warriors attacked first, breaking the enemy's ranks and making them easy prey for the well-trained Fula cavalry. With the enemy in full rout,[11] the infantry returned to their towns while the horsemen, led by Ibrahima, chased the remaining stragglers. The Fula fought their enemies with spears, bows, slings, swords, and courage.

His bearing reflected his status as the son of a major chief.

The path of pursuit led along a path that narrowed sharply as the forests thickened. The fleeing warriors disappeared into the forest that covered a sharply rising mountain. Thinking the enemy had gone for good, Ibrahima felt it would be useless to chase them further.

"We could not see them," he would write later.

But against his better judgment, he decided to look for them. The horsemen dismounted at the foot of a hill and began the steep climb on foot. Halfway up the hill the Fula realized they had been lured into a trap! Ibrahima heard the rifles firing, saw

---

9. **cavalry:** troops mounted on horses.
10. **Mandingo** (man diŋ′ gō): a tribe of West Africa.
11. **in full rout:** in complete retreat.

Words to Know and Use | **status** (stat′ əs) *n.* standing; rank
embrace (em brās′) *v.* to clasp affectionately; hug

237

the smoke from the powder and the men about him falling to the ground, screaming in agony. Some died instantly. Many horses, hit by the gunfire, thrashed about in pain and panic. The firing was coming from both sides, and Ibrahima ordered his men to the top of the hill, where they could, if time and Allah permitted it, try a charge using the speed and momentum of their remaining horses.

Ibrahima was among the first to mount and urge his animal onward. The enemy warriors came out of the forests, some with bows and arrows, others with muskets that he knew they had obtained from the Europeans. The courage of the Fula could not match the fury of the guns. Ibrahima called out to his men to save themselves, to flee as they could. Many tried to escape, rushing madly past the guns. Few survived.

Those who did clustered about their young leader, determined to make one last, desperate stand. Ibrahima was hit in the back by an arrow, but the aim was not true and the arrow merely cut his broad shoulder. Then something smashed against his head from the rear.

The next thing Ibrahima knew was that he was choking. Then he felt himself being lifted from water. He tried to move his arms, but they had been fastened securely behind his back. He had been captured.

predict   What will happen to Ibrahima?

When he came to his full senses, he looked around him. Those of his noble cav-

alry who had not been captured were already dead. Ibrahima was unsteady on his legs as his clothes and sandals were stripped from him. The victorious Mandingo warriors now pushed him roughly into file with his men. They began the long trek that would lead them to the sea.

In Fouta Djallon, being captured by the enemy meant being forced to do someone else's bidding,[12] sometimes for years. If you could get a message to your people, you could, perhaps, buy your freedom. Otherwise, it was only if you were well liked or if you married one of your captor's women that you would be allowed to go free or to live like a free person.

Ibrahima sensed that things would not go well for him.

The journey to the sea took weeks. Ibrahima was tied to other men, with ropes around their necks. Each day they walked from dawn to dusk. Those who were slow were knocked brutally to the ground. Some of those who could no longer walk were speared and left to die in agony. It was the lucky ones who were killed outright if they fell.

When they reached the sea, they remained bound hand and foot. There were men and women tied together. Small children clung to their mothers as they waited for the boats to come and the bargaining to begin.

Ibrahima, listening to the conversations of

---

12. do someone else's bidding: follow another's orders.

Words to Know and Use | **trek** (trek) *n.* a slow, difficult journey

the men who held him captive, could understand those who spoke Arabic. These Africans were a low class of men, made powerful by the guns they had been given, made evil by the white man's goods. But it didn't matter who was evil and who was good. It only mattered who held the gun.

Ibrahima was inspected on the shore, then put into irons and herded into a small boat that took him out to a ship that was larger than any he had ever seen.

The ship onto which Ibrahima was taken was already crowded with black captives. Some shook in fear; others, still tied, fought by hurling their bodies at their captors. The beating and the killing continued until the ones who were left knew that their lot was hopeless.

On board the ship there were more whites with guns, who shoved them toward the open hatch. Some of the Africans hesitated at the hatch and were clubbed down and pushed below decks.

It was dark beneath the deck and difficult to breathe. Bodies were pressed close against other bodies. In the section of the ship he was in, men prayed to various gods in various languages. It seemed that the whites would never stop pushing men into the already crowded space. Two sailors pushed the Africans into position so that each would lie in the smallest space possible. The sailors panted and sweated as they untied the men and then chained them to a railing that ran the length of the ship.

The ship rolled against its mooring as the anchor was lifted, and the journey began. The boards of the ship creaked and moaned as it lifted and fell in the sea. Some of the men got sick, vomiting upon themselves in the wretched darkness. They lay cramped, muscles aching, irons cutting into their legs and wrists, gasping for air.

Once a day they would be brought out on deck and made to jump about for exercise. They were each given a handful of either beans or rice cooked with yams, and water from a cask. The white sailors looked hardly better than the Africans, but it was they who held the guns.

Illness and the stifling conditions on the ships caused many deaths. How many depended largely on how fast the ships could be loaded with Africans and how long the voyage from Africa took. It was not unusual for 10 percent of the Africans to die if the trip took longer than the usual twenty-five to thirty-five days.

Ibrahima, now twenty-six years old, reached Mississippi in 1788. As the ship approached land, the Africans were brought onto the deck and fed. Some had oil put on their skins so they would look better; their sores were treated or covered with pitch. Then they were given garments to wear in an obvious effort to improve their appearance.

Although Ibrahima could not speak English, he understood he was being bargained for. The white man who stood on the platform with him made him turn around, and several other white men neared him, touched his limbs, examined his teeth, looked into his eyes, and made him move about.

Thomas Foster, a tobacco grower and a hard-working man, had come from South Carolina with his family and had settled on the rich lands that took their minerals from the Mississippi River. He already held one captive, a young boy. In August 1788 he bought two more. One of them was named Sambo, which means "second son." The other was Ibrahima.

Foster agreed to pay $930 for the two Africans. He paid $150 down and signed an agreement to pay another $250 the following January and the remaining $530 in January of the following year.

When Ibrahima arrived at Foster's farm, he tried to find someone who could explain to the white man who he was—the son of a chief. He wanted to offer a ransom for his own release, but Foster wasn't interested. He understood, perhaps from the boy whom he had purchased previously, that this new African was claiming to be an important person. Foster had probably never heard of the Fula or their culture; he had paid good money for the African and wasn't about to give him up. Foster gave Ibrahima a new name: He called him Prince.

For Ibrahima this was not life but a mockery of life.

For Ibrahima there was confusion and pain. What was he to do? A few months before, he had been a learned man and a leader among his people. Now he was a captive in a strange land where he neither spoke the language nor understood the customs. Was he never to see his family again? Were his sons forever lost to him?

As a Fula, Ibrahima wore his hair long; Foster insisted that it be cut. Ibrahima's clothing had been taken from him, and his sandals. Now the last remaining symbol of his people, his long hair, had been taken as well.

He was told to work in the fields. He refused, and he was tied and whipped. The sting of the whip across his naked flesh was terribly painful, but it was nothing like the pain he felt within. The whippings forced him to work.

For Ibrahima this was not life but a mockery of life. There was the waking in the morning and the sleeping at night; he worked, he ate, but this was not life. What was more, he could not see an end to it. It was this feeling that made him attempt to escape.

Ibrahima escaped to the backwoods regions of Natchez.[13] He hid there, eating wild berries and fruit, not daring to show his face to any man, white or black. There was no telling who could be trusted. Sometimes he saw men with dogs and knew they were searching for runaways, perhaps him.

Where was he to run? What was he to do? He didn't know the country, he didn't know how far it was from Fouta Djallon or how to get back to his homeland. He could tell that this place was ruled by white men who held him in captivity. The other blacks he had seen were from all parts of Africa. Some he recognized by their tribal markings, some he did not. None were allowed to speak their native tongues around the white men. Some already knew nothing of the languages of their people.

As time passed, Ibrahima's despair deepened. His choices were simple. He could stay in the woods and probably die, or he

---

13. Natchez (nach′ iz): an early settlement in what is now the state of Mississippi.

Slaves harvesting sugar cane from William Clark's *Ten Views in the Island of Antigua*, 1823.
By permission of the British Library.

could submit his body back into bondage. There is no place in Islamic law for a man to take his own life. Ibrahima returned to Thomas Foster.

Foster still owed money to the man from whom he had purchased Ibrahima. The debt would remain whether he still possessed the African or not. Foster was undoubtedly glad to see that the African had returned. Thin, nearly starving, Ibrahima was put to work.

 **Why is it impossible for Ibrahima to escape?**

Ibrahima submitted himself to the will of Thomas Foster. He was a captive, held in bondage not only by Foster but by the society in which he found himself. Ibrahima maintained his beliefs in the religion of Islam and kept its rituals as best he could. He was determined to be the same person he had always been: Abd al-Rahman Ibrahima of Fouta Djallon and of the proud Fula people.

By 1807 the area had become the Mississippi Territory. Ibrahima was forty-five and had been in bondage for twenty years. During those years he met and married a woman whom Foster had purchased, and they began to raise a family. Fouta Djallon was more and more distant, and he had become resigned to the idea that he would never see it or his family again.

*Words
to Know
and Use* | **bondage** (bän′ dij) *n.* slavery

241

Thomas Foster had grown wealthy and had become an important man in the territory. At forty-five Ibrahima was considered old. He was less useful to Foster, who now let the tall African grow a few vegetables on a side plot and sell them in town, since there was nowhere in the territory that the black man could go where he would not be captured by some other white man and returned.

It was during one of these visits to town that Ibrahima saw a white man who looked familiar. The smallish man walked slowly and with a limp. Ibrahima cautiously approached the man and spoke to him. The man looked closely at Ibrahima, then spoke his name. It was Dr. Cox.

The two men shook hands, and Dr. Cox, who now lived in the territory, took Ibrahima to his home. John Cox had not prospered over the years, but he was still hopeful. He listened carefully as Ibrahima told his story—the battle near Fouta Djallon, the defeat, the long journey across the Atlantic Ocean, and finally his sale to Thomas Foster and the years of labor.

Dr. Cox and Ibrahima went to the Foster plantation. Meeting with Foster, he explained how he had met the tall black man. Surely, he reasoned, knowing that Ibrahima was of royal blood, Foster would free him? The answer was a firm but polite no. No amount of pleading would make Foster change his mind. It didn't matter that Dr. Cox had supported what Ibrahima had told Foster so many years before, that he was a prince. To Foster the man was merely his property.

Dr. Cox had to leave the man whose people had saved his life, but he told Ibrahima that he would never stop working for his freedom.

Andrew Marschalk, the son of a Dutch baker, was a printer, a pioneer in his field, and a man of great curiosity. By the time Marschalk heard about it, Cox had told a great many people in the Natchez district the story of African royalty being held in slavery in America. Marschalk was fascinated. He suggested that Ibrahima write a letter to his people, telling them of his whereabouts and asking them to ransom him. But Ibrahima had not been to his homeland in twenty years. The people there were still being captured by slave traders. He would have to send a messenger who knew the countryside and who knew the Fula. Where would he find such a man?

For a long time Ibrahima did nothing. Finally, some time after the death of Dr. Cox in 1816, Ibrahima wrote the letter that Marschalk suggested. He had little faith in

Above, Abd al-Rahman Ibrahima from an engraving by Henry Inman in 1828. Library of Congress.

Words to Know and Use

prosper (präs′ pər) *v.* to be successful; thrive

the procedure but felt he had nothing to lose. Marschalk was surprised when Ibrahima appeared with the letter written neatly in Arabic. Since one place in Africa was the same as the next to Marschalk, he sent the letter not to Fouta Djallon but to Morocco.

The government of Morocco did not know Ibrahima but understood from his letter that he was a Moslem. Moroccan officials, in a letter to President James Monroe, pleaded for the release of Ibrahima. The letter reached Henry Clay, the American secretary of state.

The United States had recently ended a bitter war with Tripoli in North Africa and welcomed the idea of establishing good relations with Morocco, another North African country. Clay wrote to Foster about Ibrahima.

Foster resented the idea of releasing Ibrahima. The very idea that the government of Morocco had written to Clay and discussed a religion that Ibrahima shared with other Africans gave Ibrahima a past that Foster had long denied, a past as honorable as Foster's. This idea challenged a basic premise of slavery—a premise that Foster must have believed without reservation: that the Africans had been nothing but savages, with no humanity or human feelings, and therefore it was all right to enslave them. But after more letters and pressure from the State Department, Foster agreed to release Ibrahima if he could be assured that Ibrahima would leave the country and return to Fouta Djallon.

Many people who believed that slavery was wrong also believed that Africans could not live among white Americans. The American Colonization Society had been formed expressly to send freed Africans back to Africa. The society bought land, and a colony called Liberia was established on the west coast of Africa. Foster was assured that Ibrahima would be sent there.

By then Ibrahima's cause had been taken up by a number of abolitionist[14] groups in the North as well as by many free Africans. They raised money to buy his wife's freedom as well.

On February 7, 1829, Ibrahima and his wife sailed on the ship *Harriet* for Africa. The ship reached Liberia, and Ibrahima now had to find a way to reach his people again. He never found that way. Abd al-Rahman Ibrahima died in Liberia in July 1829.

Who was Ibrahima? He was one of millions of Africans taken by force from their native lands. He was the son of a chief, a warrior, and a scholar. But to Ibrahima the only thing that mattered was that he had lost his freedom. If he had been a herder in Fouta Djallon, or an artist in Benin, or a farmer along the Gambia, it would have been the same. Ibrahima was an African who loved freedom no less than other beings on earth. And he was denied that freedom. 🕊

---

14. **abolitionist** (ab′ ə lish′ ən ist): favoring the end of slavery.

Ancestors

DUDLEY RANDALL

Why are our ancestors
always kings or princes
and never the common people?

Was the Old Country a democracy
where every man was a king?
Or did the slavecatchers
take only the aristocracy[1]
and leave the fieldhands
laborers
streetcleaners
garbage collectors
dishwashers
cooks
and maids
behind?

My own ancestor
(research reveals)
was a swineherd
who tended the pigs
in the Royal Pigstye
and slept in the mud
among the hogs.

Yet I'm as proud of him
as of any king or prince
dreamed up in fantasies
of bygone glory.

---

1. aristocracy (ar´ i stä´ krə sē):
nobility.

CINQUE   about 1840   Nathaniel Jocelyn (about 1813–1879)
New Haven Colony Historical Society.

Responding to Reading

First Impressions

1. How do you feel about the life story of Abd al-Rahman Ibrahima? Use your journal or a sheet of paper to record your thoughts.

Second Thoughts

2. How would you describe Ibrahima's qualities, or **character traits?**

   Think about
   - his life and upbringing in Africa
   - his adjustment to his loss of freedom
   - how he keeps faith with his dream to return home

3. Compare Thomas Foster with Dr. John Cox. Why were they different?

4. Think about the chart you began in Enrich Your Reading on page 234. What new attitudes do you have after reading the selection?

5. Why do you think Walter Dean Myers chose to write about a prince rather than a common person like one of those described in the Insight poem "Ancestors" on page 244?

Broader Connections

6. Africans brought to this country as slaves were almost totally cut off from their language, culture, and history. How important do you think it is for people to know about their background and their ancestors? Explain your answer.

Literary Concept: Description

A writer uses **description** to create a picture of a scene, an event, or a character. In this account Walter Dean Myers creates pictures with sight and sound details. For example, during the battle with the Mandingo, Ibrahima "heard the rifles firing, saw the smoke from the powder and the men about him falling to the ground, screaming in agony." Find in the selection another example of description that you think is especially effective.

Concept Review: Biography The writer of a **biography** does research to find out about a person's life and the time in which he or she lived. What kinds of research do you think Myers had to do in order to find out about Ibrahima's life?

Writing Options

1. What do you think Ibrahima included in his letter to his people, the Fula? Write the **letter** you think he might have written.

2. Summarize Ibrahima's story for a **pamphlet** Andrew Marschalk might have printed to argue for the ending of slavery.

3. Complete the chart you began in Enrich Your Reading on page 234. Write a **summary** of the information you learned in reading this selection.

4. Use the important events of Ibrahima's life to make a **time line** stretching from his birth in 1762 to his death in Liberia in 1829. Next to each date, indicate its importance.

Vocabulary Practice

Exercise   On your paper, write the word from the list that best completes each sentence.

1. Ibrahima had been an _?_ of Fouta Djallon.

2. Timbuktu was ruled by the Songhai _?_ .

3. Most Africans did not have the same _?_ as Ibrahima, who was part of a royal family.

4. Although the condition of _?_ existed in Africa, no one became a slave just because of skin color.

5. Some African rulers saw a way to _?_ in the slave trade by supplying traders with prisoners captured in battle.

6. Enemy tribes led their prisoners on a long _?_ by foot to the African coast.

7. _?_ occurred aboard slave ships when captives tried to throw themselves overboard.

8. Slave mothers would cry and _?_ their children before being separated from them.

9. Thomas Foster believed without _?_ that Ibrahima was only a piece of property.

10. The _?_ Ibrahima followed to obtain his freedom would not have worked for most slaves, who were unable to write.

Words to Know and Use

---

bondage
chaos
dynasty
embrace
inhabitant
procedure
prosper
reservation
status
trek

Options for Learning

1 • Ancient Glory The Songhai Empire was only one of many powerful kingdoms of ancient Africa. Research the Songhai Empire, along with the kingdoms of Benin, Cush, Kanem-Bornu, Ethiopia, and Mali. On an outline map of Africa, show the region that each kingdom occupied and the time period that each existed.

2 • Free to Be Free In what way is Liberia's name related to the idea of freedom? What U.S. president supported the settlement of freed slaves in Liberia? What did these people call themselves? Answer these questions in an oral report on Liberia. Share facts about its location, government, and culture.

3 • Routes Research and make a map of some of the main routes of the slave trade. Indicate what stops slave ships made at Caribbean islands while journeying to North America. Use different colors to show the various routes on your map.

4 • A Reunion Act out the meeting between Ibrahima and Dr. John Cox in the United States. Present your dramatization to the class.

FACT FINDER SOCIAL STUDIES

Which amendment to the U.S. Constitution ended slavery?

Walter Dean Myers
1937–

The early years of Walter Dean Myers's life were marked by hardship. When this West Virginia native was three years old, his mother died, and he was put into foster care. As Myers grew into a bright and talented teenager in the Harlem district of New York City, he felt limited by a society that defined him in terms of his race rather than his abilities. He turned to writing as a way of expressing himself.

In 1970, after a brief period in the army and a series of unsatisfying jobs, Myers became an editor for a publishing company. In 1977 he became a full-time writer.

The selection "Ibrahima" is a chapter from a nonfiction book whose full title is *Now Is Your Time! The African-American Struggle for Freedom.* Through his writings Myers tries to show young people that they can succeed in life. He believes that "there is always one more story to tell, one more person whose life needs to be held up to the sun." *Now Is Your Time!,* as well as his novels *The Young Landlords* and *Motown and Didi: A Love Story,* have won the Coretta Scott King Award. His novel *Scorpions* was a 1989 Newbery Honor Book.

Drama

ᴬ*Christmas Carol*

CHARLES DICKENS
Dramatized by FREDERICK GAINES

Examine What You Know

Have you ever seen someone make a dramatic change in his or her personality? Did the change last? In small groups think of situations that lead or force people to change. Role-play one such situation for the class. As you read, compare your role-playing with what happens in this dramatization of *A Christmas Carol.*

Expand Your Knowledge

Charles Dickens published *A Christmas Carol* in 1843. At that time, about one-third of the people in London, England, lived in poverty. Factories had changed the face of London, and people flooded the city, abandoning rural areas for a new way of life. The city quickly became overcrowded, wages were low, the crime rate was high, and children were hungry. Jobs and housing were in short supply. The Poor Law of 1834 forced the homeless into workhouses, where they worked for room and board.

Enrich Your Reading

Stage Directions   The first stage directions of this play introduce you to some of the poor who were affected by the changing conditions of city life. **Stage directions** are italicized notes in the scripts of plays. They guide actors and readers by explaining the settings of scenes, the movements of actors, the tones of voice of the **dialogue,** and the sound effects. When you read a play, don't skip the stage directions. They give you information that you won't get in any other way.

■ *Author biography on Extend page*

A *Christmas Carol*

CHARLES DICKENS
Dramatized by FREDERICK GAINES

CHARACTERS

Carolers, Families, Dancers

First Boy

Second Boy

Third Boy

Girl with a doll

Ebenezer Scrooge

Bob Cratchit, Scrooge's clerk

Fred, Scrooge's nephew

Gentleman Visitor

Warder and Residents of the Poorhouse

Sparsit, Scrooge's servant

Cook

Charwoman

Jacob Marley

Leper

First Spirit (the Spirit of Christmas Past)

Jack Walton

Ben Benjamin

Child Scrooge

Fan, Scrooge's sister

Fezziwig

Dick Wilkins

Young Ebenezer

Sweetheart of Young Ebenezer

Second Spirit (the Spirit of Christmas Present)

Poorhouse Children

Mrs. Cratchit

Several Cratchit Children

Tiny Tim

Beggar Children, Hunger and Ignorance

Third Spirit (the Spirit of Christmas Yet to Come)

Peter, a Cratchit child

Boy

Butcher

Coachman

Prologue

The play begins amid a swirl of street life in Victorian London. Happy groups pass; brightly costumed Carolers *and* Families *call out to one another and sing "Joy to the World." Three* Boys *and a* Girl *are grouped about a glowing mound of coal. As the* Carolers *leave the stage, the lights dim and the focus shifts to the mound of coals, bright against the dark. Slowly, the children begin to respond to the warmth. A piano plays softly as the children talk.*

First Boy. I saw a horse in a window. *(Pause)* A dapple . . . gray and white. And a saddle, too . . . red. And a strawberry mane down to here. All new. Golden stirrups. *(People pass by the children, muttering greetings to one another.)*

Second Boy. Christmas Eve.

Third Boy. Wish we could go.

First Boy. So do I.

Third Boy. I think I'd like it.

First Boy. Oh, wouldn't I . . . wouldn't I!

Second Boy. We're going up onto the roof. *(The boys look at him quizzically.)* My father has a glass. Telescope. A brass one. It opens up and it has twists on it and an eyepiece that you put up to look through. We can see all the way to the park with it.

Third Boy. Could I look through it?

Second Boy. Maybe . . . where would you look? *(The* Third Boy *points straight up.)* Why there?

Third Boy. I'd like to see the moon. *(The boys stand and look upward as the* Girl *sings to her doll. One of the boys makes a snow angel on the ground. As snow starts to fall, he stands up and reaches out to catch a single flake.)*

Scene One: *Scrooge in His Shop*

The percussion thunders. Scrooge *hurls himself through the descending snowflakes and sends the children scattering. They retreat, watching.* Cratchit *comes in. He takes some coal from the mound and puts it*

into a small bucket; as he carries it to a corner of the stage, the stage area is transformed from street to office. Scrooge's *nephew* Fred *enters, talks with the children, gives them coins, and sends them away with a "Merry Christmas."*

Fred. A Merry Christmas, Uncle! God save you!

Scrooge. Bah! Humbug!

Fred. Christmas a humbug, Uncle? I hope that's meant as a joke.

Scrooge. Well, it's not. Come, come, what is it you want? Don't waste all the day, Nephew.

Fred. I want only to wish you a Merry Christmas, Uncle. Don't be cross.

Scrooge. What else can I be when I live in such a world of fools as this? Merry Christmas! Out with Merry Christmas! What's Christmas to you but a time for paying bills without money, a time for finding yourself a year older and not an hour richer. If I could work my will, every idiot who goes about with "Merry Christmas" on his lips should be boiled with his own pudding and buried with a stake of holly through his heart.

Fred. Uncle!

Scrooge. Nephew, keep Christmas in your own way and let me keep it in mine.

Fred. But you don't keep it.

Scrooge. Let me leave it alone then. Much good may it do you. Much good it has ever done you.

Fred. There are many things from which I might have derived good by which I have not profited, I dare say, Christmas among the rest. And though it has never put a scrap of gold in my pocket, I believe it has done me good and will do me good, and I say, God bless it!

Scrooge. Bah!

Fred. Don't be angry, Uncle. Come! Dine with us tomorrow.

Scrooge. I'll dine alone, thank you.

Fred. But why?

Scrooge. Why? Why did you get married?

Fred. Why, because I fell in love with a wonderful girl.

Scrooge. And I with <u>solitude</u>. Good afternoon.

Fred. Nay, Uncle, but you never came to see me before I was married. Why give it as a reason for not coming now?

Scrooge. Good afternoon.

Fred. I am sorry with all my heart to find you so determined; but I have made the attempt in homage to Christmas, and I'll keep that good spirit to the last. So, a Merry Christmas, Uncle.

Scrooge. Good afternoon!

Fred. And a Happy New Year!

Scrooge. Good afternoon! *(Fred hesitates as if to say something more. He sees that Scrooge has gone to get a volume down from the shelf, and so he starts to leave. As he leaves, the doorbell rings.)* Bells. Is it necessary to always have bells? *(The Gentleman Visitor enters, causing the doorbell to ring again.)* Cratchit!

Cratchit. Yes, sir?

Scrooge. The bell, fool! See to it!

Cratchit. Yes, sir. *(He goes to the entrance.)*

Scrooge *(muttering).* Merry Christmas . . . Wolves howling and a Merry Christmas . . .

Cratchit. It's for you, sir.

Scrooge. Of course it's for me. You're not receiving callers, are you? Show them in.

Cratchit. Right this way, sir. *(The Gentleman Visitor approaches Scrooge.)*

Scrooge. Yes, yes?

Gentleman Visitor. Scrooge and Marley's, I believe. Have I the pleasure of addressing Mr. Scrooge or Mr. Marley?

Scrooge. Marley's dead. Seven years tonight. What is it you want?

Gentleman Visitor. I have no doubt that his liberality is well represented by his surviving partner. Here, sir, my card. *(He hands Scrooge his business card.)*

Scrooge. Liberality? No doubt of it? All right, all right, I can read. What is it you want? *(He returns to his work.)*

Gentleman Visitor. At this festive season of the year . . .

Scrooge. It's winter and cold. *(He continues his work and ignores the Gentleman Visitor.)*

Gentleman Visitor. Yes . . . yes, it is, and the more reason for my visit. At this time of the year it is more than usually desirable to make some slight <u>provision</u> for the poor and <u>destitute</u> who suffer greatly from the cold. Many thousands are in want of common necessaries; hundreds of thousands are in want of common comforts, sir.

Words to Know and Use

solitude (säl′ ə tōōd′) *n.* the state of being alone
provision (prō vizh′ ən) *n.* a supplying of needs
destitute (des′ tə tōōt′) *n.* people lacking the necessities of life

Scrooge. Are there no prisons?

Gentleman Visitor. Many, sir.

Scrooge. And the workhouse? Is it still in operation?

Gentleman Visitor. It is; still, I wish I could say it was not.

Scrooge. The poor law is still in full vigor then?

Gentleman Visitor. Yes, sir.

Scrooge. I'm glad to hear it. From what you said, I was afraid someone had stopped its operation.

Gentleman Visitor. Under the impression that they scarcely furnish Christian cheer of mind or body to the multitude, a few of us are endeavoring to raise a fund to buy the poor some meat and drink and means of warmth. We choose this time because it is the time, of all others, when want is keenly felt and abundance rejoices. May I put you down for something, sir?

Scrooge *(retreating into the darkness temporarily)*. Nothing.

Gentleman Visitor. You wish to be anonymous?

Scrooge. I wish to be left alone. Since you ask me what I wish, sir, that is my answer. I don't make merry myself at Christmas, and I can't afford to make idle people merry. I help support the establishments I have mentioned . . . they cost enough . . . and those who are poorly off must go there.

Gentleman Visitor. Many can't go there, and many would rather die.

Scrooge. If they would rather die, they had better do it and decrease the surplus population. That is not my affair. My business is. It occupies me constantly. *(He talks both to the* Gentleman Visitor *and to himself while he thumbs through his books.)* Ask a man to give up life and means . . . fine thing. What is it, I want to know? Charity? *(His nose deep in his books, he vaguely hears the dinner bell being rung in the workhouse; he looks up as if he has heard it but never focuses on the actual scene. The* Warder *of the poorhouse stands in a pool of light at the far left, slowly ringing a bell.)*

Warder. Dinner. All right. Line up. *(The poorly clad, dirty* Residents *of the Poorhouse line up and file by to get their evening dish of gruel,[1] wordlessly accepting it and going back to eat listlessly in the gloom.* Scrooge *returns to the business of his office. The procession continues for a moment, then the image of the poorhouse is obscured by darkness. The dejected* Gentleman Visitor *exits.)*

Scrooge. Latch the door, Cratchit. Firmly, firmly. Draft as cold as Christmas blowing in here. Charity! *(Cratchit goes to the door, starts to close it, then sees the little* Girl *with the doll. She seems to beckon to him; he moves slowly toward her, and they dance together for a moment.* Scrooge *continues to work. Suddenly* Carolers *appear on the platform, and a few phrases of their carol are heard.* Scrooge *looks up.)*

---

1. gruel (grōō′ əl): a thin, watery food made by boiling ground grain in water or milk.

Cratchit! *(As soon as* Scrooge *shouts, the* Girl *and the* Carolers *vanish and* Cratchit *begins to close up the shop.)* Cratchit!

Cratchit. Yes, sir.

Scrooge. Well, to work then!

Cratchit. It's evening, sir.

Scrooge. Is it?

Cratchit. Christmas evening, sir.

Scrooge. Oh, you'll want all day tomorrow off, I suppose.

Cratchit. If it's quite convenient, sir.

Scrooge. It's not convenient, and it's not fair. If I was to deduct half a crown[2] from your salary for it, you'd think yourself ill-used, wouldn't you? Still you expect me to pay a day's wage for a day of no work.

Cratchit. It's only once a year, sir.

Scrooge. Be here all the earlier the next morning.

Cratchit. I will, sir.

Scrooge. Then off, off.

Cratchit. Yes, sir! Merry Christmas, sir!

Scrooge. Bah! *(As soon as* Cratchit *opens the door, the sounds of the street begin, very bright and loud.* Cratchit *is caught up in a swell of people hurrying through the street. Children pull him along to the top of an ice slide, and he runs and slides down it, disappearing in darkness as the stage suddenly is left almost empty.* Scrooge *goes around the room blowing out the candles, talking to himself.)* Christmas Eve. Carolers! Bah! There. Another day. *(He opens his door and peers out.)* Black, very black. Now where are they? *(The children are heard singing carols for a moment.)* Begging pennies for their songs, are they? Oh, boy! Here, boy! *(The little* Girl *emerges from the shadows.* Scrooge *hands her a dark lantern, and she holds it while he lights it with an ember from the pile of coals.)*

---

2. **half a crown:** an amount of British money, equal to two and a half shillings or one-eighth of a pound.

*R*esponding to Reading

1. How did you feel about the meeting between Ebenezer Scrooge and his nephew, Fred? Describe your reaction in your journal.

2. What is your opinion of Ebenezer Scrooge?

   Think about
   - his conversation with the Gentleman Visitor
   - his statements about the poor
   - his treatment of Bob Cratchit

3. Skim the **stage directions.** How is the **mood** outside Scrooge's office different from the mood within the office?

Words to Know and Use | **emerge** (ē murj') *v.* to come into sight

Scene Two: *Scrooge Goes Home*

Scrooge *(talking to the little* Girl*).* Hold it quiet! There. Off now. That's it. High. Black as pitch. Light the street, that's it. You're a bright lad! Good to see that. Earn your supper, boy. You'll not go hungry this night. Home. You know the way, do you? Yes, that's the way. The house of Ebenezer Scrooge. *(As the two find their way to* Scrooge's *house, the audience sees and hears a brief image of a cathedral interior with a living crèche and a large choir singing "Amen!" The image ends in a blackout. The lights come up immediately, and* Scrooge *is at his door.)* Hold the light up, boy, up. *(The* Girl *with the lantern disappears.)* Where did he go? Boy? No matter. There's a penny saved. Lantern's gone out. No matter. A candle saved. Yes, here's the key. *(He turns with the key toward the door, and* Marley's *face swims out of the darkness.* Scrooge *watches, unable to speak. He fumbles for a match, lights the lantern, and swings it toward the figure, which melts away. Pause.* Scrooge *fits the key in the lock and turns it as the door suddenly is opened from the inside by the porter,* Sparsit. Scrooge *is startled, then recovers.)* Sparsit?

Sparsit. Yes, sir?

Scrooge. Hurry. The door . . . close it.

Sparsit. Did you knock, sir?

Scrooge. Knock? What matter? Here, light me up the stairs.

Sparsit. Yes, sir. *(He leads* Scrooge *up the stairs. They pass the* Cook *on the way.*

Scrooge *brushes by her, stops, looks back, and she leans toward him.)*

Cook. Something to warm you, sir? Porridge?

Scrooge. Wha . . . ? No. No, nothing.

Cook *(waiting for her Christmas coin).* Merry Christmas, sir. *(Scrooge ignores the request, and the* Cook *disappears. Mumbling,* Scrooge *follows* Sparsit.*)

Scrooge *(looking back after the* Cook *is gone).* Fright a man nearly out of his life . . . Merry Christmas . . . bah!

Sparsit. Your room, sir.

Scrooge. Hmmm? Oh, yes, yes. And good night.

Sparsit *(extending his hand for his coin).* Merry Christmas, sir.

Scrooge. Yes, yes . . . *(He sees the outstretched hand; he knows what* Sparsit *wants and is infuriated.)* Out! Out! *(He closes the door after* Sparsit, *turns toward his chamber, and discovers the* Charwoman *directly behind him.)*

Charwoman. Warm your bed for you, sir?

Scrooge. What? Out! Out!

Charwoman. Aye, sir. *(She starts for the door.* Marley's *voice is heard mumbling something unintelligible.)*

Scrooge. What's that?

Charwoman. Me, sir? Not a thing, sir.

Scrooge. Then, good night.

Charwoman. Good night. *(She exits, and* Scrooge *pantomimes shutting the door behind her. The voice of* Marley *over an*

Words to Know and Use | **infuriated** (in fyoor′ ē āt′ id) *adj.* very angry **infuriate** *v.*

offstage microphone whispers and reverberates: "Merry Christmas, Scrooge!" Silence. Scrooge hears the voice but cannot account for it. He climbs up to open a window and looks down. A cathedral choir is heard in the distance. Scrooge listens a moment, shuts the window, and prepares for bed. As he pulls his nightcap from a chair, a small hand-bell tumbles off onto the floor. Startled, he picks it up and rings it for <u>reassurance</u>; an echo answers it. He turns and sees the little Girl on the street; she is swinging her doll, which produces the echo of his bell. Scrooge escapes to his bed; the Girl is swallowed up in the darkness. The bell sounds grow to a din, incoherent as in a dream, then suddenly fall silent. Scrooge sits up in bed, listens, and hears the chains of Marley coming up the stairs. Scrooge reaches for the bell pull to summon Sparsit. The bell responds with a gong, and Marley appears. He and Scrooge face one another.)

Scrooge. What do you want with me?

Marley *(in a ghostly, unreal voice)*. Much.

Scrooge. Who are you?

Marley. Ask who I was.

Scrooge. Who were you?

Marley. In life, I was your partner, Jacob Marley.

Scrooge. He's dead.

Words to Know and Use | **reassurance** (rē′ ə sho͞or′ əns) *n.* a restoring of confidence

Marley. Seven years this night, Ebenezer Scrooge.

Scrooge. Why do you come here?

Marley. I must. It is commanded me. I must wander the world and see what I can no longer share, what I would not share when I walked where you do.

Scrooge. And must go thus?

Marley. The chain? Look at it, Ebenezer, study it. Locks and vaults and golden coins. I forged it, each link, each day when I sat in these chairs, commanded these rooms. Greed, Ebenezer Scrooge, wealth. Feel them, know them. Yours was as heavy as this I wear seven years ago, and you have labored to build it since.

Scrooge. If you're here to lecture, I have no time for it. It is late; the night is cold. I want comfort now.

Marley. I have none to give. I know not how you see me this night. I did not ask it. I have sat invisible beside you many and many a day. I am commanded to bring you a chance, Ebenezer. Heed it!

Scrooge. Quickly then, quickly.

Marley. You will be haunted by three spirits.

Scrooge (scoffing). . . . Is that the chance?

Marley. Mark it.

Scrooge. I do not choose to.

Marley (ominously). Then you will walk where I do, burdened by your riches, your greed.

Scrooge. Spirits mean nothing to me.

Marley (slowly leaving). Expect the first tomorrow, when the bell tolls one, the second on the next night at the same hour, the third upon the next night when the last stroke of twelve has ended. Look to see me no more. I must wander. Look that, for your own sake, you remember what has passed between us.

Scrooge. Jacob . . . Don't leave me! . . . Jacob! Jacob!

Marley. Adieu, Ebenezer. (*At* Marley's *last words a funeral procession begins to move across the stage.* Scrooge *calls out, "Jacob, don't leave me!" as if talking in the midst of a bad dream. At the end of the procession is the little* Girl *swinging her doll and singing softly.*)

Girl. Hushabye, don't you cry,
Go to sleep, little baby.
When you wake, you shall have
All the pretty little horses,
Blacks and bays, dapples and grays,
All the pretty little horses.
(*She stops singing and looks up at* Scrooge; *their eyes meet, and she solemnly rings the doll in greeting.* Scrooge *pulls shut the bed curtains, and the* Girl *exits. The bell sounds are picked up by the bells of a* Leper *who enters, dragging himself along.*)

Leper (calling out). Leper! Leper! Stay the way! Leper! Leper! Keep away! (*He exits, and the clock begins to chime, ringing the hours.* Scrooge *sits up in bed and begins to count the chimes.*)

Scrooge. Eight . . . nine . . . ten . . . eleven . . . it can't be . . . twelve. Midnight? No. Not twelve. It can't be. I haven't slept the whole day through. Twelve? Yes, yes, twelve noon. (*He hurries to the window and looks out.*) Black. Twelve midnight. (*pause*) I must get up. A day wasted. I must get down to the office. (*Two small* *chimes are heard.)* Quarter past. But it just rang twelve. Fifteen minutes haven't gone past, not so quickly. *(Again two small chimes are heard.)* A quarter to one. The spirit . . . It's to come at one. *(He hurries to his bed as the chimes ring again.)* One.

Scene Three: *The Spirit of Christmas Past*

The hour is struck again by a large street clock, and the First Spirit *appears. It is a figure dressed to look like the little* Girl's *doll.*

Scrooge. Are you the spirit whose coming was foretold to me?

First Spirit. I am.

Scrooge. Who and what are you?

First Spirit. I am the Ghost of Christmas Past.

Scrooge. Long past?

First Spirit. Your past.

Scrooge. Why are you here?

First Spirit. Your welfare. Rise. Walk with me.

Scrooge. I am mortal still. I cannot pass through air.

First Spirit. My hand. *(Scrooge grasps the* Spirit's *hand tightly, and the doll's bell rings softly.* Scrooge *remembers a scene from his past in which two boys greet each other in the street.)*

First Voice. Halloo, Jack!

Second Voice. Ben! Merry Christmas, Ben!

Scrooge. Jack Walton. Young Jack Walton. Spirits . . . ?

First Voice. Have a good holiday, Jack.

Scrooge. Yes, yes, I remember him. Both of them. Little Ben Benjamin. He used to . . .

First Voice. See you next term, Jack. Next . . . term . . .

Scrooge. They . . . they're off for the holidays and going home from school. It's Christmas time . . . all of the children off home now . . . No . . . no, not all . . . there was one . . . *(The* Spirit *motions for* Scrooge *to turn, and he sees a young boy playing with a teddy bear and talking to it.)* Yes . . . reading . . . poor boy.

First Spirit. What, I wonder?

Scrooge. Reading? Oh, it was nothing. Fancy, all fancy[3] and make-believe and take-me-away. All of it. Yes, nonsense.

Child Scrooge. Ali Baba.[4]

Scrooge. Yes . . . that was it.

Child Scrooge. Yes, and remember . . . and remember . . . remember Robinson Crusoe?[5]

Scrooge. And the parrot!

Child Scrooge. Yes, the parrot! I love him best.

---

3. **fancy:** illusion.
4. **Ali Baba** (al′ ē bab′ ə): in *The Arabian Nights,* a woodcutter who discovers the treasure-filled cave of forty thieves.
5. **Robinson Crusoe:** in the novel *Robinson Crusoe* by Daniel Defoe, a shipwrecked sailor who survives for years on a small island.

Words to Know and Use

welfare (wel′ fer′) *n.* well-being
mortal (môr′ təl) *adj.* of the earth; not a spirit

Scrooge *(imitating the parrot).* With his stripy green body and yellow tail drooping along and couldn't sing—awk—but could talk, and a thing like a lettuce growing out the top of his head . . . and he used to sit on the very top of the tree—up there.

Child Scrooge. And Robinson Crusoe sailed around the island, and he thought he had escaped the island, and the parrot said, the parrot said . . .

Scrooge *(imitating the parrot).* Robinson Crusoe, where you been? Awk! Robinson Crusoe, where you been?

Child Scrooge. And Robinson Crusoe looked up in the tree and saw the parrot and knew he hadn't escaped and he was still there, still all alone there.

Scrooge. Poor Robinson Crusoe.

Child Scrooge *(sadly replacing the teddy bear).* Poor Robinson Crusoe.

Scrooge. Poor child. Poor child.

First Spirit. Why poor?

Scrooge. Fancy . . . fancy . . . *(He tries to mask his feelings by being brusque.)* It's his way, a child's way to . . . to lose being alone in . . . in dreams, dreams . . . Never matter if they are all nonsense, yes, nonsense. But he'll be all right, grow out of it. Yes. Yes, he did outgrow it, the nonsense. Became a man and left there and he became, yes, he became a man and . . . yes, successful . . . rich! *(The sadness returns.)* Never matter . . . never matter. *(Fan runs in and goes to Child Scrooge.)* Fan!

Fan. Brother, dear brother! *(She kisses Child Scrooge.)*

Child Scrooge. Dear, dear Fan.

Fan. I've come to bring you home, home for good and ever. Come with me, come now. *(She takes his hand, and they start to run off, but the Spirit stops them and signals for the light on them to fade. They look at the Spirit, aware of their role in the Spirit's "education" of Scrooge.)*

Scrooge. Let me watch them go? Let them be happy for a moment! *(The Spirit says nothing. Scrooge turns away from them and the light goes out.)* A delicate, delicate child. A breath might have withered her.

First Spirit. She died a woman and had, as I remember, children.

Scrooge. One child.

First Spirit. Your nephew.

Scrooge. Yes, yes, Fred, my nephew. *(Scrooge pauses, then tries to bluster through.)* Well? Well, all of us have that, haven't we? Childhoods? Sadnesses? But we grow and we become men, masters of ourselves. *(The Spirit gestures for music to begin. It is heard first as from a great distance, then Scrooge becomes aware of it.)* I've no time for it, Spirit. Music and all of your Christmas folderol. Yes, yes, I've learnt what you have to show me. *(Fezziwig, Young Ebenezer, and Dick appear, busily preparing for the party.)*

Fezziwig. Yo ho, there! Ebenezer! Dick!

Scrooge. Fezziwig! It's old Fezziwig that I 'prenticed[6] under.

First Spirit. Your master?

---

6. **'prenticed:** short for *apprenticed,* here meaning "learned a trade while working."

Scrooge. Oh, aye, and the best that any boy could have. There's Dick Wilkins! Bless me. He was very much attached to me was Dick. Poor Dick. Dear, dear.

Fezziwig. Yo ho, my boys! No more work tonight. Christmas Eve, Dick! Christmas, Ebenezer! Let's have the shutters up before a man can say Jack Robinson! *(The music continues. Chandeliers are pulled into position, and mistletoe, holly, and ivy are draped over everything by bustling servants. Dancers fill the stage for Fezziwig's wonderful Christmas party. In the midst of the dancing and the gaiety, servants pass back and forth through the crowd with huge platters of food. At a pause in the music,* Young Ebenezer, *who is dancing, calls out.)*

Young Ebenezer. Mr. Fezziwig, sir, you're a wonderful master!

Scrooge and **Young Ebenezer.** A wonderful master!

Scrooge *(echoing the phrase)*. A wonderful master! *(The music changes suddenly, and the* Dancers *jerk into distorted postures and then begin to move in slow motion. The celebrants slowly exit, performing a macabre dance to discordant sounds.)*

First Spirit. Just because he gave a party? It was very small.

Scrooge. Small!

First Spirit. He spent a few pounds[7] of your "mortal" money, three, four at the most. Is that so much that he deserves this praise?

Scrooge. But it wasn't the money. He had the power to make us happy, to make our service light or burdensome. The happi-ness he gives is quite as great as if it cost a fortune. That's what . . . a good master is.

First Spirit. Yes?

Scrooge. No, no, nothing.

First Spirit. Something, I think.

Scrooge. I should like to be able to say a word or two to my clerk just now, that's all.

First Spirit. But this is all past. Your clerk Cratchit couldn't be here.

Scrooge. No, no, of course not, an idle thought. Are we done?

First Spirit *(motioning for the waltz music to begin)*. Nearly.

Scrooge *(hearing the waltz and remembering it)*. Surely it's enough. Haven't you tormented me enough? *(Young Ebenezer is seen waltzing with his* Sweetheart.)

First Spirit. I only show the past, what it promised you. Look. Another promise.

Scrooge. Oh. Oh, yes. I had forgotten . . . her. Don't they dance beautifully? So young, so young. I would have married her if only . . .

Sweetheart. Can you love me, Ebenezer? I bring no dowry[8] to my marriage, only me, only love. It is no currency that you can buy and sell with, but we can live with it. Can you? *(She pauses, then returns the ring* Scrooge *gave her as his*

---

7. **pounds:** basic British units of money, each equal to twenty shillings.

8. **dowry:** the property a bride brings to her husband when they marry.

Words to Know and Use | **currency** (kûr′ ən sē) *n.* money

pledge.) I release you, Ebenezer, for the love of the man you once were. Will that man win me again, now that he is free?

Scrooge *(trying to speak to her).* If only you had held me to it. You should not have let me go. I was young; I did love you.

Sweetheart *(speaking to* Young Ebenezer*).* We have never lied to one another. May you be happy in the life you have chosen. Goodbye. *(She runs out.* Young Ebenezer *slowly leaves.)*

Scrooge. No, no, it was not meant that way . . . !

First Spirit. You cannot change now what you would not change then. I am your mistakes, Ebenezer Scrooge, all of the things you could have done and did not.

Scrooge. Then leave me! I have done them. I shall live with them. As I have, as I do; as I will.

First Spirit. There is another Christmas, seven years ago, when Marley died.

Scrooge. No! I will not see it. I will not! He died. I could not prevent it. I did not choose for him to die on Christmas Day.

First Spirit. And when his day was chosen, what did you do then?

Scrooge. I looked after his affairs.

First Spirit. His business.

Scrooge. Yes! His business! Mine! It was all that I had, all that I could do in this world. I have nothing to do with the world to come after.

First Spirit. Then I will leave you.

Scrooge. Not yet! Don't leave me here! Tell me what I must do! What of the other spirits?

First Spirit. They will come.

Scrooge. And you? What of you?

First Spirit. I am always with you. *(The little Girl appears with her doll; she takes Scrooge's hand and gently leads him to bed. Numbed, he follows her. She leans against the foot of the bed, ringing the doll and singing. The First Spirit exits as she sings.)*

Girl. When you wake, you shall have
All the pretty little horses,
Blacks and bays, dapples and grays,
All the pretty little horses.
(She rings the doll, and the ringing becomes the chiming of Scrooge's bell. The Girl exits. Scrooge sits upright in bed as he hears the chimes.)

Scrooge. A minute until one. No one here. No one's coming. *(A larger clock strikes one o'clock.)*

*R*esponding to Reading ————————————————————

1. Which character in Scenes Two and Three made the strongest impression on you? In your journal, jot down words and phrases to describe that character.

2. The girl with the doll appears at or near the end of each of the scenes through Scene Three. What effect do you think she has on the **mood** of the play?

3. Compare and contrast Scrooge with his late partner, Jacob Marley.

4. The Spirit of Christmas Past reveals memories of Scrooge's earlier life. What mistakes do you think Scrooge has made?

   Think about
   • his childhood
   • his sister Fan
   • his old master Fezziwig
   • his sweetheart

Scene Four: *The Spirit of Christmas Present*

A light comes on. Scrooge *becomes aware of it and goes slowly to it. He sees the* Second Spirit, *the* Spirit of Christmas Present, *who looks like* Fezziwig.

Scrooge. Fezziwig!

Second Spirit. Hello, Scrooge.

Scrooge. But you can't be . . . not Fezziwig.

Second Spirit. Do you see me as him?

Scrooge. I do.

Second Spirit. And hear me as him?

Scrooge. I do.

Second Spirit. I wish I were the gentleman, so as not to disappoint you.

Scrooge. But you're not . . . ?

Second Spirit. No, Mr. Scrooge. You have never seen the like of me before. I am the Ghost of Christmas Present.

Scrooge. But . . .

Second Spirit. You see what you will see, Scrooge, no more. Will you walk out with me this Christmas Eve?

Scrooge. But I am not yet dressed.

Second Spirit. Take my tails, dear boy, we're leaving.

Scrooge. Wait!

Second Spirit. What is it now?

Scrooge. Christmas Present, did you say?

Second Spirit. I did.

Scrooge. Then we are traveling here? In this town? London? Just down there?

Second Spirit. Yes, yes, of course.

Scrooge. Then we could walk? Your flying is . . . well, too sudden for an old man. Well?

Second Spirit. It's your Christmas, Scrooge; I am only the guide.

Scrooge *(puzzled)*. Then we can walk? *(The* Spirit *nods.)* Where are you guiding me to?

Second Spirit. Bob Cratchit's.

Scrooge. My clerk?

Second Spirit. You did want to talk to him? (Scrooge *pauses, uncertain how to answer.)* Don't worry, Scrooge, you won't have to.

Scrooge *(trying to change the subject, to cover his error)*. Shouldn't be much of a trip. With fifteen bob[9] a week, how far off can it be?

Second Spirit. A world away, Scrooge, at least that far. (Scrooge *and the* Spirit *start to step off a curb when a funeral procession enters with a child's coffin, followed by the* Poorhouse Children, *who are singing. Seated on top of the coffin is the little* Girl. *She and* Scrooge *look at one another.)* That is the way to it, Scrooge. *(The procession follows the coffin offstage;* Scrooge *and the* Spirit *exit after the procession. As they leave, the lights focus on* Mrs. Cratchit *and her* Children. Mrs. Cratchit *sings as she puts* Tiny Tim *and the other* Children *to bed, all in one bed. She pulls a dark blanket over them.)*

---

9. **bob:** a British slang term for a shilling.

Mrs. Cratchit *(singing).*

When you wake, you shall have
All the pretty little horses,
Blacks and bays, dapples and grays,
All the pretty little horses.

To sleep now, all of you. Christmas tomorrow. *(She kisses them and goes to Bob Cratchit,* who is by the hearth.*)* How did our little Tiny Tim behave?

Bob Cratchit. As good as gold and better. He told me, coming home, that he hoped the people saw him in church because he was a cripple and it might be pleasant to them to remember upon Christmas Day who made the lame to walk and the blind to see.

Mrs. Cratchit. He's a good boy. *(The* Second Spirit *and* Scrooge *enter.* Mrs. Cratchit *feels a sudden draft.)* Oh, the wind. *(She gets up to shut the door.)*

Second Spirit. Hurry. *(He nudges* Scrooge *in before* Mrs. Cratchit *shuts the door.)*

Scrooge. Hardly hospitable is what I'd say.

Second Spirit. Oh, they'd say a great deal more, Scrooge, if they could see you.

Scrooge. Oh, they should, should they?

Second Spirit. Oh yes, I'd think they might.

Scrooge. Well, I might have a word for them . . .

Second Spirit. You're here to listen.

Scrooge. Oh. Oh yes, all right. By the fire?

Second Spirit. But not a word.

Bob Cratchit (*raising his glass*). My dear, to Mr. Scrooge. I give you Mr. Scrooge, the founder of the feast.

Mrs. Cratchit. The founder of the feast indeed! I wish I had him here! I'd give him a piece of my mind to feast upon, and I hope he'd have a good appetite for it.

Bob Cratchit. My dear, Christmas Eve.

Mrs. Cratchit. It should be Christmas Eve, I'm sure, when one drinks the health of such an odious, stingy, hard, unfeeling man as Mr. Scrooge. You know he is, Robert! Nobody knows it better than you do, poor dear.

Bob Cratchit. I only know one thing on Christmas: one must be <u>charitable</u>.

Mrs. Cratchit. I'll drink to his health for your sake and the day's, not for his. Long life to him! A Merry Christmas and a Happy New Year. He'll be very merry and very happy, I have no doubt.

Bob Cratchit. If he cannot be, we must be happy for him. A song is what is needed. Tim!

Mrs. Cratchit. Shush! I've just gotten him down, and he needs all the sleep he can get.

Bob Cratchit. If he's asleep on Christmas Eve, I'll be much mistaken. Tim! He must sing, dear; there is nothing else that might make him well.

Tiny Tim. Yes, Father?

Bob Cratchit. Are you awake?

Tiny Tim. Just a little.

Bob Cratchit. A song then! (*The* Children *awaken and, led by* Tiny Tim, *sit up to sing. As they sing,* Scrooge *speaks.*)

Scrooge. Spirit. (*He holds up his hand; all stop singing and look at him.*) I . . . I have seen enough. (*When the* Spirit *signals to the* Children, *they leave the stage, singing quietly.* Tiny Tim *remains, covered completely by the dark blanket, disappearing against the black.*) Tiny Tim . . . will he live?

Second Spirit. He is very ill. Even song cannot keep him whole through a cold winter.

Scrooge. But you haven't told me!

Second Spirit (*imitating* Scrooge). If he be like to die, he had better do it and decrease the surplus population. (Scrooge *turns away.*) Erase, Scrooge, those words from your thoughts. You are not the judge. Do not judge, then. It may be that in the sight of heaven you are more worthless and less fit to live than millions like this poor man's child. To hear an insect on a leaf pronouncing that there is too much life among his hungry brothers in the dust. Goodbye, Scrooge.

Scrooge. But is there no happiness in Christmas Present?

Second Spirit. There is.

Scrooge. Take me there.

Second Spirit. It is at the home of your nephew . . .

Scrooge. No!

Second Spirit *(disgusted with* Scrooge*).* Then there is none.

Scrooge. But that isn't enough . . . You must teach me!

Second Spirit. Would you have a teacher, Scrooge? Look at your own words.

Scrooge. But the first spirit gave me more . . . !

Second Spirit. He was Christmas Past. There was a lifetime he could choose from. I have only this day, one day, and you, Scrooge. I have nearly lived my fill of both. Christmas Present must be gone at midnight. That is near now. *(He speaks to two* Beggar Children *who pause shyly at the far side of the stage. The* Children *are thin and wan; they are barefoot and wear filthy rags.)* Come. *(They go to him.)*

Scrooge. Is this the last spirit who is to come to me?

Second Spirit. They are no spirits. They are real. Hunger, Ignorance. Not spirits, Scrooge, passing dreams. They are real. They walk your streets, look to you for comfort. And you deny them. Deny them not too long, Scrooge. They will grow and multiply, and they will not remain children.

Scrooge. Have they no refuge, no resource?

Second Spirit *(again imitating* Scrooge*).* Are there no prisons? Are there no workhouses? *(tenderly to the* Children*)* Come. It's Christmas Eve. *(He leads them offstage.)*

Scene Five: The Spirit of Christmas Yet to Come

Scrooge *is entirely alone for a long moment. He is frightened by the darkness and feels it approaching him. Suddenly he stops, senses the presence of the* Third Spirit, *turns toward him, and sees him. The* Spirit *is bent and cloaked. No physical features are distinguishable.*

Scrooge. You are the third. *(The* Spirit *says nothing.)* The Ghost of Christmas Yet to Come. *(The* Spirit *says nothing.)* Speak to me. Tell me what is to happen—to me, to all of us. *(The* Spirit *says nothing.)* Then show me what I must see. *(The* Spirit *points. Light illuminates the shadowy recesses of* Scrooge's *house.)* I know it. I know it too well, cold and cheerless. It is mine. *(The* Cook *and the* Charwoman *are dimly visible in* Scrooge's *house.)* What is . . . ? There are . . . thieves! There are thieves in my rooms! *(He starts forward to accost them, but the* Spirit *beckons for him to stop.)* I cannot. You cannot tell me that I must watch them and do nothing. I will not. It is mine still. *(He rushes into the house to claim his belongings and to protect them. The two women do not notice his presence.)*

Cook. He ain't about, is he? *(The* Charwoman *laughs.)* Poor ol' Scrooge 'as met 'is end.[10] *(She laughs with the* Charwoman.*)*

Charwoman. An' time for it, too; ain't been alive in deed for half his life.

Cook. But the Sparsit's nowhere, is he . . . ?

Sparsit *(emerging from the blackness).*

---

10. 'as met 'is end: Cockney dialect for "has met his end." Cockneys (residents of the East End of London) drop the letter *h* when pronouncing words.

Lookin' for someone, ladies? *(The* Cook *shrieks, but the* Charwoman *treats the matter more practically, anticipating competition from* Sparsit.*)*

Charwoman. There ain't enough but for the two of us!

Sparsit. More 'an enough . . . if you know where to look.

Cook. Hardly decent is what I'd say, hardly decent, the poor old fella hardly cold and you're thievin' his wardrobe.

Sparsit. You're here out of love, are ya?

Charwoman. There's no time for that. *(*Sparsit *acknowledges* Scrooge *for the first time, gesturing toward him as if the living* Scrooge *were the corpse.* Scrooge *stands as if rooted to the spot, held there by the power of the* Spirit.*)*

Sparsit. He ain't about to bother us, is he?

Charwoman. Ain't he a picture?

Cook. If he is, it ain't a happy one. *(They laugh.)*

Sparsit. Ladies, shall we start? *(The three of them grin and advance on* Scrooge.*)* Cook?

Cook *(snatching the cuff links from the shirt* Scrooge *wears).* They're gold, ain't they?

Sparsit. The purest, madam.

Charwoman. I always had a fancy for that nightcap of his. My old man could use it. *(She takes the nightcap from* Scrooge's *head.* Sparsit *playfully removes* Scrooge's *outer garment, the coat or cloak that he has worn in the previous scenes.)*

Sparsit. Bein' a man of more practical tastes, I'll go for the worsted[11] and hope the smell ain't permanent. *(The three laugh.)* Cook, we go round again.

Cook. Do you think that little bell he's always ringing at me is silver enough to sell? *(The three of them move toward the night stand, and* Scrooge *cries out.)*

Scrooge. No more! No more! *(As the* Spirit *directs* Scrooge's *attention to the tableau[12] of the three thieves standing poised over the silver bell,* Scrooge *bursts out of the house, clad only in his nightshirt.)* I cannot. I cannot. The room is . . . too like a cheerless place that is familiar. I won't see it. Let us go from here. Anywhere. *(The* Spirit *directs his attention to the* Cratchit *house; the* Children *are sitting together near* Mrs. Cratchit, *who is sewing a coat.* Peter *reads by the light of the coals.)*

Peter. "And he took a child and set him in the midst of them."

Mrs. Cratchit *(putting her hand to her face).* The light tires my eyes so. *(pause)* They're better now. It makes them tired to try to see by firelight, and I wouldn't show reddened eyes to your father when he comes home for the world. It must be near his time now.

Peter. Past it, I think, but he walks slower than he used to, these last few days, Mother.

Mrs. Cratchit. I have known him to walk with . . . I have known him to walk with Tiny Tim upon his shoulder very fast indeed. *(She catches herself, then hurries on.)* But he was very light to carry, and his father loved him, so that it was no trouble, no trouble. *(She hears* Bob Cratchit *approaching.)* Smiles, everyone, smiles.

Bob Cratchit *(entering).* My dear, Peter . . .

---

11. **worsted:** a smooth woolen fabric.

12. **tableau** (tab′ lō′): a portion of a play in which the actors momentarily freeze in their positions for dramatic effect.

(He greets the other Children *by their real names.)* How is it coming?

Mrs. Cratchit *(handing him the coat).* Nearly done.

Bob Cratchit. Yes, good, I'm sure that it will be done long before Sunday.

Mrs. Cratchit. Sunday! You went today then, Robert?

Bob Cratchit. Yes. It's . . . it's all ready. Two o'clock. And a nice place. It would have done you good to see how green it is. But you'll see it often. I promised him that, that I would walk there on Sunday . . . often.

Mrs. Cratchit. We mustn't hurt ourselves for it, Robert.

Bob Cratchit. No. No, he wouldn't have wanted that. Come now. You won't guess who I've seen. Scrooge's nephew Fred. And he asked after us and said he was heartily sorry and to give his respect to my good wife. How he ever knew that, I don't know.

Mrs. Cratchit. Knew what, my dear?

Bob Cratchit. Why, that you were a good wife.

Peter. Everybody knows that.

Bob Cratchit. I hope that they do. "Heartily sorry," he said, "for your good wife, and if I can be of service to you in any way—" and he gave me his card—"that's where I live"—and Peter, I shouldn't be at all surprised if he got you a position.

Mrs. Cratchit. Only hear that, Peter!

Bob Cratchit. And then you'll be keeping company with some young girl and setting up for yourself.

Peter. Oh, go on.

Bob Cratchit. Well, it will happen one day, but remember, when that day does come—as it must—we must none of us forget poor Tiny Tim and this first parting in our family.

Scrooge. He died! No, no! *(He steps back, and the scene disappears; he moves away from the* Spirit.*)*

Responding to Reading

1. How do you feel about Scrooge's reaction to Tiny Tim's death at the end of Scene Five? Describe your feelings in your journal.

2. What effect does the Spirit of Christmas Present have on Scrooge?
   Think about
   - the spirit's appearance
   - the image the spirit shows of the Cratchit family
   - how the spirit repeats Scrooge's earlier statements

3. Look at the speech the Second Spirit makes about the beggar children near the end of Scene Four. What do you think he means?

4. Contrast the reactions and feelings surrounding Scrooge's death with those surrounding the death of Tiny Tim.

Scene Six: *Scrooge's Conversion*

Scrooge. Because he would not . . . no! You cannot tell me that he has died, for that Christmas has not come! I will not let it come! I will be there . . . It was me. Yes, yes, and I knew it and couldn't look. I won't be able to help. I won't. *(pause)* Spirit, hear me. I am not the man I was. I will not be that man that I have been for so many years. Why show me all of this if I am past all hope? Assure me that I yet may change these shadows you have shown me. Let the boy live! I will honor Christmas in my heart and try to keep it all the year. I will live in the Past, the Present, and the Future. The spirits of all three shall strive within me. I will not shut out the lessons that they teach. Oh, tell me that I am not too late! *(A single light focuses on the little* Girl, *dressed in a blue cloak like that of the Virgin Mary. She looks up, and from above a dove is slowly lowered in silence to her; she takes it and encloses it within her cloak, covering it. As soon as she does this, a large choir is heard, singing "Gloria!" and the bells begin to ring. Blackout. When the lights come up again,* Scrooge *is in bed. The* Third Spirit *and the figures in the church have disappeared.* Scrooge *awakens and looks around his room.)* The curtains! They are mine, and they are real. They are not sold. They are

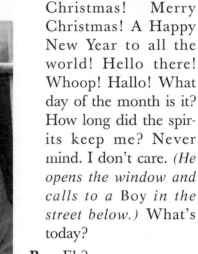

here. I am here; the shadows to come may be dispelled. They will be. I know they will be. *(He dresses himself hurriedly.)* I don't know what to do. I'm as light as a feather, merry as a boy again. Merry Christmas! Merry Christmas! A Happy New Year to all the world! Hello there! Whoop! Hallo! What day of the month is it? How long did the spirits keep me? Never mind. I don't care. *(He opens the window and calls to a* Boy *in the street below.)* What's today?

Boy. Eh?

Scrooge. What's the day, my fine fellow?

Boy. Today? Why, Christmas Day!

Scrooge. It's Christmas Day! I haven't missed it! The spirits have done it all in one night. They can do anything they like. Of course they can. Of course they can save Tim. Hallo, my fine fellow!

Boy. Hallo!

Scrooge. Do you know the poulterers[13] in the next street at the corner?

Boy. I should hope I do.

Scrooge. An intelligent boy. A remarkable boy. Do you know whether they've sold the prize turkey that was hanging up there? Not the little prize; the big one.

---

13. **poulterers** (pōl′ tər ərz): people who sell poultry.

Boy. What, the one as big as me?

Scrooge. What a delightful boy! Yes, my bucko!

Boy. It's hanging there now.

Scrooge. It is? Go and buy it.

Boy. G'wan!

Scrooge. I'm in earnest! Go and buy it and tell 'em to bring it here that I may give them the direction where to take it. Come back with the butcher and I'll give you a shilling.[14] Come back in less than two minutes and I'll give you half a crown!

Boy. Right, guv! *(He exits.)*

Scrooge. I'll send it to Bob Cratchit's. He shan't know who sends it. It's twice the size of Tiny Tim and such a Christmas dinner it will make. *(Carolers suddenly appear singing "Hark! The Herald Angels Sing." Scrooge leans out the window and joins them in the song.)* I must dress, I must. It's Christmas Day! I must be all in my best for such a day. Where is my China silk shirt? (The Boy and the Butcher run in with the turkey.)* What? Back already? And such a turkey. Why, you can't carry that all the way to Cratchit's. Here, boy, here is your half a crown and here an address in Camden Town. See that it gets there. Here, money for the cab, for the turkey, and for you, good man! *(The Boy and the Butcher, delighted, catch the money and run out. Scrooge sees the Gentleman Visitor walking by the window.)* Halloo, sir!

Gentleman Visitor *(looking up sadly, less than festive).* Hello, sir.

Scrooge. My dear sir, how do you do? I hope you succeeded yesterday. It was very kind of you to stop by to see me.

Gentleman Visitor *(in disbelief).* Mr. Scrooge?

Scrooge. Yes, that is my name, and I fear it may not be pleasant to you. Allow me to ask your pardon, and will you have the goodness to add this *(throwing him a purse)* to your good work!

Gentleman Visitor. My dear Mr. Scrooge, are you serious?

Scrooge. If you please, not a penny less. A great many back payments are included in it, I assure you. Will you do me that favor?

Gentleman Visitor. My dear sir, I don't know what I can say to such generosity.

Scrooge. Say nothing! Accept it. Come and see me. Will you come and see me?

Gentleman Visitor. I will.

Scrooge. Thank 'ee. I am much obliged to you. I thank you fifty times. God bless you and Merry Christmas!

Gentleman Visitor. Merry Christmas to you, sir!

Scrooge *(running downstairs, out of his house, and onto the street).* Now which is the way to that nephew's house. Girl! Girl!

Girl *(appearing immediately).* Yes, sir?

Scrooge. Can you find me a taxi, miss?

Girl. I can, sir. *(She rings her doll, and a Coachman appears.)*

Scrooge *(handing the Coachman a card).* Can you show me the way to this home?

Coachman. I can, sir.

Scrooge. Good man. Come up, girl. *(They mount to the top of the taxi. This action may*

---

14. **shilling:** a British coin. Five shillings equal a crown.

be stylistically suggested.) Would you be an old man's guide to a Christmas dinner?

Girl. I would, sir, and God bless you!

Scrooge. Yes, God bless us every one! *(raising his voice almost in song)* Driver, to Christmas! *(They exit, all three singing. Blackout. The lights come up for the finale at* Fred's *house. The* Cratchits *are there with* Tiny Tim. *All stop moving and talking when they see* Scrooge *standing in the center, embarrassed and humble.)* Well, I'm very glad to be here at my nephew's house! *(He starts to cry.)* Merry Christmas! Merry Christmas!

All *(softly).* Merry Christmas. *(They sing "Deck the Halls," greeting one another and exchanging gifts.* Scrooge *puts* Tiny Tim *on his shoulders.)*

Tiny Tim. God bless us every one!

Scrooge *(to the audience).* Oh, yes! God bless us every one! ❧

Responding to Reading

First Impressions

1. If you had just seen this play on stage, what is the first thing you would say to a friend about it? Write your response in your journal or on a sheet of paper.

Second Thoughts

2. What words or phrases would you use to describe the **character** of Scrooge in the last scene?

3. Which spirit made the strongest impression on you? Explain.

4. Which of the characters' lives is likely to be changed the most in the future? Explain your answer.

5. The title of this subunit is "Keeping Faith." What do the events of *A Christmas Carol* have to do with keeping faith?

Broader Connections

6. Charles Dickens wrote about many of the serious problems of his times. Are the problems of the poor today the same as or different from what they were in Dickens's time? Explain.

Literary Concept: Flashback

A **flashback** is an interruption of the order of events in a story. A flashback usually consists of a conversation or an event that happened before the beginning of the story. This background information makes a character's present actions or attitude easier to understand. In this play, the Spirit of Christmas Past allows Scrooge to look at his childhood in a flashback. How does knowing about Scrooge's past help you understand his actions as an adult?

Concept Review: Theme In a work of literature, the **theme** is the message about life or human nature that the writer presents to the reader. What do you think is the theme of *A Christmas Carol?*

Writing Options

1. What real-life actors would you choose to play Scrooge, Tiny Tim, and the spirits in a movie version of *A Christmas Carol?* Write a **memo** to the director of the movie, suggesting who should play what role and why.

2. Compose an imaginary **dialogue** in which two of the characters in this subunit discuss keeping faith.

3. Write a new **will** for Scrooge that shows his change of heart.

4. Is Scrooge permanently changed by his experience? Write a **postscript** to the play, based on what you know about Scrooge, what you know about human nature, and what you learned from the role-playing activity in Examine What You Know on page 248.

Vocabulary Practice

Exercise A On your paper, write the letter of the situation that best matches each word on the left.

1. solitude a. a filled storehouse
2. procession b. a submarine coming to the surface
3. provision c. going to your room to be alone
4. currency d. a military parade
5. emerge e. bills and coins

Exercise B On your paper, write *S* if the pair of words are *Synonyms.* Write *A* if they are *Antonyms.*

1. finale—ending
2. pledge—promise
3. surplus—lack
4. destitute—wealthy
5. infuriated—delighted
6. mortal—human
7. charitable—stingy
8. welfare—well-being
9. reassurance—discouragement
10. abundance—richness

Words to Know and Use

abundance
charitable
currency
destitute
emerge
finale
infuriated
mortal
pledge
procession
provision
reassurance
solitude
surplus
welfare

Options for Learning

1 • **Sing for Joy** What is a carol and what is the history of carols and caroling? Research this subject and present your findings to the class in the form of an oral report. If possible, include recordings or your own rendition of some of the English carols mentioned in this play.

2 • **A Christmas Play** With some classmates produce *A Christmas Carol* as a radio play. Ask some students to read parts and others to record music and create sound effects. Tape-record your drama and play it for another class.

3 • **Dickens's World** Research the clothing that the upper and lower classes wore during the time of Charles Dickens. Using your research as a guide, design and draw original costumes.

4 • **Meeting Needs** Conduct a school survey on the best ways to lessen the poverty in your community. Publish your views in your school newspaper.

FACT FINDER MATH

How much is a British pound now worth in U.S. currency?

Charles Dickens
1812–1870

Considered one of the greatest English novelists, Charles Dickens was perhaps the most popular writer of his time. When the book *A Christmas Carol* came out in 1843, six thousand copies sold the first day.

The work of Dickens is known for its "classic" or lasting quality. The books *Oliver Twist* (published in 1838), *A Tale of Two Cities* (1859), and *Great Expectations* (1860–1861) are enjoyed today even though they were written over one hundred years ago.

Dickens began contributing stories and essays about life in London while working as a newspaper reporter. By 1836 he had won great fame.

Dickens published many of his novels in parts, with a few chapters appearing each month in a magazine or newspaper. Many of the novels revealed the sufferings of the poor in the workhouses and in the slums.

Dickens's own unhappy childhood provided the material for a number of his writings. When his father was sent to prison because of debts, Dickens had to leave school at the age of twelve to work in a rat-infested factory. The hopelessness and shame he experienced deeply affected him. Of his novels, his favorite was *David Copperfield* (1849–1850), which he based partly on his experiences in the factory.

WRITER'S WORKSHOP

INFORMATIVE WRITING

"Keeping faith" means having a goal and working toward it. As you saw in this subunit, a goal may be as large as winning freedom from slavery or as small as winning a sprint. At school, extracurricular activities are one way that groups of people work together toward common goals. In this workshop, you will write a **newspaper article** about an extracurricular activity. Your topic may be a school sports event, a concert, a play, a club activity, or a student government program.

USE INFORMATIVE
WRITING FOR

essays
news articles
reports
formal letters
speeches

Here is one writer's PASSkey to this assignment.

GUIDED ASSIGNMENT: NEWSPAPER ARTICLE

Write an article about a school-related event or activity. Provide facts that inform and interest readers.

P URPOSE: To inform readers

A UDIENCE: Newspaper readers

S UBJECT: A school event

S TRUCTURE: Newspaper article

Kangaroos Hop to Victory over Redville
by Yolanda Federman

   Yesterday the Northfield Kangaroos easily
hopped to a win over the Raiders of Redville
Middle School. It was Northfield's eighth
volleyball match of the season and the fourth
one at home.
   So far the Kangaroos have had an excellent
year, with a season record of 7 wins and 1
loss. Julia Huxhold's strong serve has really
helped the team. The Kangaroos have already
improved a lot on last year's record of 4
wins and 12 losses. Coach Britton and the
team hope for a win in the regional
championship. Says Britton, "I think the

STUDENT MODEL

Before you write, read how one student responded to the assignment.

The opening sums up what happened by answering the questions *who, what, when, where,* and *how.*

players really are getting it together as a team. We have high hopes for winning the trophy."

The teams split the first two games, and the Kangaroos took the lead early on in the tiebreaker, as they had in the two earlier games of the match. Julia Huxhold scored seven points in a row. Her serves whizzed low and hard over the net. The Redville Raiders just couldn't seem to return the ball.

After the Kangaroos earned an 8-0 lead, the Raiders gained control of the ball and scored four points. Then they lost the serve when one of their forwards hit the ball into the net. Next, Cheri Patel stepped into serving position and quickly scored three points for the Kangaroos.

In the last part of the game, both teams delivered good shots but the Raiders' blocking ability seemed to fade. Center forward Holly Morito scored the winning point with a kill that landed well within bounds on the Raiders' court.

Although the hometeam crowd was small, its "oohs" and "ahhs" and victory cheers filled the gym. No wonder! If the Kangaroos keep playing this well, Coach Britton could be right. We'd better make room inside our school's display case for a regional trophy!

Notice how Yolanda returns to the topic of the volleyball game while giving additional details.

The article has informative facts and shows the writer's enthusiasm.

Yolanda wraps up the article after fully covering her topic.

WRITER'S CHOICE
Your school's current calendar may provide a list of upcoming school events. Scan the list and choose an event that you would like to cover.

Prewrite and Explore

1 **Cover your "beat"** Reporters usually have a "beat," a basic subject area or activity that they cover. Do you play or follow a particular sport? Do you belong to any clubs? Do you like attending choral concerts or school plays? As you consider a topic for your article, focus on an activity that you know about and enjoy.

2 **Study the genuine article**   Look over newspapers for articles about events similar to the one you will be writing about. The sports section, the arts and entertainment section, and the social calendar pages are good places to start. Skim several articles to learn what a news article looks like. Pay special attention to how the articles are organized. For example, the paragraphs are usually short, consisting of about two to five sentences. What **tone,** or attitude, does a writer seem to have toward a topic? How does the writer's tone affect your impressions of the article? See if there are certain words or personal statements in the article that help you to understand the writer's feelings.

◀ CUT AND PASTE
···
One way to learn how a newspaper article is constructed is to take it apart. Clip an article from the paper. Then cut it into these sections:
   leading paragraph/
      main topic
   background information
   supporting details
   conclusion
Try arranging these pieces in a different order. Is there any other way they could logically fit together?

GATHERING INFORMATION

Of course, the first step in reporting an event is to attend it. You should take detailed, on-the-spot notes that answer the questions *who, what, when, where,* and *how.* Interview people on the scene and jot down background information.

Once you have your notes, you need to narrow them down and organize them. In ordering her notes, Yolanda followed the form of a typical news story.

◀ STUDENT MODEL
···

```
MAIN TOPIC
Northfield beat Redville
final score 15-5

SUPPORTING DETAILS
Kangaroos took early lead
Huxhold served 7 points
Game picked up at 8-0
Raiders scored 4 points
Cheri Patel served 3 points
good shots on both sides
Holly Morito scored 15th point

BACKGROUND INFORMATION
Kangaroos have 7-1 record
Julia Huxhold is strong server
Coach Britton--"high hopes"

CONCLUSION
Kangaroos could win regionals
```

In a newspaper article it's important to get the most important facts up front for two reasons:
1. The reader may read only the first paragraph.
2. If the editor who is fitting all the articles onto a page runs out of space, he or she will most likely cut the last paragraphs.

Draft and Discover

1 **Write your lead**   The first paragraph of your article is called the **lead.** It should state the most important facts about your topic. When writing your lead, include information that answers at least three of the questions *who, what, when, where,* and *how.*

2 **Give the facts**   As you draft the body of your article, remember that your main purpose is to inform. Don't worry about finding the perfect adjective or comparison. Instead, concentrate on telling the facts in a clear, orderly way.

Revise Your Writing

1 **Check for organization**   Make sure your draft reads like a newspaper article. Did you get right to the point in the first paragraph? Did you follow the lead with background information, specific details, and a closing sentence or paragraph?

2 **Tune up your tone**   As a newswriter, you should sound confident, well-informed, and factual. Note how Yolanda changed these sentences to make them more factual and informative.

Before   Julia Huxhold did a really amazing job of serving. I've never seen serves as good as hers.

After   Julia Huxhold scored seven points in a row. Her serves whizzed low and hard over the net.

3 **Use a peer reader**   After you have looked over your draft, ask another student to review it. Use the following questions.

Revision Questions

For You	For a Peer Reader
1. Did I describe the event in a clear, organized way?	**1.** What else do you need to know about the topic?
2. Have I checked my facts?	**2.** Are any details unnecessary?
3. Do I sound as if I know my topic?	**3.** Is the tone both consistent and interesting?

Proofread

Check your draft for errors in grammar, punctuation, and spelling. Make sure you have capitalized all proper nouns.

NEED MORE HELP?

See the Language Workshop that follows (pages 280–282) and Section 8 in the Language Handbook.

THE EDITOR'S EYE: SUBJECT–VERB AGREEMENT

The subject and verb in a sentence must agree in number.

If a sentence has a singular subject, use a singular verb.

Coach Britton hopes to win the regional championship.

If a sentence has a compound subject joined by the word *and,* use a plural verb.

Coach Britton and *Julia Huxhold hope* to win the regional championship.

Publish and Present

Here is a suggestion for sharing your work as a class.

First Class News   Combine your articles to make a class newspaper. Work together to name your paper, write headlines, and lay out and paste up the articles. If possible, make copies of the paper to distribute among yourselves.

If your article is still timely, you might also want to send it to your school newspaper for possible publication.

◀ COMPUTER TIP
A desktop publishing program makes combining texts and headlines easy.

Reflect on Your Writing

Answer the questions below, then attach your responses to a copy of your newspaper article. Place the article in your writing portfolio.

◀ FOR YOUR PORTFOLIO

1. Did taking notes present any problems for you? What might you try next time to help you get the most from your notes?
2. Was it challenging for you to make your informative writing both factual and interesting?
3. What other newsworthy topics would you like to write about?

LANGUAGE WORKSHOP

SUBJECT AND VERB AGREEMENT

> The subject and verb in a sentence must **agree in number.**

REMINDER

A **singular noun** names one thing. A **plural noun** names more than one thing. Plural nouns usually end in *-s.*

When you write a sentence, make sure the subject and verb **agree in number.** This means that if the subject of your sentence is **singular,** the verb must also be singular. If the subject is **plural,** the verb must also be plural. Most singular third person verbs are formed by adding *-s.* Most plural verbs are formed by dropping the *-s.*

Singular	sails	listens
Plural	sail	listen

Whenever you are unsure about agreement, first find the subject of the sentence and decide whether it is singular or plural. Then make the verb match the number of the subject.

MEMORY TRICK

Can't remember the difference between singular and plural verbs? Try memorizing this rule: *S*ingular verbs often end in *-s.* *Pl*ural verbs are *pl*ain.

Singular Subjects and Verbs

The former *slave sails* to Liberia.

The *ship lands* safely.

Plural Subjects and Verbs

The former *slaves sail* to Liberia.

The *ships land* safely.

As you can see in the sentences above, in the present tense singular verbs end in *-s;* plural verbs do not.

Exceptions to the agreement rule are the singular pronouns *I* and *you,* which take plural verbs.

I sail. *You sail.*

Exercise 1   Concept Check   For each sentence write the correct verb form. Remember, the number of the verb must match the number of the subject.

1. Liberia (sit, sits) on the coast of West Africa.
2. Three countries (border, borders) Liberia.
3. A rain forest (cover, covers) about half of the country.
4. Native tribes (dwell, dwells) mainly in the rain forest.
5. Rubber trees (provide, provides) a valuable cash crop.

6. Coffee (grow, grows) well in the tropical climate.
7. Six major rivers (flow, flows) through Liberia.
8. A marshy coast (extend, extends) fifty miles inland.
9. Low mountains (dot, dots) the inland jungle.
10. Monrovia (stand, stands) as Liberia's capital city.

Sentences with Compound Subjects

Some sentences have **compound subjects.** In this kind of sentence, two or more subjects share the same verb. The parts of a compound subject are joined by the word *and, or,* or *nor.* Look at the following example of a sentence with a compound subject.

Bob Cratchit and his *wife* enjoy singing carols.

Choosing whether to use a singular or plural verb with a compound subject may seem complicated. Follow the two rules below.

1. Always use a plural verb when the parts of a compound subject are joined by *and.*

Scrooge and *Marley talk* of the past.

The *nightcap* and the *bell rest* on the nightstand.

2. When the parts of a compound subject are joined by *or, either/or,* or *neither/nor,* the verb should agree with the subject that is closest to the verb.

Bob Cratchit or *Mrs. Cratchit puts* the children to bed.

Either the *father* or the *mother checks* on Tiny Tim.

Neither *Tim* nor the *children want* to sleep.

Prepositional Phrases After the Subject

Sometimes a **prepositional phrase** comes between the subject and the verb in a sentence. Don't let these extra words mislead you. The subject is never found in a prepositional phrase. Look at this sentence. The prepositional phrase is in italics.

The little girl *in the red overalls* looks lost.

Notice on the next page how the sentence sounds complete even without the prepositional phrase.

TIP
. . . .
When a compound subject is joined by *or* or *nor,* say the sentence without the first part of the compound. Then use the verb that agrees with the simple subject. Look at this example.

Neither he nor she (see, sees) Scrooge.

She *sees* Scrooge.

Subject   Verb

The little *girl*   *looks* lost.

Girl is the subject of the sentence because it tells *whom* or *what* the sentence is about. *Girl* is also a singular noun, so it takes the singular verb *looks.*

MORE THAN MEETS
THE EAR
Don't depend only on what sounds correct to make sure subjects and verbs agree. Keep the rules in mind.

Exercise 2   Concept Check   Choose the correct verb from those in parentheses.

1. Competitors in track and field events (practice, practices) hard.

2. Either males or females (compete, competes) in races.

3. A track shoe with spikes (dig, digs) into the ground.

4. Cheap shoes or a hard road (damage, damages) runners' knees.

5. Neither the runners nor their coach (like, likes) a slippery track.

6. A runner's arms and legs (provide, provides) balance.

7. Either a jog or stretching exercises (warm, warms) up muscles before a track meet.

8. Blocks at the starting line (get, gets) runners off to a fast start.

9. Sprints or dashes (include, includes) all races up to 400 meters long.

10. Coaches and an official (keep, keeps) careful score.

11. Sprinting and hurdling (require, requires) great speed.

12. Neither children nor beginners (belong, belongs) in hurdling events.

13. A sprint relay or a distance relay (call, calls) for a team of four runners.

14. Runners on a relay team (pass, passes) a stick called a baton.

15. Devoted runners (take, takes) time and effort to learn this sport.

Exercise 3   Proofreading Skill   Rewrite the paragraph below, correcting errors in subject-verb agreement.

Books by Charles Dickens includes *David Copperfield* and *Oliver Twist.* Both books tells about young English boys. Either trouble or adventures happens to the boys at every turn. Villains and heroes appears throughout the books. Though these adventures were written over a century ago, these books still entertains readers today.

LANGUAGE HANDBOOK
For review and practice: Section 8, Subject-Verb Agreement.

Exercise 4   Revising Your Writing   Look over the newspaper article that you wrote for the Writer's Workshop on page 275. Watch for errors in subject-verb agreement. When you find an error, change the verb to the correct form.

READER'S WORKSHOP

FACT AND OPINION

What do news stories and encyclopedia articles have in common? Both contain facts. A **fact** is a statement that can be proved by checking a reference source, asking an expert, or making a personal observation. The following statement is a fact.

> Queen Victoria ruled England for sixty-three years.

An **opinion** is a statement that cannot be proved. It usually describes the writer's personal feelings about a subject. The sentence that follows is an opinion.

> Queen Victoria was England's finest queen.

An opinion cannot be proved. Opinions often contain words such as *good, best, bad, worst, I think,* and *as far as I'm concerned.* Even though an opinion cannot be proved, one opinion may be stronger than another. A sound opinion is supported with convincing evidence. The best kind of evidence is factual. An opinion that is supported only by other opinions is not really a strong argument. Suppose your friend Tyrone says, "I think owning a pet is a good idea because pets are wonderful." Tyrone's reason, "pets are wonderful," is just another opinion. It is not good support.

As you read, it is important to recognize the difference between facts and opinions. When you come across an opinion, you can evaluate it and decide whether or not it is valid.

Exercise 1   Read the following sentences. Identify each as either *Fact* or *Opinion.* Tell how you could prove each fact.

1. Charles Dickens was born on February 7, 1812.
2. Queen Victoria ruled England during most of Dickens's life.
3. Dickens had a terrible childhood.
4. *A Christmas Carol* is one of Dickens's most famous books.
5. Dickens is the finest writer who ever lived.

Exercise 2   Look over the news article that you wrote for the Writer's Workshop on page 275. Write *F* next to every sentence that is a fact. Write *O* next to every sentence that contains an opinion. Then count up how many facts and opinions are in your article. It should contain many more facts than opinions.

OPINIONATED WORDS

These words often signal opinions.

awful	lovely
bad	nice
beautiful	smart
better	terrible
excellent	ugly
fine	wonderful
good	worse
interesting	worst

HINT

When you include opinions in a factual article, make it clear that they *are* opinions. For example, introduce an opinion with a phrase like *my opinion is, I believe,* or *here is one opinion on the subject.*

WORKING IT OUT

What do you do when you have problems? Do you walk away or find someone to blame, or do you tackle problems head on and try to find solutions?

Problems come from all directions and in many forms. Social problems, like poverty or lack of education, and natural disasters, like fires or hurricanes, challenge the people they touch. Communication failures among family members, friends, or people from different cultures and social classes create tension and misunderstanding. Figuring out what to do is no easy task.

As you read the following selections, notice what the characters in the stories and the real historical characters do and what they learn as they work out the problems and challenges that enter their lives.

Fiction

The *Scribe*

KRISTIN HUNTER

*E*xamine What You Know

What problems or needs do you see in your community, and what can you do to help? In small groups identify three local problems and suggest possible ways that you and other young people can help solve those problems. Use a chart like the one below to record your ideas, and share them with the rest of the class.

Problems	Solutions
1. Litter on streets	1. Organize Saturday street cleanup patrols.

*E*xpand Your Knowledge

One problem that exists in many communities is illiteracy. An illiterate person is someone who has not learned to read and write. Because these skills are necessary for many jobs, illiterate people often have trouble finding work. In the United States, between 21 million and 25 million people are illiterate. In addition, nearly one-fifth of all working people have only minimal reading and writing skills and would benefit from additional skills.

*E*nrich Your Reading

Slang   Colorful words and expressions spoken during a particular time period or by a particular group of people are called **slang.** Slang terms can be new words or established words and phrases that have taken on new meanings. Slang terms usually go out-of-date quickly. Notice how the writer of this story puts slang expressions such as "digging the action" into the mouths of the characters in order to make them sound like real people facing real problems in a particular time and place.

■ *Author biography in Reader's Handbook*

The *Scribe*

KRISTIN HUNTER

We been living in the apartment over the Silver Dollar Check Cashing Service five years. But I never had any reason to go in there till two days ago when Mom had to go to the Wash-a-Mat and asked me to get some change.

And man! Are those people who come in there in some bad shape.

Old man Silver and old man Dollar, who own the place, have signs tacked up everywhere:

NO LOUNGING, NO LOITERING[1]

THIS IS NOT A WAITING ROOM

and

MINIMUM CHECK CASHING FEE, 50¢

and

LETTERS ADDRESSED, 50¢

and

LETTERS READ, 75¢

and

LETTERS WRITTEN, ONE DOLLAR

And everybody who comes in there to cash a check gets their picture taken like they're some kind of criminal.

After I got my change, I stood around for a while digging the action. First comes an old lady with some kind of long form to fill out. The mean old man behind the counter points to the One Dollar sign. She nods. So he starts to fill it out for her.

"Name?"

"Muskogee Marie Lawson."

"SPELL it!" he hollers.

"M, m, u, s—well, I don't exactly know, sir."

"I'll put down 'Marie,' then. Age?"

"Sixty-three my last birthday."

"Date of birth?"

"March twenty-third"—a pause—"I think, 1900."

"Look, Marie," he says, which makes me mad, hearing him first-name a dignified old gray-haired lady like that, "if you'd been born in 1900, you'd be seventy-two. Either I put that down, or I put 1910."

"Whatever you think best, sir," she says timidly.

He sighs, rolls his eyes to the ceiling, and bangs his fist on the form angrily. Then he fills out the rest.

"One dollar," he says when he's finished. She pays like she's grateful to him for taking the trouble.

Next is a man with a cane, a veteran who has to let the government know he moved. He wants old man Silver to do this for him, but he doesn't want him to know he can't do it himself.

"My eyes are kind of bad, sir. Will you fill this thing out for me? Tell them I moved from 121 South 15th Street to 203 North Decatur Street."

Old man Silver doesn't blink an eye. Just

---

1. **loitering** (loit′ ər iŋ): lingering without purpose.

fills out the form and charges the crippled man a dollar.

And it goes on like that. People who can't read or write or count their change. People who don't know how to pay their gas bills, don't know how to fill out forms, don't know how to address envelopes. And old man Silver and old man Dollar cleaning up on all of them. It's pitiful. It's disgusting. Makes me so mad I want to yell.

Mom, did you know there are hundreds of people in this city who can't read and write?

And I do, but mostly at Mom. "Mom, did you know there are hundreds of people in this city who can't read and write?"

Mom isn't upset. She's a wise woman. "Of course, James," she says. "A lot of the older people around here haven't had your advantages. They came from down South, and they had to quit school very young to go to work.

"In the old days, nobody cared whether our people got an education. They were only interested in getting the crops in." She sighed. "Sometimes I think they *still* don't care. If we hadn't gotten you into that good school, you might not be able to read so well either. A lot of boys and girls your age can't, you know."

"But that's awful!" I say. "How do they expect us to make it in a big city? You can't even cross the streets if you can't read the Walk and Don't Walk signs."

"It's hard," Mom says, "but the important

ON THE RED TABLE I 1983 Daniel Quintero
Private collection. Courtesy, Marlborough Gallery New York.

thing to remember is it's no disgrace. There was a time in history when nobody could read or write except a special class of people."

And Mom takes down her Bible. She has three Bible study certificates and is always giving me lessons from Bible history. I don't exactly go for all the stuff she believes in, but sometimes it is interesting.

"In ancient times," she says, "no one could read or write except a special class of people known as scribes. It was their job to write down the laws given by the rabbis and the judges.[2] No one else could do it.

"Jesus criticized the scribes," she goes on, "because they were so proud of themselves. But he needed them to write down his teachings."

"Man," I said when she finished, "that's something."

My mind was working double time. I'm the best reader and writer in our class. Also it was summertime. I had nothing much to do except go to the park or hang around the library and read till my eyeballs were ready to fall out, and I was tired of doing both.

So the next morning, after my parents went to work, I took Mom's card table and a folding chair down to the sidewalk. I lettered a sign with a Magic Marker, and I was in business. My sign said:

PUBLIC SCRIBE—ALL SERVICES FREE

I set my table up in front of the Silver Dollar and waited for business. Only one thing bothered me. If the people couldn't read, how would they know what I was there for?

But five minutes had hardly passed when an old lady stopped and asked me to read her grandson's letter. She explained that she had just broken her glasses. I knew she was fibbing, but I kept quiet.

I read the grandson's letter. It said he was having a fine time in California but was a little short. He would send her some money as soon as he made another payday. I handed the letter back to her.

"Thank you, son," she said, and gave me a quarter.

I handed that back to her too.

The word got around. By noontime I had a whole crowd of customers around my table. I was kept busy writing letters, addressing envelopes, filling out forms, and explaining official-looking letters that scared people half to death.

I didn't blame them. The language in some of those letters—"Establish whether your disability is one-fourth, one-third, one-half, or total, and substantiate[3] in paragraph 3 (b) below"—would upset anybody. I mean, why can't the government write English like everybody else?

Most of my customers were old, but there were a few young ones too. Like the girl who had gotten a letter about her baby from the Health Service and didn't know what "immunization" meant.

At noontime one old lady brought me some iced tea and a peach, and another gave me some fried chicken wings. I was really having a good time when the shade of all the people standing around me suddenly vanished. The sun hit me like a ton of hot bricks.

Only one long shadow fell across my table. The shadow of a tall, heavy, blue-eyed cop. In our neighborhood, when they see a

---

2. **the rabbis and the judges:** teachers and rulers of the ancient Hebrews.

3. **substantiate:** to give evidence to prove a claim.

cop, people scatter. That was why the back of my neck was burning.

"What are you trying to do here, sonny?" the cop asks.

"Help people out," I tell him calmly, though my knees are knocking together under the table.

"Well, you know," he says, "Mr. Silver and Mr. Dollar have been in business a long time on this corner. They are very respected men in this neighborhood. Are you trying to run them out of business?"

"I'm not charging anybody," I pointed out.

"That," the cop says, "is exactly what they don't like. Mr. Silver says he is glad to have some help with the letter writing. Mr. Dollar says it's only a nuisance to them anyway and takes up too much time. But if you don't charge for your services, it's unfair competition."

What did I know about licenses? I'm only thirteen, after all.

Well, why not? I thought. After all, I could use a little profit.

"All right," I tell him. "I'll charge a quarter."

"Then it is my duty to warn you," the cop says, "that it's against the law to conduct a business without a license. The first time you accept a fee, I'll close you up and run you off this corner."

He really had me there. What did I know about licenses? I'm only thirteen, after all. Suddenly I didn't feel like the big black businessman anymore. I felt like a little kid who wanted to holler for his mother. But she was at work, and so was Daddy.

"I'll leave," I said, and did, with all the cool I could muster. But inside I was burning up, and not from the sun.

One little old lady hollered "You big bully!" and shook her umbrella at the cop. But the rest of those people were so beaten down they didn't say anything. Just shuffled back on inside to give Mr. Silver and Mr. Dollar their hard-earned money like they always did.

I was so mad I didn't know what to do with myself that afternoon. I couldn't watch TV. It was all soap operas anyway, and they seemed dumber than ever. The library didn't appeal to me either. It's not air-conditioned, and the day was hot and muggy.

Finally I went to the park and threw stones at the swans in the lake. I was careful not to hit them, but they made good targets because they were so fat and white. Then after a while the sun got lower. I kind of cooled off and came to my senses. They were just big, dumb, beautiful birds and not my enemies. I threw them some crumbs from my sandwich and went home.

"Daddy," I asked that night, "how come you and Mom never cash checks downstairs in the Silver Dollar?"

"Because," he said, "we have an account at the bank, where they cash our checks free."

"Well, why doesn't everybody do that?" I wanted to know.

"Because some people want all their money right away," he said. "The bank insists that you leave them a minimum balance."

"How much?" I asked him.

"Only five dollars."

"But that five dollars still belongs to you after you leave it there?"

"Sure," he says. "And if it's in a savings account, it earns interest."

EARL'S HAIR ODYSSEY OR BUS STOP   1985   Marie E. Calloway   Courtesy of the artist.

"So why can't people see they lose money when they *pay* to have their checks cashed?"

"A lot of *our* people," Mom said, "are scared of banks, period. Some of them remember the Depression,[4] when all the banks closed and the people couldn't get their money out. And others think banks are only for white people. They think they'll be insulted, or maybe even arrested, if they go in there."

Wow. The more I learned, the more pitiful it was. "Are there any black people working at our bank?"

"There didn't used to be," Mom said, "but now they have Mr. Lovejoy and Mrs. Adams. You know Mrs. Adams; she's nice. She has a daughter your age."

"Hmmm," I said, and shut up before my folks started to wonder why I was asking all those questions.

The next morning, when the Silver Dollar opened, I was right there. I hung around near the door, pretending to read a copy of *Jet* magazine.

"Psst," I said to each person who came in. "I know where you can cash checks *free*."

It wasn't easy convincing them. A man blinked his red eyes at me like he didn't believe he had heard right. A carpenter with tools hanging all around his belt said he was on his lunch hour and didn't have time.

---

4. **Depression:** a period of decreased business activity and widespread unemployment from 1929 through the 1930s.

And a big fat lady with two shopping bags pushed past me and almost knocked me down, she was in such a hurry to give Mr. Silver and Mr. Dollar her money.

But finally I had a little group who were interested. It wasn't much. Just three people. Two men—one young, one old—and the little old lady who'd asked me to read her the letter from California. Seemed the grandson had made his payday and sent her a money order.

"How far is this place?" asked the young man.

"Not far. Just six blocks," I told him.

"Aw shoot. I ain't walking all that way just to save fifty cents."

So then I only had two. I was careful not to tell them where we were going. When we finally got to the Establishment Trust National Bank, I said, "This is the place."

"I ain't goin' in there," said the old man. "No, sir. Not me. You ain't gettin' me in *there*." And he walked away quickly, going back in the direction we had come.

To tell the truth, the bank did look kind of scary. It was a big building with tall white marble pillars. A lot of Brink's armored trucks and Cadillacs were parked out front. Uniformed guards walked back and forth inside with guns. It might as well have a "Colored Keep Out" sign.

Whereas the Silver Dollar is small and dark and funky and dirty. It has trash on the floors and tape across the broken windows. People going in there feel right at home.

I looked at the little old lady. She smiled back bravely. "Well, we've come this far, son," she said. "Let's not turn back now."

So I took her inside. Fortunately Mrs. Adams's window was near the front.

"Hi, James," she said.

"I've brought you a customer," I told her.

Mrs. Adams took the old lady to a desk to fill out some forms. They were gone a long time, but finally they came back.

"Now, when you have more business with the bank, Mrs. Franklin, just bring it to me," Mrs. Adams said.

"I'll do that," the old lady said. She held out her shiny new bankbook. "Son, do me a favor and read that to me."

"Mrs. Minnie Franklin," I read aloud. "July 9, 1972. Thirty-seven dollars."

"That sounds real nice," Mrs. Franklin said. "I guess now I have a bankbook, I'll have to get me some glasses."

Mrs. Adams winked at me over the old lady's head, and I winked back.

"Do you want me to walk you home?" I asked Mrs. Franklin.

"No, thank you, son," she said. "I can cross streets by myself all right. I know red from green."

And then she winked at both of us, letting us know she knew what was happening.

"Son," she went on, "don't ever be afraid to try a thing just because you've never done it before. I took a bus up here from Alabama by myself forty-four years ago. I ain't thought once about going back. But I've stayed too long in one neighborhood since I've been in this city. Now I think I'll go out and take a look at *this* part of town."

Then she was gone. But she had really started me thinking. If an old lady like that wasn't afraid to go in a bank and open an account for the first time in her life, why should *I* be afraid to go up to City Hall and apply for a license?

Wonder how much they charge you to be a scribe? ❧

EXPLAIN

Responding to Reading

First Impressions

1. How did you feel about James? Describe your feelings in your journal or on a sheet of paper.

Second Thoughts

2. In your opinion, what effect do James's efforts to help others have on his community?

   Think about
   - the people he helps with reading and writing
   - the people he tries to take to the bank
   - the owners of the currency exchange

3. Why do you think James wants to help people work out their problems?

4. What do you think James will do after the story ends? Make a prediction based on what you know about James's **character** and the clues at the end of the story.

Broader Connections

5. Look at the problem/solution chart you made in Examine What You Know on page 285. How do you think James might handle these situations?

Writing Options

1. In an **essay,** compare and contrast the problems of illiteracy in "The Scribe" and in "The Secret of the Wall," on page 167. How do the characters try to solve the problem of illiteracy in each story?

2. What might a typical day be like for someone in the United States who cannot read or write. In your journal, write a **narrative** that describes the difficulties and challenges that an illiterate person might face in one day.

3. Create a **slang dictionary** based on words in this story or on slang words that you know. For additional entries ask your parents for slang words they used when they were young.

Fiction

The All-American Slurp

LENSEY NAMIOKA (nä mē ō' kä)

Examine What You Know

Have you ever eaten at a restaurant or at a friend's house and not been sure of the correct table manners to use? Perhaps you were eating foreign food, or the dinner was very fancy. In your journal or on a sheet of paper, write about an embarrassing or uncomfortable moment you have had because you were not sure of proper table manners.

Expand Your Knowledge

Table manners are one aspect of etiquette, which consists of special rules of behavior or courtesy. What is polite or proper in one culture can sometimes be rude or improper in another. For example, in Vietnam it is not polite to look directly at someone who is speaking to you. It is more polite to look away from the person. In the United States, however, it's just the opposite; people think it is more polite to look at someone who is talking to you.

Enrich Your Reading

Contrasting Cultures   In the story you are about to read, the narrator compares the table manners and other aspects of Chinese culture with aspects of U.S. culture. As you read, notice the differences the narrator points out between the two families and their cultures. After you have read the story, fill in a chart like the one started below.

Cultural Differences	
Chinese Culture (The Lins)	U.S. Culture (The Gleasons)
Vegetables are always cooked.	Vegetables are eaten raw on relish trays.

■ *Author biography on Extend page*

The All-American Slurp

LENSEY NAMIOKA

The first time our family was invited out to dinner in America, we disgraced ourselves while eating celery. We had immigrated to this country from China, and during our early days here we had a hard time with American table manners.

In China we never ate celery raw, or any other kind of vegetable raw. We always had to disinfect the vegetables in boiling water first. When we were presented with our first relish tray, the raw celery caught us unprepared.

We had been invited to dinner by our neighbors, the Gleasons. After arriving at the house, we shook hands with our hosts and packed ourselves into a sofa. As our family of four sat stiffly in a row, my younger brother and I stole glances at our parents for a clue as to what to do next.

Mrs. Gleason offered the relish tray to Mother. The tray looked pretty, with its tiny red radishes, curly sticks of carrots, and long, slender stalks of pale green celery. "Do try some of the celery, Mrs. Lin," she said. "It's from a local farmer, and it's sweet."

Mother picked up one of the green stalks, and Father followed suit. Then I picked up a stalk, and my brother did too. So there we sat, each with a stalk of celery in our right hand.

Mrs. Gleason kept smiling. "Would you like to try some of the dip, Mrs. Lin? It's my own recipe: sour cream and onion flakes, with a dash of Tabasco sauce."

Most Chinese don't care for dairy products, and in those days I wasn't even ready to drink fresh milk. Sour cream sounded perfectly revolting. Our family shook our heads in unison.

Mrs. Gleason went off with the relish tray to the other guests, and we carefully watched to see what they did. Everyone seemed to eat the raw vegetables quite happily.

Mother took a bite of her celery. *Crunch.* "It's not bad!" she whispered.

Father took a bite of his celery. *Crunch.* "Yes, it *is* good," he said, looking surprised.

I took a bite, and then my brother. *Crunch, crunch.* It was more than good; it was delicious. Raw celery has a slight sparkle, a zingy taste that you don't get in cooked celery. When Mrs. Gleason came around with the relish tray, we each took another stalk of celery, except my brother. He took two.

There was only one problem: long strings ran through the length of the stalk, and they got caught in my teeth. When I help my mother in the kitchen, I always pull the strings out before slicing celery.

I pulled the strings out of my stalk.

Words to Know and Use

immigrate (im′ ə grāt′) *v.* to move to a new country

Illustration by
David Cunningham.

Z-z-zip, z-z-zip. My brother followed suit. *Z-z-zip, z-z-zip, z-z-zip*. To my left, my parents were taking care of their own stalks. *Z-z-zip, z-z-zip, z-z-zip*.

Suddenly I realized that there was dead silence except for the zipping. Looking up, I saw that the eyes of everyone in the room were on our family. Mr. and Mrs. Gleason, their daughter Meg, who was my friend, and their neighbors the Badels—they were staring at us as we busily pulled the strings of our celery.

That wasn't the end of it. Mrs. Gleason announced that dinner was served and invited us to the dining table. It was lavishly covered with platters of food, but we couldn't see any chairs around the table. So we helpfully carried over some dining chairs and sat down. All the other guests just stood there.

Mrs. Gleason bent down and whispered to us, "This is a buffet dinner. You help yourselves to some food and eat it in the living room."

Our family beat a retreat back to the sofa as if chased by enemy soldiers. For the rest of the evening, too mortified[1] to go back to the dining table, I nursed a bit of potato salad on my plate.

Next day Meg and I got on the school bus together. I wasn't sure how she would feel about me after the spectacle our family made at the party. But she was just the same as usual, and the only reference she made to the party was, "Hope you and your folks got enough to eat last night. You certainly didn't take very much. Mom never tries to figure out how much food to prepare. She just puts everything on the table and hopes for the best."

Do these incidents remind you of any of your own experiences?

connect

---

1. **mortified:** ashamed.

Words to Know and Use | **lavishly** (lav′ ish lē) *adv.* in an abundant way

295

I began to relax. The Gleasons' dinner party wasn't so different from a Chinese meal after all. My mother also puts everything on the table and hopes for the best.

Meg was the first friend I had made after we came to America. I eventually got acquainted with a few other kids in school, but Meg was still the only real friend I had.

My brother didn't have any problems making friends. He spent all his time with some boys who were teaching him baseball, and in no time he could speak English much faster than I could—not better, but faster.

I worried more about making mistakes, and I spoke carefully, making sure I could say everything right before opening my mouth. At least I had a better accent than my parents, who never really got rid of their Chinese accent, even years later. My parents had both studied English in school before coming to America, but what they had studied was mostly written English, not spoken.

Father's approach to English was a scientific one. Since Chinese verbs have no tense, he was fascinated by the way English verbs changed form according to whether they were in the present, past imperfect, perfect, pluperfect, future, or future perfect tense. He was always making diagrams of verbs and their inflections, and he looked for opportunities to show off his mastery of the pluperfect and future perfect tenses, his two favorites. "I shall have finished my project by Monday," he would say smugly.

Mother's approach was to memorize lists of polite phrases that would cover all possible social situations. She was constantly muttering things like "I'm fine, thank you. And you?" Once she accidentally stepped on someone's foot and hurriedly blurted, "Oh, that's quite all right!" Embarrassed by her slip, she resolved to do better next time. So when someone stepped on *her* foot, she cried, "You're welcome!"

In our own different ways, we made progress in learning English. But I had another worry, and that was my appearance. My brother didn't have to worry, since Mother bought him blue jeans for school and he dressed like all the other boys. But she insisted that girls had to wear skirts. By the time she saw that Meg and the other girls were wearing jeans, it was too late. My school clothes were bought already, and we didn't have money left to buy new outfits for me. We had too many other things to buy first, like furniture, pots, and pans.

The first time I visited Meg's house, she took me upstairs to her room, and I wound up trying on her clothes. We were pretty much the same size, since Meg was shorter and thinner than average. Maybe that's how we became friends in the first place. Wearing Meg's jeans and T-shirt, I looked at myself in the mirror. I could almost pass for an American—from the back, anyway. At least the kids in school wouldn't stop and stare at me in the hallways, which was what they did when they saw me in my white blouse and navy blue skirt that went a couple of inches below the knees.

When Meg came to my house, I invited her to try on my Chinese dresses, the ones with a high collar and slits up the sides. Meg's eyes were bright as she looked at her-

Words to Know and Use | **resolve** (ri zälv′) *v.* to make a firm decision

self in the mirror. She struck several sultry poses, and we nearly fell over laughing.

The dinner party at the Gleasons' didn't stop my growing friendship with Meg. Things were getting better for me in other ways too. Mother finally bought me some jeans at the end of the month, when Father got his paycheck. She wasn't in any hurry about buying them at first, until I worked on her. This is what I did. Since we didn't have a car in those days, I often ran down to the neighborhood store to pick up things for her. The groceries cost less at a big supermarket, but the closest one was many blocks away. One day, when she ran out of flour, I offered to borrow a bike from our neighbor's son and buy a ten-pound bag of flour at the big supermarket. I mounted the boy's bike and waved to Mother. "I'll be back in five minutes!"

Before I started pedaling, I heard her voice behind me. "You can't go out in public like that! People can see all the way up to your thighs!"

"I'm sorry," I said innocently. "I thought you were in a hurry to get the flour." For dinner we were going to have pot-stickers (fried Chinese dumplings), and we needed a lot of flour.

"Couldn't you borrow a girl's bicycle?" complained Mother. "That way your skirt won't be pushed up."

"There aren't too many of those around," I said. "Almost all the girls wear jeans while riding a bike, so they don't see any point buying a girl's bike."

We didn't eat pot-stickers that evening, and Mother was thoughtful. Next day we took the bus downtown, and she bought me a pair of jeans. In the same week, my brother made the baseball team of his junior high school, Father started taking driving lessons, and Mother discovered rummage sales. We soon got all the furniture we needed, plus a dart board and a 1,000-piece jigsaw puzzle (fourteen hours later, we discovered that it was a 999-piece jigsaw puzzle). There was hope that the Lins might become a normal American family after all.

Then came our dinner at the Lakeview restaurant.

The Lakeview was an expensive restaurant, one of those places where a headwaiter dressed in tails[2] conducted you to your seat and the only light came from candles and flaming desserts. In one corner of the room, a lady harpist played tinkling melodies.

Father wanted to celebrate because he had just been promoted. He worked for an electronics company, and after his English started improving, his superiors decided to appoint him to a position more suited to his training. The promotion not only brought a higher salary but was also a tremendous boost to his pride.

Up to then we had eaten only in Chinese restaurants. Although my brother and I were becoming fond of hamburgers, my parents didn't care much for Western food, other than chow mein.

But this was a special occasion, and Father asked his co-workers to recommend

---

2. tails: a formal evening suit for men.

Words to Know and Use | **co-worker** (kō′ wɨrk′ ər) *n.* a fellow worker

297

a really elegant restaurant. So there we were at the Lakeview, stumbling after the head-waiter in the murky dining room.

At our table we were handed our menus, and they were so big that to read mine I almost had to stand up again. But why bother? It was mostly in French, anyway.

Father, being an engineer, was always systematic. He took out a pocket French dictionary. "They told me that most of the items would be in French, so I came prepared." He even had a pocket flashlight, the size of a marking pen. While Mother held the flashlight over the menu, he looked up the items that were in French.

"*Pâté en croûte*,"[3] he muttered. "Let's see . . . *pâté* is paste . . . *croûte* is crust . . . hmm . . . a paste in crust."

The waiter stood looking patient. I squirmed and died at least fifty times.

At long last Father gave up. "Why don't we just order four complete dinners at random?" he suggested.

"Isn't that risky?" asked Mother. "The French eat some rather peculiar things, I've heard."

"A Chinese can eat anything a Frenchman can eat," Father declared.

The soup arrived in a plate. How do you get soup up from a plate? I glanced at the other diners, but the ones at the nearby tables were not on their soup course, while the more distant ones were invisible in the darkness.

Fortunately my parents had studied books on Western etiquette before they came to America. "Tilt your plate," whispered my mother. "It's easier to spoon the soup up that way."

She was right. Tilting the plate did the trick. But the etiquette book didn't say anything about what you did after the soup reached your lips. As any respectable Chinese knows, the correct way to eat your soup is to slurp. This helps to cool the liquid and prevent you from burning your lips. It also shows your appreciation.

We showed our appreciation. *Shloop,* went my father. *Shloop,* went my mother. *Shloop, shloop,* went my brother, who was the hungriest.

The lady harpist stopped playing to take a rest. And in the silence, our family's consumption of soup suddenly seemed unnaturally loud. You know how it sounds on a rocky beach when the tide goes out and the water drains from all those little pools? They go *shloop, shloop, shloop*. That was the Lin family, eating soup.

At the next table a waiter was pouring wine. When a large *shloop* reached him, he froze. The bottle continued to pour, and red wine flooded the table top and into the lap of a customer. Even the customer didn't notice anything at first, being also hypnotized by the *shloop, shloop, shloop*.

It was too much. "I need to go to the toilet," I mumbled, jumping to my feet. A waiter, sensing my urgency, quickly directed me to the ladies' room.

I splashed cold water on my burning face, and as I dried myself with a paper towel, I stared into the mirror. In this perfumed

---

3. *pâté en croûte* (pä tä′ än krōōt′) *French:* seasoned chopped meat in a pastry crust.

Words to Know and Use	**elegant** (el′ ə gənt) *adj.* tasteful and dignified **systematic** (sis′ tə mat′ ik) *adj.* precise and orderly **etiquette** (et′ i kit) *n.* the rules of proper social behavior

ladies' room, with its pink-and-silver wallpaper and marbled sinks, I looked completely out of place. What was I doing here? What was our family doing in the Lakeview restaurant? In America?

The door to the ladies' room opened. A woman came in and glanced curiously at me. I retreated into one of the toilet cubicles and latched the door.

Time passed—maybe half an hour, maybe an hour. Then I heard the door open again, and my mother's voice. "Are you in there? You're not sick, are you?"

There was real concern in her voice. A girl can't leave her family just because they slurp their soup. Besides, the toilet cubicle had a few drawbacks as a permanent residence. "I'm all right," I said, undoing the latch.

Mother didn't tell me how the rest of the dinner went, and I didn't want to know. In the weeks following, I managed to push the whole thing into the back of my mind, where it jumped out at me only a few times a day. Even now, I turn hot all over when I think of the Lakeview restaurant.

But by the time we had been in this country for three months, our family was definitely making progress toward becoming Americanized. I remember my parents' first PTA meeting. Father wore a neat suit and tie, and Mother put on her first pair of high heels. She stumbled only once. They met my homeroom teacher and beamed as she told them that I would make honor roll soon at the rate I was going. Of course Chinese etiquette forced Father to say that I was a very stupid girl and Mother to protest that the teacher was showing favoritism toward me. But I could tell they were both very proud.

A MEAL IN A FISHERMAN HOUSEHOLD   Chen Xiaodong
Courtesy, Foreign Languages Press   Beijing, China.

The day came when my parents announced that they wanted to give a dinner party. We had invited Chinese friends to eat with us before, but this dinner was going to be different. In addition to a Chinese-American family, we were going to invite the Gleasons.

"Gee, I can hardly wait to have dinner at your house," Meg said to me. "I just *love* Chinese food."

That was a relief. Mother was a good cook, but I wasn't sure if people who ate sour cream would also eat chicken gizzards stewed in soy sauce.

Mother decided not to take a chance with chicken gizzards. Since we had Western guests, she set the table with large dinner plates, which we never used in Chinese meals. In fact we didn't use individual plates at all but picked up food from the platters in the middle of the table and brought it directly to our rice bowls. Following the practice of Chinese-American restaurants, Mother also placed large serving spoons on the platters.

The dinner started well. Mrs. Gleason exclaimed at the beautifully arranged dishes of food: the colorful candied fruit in the sweet-and-sour pork dish, the noodle-thin shreds of chicken meat stir-fried with tiny peas, and the glistening pink prawns in a ginger sauce.

What will happen at the dinner party?

At first I was too busy enjoying my food to notice how the guests were doing. But soon I remembered my duties. Sometimes guests were too polite to help themselves, and you had to serve them more food.

I glanced at Meg to see if she needed more food, and my eyes nearly popped out at the sight of her plate. It was piled with food: the sweet-and-sour meat pushed right against the chicken shreds, and the chicken sauce ran into the prawns. She had been taking food from a second dish before she finished eating her helping from the first!

Horrified, I turned to look at Mrs. Gleason. She was dumping rice out of her bowl and putting it on her dinner plate. Then she ladled prawns and gravy on top of the rice and mixed everything together, the way you mix sand, gravel, and cement to make concrete.

I couldn't bear to look any longer, and I turned to Mr. Gleason. He was chasing a pea around his plate. Several times he got it to the edge, but when he tried to pick it up with his chopsticks, it rolled back toward the cen-ter of the plate again. Finally he put down his chopsticks and picked up the pea with his fingers. He really did! A grown man!

All of us, our family and the Chinese guests, stopped eating to watch the activities of the Gleasons. I wanted to giggle. Then I caught my mother's eyes on me. She frowned and shook her head slightly, and I understood the message: the Gleasons were not used to Chinese ways, and they were just coping the best they could. For some reason I thought of celery strings.

When the main courses were finished, Mother brought out a platter of fruit. "I hope you weren't expecting a sweet dessert," she said. "Since the Chinese don't eat dessert, I didn't think to prepare any."

"Oh, I couldn't possibly eat dessert!" cried Mrs. Gleason. "I'm simply stuffed!"

Meg had different ideas. When the table was cleared, she announced that she and I were going for a walk. "I don't know about you, but I feel like dessert," she told me when we were outside. "Come on, there's a Dairy Queen down the street. I could use a big chocolate milkshake!"

Although I didn't really want anything more to eat, I insisted on paying for the milkshakes. After all, I was still hostess.

Meg got her large chocolate milkshake, and I had a small one. Even so, she was finishing hers while I was only half done. Toward the end she pulled hard on her straws and went *shloop, shloop.*

"Do you always slurp when you eat a milk-shake?" I asked before I could stop myself.

Meg grinned. "Sure. All Americans slurp." ❧

Words to Know and Use | **cope** (kōp) *v.* to deal with difficulties

I N S I G H T

Forks in Tokyo, Chopsticks in Chicago

JAMES CROSS GIBLIN

In recent years, there's been a trend toward the transfer of eating utensils from one culture to another. Just as many Japanese now eat some foods with forks, so more and more Americans are attempting to use chopsticks

when they go out to a Chinese, Japanese, Vietnamese, or Korean restaurant or when they cook Oriental foods at home. They say that sweet-and-sour pork and sushi taste much better when eaten with chopsticks.

On the other hand, the Chinese, who invented chopsticks, are questioning whether they're always the best utensil for eating. Through the centuries Chinese families have traditionally dipped their personal chopsticks straight into a single serving pot. Now some Chinese doctors are saying that this practice helps to spread infectious diseases such as hepatitis.

The former chairman of the Chinese Communist Party, Hu Yaobang, joined in the discussion. "We should prepare more knives and forks, buy more plates, and sit around the table to eat Chinese food in the Western manner, that is, each from his own plate," Chairman Hu said in a 1984 speech. "By doing so, we can avoid many contagious diseases."

It's doubtful, however, whether the Chinese people will soon give up a style of eating that has endured for at least twenty-five hundred years. It's equally doubtful that a majority of Westerners will ever put aside their knives and forks in favor of chopsticks.

What's more likely is that people everywhere will continue to experiment with one another's table utensils. And who knows? Perhaps in time they will find a common solution to that age-old problem: how to get food as swiftly, gracefully, and neatly as possible from hand to mouth.

Responding to Reading

First Impressions

1. Which part of the story did you like best? Describe your favorite part in your journal or on a sheet of paper.

Second Thoughts

2. In your opinion, what kind of person is the narrator?

   Think about
   - how she feels about making mistakes and acting polite
   - how she tries to change
   - how she convinces her mother to buy jeans for her

3. Do you think the narrator's tensions about "working it out" and avoiding embarrassment have relaxed by the end of the story? Why or why not?

4. Do you think the Gleasons are as concerned about making etiquette errors as the Lins are? Use details from the story to support your answer.

Broader Connections

5. Complete the contrast chart described in Enrich Your Reading on page 293. What are some positive results of cultural differences?

6. The narrator and her family work hard to become "Americanized." In what ways do you think people should change when they move to a different country? Which things about themselves should they not try to change?

Literary Concept: Onomatopoeia

The use of words to imitate sounds is called **onomatopoeia** (än' ō mat' ō pē' ə). *Bang, pop, hiss,* and *sizzle* are examples of onomatopoeia. Sometimes authors even make up words to describe certain sounds. What words does the author of this story use to imitate sounds? What does the use of these words add to the story?

Concept Review: Humor An author's description of a scene can help a reader appreciate the scene's humor. What details make certain scenes in this story humorous?

Writing Options

1. This story is told from the point of view of the Chinese-American narrator. How might the story be different if it were told by another character in the story? In a **diary entry** write about a situation in the story as if you were one of the other characters.

2. Look at the journal entry you made on page 293 about table manners. Write a reassuring **letter** to the narrator comparing your experience with hers.

3. Write a **poem** about etiquette, manners, or a situation from "The All-American Slurp." Use onomatopoeia in your poem.

4. Read the Insight selection "Forks in Tokyo, Chopsticks in Chicago" on page 301. Write a **how-to speech** on the use of Western table utensils or Chinese chopsticks, directed at someone who has never used that type of utensil. Make your instructions logical and easy to follow.

Vocabulary Practice

Exercise A   An analogy contains two pairs of related words. The words in the second pair are related in the same way as those in the first pair, as in this example:

LIGHT : DARK :: up : down

Light and *dark* are opposites; *up* and *down* are also opposites. In each item below, determine how the words in the first pair are related. Then decide which word in the list best completes the second pair to express a similar relationship.

1. CLASSMATE : TEACHER :: __?__ : boss
2. QUICKLY : SLOWLY :: __?__ : simply
3. PATIENT : IMPATIENT :: __?__ : disorganized
4. CONCEAL : HIDE :: __?__ : decide
5. RULES : BASEBALL :: __?__ : eating

Exercise B   On your paper, write the word from the list that is most closely related to each situation below.

1. The Lins moved to the United States from China.
2. They had to deal with different customs.
3. Learning American table manners was one aspect of their cultural education.
4. Mr. Lin learned English from his fellow employees.
5. The table was covered with a beautiful and tasteful cloth.

> *Words to Know and Use*
>
> **cope**
> **co-worker**
> **elegant**
> **etiquette**
> **immigrate**
> **lavishly**
> **resolve**
> **systematic**

Options for Learning

1 • International Food Festival
With a group of your classmates, prepare an oral report on the foods and the table etiquette of countries or regions that are mentioned in the selections you have read in this book. Each member of the group should focus on one country or region. If possible, include demonstrations of etiquette and food preparation and samples of various dishes from each country.

2 • A Look Inside Imagine what various people at the dinner parties described in "The All-American Slurp" might have been thinking before, during, and after dinner. Create and perform a monologue for one of these characters, based on facts in the story and on how you think this person might have felt.

3 • Plan a Party Plan a party for the narrator of "The All-American Slurp" or her friend Meg. Create an invitation that would be appropriate, decide on the menus, and plan entertainment. Invite characters from stories you have read in this book or on your own. In an oral report explain your plans for the party.

4 • Art Imitates Life Draw a picture of Meg and the narrator wearing each other's clothes, the scene at one of the dinner parties, or the Lin family at the Lakeview restaurant.

FACT FINDER GEOGRAPHY
What four styles of cooking are named after regions of China?

Lensey Namioka
1929–

"The All-American Slurp" is based on an incident from Lensey Namioka's past. Like the narrator in the story, Namioka was born in China and made many adjustments when she and her family moved to the United States.

Namioka (whose maiden name was Chao) attended Radcliffe College in Massachusetts and the University of California at Berkeley. She has worked as a college math instructor and as a translator. However, when writing stories, Namioka says she doesn't turn to her math background. Instead, she draws on her Chinese heritage and on her husband's Japanese heritage.

Namioka is best known for her adventure tales of Japan. *Island of Ogres* is the latest in a series of books begun while visiting her husband's hometown of Himeji, Japan.

Other books Namioka has written include a mystery novel set in China, called *Phantom of Tiger Mountain,* and a humorous novel called *Who's Hu?* Namioka currently lives with her husband in Seattle, Washington, and is working on an autobiography about life with the Chao family.

Fiction

Fire!

JOHN D. MACDONALD

Examine What You Know

Recall a time when without thinking you did something that caused trouble. What were the consequences of your carelessness? In your journal or on a sheet of paper, describe what you did and what happened as a result.

Expand Your Knowledge

Among the most dramatic results of human carelessness are forest fires. Each year more than 100,000 forest fires rage in the United States, destroying almost 3 million acres of trees. People, either accidentally or on purpose, cause about 90 percent of these fires. To battle a forest fire, firefighters spray water or chemicals on the burning area to cool the fire and slow it down. They may also make a firebreak, a cleared strip of land, in front of the flames to keep them from spreading.

Enrich Your Reading

Cause and Effect   Events in a story are often connected as causes and effects. For example, one event (careless use of matches) may be the cause of another event (grass fire). As you read this story, look for the ways events and ideas are connected. After you read, create a cause-and-effect chart like the one started below. Keep in mind that one cause can sometimes lead to many effects and that an effect may become the cause of another effect. The chart will give you a visual picture of how cause-effect organization works in writing.

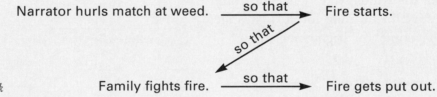

Narrator hurls match at weed. —— so that ——▶ Fire starts.

so that

Family fights fire. —— so that ——▶ Fire gets put out.

■ *Author biography in Reader's Handbook*

Fire!

JOHN D. MACDONALD

Not long ago, coming back home on a night flight, I saw the sullen ember[1] of a distant forest fire in the hills and felt a small twist of anguish. I knew it was the memory of the injustice of my grandfather toward my big brother Paul in a long-ago October.

There were seven of us children in all. Now, when we all get together with wives and husbands and children, we end up telling Grandfather stories, marveling at that strange, wild old man who raised us, with our mother acting more as referee than parent. Sometimes we judge him quite mad. At other times we think he was full of wisdom. Perhaps it was both. He never explained. Paul and I can laugh about the fire now.

It was a strange October that year. Hot and still and dry, day after day, the sun rising and setting in a weird mist. The creek ran nearly dry. We all lugged water to the growing things and worried about the well. I remember that the three littlest ones, Tom, Nan, and Bunny, volunteered to give up washing—as an effort to save water. It was denied. The woodlands which began a half dozen miles north of the farm had dozens of fires. When the winds were right, you could smell the stink of burning forest, a strange, dirty stench, somehow frightening.

BONFIRE WITH BEGGAR BUSH 1989 Mary Pratt
Courtesy, Mira Godard Gallery Toronto.

Paul was fifteen that year, and I was twelve. I did the thoughtless, stupid thing on

---

1. **sullen ember:** dismal glow.

Words to Know and Use | **anguish** (aŋ' gwish) *n.* suffering; pain
stench (stench) *n.* a strong, offensive odor

the way back from the creek. I'd gone down there with Paul on a hot Sunday afternoon to see if any fish were trapped in the pools. We were walking back. I had some kitchen matches in my pocket. When out in the wide world I liked to carry one in the corner of my mouth. I felt it gave me a certain devil-may-care[2] air.

In those years all small boys knew that if you hold a match in a certain way and throw it downward at a stone or a sidewalk, it will pop and burn. I was not skilled, but I had tried so many times it required no thought. As we passed a gray rock half buried in the dry weeds along the fence line, I hurled my match at it. It struck properly for once. The head popped and bounced into the weeds, and in an instant the sun-paled flames were high and spreading. For once Paul did not take time out to tell me how stupid I was. He yanked his shirt off and began stomping and flailing and yelled at me to run for help and water.

I was a hundred yards from the dooryard, and I think I made as good time and as much noise as a fire engine. In a very short and confusing time, all seven kids and my mother and my grandfather were out there with wet sacks and blankets. It was a very near thing. I think that if there had been eight of us instead of nine, it might have gotten away. As it was, it burned off a very large area.

Tom was nine and as responsible as any of us, and Grandfather left him out there with a bucket of water and orders to patrol the edges, looking for any spark which could have survived the battle.

When we got back to the porch, Grandfather sat down to catch his wind. He had been wonderful out in the pasture, like a great windmill hammering at the flames, yelling at them as he beat them out.

"Who was there?" he demanded.

That was one area where he had always been predictable. When any punishable <u>offense</u> occurred, Grandfather solved the problem of blame by walloping everyone who had been in the immediate area. Thus we were forever united, policing each other, with no tattletales.

"All right," he said. "Which one of you did it?"

Paul and I admitted our presence at the scene, knowing that we would sit down very carefully for the next day or so. The other kids drifted away, and we were left there facing the old man. I remember the black streaks of burned grasses on his big hands.

"All right," he said. "Which one of you did it?"

The simple question surprised us. Without warning, he had changed the rules. Paul straightened himself slightly and said, "I did it!" He was fifteen. He used a tone of voice we younger ones did not yet dare to use. Grandfather sighed, and he looked at me, blue eyes under those angry white brows. I believe I tried to speak. But the thing I had done was so shamefully stupid I wasted too

---

2. **devil-may-care:** reckless; carefree.

Words to Know and Use | **offense** (ə fens′) *n.* a violation of a rule

JONATHAN   George Labadie   Collection of Mr. and Mrs. Jonathan Blatt   Los Angeles.

much time trying to think of a way to confess which would make it believable.

Before I could find the beginning words, Grandfather got up and went into the house, Mother trotting along behind him, asking nervous questions.

I tried to explain myself to Paul, but he turned away. There was a great silence that night at the supper table. I was an outcast. I wanted the normal punishment. The change of ground rules made me feel lost and sick.

Grandfather got up from the table and looked at Paul and said, "I made some arrangements. You are excused from school. You'll get a better look at a fire, boy."

Early Monday morning one of the county trucks stopped and picked up Grandfather and Paul. There was a crew of rough, weary men aboard the truck and a crude bunch of tools in a steel drum—axes, shovels, mat-tocks.[3] I remember Mother pleading with Grandfather, saying, "But he's just a boy!"

I did not hear his answer. I know now they needed every strong pair of arms they could round up. It was a fearful time in the powder-dry forests.

I went off to school with the others. I did not hear much that day in school. I had the horrible vision of Paul encircled by a roar of flames, running and screaming. It was a horrible injustice. It was all my fault. I plotted to sneak off that night and join them in the hills. Somehow I would rescue Paul, and everyone would forgive me.

When the five of us got home from school, we learned that the well had gone dry. And that too seemed to be my fault. We

---

3. **mattocks:** digging tools having a flat blade set at a right angle to the handle.

had used a lot of water fighting that stupid grass fire. Mother got me aside and said, "What do you think we should do?"

The question astonished me. It made me realize that with Grandfather and Paul gone, I was the eldest male on the farm. I forgot the feeling of being an outcast. The creek water was sweet. The creek was nearly three hundred yards from the well. Mother had turned off the pump when it had sucked dry.

I organized the four eldest of us, Christine, Sheila, Tom, and me, into a water brigade.[4] We scoured out big containers and loaded them on the pickup, and I drove it as close to the creek as I could get it. Then we filled them, bucket by bucket, drove back, and dumped the water into the well. It was very hard work. After several loads, I primed[5] the old pump and started it again. After Tom and Sheila were too exhausted to continue, Christine and I managed two more trips by ourselves.

As I lay in my bed that moonlit night, a smell of burning forest came in the window. I was in a soft bed, while Paul and Grandfather were in the hills. There was more penance to do. I could not manage the truck system by myself, but I could carry water. I dressed and went quietly out into the night. I could not guess how many trips I made that night. Toward the end I could not manage full buckets.

I remember sitting on the edge of the well, the dawn rose-gray at the horizon line, opening and closing my aching hands, summoning up the will to make yet another trip

to the creek. I remember seeing my mother come across the side yard in her robe. She led me back to the house. I can remember fighting tears and losing just as we reached the steps.

The heavy rains began at dawn on Thursday, and before we left for school, Paul and our grandfather were home, dirty, exhausted, walking in a strange dazed, dragging way, as though they were walking uphill. When we came home from school, they were still sleeping. Grandfather got up for supper, but Paul did not, and Mother had me take him up hot soup and milk and apple pie. He told me of digging endless trenches, chopping through thousands of tough forest roots. He showed me his hands. We were friends again, somehow, but in a different way.

When I went back downstairs to my place at the table, I found Mother telling Grandfather how well I had managed the water problem. When there was a pause, I blurted, "I set that fire Sunday."

"Don't interrupt your mother," he said.

I sat with my head bowed. I could not eat. When she had finished, Grandfather said, "Mary, if I didn't think the boy could manage, I wouldn't have taken Paul with me."

He gave me a rough pat on the shoulder as he left the table. I wore it like medals. And suddenly I was hungry. Grandfather never explained, and we never knew what he would do next. He was as wild and random as the winds that blew. ❧

---

4. **brigade:** a group of persons organized for some work.
5. **primed:** poured water into a pump to start it.

Responding to Reading

First Impressions

1. In your journal, list the feelings you had as you read this story.

Second Thoughts

2. What do the narrator's attitude and actions tell about his **character?**

3. Do you think Grandfather believes Paul is guilty? Why or why not?

4. What do you think of Grandfather's method of teaching the boys a lesson? Is his way of "working it out" a good one? Why or why not?

5. What do you think the narrator learns from the effects of his actions? Use your completed cause–and–effect chart, page 305, to help you answer.

Literary Concept: Sensory Details

Sensory details help the reader see, hear, taste, smell, and feel what is being described. "When the winds were right you could smell the stink of burning forest" appeals to the sense of smell. Find other examples of sensory details in the selection.

Writing Options

1. Imagine you are Paul. Write a **note** to your brother, explaining why you took the blame for starting the fire.

2. Write a **comparison** between the grandfather in this story and the grandfather in "Two Dreamers," page 221.

Vocabulary Practice

Exercise   Write *S* for *Synonyms* or *A* for *Antonyms*.

1. offense—crime

2. stench—fragrance

3. anguish—suffering

4. random—predictable

5. penance—self-punishment

*Words
to Know
and Use*

**anguish
offense
penance
random
stench**

Nonfiction

Frontier Schools
from Children of the Wild West
RUSSELL FREEDMAN

Examine What You Know

What do you know about schools in the Wild West from movies, TV, or books? As a class create an idea map like the one below and fill in as much as you can.

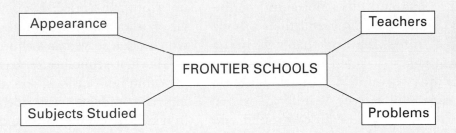

Appearance — Teachers

FRONTIER SCHOOLS

Subjects Studied — Problems

Expand Your Knowledge

The Wild West, also called the western frontier, was the area west of the Missouri River. In the 1800s most of the big cities in the United States were in the East, but many people headed west to start adventurous new lives. Life on the frontier was difficult for pioneer families. Even children worked hard and had many responsibilities. When they weren't needed at home to help with the crops and the livestock, children attended school, usually in one-room schoolhouses.

Write Before You Read

Imagine that you are a student who attends a school in the Wild West in the l870s. In your journal or on a piece of paper, describe what you think your day might be like. Think about the appearance of the school on the inside and

the outside, who your teacher is, and what you learn. As you read this story, compare your ideas with the author's description of frontier schools.

■ *Author biography on Extend page*

Frontier Schools

from Children of the Wild West

RUSSELL FREEDMAN

I remember the first school I attended, a room crowded full of big boys and girls, noise and confusion, with now and then a howl from some boy that was being whipped. I and my brother, with another boy, occupied a bench with no back, near the stove. When the stove became too warm, we whirled around and faced the other side. The boy with us wore a paddle fastened around his neck. On this paddle were posted several letters of the alphabet, and these were changed [by his parents] every day. How I envied that boy because his folks were taking so much pains with him."

Those are the memories of Roxana Rice, a pioneer girl in Kansas. With its hard wooden benches and cast-iron stove, her one-room schoolhouse resembled thousands of others on the Western frontier.

When settlers first moved into an area, there were no schools of any kind. Children were taught at home or at the home of a neighbor. A pioneer woman would take time from her endless tasks to gather a circle of children around her and teach them reading, writing, and arithmetic. Lacking a blackboard, she used a long stick to scratch out letters and numbers on the dirt floor of the family cabin.

As soon as there were enough children in an area, families would band together to put up a proper school. Everyone contributed labor and materials for the schoolhouse, which often served as a church on Sundays.

The first schoolhouse was usually a simple cabin built of logs, sod, or adobe.[1] Each morning students were called to class by the iron bell that hung outside the schoolhouse door. They came by foot, on horseback, and in wagons, carrying their books, their slates and tablets, and their dinner pails. Some of them had to travel several miles in each direction.

Youngsters of all ages were taught by a single teacher. Schools, like frontier homes, sometimes had dirt floors. Since there was no running water, everyone drank from the same bucket and dipper kept in a corner of the room. The "playground" was the field outside. The "restroom" was an outhouse. Dogs of many breeds and sizes hung around the schoolhouse, whining at the door and sneaking inside to lie at their owners' feet.

Some early schools had no blackboards; no charts, maps, or globes; no special equipment of any kind. Since textbooks were scarce, students brought whatever books they had at home. They arrived at school

---

1. **adobe** (ə dō′ bē): clay dried in the sun.

The Denver Public Library, Western History Department.

with an assortment of dictionaries, histories, encyclopedias, and storybooks. Many had copies of McGuffey's Readers,[2] popular schoolbooks of the day that were filled with inspiring stories about hard work, honesty, and piety. Other students might have only a family Bible or an old almanac for their reading lessons.

Much of the classroom time was devoted to the three R's, along with American history and geography. Students memorized grammar rules, recited history dates, practiced penmanship and arithmetic tables, read aloud, and competed in spelling bees. Since the pupils might range in age from seven or eight to sixteen or older, they were not separated into grades. The teacher worked with one or two students at a time, while the others studied by themselves. Older students often tutored younger ones.

The youngsters attended classes only as their chores and the weather allowed. On an ordinary school day, many youngsters were up at 4 A.M., milking cows, chopping wood, toting water, and helping fix breakfast before leaving for school. After a full day of classes,

---

2. **McGuffey's** (mə guf′ ēz) **Readers:** a series of schoolbooks used in the 1800s to teach reading in the United States.

Words
to Know
and Use

almanac (ôl′ mə nak′) *n.* a book that is published yearly, containing a calendar, weather forecasts, and other information
tutor (tōōt′ ər) *v.* to give additional instruction

they might do other chores by moonlight so as not to miss the next day's classes.

Since some children lived miles away from the nearest school, they might not attend classes at all until they were half grown. It was not uncommon to find youngsters twelve or fourteen years old who were just starting school for the first time. During the 1860s, fewer than half the youngsters in Oregon received any formal schooling. California did not make education compulsory until 1874, when a law was passed requiring children between the ages of eight and fourteen to attend classes during at least two-thirds of the school year.

Many frontier schools found it difficult to find and keep good teachers. The pay was low. A teacher might earn anywhere from ten dollars to thirty-five dollars a month, paid only while school was in session. In some areas, the school year lasted only three or four months.

To help make up for the low pay, teachers often received free room and board. They lived with the families of their pupils, moving from one home to another, staying longest with families that had the most children in school. Since so many pioneer families lived in small crowded cabins, this system could be tough on the teacher.

Few teachers had any formal training. To receive a teaching certificate, they had only to pass simple examinations in basic subjects. Some schools were glad to accept almost anyone who was willing to take on the job.

Teachers were especially hard to find in California's mining camps. At a mining town in Tuolumne County,[3] an unsuccessful gold-seeker named Prentice Mulford applied for a teaching job. He was examined by the school trustees—a doctor, a miner, and a saloonkeeper. "I expected a searching examination and trembled," Mulford recalled. "It was years since I had seen a schoolbook. I knew that in geography I was rusty and in mathematics musty. Before the doctor lay one thin book. It turned out to be a spelling book."

Mulford was asked to spell *cat, hat, rat,* and *mat.* When he did this perfectly, the doctor told him, "Young man, you're hired."

Not all frontier schoolteachers could spell as perfectly as young Mulford. In 1859, the superintendent of schools in Sacramento, California, complained that some teachers were misspelling the name of the state they were teaching in as *Callifornia* or *Calafornia.*

Some teachers were barely older than their pupils. Often they hoped to learn as much as they taught. In 1855, Charles A. Murdock organized the first public school in Arcata, California:

"There was no school in the town when we came. It troubled my mother that my brother and sister must be without lessons. Several other small children also were deprived of the opportunity. In the emergency we cleaned out a room in the store . . . and I organized a very primary school.

---

3. **Tuolumne** (tŏŏ äl′ ə mē) **County:** a county in east central California.

314

Roy Andrews Collection. Knight Library, University of Oregon.

"I was almost fifteen, but the children were good and manageable. I did not have very many, and fortunately I was not called upon to teach very long. There came to town a clever man, Robert Desty. He wanted to teach. There was no school building, but he built one all by his own hands. He suggested that I give up my school and become a pupil of his. I was very glad to do it. He was a good and <u>ingenious</u> teacher. I enjoyed his lessons about six months, and then I felt I must help my father."

Eventually school boards began to adopt rules that no teacher under sixteen years of age could be hired. As late as 1880, however, the United States census reported that California still had one boy and two girl teachers under sixteen.

Discipline in the classroom was not usually a serious problem for female teachers. In those days, they were respected because they were women. A male teacher, however, might have to earn the respect of his older students. He might find himself <u>confronted</u> with husky teenagers who had driven ox teams across the continent, fought Indians, mined gold, and shot grizzlies, and may have just split a cord of wood before galloping off to class that morning.

These older boys had developed the habits of frontiersmen and were not used to the discipline of a classroom. Many of them had never attended a school before. On their first day of class, they would walk around the room, talk, whistle, and throw things. When they took their seats, fistfights broke out. A school superintendent in Santa Clara, California, demanded an end to "the use of tobacco amongst the grown boys, for the smell is quite disgusting to visitors on entering. Moreover, the constant expectoration [spitting] under the desks renders the room quite filthy."

Some teachers were not reluctant to use a rawhide whip. One of them reported that he had whipped thirteen boys the first day of class. Each day thereafter he whipped fewer boys, until finally he was able to put the whip away.

At Castroville, California, a young teacher named Tom Clay had no problems at all with discipline. The first day of class, he stood up, smiled at the students before him, and placed a six-shooter on his desk. "We're here to learn," he announced. "If anyone misbehaves, there's going to be trouble." ❧

Responding to Reading

First Impressions

1. What were you thinking about when you finished this selection? Jot down your thoughts in your journal or on a sheet of paper.

Second Thoughts

2. Think about the idea map you and your classmates filled out in Examine What You Know and the journal writing you did in Write Before You Read, both on page 311. How did your ideas compare with what you learned about frontier schools from this selection?

3. What would you have liked about attending a frontier school? What would you have disliked?

4. In what ways are today's schools different from, and similar to, frontier schools?

   Think about
   - the school building and equipment
   - the subjects taught
   - the discipline
   - the characteristics of students and teachers

Broader Connections

5. Frontier schools emphasized "the three R's, along with American history and geography." In your opinion are these still the most important subjects? Explain your answer.

Literary Concept: Anecdote

An **anecdote** is a short, entertaining story, usually about a person. It is included in a larger work to amuse or to make a point. This selection ends with an anecdote about a young teacher named Tom Clay. Why do you suppose Freedman ends his chapter on frontier schools with this anecdote?

Concept Review: Nonfiction The purpose of **nonfiction** is to inform, to persuade, to express an opinion, or to entertain. What do you think was Freedman's main purpose for writing this nonfiction selection?

Writing Options

1. Write an **instruction manual** for new students attending a one-room schoolhouse. Explain what they can expect from school and what will be expected of them.

2. List the qualities that a frontier teacher needs. Then write a **help-wanted notice** for an Eastern newspaper, persuading someone to teach in your newly built schoolhouse.

3. Write a **dramatic skit** based on the information in this selection. Include dialogue and a brief description of the setting and characters.

4. In which of the selections in this subunit could you most easily imagine yourself? Write an **informative essay,** describing the personal qualities that would allow you to work out the problem or deal with the situation presented in that selection.

Vocabulary Practice

Exercise   On your paper, write the letter of the situation that best shows the meaning of the boldfaced word.

1. **almanac**

   a. Pioneers used rough maps to cross the mountains.
   b. Farmers had books with crop and weather information.
   c. Towns published newspapers full of local gossip.

2. **tutor**

   a. Students were not separated into grades.
   b. Some students had to study by themselves.
   c. Older students helped teach the younger students.

3. **compulsory**

   a. In the late 1800s, states began to require children to attend school.
   b. To own land, pioneers had to live on it for five years.
   c. Teachers lived in cabins with their students' families.

4. **ingenious**

   a. Frontier teachers were often young and inexperienced.
   b. Female teachers were respected because they were women.
   c. Good teachers came up with clever ways to teach.

5. **confronted**

   a. Rowdy frontier children stayed away from school whenever possible.
   b. A pioneer might come face to face with hardship and danger.
   c. Frontier schools were built of logs, sod, or adobe.

Options for Learning

1 • Build a Schoolhouse Build a three-dimensional model of a frontier schoolhouse. Show the materials used to build the structure and the arrangement of the furnishings. Use this selection and other research to help you design, construct, and furnish your schoolhouse.

2 • Wild West Day Research some aspect of the Wild West for an oral report. Choose from such subjects as Indian history, outlaws, cowboys, frontier women, the Oregon Trail, the California gold rush, and the railroads. Include photos, posters, and objects that demonstrate how people lived at that time.

3 • Back to the Past With a small group, act out a skit in which a present-day teacher is transported in time to teach at a frontier school. Use details from the selection to dramatize the school day.

4 • Oral History Interview grandparents and other older people about their own school experiences. Tape-record the interviews and transcribe them. Collect the class's interviews into a booklet.

FACT FINDER MATH

If a frontier student lived three miles from school, how many miles would he or she walk to and from school in a five-day week?

Russell Freedman
1929–

Russell Freedman always knew he wanted to be a writer. His first job was as a reporter. "That's where I really learned to write," he says. "I learned to organize my thoughts, respect facts, and meet deadlines." A newspaper article about a sixteen-year-old blind boy who invented a Braille typewriter inspired his first book, *Teenagers Who Made History,* and started his career as a nonfiction writer. Since then, Freedman has written on a range of subjects, from sharks and poisonous snakes to Native American chiefs and Abraham Lincoln.

Freedman won the Newbery Medal in 1988 for his photobiography of Abraham Lincoln; and *Children of the Wild West,* from which "Frontier Schools" is taken, won the Western Heritage Award of the National Cowboy Hall of Fame in 1984.

"Like every writer," Freedman says, "a nonfiction writer is essentially a storyteller. Whatever my subject, I always feel that I have a story to tell that is worth telling. I want to tell it as clearly and simply and effectively as I can, in a way that will stretch the reader's imagination and make that reader care."

WRITER'S WORKSHOP

INFORMATIVE WRITING

How do you plan a dinner party? How do you put out a grass fire? How do you start a business of your own? The characters in this subunit did each of these things. Even if you never have to do any of these, you will often need to explain how to do something. In this workshop you will have a chance to write a speech in which you describe to your classmates the step-by-step process of something you know well.

Here is one writer's PASSkey to this assignment.

GUIDED ASSIGNMENT: HOW-TO SPEECH

Write a speech that explains step-by-step how to do something. Then, deliver your speech to the class.

PURPOSE: To explain how to do something

AUDIENCE: My teacher and classmates

SUBJECT: Eating with chopsticks

STRUCTURE: How-to speech

How to Eat with Chopsticks
by Cathy Zhou

Have you ever eaten in a Chinese restaurant and wondered why some of the people were eating with chopsticks instead of with forks and knives? My grandfather says it's because Chinese food tastes better when you eat it with chopsticks. On the other hand, my mother says chopsticks are good for a person on a diet because when you use chopsticks it can take a long time to eat. Whatever the reason, I am going to explain how to eat with chopsticks, and with practice you may soon be eating as quickly as you like. Before we start, you will need a pair of chopsticks--two pencils will do--and a peanut (hand out peanuts).

STUDENT MODEL

◀ Before you write, read how one student responded to the assignment.

◀ The goal is clearly stated.

◀ Cathy won't read the comments in parentheses. They are reminders of what to do next.

First, take one of the chopsticks and hold it between your thumb and index finger at the base of your thumb, like this (hold up chopstick). It's important to keep the chopstick pointing straight out instead of having it cross the palm of your hand, so curl your fourth finger down to brace the chopstick and keep it straight. Now, make sure about three or four inches of the chopstick are sticking out at the front. Of course, since you're using pencils, you won't have this much sticking out in front, but at least you'll know what to do.

Next, hold the other chopstick with your index finger and your thumb, sort of like you are going to write (show chopsticks in correct position). Now, move the top chopstick by pressing your index finger down. However, don't worry about moving the one on the bottom--just hold it where it is.

Now, why are we going to practice with peanuts? Because it's difficult! My grandfather says, "If you can master a peanut, you can eat anything!" Try picking up the peanut by pressing the chopsticks together around it. Then move it to your mouth, but don't eat it or you won't be able to practice anymore. This is the basic way of eating most things with chopsticks. However, when you eat rice, you should just slide the chopsticks under the rice and pick some up to eat. Do not try to press the chopsticks together.

At first, you may have some trouble eating with chopsticks. However, with practice you will improve. Finally, remember what my mother says: "If at first you don't succeed, use a fork."

Prewrite and Explore

1 **How to pick a "how-to"**   Think small! Choose a process that has a clearly defined beginning and ending. Examples include flossing your teeth, making pancakes, raking leaves, cleaning a bird cage, building a model, oiling a baseball mitt, or braiding hair. In the model, Cathy explains something she learned from her grandfather.

2 **Make a list**   Once you have decided on your topic, ask yourself, "What are all the steps involved?" Think through the process from beginning to end.

◀ **WHAT DO YOU KNOW?**
....
Make a list that begins, "I know how to . . . ." Choose one item from your list as the subject for your speech.

GATHERING INFORMATION

Write each step in a single, clear sentence. Don't worry about getting them all in perfect order, but make sure you include each step. Imagine that someone who does not know anything about your topic is asking you questions. When you have finished your list, reread it. Make sure the steps are in the correct order.

```
        Steps for Eating with Chopsticks

Hold one chopstick with thumb

Brace chopstick with fourth finger

Hold other chopstick like a pencil

Move top chopstick only

Eat rice by sliding chopsticks underneath

Eat big pieces of food by pressing chopsticks
    together
```

◀ **STUDENT MODEL**
....

Draft and Discover

1 **Trace your steps**   Begin by introducing your topic and listing all the materials needed. Then, lead your listeners through the process step by step. Be sure to stop and identify unfamiliar terms or explain an unusual step.

GATHER WHAT YOU NEED
....
List the materials you need to demonstrate your process. Check to make sure you have not forgotten anything.

HELP WITH SIGNAL
WORDS
For more information
on signal words, see
The Editor's Eye,
page 323.

2 **Use signal words**   Signal words help guide the listener through the steps. For example, Cathy always lets her listeners know when she is moving to a new step. She uses transition words such as *first, then,* and *now.* She also uses the word *finally* to signal the last step of the process.

3 **Show and tell**   What visual materials would help your audience understand the process? For her speech, Cathy brings chopsticks and peanuts. She suggests that her listeners practice with pencils in place of chopsticks.

Revise Your Writing

COMPUTER TIP
Use bold or italic type
for words you want to
stress. In brackets,
type any additional
directions, such as
places to pause.

1 **Keep your steps clear and simple**   Break down any steps that may be too complicated or unclear.

Before   It's important to keep the chopstick pointing straight out.

After   It's important to keep the chopstick pointing straight out instead of having it cross the palm of your hand, so curl your fourth finger down to brace the chopstick and keep it straight.

SPEAK UP!
For more tips on how
to give a talk, see the
Speaking and
Listening Workshop on
page 327.

2 **Practice makes perfect**   Speeches are more effective when they are not read word by word. After you have written your speech, take some time to outline the main points on three-by-five-inch note cards. Use your note cards and practice giving your speech until you are comfortable. If you are stumbling over certain parts, change the wording to something that is easier to say. If you are demonstrating something, gather all the materials you need. Practice the demonstration along with the speech until both parts flow smoothly.

Revision Questions

For You	For a Peer Reader
1. Are my steps clear and understandable?	**1.** Can you follow the steps of the process easily?
2. Is the process complete?	**2.** Was any step unclear?
	3. What did you like best about the speech?

HE EDITOR'S EYE: SIGNAL WORDS AND PHRASES

Use signal words to explain your process.

Transitions are verbal bridges that get you from one place to another in your writing. **Signal words** can signal a new idea, help your sentences flow together smoothly, and show how one idea is tied to another. The following are examples of different kinds of signal words.

Time   first, second, then

Space   above, below, around

Comparison/Contrast   however, on the other hand, but

Importance   mainly, primarily, finally

Cause and Effect   therefore, as a result, so

Publish and Present

Here is a suggestion for sharing your work with others

Speakers' Bureau   Organize the speeches by subject area and create a list that can be circulated to other classes. Ask these classes to circle the names of any of the how-to speeches they are interested in hearing. Appoint a class committee to handle the scheduling arrangements. You might also videotape your speeches. Make the tape available as a reference in your school library.

Reflect on Your Writing

Write answers to the questions below. Include your answers with your speech when you put it in your writing portfolio.

◀ FOR YOUR PORTFOLIO
. . . .

1. How did the audience respond?
2. What did I learn from writing this speech that might help me with other assignments?

LANGUAGE WORKSHOP

USING SIGNAL WORDS AND PHRASES

Signal words and phrases can help you write more clearly by connecting the ideas in your sentences and paragraphs. Also called **transitions,** signal words and phrases help your readers understand how your ideas fit together.

Signal Words and Phrases That Show Time and Space

Signal words and phrases, also called **transitions,** are used to clarify and make connections in writing and speaking. This workshop presents a look at different types of signal words and phrases and shows how they are used. In the following passage, notice how signal words help explain the prewriting process of a student writing a how-to speech.

> **First,** Rick made a list of everyday processes and **then** he chose one in particular for his how-to speech. **Next,** he listed the steps of the process. **Alongside** each step he wrote the questions he thought his audience might have. **Below** the list he wrote detailed explanations to each of these questions. **Finally,** he thought about the signal words that would help make his speech clearer.

WHAT TIME IS IT?
Signal words and phrases that show time order are particularly useful for explaining a process or for keeping the order of events straight in fiction.

Signal Words That Show Time   If you are writing about an incident, an event, or a process, you may want to organize your sentences in **chronological,** or **time, order.** That means you tell about the details of an experience in the order that they happened, from the beginning to the end. The following signal words and phrases show time: *before, during, after, first, second, next, finally, while, sometimes, often, whenever, immediately, at first, at last, then, meanwhile, soon, always, later.*

Signal Words That Show Space   When you use **spatial order,** you show where each detail is located in space. Signal words can help you describe something from bottom to top, left to right, front to back, inside to outside, or the reverse of any of these. The list that follows gives examples of signal words and phrases that show spatial relationships: *above, below, on top, around, inside, outside, alongside, under, over, at first, at last, within, to the right, on the left side, in between, in the back, behind, beyond.*

COMMA COMMENT
You may have noticed that when a signal word or phrase begins a sentence, it is usually followed by a comma.

Exercise 1   Concept Check   Read the following sentences. Write the best signal word or phrase from the two shown in parentheses. Keep in mind that all five sentences are part of one passage.

1. (First, Outside) the firefighters spray water or chemicals over the burning area in order to slow the fire's progress.
2. (Next, At last) they begin to clear away the dried twigs, leaves, and other materials that make up the fire's "fuel."
3. (Under, Alongside) the space they have cleared, the firefighters dig a "fire line" by scraping, sweeping, and digging away more dried material.
4. (After, While) the fire line is finished, the firefighters set fires on purpose in order to burn away the fuel lying between the fire line and the flames.
5. (Meanwhile, At last) when the forest fire is out, the firefighters clear away even more material so that the fire cannot break out again.

Other Types of Signal Words

Three other types of signal words and phrases can help you compare one idea with another, emphasize one idea over another, and show the relationship between two ideas or events.

Signal Words That Show Comparison/Contrast   When you need to show how two things are similar or different, use comparison/contrast signal words. For example, when a sentence begins with "On the other hand" you expect to read something that is different from, or in contrast to, what you have just read. "On the other hand" gives you a clear signal of what to expect next. The following signal words and phrases will help you show comparison/contrast: *similarly, likewise, also, in comparison, in the same way, too, but, by contrast, on the other hand, unlike, however, otherwise.*

Signal Words That Show Order of Importance   When you want to clearly indicate that one idea is more important than another, use signal words that show the order of importance. If, for example, you were writing an essay about the hardships of frontier schools, you might want to signal your most important point with the word *primarily*. Other signal words and phrases that show order of importance include the following: *at first, first, most important, primarily, second, last, former, latter.*

Signal Words That Show Cause and Effect   To explain the connection between an event and its causes or between an event and its effects, use cause-and-effect signal words. Science or social studies classes are places where you frequently need to explain why something

WRITING ABOUT
CHOICES
Comparison/contrast signal words and phrases are particularly useful in writing evaluations.

TWO MEANINGS
As you can see by this list, some words, such as *first, second,* or *finally,* can refer to either time order or the order of importance.

happened or what happened as the result of some other event. Cause-and-effect signal words and phrases include the following: *as a result, because, therefore, so, for that reason.*

Exercise 2   Concept Check   Complete each sentence by adding the best signal word or phrase from the list below. Use each word or phrase only once, although you will find that some sentences could be completed with more than one of the signal words and phrases.

first	as a result
most important	on the other hand
because	however
otherwise	likewise
therefore	in comparison

1. There were a number of reasons why people headed west so quickly in 1849. _?_ , there was the California gold rush.

2. The gold rush took place during 1849. _?_ , gold miners were called "Forty-Niners."

3. Most of the western settlers were men. _?_ , some were women.

4. Mark Twain wrote humorous stories of the Old West. _?_ , Bret Harte was a popular writer of the time.

5. Pioneers could head west by the northern route, called the Oregon Trail. _?_ , they could head south along the Santa Fe Trail.

6. The pioneers were newcomers to the West. _?_ , Native Americans, such as the Apaches and Hopis, had been in the area for centuries.

7. In the 1840s, a trip from Missouri to California took months to complete. _?_ of this, it was important to plan well.

8. Pioneers had to consider many things before starting out West. _?_ , was the weather.

9. Settlers had to begin a trip by May. _?_ , they had to wait another year.

10. California became a state in 1850. _?_ , new settlers were no longer moving into a "foreign country."

Exercise 3   Looking at Style   Skim the Insight selection, "Forks in Tokyo, Chopsticks in Chicago" on page 301. Find at least three examples of signal words and phrases. Write the sentence in which each example occurs and identify the type of signal word that is used. Explain why you think the writer used this particular signal word or phrase.

Exercise 4   Revising Your Writing   Read over your how-to speech, paying close attention to the signal words and phrases you used. Add transitions to help your sentences flow together more smoothly.

SPEAKING AND LISTENING
WORKSHOP

GIVING A TALK

Giving a talk may seem frightening, but with preparation and practice, you can relax. Follow these suggestions for a talk.

1. Practice, practice, practice. After you have prepared your talk, practice it out loud. Don't read your speech word for word. Create note cards instead and refer to them as necessary. Ask friends or family members to listen and give constructive criticism.

2. Stand tall. Stand straight and still, but don't be a lifeless statue. Feel free to shift your weight or to take a step now and then. Take a deep breath before you begin.

3. Look at your listeners. Make eye contact with your audience. Don't stare at the ceiling or at the floor. Know your speech well enough so your eyes aren't glued to your notes. Your listeners want to feel connected with you.

4. Express yourself. *Before* you give your talk, think about what you want to express. For example, you might want to convey enthusiasm or humor at particular points. You may also want to make specific gestures such as shrugging your shoulders or holding up two fingers when you say, "The second step is . . ."

5. Use your voice effectively. Although you don't need to shout, make sure you are speaking loudly enough to be heard in the back of the room. Speak slowly and keep your words clear and distinct.

6. Use visual aids. If there are any maps, charts, pictures, or other objects that may help your audience understand your subject, make use of them. For a how-to speech, you may want to draw up a large chart showing the various steps of the process.

Exercise 1   Prepare a one- to two-minute talk on something interesting that you have seen. It could be an unusual store, toy, or event, or a television program. Write notes on three-by-five-inch cards. Keep the above guidelines in mind as you prepare.

Exercise 2   Practice your talk in a small group of four or five students. Comment on each talk presented in your group. Give at least two helpful suggestions for each talk.

BREATHE!

Take a deep breath before speaking and whenever you feel nervous. Everybody who speaks in public, from politicians to actors knows this secret. Since running out of air can make you more nervous, a breath of fresh air may really help!

TIP

Tape-record a practice version of your speech (don't worry, everyone sounds different on tape) so you can make changes ahead of time. Notice unnecessary "ums" and "you knows" and try to avoid them next time.

Reading on Your Own

Suggested Novels for Unit Three

Characters confront danger and adventure in novels that reflect the Unit Three theme, "Face to Face."

CALL IT COURAGE

ARMSTRONG SPERRY ©1939

When high waves strike the shore of Mafatu's South Pacific island, a "terrible trembling" seizes him. He remembers the hurricane that overturned his mother's canoe and drowned her. The meaning of Mafatu's name is "stout heart," but this chief's son is seen as a coward and a jinx. His fear has no place among people fierce of heart and dependent on fishing, so Mafatu sets out to prove he is worthy of his name. Preparing to "face the thing he fears the most," he takes a canoe and shoves off. With white knuckles gripping the paddle, Mafatu steers the canoe out into the open sea. Read this story to discover . . .

- the frightening encounters Mafatu has at sea

- the dangers he finds on a forbidden island

- the struggles Mafatu has with himself

Call it Courage

ARMSTRONG SPERRY

HIDE AND SEEK
IDA VOS ©1991

The Germans invade Holland in 1940, bringing disturbing changes into Rachel Hartog's everyday life. Soon Jewish children are forbidden to play in the park or to attend school with non-Jewish children. All citizens who are Jews must wear a label—a big yellow star—to identify themselves. When several children are taken away by German authorities, the simple game of hide-and-seek becomes a frightening reality. Rachel's family, as well as many other families, goes into hiding. As you read this historical novel about one part of World War II, imagine how you might feel in Rachel's place and think about these questions:

• What steps must the Hartog family take to avoid the danger of discovery?

• How does living with constant fear affect Rachel?

• What are the effects of the war on her family?

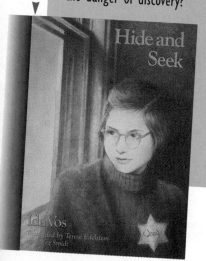

SHADOW OF A BULL
MAIA WOJCIECHOWSKA ©1964

Juan Olivar was a Spanish torero, a bullfighter so legendary that a statue and museum honor his victories in the bullring. Everyone expects young Manolo to take his dead father's place. "It is his fate" is whispered so often by the townspeople that Manolo keeps his fear a secret, even after he has found a new direction for his future. The fateful day has come for ten-year-old Manolo to fight the bull picked especially for the son of Juan Olivar. How will Manolo meet his destiny? As you read, think about . . .

• the proud traditions cherished by the people of Manolo's world

• how Manolo comes to know his dead father

• what Manolo discovers about the true nature of fear and bravery

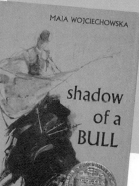

Other Recommended Books

In the Year of the Boar and Jackie Robinson by Bette Bao Lord (©1984). In this lighthearted novel, what does Shirley Temple Wong, a young Chinese immigrant, do to adjust to her new life in the United States? Play ball!

Hugh Glass, Mountain Man by Robert M. McClung (©1990). In this historical novel set in the 1800s, a fur trapper struggles to survive the attack of a giant grizzly bear and to understand his abandonment by his companions.

Anne of Green Gables by L. M. Montgomery (©1908, ©1935, ©1983). In this classic novel, a spunky orphan girl brings changes—some welcome, some upsetting—to the lives of her foster parents.

Justin and the Best Biscuits in the World by Mildred Pitts Walter (©1986). Justin feels out of place both at school and at home. See how, in this novel, time at Grandpa's ranch and a new understanding of his African-American heritage affect Justin.

IN AND
OUT OF
CONTROL

Have faith

and pursue

the unknown end.

Oliver Wendell Holmes

FOOTBALL 1979
Graciela Rodo Boulanger
Oil on canvas, 1.62 x 1.30m.

331

TAKING CHARGE

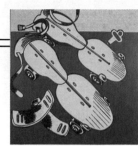

Taking charge is the positive side of "In and Out of Control," the theme of Unit Four. When you are the captain of a sports team or agree to look after your little brother, taking charge can be easy.

There are times, however, when taking charge is impossible. What does it mean to take charge when a problem seems bigger than the world or when someone demands of you more than you ask of yourself? How can you take charge when scary things occur, when your next step could bring more struggle, or when disturbing, confusing events stir up your emotions?

As you read the selections in this subunit, discover what the characters learn as they struggle to understand the world and to take charge of their little corner of it.

Nonfiction *from* Save the Earth

BETTY MILES

Examine What You Know

What are some of the environmental problems in the world today? What are some of the environmental problems in your community? In your journal or on a sheet of paper, copy and fill out webs like the ones started below.

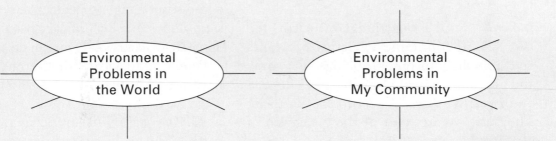

Environmental Problems in the World

Environmental Problems in My Community

Expand Your Knowledge

After World War II ended in 1945, industry boomed and technology advanced. Growing cities poured waste materials into the nearest bodies of water. Smoke, gases, and other polluting substances rose into the air from factories, car exhausts, and burning garbage. Alarm over this pollution led to the first Earth Day on April 22, 1970. The event was the start of today's environmental movement. On April 22, 1990, about 200 million people celebrated Earth Day worldwide.

Enrich Your Reading

Fact and Opinion A **fact** is a statement that can be proved, such as "Earth is the third planet from the sun." An **opinion** is a statement that cannot be proved, such as "Environmental problems are the most important problems in the world." The opinions of the writer of this selection might be summed up in this statement: "Thinking globally, acting locally, we can save the earth—starting right now." As you read, notice how the writer uses facts and examples to support her opinion. For more information about fact and opinion, see page 283.

■ *Author biography on Extend page*

from Save the Earth

BETTY MILES

All people on earth share one home: our bright, fragile planet, circling the sun in the vast blue darkness of space.

All living things on earth—the uncountable varieties of plants and animals and human beings that grow and reproduce themselves and die—depend on the earth's environment to <u>sustain</u> them. They are—*we* are—part of the great web of life that has existed for millions of years, and will keep on existing for as long as the earth can support it.

Australian aboriginal[1] Bill Neidjie of the Bunitz clan expresses the idea this way:

> *Tree . . .*
> *he watching you.*
> *You look at tree,*
> *he listen to you.*
> *He got no finger,*
> *he can't speak.*
> *But that leaf . . .*
> *he pumping, growing,*
> *growing in the night.*
> *While you sleeping*
> *you dream something.*
> *Tree and grass same thing.*
> *They grow with your body,*
> *with your feeling.*

Think Globally, Act Locally

The earth's grave problems, like overflowing landfills,[2] oil spills, and acid rain,[3] are huge and discouraging. Sometimes these problems seem impossible for ordinary people to solve. You may wonder what you can do.

People who work for the environment have a saying that may be helpful to you: *Think globally, act locally.*

Thinking globally means being aware of the earth's big problems—understanding that they're connected, that they're influenced by forces like politics and population and poverty, and that no matter where they occur, they can affect everyone on earth.

Thinking globally is like looking at a whole forest and seeing beyond the beauty of the trees. It means thinking about the forest's history, its wildlife, the resources it provides, the people it supports. When you think globally, you think about the forest's effect on the climate around it, about overlogging, acid rain, and soil <u>erosion</u>. You think about worldwide action to preserve forests and provide jobs for people who

---

1. aboriginal (ab′ ə rij′ ə nəl): a descendant of the native people of Australia.
2. landfills: places where garbage is buried; dumps.
3. acid rain: rain that contains acid because of mixing with air pollution.

Words to Know and Use

sustain (sə stān′) *v.* to keep alive
erosion (ē rō′ zhən) *n.* the wearing away of something

334

depend on them for a living. That's taking a global view.

When you start thinking globally, it's easier to see how *acting locally* fits in. Acting locally is planting one small tree, and caring for it, and then planting another one. It's getting a friend to plant a tree, too—maybe getting everyone in your town to plant trees. Acting locally means doing what you can, where you are, to help the environment.

The earth is always changing. Storms and fires, winds and droughts, earthquakes and floods, and the slow, strong force of water over rock change the land and seas and the climate around them. Over long periods of time these natural changes have affected all life on earth.

Today people are changing the earth faster and more drastically than any force of nature. There are so many of us—more than five billion now, and thousands more being born every hour. Each one of these human beings needs food and shelter and security. But we haven't yet learned how to manage the earth's resources so that everyone can have these basic things. We are using up the earth's resources, like clean air and fresh water, before we have learned to distribute them fairly among all people. We are damaging the earth's environment before we have learned how to restore it. We are changing the earth in ways that may never be undone.

But we are also learning to save it.

Around the world, people are becoming aware of the urgent need to stop destroying the environment and start restoring it—now, before it is too late. In the United Nations and in individual countries, in political parties, in large organizations and in small community groups, people are beginning to understand the connections between their own needs and wants and the health of the whole planet. They are marching, protesting, working, and finding others to work with them. They are learning how to save the earth.

Saving the Coast

There are 260 miles of coastline in the state of Delaware. Every year, kids from schools around the state come to Lewes Beach to save one small part of this coastline and to learn how to preserve all of it.

They come to the Children's Beach House, a place where kids study the ocean by wading into it. Kids who can't wade in ride wheelchairs to the water's edge, pulling crab traps along to collect live sea creatures, like crabs, snails, starfish, and minnows.

Everyone learns about the coastal environment of Delaware—a state where no place is more than eight miles away from tidal water. They learn about the tidal marshes that nourish ocean life and about the sand dunes that protect beaches from storm tides and high waves. They hear about the birds and sea animals that die when they get caught in six-pack rings or swallow plastic bags, and they see for themselves how litter and pollution can spoil the beach's beauty.

Then they set to work.

Every group that comes to the Beach House helps to clean up a stretch of public beach nearby. They collect the trash that

---

Words	**drought** (drout) *n.* a long period of little or no rain
to Know	**drastically** (dras' tik lē) *adv.* in a severe way
and Use	**restore** (ri stôr') *v.* to bring back to an original condition; repair
	dune (dōōn) *n.* a rounded hill

people have dropped carelessly, stuffing what they find into bags and pails.

Some groups work on the sand dunes. They've learned that even large dunes will shift and disappear as the wind blows sand off them unless there is something to hold the sand in place.

Beach grass will hold it. Grass slows the force of the wind and traps the windblown sand grains, making the dunes grow higher. Underground, a network of beach-grass rhizomes, or stems, helps to hold the dune in place.

Beach-grass rhizomes spread naturally by themselves, but they don't spread fast enough to keep up with wind erosion. To stop this erosion, you have to plant a lot of beach grass. On Lewes Beach you can't plant it by machines—that only works in large, flat places. Most dune erosion in Delaware is in small, sloping areas. So kids plant the grass themselves. They do it in teams of four: a plant bucket carrier, a spader, a plant feeder, and a planter.

First, they mark a straight row with string. Then the spader digs a hole twelve to fourteen inches deep, holding the spade in it to keep the sand out. The plant feeder measures out fertilizer and spreads it in a circle around the hole. The plant bucket carrier gives three grass plants to the planter, who sets them in the hole. The spader pulls out the spade. The planter packs the sand around the plants until it's so firm that they won't come out.

That's how you do one plant. After they've planted a whole row, the team moves the marker and starts on a new one. They keep going like this, changing jobs every thirty plants, until they have planted 120.

It's hard work. But it's good.

"We helped to save the beach," one planter said afterward.

"We put our names in the sand," said the spader.

"We had a good time," said the plant bucket carrier.

"I hope we can go back to plant more grass," said the plant feeder.

They are going back. They're going to see how the grass they planted has spread over the sand of their Delaware beach. They're going to plant more grass, to save more dunes for the future.

Workers at a Delaware beach.
© Mary V. Sprague.

The Toxic Avengers.
© Dirk Westphal.

The Toxic Avengers of El Puente

The Toxic Avengers are a group of young people who live in Brooklyn, New York, and meet at *El Puente,* a neighborhood center. They're fighting <u>toxic</u> waste. They're also fighting what they call "environmental racism"—allowing factories that pollute to exist in poor and <u>minority</u> neighborhoods.

The founding members of the group discovered pollution in their own neighborhood as part of a class project. With their teacher, José Morales, they took samples of waste from a street gutter near the vacant lot where a local factory kept chemical waste in barrels. Their laboratory <u>analysis</u> showed the samples to be toxic and flammable. They then learned that a local warehouse stored hazardous and radioactive waste. They wondered: do polluters think that in a Hispanic neighborhood, people won't care?

The Toxic Avengers of *El Puente* set out to show that people *do* care. They began to challenge the polluters. When they organized a demonstration against the hazardous-waste warehouse, community leaders and citizens of all ages turned out to demonstrate with them. The Avengers intend to keep up the pressure until they get the warehouse out of their neighborhood.

The Avengers believe that too many major environmental groups ignore what's going on in poor and minority communities. They don't know of another group like theirs—but they don't let that stop them. They don't let the fact that they're not adults stop them from speaking out and organizing.

The Toxic Avengers think young people in other neighborhoods should be aware of environmental issues that affect them.

"Know what you're doing," says member Rosa Rivera, "and don't be <u>intimidated</u> by adults who try to put you down. By working together, you can really make a difference."

Cleaning up Adobe Creek. © 1989 Ann Dowie.

Fish Story

Ninety years ago, the last steelhead spawned in Adobe Creek in Petaluma, California. The steelhead is a silvery rainbow trout that migrates to the Pacific before returning to fresh water to spawn. Ninety years ago the city diverted the stream's water for its use, leaving the creek only spillage[4] from winter rains. Adobe Creek was dry and dead, a dump for the trash people tossed into it—tires, mattresses, appliances, garbage.

Five years ago, a group of Casa Grande High School students called the United Anglers were determined to bring the steelhead back to Adobe Creek. Working on weekends, they cleared away the tons of garbage, piece by piece. They planted hundreds of young trees to stop shore erosion. They dug out the gravel creekbed to create safe spawning grounds. Finally, they turned an unused greenhouse behind the school into a fish hatchery. Several thousand finger-lings hatched from the first batch of eggs, and on a day when winter runoff filled the creek, the Anglers notched the fish's fins for identification and let them go.

On a rainy spring day, three students walking on the bank saw a flitting shadow in the ripples. A fish! As the United Anglers gathered at the creek, they saw a notch in the fish's fin—proof that it was one they had released. They had brought the steelhead back.

Now the Anglers have begun a new project—building a new fish hatchery. With car washes and other projects, they have raised half the money it will cost, and construction has begun. Meanwhile, more than half of the original group have gone on to college to prepare for environmental careers. All of them are committed to preserving the environment.

They know how to do it. They know they *can* do it. ❧

---

4. **spillage** (spil′ ij): the amount left over after liquid has been absorbed.

from Wisdomkeepers

HARRIETT STARLEAF GUMBS
Interviewed by HARVEY ARDEN and STEVE WALL

Starleaf is the Native American name of Harriett Gumbs. She is a teacher, historian, and a tribal leader on the four-hundred-acre Shinnecock Indian Reservation, located on eastern Long Island in New York. Because Long Island is a popular vacation area, the Shinnecocks have received offers of millions of dollars to relocate. They have refused all offers. "Our ancestors called this place Sea-wan-hac-hee, or Shell Heaven," Starleaf says. "This land is ours forever—and we're not leaving."

"When I was a girl, the water was so clean and clear we bathed and washed our clothes in it. Now there's so much pollution no one wants to set foot in it. What a difference between White Man's way and the Indian way! We lived here since time began and the only waste we left behind was the oyster-shell middens[1] on the shore. But what will future archaeologists find when they unearth today's civilization? Generations to come will look back and see how twentieth-century Americans were the garbage-makers, the poison-producers, the carcinogen[2]-creators."

• • • • • • • • • •

"There used to be so many clams on the beach you only had to kick the sand to find them. You could dig them up with your toes. Now they're scarce. Commercial clammers rake the shore right up to the tideline. When I was a girl, the sand was pearly white. Now it's covered with that green algae—from pollution, they say. The pesticides and herbicides and fertilizers run down from the potato fields. Still, isn't it beautiful? This is where the Creator intended us to live."

---

1. **middens** (mid' 'nz): piles.
2. **carcinogen** (kär sin' ə jən): a substance that causes cancer.

*R*esponding to Reading

First Impressions

1. After reading this selection, how do you feel about saving the earth? Describe these feelings in your journal or on a sheet of paper.

Second Thoughts

2. Compare and contrast the three projects described in this selection. What are their similarities and differences?

> **Think about**
> - the location of each project
> - what is involved in each project
> - the young people who are involved in each project

3. Which group do you think has the most difficult task in taking charge of the environment?

> **Think about**
> - each group's goals
> - the amount of organization and work needed

4. Do you think Betty Miles's opinions on saving the earth are convincing? Why or why not?

Broader Connections

5. The author explains the saying "Think globally, act locally" and provides examples of young people taking action in their local areas. Look over the word webs you made before reading the selection. Focus on a single problem in your community. Describe one step that you or others in your community can take to help solve the problem.

*L*iterary Concept: Author's Purpose

An **author's purpose** in writing can be to inform, to persuade, to entertain, or to give an opinion. Often a writer has more than one purpose for writing. What might Betty Miles's purposes in writing *Save the Earth* have been?

Concept Review: Audience Betty Miles wrote *Save the Earth* for young people. In what ways does this excerpt from the book show that Miles kept her audience in mind while writing?

Writing Options

1. Imagine that you are a member of the Toxic Avengers. Write an opening statement for a **petition** that contains the signatures of people who want the warehouse to move. Title your petition, identify who you are, and describe both the problem and the plan you are proposing.

2. If the earth could talk, what might she say to people? Write a **letter** from the earth to humans, beginning "Dear Children."

3. Look at the poem on page 334 and the Insight selection on page 339. Write a **poem** that praises the earth for its beauty and its many benefits to humans.

4. Write a radio **public-service announcement** that describes one of the projects discussed in the selection. Persuade listeners to support the project. Include quotations from the young workers involved in the project.

Vocabulary Practice

Exercise   On your paper, write the word that best completes each sentence.

1. People are trying to learn how to _?_ themselves without using up the earth's resources.

2. You can ask your local water company for the most recent _?_ of the chemicals in your drinking water.

3. Soil _?_ by water or wind can be prevented by planting trees or grasses, which hold the soil in place.

4. Chemicals in the _?_ waste that is dumped into oceans can kill marine life and poison human beings.

5. The size of rain forests is being _?_ reduced; every hour 500,000 rain-forest trees are cut down.

6. Planting beach grass can help keep a _?_ from drifting.

7. Use less water in your garden by growing plants that originate in dry climates and can thrive even during a _?_ .

8. Composting is a natural way to _?_ nutrients to damaged soil.

9. People in _?_ neighborhoods are taking a stand against factories that pollute their communities.

10. Industries that pollute a community can sometimes _?_ people who are trying to clean up the environment.

> *Words to Know and Use*
>
> ---
>
> **analysis**
> **drastically**
> **drought**
> **dune**
> **erosion**
> **intimidate**
> **minority**
> **restore**
> **sustain**
> **toxic**

Options for Learning

1 • Earth Day Hold an Earth Day celebration at your school. With your classmates, research a variety of issues, such as garbage dumping, global warming, solar and wind power, and rain forests. Write and distribute pamphlets or "fact sheets"; give speeches and hands-on demonstrations; create posters and other displays. At the end of the day, hold a discussion about what you have learned.

2 • News Update Take the role of a TV reporter covering the progress of one of the projects described in the selection. Stage imaginary interviews with students involved in the project. Discuss what action has been taken, what difficulties were encountered, and how successful the project has been.

3 • Become Streetwise Under your teacher's supervision, form investigative teams to check out environmental conditions in your neighborhood. On your trip, observe and take notes. Return to school to compare observations and to brainstorm a plan of action.

4 • Crafty Recycling How could a plastic milk bottle be made into a birdhouse? How could you change cereal boxes into file boxes for your written work? Explore creative and practical new uses for disposable objects in your home or school. Explain how to make your creations.

 FACT FINDER MATH

People in the United States use 2.5 million plastic bottles every hour. How many plastic bottles do we use each year?

Betty Miles
1928–

Betty Miles is the author of many popular books for young people, including the novels *The Real Me* and *The Secret Life of the Underwear Champ* and the ecology handbook *Save the Earth* from which this selection is taken. Miles says that one reason she wrote *Save the Earth* was to show "how knowledge, forward planning, and hard work can lead to useful solutions. I do believe that though it will be complicated and difficult, people can cooperate to save the earth."

About her writing, Miles says, "I can only write about subjects that interest me and things I care about as an adult; but I am always aware that I am writing for kids, and I work hard to find the tone and style that's appropriate to them."

Miles hopes that readers of her books will understand and share her ideas and feelings. She teaches and writes about children's literature and visits schools to talk to students, teachers, and parents about books.

Fiction

Miss Awful

ARTHUR CAVANAUGH

Examine What You Know

What conditions help you learn best in school? Do you prefer a classroom with strict discipline, one with relaxed discipline, or one that is somewhere in between? In your journal or on a sheet of paper, describe the classroom atmosphere that you consider ideal.

Expand Your Knowledge

In schools of the 1800s, teachers stressed memorization and strict discipline. Students sat in rows and could not move or talk without permission. This method of teaching was known as traditional education. In the early 1900s, teachers who preferred more relaxed methods turned toward a method of teaching that became known as progressive education. These teachers believed that students learn best when they can move about and work at their own pace. Creativity was highly valued. Many schools today practice some combination of these two methods.

Enrich Your Reading

Challenging Vocabulary As you read this story, you may come across words and phrases that are unfamiliar to you. At the same time, however, you will probably be caught up and pulled along very quickly by the plot of the story. An important point to remember in reading any piece of writing is that you do not need to understand every word. In this story the footnotes and the Words to Know and Use will define the difficult words and phrases that are most important to your understanding of the story. Do not let yourself be slowed down by other words or phrases that you may not recognize. Just keep reading and enjoy the story! Later, you can go back and enrich your vocabulary by looking up the words you didn't know.

■ *Author biography in Reader's Handbook*

Miss Awful

ARTHUR CAVANAUGH

The whole episode of Miss Awful began for the Clarks at their dinner table one Sunday afternoon. Young Roger Clark was explaining why he could go to Central Park with his father instead of staying home to finish his homework—Miss Wilson, his teacher, wouldn't be at school tomorrow, so who'd know the difference? "She has to take care of a crisis," Roger explained. "It's in Omaha."[1]

"What is?" his older sister, Elizabeth, inquired. "For a kid in third grade, Roger, you talk dopey. You fail to make sense."

Roger ignored the insult. His sister was a condition of life he had learned to live with, like lions. Or snakes. Poisonous ones. Teetering, as always, on the tilted-back chair, feet wrapped around the legs, he continued, "Till Miss Wilson gets back, we're having some other teacher. She flew to Omaha yesterday." He pushed some peas around on his plate and was silent a moment. "I hope her plane don't crash," he said.

Roger's mother patted his hand. A lively, outgoing youngster, as noisy and rambunctious as any seven-year-old, he had another side to him, tender and soft, which worried about people. Let the blind man who sold pencils outside the five-and-ten on Broadway be absent from his post, and Roger worried that catastrophe had overtaken him. When Mrs. Loomis, a neighbor of the Clarks in the Greenwich Village brownstone,[2] had entered the hospital, Roger's anxious queries had not ceased until she was discharged. And recently there was the cat, which had nested in the downstairs doorway at night. Roger had carried down saucers of milk, clucking with concern. "Is the cat run away? Don't it have a home?"

Virginia Clark assured her son, "You'll have Miss Wilson safely back before you know it. It's nice that you care so."

Roger beamed with relief. "Well, I like Miss Wilson; she's fun. Last week, for instance, when Tommy Miller got tired of staying in his seat and lay down on the floor—"

"He did what?" Roger's father was roused from his postdinner torpor.[3]

"Sure. Pretty soon the whole class was lying down. Know what Miss Wilson did?"

---

1. **Omaha** (ō′ mə hô): a city in Nebraska.
2. **Greenwich** (gren′ ich) **Village brownstone:** a sandstone apartment building in a section of the lower west side of Manhattan Island in New York City.
3. **torpor** (tôr′ pər): a state of inactivity; sluggishness.

"If you'll notice, Mother," Elizabeth interjected, "he hasn't touched a single pea."

"*She* lay down on the floor, too," Roger went on ecstatically. "She said we'd *all* have a rest. It was perfectly normal in the middle of the day. That's what I love about St. Geoff's.[4] It's fun."

"Fun," snorted his sister. "School isn't supposed to be a fun fest. It's supposed to be filling that empty noodle of yours."

"Miss Wilson got down on the floor?" Mr. Clark repeated. He had met Roger's teacher on occasion; she had struck him as capable but excessively whimsical.[5] She was a large woman to be getting down on floors, Mr. Clark thought. "What did the class do next?" he asked.

"Oh, we lay there a while, then got up and did a Mexican hat dance," Roger answered. "It was swell."

"I'm sure not every day is as frolicsome," Mrs. Clark countered, slightly anxious. She brought in dessert, a chocolate mousse. Roger's story sounded typical of St. Geoffrey's. Not that she was unhappy with his school. A small private institution, while it might be called overly permissive, it projected a warm, homey atmosphere which Mrs. Clark found appealing. It was church affiliated, which she approved of, and heaven knows its location a few blocks away from the brownstone was convenient. True, Roger's scholastic progress wasn't notable—his spelling, for example, remained atrocious.[6] Friendly as St. Geoffrey's was, Mrs. Clark sometimes *did* wish . . .

Roger attacked dessert with a lot more zest than he had shown the peas. "So can I go to the park with you, Dad? I've only got spelling left, and who cares about that?" Before his mother could comment, he was up from the table and racing toward the coat closet. "OK, Dad?"

"I didn't say you could go. I didn't even say I'd take you," Mr. Clark objected. He happened, at that moment, to glance at his waistline and reflect that a brisk hike might do him some good. He pushed back his chair. "All right, but the minute we return, it's straight to your room to finish your spelling."

"Ah, thanks, Dad. Can we go to the boat pond first?"

"We will not," cried Elizabeth, elbowing into the closet. "We'll go to the Sheep Meadow first."

Roger was too happy to argue. Pulling on his jacket, he remarked, "Gee, I wonder what the new teacher will be like. Ready for your coat, Dad?"

It was just as well that he gave the matter no more thought. In view of events to come, Roger was entitled to a few carefree hours.

Monday morning at school started off with perfect normalcy. It began exactly like any other school morning. Elizabeth had long since departed for the girls' school she attended uptown when Mrs. Clark set out with Roger for the short walk to St. Geoff's. She didn't trust him with the Fifth Avenue traffic yet. They reached the school corner,

---

4. **St. Geoff's** (jefs): a school.
5. **whimsical:** imaginative and playful.
6. **atrocious** (ə trō′ shəs): extremely bad.

Words to Know and Use

interject (in′ tər jekt′) *v.* to say as an interruption
ecstatically (ek stat′ ik lē) *adv.* with great joy

MRS. C. E. ETNIER Franklin C. Watkins Courtesy, David and John Etnier.

and Roger skipped away eagerly from her. The sidewalk in front of school already boasted a large, jostling throng of children, and his legs couldn't hurry Roger fast enough to join them. Indeed, it was his reason for getting to school promptly: to have time to play before the 8:45 bell. Roger's school bag was well equipped for play. As usual, he'd packed a supply of baseball cards for trading opportunities; a spool of string, in case anybody brought a kite; a water pistol for possible use in the lavatory; and a police whistle for sheer noise value. Down the Greenwich Village sidewalk he galloped, shouting the names of his third-grade friends

as he picked out faces from the throng. "Hiya, Tommy. Hey, hiya, Bruce. Hi, Steve, you bring your trading cards?"

By the time the 8:45 bell rang—St. Geoff's used a cowbell, one of the homey touches—Roger had finished a game of tag, traded several baseball cards, and was launched in an exciting jump-the-hydrant contest. Miss Gillis, the school secretary, was in charge of the bell, and she had to clang it extensively before the student body took notice. Clomping up the front steps, they spilled into the downstairs hall, headed in various directions. Roger's class swarmed up the stairs in rollicking spirits—Tommy Miller,

Bruce Reeves, Joey Lambert, with the girls forming an untidy rear flank behind them, shrill with laughter.

It wasn't until the front ranks reached the third-grade classroom that the first ominous note was struck.

"Hey, what's going on?" Jimmy Moore demanded, first to observe the changed appearance of the room. The other children crowded behind him in the doorway. Instead of a cozy semicircle—"As though we're seated around a glowing hearth," Miss Wilson had described it—the desks and chairs had been rearranged in stiff, rigid rows. "Gee, look, the desks are in rows," commented Midge Fuller, a plump little girl who stood blocking Roger's view. Midge was a child given to unnecessary statements. "It's raining today," she would volunteer to her classmates, all of them shod in slickers and rubbers. Or, "There's the lunch bell, gang." The point to Roger wasn't that the desks had been rearranged. The point was, *why?* As if in answer, he heard two hands clap behind him as loud and menacing as thunder.

"What's this, what's this?" barked a stern, raspish voice. "You are not cattle milling in a pen. Enough foolish gaping! Come, come, form into lines."

Heads turned in unison, mouths fell agape. The children of St. Geoffrey's third grade had never formed into lines of any sort, but this was not the cause of their shocked inertia.[7] Each was staring, with a sensation similar to that of drowning, at the owner of the raspish voice. She was tall and straight as a ruler and was garbed in an ancient tweed suit whose skirt dipped nearly to the ankles. She bore a potted plant in one arm and Miss Wilson's roll book in the

other. Rimless spectacles glinted on her bony nose. Her hair was gray, like a witch's, skewered in a bun, and there was no question that she had witch's eyes. Roger had seen those same eyes leering from the pages of *Hansel and Gretel*—identical, they were. He gulped at the terrible presence.

Sloppiest group I've ever beheld. March!

"Are you a class of deaf mutes?" he heard with a start. "Form lines, I said. Girls in one, boys in the other." Poking, prodding, patrolling back and forth, the new teacher kneaded the third grade into position and ruefully inspected the result. "Sloppiest group I've ever beheld. *March!*" She clapped time with her hands, and the stunned ranks trooped into the classroom. *"One,* two, three, *one,* two—girls on the window side, boys on the wall. Stand at your desks. Remove your outer garments. You, little miss, with the vacant stare. What's your name?"

"Ja-ja—" a voice squeaked.

"Speak up. I won't have mumblers."

"Jane Douglas."

"Well, Jane Douglas, you will be coat monitor. Collect the garments a row at a time and hang them neatly in the cloakroom. Did you hear me, child? Stop staring." Normally slow-moving, Jane Douglas became a whirl of activity, charging up and down the aisles, piling coats in her arms. The new teacher tugged at her tweed jacket. "Class be seated, hands folded on desks," she barked, and there was immediate

---

7. **inertia** (in ur′ shə): an inability to move.

compliance.[8] She next paraded to the windows and installed the potted plant on the sill. Her witch's hands fussed with the green leaves, straightening, pruning. "Plants and children belong in classrooms," she declared, spectacles sweeping over the rows. "Can someone suggest why?"

There was total silence, punctured by a deranged giggle, quickly suppressed.

"Very well, I will tell you. Plants and children are living organisms. Both will grow with proper care. Repeat, *proper*. Not indulgent fawning or giving in to whims—scrupulosity!"[9] With another tug at the jacket, she strode, ruler straight, to the desk in the front of the room. "I am Miss Orville. O-r-v-i-l-l-e," she spelled. "You are to use my name in replying to all questions."

In the back of the room, Jimmy Moore whispered frantically to Roger. "What did she say her name is?"

Miss Orville rapped her desk. "Attention, please, no muttering in the back." She cleared her voice and resumed. "Prior to my retirement I taught boys and girls for forty-six years," she warned. "I am beyond trickery, so I advise you to try none. You are to be in my charge until the return of Miss Wilson, however long that may be." She clasped her hands in front of her and trained her full scrutiny on the rows. "Since I have no knowledge of your individual abilities, perhaps a look at the weekend homework will shed some light. Miss Wilson left me a copy of the assignment. You have all completed it, I trust? Take out your notebooks, please. At once, at once, I say."

Roger's head spun dizzily around. He gaped at the monstrous tweed figure in dis-

may. Book bags were being clicked open, notebooks drawn out—what was he to do? He had gone to his room after the outing in the park yesterday, but alas, it had not been to complete his assignment. He watched, horrified, as the tweed figure proceeded among the aisles and inspected notebooks. What had she said her name was? Awful—was that it? Miss Awful! Biting his lip, he listened to her scathing comments.

"You call this chicken scrawl penmanship?" R-r-rip! A page was torn out and thrust at its owner. "Redo it at once; it assaults the intelligence." Then, moving on, "What is this maze of ill-spelled words? Not a composition, I trust."

Ill-spelled words! He was in for it for sure. The tweed figure was heading down his aisle. She was three desks away, no escaping it. Roger opened his book bag. It slid from his grasp and, with a crash, fell to the floor. Books, pencil case spilled out. Baseball cards scattered, the water pistol, the police whistle, the spool of string . . .

"Ah," crowed Miss Awful, instantly at his desk, scooping up the offending objects. "We have come to play, have we?"

And she fixed her witch's gaze on him.

Long before the week's end, it was apparent to Virginia Clark that something was drastically wrong with her son's behavior. The happy-go-lucky youngster had disappeared, as if down a well. Another creature had replaced him, nervous, harried, continuously glancing over his shoulder

---

8. **compliance** (kəm plī′ əns): the carrying out of a request or command.

9. **scrupulosity** (skrōō′ pyə läs′ ə tē): extremely careful and proper behavior.

in the manner of one being followed. Mrs. Clark's first inkling of change occurred that same Monday. She had been chatting with the other mothers who congregated outside St. Geoffrey's at three every afternoon to pick up their offspring. A casual assembly, the mothers were as relaxed and informal as the school itself, lounging against the picket fence, exchanging small talk and anecdotes.

"That darling cowbell," laughed one of the group at the familiar clang. "Did I tell you Anne's class is having a taffy pull on Friday? Where else, in the frantic city of New York . . ."

The third grade was the last class to exit from the building on Monday. Not only that, but Mrs. Clark noted that the children appeared strangely subdued. Some of them were actually reeling, all but dazed. As for Roger, eyes taut and pleading, he quickly pulled his mother down the block, signaling for silence. When enough distance had been gained, words erupted from him.

"No, we don't have a new teacher," he flared wildly. "We got a *witch* for a new teacher. It's the truth. She's from *Hansel and Gretel,* the same horrible eyes—and she steals toys. *Yes,"* he repeated in mixed outrage and hurt. "By accident you happen to put some toys in your book bag, and she *steals* 'em. I'll fool her! I won't *bring* any more toys to school," he howled. "Know what children are to her? Plants! She did, she called us plants. Miss Awful, that's her name."

Such was Roger's distress that his mother offered to stop at the Schrafft's on Thirteenth Street and treat him to a soda. "Who's got time for sodas?" he bleated. "I have homework to do. Punishment home-

NEAR THE WINDOW (CERCA DE LA VENTANA) 1983
Daniel Quintero Courtesy, Marlborough Gallery New York.

work. Ten words, ten times each. On account of the witch's spelling test."

"Ten words, ten times each?" Mrs. Clark repeated. "How many words were on the test?"

"Ten," moaned Roger. "Every one wrong. Come on. I've got to hurry home. I don't have time to waste." Refusing to be consoled, he headed for the brownstone and the desk in his room.

On Tuesday, together with the other mothers, Mrs. Clark was astonished to see the third grade march down the steps of St. Geoffrey's in military precision. Clop, clop, the children marched, looking neither to the left nor right, while behind them came a stiff-backed, iron-haired woman in a pepper-and-salt suit. *"One,* two, three, *one,* two, three," she counted, then clapped her hands in dismissal. Turning, she surveyed the assemblage of goggle-eyed mothers. "May I inquire if the mother of Joseph Lambert is among you?" she asked.

"I'm Mrs. Lambert," replied a voice meekly, whereupon Miss Orville paraded directly up to her. The rest of the mothers looked on, speechless.

"Mrs. Lambert, your son threatens to grow into a useless member of society," stated Miss Orville in ringing tones that echoed down the street. "That is, unless you term watching television useful. Joseph has confessed that he views three hours per evening."

"Only after his homework's finished," Margery Lambert allowed.

"Madame, he does not finish his homework. He idles through it, scattering mistakes higgledy-piggledy. I suggest you give him closer supervision. Good day." With a brief nod, Miss Orville proceeded down the street, and it was a full minute before the mothers had recovered enough to comment. Some voted in favor of immediate protest to Dr. Jameson, St. Geoffrey's headmaster, on the hiring of such a woman, even on a temporary basis. But since it was temporary, the mothers concluded it would have to be tolerated.

Nancy Reeves, Bruce's mother, kept staring at the retreating figure of Miss Orville, by now far down the block. "I know her from somewhere, I'm sure of it," she insisted, shaking her head.

The next morning, Roger refused to leave for school. "My shoes aren't shined," he wailed. "Not what Miss Awful calls shined. Where's the polish? I can't leave till I do 'em over."

"Roger, if only you'd thought of it last night," sighed Mrs. Clark.

"You sound like her," he cried. "That's what *she'd* say," and it gave his mother something to puzzle over for the rest of the day. She was still thinking about it when she joined the group of mothers outside St. Geoffrey's at three. She had to admit it was sort of impressive, the smart, martial[10] air exhibited by the third grade as they trooped down the steps. There was to be additional ceremony today. The ranks waited on the sidewalk until Miss Orville passed back and forth in inspection. Stationing herself at the head of the columns, she boomed, "Good afternoon, boys and girls. Let us return with perfect papers tomorrow."

"Good aaaaafternoon, Miss Orville," the class sang back in unison, after which the ranks broke. Taking little Amy Lewis in tow, Miss Orville once more nodded at the mothers. "Which is she?" she asked Amy.

Miss Orville approached the trapped Mrs. Lewis. She cleared her throat, thrust back her shoulders. "Amy tells me she is fortunate enough to enjoy the services of a full-time domestic[11] at home," said Miss Orville.

---

10. **martial** (mär′ shəl): military.
11. **domestic:** a servant.

"May I question whether she is fortunate—or deprived? I needn't lecture you, I'm sure, Mrs. Lewis, about the wisdom of assigning a child tasks to perform at home. Setting the table, tidying up one's room, are lessons in self-reliance for the future. Surely you agree." There was a nod from Mrs. Lewis. "Excellent," smiled Miss Orville. "Amy will inform me in the morning the tasks you have assigned her. Make them plentiful, I urge you."

The lecturing, however, was not ended. Turning from Mrs. Lewis, Miss Orville cast her gaze around and inquired, "Is Roger Clark's mother present?"

"Yes?" spoke Virginia Clark, reaching for Roger's hand. "What is it?"

Miss Orville studied Roger silently for a long moment. "A scallywag,[12] if ever I met one," she pronounced. The rimless spectacles lifted to the scallywag's mother. "You know, of course, that Roger is a prodigy,"[13] said Miss Orville. "A prodigy of misspelling. Roger, spell *flower* for us," she ordered. "Come, come, speak up."

Roger kept his head lowered. "F," he spelled. "F-l-o-r."

"Spell *castle*."

"K," spelled Roger. "K-a-z-l."

Miss Orville's lips parted grimly. "Those are the results, mind you, of an hour's solid work with your son, Mrs. Clark. He does not apply himself. He wishes to remain a child at play, absorbed in his toys. Is that what you want for him?"

"I–I–" Virginia Clark would have been grateful if the sidewalk had opened up to receive her.

As she reported to her husband that evening, she had never in her life been as mortified. "Spoke to me in front of all the other mothers in loud, clarion tones," she described the scene. "Do I want Roger to remain a child at play. Imagine."

"By the way, where is Roge?" Mr. Clark asked, who had come home late from the office. "He's not watching television or busy with his airplanes—"

"In his room, doing over his homework for the ninety-eighth time. It has to be perfect, he says. But really, Charles, don't you think it was outrageous?"

*H*e's cute and all, but I wouldn't want to be in a shipwreck with him.

Mr. Clark stirred his coffee. "I bet Miss Orville doesn't get down on the floor with the class. Or do Mexican hat dances with them."

"If that's meant to disparage[14] Miss Wilson—" Virginia Clark stacked the dinner dishes irritably. She sometimes found her husband's behavior maddening. Especially when he took to grinning at her, as he was presently doing. She also concluded that she'd had her fill of Elizabeth's attitude on the subject. "At least some teacher's wised up to Roge," had been the Clarks' daughter's comment. "He's cute and all, but I wouldn't want to be in a shipwreck with him." Washing dishes in the kitchen, Mrs. Clark considered that maybe she wouldn't meet Roger in *front* of school tomorrow.

---

12. **scallywag** (skal′ ē wag′): a form of *scalawag,* meaning "rascal."
13. **prodigy** (präd′ ə jē): a child with unusual talent.
14. **disparage** (di spar′ ij): to belittle; show no respect for.

Maybe she'd wait at the corner instead. "His shoes," she gasped, and hurried to remind her son to get out the polishing kit. The spelling, too, she'd better work on that . . .

It was on Thursday that Nancy Reeves finally remembered where, previously, she had seen Miss Orville. Perhaps it was from the shock of having received a compliment from the latter.

"Mrs. Reeves, I rejoice to inform you of progress," Miss Orville had addressed her after the third grade had performed its military display for the afternoon. "On Monday, young Bruce's penmanship was comparable to a chicken's—if a chicken could write. Today, I was pleased to award him an A."

A tug at the tweed jacket, and the stiff-backed figure walked firmly down the street. Nancy Reeves stared after her until Miss Orville had merged into the flow of pedestrians and traffic. "I know who she is," Nancy suddenly remarked, turning to the other mothers. "I knew I'd seen her before. Those old ramshackle buildings near us on Hudson Street—remember when they were torn down last year?" The other mothers formed a circle around her. "Miss Orville was one of the tenants," Nancy Reeves went on. "She'd lived there for ages and refused to budge until the landlord got a court order and deposited her on the sidewalk. I *saw* her there, sitting in a rocker on the sidewalk surrounded by all this furniture and plants. Her picture was in the papers. Elderly retired schoolteacher . . . they found a furnished room for her on Jane

Street, I think. Poor old thing, evicted like that . . . I remember she couldn't keep any of the plants . . ."

On the way home, after supplying a lurid account of the day's tortures—"Miss Awful made Walter Meade stand in the corner for saying a bad word"—Roger asked his mother, "Eviction. What does that mean?"

"It's when somebody is forced by law to vacate an apartment. The landlord gets an eviction notice, and the person has to leave."

"Kicked her out on the street. Is that what they did to the witch?"

"Don't call her that; it's rude and impolite," Mrs. Clark said as they turned into the brownstone doorway. "I can see your father and I have been too easygoing where you're concerned."

"Huh, we've got worse names for her," Roger retorted. "*Curse* names; you should hear 'em. We're planning how to get even with Miss Awful, just you see." He paused as his mother opened the downstairs door with her key. "That's where the cat used to sleep, remember?" he said, pointing at a corner of the entryway. His face was grave and earnest. "I wonder where that cat went to. Hey, Mom," he hurried to catch up. "Maybe *it* was evicted, too."

Then it was Friday at St. Geoffrey's. Before lunch, Miss Orville told the class, "I am happy to inform you that Miss Wilson will be back on Monday." She held up her hand for quiet. "This afternoon will be my final session with you. Not that discipline will relax, but I might read you a story. Robert Louis Stevenson, perhaps. My boys

Words to Know and Use | **evicted** (ē vict′ id) *adj.* legally removed from a rented house or apartment **evict** *v.*

SONDRA'S L'ATELIER   Irene Ingalls   Courtesy of the artist.
Photograph by Bill Ashe Studio.

and girls always enjoyed him so. Forty-six years of them . . . Joseph Lambert, you're not sitting up straight. You know I don't permit slouchers in my class."

It was a mistake to have told the class that Miss Wilson would be back on Monday, that only a few hours of the terrible reign of Miss Awful were left to endure. Even before lunch recess, a certain spirit of challenge and defiance had infiltrated into the room. Postures were still erect but not quite as erect. Tommy Miller dropped his pencil case on the floor and did not request permission to pick it up.

"Ahhh, so what," he mumbled when Miss Orville remonstrated[15] with him.

---

15. **remonstrated** (ri män′ strāt′ id): argued.

353

"What did you say?" she demanded, drawing herself up.

"I said, so what," Tommy Miller answered, returning her stare without distress.

Roger thought that was neat of Tommy, talking fresh like that. He was surprised, too, because Miss Awful didn't yell at Tommy or anything. A funny look came into her eyes, he noticed, and she just went on with the geography lesson. And when Tommy dropped his pencil case again and picked it up without asking, she said nothing. Roger wasn't so certain that Tommy should have dropped the pencil case a second time. The lunch bell rang then, and he piled out of the classroom with the others, not bothering to wait for permission.

At lunch in the basement cafeteria, the third grade talked of nothing except how to get even with Miss Awful. The recommendations showed daring and imagination.

"We could beat her up," Joey Lambert suggested. "We could wait at the corner till she goes by and throw rocks at her."

"We'd get arrested," Walter Meade pointed out.

"Better idea," said Bruce Reeves. "We could go upstairs to the classroom before she gets back and tie a string in front of the door. She'd trip and break her neck."

"She's old," Roger Clark protested. "We can't hurt her like that. She's too old."

It was one of the girls, actually, who thought of the plant. "That dopey old plant she's always fussing over," piped Midge Fuller. "We could rip off all the dopey leaves. That'd show her."

Roger pushed back his chair and stood up from the table. "We don't want to do that," he said, not understanding why he objected. It was a feeling inside he couldn't explain . . . "Aw, let's forget about it," he said. "Let's call it quits."

"The plant, the plant," Midge Fuller squealed, clapping her hands.

Postures were a good deal worse when the third grade reconvened after lunch. "Well, you've put in an industrious week, I dare say . . . ," Miss Orville commented. She opened the frayed volume of *Treasure Island* which she had brought from home and turned the pages carefully to Chapter One. "I assume the class is familiar with the tale of young Jim Hawkins, Long John Silver, and the other wonderful characters."

"No, I ain't," said Tommy Miller.

"Ain't. What word is that?"

"It's the word *ain't*," answered Tommy.

"Ain't, ain't," somebody jeered.

Miss Orville lowered the frayed volume. "No, children, you mustn't do this," she said with force. "To attend school is a privilege you must not mock. Can you guess how many thousands of children in the world are denied the gift of schooling?" Her lips quavered. "It is a priceless gift. You cannot permit yourselves to squander a moment of it." She rose from her desk and looked down at the rows of boys and girls. "It isn't enough any longer to accept a gift and make no return for it, not with the world in the shape it's in," she said, spectacles trembling

Words to Know and Use | **recommendation** (rek′ ə mən dā′ shən) *n.* a suggestion

on her bony nose. "The world isn't a play box," she said. "If I have been severe with you this past week, it was for your benefit. The world needs good citizens. If I have helped one of you to grow a fraction of an inch, if just *one* of you—"

She stopped speaking. Her voice faltered, the words dammed up. She was staring at the plant on the windowsill, which she had not noticed before. The stalks twisted up bare and naked where the leaves had been torn off. "You see," Miss Orville said after a moment, going slowly to the windowsill. "You *see* what I am talking about? To be truly educated is to be civilized. Here, you may observe the opposite." Her fingers reached out to the bare stalks. "Violence and destruction . . ." She turned and faced the class, and behind the spectacles her eyes were dim and faded. "Whoever is responsible, I beg of you only to be sorry," she said. When she returned to her desk, her back was straighter than ever, but it seemed to take her longer to cover the distance.

At the close of class that afternoon, there was no forming of lines. Miss Orville merely dismissed the boys and girls and did not leave her desk. The children ran out, some in regret, some silent, others cheerful and scampering. Only Roger Clark stayed behind.

He stood at the windows, plucking at the naked plant on the sill. Miss Orville was emptying the desk of her possessions, books, pads, a folder of maps. "These are yours, I believe," she said to Roger. In her hands were the water pistol, the baseball cards, the spool of string. "Here, take them," she said.

Roger went to the desk. He stuffed the toys in his coat pocket without paying attention to them. He stood at the desk, rubbing his hand up and down his coat.

"Yes?" Miss Orville asked.

Roger stood back, hands at his side, and lifted his head erectly. "Flower," he spelled. "F-l-o-w-e-r." He squared his shoulders and looked at Miss Orville's brimming eyes. "Castle," Roger spelled. "C-a-s-t-l-e."

Then he walked from the room. ❧

INSIGHT

The Spelling Test

KAYE STARBIRD

One morning in a spelling test
The teacher said to Hugh:
"I have a word for you to spell
The word is 'kangaroo.'"
But Hugh was puzzled by the word
Which wasn't one he knew,
So, when he wrote it on the board,
He printed "hannagrue."

"No, No! Go take your seat again,"
The teacher said to Hugh,
"And take along this copy card.
The card says 'kangaroo,'
Then get your pencil out," she said,
"And get your notebook, too.
And write the word a hundred times
And tell me when you're through."

So Hugh did just exactly what
The teacher told him to,
And, when he handed in his work,
The teacher said to Hugh:
"I hope you know your spelling now."
And Hugh said, "Yes, I do,"
Then—walking bravely to the board—
He printed "kannagrue."

Kangaroo sculpture   Louie Pwerle
Collection, Utopia Art   Sydney, Australia.

Responding to Reading

First Impressions

1. How did you feel about Roger's spelling of the words *flower* and *castle* at the end of the story? Describe your feelings in your journal or on a sheet of paper.

Second Thoughts

2. Did your opinion of Miss Orville change as you read the selection? Explain why or why not.

> **Think about**
> • her way of taking charge of the class
> • her life outside school
> • her response to the leafless plant
> • her response to Roger's spelling

3. Why does Roger change his attitude toward Miss Orville?

4. How did you feel about the students' destruction of the plant and their behavior toward Miss Orville on the last day?

5. In your opinion, is Miss Wilson or Miss Orville the better teacher? Why?

> **Think about**
> • how students and parents feel about each teacher
> • how students learn under each teacher

Broader Connections

6. The characters in "Miss Awful" have different attitudes toward school discipline. Think about what you wrote about discipline before reading the story. Has this story changed your opinion about what style of discipline is best? Explain.

Literary Concept: External Conflict

An **external conflict** is a struggle between a character and an outside force, such as another character. A character may face more than one external conflict. For example, Miss Orville is in conflict with the third-grade students. What other external conflicts does Miss Orville face?

*W*riting Options

1. Write a **proposal** to the principal of St. Geoffrey's. Describe recommendations you would make for improving the school.

2. What if Miss Wilson were not able to return the following Monday and Miss Orville came back again as the substitute? Write a **monologue** describing one character's view of the happenings of that day.

3. Write a **dialogue** between Roger and Hugh of "The Spelling Test," the Insight poem on page 356. Have them discuss their feelings about learning to spell.

4. Is Miss Orville really "Miss Awful"? Write a **speech** in which you defend or criticize Miss Orville's teaching. Support your opinion with examples from the story.

*V*ocabulary Practice

Exercise A   In each item below, determine how the words in the capitalized pair are related. Then decide which word from the list best completes the second pair to show a similar relationship.

1. MAMMAL : WHALE :: __?__ : hurricane
2. ORDER : CONFUSION :: __?__ : answer
3. DIFFICULT : EASY :: __?__ : calm
4. HAPPENING : EVENT :: __?__ : suggestion
5. PRIDE : SHAME :: __?__ : obedience
6. WORRY : DISTURB :: __?__ : fire
7. DECAYED : ROTTED :: __?__ : kicked out
8. TERM IN OFFICE : PRESIDENT :: __?__ : king
9. THOUGHTFULLY: CONSIDERATELY :: __?__ : joyfully
10. PRETEND : IMAGINE :: __?__ : interrupt

> *Words to Know and Use*
> ──────
> **catastrophe**
> **defiance**
> **discharge**
> **ecstatically**
> **evicted**
> **interject**
> **query**
> **rambunctious**
> **recommendation**
> **reign**

Exercise B   In small groups follow these steps.

1. Skim through the selection for additional unfamiliar words; make a list of all of these words.

2. Ask members of the group to define any words on the list that they know. Write down the definitions.

3. In a dictionary look up words that no one knows or that no one can define with certainty.

4. Add the new vocabulary words and their definitions to your personal word lists or write them in your journals.

Poetry

Life Doesn't Frighten Me
MAYA ANGELOU

74th Street
MYRA COHN LIVINGSTON

Examine What You Know

In your opinion, what are some attitudes a person needs to face life's fears and challenges successfully? Draw a priority scale like the one below. Number the attitudes in order of their importance to you, with number 1 being the most important.

1.

2.

3.

4.

5.

Expand Your Knowledge

In these two poems, the speakers face different kinds of fears and challenges. Each poem has a slightly different tone. **Tone** is the attitude a writer, in this case a poet, has toward a subject. The tone of a poem might be humorous, serious, angry, or sentimental. In these poems, the writers reveal their attitudes through their word choice and repetition of certain words and phrases.

Write Before You Read

■ *Author biographies on Extend page*

In your journal, write about a time you tried to overcome your fear of something or to master a challenging skill. As you read the poems, compare your feelings and experiences with the speakers'.

Life Doesn't Frighten Me

MAYA ANGELOU

Shadows on the wall
Noises down the hall
Life doesn't frighten me at all
Bad dogs barking loud
5 Big ghosts in a cloud
Life doesn't frighten me at all.

Mean old Mother Goose
Lions on the loose
They don't frighten me at all
10 Dragons breathing flame
On my counterpane[1]
That doesn't frighten me at all.

I go boo
Make them shoo
15 I make fun
Way they run
I won't cry
So they fly
I just smile
20 They go wild
Life doesn't frighten me at all.

Tough guys in a fight
All alone at night
Life doesn't frighten me at all.
25 Panthers in the park
Strangers in the dark
No, they don't frighten me at all.

---

1. counterpane: bedspread; quilt.

That new classroom where
Boys all pull my hair
30 (Kissy little girls
With their hair in curls)
They don't frighten me at all.

Don't show me frogs and snakes
And listen for my scream,
35 If I'm afraid at all
It's only in my dreams.

I've got a magic charm
That I keep up my sleeve,
I can walk the ocean floor
40 And never have to breathe.

Life doesn't frighten me at all
Not at all
Not at all.
Life doesn't frighten me at all.

Responding to Reading

First Impressions of "Life Doesn't Frighten Me"

1. What are your impressions of the speaker of this poem? Describe your impressions in your journal or on a sheet of paper.

Second Thoughts on "Life Doesn't Frighten Me"

2. Do the speaker's methods of taking charge seem effective to you? Why or why not?

3. Do you think the speaker is as fearless as she says she is? Explain your thoughts.

> **Think about**
> • the **tone** of the poem
> • your feelings about overcoming fear

4. How do the fears or challenges faced by the speaker compare with the fears or challenges you face?

74th Street

MYRA COHN LIVINGSTON

Hey, this little kid gets roller skates.
She puts them on.
She stands up and almost
flops over backwards.
5   She sticks out a foot like
she's going somewhere and
falls down and
smacks her hand. She
grabs hold of a step to get up and
10   sticks out the other foot and
slides about six inches and
falls and
skins her knee.

And then, you know what?

15   She brushes off the dirt and the
blood and puts some
spit on it and then
sticks out the other foot

again.

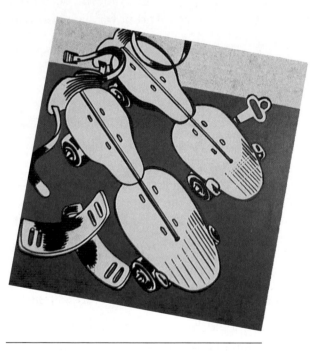

ROLLERSKATES   © Roy Lichtenstein   Courtesy of the artist.

E X P L A I N

Responding to Reading

First Impressions of "74th Street"

1. How did this poem make you feel? Write your feelings in your journal.

Second Thoughts on "74th Street"

2. How do you think the speaker feels about the skater?

> **Think about**
> - the speaker's **tone**
> - the **word choice** at the end of the poem

3. Predict what kind of person the skater will be when she gets older.

Comparing the Poems

4. Which poem do you think has more to say about how a person should respond to the fears and challenges of life?

Literary Concept: Refrain

A **refrain** consists of a word, line, or group of lines that is repeated regularly in a poem or song. Such repetition is often used to emphasize the main idea and create rhythm. What is the refrain in "Life Doesn't Frighten Me"? How does the refrain help you understand or visualize the speaker?

Writing Options

1. Imagine that each year a Try, Try Again Award is presented to individuals who show determination. Write an **award nomination** for the skater in "74th Street."

2. Write a short **profile** of the speaker of "Life Doesn't Frighten Me" for a magazine article about how young people take charge of fears and challenges.

3. Create a **free-verse poem** about a fear or challenge you have overcome. As a guide to the attitudes that helped you, use the priority scale you made on page 359.

4. Write roller-skating **instructions** that the skater in "74th Street" could use before her next attempt at skating.

*O*ptions for Learning

1 • **On the Roll Again** Practice and perform a pantomime of "74th Street." Have a classmate read the poem as you act it out.

2 • **Choral Reading** Working in a small group, present the Angelou poem to your class. Capture the speaker's tone with your voice and hand gestures.

*M*aya Angelou 1928–

The life of Maya Angelou reflects her belief that "all things are possible for a human being, and I don't think there's anything in the world I can't do." Angelou grew up in the racially divided town of Stamps, Arkansas. In 1940 she moved away from home and finished high school. Over the next three decades, Angelou became a dancer, singer, composer, stage and screen performer, playwright, writer, poet, editor, and teacher.

I Know Why the Caged Bird Sings, her first autobiographical work, earned a National Book Award nomination in 1970. Angelou is best known for this book and has continued her life story in four more books. A collection of her poems received a Pulitzer Prize nomination in 1972. Angelou was honored in 1993 by being asked to read an original poem at the presidential inauguration of Bill Clinton.

*M*yra Cohn Livingston 1926–

Myra Cohn Livingston has spent most of her career writing poetry and helping young people learn to write. Livingston says she had an "ideal, happy childhood" while growing up in Omaha, Nebraska. She lived on a block with many children, with whom she would "make mud pies, put on plays, swing into the apple tree, [and] play games each night in the empty lot after supper."

Livingston has kept a journal since she was ten years old. Describing it, she says, "All of the feelings and observations I have go into that journal. Some eventuallly come out as poems, others are snatches of conversations or ideas that I may use someday."

Livingston has published many volumes of her own poetry, including *O Sliver of Liver.* She has also edited collections of poetry written by others.

Nonfiction

from Sweet Summer

BEBE MOORE CAMPBELL

Examine What You Know

In this excerpt from an autobiography, Bebe Moore Campbell describes what it was like to be a sixth grader affected by the events of the early 1960s. In your journal, jot down some big issues or events that concern people today. In a few sentences explain how one of these issues or events has touched your life or affected your family.

Expand Your Knowledge

A major issue of the 1950s and 1960s was the struggle of African Americans for civil rights. Among these basic rights were the right to eat at any lunch counter, the right to attend any public school, and the right to vote. Civil-rights groups, led by Dr. Martin Luther King, Jr., and others, relied on nonviolent forms of protest—marches, boycotts, and sit-ins—to achieve their goal of equality for all U.S. citizens. Daily news reports showed violent attacks against the protesters. The Civil Rights Acts of 1964 and 1968 and the Voting Rights Act of 1965 were direct results of the civil-rights movement.

Enrich Your Reading

Exploring Motives   The reason a person does something or acts in a certain way is called a **motive.** The motives of the people in this selection are based on personal feelings and reactions to the civil-rights movement. After reading, copy and complete three or more sets of boxes like the ones below. In each set of boxes, describe one action presented in the selection and the possible motive or motives behind this action.

Action	Motive(s)
Bebe pretends to say the Pledge of Allegiance	anger over the way African Americans are treated

■ *Author biography on Extend page*

from *Sweet Summer*

BEBE MOORE CAMPBELL

This selection is a chapter from Bebe Moore Campbell's autobiography, Sweet Summer. *As a child, Bebe spent each summer with her wheelchair-bound father and her grandma Mary in a small town in North Carolina. At the start of each school year, she returned north to Philadelphia, Pennsylvania, and her life with her mother, grandmother Nana, cousin Michael, and neighbor Pete.*

The blare of Monday's late bell jolted the last vestiges of torpor from my bones. In September I had entered 5A. In January 1961 I skipped 5B and went to the sixth grade. Most of my fifth-grade classmates accompanied me to Miss Tracy's room. The Philadelphia school system, in order to end midyear graduations, had abandoned the A/B grade levels. In January most students were skipped into the next grade, although some were retained.

Miss Tracy nodded her head and held out her hands, letting her palms face her students; she drew her hands upward. I rose with the rest of the class and placed my hand over my heart, shifting my weight from foot to foot and staring straight ahead at the bulletin boards, which were still covered with red and green construction-paper Santa Clauses and Christmas trees. I acted as if I were speaking, but when the rest of the class said, "I pledge allegiance to the flag . . ." I only mouthed the words. Months before, Reverend Lewis had told the congregation that Negroes in the South were being beaten by white people because they wanted to integrate lunch counters at drugstores. A few weeks earlier, while Mommy, Nana, Michael, and I were sitting in the living room watching television, the show was interrupted; the announcer showed colored people trying to march and white policemen coming after them with giant German shepherds.

When did this take place? *question*

"Now you know that ain't right," Nana had said angrily.

The day after I saw that news bulletin, I was saying the Pledge of Allegiance in class, and right in the middle of it my head started hurting so bad I thought it was gonna fall off, and I felt so mad I wanted to punch

---

Words to Know and Use | **integrate** (in′ tə grāt′) *v.* to make available to people of all races

Civil-rights protesters in
Albany, Georgia, in 1962.

somebody. I didn't want to say the pledge, that was the problem. I was afraid not to say anything, so I just kept opening my mouth, but nothing came out. After that I only pretended to say the words. If they were gonna sic dogs on Negroes, then I wasn't gonna say some pledge, and I wasn't gonna sing "The Star-Spangled Banner" neither. Not for them, I wasn't.

Sixth grade was rough. In the first place, I didn't like Miss Tracy. None of my friends liked her either. She was the meanest teacher I ever had, so full of rules and ultimatums. No talking. No erasures on spelling tests. No going to the bathroom except at recess. No this, no that. Always use her name when addressing her. No, Miss Frankenstein. Yes, Miss Frankenstein. She sent Linda out of the room just because she said "Excuse me" to me when she dropped my spelling paper. I mean . . . really. I could see Linda through the small glass window in

the door, standing outside in the hall crying while we graded the spelling papers. Causing my best friend's tears was enough for me to start hating Miss Tracy, but I had other reasons.

It was a year of hot breathing and showdowns at Logan. We were sixth graders, on our way out the door and feeling our oats every step of the way. Some of the boys began to sound a little bit like men, their upper lips darkened and their chests expanded. Among the girls, an epidemic of hard little bumps popped out on our chests. First Carol, then Linda, then me. We were embarrassed; we were proud. But the little band of Negroes at Logan felt something more than puberty. Fierce new rhythms—bam de bam de *bam bam bam!*—were welling up inside us. We were figuring things out. At home in the living room with our parents, we watched the nightly news—the dogs, the hoses, and nightsticks against black flesh—and we seethed; we brought our anger to school. The rumor flew around North Philly, West Philly, and Germantown[1] that Elvis Presley had said, "All colored people can do for me is buy my records and shine my shoes." In the schoolyard and the classroom we saw the sea of white surrounding us, and we drew in closer. We'd been fooling ourselves. It didn't matter how capable we were: it was *their* school, *their* neighborhood, *their* country, *their* planet. We were the outsiders, and they looked down on us. Our bitterness exploded like an overdue time bomb.

"Miss Tracy doesn't like Negroes," I announced to Carol and Linda when we sat under the poplar tree at recess.

Linda got excited. "How do you know that?"

"You ever notice how she never picks us to do anything? And she's always putting our names on the board for talking, and she doesn't ever put David's name on the board, and all he does is run his mouth and eat boogers."

"And try to act like he's Elvis Presley," Carol added. "Miss Tracy's always calling us 'you people.' And remember that time she sent Wallace to the office when that white boy stepped on his foot?"

"That doesn't mean she doesn't like Negroes," Linda said doubtfully. Carol and I looked at each other and shook our heads. What a baby.

"Well, what does it mean, then?" I asked Linda sarcastically.

"It means she doesn't like the Negroes in her room," Carol said dryly.

The skirmishes were slight affairs, noth-ing anyone could really put a finger on. A black boy pushed a white boy in line. A black girl muttered "cracker"[2] when a white girl touched her accidentally. One afternoon when David was walking past our tree, Carol yelled, "Elvis Presley ain't doing nothing but imitating colored people. And he can't even sing." David looked at her in astonishment. She put her hands on her hips and declared, "I ain't buying his records, and I ain't shining his shoes neither!"

Something hot and electric was in the air.

"Boys and girls, you're growing up," Miss Tracy said to the class one afternoon. Yes, we were. Something hot and electric was in the air.

The winter before I graduated from Logan Elementary, there was a disturbance in my class. Miss Tracy was absent, and we had a substitute, a small, pretty woman named Mrs. Brown. She had taught us before, and all of us liked her because if we finished our work, she would let us play hangman. We were spelling that day, going through our list of words in the usual, bor-ing way. Mrs. Brown picked someone, and the person had to go to the blackboard and write a sentence using the spelling word. We

---

1. **North Philly, West Philly, and Germantown:** sections of the city of Philadelphia, Pennsylvania.
2. **"cracker":** an insulting slang term for a poor white person living in a rural Southern state.

Words to Know and Use

368

skirmish (skʉr′ mish) *n.* a minor conflict

had three more words to go, and I'd already been picked, so my interest in the whole process was waning. Hurry up, I thought. I was only half listening when I heard Mrs. Brown ask Clarence, who was wearing his everyday uniform, a suit and a tie, to stop talking. Clarence turned a little in his chair and frowned. He continued to talk.

"Did you hear me, Clarence?" Mrs. Brown asked.

"No."

Everybody turned to stare at Clarence and to check him for any outward signs of mental instability. Nobody talked back to teachers at Logan. Mrs. Brown coughed for a full minute, then stood up and asked Clarence to go to the board. Her voice was sharp. Clarence slouched in his seat. "No," he said almost lazily. Nobody breathed. Mrs. Brown said he would have to go to the principal's office if he wouldn't behave. All of us in class shuddered as if we were one body. Was Clarence crazy? I thought of my own dark trek to the principal's office. Nobody wanted to visit Jennie G. Clarence glared at Mrs. Brown so forcefully that she turned away from him. Clarence said slowly, "Later for the principal. Later for you. Later for all y'all white people. Send me to the principal. That don't cut no cheese with me."

Everything happened fast after that, after it was clear that Clarence had lost his mind. Mrs. Brown quickly dispatched one of the boys to bring Mr. Singer, who appeared moments later at the door. Mrs. Brown conferred with Mr. Singer hastily, and then he took Clarence by the arm and ushered him out of the room. Clarence did a diddy-bop hoodlum stroll[3] and showed not one bit of remorse as he left.

As soon as he was gone, Mrs. Brown leaned back in her chair and put the sides of her hands to her temples. The small diamond on her finger glittered in the sunlight. "Why would he say such awful things to me? Why?" she demanded, looking at the class. "Why?" she repeated, her eyes now focusing on every dark face in the class as if we alone knew the answer. Everyone was looking at Linda, Carol, Wallace, and me, I realized. And they were . . . scared. Their eyes asked: Are you like Clarence? Are you angry too? Mrs. Brown tried to start the lesson again, but nobody was concentrating. Linda, Carol, and I looked at each other cautiously. It was silently agreed: we wouldn't explain anything.

"That nigger's[4] crazy!" Wallace whispered as we filed outside for recess. There was no more that could be said.

In the schoolyard, in our compact circle, we whooped like renegades. "He sure told Mrs. Brown off!" we exclaimed, falling all over each other in our excitement. "Later for all y'all white people." We repeated that single line, giggling as we slapped each other's thighs. I thought not of the dogs and the nightsticks but of the ponytails and poodle

---

3. **diddy-bop hoodlum stroll:** a rhythmic walk, the head moving forward with each step, used by some street-gang members looking for a fight.

4. **nigger:** *slang,* a derogatory name for an African American. The word is considered to be extremely offensive, even though it is sometimes used by African Americans themselves.

Words to Know and Use

instability (in' stə bil' ə tē) n. a state of being out of control
shudder (shud' ər) v. to tremble violently
remorse (ri môrs') n. regret for a wrongdoing
renegade (ren' ə gād') n. a person who rejects lawful behavior

Bebe and her father.

skirts on *Bandstand,* bobbing and swishing off beat, twisting and turning so happily. Carol, Linda, and I nodded at each other. The single vein of anger that was growing in us all had been acknowledged this day. We had a crazy nigger in our midst, close enough for comfort.

Clarence, of course, was suspended. A much more subdued boy returned to school, flanked by his mother and father. The grapevine[5] said that Jennie G. had said sternly to his parents, "We will not tolerate that kind of rude, uncivilized behavior at Logan. Is that clear?" When it was all over, Clarence had to apologize to Mrs. Brown and tell her he didn't know what on earth had gotten into him. But I knew.

I turned eleven in February. My father drove to Philadelphia to celebrate, and he took my mother and me to dinner at Horn & Hardart because the aisles were wide enough for his wheelchair. After we ate, I got behind Daddy and pushed him, and we all went around the corner to the movies. The usher stared when Daddy came in and said, "Now you aren't gonna block up the aisle, are you?"

Mommy looked straight ahead past the man. Daddy stuck out his chin a little, laughed and said, "Where would you like me to sit, mister?" I could tell he was mad. We ended up sitting in the back. Daddy hopped into the aisle chair and folded up his chair and leaned it against the outside of his seat. I sat next to him, and every time some-

What was really happening with Clarence?

---

5. **grapevine:** an informal way of spreading news from person to person.

thing funny or exciting happened, I squeezed Daddy's hand until I was sure he wasn't angry anymore.

We came straight home after the movie. After my father parked the car in front of our house, my parents handed me a small box. Inside was a thin Timex watch with a black strap. I gasped with happiness and excitement. I was sitting between my mother and father, admiring my watch, basking in their <u>adoration</u>. I'd forgotten all about the usher. This is the way it should always be, I thought. When my mother said it was time for us to go in, I said, "Kiss Daddy."

Mommy paused for a moment. My father looked awkward. He leaned toward my mother. She pecked him on the cheek.

"No. Not like that," I chided them. "Kiss on the lips."

They obeyed me and gave each other another brief, chaste peck. Why couldn't they kiss better than that? Mr. Johnston wasn't my mother's boyfriend anymore. He hadn't been around for several months. Why couldn't she love my daddy again? My mother and father didn't look at each other as they moved away.

I wanted magic from them, a kiss that would ignite their love, reunite all three of us. As my father drove off I looked down at my watch and stared at the minute hand ticking away.

Miss Tracy worked our butts off until just before graduation. She assigned us a health report and an arithmetic project, and we had to write a creative story using all the spelling words we'd had since January. On top of everything else, she gave us a book report.

Miss Tracy took our class to the school library and told us to find the book we wanted to do a report on and to make sure we told her what it was. I turned the library inside out trying to find a book I liked. The problem was, I'd read all the good stuff. So I asked Miss Tracy if I could get my book from the public library; she said that was fine with her.

Michael, Mommy, and I went to the downtown library one Sunday after church. I searched in the young adult section for an interesting title. Then I went to where the new books were displayed and picked up one with a picture of an earnest-looking black boy in the foreground and a small town in the background. I started leafing through some of the pages, and I couldn't put it down. The book was about Negroes trying to win their rights in a small Southern town and how they struggled against bad white people and were helped by good ones. There weren't any bad Negroes, and that fit my mood perfectly. As I was reading it, the thought hit me instantly: Miss Tracy wouldn't want me to do my report on *South Town*. She'd tell me it wasn't "suitable." I decided I wouldn't tell Miss Tracy; I'd just do the report.

The day I stood in front of the class to give my report, my mouth was dry and my hands were moist. "My book is called *South Town,*" I said, holding the book up so everybody could see the cover. The whole class got quiet as they studied the black boy's serious face; Miss Tracy's head jerked up

371

straight. "This was a very exciting, dramatic book, and I liked it a lot because every summer I live in a place exactly like the town that was described in this book," I said, my voice rising. I had my entire book report memorized, and after a while everything came easily. I walked across the room, raising my hand for dramatic <u>flair</u>, feeling like a bold renegade telling my people's struggle to the world. I whispered when I described a sad part of the book. I finished with a flourish. "I recommend this book for anyone interested in the struggle for Negroes to gain equal rights in America. Thank you."

As soon as I sat down, I could feel Miss Tracy's breath on my neck. "You didn't ask my permission to do that report," she said. Her hazel eyes were as cold as windowpanes in February. I had forgotten how terrifying Miss Tracy's rage could be. What if she gave me an F? Or sent me to the principal's office? Oh, Lordy.

"I'm sorry," I said, my voice drained of dramatic flair. I didn't feel like such a bold renegade anymore. I was scared.

Miss Tracy turned away without saying a word. Three days later she returned the reports. At the bottom in the right-hand corner of mine, there was a small B. Emblazoned across the top in fierce red ink were the words: "Learn to follow directions."

I took the report home and gave it to my mother, who, of course, asked, "What directions didn't you follow?" I told her the whole story, then I held my breath. The last thing I wanted to hear was, "Bebe, I'm disappointed in you." Mommy didn't say that; she just looked at Miss Tracy's comments again. Then she said, "Sometimes you eat the bear; sometimes the bear eats you," which sounded kinda strange coming from her because Mommy wasn't one for a lot of down-home sayings. She put the report in the bottom drawer of her bureau, where she kept my school papers and grades. "Don't worry about it," Mommy said.

Three weeks later I sat on the stage of the school auditorium in the green chiffon dress my mother made me, underneath it a brand-new Littlest Angel bra identical to the one Linda's mother had bought her. The straps cut into my shoulders, but my mind was too crowded with thoughts for me to feel any pain. As Nana, Mommy, Michael, and Pete watched, I walked across the stage to receive my certificate. Pete took pictures. I wanted my father to be there, but at least I could show him the photos.

Two weeks later I kissed Mommy, Nana, and Michael goodbye and climbed into my father's newest <u>acquisition</u>, a blue Impala convertible. "BebebebebebebebeMoore," Daddy sang out when he saw me, then, "I guess you're getting too big for that stuff, huh?" His eyes were questioning, searching. I didn't know what to say, afraid that if I said yes, Daddy would never again make a song of my name, and if I said no, he'd think of me as a baby forever. So I leaned my head back against the seat and smiled. The wind was in my face, and I was heading toward a North Carolina summer that would deliver a heartbreak and a promise. ❧

Words to Know and Use

flair (fler) *n.* a sense of style
acquisition (ak′ wə zish′ ən) *n.* something that has been obtained

*R*esponding to Reading

First Impressions

1. How did you react to the experiences described by Bebe Moore Campbell? Jot down your reactions in your journal or notebook.

Second Thoughts

2. What kind of person is Bebe?

Think about
- her reactions to attacks on civil-rights workers
- her reaction to Clarence's outburst
- her birthday celebration with her divorced parents

3. Did you agree or disagree with Bebe's way of taking charge of the book-report assignment? Explain.

Think about
- the kind of book Bebe chooses
- whether Miss Tracy would have given Bebe permission
- Mrs. Moore's reaction

4. How is Bebe's giving the book report similar to and different from Clarence's outburst?

5. Look over your chart of actions and **motives** on page 365. How did considering the motive behind a person's action affect your feelings about him or her?

Broader Connections

6. Bebe keeps looking for the "magic" that will reunite her divorced parents. In your opinion should divorced parents celebrate occasions like their children's birthdays together? How can divorced parents be on friendly terms without raising their children's hopes of a reunion?

*L*iterary Concept: Autobiography

An **autobiography** is a story a person writes about his or her own life. It is usually told from a first-person point of view, using the first-person pronouns *I, we, me,* and *us.* Since the writer is writing about himself or herself, an autobiography can provide information that only the writer knows. From reading the selection, what do you learn about Campbell that you might not have learned if someone else had told her story?

Writing Options

1. Imagine Bebe's mother at a parent-teacher conference with Miss Tracy after Bebe's book report. Write the **dialogue** that might take place.

2. Which of the characters in this sub-unit is the most successful in taking charge of situations? Write an **evaluation,** ranking the characters according to how effective you think they are and explaining which, in your opinion, handles his or her situation best.

3. Review the story "Miss Awful" on page 343 or "Eleven" on page 68. Write an **essay** comparing and contrasting Bebe's feelings about Miss Tracy with Roger's or Rachel's feelings about a teacher.

4. How much progress has been made in civil rights since the 1960s? Compare the issues of the 1960s with those of today. Give your opinion in a **television editorial.**

Vocabulary Practice

Exercise   On your paper, write the word from the list that best completes each sentence.

1. A 1954 Supreme Court decision said that states should _?_ their public schools.

2. Arkansas governor Orval Faubus showed no _?_ about refusing to obey a federal order allowing African Americans to attend Little Rock Central High School.

3. At any newly integrated school, a _?_, with name-calling or pushing and shoving among students, could break out.

4. School officials would _?_ children from school for disorderly behavior.

5. A nonviolent civil-rights protester who was white was often treated as a _?_ by white Southerners.

6. Watching 1960s television documentaries showing police dogs attacking protesters might make you _?_ .

7. The 1965 riot in the Watts section of Los Angeles revealed the _?_ of the times.

8. The _?_ of equal treatment under the law was a goal of the civil-rights movement.

9. Martin Luther King, Jr., and Malcolm X were two leaders who had a dramatic _?_ for public speaking.

10. Civil-rights leaders felt the hate of some people and the _?_ of others.

> *Words to Know and Use*
>
> ___
>
> **acquisition**
> **adoration**
> **flair**
> **instability**
> **integrate**
> **remorse**
> **renegade**
> **shudder**
> **skirmish**
> **suspend**

Options for Learning

1 • **Form a Line** As a class, prepare a time line of the civil-rights movement from 1955 to 1965. Each student should then select a subject (a person or an event) from the time line to research independently. Present your individual oral reports in the correct time order.

2 • **January of 1961** Search library microfilms for newspapers from January 1961. Photocopy news items that you think might have affected young Bebe. Then create a "Day in the Life of Bebe" collage that includes parts of the news items and reflects your own feelings about the issues of that time.

3 • **Following Directions** As Mrs. Moore looks over Bebe's book report, she asks, "What directions didn't you follow?" Improvise the scene in which Bebe discusses her grade with her mother.

4 • **"We Shall Overcome"** Explore the origins of the civil-rights movement's freedom songs. Play recordings of or sing some of the songs, and discuss how they might have encouraged those who struggled for freedom.

FACT FINDER HISTORY

What African-American woman was arrrested in 1955 for refusing to give up her seat on a bus in Montgomery, Alabama?

Bebe Moore Campbell
1950–

The full title of Bebe Moore Campbell's autobiography is *Sweet Summer: Growing Up With and Without My Dad*. The cherished daughter of divorced parents, young Bebe had a life divided between two places that seemed worlds apart.

Summer was sweet because it was a time she grew close to her father in North Carolina. She spent the rest of the year in the city of Philadelphia, Pennsylvania, where her mother stressed the importance of a good education. Campbell says, "I had much to be proud of—my father, my mother, my family, the way I grew up. Things that might have destroyed me didn't, because my family had empowered me. There's strength in that which can help you rise above circumstance."

Campbell attended the University of Pittsburgh and went on to work as a teacher and a writer. In addition to producing articles for magazines, she has written two other books. She is currently working as a journalist and living in Los Angeles with her husband, daughter, and stepson.

PERSUASIVE WRITING

USE PERSUASIVE
WRITING FOR
debate notes
advertisements
letters to the editor
petitions
opinion papers

From fighting toxic waste to expressing feelings about equal rights, the people in this subunit take charge. Far from being quiet bystanders, they are *doers* who expect results. What local issue do you have strong feelings about? What should be done about the situation? In this workshop, you will plan, organize, and write a **brochure** that deals with a community issue or problem. In your brochure you will use **persuasive writing** to convince readers that your way of solving the problem is the best way.

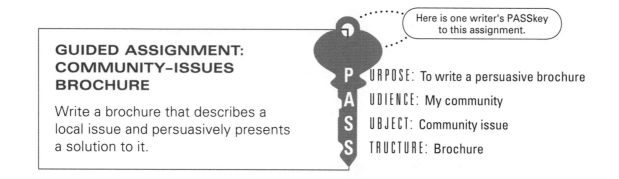

Here is one writer's PASSkey to this assignment.

GUIDED ASSIGNMENT:
COMMUNITY–ISSUES
BROCHURE

Write a brochure that describes a local issue and persuasively presents a solution to it.

PURPOSE: To write a persuasive brochure

AUDIENCE: My community

SUBJECT: Community issue

STRUCTURE: Brochure

STUDENT MODEL

Before you write, read how one student responded to the assignment.

▶

The writer starts by defining the issue.

▶

> ### Let's Limit, Not Ban, Skateboard Use
> #### by Brent Pappas
>
> #### The Skateboard Issue
>
> A number of adults in Bingham have been complaining about kids riding skateboards on the sidewalks downtown. They say that skateboarders interfere with pedestrian traffic and sometimes even sideswipe pedestrians. No one has bothered to talk to the people causing the problem--the skateboarders themselves. Instead, the town leaders are sidestepping kids to make an ordinance banning all skateboarding in downtown Bingham.

There Is a Better Solution

The proposed "No Skateboard" ordinance is too extreme and definitely unfair to kids. After all, Pondview Park, the biggest park in Bingham, is in the heart of downtown. Pondview is also the favorite park of the skateboarders. The solution to the problem is simple: Allow skateboarding in Pondview Park but don't allow it on downtown sidewalks. Those who skateboard where it is not permitted would be grounded. They would be required to turn over their skateboards for at least one week to recreation department officials.

The Pros Outnumber the Cons

Allowing skateboards in limited areas is a good idea because everyone wins. Adults downtown can keep walking, free from the fear of being run down by a crazy skateboarder. Kids who love skateboarding can keep rolling in the main park downtown.

Those who use the park or bike paths might say they don't want skateboards in their way, either. However, the paths are wide enough for bikers, joggers, and skateboarders. The paths are safer than narrow, crowded sidewalks. Skateboarders in these areas should yield to pedestrians and behave responsibly, as bikers are expected to do.

How Can You Help?

With your support, these ideas can be put to work. Please write to Mayor Nora Flannery. Speak out against the "No Skateboard" ordinance and let her know you are in favor of limited skateboarding downtown. A big public response could lead to a town meeting, where both sides of the issue can be heard. By working together, we can have the best of both worlds.

◀ Notice how headings set off main points and make the brochure easier to read.

◀ Brent proposes a way to solve the skateboarding issue.

◀ Brent argues in favor of his idea. Notice how he appeals to people on both sides of the issue.

◀ The writer addresses possible doubts and tries to put them to rest.

◀ The conclusion urges readers to take specific action.

Prewrite and Explore

WRITER'S CHOICE
Read the Letters to the Editor column in your newspaper for a week. Jot down possible issues that you might address.

1 **Take on an issue** Think about problems or needs in your neighborhood, town, or school. Is your local park unsafe or unclean? Do kids in your school need extra tutoring? Make a list of community issues like these. Then choose the issue that you care most about and want to help solve.

2 **Find a solution** Brainstorm for ways to solve the issue. List as many solutions as you can. Then settle on the plan that will work best. Also think about what practical actions you want your readers to take.

STUDENT MODEL

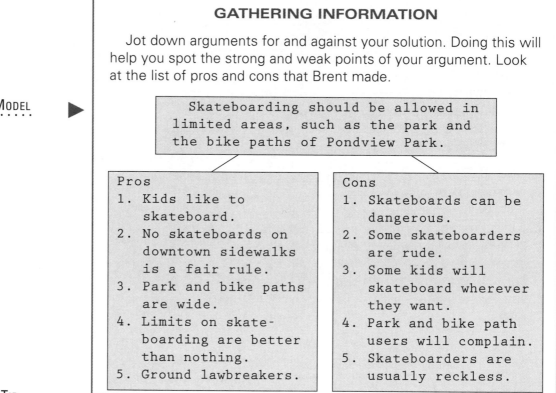

GATHERING INFORMATION

Jot down arguments for and against your solution. Doing this will help you spot the strong and weak points of your argument. Look at the list of pros and cons that Brent made.

> Skateboarding should be allowed in limited areas, such as the park and the bike paths of Pondview Park.

Pros	Cons
1. Kids like to skateboard.	1. Skateboards can be dangerous.
2. No skateboards on downtown sidewalks is a fair rule.	2. Some skateboarders are rude.
3. Park and bike paths are wide.	3. Some kids will skateboard wherever they want.
4. Limits on skateboarding are better than nothing.	4. Park and bike path users will complain.
5. Ground lawbreakers.	5. Skateboarders are usually reckless.

COMPUTER TIP
Experiment with these formatting features:
• margins • type styles
• italics and boldface
If you add graphics, remember that too much variety can be distracting.

3 **Sketch out the brochure** Think about how you want your brochure to look. Would it look better on a-folded or an unfolded sheet of paper? What size and color should it be? On a piece of paper, sketch a design for your brochure. Aim for a design that will not cost much to produce—but one that will attract and hold your readers' attention.

Draft and Discover

1 Organize your draft Present your ideas clearly and logically. You may want to organize your arguments from the least persuasive to the most persuasive. Another way is to first attack opposing views, then present alternatives.

2 Write persuasively Use solid facts and persuasive language to get your message across. Choose words that strongly express feelings. In the excerpt notice how the words in italics show a sense of alarm.

> Around the world, people are becoming aware of the *urgent* need to stop *destroying* the environment and start restoring it— now, *before it is too late.*

◀ **LITERARY MODEL** ·················
from *Save the Earth*
by Betty Miles

Revise Your Writing

1 Read with a disbelieving eye Imagine that you are the kind of person who always has a thousand reasons for why any new idea won't work. What would this person say after reading your draft? Note how Brent used this process to improve his writing.

Before Allowing skateboards in limited areas is a good idea because it just is. Besides, kids really enjoy skateboarding.

After Allowing skateboards in limited areas is a good idea because everyone wins. Adults downtown can keep walking, free from the fear of being run down by a crazy skateboarder. Kids who love skateboarding can keep rolling in the main park downtown.

◀ **STUDENT MODEL** ·················

2 Use a peer reader Review your draft, then ask a classmate to read it and respond. Use the following questions.

Revision Questions	
For You	**For a Peer Reader**
1. How clearly did I describe the issue or problem?	1. Did I convince you that my solution is best?
2. Do I address both sides of the issue?	2. Which argument is weakest? strongest?
3. Could my solution work?	3. Is my message clear?

◀ **ASK FOR HELP** ·················
Have a classmate write two lists about your draft: a list of reasons why your solution will work and a list of reasons why it won't work. Use these lists to strengthen your arguments.

Proofread

Your community-issues brochure might be widely read, so proofread it carefully. Use a spellchecker if you are writing on a computer. Ask two or three other people to read your brochure for mistakes in spelling, capitalization, grammar, and punctuation.

NEED MORE HELP?
See the Language Workshop that follows (pages 381–383) and Section 10 in the Language Handbook.

THE EDITOR'S EYE: USING COMMAS

When you list three or more items in a series, place a comma after each item except the last.

Commas tell readers when to pause. If you leave out commas, readers could run words together and become confused.

Incorrect	The paths are wide enough for bikers joggers *and* skateboarders.
Correct	The paths are wide enough for bikers**,** joggers**,** *and* skateboarders.

Publish and Present

Here is a suggestion for sharing your work with others.

Spread the Word   Have copies of your brochure printed. Then deliver them door-to-door in your neighborhood, or distribute them at school. You might also leave stacks of brochures in high-traffic locations such as libraries, supermarkets, video stores, and community centers. Be sure to get permission first from those in charge.

Reflect on Your Writing

Answer the questions below. Attach your answers to a copy of your community-issues brochure and place it in your writing portfolio.

FOR YOUR PORTFOLIO ▶

1. What was the reaction to your brochure?
2. What did you learn in this assignment about writing persuasively?

USING COMMAS CORRECTLY

> Use **commas** to separate ideas within a sentence.

Commas That Separate Ideas

To express your ideas clearly, you need to use **commas** in your writing. Commas are like traffic signals in a sentence. They let readers know when to slow down, pause, or shift to a new idea. The following rules will help you use commas correctly and keep your readers on track.

Use a comma to separate the items in a series.

A **series** consists of three or more items. Use a comma after every item in a series except the last.

> Fires, earthquakes, droughts, and floods keep the earth changing.

> We are quickly using up such resources as clean air, fresh water, and forests.

When you combine two sentences with the conjunctions *and, but,* or *or,* use a comma before the conjunctions.

> We are drastically changing the earth. We are also learning to save it.

> We are drastically changing the earth, but we are also learning to save it.

Some sentences can be misunderstood if no commas are used. In these cases, use commas to avoid confusing your readers.

| **Confusing** | On the beach grass protects sand from erosion. |
| **Clear** | On the beach, grass protects sand from erosion. |

| **Confusing** | Blowing hard winds scattered the sand. |
| **Clear** | Blowing hard, winds scattered the sand. |

◄ REMINDERS
Clean air and fresh water are each one item. The words clean and fresh are adjectives. They describe air and water, the nouns they precede.

Exercise 1   Concept Check   Write these sentences. Insert commas where they are needed.

1. Fumes smog and acid rain are killing our trees.
2. We can ignore the problem or we can make a difference.
3. People in Atlanta Chicago and Detroit are volunteering.
4. For each dying tree volunteers plant a new tree.
5. Planting a tree can be fun and it can reduce carbon dioxide in the air.
6. Maples oaks elms and pines are now springing up in cities.
7. Many trees have been planted but there is more work to be done.
8. By the year 2000 400 million to 600 million trees must be planted.

Commas That Set Off Special Elements

> Use commas to set off introductory words, names of persons spoken to, appositives, and the parts of dates and addresses. Use a comma to set off a direct quotation.

LETTER PERFECT
In a friendly letter, use a comma after the greeting and the closing.
    Dear Hector,
    Yours truly,

Use a comma after introductory words such as *yes, no,* or *well* when such words begin a sentence.

Yes, my report is done.   Well, I'll read it aloud.

Use commas to set off the names of persons spoken to directly.

When a name begins or ends a sentence, use one comma. Use two commas when a name appears in the middle of a sentence.

Maia, it's your turn to speak.   Will you go next, Lee?

Sure, Mr. Wilson, I'll be ready.

Use commas to set off an appositive.

An **appositive** follows a noun and renames the noun. An appositive gives more information about a noun.

The book I just read, *Freedom Trail,* tells about Harriet Tubman.

Use commas to separate the parts of a date.

When a date appears in the middle of a sentence, a comma follows the last part of the date.

Summer vacation ends on Tuesday, September 7.

On April 15, 1865, President Lincoln died.

Use a comma to separate the name of a city from the name of a state or country.

When a place name appears in the middle of a sentence, a comma follows the last part of the name.

My grandparents live in Selma, Alabama.

We moved here from Lagos, Nigeria, in 1987.

Use a comma to set off the explanatory words that come before or after a direct quotation.

◀ REMINDER
. . . .
Explanatory words are statements such as *she said*, *Al answered*, and *Mimi explained.*

Ms. Maki said, "Class will begin in five minutes."

"I heard the bell ring," Terry commented.

"Somebody here," the teacher said, "took my chalk."

Exercise 2   Concept Check   Write these sentences. Add commas where they are needed.

1. On December 1 1955 Rosa Parks a seamstress was returning home.
2. In Rosa Parks's home town of Montgomery Alabama African Americans were not allowed to sit in the front section of the bus if a white person asked them to move to the back.
3. Another passenger a white man asked Rosa for her seat.
4. "If you don't move" the driver said "I'll call the police."
5. "Rosa Parks you are under arrest" the police said.
6. On Monday December 4 the African-American community stopped riding Montgomery's buses.
7. Yes Rosa Parks's refusal to give up her seat triggered a new stage in the civil-rights movement.
8. Thank you Rosa Parks for your courage.

DON'T OVERDO IT!
. . . .
Use commas only when you need to separate or set off ideas. Too many commas in a sentence make it harder—not easier—to read.

Exercise 3   Revision Skill   Rewrite the editorial below, adding commas as needed.

On June 15 1993 a recycling center was opened here in Meadville Idaho. Mayor Martin a strong supporter of the center attended the opening ceremony. "Today" he said "we can all start recycling." Well where are you now Mayor Martin? Where are all the kids grown-ups and officials who vowed to use the center? Yes Meadville has a place for recycling but nobody uses it. What will it take to get people to start recycling their cans bottles paper and plastic?

Exercise 4   Revising Your Writing   Reread the brochure you wrote on page 376. Make sure that you have included commas in the right places.

READER'S WORKSHOP

MAIN IDEA

IN OTHER CLASSES

Identifying the main idea is most important when reading nonfiction. Look for the main idea when you read lessons in your social studies and science textbooks.

When you read an article or essay, you need to understand its main idea. Writers of both fiction and nonfiction organize their ideas in paragraphs. A **paragraph** is a group of sentences about one idea. This idea is the **main idea.** The main idea can be stated directly, or it can be implied.

In some paragraphs, the main idea is stated in one sentence called the **topic sentence.** The topic sentence is often the first sentence in a paragraph, but it can be any sentence. Sometimes a writer uses more than one paragraph to develop a main idea. To find the main idea, ask yourself, What is this selection mainly about? Look at the excerpt below from *Save the Earth.* What is the main idea of this paragraph?

LITERARY MODEL

from *Save the Earth* by Betty Miles

> Five years ago, a group of Casa Grande High School students called the United Anglers were determined to bring the steelhead back to Adobe Creek. Working on weekends, they cleared away the tons of garbage, piece by piece. They planted hundreds of young trees to stop shore erosion. They dug out the gravel creekbed to create safe spawning grounds. Finally, they turned an unused greenhouse behind the school into a fish hatchery.

If you said this paragraph is mainly about students' efforts to bring steelhead trout back to Adobe Creek, you have identified its main idea.

Wherever you find a main idea, you should also find **supporting details.** Supporting details give more information about the main idea. In the excerpt from *Save the Earth,* all of the sentences except the first one are supporting details. These sentences tell exactly what the students did—cleared garbage, dug out the creekbed, and so on—to bring steelhead back to Adobe Creek. To find supporting details in a selection, find the details that support and develop the main idea.

Exercise   Exchange the community-issues brochure that you wrote in the Writer's Workshop on page 376 with a classmate. After reading your classmate's brochure, write down its main idea. List any supporting details that you can find.

WHO CAN EXPLAIN?

Who can explain the mysteries of the universe or the human spirit? Some mysteries can be explained by facts, some can be accepted on faith, and others may remain mysterious forever. In fact, some mysteries seem to be never ending. When we solve one, we often find another one following right behind.

Literature provides an opportunity to examine mysteries in depth. Stories, poems, plays, and nonfiction all help us to ask new questions and to explore new answers.

Each of the selections in this subunit presents some kind of mystery about the world or human nature. What makes a person change? Can your senses play tricks on you? Can flowers talk? Is war ever worth its cost in human lives? As you read, see what you can—and cannot—explain.

Fiction

The *Gold Coin*

ALMA FLOR ADA

Examine What You Know

Make a list of the things you treasure. You may want to include things, such as friendship, that cannot be bought with money, as well as things that can. List your treasures in order of importance, with number 1 being the treasure you consider most important. As you read this story, review your list in light of what the main character learns as he pursues the treasure of the gold coin.

Expand Your Knowledge

Alma Flor Ada wrote "The Gold Coin" as a result of meeting a group of poor farm workers. Ada was very impressed by the farm workers—their hard work, their dignity, and the things they considered important. She says, "I felt extremely moved and enriched from knowing them and . . . felt as if, in our encounters, I had received a valuable treasure." In "The Gold Coin" she uses these people as characters to tell what some people would call a modern-day **parable,** a short story used to teach a moral or religious lesson.

Enrich Your Reading

Sequence   The order in which events occur or ideas are presented is called **sequence.** A writer of fiction, for example, often uses time order to narrate the events of his or her story. In this story Alma Flor Ada uses words and phrases, such as *one night, a few minutes later, finally,* and *the following day,* to signal the time order, or sequence, of events that lead Juan to discover the treasures of life.

■ *Author biography in Reader's Handbook*

The Gold Coin

ALMA FLOR ADA

Juan[1] had been a thief for many years. Because he did his stealing by night, his skin had become pale and sickly. Because he spent his time either hiding or sneaking about, his body had become shriveled and bent. And because he had neither friend nor relative to make him smile, his face was always twisted into an angry frown.

One night, drawn by a light shining through the trees, Juan came upon a hut. He crept up to the door and through a crack saw an old woman sitting at a plain, wooden table.

What was that shining in her hand? Juan wondered. He could not believe his eyes: it was a gold coin. Then he heard the woman say to herself, "I must be the richest person in the world."

Juan decided instantly that all the woman's gold must be his. He thought that the easiest thing to do was to watch until the woman left. Juan hid in the bushes and huddled under his poncho, waiting for the right moment to enter the hut.

Juan was half asleep when he heard knocking at the door and the sound of insistent voices. A few minutes later, he saw the woman, wrapped in a black cloak, leave the hut with two men at her side.

Here's my chance! Juan thought. And forcing open a window, he climbed into the empty hut.

He looked about eagerly for the gold. He looked under the bed. It wasn't there. He looked in the cupboard. It wasn't there, either. Where could it be? Close to despair, Juan tore away some beams supporting the thatch roof.

Finally, he gave up. There was simply no gold in the hut.

All I can do, he thought, is to find the old woman and make her tell me where she's hidden it.

So he set out along the path that she and her two companions had taken.

It was daylight by the time Juan reached the river. The countryside had been deserted, but here along the riverbank were two huts. Nearby, a man and his son were hard at work, hoeing potatoes.

It had been a long, long time since Juan had spoken to another human being. Yet his desire to find the woman was so strong that he went up to the farmers and asked, in a hoarse, raspy voice, "Have you seen a short, gray-haired woman, wearing a black cloak?"

"Oh, you must be looking for Doña Josefa,"[2] the young boy said. "Yes, we've seen her. We went to fetch her this morning, because my grandfather had another attack of—"

"Where is she now?" Juan broke in.

---

1. **Juan** (hwän).
2. **Doña Josefa** (dô′ nyä hō sä′ fä).

"She is long gone," said the father with a smile. "Some people from across the river came looking for her, because someone in their family is sick."

"How can I get across the river?" Juan asked anxiously.

"Only by boat," the boy answered. "We'll row you across later, if you'd like." Then turning back to his work, he added, "But first we must finish digging up the potatoes."

The thief muttered, "Thanks." But he quickly grew impatient. He grabbed a hoe and began to help the pair of farmers. The sooner we finish, the sooner we'll get across the river, he thought. And the sooner I'll get to my gold!

It was dusk when they finally laid down their hoes. The soil had been turned, and the wicker baskets were brimming with potatoes.

"Now can you row me across?" Juan asked the father anxiously.

"Certainly," the man said. "But let's eat supper first."

Juan had forgotten the taste of a home-cooked meal and the pleasure that comes from sharing it with others. As he sopped up the last of the stew with a chunk of dark bread, memories of other meals came back to him from far away and long ago.

By the light of the moon, father and son guided their boat across the river.

"What a wonderful healer Doña Josefa is!" the boy told Juan. "All she had to do to make Abuelo[3] better was give him a cup of her special tea."

"Yes, and not only that," his father added, "she brought him a gold coin."

Juan was stunned. It was one thing for Doña Josefa to go around helping people. But how could she go around handing out gold coins—*his gold coins?*

When the threesome finally reached the other side of the river, they saw a young man sitting outside his hut.

"This fellow is looking for Doña Josefa," the father said, pointing to Juan.

"Oh, she left some time ago," the young man said.

"Where to?" Juan asked tensely.

"Over to the other side of the mountain," the young man replied, pointing to the vague outline of mountains in the night sky.

"How did she get there?" Juan asked, trying to hide his impatience.

"By horse," the young man answered. "They came on horseback to get her because someone had broken his leg."

"Well, then, I need a horse, too," Juan said urgently.

Each ear of corn that he picked seemed to bring him closer to his treasure.

"Tomorrow," the young man replied softly. "Perhaps I can take you tomorrow, maybe the next day. First I must finish harvesting the corn."

So Juan spent the next day in the fields, bathed in sweat from sunup to sundown.

Yet each ear of corn that he picked seemed to bring him closer to his treasure. And later that evening, when he helped the

---

3. **Abuelo** (ä bwā′ lō) *Spanish*: Grandfather.

young man husk several ears so they could boil them for supper, the yellow kernels glittered like gold coins.

While they were eating, Juan thought about Doña Josefa. Why, he wondered, would someone who said she was the world's richest woman spend her time taking care of every sick person for miles around?

The following day, the two set off at dawn. Juan could not recall when he last had noticed the beauty of the sunrise. He felt strangely moved by the sight of the mountains, barely lit by the faint rays of the morning sun.

As they neared the foothills, the young man said, "I'm not surprised you're looking for Doña Josefa. The whole countryside needs her. I went for her because my wife had been running a high fever. In no time at all, Doña Josefa had her on the road to recovery. And what's more, my friend, she brought her a gold coin!"

Juan groaned inwardly. To think that someone could hand out gold so freely! What a strange woman Doña Josefa is, Juan thought. Not only is she willing to help one person after another, but she doesn't mind traveling all over the countryside to do it!

"Well, my friend," said the young man finally, "this is where I must leave you. But you don't have far to walk. See that house over there? It belongs to the man who broke his leg."

The young man stretched out his hand to say good-bye. Juan stared at it for a moment. It had been a long, long time since the thief had shaken hands with anyone. Slowly, he pulled out a hand from under his poncho. When his companion grasped it firmly in his own, Juan felt suddenly warmed, as if by the rays of the sun.

But after he thanked the young man, Juan ran down the road. He was still eager to catch up with Doña Josefa. When he reached the house, a woman and a child were stepping down from a wagon.

"Have you seen Doña Josefa?" Juan asked.

"We've just taken her to Don Teodosio's,"[4] the woman said. "His wife is sick, you know—"

"How do I get there?" Juan broke in. "I've got to see her."

"It's too far to walk," the woman said amiably. "If you'd like, I'll take you there tomorrow. But first I must gather my squash and beans."

So Juan spent yet another long day in the fields. Working beneath the summer sun, Juan noticed that his skin had begun to tan. And although he had to stoop down to pick the squash, he found that he could now stretch his body. His back had begun to straighten too.

Later, when the little girl took him by the hand to show him a family of rabbits burrowed under a fallen tree, Juan's face broke into a smile. It had been a long, long time since Juan had smiled.

Yet his thoughts kept coming back to the gold.

The following day, the wagon carrying Juan and the woman lumbered along a road lined with coffee fields.

The woman said, "I don't know what we would have done without Doña Josefa. I sent my daughter to our neighbor's house,

---

4. **Don Teodosio** (dôn tā´ ô dô´ sē ô).

CUADRILLAS   Edmundo Otoniel Mejia   Courtesy, Galleria 123   Middleburg, Virginia.

who then brought Doña Josefa on horseback. She set my husband's leg and then showed me how to brew a special tea to lessen the pain."

Getting no reply, she went on. "And, as if that weren't enough, she brought him a gold coin. Can you imagine such a thing?"

Juan could only sigh. No doubt about it, he thought, Doña Josefa is someone special. But Juan didn't know whether to be happy that Doña Josefa had so much gold she could freely hand it out, or angry for her having already given so much of it away.

When they finally reached Don Teodosio's house, Doña Josefa was already gone. But here, too, there was work that needed to be done. . . .

Juan stayed to help with the coffee harvest. As he picked the red berries, he gazed up from time to time at the trees that grew, row upon row, along the hillsides. What a calm, peaceful place this is! he thought.

The next morning, Juan was up at daybreak. Bathed in the soft dawn light, the mountains seemed to smile at him. When Don Teodosio offered him a lift on horseback, Juan found it difficult to have to say good-bye.

"What a good woman Doña Josefa is!" Don Teodosio said, as they rode down the hill toward the sugarcane fields. "The minute she heard about my wife being sick, she came with her special herbs. And as if that weren't enough, she brought my wife a gold coin!"

In the stifling heat, the kind that often signals the approach of a storm, Juan simply sighed and mopped his brow. The pair continued riding for several hours in silence.

Juan then realized he was back in familiar territory, for they were now on the stretch of road he had traveled only a week ago—though how much longer it now seemed to him. He jumped off Don Teodosio's horse and broke into a run.

This time the gold would not escape him! But he had to move quickly, so he could find shelter before the storm broke.

Out of breath, Juan finally reached Doña Josefa's hut. She was standing by the door, shaking her head slowly as she surveyed the ransacked house.

"So I've caught up with you at last!" Juan shouted, startling the old woman. "Where's the gold?"

"The gold coin?" Doña Josefa said, surprised and looking at Juan intently. "Have you come for the gold coin? I've been trying hard to give it to someone who might need it," Doña Josefa said. "First to an old man who had just gotten over a bad attack. Then to a young woman who had been running a fever. Then to a man with a broken leg. And finally to Don Teodosio's wife. But none of them would take it. They all said, 'Keep it. There must be someone who needs it more.'"

Juan did not say a word.

"You must be the one who needs it," Doña Josefa said.

She took the coin out of her pocket and handed it to him. Juan stared at the coin, speechless.

"*So I've caught up with you at last!*" *Juan shouted.*

At that moment a young girl appeared, her long braid bouncing as she ran. "Hurry, Doña Josefa, please!" she said breathlessly. "My mother is all alone, and the baby is due any minute."

"Of course, dear," Doña Josefa replied. But as she glanced up at the sky, she saw nothing but black clouds. The storm was nearly upon them. Doña Josefa sighed deeply.

"But how can I leave now? Look at my house! I don't know what has happened to the roof. The storm will wash the whole place away!"

And there was a deep sadness in her voice.

Juan took in the child's frightened eyes, Doña Josefa's sad, distressed face, and the ransacked hut.

"Go ahead, Doña Josefa," he said. "Don't worry about your house. I'll see that the roof is back in shape, good as new."

The woman nodded gratefully, drew her cloak about her shoulders, and took the child by the hand. As she turned to leave, Juan held out his hand.

"Here, take this," he said, giving her the gold coin. "I'm sure the newborn will need it more than I." ❧

Love and the Cabbie

ART BUCHWALD

I was in New York the other day and rode with a friend in a taxi. When we got out, my friend said to the driver, "Thank you for the ride. You did a superb job of driving."

The taxi driver was stunned for a second. Then he said:

"Are you a wise guy or something?"

"No, my dear man, and I'm not putting you on. I admire the way you keep cool in heavy traffic."

"Yeh," the driver said and drove off.

"What was that all about?" I asked.

"I am trying to bring love back to New York," he said. "I believe it's the only thing that can save the city."

"How can one man save New York?"

"It's not one man. I believe I have made the taxi driver's day. Suppose he has twenty fares. He's going to be nice to those twenty fares because someone was nice to him. Those fares in turn will be kinder to their employees or shopkeepers or waiters or even their own families. Eventually the goodwill could spread to at least one thousand people. Now that isn't bad, is it?"

"But you're depending on that taxi driver to pass your goodwill to others."

"I'm not depending on it," my friend said. "I'm aware that the system isn't foolproof, so I might deal with ten different people today. If out of ten, I can make three happy, then even-tually I can indirectly influence the attitudes of three thousand more."

"It sounds good on paper," I admitted, "but I'm not sure it works in practice."

"Nothing is lost if it doesn't. I didn't take any of my time to tell that man he was doing a good job. He neither received a larger tip nor a smaller tip. If it fell on deaf ears, so what? Tomorrow there will be another taxi driver whom I can try to make happy."

"You're some kind of a nut," I said.

"That shows you how cynical you have become. I have made a study of this. The thing that seems to be lacking, besides money of course, for our postal employees is that no one tells people who work for the post office what a good job they're doing."

"But they're not doing a good job."

"They're not doing a good job because they feel no one cares if they do or not. Why shouldn't someone say a kind word to them?"

We were walking past a structure in the process of being built and passed five work-men eating their lunch. My friend stopped. "That's a magnificent job you men have done. It must be difficult and dangerous work."

The five men eyed my friend suspiciously.

"When will it be finished?"

"June," a man grunted.

"Ah. That really is impressive. You must all be very proud."

We walked away. I said to him, "I haven't seen anyone like you since *The Man from La Mancha*."[1]

"When those men digest my words, they will feel better for it. Somehow the city will benefit from their happiness."

"But you can't do this all alone!" I protested. "You're just one man."

"The most important thing is not to get discouraged. Making people in the city become kind again is not an easy job, but if I can enlist other people in my campaign . . ."

"You just winked at a very plain-looking woman," I said.

"Yes, I know," he replied. "And if she's a schoolteacher, her class will be in for a fantastic day."

---

1. ***The Man from La Mancha:*** A reference to *Man of La Mancha,* a musical about Don Quixote, a famous character from literature who thought he was a knight and fought against evil.

E X P L A I N

Responding to Reading

First Impressions

1. How did you feel about Juan as you read this story? Take a minute to describe your thoughts in your journal.

Second Thoughts

2. "Who Can Explain?" is the title of this subunit. How would you explain the changes in Juan's character?

    Think about
    - the effects of his contact with people and nature
    - the effects of hard work
    - what he learns from Doña Josefa

3. Doña Josefa says, "I must be the richest person in the world." Why do you think she says that?

4. What do you think is the lesson, or moral, of this story?

Broader Connections

5. Both "The Gold Coin" and the Insight selection on page 392 describe a chain of events in which goodwill spreads from one person to many more. Is this an accurate or an exaggerated picture of what happens in real life? Explain.

Writing Options

1. If you have read *A Christmas Carol,* on page 248, write an **essay** comparing and contrasting the change in Juan with the change in Ebenezer Scrooge.

2. Write an **epilogue** to this story. Start with the end of the story and imagine what Juan might do next.

3. Look at the list you made on page 386 before reading this story. Choose the thing you consider most valuable after reading the story and the Insight selection, and write your own modern-day **parable** about this item.

Nonfiction

Hiroshima No Pika

TOSHI MARUKI (tō′ shē mä rōō′ kē)

Examine What You Know

Have you ever experienced a disaster such as a fire, a hurricane, an earthquake, or a war? In your journal or on a sheet of paper, write down your feelings about a disaster you have experienced, one you have heard about, or even one you have only imagined.

Expand Your Knowledge

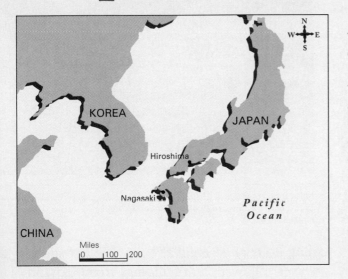

On the morning of August 6, 1945, the people of Hiroshima, Japan, experienced disaster on a vast scale. In an attempt to end World War II, the United States dropped the first atomic bomb on this city. In seconds the explosion destroyed about five square miles of the city and killed between 70,000 and 100,000 people. Another 70,000 died by the end of the year. Thousands more died later from radiation sickness. Three days later, the United States dropped a second atomic bomb, on Nagasaki, Japan. A week later, World War II ended.

Enrich Your Reading

Chronological Order   The order in which events happen in time is called time order or **chronological order.** The events in this selection are in chronological order, but because of the disaster, time passes both quickly and slowly. As you read, notice that the author follows chronological order in describing most of the events and also uses paragraphs to show how quickly or slowly time is moving. Some paragraphs describe events taking place in just a few seconds; other paragraphs cover longer periods of time.

■ *Author biography in Reader's Handbook*

Hiroshima No Pika

TOSHI MARUKI

That morning in Hiroshima[1] the sky was blue and cloudless. The sun was shining. Streetcars had begun making rounds, picking up people who were on their way to work. Hiroshima's seven rivers flowed quietly through the city. The rays of the midsummer sun glittered on the surface of the rivers.

In Tokyo, Osaka, Nagoya,[2] and many other Japanese cities there had been air raids. The people of Hiroshima wondered why their city had been spared. They had done what they could to prepare for an air raid. To keep fire from spreading, they had torn down old buildings and widened streets. They had stored water and decided where people should go to avoid the bombs. Everyone carried small bags of medicine and, when they were out of doors, wore air-raid hats or hoods to protect their heads.

Mii[3] was seven years old and lived in Hiroshima with her mother and father. She and her parents were breakfasting on sweet potatoes, which had been brought in the day before by cousins who lived in the country. Mii was very hungry this morning and exclaimed about how good the sweet potatoes tasted. Her father agreed that they made a delicious breakfast, though they weren't the rice he preferred.

Then it happened. A sudden, terrible light flashed all around. The light was bright orange—then white, like thousands of light-

Illustration copyright © 1980 by Toshi Maruki. By permission of Lothrop, Lee & Shepard Books, a division of William Morrow Company, Inc.

ning bolts all striking at once. Violent shock waves followed, and buildings trembled and began to collapse.

Moments before the Flash, United States Air Force bomber *Enola Gay* had flown over the city and released a top-secret explosive. The explosive was an atomic bomb, which had been given the name "Little Boy" by the B-29's crew.

1. **Hiroshima** (hir′ ə shē′ mə): city in Japan.
2. **Tokyo** (tō′ kē ō′), **Osaka** (ô′ sä kä′), **Nagoya** (nä′ gō yä′).
3. **Mii** (mē).

"Little Boy" fell on Hiroshima at 8:15 on the morning of August 6, 1945.

Mii was knocked unconscious by the force of the Flash, and when she woke up everything around her was still and dark. At first she couldn't move, and she heard crackling sounds that frightened her. Far off in the darkness she could see a red glow. Her mother's voice penetrated the dark, calling her.

Mii struggled out from under the heavy boards that had fallen on top of her. Her mother rushed to her and drew her close and hugged her. "We must hurry," she said. "The fire . . . your father is caught in the flames!"

Mii and her mother faced the fire and began to pray. Then Mii's mother leaped into the flames and pulled her husband to safety.

Mii watched as her mother examined her father. "He's hurt badly," she said. She untied the sash from her kimono and wrapped it around her husband's body as a bandage. Then she did something amazing. She lifted him onto her back and, taking Mii by the hand, started running.

"The river. We must reach the river," Mother directed.

The three of them tumbled down the riverbank and into the water. Mii lost hold of her mother's hand.

"Mii-chan! Hang on to me!" her mother shouted.

There were crowds of people fleeing the fire. Mii saw children with their clothes burned away, lips and eyelids swollen. They were like ghosts, wandering about, crying in weak voices. Some people, all their strength gone, fell face down on the ground, and others fell on top of them. There were heaps of people everywhere.

Mii and her mother and father continued their escape and crossed another river. When they reached the far bank, Mii's mother put her husband down and collapsed on the ground beside him.

There were crowds of people fleeing the fire.

Mii felt something moving past her feet. Hop . . . hop. . . . It was a swallow. Its wings were burned, and it couldn't fly. Hop . . . hop . . .

She saw a man floating slowly down the river. Floating behind him was the body of a cat.

Mii turned and saw a young woman holding a baby and crying. "We escaped this far and then I stopped to feed him," she said. "But he wouldn't take his milk. He's dead." The young woman, still holding her baby, waded into the river. She waded deeper and deeper, until Mii couldn't see her anymore.

The sky grew dark, and there was a rumble of thunder. It began to rain. Though it was midsummer, the air turned very cold, and the rain was black and sticky.

Then a rainbow arched across the sky, pushing the dark away. It gleamed brightly over the dead and wounded.

Mii's mother lifted Father onto her back again. She took Mii by the hand, and they began to run. Fire was moving toward them at a terrible speed. They ran among piles of cracked roof tiles, over fallen telephone poles and wires. Houses were burning on every side. They came to another river, and once in the water Mii felt suddenly sleepy. Before she knew it, she had gulped down mouthfuls of water. Her mother pulled her head above the water. They reached the other side and kept running.

At long last they reached the beach outside Hiroshima. They could see Miyajima[4] island, wrapped in purple mist, across the water. Mii's mother had hoped they could cross over to the island by boat. Miyajima was covered with beautiful pine and maple trees and surrounded by clear water. Thinking that safety was not far away, Mii and her mother and father fell asleep.

The sun went down. Night came and went. The sun rose, then set. It rose and set again, then rose for the third time.

"Please, tell me what day it is," Mii's mother asked a man who was passing by. He had been looking over the people lying on the beach.

"It's the ninth," he answered.

Mother counted on her fingers. "Four days!" she cried out in amazement. "We've been here four days?"

Mii started to cry softly. An old woman who was lying nearby sat up and took a rice ball out of her bag and gave it to Mii. When Mii took it from her, the woman fell down again. This time she didn't move.

"Mii-chan! You're still holding your chopsticks!" her mother exclaimed. "Here, let me have them." But Mii's hand wouldn't open. Her mother pried her fingers open one by one. Four days after the bomb, Mii let go of her chopsticks.

Firemen came from a nearby village to help them. Soldiers came and took the dead away. A school building that was still standing had been turned into a hospital, and they took Father there. There were no doctors, no medicine, no bandages—only shelter.

With Father as safe as possible in the hospital, Mii and her mother decided to go back into the city to see if anything was left of their home. There were neither grass nor trees nor houses left in Hiroshima. A burnt-out wasteland stretched before them as far as the eye could see. Mii and her mother found everything destroyed. The only thing left to remind them they had ever lived there was Mii's rice bowl. Bent and broken, it still contained some sweet potatoes.

That day, August 9, 1945, as Mii and her mother looked at the rubble that had been Hiroshima, an atomic bomb was dropped on Nagasaki.[5] And there, as in Hiroshima, thousands of people died, and anyone who survived was left homeless. Among the victims, in addition to the Japanese, were people from many other countries, such as Korea, China, Russia, Indonesia, and the United States.

The atomic bomb was unlike any explosive ever used before. The destruction on impact was greater than thousands of conventional bombs exploding all at once, and it also contaminated the area with radiation that caused deaths and illnesses for many years following the explosion.

Mii never grew after that day. Many years have passed, and she is still the same size she was when she was seven years old. "It is because of the Flash from the bomb," her mother says. Sometimes Mii complains that her head itches, and her mother parts her hair, sees something shiny, and pulls it out of her scalp with a pair of tweezers. It's a

---

4. **Miyajima** (mē′ yə jē′ mə): island, part of Japan.
5. **Nagasaki** (nä′ gə sä′ kē): city in Japan.

Illustration copyright © 1980 by Toshi Maruki. By permission of Lothrop, Lee & Shepard Books, a division of William Morrow Company, Inc.

sliver of glass, imbedded when the bomb went off years ago, that has worked its way to the surface.

Mii's father had seven wounds in his body, but they healed and for a while he thought he was getting well. Then one day in autumn after the Flash, his hair fell out and he began coughing blood. Purple spots appeared all over his body, and he died.

Many of the people who had said, "Thank God, our lives were spared," later became ill with radiation sickness. Though this happened in 1945, some of these people are still in hospitals. There is no cure for their disease.

Every year on August 6 the people of Hiroshima inscribe the names of loved ones who died because of the bomb on lanterns. The lanterns are lit and set adrift on the seven rivers that flow through Hiroshima. The rivers flow slowly to the sea, carrying the lanterns in memory of those who died.

Mii, who is still like a small child after all these years, writes "Father" on one lantern and "The Swallow" on another. Her mother's hair has now turned white, and she watches sorrowfully as her daughter sets the lanterns afloat.

"It can't happen again," she says, "if no one drops the bomb." ❧

Responding to Reading

First Impressions

1. What words describe your feelings as you read about the destruction of Hiroshima? Record these words in your journal or on a sheet of paper.

Second Thoughts

2. Look back at the pictures that the author drew to illustrate this selection. What effect do they have on your feelings about the story?

3. How can you explain the way Mii's mother reacts to the disaster?

   Think about
   • her immediate reactions to the explosion
   • her physical strength

4. Every year Mii lights one lantern for her father and one for the injured swallow. What do you think the swallow might represent to Mii?

Broader Connections

5. Every year the city of Hiroshima hosts a ceremony on August 6 to remember the explosion. Thousands of people from around the world attend. Why do you think people want to remember a tragedy that happened so many years ago?

Writing Options

1. Write a **note** Mii might attach to one of her lanterns for the memorial ceremony.

2. In concrete poetry the words are arranged to form a shape or pattern. Write a **concrete poem** about the atomic bomb dropped on Hiroshima or about the disaster that you described in Examine What You Know on page 395. (For an example of concrete poetry, see the poem "Crystal Rowe (Track Star)" on page 230.)

3. Write a **persuasive speech** for a debate in which you support or oppose nuclear weapons. Explain how *Hiroshima No Pika* influenced your opinion.

Poetry

Forgotten Language
SHEL SILVERSTEIN

Petals
PAT MORA

Examine What You Know

Think of your earliest experiences of nature. Do you remember lying on the ground and watching ants or caterpillars or staring in wonder at the inside of a flower? Was there ever a time when you felt you could talk and understand the "language" of plants or animals? In your journal, write or draw a picture about an early experience that you had in the world of nature.

Expand Your Knowledge

Poets often use images from nature in their poetry. For example, a poet may use an image of a flower to suggest beauty or the image of a tiger to suggest power and danger. Poets sometimes express their observations by means of contrasts, comparisons, and descriptions. In the poems you are about to read, the poets use images of flowers and other things in the natural world to make observations about growing older and remembering the past.

Enrich Your Reading

Understanding Poetry   Because poets pack a lot of ideas into a few lines, special reading strategies can help you discover what a poem means. To understand these two poems about people and nature, try the following techniques:

1. Read through each poem several times to get its general meaning. Pay attention to punctuation. The second poem, "Petals," is one long sentence beginning with the title. Pay special attention to each mark of punctuation in this poem.

2. Read each poem slowly, line by line or image by image. Stop at the end of each line or phrase to determine what the line or phrase is about. Picture the images that the poet creates.

3. Read the poem aloud. A poet often arranges words so that their sounds are pleasing in some way. Listen to how the words sound. Experiment with the expression of your voice.

■ *Author biographies on Extend page*

Forgotten Language

SHEL SILVERSTEIN

Once I spoke the language of the flowers,
Once I understood each word the caterpillar said,
Once I smiled in secret at the gossip of the starlings,[1]
And shared a conversation with the housefly
5 in my bed.
Once I heard and answered all the questions
  of the crickets,
And joined the crying of each falling dying
  flake of snow,
10 Once I spoke the language of the flowers . . .
   How did it go?
   How did it go?

_____

1. starlings: a kind of bird.

*R*esponding to Reading

First Impressions of "Forgotten Language"

1. What images does this poem bring to mind? In your journal or on a sheet of paper, draw an image from the poem.

Second Thoughts on "Forgotten Language"

2. What do you think "the language of the flowers" is?

3. Why do you think the speaker has forgotten the language of the flowers?

> **Think about**
> * how the speaker may have changed
> * what the repetition of the word *once* may mean

4. Think about the experience of nature that you described before reading the poem. How do you think the speaker might have communicated with nature when he was younger?

Petals

PAT MORA

have calloused[1] her hands,
brightly colored crepe paper: turquoise,
yellow, magenta,[2] which she shapes
into large blooms for bargain-hunting tourists
5 who see her flowers, her puppets, her baskets,
but not her—small, gray-haired woman
wearing a white apron, who hides behind
blossoms in her stall at the market,
who sits and remembers collecting wildflowers
10 as a girl, climbing rocky Mexican hills
to fill a straw hat with soft blooms
which she'd stroke gently, over and over again
with her smooth fingertips.

---

1. **calloused**: made the skin tough and thick.
2. **magenta**: a bright purplish-red color.

SPRING PROMISE   Sylvia Frattini   from *Painting the Enchanted World of Nature* by James Lester and Sylvia Frattini. Used by permission of Search Press, Ltd.

*R*esponding to Reading

First Impressions of "Petals"

1. Describe your feelings about the woman in the poem.

Second Thoughts on "Petals"

2. Why do you think the tourists see only the flowers and not the woman who makes them?

> **Think about**
> • the description of the woman and the flowers
> • what tourists might value

3. How do you think the speaker of the poem feels about the woman who makes flowers?

Comparing the Poems

4. Compare and contrast the speakers in the two poems.

5. How do you think the woman in "Petals" would describe the language of the flowers?

*L*iterary Concept: Personification

The giving of human qualities to an animal, object, or idea is called **personification.** For example, in "Forgotten Language" the starlings are described as gossiping. Why do you think the poet uses personification in "Forgotten Language"?

Concept Review: Imagery "Petals" begins and ends with imagery that appeals to the sense of touch. Why do you think the poet might have used this type of imagery to begin and end her poem?

*W*riting Options

1. Imagine that you are one of the tourists in the marketplace in "Petals." Write a **letter** to a friend at home, describing the scene.

2. Write a **dialogue** between the speaker of "Forgotten Language" and the woman in "Petals." Have them discuss their pasts, the present, or their attitudes toward flowers and nature.

E X T E N D

Options for Learning

1 • **Poetic Mysteries** With a small group create a poetry anthology based on the title of this subunit, "Who Can Explain?" Include poems from this book and elsewhere that deal with the mysteries of the world and human nature. Illustrate the poems with drawings or pictures.

2 • **Paper Flowers** Learn how to make flowers out of crepe paper, and demonstrate the technique to other students in your class. Present the flowers you make to elderly people in hospitals or nursing homes in your community.

Shel Silverstein 1932–

Besides writing poetry, songs, and stories, Shel Silverstein draws cartoons, sings, and plays the guitar. He started writing and drawing when he was around twelve, although, he says, "I would much rather have been a good baseball player."

Silverstein's work is popular with people of all ages. His books include *Where the Sidewalk Ends* and *A Light in the Attic.*

Silverstein lives on a houseboat in California but travels often. He says, "I want to go everywhere, look at and listen to everything. You can go crazy with some of the wonderful stuff there is in life. I have ideas, and ideas are too good not to share."

Pat Mora 1942–

Pat Mora was born and raised in El Paso, Texas, where she experienced a blending of Mexican and U.S. cultures. As a child she felt embarrassed by her Hispanic heritage: "I spoke Spanish at home to my grandmother and aunt, but I didn't always want my friends at school to know that I spoke Spanish.

As an adult Mora takes pride in being a Hispanic writer. She says it is very difficult for people to feel good about themselves when television commercials are always telling them to buy something new to improve their appearance. For Mora, the real improvements start with knowing yourself. "I write because I am curious," she says. "I am curious about me. Writing is a way of finding out how I feel about anything and everything."

Fiction

Lob's Girl

JOAN AIKEN

Examine What You Know

Have you heard of cats or dogs or other animals that rescued people from fires or drowning? Do you know of pets that traveled many miles to be reunited with their owners? Stage a talk show in front of the class. Select a host to interview classmates who know true stories of devoted and loyal pets that did extraordinary things.

Expand Your Knowledge

This story about a dog's devotion to a girl is set in Cornwall, a county in southwestern England. Cornwall is known for the beauty of its high, sheer cliffs and its many tiny fishing villages along the coast. A typical village in Cornwall has white cottages lining steep, narrow streets that wind down to a harbor filled with fishing boats. The region is a very popular vacation spot. An English tradition mentioned in the story is taking a break for tea in the afternoon. A proper tea often includes scones (which are like biscuits) and butter.

Enrich Your Reading

Reviewing Reading Strategies As you read this story, you will see questions based on the reading strategies you learned on page 6: **questioning, connecting, predicting, reviewing,** and **evaluating.** Review your understanding of these strategies. To improve your reading, use these strategies whenever you read. In your journal, jot down your responses to the reading-strategy questions that are inserted in this story.

■ *Author biography on Extend page*

Lob's Girl

JOAN AIKEN

Some people choose their dogs, and some dogs choose their people. The Pengelly family had no say in the choosing of Lob; he came to them in the second way, and very decisively.

It began on the beach, the summer when Sandy was five, Don, her older brother, twelve, and the twins were three. Sandy was really Alexandra, because her grandmother had a beautiful picture of a queen in a diamond tiara and high collar of pearls. It hung by Granny Pearce's kitchen sink and was as familiar as the doormat. When Sandy was born everyone agreed that she was the living spit[1] of the picture, and so she was called Alexandra, and Sandy for short.

On this summer day she was lying peacefully reading a comic and not keeping an eye on the twins, who didn't need it because they were occupied in seeing which of them could wrap the most seaweed around the other one's legs. Father—Bert Pengelly—and Don were up on the Hard[2] painting the bottom boards of the boat in which Father went fishing for pilchards.[3] And Mother—Jean Pengelly—was getting ahead with making the Christmas puddings because she never felt easy in her mind if they weren't made and safely put away by the end of August.

As usual, each member of the family was happily getting on with his or her own affairs. Little did they guess how soon this state of things would be changed by the large new member who was going to erupt into their midst.

Sandy rolled onto her back to make sure that the twins were not climbing on slippery rocks or getting cut off by the tide. At the same moment a large body struck her forcibly in the midriff, and she was covered by flying sand. Instinctively she shut her eyes and felt the sand being wiped off her face by something that seemed like a warm, rough, damp flannel. She opened her eyes and looked. It was a tongue. Its owner was a large and bouncy young Alsatian, or German shepherd, with topaz eyes, black-tipped prick ears, a thick, soft coat, and a bushy, black-tipped tail.

Whose dog is this? *question*

"Lob!" shouted a man farther up the beach. "Lob, come here!"

---

1. **the living spit:** an exact likeness; a perfect copy.
2. **Hard:** a solid landing place for boats.
3. **pilchards:** small fish, similar to sardines.

Words to Know and Use	**midriff** (mid′ rif) *n.* the upper part of the stomach **topaz** (tō′ paz′) *adj.* yellow-gold, like the topaz stone

But Lob, as if trying to atone for the surprise he had given her, went on licking the sand off Sandy's face, wagging his tail so hard while he kept on knocking up more clouds of sand. His owner, a gray-haired man with a limp, walked over as quickly as he could and seized him by the collar.

"I hope he didn't give you a fright?" the man said to Sandy. "He meant it in play—he's only young."

"Oh, no, I think he's beautiful," said Sandy truly. She picked up a bit of driftwood and threw it. Lob, whisking easily out of his master's grip, was after it like a sand-colored bullet. He came back with the stick, beaming, and gave it to Sandy. At the same time he gave himself, though no one else was aware of this at the time. But with Sandy, too, it was love at first sight, and when, after a lot more stick throwing, she and the twins joined Father and Don to go home for tea, they cast many a backward glance at Lob being led firmly away by his master.

"I wish we could play with him every day," Tess sighed.

"Why can't we?" said Tim.

Sandy explained. "Because Mr. Dodsworth, who owns him, is from Liverpool, and he is only staying at the Fisherman's Arms till Saturday."

"Is Liverpool a long way off?"

"Right at the other end of England from Cornwall, I'm afraid."

It was a Cornish fishing village where the Pengelly family lived, with rocks and cliffs and a strip of beach and a little round harbor, and palm trees growing in the gardens of the little whitewashed stone houses. The village was approached by a narrow, steep, twisting hillroad and guarded by a notice that said LOW GEAR FOR $1\frac{1}{2}$ MILES, DANGEROUS TO CYCLISTS.

The Pengelly children went home to scones[4] with Cornish cream and jam, thinking they had seen the last of Lob. But they were much mistaken. The whole family was playing cards by the fire in the front room after supper when there was a loud thump and a crash of china in the kitchen.

"My Christmas puddings!" exclaimed Jean, and ran out.

"Did you put TNT in them, then?" her husband said.

But it was Lob, who, finding the front door shut, had gone around to the back and bounced in through the open kitchen window, where the puddings were cooling on the sill. Luckily only the smallest was knocked down and broken.

Lob stood on his hind legs and plastered Sandy's face with licks. Then he did the same for the twins, who shrieked with joy.

"Where does this friend of yours come from?" inquired Mr. Pengelly.

"He's staying at the Fisherman's Arms—I mean his owner is."

"Then he must go back there. Find a bit of string, Sandy, to tie to his collar."

"I wonder how he found his way here," Mrs. Pengelly said, when the reluctant Lob had been led whining away and Sandy had explained about their afternoon's game on the beach. "Fisherman's Arms is right round the other side of the harbor."

Lob's owner scolded him and thanked Mr. Pengelly for bringing him back. Jean Pengelly warned the children that they had

---

4. **scones** (skōnz): English biscuits.

TWO GIRLS ON A CLIFF c.1917 Laura Knight Reproduced by permission of John Farquharson, Ltd., London. Courtesy, Sotheby's London.

better not encourage Lob any more if they met him on the beach, or it would only lead to more trouble. So they dutifully took no notice of him the next day until he spoiled their good resolutions by dashing up to them with joyful barks, wagging his tail so hard that he winded Tess and knocked Tim's legs from under him.

They had a happy day, playing on the sand.

The next day was Saturday. Sandy had found out that Mr. Dodsworth was to catch the half-past-nine train. She went out secretly, down to the station, nodded to Mr. Hoskins, the stationmaster, who wouldn't dream of charging any local for a platform ticket, and climbed up on the footbridge that led over the tracks. She didn't want to be seen, but she did want to see. She saw Mr. Dodsworth get on the train, accompanied by an unhappy-looking Lob with drooping ears and tail. Then she saw the train slide away out of sight around the next headland, with a melancholy wail that sounded like Lob's last good-bye.

How would you feel in Sandy's situation?

connect

Sandy wished she hadn't had the idea of coming to the station. She walked home miserably, with her shoulders hunched and her hands in her pockets. For the rest of the day, she was so cross and unlike herself that Tess and Tim were quite surprised, and her mother gave her a dose of senna.[5]

A week passed. Then, one evening, Mrs. Pengelly and the younger children were in the front room playing snakes and ladders. Mr. Pengelly and Don had gone fishing on the evening tide. If your father is a fisherman, he will never be home at the same time from one week to the next.

Suddenly, history repeating itself, there was a crash from the kitchen. Jean Pengelly leaped up, crying, "My blackberry jelly!" She and the children had spent the morning picking and the afternoon boiling fruit.

But Sandy was ahead of her mother. With flushed cheeks and eyes like stars, she had darted into the kitchen, where she and Lob were hugging one another in a frenzy of joy. . . .

"Good heavens!" exclaimed Jean. "How in the world did he get here?"

"He must have walked," said Sandy. "Look at his feet."

They were worn, dusty, and tarry. One had a cut on the pad.

"They ought to be bathed," said Jean

---

5. **senna:** a medicine made from senna plants.

KATHY'S WINDOW 1969
John Chumley Private collection.
Photo by Johnny Meeks.

Pengelly. "Sandy, run a bowl of warm water while I get the disinfectant."

"What'll we do about him, Mother?" said Sandy anxiously.

Mrs. Pengelly looked at her daughter's pleading eyes and sighed.

"He must go back to his owner, of course," she said, making her voice firm. "Your dad can get the address from the Fisherman's tomorrow and phone him or send a telegram. In the meantime he'd better have a long drink and a good meal."

Lob was very grateful for the drink and the meal and made no objection to having his feet washed. Then he flopped down on the hearth rug and slept in front of the fire they had lit because it was a cold, wet evening, with his head on Sandy's feet. He was a very tired dog. He had walked all the way from Liverpool to Cornwall, which is more than four hundred miles.

The next day Mr. Pengelly phoned Lob's owner, and the following morning Mr. Dodsworth arrived off the night train, decidedly put out, to take his pet home. That parting was worse than the first. Lob whined, Don walked out of the house, the twins burst out crying, and Sandy crept up to her bedroom afterward and lay with her face pressed into the quilt, feeling as if she were bruised all over.

Jean Pengelly took them all into Plymouth to see the circus on the next day, and the twins cheered up a little, but even the hour's ride in the train each way and the Liberty horses and performing seals could not cure Sandy's sore heart.

She need not have bothered, though. In ten days' time Lob was back—limping this time, with a torn ear and a patch missing out of his furry coat, as if he had met and tangled with an enemy or two in the course of his four-hundred-mile walk.

Bert Pengelly rang up Liverpool again. Mr. Dodsworth, when he answered, sounded weary. He said, "That dog has already cost me two days that I can't spare away from my work—plus endless time in police stations and drafting newspaper advertisements. I'm too old for these ups and downs. I think we'd better face the fact, Mr. Pengelly, that it's your family he wants to stay with—that is, if you want to have him."

Bert Pengelly gulped. He was not a rich man, and Lob was a pedigreed dog. He said cautiously, "How much would you be asking for him?"

"Good heavens, man, I'm not suggesting I'd sell him to you. You must have him as a gift. Think of the train fares I'll be saving. You'll be doing me a good turn."

"Is he a big eater?" Bert asked doubtfully.

By this time the children, breathless in the background listening to one side of this conversation, had realized what was in the wind and were dancing up and down with their hands clasped beseechingly.

"Oh, not for his size," Lob's owner assured Bert. "Two or three pounds of meat a day and some vegetables and gravy and biscuits—he does very well on that."

Alexandra's father looked over the telephone at his daughter's swimming eyes and trembling lips. He reached a decision. "Well,

Words to Know and Use | **pedigreed** (ped' ə grēd') *adj.* having papers showing that all of the animal's ancestors were the same breed

411

© 1988 Michael Garland / The Image Bank.

then, Mr. Dodsworth," he said briskly, "we'll accept your offer and thank you very much. The children will be overjoyed and you can be sure Lob has come to a good home. They'll look after him and see he gets enough exercise. But I can tell you," he ended firmly, "if he wants to settle in with us, he'll have to learn to eat a lot of fish."

So that was how Lob came to live with the Pengelly family. Everybody loved him and he loved them all. But there was never any question who came first with him. He was Sandy's dog. He slept by her bed and followed her everywhere he was allowed.

What kind of family are the Pengellys?

Nine years went by, and each summer Mr. Dodsworth came back to stay at the Fisherman's Arms and call on his erstwhile dog. Lob always met him with recognition and dignified pleasure, accompanied him for a walk or two—but showed no signs of wishing to return to Liverpool. His place, he intimated, was definitely with the Pengellys.

In the course of nine years, Lob changed less than Sandy. As she went into her teens he became a little slower, a little stiffer, there was a touch of gray on his nose, but he was still a handsome dog. He and Sandy still loved one another devotedly.

One evening in October all the summer visitors had left, and the little fishing town looked empty and secretive. It was a wet, windy dusk. When the children came home from school—even the twins were at high school now, and Don was a full-fledged fisherman—Jean Pengelly said, "Sandy, your Aunt Rebecca says she's lonesome because Uncle Will Hoskins has gone out trawling, and she wants one of you to go and spend the evening with her. You go, dear; you can take your homework with you."

Sandy looked far from enthusiastic.

"Can I take Lob with me?"

"You know Aunt Becky doesn't really like dogs—Oh, very well." Mrs. Pengelly sighed. "I suppose she'll have to put up with him as well as you."

Reluctantly Sandy tidied herself, took her

Words to Know and Use | **dignified** (dig' nə fīd') *adj.* majestic and restrained

schoolbag, put on the damp raincoat she had just taken off, fastened Lob's lead[6] to his collar, and set off to walk through the dusk to Aunt Becky's cottage, which was five minutes' climb up the steep hill.

The wind was howling through the shrouds[7] of boats drawn up on the Hard.

"Put some cheerful music on, do," said Jean Pengelly to the nearest twin. "Anything to drown that <u>wretched</u> sound while I make your dad's supper." So Don, who had just come in, put on some rock music, loud. Which was why the Pengellys did not hear the truck hurtle down the hill and crash against the post office wall a few minutes later.

Dr. Travers was driving through Cornwall with his wife, taking a late holiday before patients began coming down with winter colds and flu. He saw the sign that said STEEP HILL. LOW GEAR FOR $1^1/_2$ MILES. Dutifully he changed into second gear.

"We must be nearly there," said his wife, looking out of her window. "I noticed a sign on the coast road that said the Fisherman's Arms was two miles. What a narrow, dangerous hill! But the cottages are very pretty— Oh, Frank, stop, stop! There's a child, I'm sure it's a child—by the wall over there!"

Dr. Travers jammed on his brakes and brought the car to a stop. A little stream ran down by the road in a shallow stone <u>culvert</u>, and half in the water lay something that looked, in the dusk, like a pile of clothes—or was it the body of a child? Mrs. Travers was out of the car in a flash, but her husband was quicker.

"Don't touch her, Emily!" he said sharply. "She's been hit. Can't be more than a few minutes. Remember that truck that overtook us half a mile back, speeding like the devil? Here, quick, go into that cottage and phone for an ambulance. The girl's in a bad way. I'll stay here and do what I can to stop the bleeding. Don't waste a minute."

There's a child, I'm sure it's a child—by the wall over there!

Doctors are expert at stopping dangerous bleeding, for they know the right places to press. This Dr. Travers was able to do, but he didn't dare do more; the girl was lying in a queerly crumpled heap, and he guessed she had a number of bones broken and that it would be highly dangerous to move her. He watched her with great concentration, wondering where the truck had got to and what other damage it had done.

Mrs. Travers was very quick. She had seen plenty of accident cases and knew the importance of speed. The first cottage she tried had a phone; in four minutes she was back, and in six an ambulance was wailing down the hill. Its attendants lifted the child onto a stretcher as carefully as if she were made of fine thistledown. The ambulance sped off to Plymouth—for the local cottage hospital did not take serious accident cases— and Dr. Travers went down to the police station to report what he had done.

---

6. **lead:** a leash.
7. **shrouds:** ropes on a boat's mast.

413

He found that the police already knew about the speeding truck—which had suffered from loss of brakes and ended up with its radiator halfway through the post office wall. The driver was concussed[8] and shocked, but the police thought he was the only person injured—until Dr. Travers told his tale.

Terrible thing, poor little soul, and they don't know if she's likely to live.

At half past nine that night Aunt Rebecca Hoskins was sitting by her fire thinking aggrieved thoughts about the inconsiderateness of nieces who were asked to supper and never turned up, when she was startled by a neighbor, who burst in, exclaiming, "Have you heard about Sandy Pengelly, then, Mrs. Hoskins? Terrible thing, poor little soul, and they don't know if she's likely to live. Police have got the truck driver that hit her—ah, it didn't ought to be allowed, speeding through the place like that at umpty miles an hour, they ought to jail him for life—not that that'd be any comfort to poor Bert and Jean."

Horrified, Aunt Rebecca put on a coat and went down to her brother's house. She found the family with white shocked faces; Bert and Jean were about to drive off to the hospital where Sandy had been taken, and the twins were crying bitterly. Lob was nowhere to be seen. But Aunt Rebecca was not interested in dogs; she did not inquire about him.

"Thank the Lord you've come, Beck," said her brother. "Will you stay the night with Don and the twins? Don's out looking for Lob, and heaven knows when we'll be back; we may get a bed with Jean's mother in Plymouth."

"Oh, if only I'd never invited the poor child," wailed Mrs. Hoskins. But Bert and Jean hardly heard her.

That night seemed to last forever. The twins cried themselves to sleep. Don came home very late and grim-faced. Bert and Jean sat in a waiting room of the Western Counties Hospital, but Sandy was unconscious, they were told, and she remained so. All that could be done for her was done. She was given <u>transfusions</u> to replace all the blood she had lost. The broken bones were set and put in slings and cradles.

Will Sandy survive?    *predict*

"Is she a healthy girl? Has she a good constitution?"[9] the emergency doctor asked.

"Aye, Doctor, she is that," Bert said hoarsely. The lump in Jean's throat prevented her from answering; she merely nodded.

"Then she ought to have a chance. But I won't conceal from you that her condition is very serious, unless she shows signs of coming out from this <u>coma</u>."

But as hour succeeded hour, Sandy showed no signs of recovering conscious-

---

8. **concussed:** suffering from a concussion, an injury that results from being struck in the head.

9. **constitution:** the physical condition of a person.

ness. Her parents sat in the waiting room with haggard faces; sometimes one of them would go to telephone the family at home, or to try to get a little sleep at the home of Granny Pearce, not far away.

At noon next day Dr. and Mrs. Travers went to the Pengelly cottage to inquire how Sandy was doing, but the report was gloomy: "Still in a very serious condition." The twins were miserably unhappy. They forgot that they had sometimes called their elder sister bossy and only remembered how often she had shared her pocket money with them, how she read to them and took them for picnics and helped with their homework. Now there was no Sandy, no Mother and Dad, Don went around with a gray, shuttered face, and worse still, there was no Lob.

The Western Counties Hospital is a large one, with dozens of different departments and five or six connected buildings, each with three or four entrances. By that afternoon it became noticeable that a dog seemed to have taken up position outside the hospital, with the fixed intention of getting in. Patiently he would try first one entrance and then another, all the way around, and then begin again. Sometimes he would get a little way inside, following a visitor, but animals were of course forbidden, and he was always kindly but firmly turned out again. Sometimes the guard at the main entrance gave him a pat or offered him a bit of sandwich—he looked so wet and beseeching and desperate. But he never ate the sandwich. No one seemed to own him or to know where he came from; Plymouth is a large city, and he might have belonged to anybody.

At teatime Granny Pearce came through the pouring rain to bring a flask of hot tea to her daughter and son-in-law. Just as she reached the main entrance, the guard was gently but forcibly shoving out a large, agitated, soaking-wet Alsatian dog.

"No, old fellow, you cannot come in. Hospitals are for people, not for dogs."

"Why, bless me," exclaimed old Mrs. Pearce. "That's Lob! Here, Lob, Lobby boy!"

Lob ran to her, whining. Mrs. Pearce walked up to the desk.

"I'm sorry, madam, you can't bring that dog in here," the guard said.

Mrs. Pearce was a very determined old lady. She looked the porter in the eye.

"Now, see here, young man. That dog has walked twenty miles from St. Killan to get to my granddaughter. Heaven knows how he knew she was here, but it's plain he knows. And he ought to have his rights! He ought to get to see her! Do you know," she went on, bristling, "that dog has walked the length of England—twice—to be with that girl? And you think you can keep him out with your fiddling rules and regulations?"

"I'll have to ask the medical officer," the guard said weakly.

"You do that, young man." Granny Pearce sat down in a determined manner, shutting her umbrella, and Lob sat patiently dripping at her feet. Every now and then he shook his head, as if to dislodge something heavy that was tied around his neck.

Words to Know and Use | **agitated** (aj′ i tāt′ id) *adj.* excited, nervous

415

Presently a tired, thin, intelligent-looking man in a white coat came downstairs, with an impressive, silver-haired man in a dark suit, and there was a low-voiced discussion. Granny Pearce eyed them, biding her time.

"Frankly . . . not much to lose," said the older man. The man in the white coat approached Granny Pearce.

"It's strictly against every rule, but as it's such a serious case we are making an exception," he said to her quietly. "But only outside her bedroom door—and only for a moment or two."

Without a word, Granny Pearce rose and stumped upstairs. Lob followed close to her skirts, as if he knew his hope lay with her.

review   Why has Lob come to the hospital?

They waited in the green-floored corridor outside Sandy's room. The door was half-shut. Bert and Jean were inside. Everything was terribly quiet. A nurse came out. The white-coated man asked her something, and she shook her head. She had left the door ajar, and through it could now be seen a high, narrow bed with a lot of gadgets around it. Sandy lay there, very flat under the covers, very still. Her head was turned away. All Lob's attention was riveted on the bed. He strained toward it, but Granny Pearce clasped his collar firmly.

"I've done a lot for you, my boy, now you behave yourself," she whispered grimly. Lob let out a faint whine, anxious and pleading.

At the sound of that whine, Sandy stirred just a little. She sighed and moved her head the least fraction. Lob whined again. And then Sandy turned her head right over. Her eyes opened, looking at the door.

"Lob?" she murmured—no more than a breath of sound. "Lobby boy?"

The doctor by Granny Pearce drew a quick, sharp breath. Sandy moved her left arm—the one that was not broken—from below the covers and let her hand dangle down, feeling, as she always did in the mornings, for Lob's furry head. The doctor nodded slowly.

"All right," he whispered. "Let him go to the bedside. But keep ahold of him."

Granny Pearce and Lob moved to the bedside. Now she could see Bert and Jean, white faced and shocked, on the far side of the bed. But she didn't look at them. She looked at the smile on her granddaughter's face as the groping fingers found Lob's wet ears and gently pulled them. "Good boy," whispered Sandy, and fell asleep again.

Granny Pearce led Lob out into the passage again. There she let go of him, and he ran off swiftly down the stairs. She would have followed him, but Bert and Jean had come out into the passage, and she spoke to Bert fiercely.

"I don't know why you were so foolish as not to bring the dog before! Leaving him to find the way here himself—"

"But, Mother!" said Jean Pengelly. "That can't have been Lob. What a chance to take! Suppose Sandy hadn't—" She stopped, with her handkerchief pressed to her mouth.

"Not Lob? I've known that dog nine years! I suppose I ought to know my own granddaughter's dog?"

"Listen, Mother," said Bert. "Lob was killed by the same truck that hit Sandy. Don found him—when he went to look for Sandy's schoolbag. He was—he was dead. Ribs all smashed. No question of that. Don told me on the phone—he and Will Hoskins rowed a half mile out to sea and sank the dog with a lump of concrete tied to his collar. Poor old boy. Still—he was getting on. Couldn't have lasted forever."

"Sank him at sea? Then what—?"

Slowly old Mrs. Pearce, and then the other two, turned to look at the trail of dripping-wet footprints that led down the hospital stairs.

In the Pengellys' garden they have a stone, under the palm tree. It says: "Lob. Sandy's dog. Buried at sea." ❧

I N S I G H T

Little Short Legs

CYNTHIA RYLANT

Little black dog
down the road
we called
Little Short Legs.
One day
my mother late for work
went driving hard
down that dirt road.
Ran over Little Short Legs.
Never knew a grown-up could
make such a mistake.
Never knew one could make it
and say it was so
and feel sorry.
But she did.
And nothing for me to say
but
it's all right, Mom.
It's all right.

STANLEY   David Hockney
Courtesy, David Hockney Studio.

*R*esponding to Reading

First Impressions

1. How did you react to the ending of this story? Jot down a few sentences in your journal or on a sheet of paper.

Second Thoughts

2. Why do you think Lob chooses to be with Sandy and the Pengelly family instead of Mr. Dodsworth?

> **Think about**
> • how Sandy and Lob get along
> • the differences between the Pengellys and Mr. Dodsworth
> • the bonds between certain people and pets

3. The title of this subunit is "Who Can Explain?" How do you explain the presence of Lob at the hospital?

Broader Connections

4. Granny Pearce recognizes the help Lob might be to Sandy's recovery. Why do you think animals can sometimes help people recover from physical and emotional problems?

*L*iterary Concept: Plot

The **plot** of a story consists of the events the story describes. In "Lob's Girl" the plot is actually in two parts. In the first part Sandy meets Lob, and Lob becomes part of the Pengelly household. Then several years pass, and in the second part of the plot, Sandy and Lob are involved in the truck accident. Why do you think the author leaves out details of the years between Sandy's meeting Lob and the accident?

Concept Review: Setting "Lob's Girl" has several settings: the beaches of Cornwall, the sea, a steep and winding road, a rainy night, and a hospital. What role do the settings play in the events of the story?

Writing Options

1. Write a **newspaper article** about the mystery of Lob's appearance. Include interviews with members of the Pengelly family, Mr. Dodsworth, the police, and the hospital staff.

2. What would "Lob's Girl," "The Gold Coin," or *Hiroshima No Pika* be like if it was written as a poem? Write a **poem** based on one of these selections. As the title of your poem, use the title of this subunit, "Who Can Explain?"

3. Write a **short story** describing what occurred on Lob's second journey from Liverpool to St. Killan. Imagine the reasons for his limp, his torn ear, and his missing patch of fur.

4. Write an **editorial** in which you express your opinion on the subject of reckless driving. Use details from "Lob's Girl" and the Insight poem on page 417 to support your opinion. Also include recommendations on how to help solve this problem.

Vocabulary Practice

Exercise A   On your paper, write the letter of the word or phrase that best completes the sentence.

1. A person in a **coma** appears (a) active and dangerous (b) in great pain (c) unconscious.

2. Hospitalized patients feel **wretched** when (a) they are comfortable (b) they are in pain (c) they are told they can go home.

3. An accident victim needs a **transfusion** to (a) replace blood he or she has lost (b) set broken bones (c) start breathing again.

4. Something that is **topaz** looks like (a) a yellow gemstone (b) a red gemstone (c) a blue gemstone.

5. In a **culvert** you would expect to find (a) trees (b) water (c) boats.

Words to Know and Use

agitated
coma
culvert
dignified
melancholy
midriff
pedigreed
topaz
transfusion
wretched

Exercise B   On your paper, write the word from the list that is most clearly related to each sentence below.

1. Records are kept of the names of some purebred dogs' ancestors.

2. The Great Dane is noted for its proud and serious appearance.

3. Many dogs will growl or bite if they become disturbed or upset.

4. A basset hound's droopy eyes look sad and thoughtful.

5. Dachshunds are sometimes called wiener dogs because of the length of their chests and bellies.

Options for Learning

1 • Animals to the Rescue
Think about the talk show that you and your classmates staged before reading this story. Use the *Readers' Guide to Periodical Literature* to find magazine articles on the ways animals help people who have special physical or emotional needs. Present information from the articles in an oral report.

2 • First Help If you come across an accident victim who is unconscious or who may have broken bones, what should you do and not do? Research up-to-date first-aid manuals and medical books for information, or talk to a doctor, nurse, or paramedic. Present your information to the class in the form of a demonstration.

3 • An Incredible Journey
Using an atlas from the library, draw a map showing the possible route that Lob traveled from Liverpool to Cornwall. Include geographical features, such as rivers, as well as the towns he passed along the way.

4 • Caring for Your Dog How much does it cost to own a dog? What kinds of care and exercise do different dogs need? How do you train a dog? Gather information and present a "dog seminar" to your class.

FACT FINDER SCIENCE
How many pints of blood are in an average human being?

Joan Aiken
1924–

Joan Aiken, the daughter of the U.S. poet Conrad Aiken, was born in Rye, England, and grew up as a British citizen. Her parents divorced when she was four, and her mother taught her at home until the age of twelve.

Since there were no children of her age in the neighborhood, Aiken spent much of her time reading and making up stories to amuse herself and her younger stepbrother. She says, "I knew from the age of five that I was going to be a writer. . . ."

When her own children were young, their father died and Aiken had to work to support her family. After jobs at a magazine and an advertising agency, she decided to become a full-time writer. Aiken has since written dozens of children's books.

Aiken explains her writing habits this way: "Generally, I'll start rather slowly, with a lot of revising and going back and crossing out words. As I get warmed up, it may come out faster and faster." About her story ideas she says, "Often I just get ideas from things I hear or read. I keep a little notebook."

WRITER'S WORKSHOP

PERSUASIVE WRITING

The selections in this subunit touch on some of the hard questions of life. What makes people change? How can people get along? In this workshop you will write a **letter to the editor** on a subject that you feel strongly about. Through forceful, persuasive writing, you will try to build a strong case for your point of view.

USE PERSUASIVE WRITING FOR

letters to the editor
petitions
brochures
essays
speeches
advertisements

Here is one writer's PASSkey to this assignment.

GUIDED ASSIGNMENT: LETTER TO THE EDITOR

Write a persuasive letter to the editor of your local or school newspaper. You may wish to write your letter in response to a newspaper or magazine article.

PURPOSE: To write a persuasive letter to the editor
AUDIENCE: Newspaper readers
SUBJECT: Homeless shelter
STRUCTURE: Formal letter

STUDENT MODEL

Ellie uses business-letter form for her letter. This includes a **heading**, an **inside address**, a **salutation**, a **body**, a **closing**, and a **signature**.

Heading
```
                              14 Willow Road
                              Hudson, Kansas 67523
                              January 15, 19--
```

Inside Address
The Hudson Gazette
623 Main Street
Hudson, Kansas 67523

Salutation
To the Editor:

Body

I was really upset by the article "No Hope for Homeless" that was in your paper last week. The story said that Jessie's House, our local shelter for homeless people, will shut down because the town can't afford to run it anymore. I am writing to protest this and to give some reasons why I think we should try to keep Jessie's House open.

◀ Ellie clearly states her opinion and her reason for writing the letter.

The writer begins with her strongest supporting argument. Note how these details appeal to readers' emotions.

First and most important, if Jessie's House closes, people without homes would have nowhere to go. Try putting yourself in these people's shoes. What would you do if you didn't have a job or an apartment? I know I would want a place like Jessie's House to go to for food and a warm bed.

Ellie uses signal words like *first and most important, second,* and *last of all* to show the order of importance of her ideas.

Second, closing the shelter would cause more problems than it would solve. Without the shelter, our homeless people will never get back on their feet or get a job. Their kids won't be able to go to school because they'll be moving around all the time. Some people might end up begging or stealing. Some could even die--especially in this weather.

The writer uses a personal experience to back up her argument.

Last of all, running Jessie's House doesn't have to be expensive. The town should tell us what it costs to run the shelter. Many people would help out if they knew that if they didn't, the shelter would close. Your story said that when the shelter first opened, there were lots of volunteers, but now people have kind of forgotten about it. Remind us! If you explain the situation, I think lots of people will volunteer to help.

Ellie ends by restating her opinion and telling readers what to do.

I believe that closing Jessie's House would be like closing our hearts to people in trouble. Please, everybody, let's keep the doors to Jessie's House open.

Closing   Sincerely,

Signature   *Ellie Lightfoot*

THE LITERATURE CONNECTION

Skim the selections in this subunit for possible topics. For example, does *Hiroshima No Pika* convince you that nuclear weapons should be banned?

Prewrite and Explore

1 **Pick a topic**   Learn about current events by reading magazines and newspapers. Watch the news, listen to talk shows, and discuss "hot" issues. As you read and listen, jot down the topics that you feel strongly about. You'll have more success in convincing others if you have strong personal beliefs about a particular subject. Choose one of these issues as the topic for your letter.

2 **Examine your purpose**   Think about your purpose for writing the letter. Do you simply want to change readers' minds, or do you also want them to take action? Then consider how you will persuade readers to accept your views.

GATHERING INFORMATION

To make your opinion persuasive, you need to back it up with strong arguments. Here's one way to explore your ideas:

1. Write your opinion at the top of a page.
2. Brainstorm for arguments that support your opinion.
3. Go back and underline your two or three strongest arguments.

Following these steps, Ellie ended up with the notes below.

> I think Jessie's House should stay open.
> We give pets food and shelter--why not people?
> <u>The homeless need a place to go.</u>
> It's so cold outside in winter.
> We can find the money to run the shelter.
> <u>Closing the shelter could cause more crime,
> hunger, and begging.</u>
> Jessie's House has been open for three years.
> <u>We could use volunteers and donated stuff to
> cut costs.</u>

◀ STUDENT MODEL ....

Draft and Discover

1 **Introduce your topic**   Start with a paragraph that explains why you are writing the letter. If you are responding to an article, describe what part of it you disagree or agree with.

2 **Organize your draft**   Look over the supporting arguments you underlined in your prewriting notes. You might want to turn each argument into a separate paragraph in your letter.

3 **Add supporting details**   Back up each of your reasons or arguments with details. Your details may be examples, stories, facts, statistics, or a reasonable line of thinking. On the next page, look at examples from Ellie's letter.

FACT OR OPINION?
. . . .
Knowing the difference between a fact and an opinion is especially important in persuasive writing. Not knowing this may lead you to a false conclusion. For more information on this, see the Reader's Workshop, page 283.

> --Closing the shelter causes more problems
>   than it solves.
> --Without a home base, people will be unable
>   to get a job.
> --Kids will be unable to attend school.
> --People could be forced to beg or steal.
> --People could die.

4 **Make a final appeal** Wrap up your draft with a main thought or recommendation. You might want to add a strong emotional appeal at this point.

Revise Your Writing

REMINDER
To learn about signal words, see the Language Workshop on pages 324–326.

1 **Examine the order of your letter** Make sure that your main points are in a logical order. Have you listed your strongest argument first or last? Using signal words will help you connect the main points in your letter. Check to see if your paragraphs begin with signal words like the following: *first, second, next, more important, most important, in addition, moreover, last, finally.*

2 **Strengthen your case** Look at your letter as if you were someone on the other side of the argument. What arguments are weak or purely emotional? Revise your draft as needed to make your opinion more persuasive.

COMPUTER TIP
Put each supporting argument in a separate paragraph. Organize them by **order of importance,** from strongest to weakest or from weakest to strongest. Try moving these paragraphs around until you find the order that works best.

3 **Use a peer reader** Reread your draft. Then ask a peer reader to review it and respond. Use the following questions.

Revision Questions

For You

1. How accurately did I describe the article or topic that I'm responding to?
2. Did I support my opinion with strong arguments?
3. Is my letter too emotional and lacking in facts?

For a Peer Reader

1. Does my letter persuade you to agree with me?
2. Where can I add more details and examples?
3. Does my letter sound whiny or bad-tempered? If so, where?

Proofread

Check your draft carefully for errors in grammar, punctuation, capitalization, and spelling. If your letter is not free of careless errors, how can an editor be sure it is not full of factual errors? Also, make sure you use correct letter form. Your letter should have a heading, an inside address, a salutation, a body, a closing, and a signature.

◄ WRITE RIGHT
For more information on correct business-letter style, see page 648 in the Writer's Handbook.

THE EDITOR'S EYE: CAPITALIZATION

Capitalize geographical names and the names of streets, parks, and buildings.

Problem   The heading in Ellie's letter was as follows:

> 14 Willow road
> Hudson, Kansas 67523

Revised   While proofreading, Ellie realized that the word *road* in her address also needed to be capitalized.

> 14 Willow **R**oad
> Hudson, Kansas 67523

NEED MORE HELP
See the Language Handbook that follows (pages 426–428).

Publish and Present

Here are two suggestions for sharing your work with others.

Post it   Mail your letter to your school or local newspaper. Check the "Letters to the Editor" section of that publication for the next few weeks. You may have the thrill of seeing your name and your opinions in print!

Speak up!   Your opinions are important. Send a copy of your letter to an official in your town or a member of your state or federal government. You may very well get a response.

Reflect on Your Writing

Answer the following questions. Include your answers with a copy of your letter when you put it in your writing portfolio.

◄ FOR YOUR PORTFOLIO

1. Did you learn anything new about your issue as you were writing about it?
2. What else can you do about the situation you wrote about?

LANGUAGE WORKSHOP

CAPITALIZATION

> Capitalize **proper nouns** and **proper adjectives,** including names, titles of people, and the word *I*.

A **common noun** is a general name of a person, a place, a thing, or an idea. A **proper noun** names a particular person, place, thing, or idea. A **proper adjective** is an adjective formed from a proper noun. Capitalize every important word in a proper noun or adjective.

► | **Common Noun** | **Proper Noun** | **Proper Adjective** |
|---|---|---|
| continent | Asia | Asian |
| character | Hercules | Herculean |
| holiday | Fourth of July | |

Proper adjectives are often used with common nouns. In these cases, capitalize only the proper adjective. Do not capitalize the common noun.

Irish setter   **F**rench toast   **K**orean flag

Capitalize the names of people and pets. Also capitalize the initials that stand for people's names.

W.C. Fields   **S**ally **K. R**ide   **R**over

Capitalize a title used before a person's name. Also capitalize the short forms, or abbreviations, used for titles.

Mayor Polk   **M**rs. Alverio   **D**r. Glassman

Capitalize the word *I*.

My brothers and *I* started a band.

Exercise 1   Concept Check   Write the words that need to be capitalized in these sentences. Change small letters to capitals wherever necessary.

1. My friend wesley and i wrote a report about famous dogs.
2. Our school librarian, ms. lefleur, was very helpful.
3. She said, "i know of several articles about unusual dogs."
4. We learned about bobbie, a dog who walked three thousand miles to his oregon home.

5. Later col. e. hofer retraced bobbie's path and found many people who remembered him.

6. A dog named chips helped american troops capture german soldiers in 1943.

7. Two russian huskies, strelka and belka, orbited the earth in a satellite.

8. After strelka had puppies, one was given to president john f. kennedy.

9. A cocker spaniel named millie wrote a book about her life.

10. Millie's owner, mrs. barbara bush, actually wrote the book.

Capitalize the names of places, days, months, holidays, races, languages, and organizations.

Capitalize geographical names and the names of streets, bridges, parks, and buildings.

South **A**merica	**M**ain **S**treet	**Y**ellowstone **N**ational **P**ark
Atlanta, **G**eorgia	**G**olden **G**ate **B**ridge	the **W**hite **H**ouse

Capitalize the names of months, days, and holidays, but not seasons.

June	**M**onday	**V**eteran's **D**ay	spring

Capitalize the names of races, religions, nationalities, and languages.

African **A**merican	**B**uddhism	**G**erman	**A**rabic
Chinese	**C**hristianity	**M**exican	**S**wahili

Capitalize words referring to God and to religious scriptures.

the **A**lmighty	the **B**ible	the **L**ord	the **T**almud
the **O**ld **T**estament	**A**llah	the **B**hagavad **G**ita	

Capitalize the names of clubs, organizations, and businesses.

Girl **S**couts of **A**merica	**D**emocratic **P**arty
Stamp **C**ollectors **S**ociety	**A**ssociated **W**reckers, **I**nc.

DIRECTIONS VS. REGIONS

Do not capitalize *north, south, east,* or *west* when they refer to directions.

Turn west at the stoplight.

Capitalize these words when they name a particular region of the country or world.

California is part of the **W**est.

Exercise 2 Concept Check Write the words that need to be capitalized in these sentences. Change small letters to capitals wherever necessary.

1. On friday the foreign studies club learned about japan.

2. In square miles, japan is slightly smaller than california.

3. Near the capital city of tokyo stands mt. fuji.

4. Most japanese citizens are of asian descent.

5. The main religions are buddhism and shintoism.

6. Many of the people speak english as well as japanese.

7. Like americans, they observe new year's day on january 1.

8. On april 23 a holiday called emperor's birthday is held.

9. Two monuments in hiroshima are peace park and peace tower.

10. One famous japanese company is the sony corporation.

> Capitalize the first words of sentences and lines of poetry. Capitalize all important words in a title.

Capitalize the first word of every sentence.

Have you eaten lunch?   **T**he plane leaves at noon.

Capitalize the first word in most lines of poetry.

LITERARY MODEL
from "The Walrus and the Carpenter" by Lewis Carroll

The sun was shining on the sea,

Capitalize the first word, last word, and all important words in a title. Do not capitalize articles (*a, an, the*) or short prepositions unless they come first or last.

BREAKING THE RULES
Sometimes, especially in modern poetry, the lines of a poem may not begin with a capital letter. Look at "Petals" on page 403.

The Sound of Music (movie)

"**S**topping by **W**oods on a **S**nowy **E**vening" (poem)

Minneapolis Star Tribune (newspaper)

Exercise 3   Proofreading   Rewrite the following passage, using proper capitalization.

> shel silverstein was born in chicago, illinois. his books include *who wants a cheap rhinoceros?* and *the giving tree.* in 1974 silverstein wrote a poetry book called *where the sidewalk ends.* it contains funny poems like "sarah cynthia sylvia stout would not take the garbage out" and "recipe for a hippopotamus sandwich."

LANGUAGE HANDBOOK
For review and practice: Section 9, Capitalization.

Exercise 4   Revising Your Writing   Review your letter to the editor for errors in capitalization. Correct any errors that you find.

VOCABULARY
WORKSHOP

PREFIXES AND SUFFIXES

Many words that you read are made up of smaller parts. Usually there is a **base word,** or main word. This base word may have a **prefix** added to the beginning, or it may have a **suffix** added to the end. Sometimes you can figure out the meaning of an unfamiliar word by studying its parts. Look at this example of a word with a prefix.

Prefix	+	Base Word	=	New Word
im-		pure		impure

The prefix *im-* means "not." Therefore, *impure* means "not pure." Next, look at a word with a suffix.

Base Word	+	Suffix	=	New Word
hate		-ful		hateful

The suffix *-ful* means "full of" or "having." Thus, someone who is *hateful* is "full of hate." To learn the meanings of other common prefixes and suffixes, study the chart below.

Prefixes	Meaning	Suffixes	Meaning
im-, in-	not	*-able, -ible*	can be, having this feature
mis-	wrong	*-er, -or*	one who does something
non-	not	*-ful*	full of, having
pre-	before	*-less*	without
re-	back, again	*-ous*	full of, having
un-	opposite of		

Exercise   Copy these words. After each word, write the base word and the suffix or prefix that was added. Remember that sometimes the spelling of the base word has been changed. Then write the meaning of each word.

Example   protector = protect + *-or;* one who protects

1. nonrigid
2. spiteful
3. reorganize
4. surveyor
5. immobile
6. painless
7. prearrange
8. digestible
9. unaware
10. odorous
11. misjudge
12. rancher
13. insecure
14. floatable
15. rebuckle

◀ IS IT A PREFIX?
Not everything that looks like a prefix is one. For example, the letters *mis* in *mission* and the letters *re* in *relative* are not prefixes. How can you tell? Neither *sion* nor *lative* is a word that can stand alone.

SPELLING TIP
Adding a prefix never changes the spelling of the base word. Adding a suffix, however, may change the spelling of the base word. Look at these examples of words with suffixes.
reverse + *-ible* = reversible
knit + *-er* = knitter

If you're not sure how to spell a word with a suffix, check the dictionary.

Reading on Your Own

Suggested Novels for Unit Four

Experiences of being "In and Out of Control," the theme of Unit Four, are portrayed in the novels introduced on these pages.

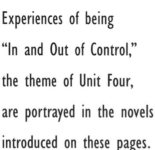

BRIDGE TO TERABITHIA

KATHERINE PATERSON ©1977

Leslie, the new kid at Lark Creek Elementary School, is an outsider. Without even trying, she has outrun all the boys, become the teacher's pet, and made all the girls jealous. Only Jess understands Leslie. He is the "crazy little kid that draws all the time," a boy who despite many efforts can't seem to please his father. "Do you know what we need?" Leslie asks her only friend one day. "We need a place just for us." Swinging across a creek bed on an "enchanted" rope, Jess and Leslie reach a secret spot in the woods, which they pretend is the kingdom of Terabithia. Here the friends escape the hurts of the real world. As you read this story, think about these questions:

- Does the real world remain outside Terabithia?

- How do Jess and Leslie grow close in spite of their many differences?

- How does knowing Leslie affect Jess's feelings and fears?

THE WHIPPING BOY

BY SID FLEISCHMAN ©1986

"Fetch the whipping boy!" echoes throughout the castle each time Prince Brat misbehaves. For Jemmy, who is the whipping boy, this command comes far too often. The time of this novel is the distant past, a time when commoners were punished in place of royal children who misbehaved. In his free time Jemmy learns reading, writing, and other kingly skills that Prince Brat avoids. How might Jemmy use them when outlaws capture both boys and discover that one might be the prince? As you read and are drawn into the boys' adventures, think about . . .

- what each boy comes to realize about himself

- the surprises Prince Brat has for the outlaws and for Jemmy

- the different kinds of people who inhabit Prince Brat's kingdom

SWEETGRASS

JAN HUDSON ©1989

The title character of this historical novel is a Native American girl of the 1800s. "Sweetgrass will be a warrior woman," her wise grandmother declares about the fifteen-year-old. No one else is as certain, since Sweetgrass has struggled only with the daily frustrations of family life. Then a harsh winter brings hunger, and the disease of smallpox brings death to the Blackfoot tribe. Untouched when the disease strikes members of her family, Sweetgrass is the only one who can fight for their survival. As you read this book, consider these questions:

- What was daily life like 150 years ago on the Canadian prairies?

- What changes occur in Sweetgrass's relationship with Otter, her younger brother?

- What sacrifices does Sweetgrass make to save her family?

Other Recommended Books

Other Bells for Us to Ring by Robert Cormier (©1990). The period of World War II is the setting of this historical novel. Eleven-year-old Darcy makes discoveries about friendship and miracles.

Afternoon of the Elves by Janet Taylor Lisle (©1989). Was the miniature village in Sara-Kate's back yard really built by elves? Hillary believes Sara-Kate's claim. As this novel unfolds, Hillary learns much more about her unusual new friend.

Tom's Midnight Garden by Philippa Pearce (©1958). In this classic fantasy, Tom finds himself in an enchanted garden when a clock strikes thirteen. Through his experiences Tom learns that people and things are not always what they seem to be.

The Sign of the Beaver by Elizabeth George Speare (©1983). This historical novel portrays the friendship that slowly forms between a pioneer boy and a Native American boy of the Penobscot tribe in Maine in the 1700s.

WHAT MATTERS MOST

*A*lways remember that

you are never alone.

Marian Wright Edelman

THE HEART'S DESIRE

"What Matters Most" is the theme of Unit Five. If this theme were phrased as a question, how would you answer? Your first response might be "Success," "Fame," "Money," or "Happiness."

On second thought, you may come up with different answers. Perhaps deep down in your heart you have always wanted to have a pet, a special friend, a real home, or a trip to the mountains or the seashore. In this subunit, the characters reveal their hearts' desires. Often however, you must look beyond what a character says to discover an unspoken need that is truly his or her heart's desire.

Fiction

The *Circuit*

FRANCISCO JIMÉNEZ (frän sēs' kỏ hē mē' nes)

*E*xamine What You Know

What are some of the effects that frequent moves to new homes and towns might have on your life? Think about the effects on your feelings, your experiences in school, and your friendships. Jot down these feelings in your journal or on a piece of paper.

*E*xpand Your Knowledge

This story is about the problems that frequent moves cause for Panchito, a young Mexican boy in a family of migrant farm workers in California. Migrant farm workers are laborers who migrate, or move, from one agricultural area to another in search of work. The workers often move in a *circuit,* a regular route of travel, that follows the harvest seasons in different places. Most migrant workers work hard for low pay. Children as well as adults work in the fields. The many hours of work and constant moving make regular attendance at school difficult.

*E*nrich Your Reading

Evaluating   When you evaluate literature, you form opinions about it. As you read the following story, think about the author's purpose. Why do you think Jiménez wrote about the difficulties a young migrant worker has with moving? After you have read the story, decide how well Jiménez used character, setting, plot, and theme to achieve his purpose.

■ *Author biography on Extend page*

The Circuit

FRANCISCO JIMÉNEZ

It was that time of year again. Ito, the strawberry sharecropper, did not smile. It was natural. The peak of the strawberry season was over, and the last few days the workers, most of them *braceros*,[1] were not picking as many boxes as they had during the months of June and July.

As the last days of August disappeared, so did the number of *braceros*. Sunday, only one—the best picker—came to work. I liked him. Sometimes we talked during our half-hour lunch break. That is how I found out he was from Jalisco,[2] the same state in Mexico my family was from. That Sunday was the last time I saw him.

When the sun had tired and sunk behind the mountains, Ito signaled us that it was time to go home. *"Ya esora,"*[3] he yelled in his broken Spanish. Those were the words I waited for twelve hours a day, every day, seven days a week, week after week. And the thought of not hearing them again saddened me.

As we drove home, Papa did not say a word. With both hands on the wheel, he stared at the dirt road. My older brother, Roberto, was also silent. He leaned his head back and closed his eyes. Once in a while he cleared from his throat the dust that blew in from outside.

Yes, it was that time of year. When I opened the front door to the shack, I stopped. Everything we owned was neatly packed in cardboard boxes. Suddenly I felt even more the weight of hours, days, weeks, and months of work. I sat down on a box. The thought of having to move to Fresno, and knowing what was in store for me there, brought tears to my eyes.

Everything we owned was neatly packed in cardboard boxes.

That night I could not sleep. I lay in bed thinking about how much I hated this move.

A little before five o'clock in the morning, Papa woke everyone up. A few minutes later, the yelling and screaming of my little brothers and sisters, for whom the move was a great adventure, broke the silence of dawn. Shortly, the barking of the dogs accompanied them.

While we packed the breakfast dishes, Papa went outside to start the "Carcanchita." That was the name Papa gave his old '38 black Plymouth. He bought it in a used-car lot in Santa Rosa in the winter of 1949.

---

1. *braceros* (brä se′ rôs) *Spanish:* Hispanic farm workers.
2. **Jalisco** (hä lēs′ ko).
3. *Ya esora:* a made-up spelling for the sharecropper's incorrect pronunciation of the Spanish expression *ya es hora* (yä′ es hô′ rä), which means "it is time."

Papa was very proud of his car. *"Mi Carcanchita,"*[4] my little jalopy, he called it. He had a right to be proud of it. He spent a lot of time looking at other cars before buying this one. When he finally chose the "Carcanchita," he checked it thoroughly before driving it out of the car lot. He examined every inch of the car. He listened to the motor, tilting his head from side to side like a parrot, trying to detect any noises that spelled car trouble. After being satisfied with the looks and sounds of the car, Papa then insisted on knowing who the original owner was. He never did find out from the car salesman. But he bought the car anyway. Papa figured the original owner must have been an important man, because behind the rear seat of the car he found a blue necktie.

Papa parked the car out in front and left the motor running. *"Listo,"*[5] he yelled. Without saying a word, Roberto and I began to carry the boxes out to the car. Roberto carried the two big boxes, and I carried the smaller ones. Papa then threw the mattress on top of the car roof and tied it with ropes to the front and rear bumpers.

Everything was packed except Mama's pot. It was an old, large, galvanized pot she had picked up at an army surplus store in Santa Maria the year I was born. The pot was full of dents and nicks, and the more dents and nicks it had, the more Mama liked it. *"Mi olla,"*[6] she used to say proudly.

I held the front door open as Mama carefully carried out her pot by both handles, making sure not to spill the cooked beans. When she got to the car, Papa reached out to help her with it. Roberto opened the rear car door, and Papa gently placed it on the floor behind the front seat. All of us then climbed in. Papa sighed, wiped the sweat off his forehead with his sleeve, and said wearily: *"Es todo."*[7]

As we drove away, I felt a lump in my throat. I turned around and looked at our little shack for the last time.

At sunset we drove into a labor camp near Fresno. Since Papa did not speak English, Mama asked the camp foreman if he needed any more workers. "We don't need no more," said the foreman, scratching his head. "Check with Sullivan down the road. Can't miss him. He lives in a big white house with a fence around it."

When we got there, Mama walked up to the house. She went through a white gate, past a row of rose bushes, up the stairs to the front door. She rang the doorbell. The porch light went on, and a tall, husky man came out. They exchanged a few words. After the man went in, Mama clasped her hands and hurried back to the car. "We have work! Mr. Sullivan said we can stay there the whole season," she said, gasping and pointing to an old garage near the stables.

The garage was worn out by the years. It had no windows. The walls, eaten by termites, strained to support the roof full of holes. The loose dirt floor, populated by earthworms, looked like a gray road map.

That night, by the light of a kerosene lamp, we unpacked and cleaned our new home. Roberto swept away the loose dirt, leaving the hard ground. Papa plugged the holes in the walls with old newspapers and tin can tops. Mama fed my little brothers

---

4. *Mi Carcanchita* (mē kä*r* kän chē′ tä).
5. *Listo* (lē′ stô) *Spanish:* Ready.
6. *Mi olla* (mē ô′ yä) *Spanish:* My pot.
7. *Es todo* (es tô′ dô) *Spanish:* That's everything.

GRAPEPICKERS Vernon Nye
Gallery on Main Street St. Helena, California.

and sisters. Papa and Roberto then brought in the mattress and placed it in the far corner of the garage. "Mama, you and the little ones sleep on the mattress. Roberto, Panchito, and I will sleep outside under the trees," Papa said.

Early next morning Mr. Sullivan showed us where his crop was, and after breakfast, Papa, Roberto, and I headed for the vineyard to pick.

Around nine o'clock the temperature had risen to almost one hundred degrees. I was completely soaked in sweat, and my mouth felt as if I had been chewing on a handkerchief. I walked over to the end of the row, picked up the jug of water we had brought, and began drinking. "Don't drink too much; you'll get sick," Roberto shouted. No sooner had he said that than I felt sick to my stomach. I dropped to my knees and let the jug roll off my hands. I remained motionless with my eyes glued on the hot, sandy ground. All I could hear was the drone of insects. Slowly I began to recover. I poured water over my face and neck and watched the black mud run down my arms and hit the ground.

I still felt a little dizzy when we took a break to eat lunch. It was past two o'clock, and we sat underneath a large walnut tree that was on the side of the road. While we ate, Papa jotted down the number of boxes we had picked. Roberto drew designs on the ground with a stick. Suddenly I noticed Papa's face turn pale as he looked down the road. "Here comes the school bus," he whispered loudly in alarm. Instinctively, Roberto and I ran and hid in the vineyards. We did not want to get in trouble for not going to school. The yellow bus stopped in front of Mr. Sullivan's house. Two neatly dressed boys about my age got off. They carried books under their arms. After they crossed the street, the bus drove away. Roberto and I came out from hiding and joined Papa. *"Tienen que tener cuidado,"*[8] he warned us.

After lunch we went back to work. The sun kept beating down. The buzzing insects, the wet sweat, and the hot, dry dust made the afternoon seem to last forever. Finally the mountains around the valley reached out and swallowed the sun. Within an hour it was too dark to continue picking. The vines blanketed the grapes, making it difficult to see the bunches. *"Vámonos,"*[9] said Papa, signaling to us that it was time to quit work. Papa then took out a pencil and began to figure out how much we had earned our first day. He wrote down numbers, crossed some out, wrote down some more. *"Quince,"*[10] he murmured.

When we arrived home, we took a cold shower underneath a waterhose. We then sat down to eat dinner around some wooden

---

8. ***Tienen que tener cuidado*** (tye nen′ kā te ner′ kwē dä′ dô) *Spanish:* You have to be careful.

9. ***Vámonos*** (vä′ mô nôs) *Spanish:* Let's go.

10. ***Quince*** (kēn′ sā) *Spanish:* fifteen.

crates that served as a table. Mama had cooked a special meal for us. We had rice and tortillas with *carne con chile,*[11] my favorite dish.

The next morning I could hardly move. My body ached all over. I felt little control over my arms and legs. This feeling went on every morning for days, until my muscles finally got used to the work.

It was Monday, the first week of November. The grape season was over, and I could now go to school. I woke up early that morning and lay in bed, looking at the stars and savoring the thought of not going to work and of starting sixth grade for the first time that year. Since I could not sleep, I decided to get up and join Papa and Roberto at breakfast. I sat at the table across from Roberto, but I kept my head down. I did not want to look up and face him. I knew he was sad. He was not going to school today. He was not going tomorrow, or next week, or next month. He would not go until the cotton season was over, and that was sometime in February. I rubbed my hands together and watched the dry, acid-stained skin fall to the floor in little rolls.

When Papa and Roberto left for work, I felt relief. I walked to the top of a small grade next to the shack and watched the "Carcanchita" disappear in the distance in a cloud of dust.

Two hours later, around eight o'clock, I stood by the side of the road waiting for school bus number twenty. When it arrived, I climbed in. No one noticed me. Everyone was busy either talking or yelling. I sat in an empty seat in the back.

When the bus stopped in front of the school, I felt very nervous. I looked out the bus window and saw boys and girls carrying books under their arms. I felt empty. I put my hands in my pants pockets and walked to the principal's office. When I entered, I heard a woman's voice say: "May I help you?" I was startled. I had not heard English for months. For a few seconds I remained speechless. I looked at the lady who waited for an answer. My first instinct was to answer her in Spanish, but I held back. Finally, after struggling for English words, I managed to tell her that I wanted to enroll in the sixth grade. After answering many questions, I was led to the classroom.

Mr. Lema, the sixth-grade teacher, greeted me and assigned me a desk. He then introduced me to the class. I was so nervous and scared at that moment when everyone's eyes were on me that I wished I were with Papa and Roberto picking cotton. After taking roll, Mr. Lema gave the class the assignment for the first hour. "The first thing we have to do this morning is finish reading the story we began yesterday," he said enthusiastically. He walked up to me, handed me an English book, and asked me to read. "We are on page 125," he said politely. When I heard this, I felt the blood rush to my head. I felt dizzy. "Would you like to read?" he asked hesitantly. I opened the book to page 125. My mouth was dry. My eyes began to water. I could not begin. "You can read later," Mr. Lema said understandingly.

For the rest of the reading period, I kept getting angrier and angrier with myself. I should have read, I thought to myself.

During recess I went into the restroom

---

11. **tortillas with *carne con chile*** (tôr tē′ yäs, kär′ nā kôn chē′ lä) *Spanish:* flat, round cornmeal cakes and a mixture of meat and red peppers.

and opened my English book to page 125. I began to read in a low voice, pretending I was in class. There were many words I did not know. I closed the book and headed back to the classroom.

Mr. Lema was sitting at his desk correcting papers. When I entered he looked up at me and smiled. I felt better. I walked up to him and asked if he could help me with the new words. "Gladly," he said.

The rest of the month I spent my lunch hours working on English with Mr. Lema, my best friend at school.

One Friday during lunch hour, Mr. Lema asked me to take a walk with him to the music room. "Do you like music?" he asked me as we entered the building.

"Yes, I like Mexican *corridos*,"[12] I answered.

He then picked up a trumpet, blew on it, and handed it to me. The sound gave me goose bumps. I knew that sound. I had heard it in many Mexican *corridos*. "How would you like to learn how to play it?" he asked. He must have read my face, because before I could answer, he added: "I'll teach you how to play it during our lunch hours."

That day I could hardly wait to get home to tell Papa and Mama the great news. As I got off the bus, my little brothers and sisters ran up to meet me. They were yelling and screaming. I thought they were happy to see me, but when I opened the door to our shack, I saw that everything we owned was neatly packed in cardboard boxes. ❧

---

12. *corridos* (kô rē′ dôs) *Spanish:* slow, romantic songs.

INSIGHT

The 1st

LUCILLE CLIFTON

What I remember about that day
is boxes stacked across the walk
and couch springs curling through the air
and drawers and tables balanced on the curb
and us, hollering,
leaping up and around
happy to have a playground;

nothing about the emptied rooms
nothing about the emptied family

Responding to Reading

First Impressions

1. How did you feel about the end of the story? Use your journal to explore your thoughts and feelings.

Second Thoughts

2. How would you describe Panchito, the **narrator** of the story?

   Think about
   - his attitude toward school and work
   - his feelings about his brother Roberto
   - his feelings about moving

3. Why do you think Mama is so fond of her cooking pot and Papa is so proud of his car?

4. Do you think the narrator's friendship with Mr. Lema will have a lasting effect? Why or why not?

5. The author uses many **sensory details** to describe how things look, feel, taste, smell, and sound. Which descriptions best help you to understand the hardships of migrant life?

Broader Connections

6. Only about twenty percent of migrant workers go beyond sixth grade in school. From your reading of "The Circuit," what are the reasons for this? How do you think this situation could be changed?

Writing Options

1. Both "The Circuit" and the Insight poem "The 1st" on page 440 describe the difficulties of moving. In an **essay,** compare and contrast the narrator of "The Circuit" with the speaker of "The 1st."

2. Write a **prediction** of what life will be like for the narrator of "The Circuit" ten years later. Give reasons for your prediction.

3. Write the **letter** the narrator writes to Mr. Lema from the next town along "the circuit."

4. Review Enrich Your Reading on page 435. Then write an **evaluation** of "The Circuit."

Options for Learning

1 • Moving Experiences Take a poll of your classmates or the people in your neighborhood. Find out how many times they have moved, the places they have moved from, and the reasons for moving. Ask them to describe the positive and negative sides of moving. Share your findings in an oral report.

2 • Photo Exhibit Create a display of photographs that document the history and the lifestyle of U.S. migrant farm workers. Photocopy pictures from books, newspapers, and magazines showing various aspects of migrant workers' lives. Add captions to explain your pictures to your audience.

3 • Play Corridos! Mexican *corridos* are folk ballads. They may tell of an event in the Mexican Revolution, the adventures of a bandit, or the death of a local hero. Check out a recording of Mexican *corridos* from the library and play it for the class.

4 • Family Budget Imagine that a migrant farm worker family of six earns $9,000 a year. Create a monthly family budget that includes groceries, clothing, gasoline, medicine, a small rent and utility bill, and a fund for emergencies such as car repairs or doctor visits.

FACT FINDER HISTORY

Who was Cesar Chavez and how has he affected the lives of migrant farm workers?

Francisco Jiménez
1943–

Francisco Jiménez was born in Mexico and immigrated to the United States in 1947 with his parents. His mother worked in a factory, and his father was a farm worker. Jiménez is now a professor at the University of Santa Clara in California, teaching literature. He has written articles and stories for periodicals and has coauthored two textbooks on Spanish.

Jiménez says that his primary goal in writing "is to fill the need for cultural and human understanding, between the United States and Mexico in particular. I write in both English and Spanish. The language I use is determined by what period in my life I write about. Since Spanish was the dominant language during my childhood, I generally write about those experiences in Spanish" (he translated "The Circuit" from the original Spanish). Jiménez considers it a privilege to be able to move in and out of both U.S. and Mexican cultures with ease and to be able to write stories in both languages. Jiménez's most recent book, *Migrant Child*, is a collection of autobiographical short stories.

Fiction

Flowers and Freckle Cream

ELIZABETH ELLIS

Examine What You Know

About how much money do you receive or earn in a typical month? How do you spend it? Make a pie chart like the one on your right. Divide the pie to show approximately how you spend your money in a typical month. Use these categories or categories of your own choosing.

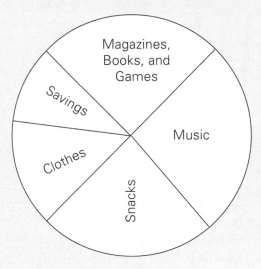

Expand Your Knowledge

In the United States, The total buying power of young people between the ages of eight and seventeen is over twenty-two billion dollars a year. This income is either earned or received as allowances or gifts. Mail-order businesses (those that deliver products through the mail) often target young people. Attractive advertisements appear on TV and radio, in newspapers and magazines, and even on cereal boxes. Though many fine products are advertised and sold by mail, other products are falsely advertised. Some of these products are health and beauty items that are worthless.

Enrich Your Reading

Making Connections   This narrative is based on an experience the writer had with a mail-order company when she was twelve years old. She saved her money and bought a product that she hoped would change her life. As you read, make connections between the narrator's experiences and feelings and your own.

■ *Author biography in Reader's Handbook*

Flowers and Freckle Cream

ELIZABETH ELLIS

When I was a kid about twelve years old, I was already as tall as I am now, and I had a lot of freckles. I had reached the age when I had begun to really look at myself in the mirror, and I was underwhelmed.[1] Apparently my mother was too, because sometimes she'd look at me and shake her head and say, "You can't make a silk purse out of a sow's ear."[2]

I had a cousin whose name was Janette Elizabeth, and Janette Elizabeth looked exactly like her name sounds. She had a waist so small that men could put their hands around it . . . and they did. She had waist-length naturally curly blond hair too, but to me her unforgivable sin was that she had a flawless peaches-and-cream complexion. I couldn't help comparing myself with her and thinking that my life would be a lot different if I had beautiful skin too—skin that was all one color.

And then, in the back pages of Janette Elizabeth's *True Confessions* magazine, I found the answer: an advertisement for freckle-remover cream. I knew that I could afford it if I saved my money, and I did. The ad assured me that the product would arrive in a "plain brown wrapper." Plain brown freckle color.

For three weeks I went to the mailbox every day precisely at the time the mail was delivered. I knew that if someone else in my family got the mail, I would never hear the end of it. There was no way that they would let me open the box in private. Finally, after three weeks of scheduling my entire day around the mail truck's arrival, my package came.

I went to my room with it, sat on the edge of my bed, and opened it. I was sure that I was looking at a miracle. But I had gotten so worked up about the magical package that I couldn't bring myself to put the cream on. What if it didn't work? What would I do then?

I was sure that I was looking at a miracle.

I fell asleep that night without even trying the stuff. And when I got up the next morning and looked at my freckles in the mirror, I said, "Elizabeth, this is silly. You have to do it now!" I smeared the cream all over my body. There wasn't as much of it as I had thought there would be, and I could see that I was going to need a part-time job to keep me in freckle remover.

---

1. **underwhelmed**: the author's humorous way of saying that she is not impressed.
2. **a silk purse out of a sow's ear**: something fine or beautiful from something inferior or ugly.

SIRI   1970   Andrew Wyeth   Tempera on panel, 30 x 30½ inches (76.2 x 77.5 cm)
Collection of the Brandywine River Museum, Chadds Ford, Pennsylvania.   Photo courtesy of the Brandywine River Museum.

Later that day I took my hoe and went with my brother and cousins to the head of the holler[3] to hoe tobacco, as we did nearly every day in the summer. Of course, when you stay out hoeing tobacco all day, you're not working in the shade. And there was something important I hadn't realized about freckle remover: if you wear it in the sun, it seems to have a reverse effect. Instead of developing a peaches-and-cream complexion, you just get more and darker freckles.

By the end of the day, I looked as though I had leopard blood in my veins, although I didn't realize it yet. When I came back to the house, my family, knowing nothing about the freckle-remover cream, began to say things like, "I've never seen you with that many freckles before." When I saw myself in the mirror, I dissolved into tears and hid in the bathroom.

My mother called me to the dinner table, but I ignored her. When she came to the bathroom door and demanded that I come out and eat, I burst out the door and ran by her, crying. I ran out to the well house[4] and threw myself down, and I was still sobbing when my grandfather came out to see what was wrong with me. I told him about how I'd sent for the freckle remover, and he didn't laugh—though he did suggest that one might get equally good results from burying a dead black cat when the moon was full.

It was clear that Grandpa didn't understand, so I tried to explain why I didn't want to have freckles and why I felt so inadequate when I compared my appearance with Janette Elizabeth's. He looked at me in stunned surprise, shook his head, and said, "But child, there are all kinds of flowers, and they are all beautiful." I said, "I've never seen a flower with freckles!" and ran back to my room, slamming the door.

When my mother came and knocked, I told her to go away. She started to say the kinds of things that parents say at times like that, but my grandfather said, "Nancy, leave the child alone." She was a grown-up, but he was her father. So she left me alone.

I don't know where Grandpa found it. It isn't at all common in the mountains where we lived then. But I know he put it in my room, because my mother told me later. I had cried myself to sleep that night, and when I opened my swollen, sticky eyes the next morning, the first thing I saw, lying on the pillow next to my head, was a tiger lily. ❧

---

3. **head of the holler:** dialect for "head of the hollow," the end of a small valley.

4. **well house:** a shed covering a deep hole from which water is drawn.

DAYBREAK (DAYLILIES) 1985 © Gary Bukovnik. Collection, Brian Lewis Los Gatos, California.

Responding to Reading

First Impressions

1. What feelings does Elizabeth's experience trigger in you? Describe them briefly in your journal.

Second Thoughts

2. What thoughts do you think went through the narrator's mind when she saw the tiger lily?

3. What kind of person is Grandpa?

   Think about
   - why Elizabeth confides in him
   - how he first responds to her problem
   - how and where he finds the flower

4. What if the freckle cream had worked? In your opinion, would Elizabeth's life have changed? Explain.

Broader Connections

5. Having "skin that was all one color" seemed to be Elizabeth's heart's desire. How far do you think a person should go to look the way he or she wants to look?

Literary Concept: Symbol

A **symbol** is a person, a place, or a thing that stands for something beyond itself, such as an idea or a feeling. For example, the boxes at the end of "The Circuit" might symbolize moving. What might the tiger lily in this story symbolize?

Writing Options

1. Write the **magazine advertisement** that persuades Elizabeth to send for the freckle cream.

2. Look at the chart you made of your monthly spending for Examine What You Know on page 443. What changes would you like to make? Create a budget for yourself. Write a **summary** of your new plan.

Poetry

Mama Is a Sunrise

EVELYN TOOLEY HUNT

Common Bond

KIMI NARIMATSU

(kē mē nä rē mät′ sōō)

Examine What You Know

Make a list of the people who have been positive role models in your life. Choose one of these people to use as the subject of a web like the one below. In your journal or on a sheet of paper, create a web with the categories that are listed. In the middle rectangle, write the person's name. Then fill in your response to each category.

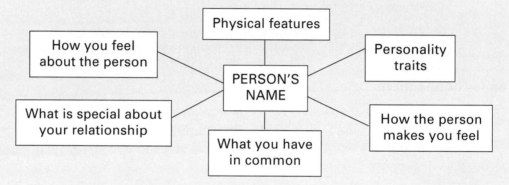

Expand Your Knowledge

Often, a poem grows out of a strong desire to express a feeling. In the two poems that follow, the poets write about mothers who are positive role models. One of the ways a poet can express feelings is through a speaker. The **speaker** is the voice that talks to the reader. However, the speaker is not necessarily the poet, even in a poem that uses the words *I* and *me*.

Write Before You Read

Use the ideas in the web that you created for Examine What You Know to write a poem about the person that you selected as the subject of your web.

■ *Author biographies in Reader's Handbook*

Mama Is a Sunrise

EVELYN TOOLEY HUNT

When she comes slip-footing through the door,
　　she kindles[1] us
　　like lump coal lighted,
　　and we wake up glowing.
5 She puts a spark even in Papa's eyes
and turns out all our darkness.

When she comes sweet-talking in the room,
　　she warms us
　　like grits[2] and gravy,
10　　and we rise up shining.
Even at night-time Mama is a sunrise
that promises tomorrow and tomorrow.

---

1. kindles: lights a fire in.
2. grits: coarsely ground corn cooked like oatmeal.

MASAI WOMEN　Ed Dwight
Courtesy, Bryant Galleries　Jackson, Miss.

*R*esponding to Reading

First Impressions of "Mama Is a Sunrise"

1. What is your favorite image in the poem? Jot it down in your journal.

Second Thoughts on "Mama Is a Sunrise"

2. In your opinion, how old is the speaker? Give reasons for your answer.

3. Think about the qualities of a sunrise. How does the comparison of Mama to a sunrise help you understand the speaker's feelings about his or her mother?

Common Bond

KIMI NARIMATSU

My mother,
not so close are we,
yet we share a common bond,
    a goal,
5   a unity.
Not because she is my mother,
and I her daughter
But because we are both Asian,
in a world of prejudices and hate.
10 We need to stay together as one,
    to survive,
    to love,
    to live.
We need to fight for our rights.
15 My mother,
she lives in a world as a person.
She fights for what she knows is right.
She works so hard to give me what I need.
    I give her in return what she needs,
20   love,
     peace,
     understanding,
     and the will to live as an Asian
      and person.
25 Together, my mother and I are one.

Responding to Reading

First Impressions of "Common Bond"

1. In your journal or on a sheet of paper, write down a few words that describe the speaker's relationship with her mother.

Second Thoughts on "Common Bond"

2. How would you describe the speaker of the poem?

3. How might living "in a world of prejudices and hate" bring a mother and child closer together?

Comparing the Poems

4. Compare and contrast the speakers in these two poems.

5. If these poems were about fathers instead of about mothers, how might the poems be different? How might they be similar?

Literary Concepts: Simile and Metaphor

A **simile** (sim' ə lē) uses the words *like, as, than,* or *resembles* to compare two unlike things that have something in common. For example, "My love is *like* a red, red rose" is a simile that compares love to a rose.

A **metaphor** compares two unlike things directly without using words such as *like* or *as*. Instead, a metaphor says that one thing *is* another as in this example: "Life is a dream." Find a metaphor and a simile in the poem, "Mama Is a Sunrise." How does the poet's use of metaphor and simile help you understand the speaker's feelings?

Writing Options

1. Use ideas from the poem you wrote on page 448, as well as from the two poems you have just read to create a **dialogue** among the speakers in the three poems. Make the subject of the dialogue the theme of Unit Five, "What Matters Most."

2. Prepare a **report card** for Hunt and Narimatsu in which you evaluate each of their poems. Use these categories: theme, figurative language such as similes and metaphors, word choice, and overall quality.

Nonfiction

Carrying the Running-Aways

VIRGINIA HAMILTON

Examine What You Know

The man who tells the following narrative says that his youngest grandchildren never got tired of hearing how their grandfather helped bring slaves to freedom on the Underground Railroad. Think of a story in your family's history that is retold with pride. Share this story with your classmates.

Expand Your Knowledge

The Underground Railroad, which is portrayed in the quilt on the right, was, in fact, neither a railroad nor underground. It was a secret network of escape routes and people, both black and white. Thousands of slaves used the Underground Railroad to reach freedom in the northern states, in Canada, and in Mexico. Railroad terms were used as code words. *Station,* for example, referred to a hiding place. *Conductor* was the word that was used for a person who helped transport slaves. White people risked fines or jail sentences to help slaves escape. Black helpers risked freedom, severe beatings, and their lives.

Enrich Your Reading

■ *Author biography in Reader's Handbook*

Slave Narrative   The following selection about the Underground Railroad is a slave narrative, a true account told by a former slave. As you read the narrative, pay attention to the direct way it "speaks" to you. Try to "hear" the dialect, the speech pattern of the person who narrates this account.

Carrying the Running-Aways

VIRGINIA HAMILTON

Never had any idea of carryin' the runnin'-away slaves over the river. Even though I was right there on the plantation, right by that big river, it never got in my mind to do somethin' like that. But one night the woman whose house I had gone courtin' to said she knew a pretty girl wanted to cross the river and would I take her. Well, I met the girl and she was awful pretty. And soon the woman was tellin' me how to get across, how to go, and when to leave.

Well, I had to think about it. But each day, that girl or the woman would come around, ask me would I row the girl across the river to a place called Ripley. Well, I finally said I would. And one night I went over to the woman's house. My owner trusted me and let me come and go as I pleased, long as I didn't try to read or write anythin'. For writin' and readin' was forbidden to slaves.

Now, I had heard about the other side of the river from the other slaves. But I thought it was just like the side where we lived on the plantation. I thought there were slaves and masters over there, too, and overseers and rawhide whips they used on us. That's why I was so scared. I thought I'd land the girl over there and some overseer didn't know us would beat us for bein' out at night. They could do that, you know.

Well, I did it. Oh, it was a long rowin' time in the cold, with me worryin'. But pret-ty soon I see a light way up high. Then I remembered the woman told me to watch for a light. Told me to row to the light, which is what I did. And when I got to it, there were two men. They reached down and grabbed the girl. Then one of the men took me by the arm. Said, "You about hungry?" And if he hadn't been holdin' me, I would of fell out of that rowboat.

Well, that was my first trip. I was scared for a long time after that. But pretty soon I got over it, as other folks asked me to take them across the river. Two and three at a time, I'd take them. I got used to makin' three or four trips every month.

Now it was funny. I never saw my passengers after that first girl. Because I took them on the nights when the moon was not showin', it was cloudy. And I always met them in the open or in a house with no light. So I never saw them, couldn't recognize them, and couldn't describe them. But I would say to them, "What you say?" And they would say the password. Sounded like "Menare." Seemed the word came from the Bible somewhere, but I don't know. And they would have to say that word before I took them across.

Well, there in Ripley was a man named Mr. Rankins; the rest was John, I think. He had a "station" there for escaping slaves. Ohio was a free state, I found out, so once they got across, Mr. Rankins would see to

ON TO LIBERTY   1867   Theodor Kaufmann   The Metropolitan Museum of Art, New York.   Gift of Erving and Joyce Wolf, 1982.

them. We went at night so we could continue back for more and to be sure no slave catchers would follow us there.

Mr. Rankins had a big light about thirty feet high up, and it burned all night. It meant freedom for slaves if they could get to that bright flame.

I worked hard and almost got caught. I'd been rowin' fugitives for almost four years. It was in 1863, and it was a night I carried twelve runnin'-aways across the river to Mr. Rankins's. I stepped out of the boat back in Kentucky, and they were after me. Don't know how they found out. But the slave catchers, didn't know them, were on my trail. I ran away from the plantation and all who I knew there. I lived in the fields and in the woods. Even in caves. Sometimes I slept up in the tree branches. Or in a hay pile. I couldn't get across the river now, it was watched so closely.

Finally, I did get across. Late one night me and my wife went. I had gone back to

the plantation to get her. Mr. Rankins had him a bell by this time, along with the light. We were rowin' and rowin'. We could see the light and hear that bell, but it seemed we weren't gettin' any closer. It took forever, it seemed. That was because we were so scared and it was so dark and we knew we could get caught and never get gone.

Well, we did get there. We pulled up there and went on to freedom. It was only a few months before all the slaves was freed.

We didn't stay on at Ripley. We went on to Detroit, because I wasn't takin' any chances. I have children and grandchildren now. Well, you know, the bigger ones don't care so much to hear about those times. But the little ones, well, they never get tired of hearin' how their grandpa brought emancipation[1] to loads of slaves he could touch and feel in the dark but never ever see. 🐦

_____

1. **emancipation:** freedom.

"Carrying the Running-Aways" is a reality tale of freedom, a true slave narrative. The former slave who first told the tale was an actual person, Arnold Gragston, a slave in Kentucky. His story of rowing runaways across the Ohio River represents thousands of such stories of escape to freedom.

The abolitionist who helped the runaways once they were across the river was John Rankin, a Presbyterian minister and a southerner who lived in Ripley, Ohio. The town is still there, situated on the great river. A rickety wood staircase leads up Liberty Hill from Ohio River bottom lands to the Underground "station" house of the Rankin family. From 1825 to 1865, more than two thousand slaves were sheltered at the house and guided on by the family. Today, the Rankin house is a State Memorial open to the public from April through October.

Another fugitive, Levi Perry, born a slave, crossed the Ohio River into freedom with his mother about 1854. They were rescued by John Rankin and were taken in and taken care of at the house with the light. Years later, every six months or so, Levi Perry would settle his ten children around him and he would begin: "Now listen, children. I want to tell you about slavery and how my mother and I ran away from it. So you'll know and never let it happen to you." This tale was told to me recently by my mother, Etta Belle Perry Hamilton, who is 92 years old and Levi Perry's oldest daughter.

INSIGHT

Words Like Freedom

LANGSTON HUGHES

There are words like *Freedom*
Sweet and wonderful to say.
On my heartstrings freedom sings
All day everyday.

There are words like *Liberty*
That almost make me cry.
If you had known what I know
You would know why.

Free-slave badge.

Responding to Reading

First Impressions

1. What do you think of the events described in this selection? Jot down your response in your journal or on a piece of paper.

Second Thoughts

2. Describe the narrator, based on his words and actions.

   Think about
   - how he continues rowing runaways after his first trip
   - the **tone** of his narrative
   - his own experiences as a runaway

3. Why do you think reading and writing were forbidden to slaves?

4. What if the narrator had seen the people he carried to freedom? What difference might this have made?

5. "Ibrahima" on page 234 and many other accounts about slaves make it clear that their hearts' desire was freedom. Why do you think the narrator in this account does not talk about his feelings?

Broader Connections

6. Langston Hughes, the author of the Insight poem on page 455, died over a hundred years after the slaves in the United States gained freedom. Why do you think he says that words like *Liberty* almost make him cry?

Writing Options

1. Write a **folk song** that pays tribute to the narrator's actions.

2. Imagine that the narrator has just rowed himself and his wife to freedom and has met Mr. Rankins. Compose the **dialogue** that might have taken place.

3. Look back at the family event that you described in Examine What You Know on page 452. Write a **first-person narrative** from the point of view of the person who experienced this event. Use dialect or any expressions that will make the narrative sound realistic.

Fiction

My Friend Flicka

MARY O'HARA

Examine What You Know

Have you ever made a decision that you knew was right, but everyone else felt was wrong? Record the situation and your feelings about it in your journal or on a sheet of paper. Discover what happens in this story when a boy named Kennie makes a major decision.

Expand Your Knowledge

"My Friend Flicka" takes place around 1940 on a Wyoming horse ranch where the careful breeding of horses is essential to success. A purebred horse is one that belongs to a recognized breed. Owners carefully select stallions (male horses) and mares (female horses) to produce colts that have traits the owners want, such as speed, strength, or size. The height of a horse is measured by the basic width of an adult hand (four inches) from the withers (the ridge between a horse's shoulder blades) to the ground.

Enrich Your Reading

Making Predictions When you read a suspenseful story, you often predict what will happen next. Making predictions helps you get involved in a story and enjoy it more fully. As you read this story, try to predict what will result from the characters' decisions and actions. When you come to a suspenseful moment, pause and record your prediction on a chart like the one below. Then read on to see what happens.

Suspenseful moment	Prediction	What actually occurs

■ *Author biography on Extend page*

My Friend Flicka

MARY O'HARA

Report cards for the second semester were sent out soon after school closed in mid-June.

Kennie's was a shock to the whole family.

"If I could have a colt all for my own," said Kennie, "I might do better."

Rob McLaughlin glared at his son. "Just as a matter of curiosity," he said, "how do you go about it to get a *zero* in an examination? Forty in arithmetic; seventeen in history! But a *zero*? Just as one man to another, what goes on in your head?"

"Yes, tell us how you do it, Ken," chirped Howard.

"Eat your breakfast, Howard," snapped his mother.

Kennie's blond head bent over his plate until his face was almost hidden. His cheeks burned.

McLaughlin finished his coffee and pushed his chair back. "You'll do an hour a day on your lessons all through the summer."

Nell McLaughlin saw Kennie wince as if something had actually hurt him.

Lessons and study in the summertime, when the long winter was just over and there weren't hours enough in the day for all the things he wanted to do!

Kennie took things hard. His eyes turned to the wide-open window with a look almost of despair.

The hill opposite the house, covered with arrow-straight jack pines, was sharply etched in the thin air of the eight-thousand-foot altitude. Where it fell away, vivid green grass ran up to meet it; and over range and upland poured the strong Wyoming sunlight that stung everything into burning color. A big jack rabbit sat under one of the pines, waving his long ears back and forth.

Ken had to look at his plate and blink back tears before he could turn to his father and say carelessly, "Can I help you in the corral with the horses this morning, Dad?"

"You'll do your study every morning before you do anything else." And McLaughlin's scarred boots and heavy spurs clattered across the kitchen floor. "I'm disgusted with you. Come, Howard."

Howard strode after his father, nobly refraining from looking at Kennie.

"Help me with the dishes, Kennie," said Nell McLaughlin as she rose, tied on a big apron, and began to clear the table.

Kennie looked at her in despair. She poured steaming water into the dishpan and sent him for the soap powder.

"If I could have a colt," he muttered again.

"Now get busy with that dish towel, Ken. It's eight o'clock. You can study till nine and then go up to the corral. They'll still be there."

At supper that night Kennie said, "But Dad, Howard had a colt all of his own when

YOUNG PETER Henriette Wyeth
The OS Ranch Foundation Museum
Post, Texas.

he was only eight. And he trained it and schooled it all himself; and now he's eleven, and Highboy is three, and he's riding him. I'm nine now, and even if you did give me a colt now I couldn't catch up to Howard, because I couldn't ride it till it was a three-year-old, and then I'd be twelve."

Nell laughed. "Nothing wrong with that arithmetic."

But Rob said, "Howard never gets less than seventy-five average at school and hasn't disgraced himself and his family by getting more <u>demerits</u> than any other boy in his class."

Kennie didn't answer. He couldn't figure it out. He tried hard; he spent hours poring over his books. That was supposed to get you good marks, but it never did. Everyone said he was bright. Why was it that when he studied he didn't learn? He had a vague feeling that perhaps he looked out the window too much, or looked through the walls to see clouds and sky and hills and wonder what was happening out there. Sometimes it wasn't even a wonder, but just a pleasant drifting feeling of nothing at all, as if nothing mattered, as if there was always plenty of time, as if the lessons would get done of themselves. And then the bell would ring, and study period was over.

If he had a colt. . . .

When the boys had gone to bed that

Words to Know and Use

demerit (dē mer' it) *n.* a mark in a student's record for poor work or for misbehavior

459

night, Nell McLaughlin sat down with her overflowing mending basket and glanced at her husband.

He was at his desk as usual, working on account books and <u>inventories</u>.

Nell threaded a darning needle and thought, "It's either that whacking big bill from the vet for the mare that died or the last half of the tax bill."

It didn't seem just the auspicious moment to plead Kennie's cause. But then, these days there was always a line between Rob's eyes and a harsh note in his voice.

"Rob," she began.

He flung down his pencil and turned around.

"Darn that law!" he exclaimed.

"What law?"

"The state law that puts high taxes on pedigreed stock. I'll have to do as the rest of 'em do—drop the papers."

"Drop the papers! But you'll never get decent prices if you don't have registered horses."

"I don't get decent prices now."

"But you will someday if you don't drop the papers."

"Maybe." He bent again over the desk.

Rob, thought Nell, was a lot like Kennie himself. He set his heart. Oh, how stubbornly he set his heart on just some one thing he wanted above everything else. He had set his heart on horses and ranching way back when he had been a crack rider at West Point; and he had resigned and thrown away his army career just for the horses. Well, he'd got what he wanted. . . .

She drew a deep breath, snipped her thread, laid down the sock, and again looked across at her husband as she unrolled another length of darning cotton.

To get what you want is one thing, she was thinking. The three-thousand-acre ranch and the hundred head of horses. But to make it pay—for a dozen or more years they had been trying to make it pay. People said ranching hadn't paid since the beef barons ran their herds on public land; people said the only prosperous ranchers in Wyoming were the dude ranchers; people said . . .

But suddenly she gave her head a little <u>rebellious</u>, gallant shake. Rob would always be fighting and struggling against something, like Kennie—perhaps like herself, too. Even those first years when there was no water piped into the house, when every day brought a new difficulty or danger, how she had loved it! How she still loved it!

She ran the darning ball into the toe of a sock, Kennie's sock. The length of it gave her a shock. Yes, the boys were growing up fast, and now Kennie—Kennie and the colt . . .

After a while she said, "Give Kennie a colt, Rob."

"He doesn't deserve it." The answer was short. Rob pushed away his papers and took out his pipe.

"Howard's too far ahead of him, older and bigger and quicker, and has his wits about him, and—"

"Ken doesn't half try, doesn't stick at anything."

She put down her sewing. "He's crazy for

460

a colt of his own. He hasn't had another idea in his head since you gave Highboy to Howard."

"I don't believe in bribing children to do their duty."

"Not a bribe." She hesitated.

"No? What would you call it?"

She tried to think it out. "I just have the feeling Ken isn't going to pull anything off, and"—her eyes sought Rob's—"it's time he did. It isn't the school marks alone, but I just don't want things to go on any longer with Ken never coming out at the right end of anything."

"I'm beginning to think he's just dumb."

"He's not dumb. Maybe a little thing like this—if he had a colt of his own, trained him, rode him—"

Rob interrupted. "But it isn't a little thing, nor an easy thing, to break and school a colt the way Howard has schooled Highboy. I'm not going to have a good horse spoiled by Ken's careless ways. He goes woolgathering.[1] He never knows what he's doing."

"But he'd *love* a colt of his own, Rob. If he could do it, it might make a big difference in him."

"*If* he could do it! But that's a big if."

How would Kennie act if he had a colt?

At breakfast next morning Kennie's father said to him, "When you've done your study, come out to the barn. I'm going in the car up to section twenty-one this morning to look over the brood mares. You can go with me."

"Can I go, too, Dad?" cried Howard.

McLaughlin frowned at Howard. "You turned Highboy out last evening with dirty legs."

Howard wriggled. "I groomed him—"

"Yes, down to his knees."

"He kicks."

"And whose fault is that? You don't get on his back again until I see his legs clean."

The two boys eyed each other, Kennie secretly triumphant and Howard chagrined. McLaughlin turned at the door. "And, Ken, a week from today I'll give you a colt. Between now and then you can decide what one you want."

Kennie shot out of his chair and stared at his father. "A—a spring colt, Dad, or a yearling?"[2]

McLaughlin was somewhat taken aback, but his wife concealed a smile. If Kennie got a yearling colt, he would be even up with Howard.

"A yearling colt, your father means, Ken," she said smoothly. "Now hurry with your lessons. Howard will wipe."

Kennie found himself the most important personage on the ranch. Prestige lifted his head, gave him an inch more of height and a bold stare, and made him feel different all the way through. Even Gus and Tim Murphy, the ranch hands, were more interested in Kennie's choice of a colt than anything else.

Howard was fidgety with suspense. "Who'll you pick, Ken? Say—pick Doughboy,

---

1. **woolgathering:** daydreaming.
2. **yearling:** a one-year-old horse.

Words to Know and Use | **fidgety** (fij′ it ē) *adj.* moving restlessly

461

why don't you? Then when he grows up he'll be sort of twins with mine, in his name anyway. Doughboy, Highboy, see?"

The boys were sitting on the worn wooden step of the door which led from the tack room[3] into the corral, busy with rags and polish, shining their bridles.

Ken looked at his brother with scorn. Doughboy would never have half of Highboy's speed.

"Lassie, then," suggested Howard. "She's black as ink, like mine. And she'll be fast—"

"Dad says Lassie'll never go over fifteen hands."

Nell McLaughlin saw the change in Kennie, and her hopes rose. He went to his books in the morning with determination and really studied. A new alertness took the place of the day-dreaming. Examples in arithmetic were neatly written out, and as she passed his door before breakfast, she often heard the monotonous drone of his voice as he read his American history aloud.

Each night when he kissed her, he flung his arms around her and held her fiercely for a moment, then, with a winsome and <u>blissful</u> smile into her eyes, turned away to bed.

He spent days inspecting the different bands of horses and colts. He sat for hours on the corral fence, very important, chewing straws. He rode off on one of the ponies for half the day, wandering through the mile-square pastures that ran down toward the Colorado border.

And when the week was up he announced his decision. "I'll take that yearling filly of Rocket's. The sorrel[4] with the cream tail and mane."

His father looked at him in surprise. "The one that got tangled in the barbed wire? That's never been named?"

In a second all Kennie's new pride was gone. He hung his head defensively. "Yes."

"You've made a bad choice, son. You couldn't have picked a worse."

"She's fast, Dad. And Rocket's fast—"

"It's the worst line of horses I've got. There's never one amongst them with real sense. The mares are hellions and the stallions outlaws; they're untamable."

"I'll tame her."

Rob guffawed. "Not I, nor anyone, has ever been able to really tame any one of them."

Kennie's chest heaved.

"Better change your mind, Ken. You want a horse that'll be a real friend to you, don't you?"

"Yes." Kennie's voice was unsteady.

"Well, you'll never make a friend of that filly. She's all cut and scarred up already with tearing through barbed wire after that mother of hers. No fence'll hold 'em—"

"I know," said Kennie, still more faintly.

"Change your mind?" asked Howard briskly.

"No."

Rob was grim and put out. He couldn't go back on his word. The boy had to have a reasonable amount of help in breaking and taming the filly, and he could envision

---

3. **tack room:** a room in which saddles and other horse gear is stored.
4. **sorrel** (sôr′ əl): a horse with a light reddish-brown color.

Words to Know and Use | **blissful** (blis′ fəl) *adj.* very happy

precious hours, whole days, wasted in the struggle.

Nell McLaughlin despaired. Once again Ken seemed to have taken the wrong turn and was back where he had begun; stoical, silent, defensive.

But there was a difference that only Ken could know. The way he felt about his colt. The way his heart sang. The pride and joy that filled him so full that sometimes he hung his head so they wouldn't see it shining out of his eyes.

He had known from the very first that he would choose that particular yearling because he was in love with her.

The year before, he had been out working with Gus, the big Swedish ranch hand, on the irrigation ditch, when they had noticed Rocket standing in a gully on the hillside, quiet for once and eyeing them cautiously.

"Ay bet she got a colt," said Gus, and they walked carefully up the draw. Rocket gave a wild snort, thrust her feet out, shook her head wickedly, then fled away. And as they reached the spot, they saw standing there the wavering, pinkish colt, barely able to keep its feet. It gave a little squeak and started after its mother on crooked, wobbling legs.

"Yee whiz! Luk at de little *flicka*!" said Gus.

"What does *flicka* mean, Gus?"

"Swedish for little gurl, Ken."

Ken announced at supper, "You said she'd never been named. I've named her. Her name is Flicka."

The first thing to do was to get her in. She was running with a band of yearlings on the saddleback,[5] cut with ravines and gullies, on section twenty.

They all went out after her, Ken, as owner, on old Rob Roy, the wisest horse on the ranch.

Ken was entranced to watch Flicka when the wild band of youngsters discovered that they were being pursued and took off across the mountain. Footing made no difference to her. She floated across the ravines, always two lengths ahead of the others. Her pink mane and tail whipped in the wind. Her long, delicate legs had only to aim, it seemed, at a particular spot for her to reach it and sail on. She seemed to Ken a fairy horse.

She floated across the ravines, always two lengths ahead of the others.

He sat motionless, just watching and holding Rob Roy in, when his father thundered past on Sultan and shouted, "Well, what's the matter? Why didn't you turn 'em?"

Kennie woke up and galloped after.

Rob Roy brought in the whole band. The corral gates were closed, and an hour was spent shunting the ponies in and out and through the chutes, until Flicka was left alone in the small round corral in which the baby colts were branded. Gus drove the others away, out the gate, and up the saddleback.

---

5. **saddleback:** a ridge with a sunken top.

Words to Know and Use | **pursue** (pər sōō´) *v.* to chase after

But Flicka did not intend to be left. She hurled herself against the poles which walled the corral. She tried to jump them. They were seven feet high. She caught her front feet over the top rung, clung, scrambled, while Kennie held his breath for fear the slender legs would be caught between the bars and snapped. Her hold broke; she fell over backward, rolled, screamed, tore around the corral. Kennie had a sick feeling in the pit of his stomach, and his father looked disgusted.

One of the bars broke. She hurled herself again. Another went. She saw the opening and, as neatly as a dog crawls through a fence, inserted her head and forefeet, scrambled through, and fled away, bleeding in a dozen places.

As Gus was coming back, just about to close the gate to the upper range, the sorrel whipped through it, sailed across the road and ditch with her inimitable floating leap, and went up the side of the saddleback like a jack rabbit.

From way up the mountain Gus heard excited whinnies as she joined the band he had just driven up, and the last he saw of them they were strung out along the crest, running like deer.

"Yee whiz!" said Gus, and stood motionless and staring until the ponies had disappeared over the ridge. Then he closed the gate, remounted Rob Roy, and rode back to the corral.

Rob McLaughlin gave Kennie one more chance to change his mind. "Last chance, son. Better pick a horse that you have some hope of riding one day. I'd have got rid of this whole line of stock if they weren't so fast that I've had the fool idea that someday there might turn out one gentle one in the lot—and I'd have a racehorse. But there's never been one so far, and it's not going to be Flicka."

"It's not going to be Flicka," chanted Howard.

"Perhaps she *might* be gentled," said Kennie; and Nell, watching, saw that although his lips quivered, there was fanatical determination in his eye.

"Ken," said Rob, "it's up to you. If you say you want her, we'll get her. But she wouldn't be the first of that line to die rather than give in. They're beautiful, and they're fast, but let me tell you this, young man, they're *loco!*"[6]

Kennie flinched under his father's direct glance.

"If I go after her again, I'll not give up whatever comes; understand what I mean by that?"

"Yes."

"What do you say?"

"I want her."

They brought her in again. They had better luck this time. She jumped over the Dutch half door of the stable and crashed inside. The men slammed the upper half of the door shut, and she was caught.

The rest of the band was driven away, and Kennie stood outside of the stable, listening to the wild hoofs beating, the screams, the crashes. His Flicka inside there! He was drenched with perspiration.

"We'll leave her to think it over," said Rob when dinnertime came. "Afterward we'll go up and feed and water her."

But when they went up afterward, there was no Flicka in the barn. One of the windows, higher than the mangers, was broken.

The window opened onto a pasture an eighth of a mile square, fenced in barbed wire six feet high. Near the stable stood a wagonload of hay. When they went around the back of the stable to see where Flicka had hidden herself, they found her between the stable and the hay wagon, eating.

At their approach she leaped away, then headed east across the pasture.

"If she's like her mother," said Rob, "she'll go right through the wire."

"Ay bet she'll go over," said Gus. "She yumps like a deer."

"No horse can jump that," said McLaughlin.

Kennie said nothing because he could not speak. It was, perhaps, the most terrible moment of his life. He watched Flicka racing toward the eastern wire.

A few yards from it she swerved, turned, and raced diagonally south.

"It turned her! It turned her!" cried Kennie, almost sobbing. It was the first sign of hope for Flicka. "Oh, Dad! She has got sense. She has! She has!"

Flicka turned again as she met the southern boundary of the pasture, again at the northern; she avoided the barn. Without abating anything of her whirlwind speed, following a precise, accurate calculation and turning each time on a dime, she investi-

---

6. **loco** (lō′ cō): slang for crazy.

465

gated every possibility. Then, seeing that there was no hope, she raced south toward the range where she had spent her life, gathered herself, and shot into the air.

Each of the three men watching had the impulse to cover his eyes, and Kennie gave a sort of a howl of despair.

Twenty yards of fence came down with her as she hurled herself through. Caught on the upper strands, she turned a complete somersault, landing on her back, her four legs dragging the wires down on top of her, and tangling herself in them beyond hope of escape. . . .

Kennie followed the men miserably as they walked to the filly. They stood in a circle watching while she kicked and fought and thrashed until the wire was tightly wound and knotted about her, cutting, piercing, and tearing great three-cornered pieces of flesh and hide. At last she was unconscious, streams of blood running on her golden coat and pools of crimson widening and spreading on the grass beneath her.

With the wire cutter which Gus always carried in the hip pocket of his overalls, he cut all the wire away, and they drew her into the pasture, repaired the fence, placed hay, a

BAREBACK #3   Bud Helbig   Courtesy of the artist.

box of oats, and a tub of water near her, and called it a day.

"I don't think she'll pull out of it," said McLaughlin.

 What do you think of Kennie's choice of Flicka for his colt?

Next morning Kennie was up at five, doing his lessons. At six he went out to Flicka.

She had not moved. Food and water were untouched. She was no longer bleeding, but the wounds were swollen and caked over.

Kennie got a bucket of fresh water and poured it over her mouth. Then he leaped away, for Flicka came to life, scrambled up, got her balance, and stood swaying.

Kennie went a few feet away and sat down to watch her. When he went in to breakfast she had drunk deeply of the water and was mouthing the oats.

There began then a sort of recovery. She ate, drank, limped about the pasture, stood for hours with hanging head and weakly splayed-out[7] legs under the clump of cotton-wood trees. The swollen wounds scabbed and began to heal.

Kennie lived in the pasture too. He followed her around; he talked to her. He, too, lay snoozing or sat under the cottonwoods; and often, coaxing her with hand outstretched, he walked very quietly toward her. But she would not let him come near her.

Often she stood with her head at the south fence, looking off to the mountain. It made the tears come to Kennie's eyes to see the way she longed to get away.

Still Rob said she wouldn't pull out of it. There was no use putting a halter on her. She had no strength.

One morning as Ken came out of the house, Gus met him and said, "De filly's down."

Kennie ran to the pasture, Howard close behind him. The right hind leg, which had been badly swollen at the knee joint, had opened in a festering wound, and Flicka lay flat and motionless, with staring eyes.

"Don't you wish now you'd chosen Doughboy?" asked Howard.

"Go away!" shouted Ken.

*F*licka lay flat and motionless, with staring eyes.

Howard stood watching while Kennie sat down on the ground and took Flicka's head on his lap. Though she was conscious and moved a little, she did not struggle or seem frightened. Tears rolled down Kennie's cheeks as he talked to her and petted her. After a few moments Howard walked away.

"Mother, what do you do for an infection when it's a horse?" asked Kennie.

"Just what you'd do if it was a person. Wet dressings. I'll help you, Ken. We mustn't let those wounds close or scab over until they're clean. I'll make a poultice[8] for that hind leg and help you put it on. Now that she'll let us get close to her, we can help her a lot."

"The thing to do is see that she eats," said Rob. "Keep up her strength."

---

7. **splayed-out:** turned outward.

8. **poultice** (pōl′ tis): medicine spread on a cloth and applied to a sore.

But he himself would not go near her. "She won't pull out of it," he said. "I don't want to see her or think about her."

Kennie and his mother nursed the filly. The big poultice was bandaged on the hind leg. It drew out much poisoned matter, and Flicka felt better and was able to stand again.

She watched for Kennie now and followed him like a dog, hopping on three legs, holding up the right hind leg with its huge knob of a bandage in comical fashion.

"Dad, Flicka's my friend now; she likes me," said Ken.

His father looked at him. "I'm glad of that, son. It's a fine thing to have a horse for a friend."

Kennie found a nicer place for her. In the lower pasture the brook ran over cool stones. There was a grassy bank the size of a corral, almost on a level with the water. Here she could lie softly, eat grass, drink fresh running water. From the grass a twenty-foot hill sloped up, crested with overhanging trees. She was enclosed, as it were, in a green open-air nursery.

Kennie carried her oats morning and evening. She would watch for him to come, eyes and ears pointed to the hill. And one evening, Ken, still some distance off, came to a stop, and a wide grin spread over his face. He had heard her nicker. She had caught sight of him coming and was calling to him!

He placed the box of oats under her nose, and she ate while he stood beside her, his hand smoothing the satin-soft skin under her mane. It had a nap[9] as deep as plush. He played with her long, cream-colored tresses,

arranged her forelock neatly between her eyes. She was a bit dish faced, like an Arab,[10] with eyes set far apart. He lightly groomed and brushed her while she stood turning her head to him whichever way he went.

He spoiled her. Soon she would not step to the stream to drink but he must hold a bucket for her. And she would drink, then lift her dripping muzzle, rest it on the shoulder of his blue chambray shirt, her golden eyes dreaming off into the distance, then daintily dip her mouth and drink again.

When she turned her head to the south and pricked her ears and stood tense and listening, Ken knew she heard the other colts galloping on the upland.

"You'll go back there someday, Flicka," he whispered. "You'll be three, and I'll be eleven. You'll be so strong you won't know I'm on your back, and we'll fly like the wind. We'll stand on the very top where we can look over the whole world and smell the snow from the Neversummer Range. Maybe we'll see antelope. . . ."

This was the happiest month of Kennie's life.

With the morning, Flicka always had new strength and would hop three-legged up the hill to stand broadside to the early sun, as horses love to do.

The moment Ken woke he'd go to the window and see her there, and when he was dressed and at his table studying, he sat so that he could raise his head and see Flicka.

---

9. nap: a soft, fuzzy surface formed by brushing hairs or fibers.

10. Arab (ar′ əb): a breed of horse native to Arabia and noted for its speed and grace.

After breakfast she would be waiting for him and the box of oats at the gate, and for Nell McLaughlin with fresh bandages and buckets of disinfectant; and all three would go together to the brook, Flicka hopping along ahead of them as if she were leading the way.

But Rob McLaughlin would not look at her.

One day all the wounds were swollen again. Presently they opened one by one, and Kennie and his mother made more poultices.

Still the little filly climbed the hill in the early morning and ran about on three legs. Then she began to go down in flesh and almost overnight wasted away to nothing. Every rib showed; the glossy hide was dull and brittle and was pulled over the skeleton as if she were a dead horse.

Gus said, "It's de fever. It burns up her flesh. If you could stop de fever she might get vell."

T hen she began to go down in flesh and almost overnight wasted away to nothing.

McLaughlin was standing in his window one morning and saw the little skeleton hopping about three-legged in the sunshine, and he said, "That's the end. I won't have a thing like that on my place."

Kennie had to understand that Flicka had not been getting well all this time; she had been slowly dying.

"She still eats her oats," he said mechanically.

They were all sorry for Ken. Nell McLaughlin stopped disinfecting and dressing the wounds. "It's no use, Ken," she said gently, "you know Flicka's going to die, don't you?"

"Yes, Mother."

Ken stopped eating. Howard said, "Ken doesn't eat anything any more. Don't he have to eat his dinner, Mother?"

But Nell answered, "Leave him alone."

How has Kennie changed since the beginning of the story?

evaluate

Because the shooting of wounded animals is all in the day's work on the western plains, and sickening to everyone, Rob's voice, when he gave the order to have Flicka shot, was as flat as if he had been telling Gus to kill a chicken for dinner.

"Here's the Marlin, Gus. Pick out a time when Ken's not around and put the filly out of her misery."

Gus took the rifle. *"Ja,* boss. . . ."

Ever since Ken had known that Flicka was to be shot, he had kept his eye on the rack which held the firearms. His father allowed no firearms in the bunkhouse. The gun rack was in the dining room of the ranch house, and going through it to the kitchen three times a day for meals, Ken's eye scanned the weapons to make sure that they were all there.

That night they were not all there. The Marlin rifle was missing.

When Kennie saw that, he stopped walking. He felt dizzy. He kept staring at the gun rack, telling himself that it surely was there—he counted again and again—he couldn't see clearly. . . .

Then he felt an arm across his shoulders and heard his father's voice.

"I know, son. Some things are awful hard to take. We just have to take 'em. I have to, too."

Kennie got hold of his father's hand and held on. It helped steady him.

Finally he looked up. Rob looked down and smiled at him and gave him a little shake and squeeze. Ken managed a smile too.

"All right now?"

"All right, Dad."

They walked in to supper together.

Ken even ate a little. But Nell looked thoughtfully at the ashen color of his face and at the little pulse that was beating in the side of his neck.

After supper he carried Flicka her oats, but he had to coax her, and she would only eat a little. She stood with her head hanging, but when he stroked it and talked to her, she pressed her face into his chest and was content. He could feel the burning heat of her body. It didn't seem possible that anything so thin could be alive.

Presently Kennie saw Gus come into the pasture carrying the Marlin. When he saw Ken he changed his direction and <u>sauntered</u> along as if he was out to shoot some cottontails.

Ken ran to him. "When are you going to do it, Gus?"

"Ay was goin' down soon now, before it got dark. . . ."

"Gus, don't do it tonight. Wait till morning. Just one more night, Gus."

"Vell, in de morning den, but it got to be done, Ken. Yer fader gives de order."

"I know. I won't say anything more."

An hour after the family had gone to bed, Ken got up and put on his clothes. It was a warm, moonlit night. He ran down to the brook, calling softly. "Flicka! Flicka!"

But Flicka did not answer with a little nicker; and she was not in the nursery nor hopping about the pasture. Ken hunted for an hour.

At last he found her down the creek, lying in the water. Her head had been on the bank, but as she lay there the current of the stream had sucked and pulled at her, and she had had no strength to resist; and little by little her head had slipped down, until when Ken got there only the muzzle was resting on the bank, and the body and legs were swinging in the stream.

Kennie slid into the water, sitting on the bank, and he hauled at her head. But she was heavy, and the current dragged like a weight; and he began to sob because he had no strength to draw her out.

Then he found a leverage for his heels against some rocks in the bed of the stream, and he braced himself against these and pulled with all his might; and her head came up onto his knees, and he held it cradled in his arms.

He was glad that she had died of her own accord, in the cool water, under the moon, instead of being shot by Gus. Then, putting his face close to hers and looking searchingly into her eyes, he saw that she was alive and looking back at him.

And then he burst out crying and hugged her and said, "Oh, my little Flicka, my little Flicka."

Words to Know and Use | **saunter** (sôn′ tər) *v.* to walk leisurely

The long night passed.

The moon slid slowly across the heavens.

The water rippled over Kennie's legs and over Flicka's body. And gradually the heat and fever went out of her. And the cool running water washed and washed her wounds.

When Gus went down in the morning with the rifle they hadn't moved. There they were, Kennie sitting in water over his thighs and hips, with Flicka's head in his arms.

Gus seized Flicka by the head and hauled her out on the grassy bank and then, seeing that Kennie couldn't move, cold and stiff and half paralyzed as he was, lifted him in his arms and carried him to the house.

"Gus," said Ken through chattering teeth, "don't shoot her, Gus."

"It ain't fur me to say, Ken. You know dat."

"But the fever's left her, Gus."

"Ay wait a little, Ken. . . ."

Rob McLaughlin drove to Laramie to get the doctor, for Ken was in violent chills that would not stop. His mother had him in bed wrapped in hot blankets when they got back.

He looked at his father imploringly as the doctor shook down the thermometer.

"She might get well now, Dad. The fever's left her. It went out of her when the moon went down."

"All right, son. Don't worry. Gus'll feed her, morning and night, as long as she's—"

"As long as I can't do it," finished Kennie happily.

The doctor put the thermometer in his mouth and told him to keep it shut.

All day Gus went about his work, thinking of Flicka. He had not been back to look

at her. He had been given no more orders. If she was alive, the order to shoot her was still in effect. But Kennie was ill, McLaughlin making his second trip to town, taking the doctor home, and would not be back till long after dark.

After their supper in the bunkhouse, Gus and Tim walked down to the brook. They did not speak as they approached the filly, lying stretched out flat on the grassy bank, but their eyes were straining at her to see if she was dead or alive.

She raised her head as they reached her.

"By the powers!" exclaimed Tim. "There she is!"

She dropped her head, raised it again, and moved her legs and became tense as if struggling to rise. But to do so she must use her right hind leg to brace herself against the earth. That was the damaged leg, and at the first bit of pressure with it she gave up and fell back.

"We'll swing her onto the other side," said Tim. "Then she can help herself."

"Ja . . . ."

Standing behind her, they leaned over, grabbed hold of her left legs, front and back, and gently hauled her over. Flicka was as lax and willing as a puppy. But the moment she found herself lying on her right side, she began to scramble, braced herself with her good left leg, and tried to rise.

"Yee whiz!" said Gus. "She got plenty strength yet."

"Hi!" cheered Tim. "She's up!"

But Flicka wavered, slid down again, and lay flat. This time she gave notice that she would not try again by heaving a deep sigh and closing her eyes.

Gus took his pipe out of his mouth and thought it over. Orders or no orders, he would try to save the filly. Ken had gone too far to be let down.

"Ay'm goin' to rig a blanket sling fur her, Tim, and get her on her feet and keep her up."

There was bright moonlight to work by. They brought down the posthole digger and set two aspen poles deep into the ground either side of the filly, then, with ropes attached to the blanket, hoisted her by a pulley.

Not at all disconcerted, she rested comfortably in the blanket under her belly, touched her feet on the ground, and reached for the bucket of water Gus held for her.

Kennie was sick a long time. He nearly died. But Flicka picked up. Every day Gus passed the word to Nell, who carried it to Ken. "She's cleaning up her oats." "She's out of the sling." "She bears a little weight on the bad leg."

Tim declared it was a real miracle. They argued about it, eating their supper.

"Na," said Gus. "It was de cold water, washin' de fever outa her. And more dan dat—it was Ken—you tink it don't count? All night dot boy sits dere and says, 'Hold on, Flicka, Ay'm here wid you. Ay'm standin' by, two of us togedder'. . . ."

Tim stared at Gus without answering, while he thought it over. In the silence a coyote yapped far off on the plains, and the wind made a rushing sound high up in the jack pines on the hill.

Gus filled his pipe.

"Sure," said Tim finally. "Sure. That's it."

Then came the day when Rob McLaughlin stood smiling at the foot of Kennie's bed and said, "Listen! Hear your friend?"

Ken listened and heard Flicka's high, eager whinny.

"She don't spend much time by the brook any more. She's up at the gate of the corral half the time, nickering for you."

"For me!"

Rob wrapped a blanket around the boy and carried him out to the corral gate.

Kennie gazed at Flicka. There was a look of marveling in his eyes. He felt as if he had been living in a world where everything was dreadful and hurting but awfully real; and *this* couldn't be real; this was all soft and happy, nothing to struggle over or worry about or fight for any more. Even his father was proud of him! He could feel it in the way Rob's big arms held him. It was all like a dream and far away. He couldn't, yet, get close to anything.

But Flicka—Flicka—alive, well, pressing up to him, recognizing him, nickering. . . .

Kennie put out a hand—weak and white—and laid it on her face. His thin little fingers straightened her forelock the way he used to do, while Rob looked at the two with a strange expression about his mouth and a glow in his eyes that was not often there.

"She's still poor, Dad, but she's on four legs now."

"She's picking up."

Ken turned his face up, suddenly remembering. "Dad! She did get gentled, didn't she?"

"Gentle—as a kitten. . . ."

They put a cot down by the brook for Ken, and boy and filly got well together. ❧

Responding to Reading

First Impressions

1. What image from the story had the greatest impact on you? In your journal, briefly describe the image and how you felt about it.

Second Thoughts

2. Evaluate Kennie's decision to choose Flicka. Was he blinded by his own stubbornness? Explain.

3. How would you describe Kennie's relationship with his mother and father?

4. In your opinion, how does Kennie change during the story?

   Think about
   - his feelings about himself
   - his care of Flicka

5. If Flicka had died, do you think the lessons Kennie learned from her would have died too? Why or why not?

Broader Connections

6. At one point, Rob McLaughlin says about his son, "Ken doesn't half try, doesn't stick to anything." How important do you think it is for a nine-year-old child to persist at an activity?

Literary Concept: Conflict

The plot of a story usually centers around a problem or conflict and the actions a character takes to solve the **conflict.** "My Friend Flicka" has multiple conflicts. One of the conflicts is Flicka's unwillingness to be tamed. Describe another conflict and explain why this conflict is important to the story.

Concept Review: Suspense As you know, **suspense** is the feeling of excitement that grows when the reader wants to know how a situation will turn out. Flicka's attempt to jump over the fence, for example, is a moment of suspense. Use the prediction chart you made to describe another suspenseful part of the story.

*W*riting Options

1. Imagine that you have been asked to write an episode of the television series "My Friend Flicka." Write a **plot summary** of a half-hour show.

2. In an **essay,** compare Kennie and Flicka's relationship to the human-animal relationship described in "A Secret for Two," "Lob's Girl," or another story you have read in this book or on your own.

3. Based on Kennie's experiences with Flicka, write a **guidebook** on choosing and taking care of a colt.

4. Compare and contrast Kennie's mother with one of the other mothers in this subunit. Write an **evaluation** in which you explain which mother does the best job of recognizing the heart's desire of her child.

*V*ocabulary Practice

Exercise On your paper, write the letter of the word that is least like the other words in the set.

1. (a) award (b) recommendation (c) demerit (d) compliment

2. (a) stock (b) invention (c) list (d) inventory

3. (a) rebellious (b) disobedient (c) uncontrollable (d) cautious

4. (a) calm (b) fidgety (c) restless (d) nervous

5. (a) sad (b) gloomy (c) blissful (d) miserable

6. (a) pursue (b) chase (c) seek (d) escape

7. (a) extreme (b) careful (c) fanatical (d) intense

8. (a) careless (b) precise (c) exact (d) accurate

9. (a) stroll (b) walk (c) run (d) saunter

10. (a) worry (b) tension (c) calculation (d) stress

Words to Know and Use

blissful
calculation
demerit
fanatical
fidgety
inventory
precise
pursue
rebellious
saunter

EXTEND

Options for Learning

1 • Act It Out With a group of classmates, choose one or two scenes from the story to act out before the class. Look at the story for dialogue, but feel free to add lines of your own. Try to convey the mood of each scene through the expression in your voice and the interaction of the characters. Choose a director and rehearse together before presenting your scene.

2 • Hey, Dude Imagine the McLaughlins have turned their place into a dude ranch (a ranch that is operated for people on vacation). Create a travel brochure for the McLaughlin Dude Ranch. Include descriptions of the ranch, the scenery along the trails, the variety of horses available, the helpfulness of the staff, and other information for those who want to experience life on a Western ranch.

3 • Flicka: The Movie Design a poster to advertise a new movie version of "My Friend Flicka." Using hand-drawn art or magazine pictures, try to capture the mood of the story in a visual illustration.

4 • A Book of Horses The word *yearling* is one of many special terms in the story that relate to horses. Review the story and make a list of the specialized vocabulary words. Using reference materials, define the words and list them alphabetically. Combine your definitions with illustrations to create a pocket dictionary of horse terms to accompany the story.

FACT FINDER MATH

Kennie tells Howard that Lassie "will never go over fifteen hands." What is this measurement in feet?

Mary O'Hara
1885–1980

Mary O'Hara Alsop began her career as a scriptwriter in the 1920s, the early days of motion pictures. In 1931 she gave up screenwriting and moved with her husband to a sheep ranch in Wyoming. O'Hara found herself in a "different world. Vast. Empty. Glowing with heavenly colors."

As O'Hara struggled with a story idea that was not working out, she recalled that when she told stories about her many animals, people always seemed to listen. "How easy it would be," she thought, to write a story "about that little filly, for instance, the one that got caught in the barbed wire." Within twenty-four hours, she wrote the notes and a few scenes for a short story called "My Friend Flicka."

In 1941 O'Hara expanded the short story into a novel. O'Hara continued the story of the McLaughlin family in the novels *Thunderhead* (1943) and *Green Grass of Wyoming* (1946). All three books were made into movies in the 1940s.

WRITER'S WORKSHOP

WRITING ABOUT LITERATURE

WRITING ABOUT LITERATURE INCLUDES
book reviews
essays
literary reviews

In terms of reading choices, what is your heart's desire? In this workshop you will have a chance to review your most favorite, or least favorite, selections from this book. Now's your chance to explain why some selections deserve a "thumbs up" or a "thumbs down"!

Here is one writer's PASSkey to this assignment.

GUIDED ASSIGNMENT: THUMBS UP! THUMBS DOWN!

Write a review that compares two or more selections from this book.

P URPOSE: To write a comparison of selections

A UDIENCE: Teacher and classmates

S UBJECT: Two or more selections

S TRUCTURE: Comparison/contrast review

STUDENT MODEL

► Before you write, read how one student responded to the assignment.

► Katrina explains which selections she's comparing and how she feels about them.

► The writer explains what she likes about the first selection and gives examples. She copies direct quotations exactly.

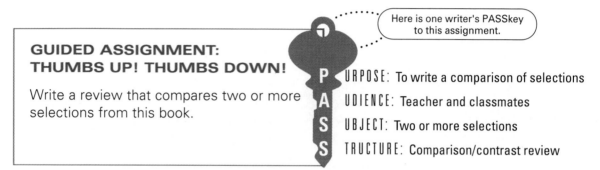

```
           The Real Thing
          by Katrina Larson

   I like realistic stories, so it should not
be a surprise that I liked "Flowers and
Freckle Cream" better than "Playing for
Keeps," which is a science fiction story and
not very realistic. I think "Flowers and
Freckle Cream" is very realistic and has a
good ending, and I think "Playing for Keeps" is
very unrealistic and has a ridiculous ending.
   One of the things I like about "Flowers and
Freckle Cream" is when Elizabeth says she was
"underwhelmed" instead of "overwhelmed" when
she looked in the mirror. I could also relate
to the character when she says to herself,
"Elizabeth, this is silly. You have to do it
now!" She doesn't try the freckle cream right
away because she is too nervous. I know
exactly how she must have felt.
```

Finally, I really like the ending of this story. When Elizabeth's grandfather leaves the tiger lily on her pillow, I think it really makes her feel better. Her grandfather understands her much better than her mother does, and I think this is also true-to-life. He shows how much he loves Elizabeth by looking all over the mountains for this particular flower.

"Playing for Keeps," on the other hand, is a very different kind of story. For one thing, it's science fiction, so none of it could ever happen. I think the story mixes up what's going on in the boy's imagination and an alien invasion that is supposed to actually happen. It is also hard to understand when the story is serious and when it isn't. For example, in one scene it says, "Sara shuddered at the memory of the bomb squad marching through their living room in knee-deep water." Is this real or not?

In conclusion, I think that the most realistic selections in the book are the best ones. "Flowers and Freckle Cream" makes me think of real problems and a good solution, but "Playing for Keeps" doesn't make me think of anything but aliens and marbles.

◀ Katrina describes her second selection. She explains her opinion and compares the two selections.

◀ Katrina concludes her review by discussing her general views about both choices.

Prewrite and Explore

1 **Search for selections** Look over the table of contents and flip through this book to find selections you especially liked or disliked. You can also read your journal to see which selections affected you the most. Choose two or more selections to review and compare.

2 **Find common ground** Whatever you choose—stories, poems, plays, nonfiction, or a mix—think about their features. What elements or characteristics do the selections share? Which of these elements do you think are worth writing about? Jot down the elements that interest you.

GATHERING INFORMATION

Make a chart like the one below. On the left, list the features, or elements, that you are comparing. On the right, jot down key words or phrases from the two selections you are comparing. Decide which features and quotes you want to discuss in your review. Circle those items.

STUDENT MODEL ▶

REVIEW THE ELEMENTS
Elements of Fiction, pages 15–16
Elements of Nonfiction, pages 48–49
Elements of Poetry, pages 89–90
Elements of Drama, pages 188–189

Features	"Flowers and Freckle Cream"	"Playing for Keeps"
Main character	likeable	imaginative
Plot	realistic	unrealistic
Point of view	first-person	third-person
Mood	sad, but with a happy ending	weird
Theme	everything is beautiful	can't tell
Setting	Grandpa's house	back yard
Quotes	"underwhelmed" "this is silly"	"bomb-squad" "Lone Ranger"

Draft and Discover

1 Draft an introduction   Tell which selections you are comparing. In a few sentences give your honest opinion of these selections.

2 Move through a pattern of comparison   Use the chart from your prewriting notes to compare and contrast the elements in both selections. To organize your comparison, use one of these two basic patterns:

Block pattern of comparison   Cover all the features of one selection, then cover all the same features of the other selection. For example, discuss the first selection in the first paragraph after the introduction, then begin a new paragraph and discuss the next selection.

Alternating pattern of comparison   Move back and forth between the selections, comparing and contrasting each feature. For example, in

WRITER'S CHOICE ▶
Katrina used the block pattern to compare her selections. Which pattern of comparison works best for your review?

your first paragraph after the introduction, discuss both selections at once, but only consider one feature, such as plot. Then, in the next paragraph, discuss both selections again, but this time focus on a different feature, such as dialogue.

3 **Draw examples from the selection**   Use quotations, examples, and details to support your opinions about the selections. For instance, Katrina states that she could relate to Elizabeth's nervousness, and she uses the following quotation to show what she means: "Elizabeth, this is silly. You have to do it now!"

4 **Use signal words and phrases**   Use the following words to help point out how features are similar or different. Notice that many of these can be very helpful for beginning paragraphs, since transitions and signal words let your reader know what to expect.

Words That Show Similarities	**Words That Show Differences**
likewise both similarly in the same way	but instead however on the other hand

◄ **COMPUTER TIP** . . . .
Keep a running list of your favorite quotations from the selections. Insert appropriate ones into your main text.

◄ **KEEP YOUR SIGNALS STRAIGHT**
. . . .
For help with making the direction of your writing clear, see the Tips for Better Paragraphs in the Writer's Handbook, and the Language Workshop on using signal words on pages 324–326.

Revise Your Writing

1 **Did you cover the main points?**   Go though your prewriting chart. Check to see if each circled feature in the chart is covered in your draft. Do you need to add any points of comparison? Could you use more descriptions, details, or quotations?

2 **Use a peer reader**   Look over your draft, then share it with a classmate. Use the questions below to guide your revision.

Revision Questions

For You	For a Peer Reader
1. Are my opinions about the selections clear?	1. Can you tell what I liked best about these selections?
2. Did I offer support for my opinions?	2. Are my comparisons clear?
3. Did I show how the selections are alike? different?	3. Did I include enough quotations and details about the selections?

Proofread

After you have finished revising your essay, proofread it carefully. Look for mistakes in grammar, punctuation, spelling, and capitalization. Make sure you put quotation marks around story and poem titles as well as around quotations.

THE EDITOR'S EYE: COMPARISONS

When you compare two things, use the comparative form of an adjective. To make the comparative form of most short adjectives, add -er. If the adjective ends in y, drop the y and add -ier.

Adjective	Comparative Form
small	smaller
funny	funnier

Never put the word *more* before an adjective that uses the *-er* ending.

Incorrect	I liked "Flowers and Freckle Cream" more better than "Playing for Keeps."
Correct	I liked "Flowers and Freckle Cream" better than "Playing for Keeps."

NEED MORE HELP?
See the Language Workshop that follows (pages 481–483) and Section 7 in the Language Handbook.

Publish and Present

CRITICAL DUOS
Film critics Gene Siskel and Roger Ebert review movies together on TV. With a classmate, try presenting your review in the same style.

Co-Review   If possible, find a classmate who has reviewed the same selections as you and discuss how your reviews are the same or different. Present your reviews orally in the form of a dialogue for your class.

Reflect on Your Writing

FOR YOUR PORTFOLIO

Write your answers to the questions below. Place the answers in your writing portfolio, along with a copy of your review.

1. Will this review make other people want to read the selections, or not?
2. Can you think of other cases where a comparison pattern might be helpful in an essay?

LANGUAGE WORKSHOP

MAKING CORRECT COMPARISONS

Use the **comparative form** of an adjective to compare two things. Use the **superlative form** of an adjective to compare three or more things.

Adjectives

A fly, a mouse, and a squirrel are all small creatures. You can show the differences in size by using special forms of adjectives. Use the word *smaller* to compare two things. *Smaller* is the **comparative form** of *small.*

A mouse is *smaller* than a squirrel.

Use *smallest* to compare three or more things. *Smallest* is the **superlative form** of small.

A fly is the *smallest* of the three creatures.

Follow the rules below to make the comparative and superlative forms of adjectives.

1. **To make the comparative form of most short adjectives, add *-er.***
2. **To make the superlative form of most short adjectives, add *-est.***

Adjective	Comparative Form	Superlative Form
long	longer	longest
sad	sadder	saddest
fine	finer	finest
funny	funnier	funniest

Not all adjectives use *-er* or *-est* to make the comparative or superlative form. For longer adjectives, use the word *more* before the adjective to make the comparative form. Use the word *most* before longer adjectives to make the superlative form.

Adjective	Comparative Form	Superlative Form
thoughtful	more thoughtful	most thoughtful
important	more important	most important
agreeable	more agreeable	most agreeable

◀ **REMINDER**
An **adjective** is a word that describes a noun or a pronoun.

SPELLING TIP
When an adjective ends in silent *e,* as in *fine,* drop the *e* before adding the ending. When the adjective ends in a *y* that follows a consonant, as in *funny,* change the *y* to *i* before adding the ending: *funniest.*

◀ **DON'T DO TWO!**
Never use both *-er* and *more* or both *-est* and *most.*
Incorrect Kennie was *more sadder* than Howard.
Correct Kennie was *sadder* than Howard.

Irregular Comparison Forms

Some adjectives use completely new words for their comparative and superlative forms. The chart below shows some of these forms.

Adjective	Comparative Form	Superlative Form
good	better	best
bad	worse	worst
little	less	least
much	more	most

Exercise 1   Concept Check   Read each sentence. Write the correct form of the adjective in parentheses.

1. Mary O'Hara is one of the (talented) authors of books about horses.
2. Mary was the (creative) of the four children in her family.
3. Writing was (enjoyable) to Mary than doing housework.
4. As a child, Mary was the (good) writer in her class.
5. As an adult, Mary was (happy) living on a ranch than in the city.
6. Of the three books she wrote, *My Friend Flicka* is the (good).
7. In *Thunderhead,* Flicka has a colt who is even (wild) than Flicka.
8. Flicka's colt is the (fast) horse on the ranch.
9. *Green Grass of Wyoming* is a (challenging) book to read than *My Friend Flicka.*
10. In *Green Grass of Wyoming,* Ken McLaughlin is seven years (old) than he is in *My Friend Flicka.*

REMINDER
An **adverb** describes a verb, an adjective, or another adverb. Adverbs tell *how, when, where,* or *to what degree.*

▶ Adverbs

Use the **comparative form** of an adverb to compare two actions. Use the **superlative form** of an adverb to compare three or more actions.

Adverbs can also be changed to either the comparative or superlative form. When you compare two actions, use the **comparative form.**

Mama wakes up *earlier* than I do.

When you compare three or more actions, use the **superlative form.**

Of all of us, Mama wakes up the *earliest.*

Follow the rules on the next page to use the correct forms of adverbs.

1. **To make the comparative form of most short adverbs, add -er. To make the superlative form of most short adverbs, add -est.**

Adverb	Comparative	Superlative
late	later	latest
hard	harder	hardest

2. **For adverbs that end in -ly, use the word *more* before the adverb to make the comparative form. Use the word *most* to make the superlative form.**

Adverb	Comparative	Superlative
gently	more gently	most gently
happily	more happily	most happily

3. **Some adverbs change completely for their comparative and superlative forms.**

Adverb	Comparative	Superlative
well	better	best
badly	worse	worst
much	more	most
little	less	least

◄ CAUTION! . . . .
As with adjectives, never use both -er and *more,* or both -est and *most,* when you form the comparative or superlative of an adverb.
Incorrect Flicka ran *more faster* than Doughboy.
Correct Flicka ran *faster* than Doughboy.

Exercise 2   Concept Check   Read each sentence. Write the correct form of the adverb in parentheses.

1. You must pick peaches (carefully) than apples.
2. Of all fruits, bananas bruise the (easily).
3. The strawberries grew (well) than the raspberries this year.
4. Of the four ladders, this one reaches (high).
5. The bees in the orchard bother us (little) than the heat.
6. Because of rain, the grapes grew the (slowly) of all the crops.

LANGUAGE HANDBOOK . . . .
For review and practice: Section 7, Adjectives and Adverbs.

Exercise 3   Proofreading Skill   Rewrite the paragraph below, correcting errors in comparisons.

(1) Of all slaves' escapes on the Underground Railroad, Henry Brown's was the unusuallest. (2) Brown made a box that was more bigger than he. (3) Brown got inside the box and a friend nailed it closed, then loaded it onto the most fast train from Virginia to Philadelphia. (4) That night was the longer night of Brown's life. (5) He reached Philadelphia safely, however. The worse part of his life was behind him.

◄ TRUE STORY . . . .
Henry Brown's story is told in a book by Henrietta Buckmaster, *Flight to Freedom: The Story of the Underground Railroad.*

Exercise 4   Revising Your Writing   Check the review you wrote on page 476. Correct any comparison errors you find.

READER'S WORKSHOP

MAKING INFERENCES

Have you ever heard of "reading between the lines"? That's just what you're doing when you make **inferences.** Inferences are smart guesses based on facts and common sense. Making inferences allows you to use clues in a reading passage to figure out information that is not stated directly. For example, look at the paragraph below.

LITERARY MODEL
from "The Circuit" by
Francisco Jiménez

▶ It was Monday, the first week of November. The grape season was over, and I could now go to school. I woke up early that morning and lay in bed, looking at the stars and savoring the thought of not going to work and of starting sixth grade for the first time that year.

TIP

To make inferences, first gather all the facts you can. Then think about what bigger ideas or conclusions these facts lead you to. Base your inference *only* on the facts that you have.

▶ From the facts in this paragraph, you can infer even more information. In the chart below, the simple facts are listed in one column. In the other column are the inferences that can be made from the facts.

Fact	Inference
the grape season is over	he is finished with work
starting sixth grade	he is about eleven years old
"savoring the thought"	he is excited about school

Making inferences like these helps you get the most out of what you read. Through inferences, you can figure out settings, characters' feelings, and other important details.

Exercise   Read the paragraph. Then use inferences to answer the questions below.

LITERARY MODEL
from "Carrying the
Running-Aways" by
Virginia Hamilton

▶ Well, I did it. Oh, it was a long rowin' time in the cold, with me worryin'. But pretty soon I see a light way up high. Then I remembered the woman told me to watch for a light. Told me to row to the light, which is what I did. And when I got to it, there were two men. They reached down and grabbed the girl. Then one of the men took me by the arm. Said, "You about hungry?" And if he hadn't been holdin' me, I would of fell out of that rowboat.

1. What is the purpose of the light? Which clues tell you this?
2. How do the actions of the two men tell you that they are friendly?
3. How does the speaker feel after he has rowed the boat across the river? How do you know?

ALL YOU EVER WANTED

CHARLIE BROWN © 1950
United Feature Syndicate, Inc.

Nearly everyone has had this thought: If only things were just the way *I* want them, then everything would be fine and there wouldn't be any problems. Yet what one person wants may be different from what another person wants. What makes one person happy may not make another person happy at all. Luckily, happiness doesn't wait for everyone to agree before it shows up. People usually find ways of being happy as they pass through their ordinary days.

In this subunit you will read a musical play with very familiar characters. These characters spend their day exchanging views and fears, hopes and disappointments. Through it all, they find happiness appearing and disappearing and then appearing again. As you read, think about "all you ever wanted." Is happiness related to personal goals or to feeling good about yourself? Is happiness working together with other people to make life better? Is happiness something you find, or does happiness find you?

Drama

You're a Good Man, Charlie Brown

CLARK GESNER

Based on the comic strip Peanuts *by*

CHARLES M. SCHULZ

Examine What You Know

Take a survey of your classmates to find out how they would complete the sentence "Happiness is . . . ." Compare the responses you gather to the responses of the characters in this play.

Expand Your Knowledge

The characters in the comic strip *Peanuts* have been pursuing happiness in their own way for over forty years. Today, *Peanuts* is the most popular comic strip in U.S. history. *Peanuts* appears in more than two thousand newspapers worldwide and is translated into twenty-four languages. Charles Schulz first created the characters of Charlie Brown, Snoopy, Shermy, and Patty (not Peppermint Patty) for a comic strip he called *Li'l Folks* in 1948. The name of the strip was changed to *Peanuts* in 1950.

Enrich Your Reading

Examining Characters   Playwrights rely on **dialogue** to develop their characters. As they speak, characters often state how they feel about others; however, they usually reveal their own personalities indirectly. The audience must infer what the characters are like from the way they react to each other as well as from the things they say and do. Create a chart like the one started below. After each act, record two or three things that each character says and does. In this way, you can more clearly see what makes each character unique and what makes each character happy or unhappy.

Charlie Brown	Lucy	Linus	Schroeder	Patty	Snoopy

■ *Author biographies on Extend page*

You're a Good Man, Charlie Brown

CLARK GESNER
Based on the comic strip Peanuts *by* CHARLES M. SCHULZ

CHARLIE BROWN   © 1950 United Feature Syndicate, Inc.

CAST OF CHARACTERS

Linus

Charlie Brown

Patty

Schroeder

Snoopy

Lucy

TIME: *An average day in the life of* Charlie Brown.

ACT ONE

Just as the audience is beginning to be aware that there is the faint sound of a funny little waltz coming from somewhere, the house lights begin to dim. The darkness increases, the waltz moves and grows, and then a single light picks out a small face at center stage. It is Charlie Brown. *Suddenly*

Acknowledgment
YOU'RE A GOOD MAN, CHARLIE BROWN by Clark Gesner. Copyright 1967 by Clark Gesner. Copyright 1965, 1966, 1967 by Jeremy Music, Inc. Reprinted by permission of Random House, Inc. Professionals and amateurs are hereby warned that YOU'RE A GOOD MAN, CHARLIE BROWN is fully protected under the Universal Copyright Convention, Berne Convention and Pan-American Copyright Convention and is subject to royalty. All rights are strictly reserved including professional, amateur, motion picture, television, radio, recitation, lecturing, public reading, and foreign translation and none such rights can be exercised or used without written permission from the copyright holder. All inquiries for licenses or permissions for stock and amateur uses should be addressed to Tams-Witmark Music Library, 560 Lexington Avenue, New York, New York 10022.

the music stops, and a voice pipes up from the darkness behind him.

Linus. I really don't think you have anything to worry about, Charlie Brown. After all, science has shown that a person's character isn't really established until he's at least five years old.

Charlie Brown. But I *am* five. I'm more than five.

Linus. Oh. Well that's the way it goes.

(The waltz continues. It glides forward, rises, then stops again.)

Patty *(from another section of the darkness).* The only thing wrong with Charlie Brown is his lack of confidence. *(She thinks a moment.)* His inferiority and his lack of confidence. *(She thinks again.)* His clumsiness, his inferiority, and his lack of confidence. *(She pauses again.)* His stupidity, his clumsiness, his inferiority, and his . . . .

(The music mercifully begins again, cutting off her speech. It trickles along briefly, then stops.)

Schroeder. Did you know that Charlie Brown has never pitched a winning baseball game, never been able to keep a kite in the air, never won a game of checkers, and never successfully punted a football? Sometimes I marvel at his consistency.

(The music begins again. It rises to a brief pause.)

Linus. I think Charlie Brown has nice hands.

(The music continues to another stopping place.)

Snoopy. It is truly a dog's life. I feel so neglected. Charlie Brown never brings me coffee in the morning.

(The music is heard for another moment.)

Lucy. Now, Linus, I want you to take a good look at Charlie Brown's face. Would you please hold still a minute, Charlie Brown; I want Linus to study your face. Now this is what you call a Failure Face, Linus. Notice how it has failure written all over it. Study it carefully, Linus; you rarely get to see such a good example. Notice the deep lines, the dull, vacant look in the eyes. Yes, I would say this is one of the finest examples of a Failure Face that you're liable to see for a long while.

(The music fades as Charlie Brown *stirs himself to speak.)*

Charlie Brown. Some days I wake up early to watch the sunrise, and I think how beautiful it is and how my whole life lies before me, and I get a very positive feeling about things. Like this morning, for instance. The sky's so clear and the sun's so bright. How can anything go wrong on a day like this?

(His question is answered by an ominous and energetic imitation of drum taps from Schroeder *and* Linus. *The stage is suddenly filled with light, and we at last can see its contents: several oversized, brightly painted*

Words to Know and Use

inferiority (in fir′ ē ôr′ ə tē) *n.* a lack of worth or excellence
consistency (kən sis′ tən sē) *n.* the condition of always behaving in the same way

objects in simple geometric shapes and six undersized, simply dressed people of straightforward, uncomplicated character. As the music swings into a march, the people begin parading around and about the rather nonplused[1] fellow at center stage. They sing "You're a Good Man, Charlie Brown.")

All (*except* Charlie Brown*).*
You're a good man, Charlie Brown;
You're the kind of reminder we need.
You have humility, nobility, and a sense
  of honor
That are very rare indeed.

You're a good man, Charlie Brown,
And we know you will go very far.
Yes, it's hard to believe,
Almost frightening to conceive,
What a good man you are.
You are kind to all the animals
And ev'ry little bird.
With a heart of gold you believe what
  you're told.

Lucy. Ev'ry single solitary word.

All. You bravely face adversity;[2]
You're cheerful through the day;
You're thoughtful, brave, and courteous.

Lucy. And you also have some faults,
    but for the
Moment let's just say . . .

All. That you're a good man, Charlie Brown;

(They break into a boisterous march.)

You're a good man, Charlie Brown;
You're a prince, and a prince could be
  king.

With a heart such as yours
You could open any doors,
You could go out and do anything.
You could be king, Charlie Brown,
You could be king!

Lucy. If only you weren't so wishy-washy.

(The music and the marchers disappear as quickly as they arrived, and as the sound of a jangling school bell cuts through the fading voices, Charlie Brown *is left alone at center stage, seated, clutching a paper bag.)*

Charlie Brown. I think lunch time is about the worst time of the day for me. Always having to sit here alone. Of course, sometimes mornings aren't so pleasant either—waking up and wondering if anyone would really miss me if I never got out of bed. Then there's the night too—lying there and thinking about all the stupid things I've done during the day. And all those hours in between—when I do all those stupid things. Well, lunch time is *among* the worst times of the day for me.

Well, I guess I'd better see what I've got. *(He opens the bag, unwraps a sandwich, and looks inside.)* Peanut butter. *(He bites and chews.)* Some psychiatrists say that people who eat peanut butter sandwiches are lonely. I guess they're right. And if you're really lonely, the peanut butter sticks to the roof of your mouth. *(He munches quietly, idly fingering the bench.)* Boy, the PTA sure did a good job

---

1. **nonplused** (nän ploost′): puzzled; confused
2. **adversity**: trouble or misfortune

Words to Know and Use

humility (hyo͞o mil′ ə tē) *n.* a lack of pride
nobility (nō bil′ ə tē) *n.* a greatness of character

489

of painting these benches. *(He looks off to one side.)* There's that cute little redheaded girl eating her lunch over there. I wonder what she'd do if I went over and asked her if I could sit and have lunch with her. She'd probably laugh right in my face. It's hard on a face when it gets laughed in. There's an empty place next to her on the bench. There's no reason why I couldn't just go over and sit there. I could do that right now. All I have to do is stand up. *(He stands.)* I'm standing up. *(He sits.)* I'm sitting down. I'm a coward. I'm so much of a coward she wouldn't even think of looking at me. She hardly ever *does* look at me. In fact, I can't remember her ever looking at me. Why shouldn't she look at me? Is there any reason in the world why she shouldn't look at me? Is she so great and am I so small that she couldn't spare one little moment just to . . . *(He freezes.)* She's looking at me. *(In terror he looks one way, then another.)* She's *looking* at me.

(His head looks all around, frantically trying to find something else to notice. His teeth clench. Tension builds. Then, with one motion, he pops the paper bag over his head. Lucy *and* Patty *enter.)*

Lucy. No, Patty, you're thinking of that other dress, the one I wore to Lucinda's party. The one I'm talking about was this very light blue one and had a design embroidered around the waist.

Patty. I don't remember that dress.

Lucy *(takes a pencil and draws matter-of-factly on the bottom of the paper bag).* Something like this. The skirt went out like this, and it had these puffy sleeves and a sash like this.

Patty. Oh, yes, I remember.

Lucy. Yes, well, *that* was the dress I was wearing last week when I met Frieda and she told me she'd seen one just like it over at . . . .

(The girls have exited. Charlie Brown *sits immobile as their voices fade.)*

Charlie Brown *(the paper bag still pulled over his head).* Lunch time *is* among the worst times of the day for me. If that little redheaded girl is looking at me with this stupid bag on my head, she must think I'm the biggest fool alive. But if she isn't looking at me, then maybe I could take it off quickly and she'd never notice it. On the other hand, I can't tell if she's looking until I take it off. Then again, if I *never* take it off, I'll never have to know if she was looking or not. On the other hand, it's very hard to breathe in here. *(There is a moment of tense silence. Then his hand rises slowly, jerks the bag from his head and folds it quickly as he glances furtively in the direction of the little girl. He smiles.)* She's not looking at me. *(He looks concerned.)* I wonder why she never looks at me. *(The school bell jangles once again.)* Oh, well, another lunch hour over with. Only two thousand eight hundred and sixty-three to go.

(As he makes his way offstage, the opening bars of Beethoven's "Moonlight" Sonata are heard, and a change in lighting reveals Schroeder *and* Lucy *on another part of the stage.* Schroeder *is seated at one of the shapes, which somewhat resembles a piano. He is engrossed in his playing.* Lucy *is leaning contentedly against the "piano," listen-*

Above, Schroeder and Lucy in the original off-Broadway production of the play.
Courtesy of Max Eiser. *Right*, PEANUTS characters © 1951, 1952   United Feature Syndicate, Inc.

ing. In counterpoint³ to the continuing sonata, she sings "Schroeder.")

Lucy *(singing).*

D'ya know something, Schroeder?
I think the way you play the piano is nice.
D'ya know something else?
It's always been my dream that I'd marry
A man who plays the piano.
At parties he'd play something nice
Like "April Showers."
I'm sure you could play something nice
Like "April Showers."
Or even "Frère Jacques."
Beethoven's nice, too.
Just imagine.
What would you think if someday you
    and I should get married?
Wouldn't you like that if someday we two
    should get married?

(Schroeder hasn't heard a word she's said.

His playing finally reaches a pause in the music.)

Lucy. My Aunt Marion was right. Never try to discuss marriage with a musician.

(With the final chords of the piece, the light slowly fades. Then, upstage, suddenly there is Patty.*)*

Patty *(standing at attention with her hand over her heart).* I pledge allegiance to the flag of the United States of America, and to the Republic for which it stands. One nation, under God, indivisible, with liberty and justice for all. *(She sits, then quickly stands again.)* Amen.

(Charlie Brown and Linus *enter at another corner of the stage. Charlie Brown is look-*

---

3. counterpoint: the playing or singing of two melodies at the same time.

ing at a large, stiff, brightly colored square of board, which is, of course, a newspaper.)

Charlie Brown. I think most of us take newspapers too much for granted. We don't really appreciate the miracle that is the modern daily newspaper. Of course, it's difficult to put into words just why one likes a newspaper.

Linus. I like a newspaper because you don't have to dial it.

(Charlie Brown exits. Linus, holding his blanket, sits quietly at center stage. Lucy casually wanders by, then makes a quick grab for his blanket and takes off with it.)

Lucy. I got it! I got it!

Linus *(going after her like a shot)*. You give me back my blanket.

Lucy. No! I've got it and I'm going to keep it. *(They stop running.)* This is just the start you need to help you break this disgusting habit.

Linus. Apparently you haven't read the latest scientific reports. A blanket is as important to a child as a hobby is to an adult. Many a man spends his time restoring antique automobiles or building model trains or collecting old telephones or even studying about the Civil War. This is called playing with the past.

Lucy. Really?

Linus. Certainly. And this is good, for it helps these men to cope with their everyday problems. Now, I feel that it is going to be absolutely necessary for me to get my blanket back, so I'm just going to have to give it a good YANK! *(He quickly*

pulls the blanket away from her.) It's surprising what you can accomplish with a little smooth talking and some fast action.

(From behind the largest object on the stage, something that could easily be mistaken for a doghouse, Snoopy appears. He is a human being, like any other dog, and he happens to be wearing a white turtleneck sweater, black pants, and sneakers. He yawns, stretches, and walks downstage, where Patty sees him.)

Patty. Oh, Snoopy, you're such a sweet doggy. I'd love to give you a great big kiss. *(Snoopy offers a pucker.)* But of course I can't. *(She quickly crosses away.)*

Snoopy. The curse of a fuzzy face.

(He sinks into a resigned heap on the floor. The light reveals Patty and Linus seated together.)

Linus. Happiness is a fleeting thing, Patty, but I think that a man can really come closer to it by directing the forces of his life toward a single goal that he believes in. And I think that a man's personal search for happiness is not really a selfish thing either, because by achieving happiness himself, he can help others to find it. Does that make sense to you?

Patty. We had spaghetti at our house three times this week.

(A burst of virtuoso[4] piano playing mercifully draws our attention to another part of the stage, where Schroeder is once again practicing and Lucy is once again talking.)

---

4. virtuoso (vʉr′ choo ō′ sō): done with great skill.

Lucy. What would you think, Schroeder, if someday you and I got married and we were so poor you had to sell the piano to buy me saucepans?

(The music comes to a sour halt.)

Schroeder. Saucepans?

Lucy. Well, sure. You don't expect me to set up housekeeping without a good set of saucepans, do you?

Schroeder. Saucepans?

Lucy. Well, girls have to think about those things. Boys are lucky. Boys never have to think about things like saucepans.

Schroeder *(rises, crosses slowly away)*. I can't stand it. I just can't stand it. *(He collapses with his head in his hands.)*

Snoopy. *(Moving forward, jaw jutting, brow furrowed. He draws himself up to his full height.)* Here is the fierce jungle ape pounding his mighty chest while the other animals cower in the distance. Now he throws back his head and emits a terrifying roar . . . arf! (He collapses in complete chagrin.⁵) How humiliating.*

(He drags himself up onto his doghouse. Patty enters, walking slowly, staring at the limp jump-rope she holds in her hand.)

Schroeder. What's the matter, Patty?

Patty. Well, I don't know. I was jumping rope. Everything was all right, and suddenly, it all seemed so <u>futile</u>.

(She exits. Snoopy rises on his doghouse and, with musical support, assumes three highly dramatic and impressive poses. Then he stops.)

Snoopy. I would have made a terrific trophy.

(He lies down. Lucy enters, fit to be tied, and shouting angrily offstage.)

Lucy. It's not fair! You promised me a birthday party, and now you say I can't have one. It's not fair! IT IS NOT FAIR!

Linus. You're not using the right strategy.

Lucy. What?

Linus. The more you fuss, the worse off you'll be. Why not admit it was all your own fault. Why not go up to Mom and say to her, "I'm sorry, dear Mother. I admit I've been bad and you were right to cancel my party. From now on I shall try to be good." That's much better than ranting and raving. All that does is prove her point.

Lucy *(thinks a moment, then tries it on for size)*. "I'm sorry, dear Mother. I admit I've been bad and you were right to cancel my party. From now on I shall try to be good." *(She smiles at the effort, starts offstage, stops, and then returns to* Linus.*)* I'D RATHER DIE!

(They exit. Schroeder is left on the stage, which he paces contentedly.)

Schroeder. Beethoven loved the country. He quite often liked to take long strolls into

---

5. **chagrin** (shə grin′): embarrassment.

Words to Know and Use | **futile** (fyo͞ot′ ′l) *adj.* useless

493

the countryside. He loved the peace and quiet of the country. They were an inspiration to him.

Lucy *(offstage).* Gimme that ball, you block-head!

Schroeder. Beethoven had it nice.

(The lights dim as he exits. Then Snoopy, *asleep on the doghouse, can be seen squirming and whimpering with delight at the sound of the following dialogue, which, at the moment, is brightening his dreams.)*

Charlie Brown *(offstage).* Hey, Snoopy, we're home from school. Hi there, fella. Gosh, it's good to see you.

Lucy *(offstage).* Oh, Snoopy, you're so adorable. Mm-mm!

Charlie Brown. Okay, Snoopy, get back on your doghouse. I'll be out later with your supper.

Lucy. I think Snoopy's such a wonderful dog.

Charlie Brown. I do too. He's just about the best there is.

(The music begins; the lights grow. Snoopy *stirs, stretches, and happily considers his situation. He sings "Snoopy.")*

Snoopy *(singing).*
They like me,
I think they're swell.
Isn't it remarkable
How things work out so well?
Pleasant day, pretty sky,
Life goes on, here I lie.
Not bad, not bad at all.
Cozy home, board and bed,
Sturdy roof beneath my head.
Not bad, not bad at all.

Faithful friends always near me,
Bring me bones, scratch my ear.
Little birds come to cheer me,
Every day
Sitting here
On my stomach,
With their sharp little claws,
Which are usually cold
And occasionally painful,
And sometimes there are so many
That I can hardly stand it . . . .

Rats!
I feel ev'ry now and then that I gotta bite
    someone.
I know ev'ry now and then what I
    wanna be,
A fierce jungle animal crouched on the
    limb of a tree.
I'd stay very very still till I see a victim
    come.
I'd wait, knowing very well ev'ry second
    counts,
And then, like the fierce jungle creature
    I am,
I would pounce.
I'd pounce.
I'd pounce.
I'd . . . .
You know, I never quite realized it was so far down to the ground from here. Hm.
    Let me see, where was I?
    Oh, that's right. The pretty sky.
    Not bad, not bad at all.
I wonder if it will snow tonight.

(He grumbles a moment to himself, then falls asleep. The lights change. Charlie Brown *enters, holding his paper bag.)*

Charlie Brown. I think I'll walk right up to that little redheaded girl and introduce myself. I think I'll introduce myself and then I think I'll ask her to come over here and sit by me. I think I'll ask her to sit by me and then I think I'll tell her how much I've always admired her. . . . I think I'll flap my arms and fly to the moon.

(He exits. Snoopy rouses himself and starts to ease over the rear edge of his house, pondering as he goes.)

Snoopy. Yesterday I was a dog. Today I'm a dog. Tomorrow I'll probably still be a dog. There's just so little hope of advancement.

(He is gone. The lights ruminate a moment, then reveal a shadowy figure with a blanket. After ably dispatching[6] an invisible insect with a quick snap of the blanket, Linus settles down with his woolly companion in front of the TV set. The music of "My Blanket and Me" begins. The first pause of the song is punctuated by his contented sigh; the second, by his murmuring, "Delightful," as he fondles the blanket. Eventually he is moved to sing.)

Linus *(singing).*
It's a cozy sanctuary
But it's far from necessary,
'Cause I'm just as self-reliant as before.
As a simple demonstration
Of my independent station
I will go and leave my blanket on the floor.
Yes, I'll walk away and leave it,
Though I know you won't believe it,
I'll just walk away and leave it on the floor.

(He saunters away, humming. The hum grows tenser, however, and soon, unable to bear the separation any longer, he makes a desperate grab for the blanket.)

Don't ever let me do that again.

(The music resumes. Linus dances with his "friend.")

Got you back again.

(The music continues and grows. Finally . . . .)

It's foolish, I know it,
I'll try to outgrow it,
But meanwhile
There's my blanket and me.

(He sighs. As the song ends, Linus is once again settled in front of the TV. Lucy enters and watches with him for a moment.)

Lucy. OK, switch channels.

Linus. Are you kidding? What makes you think you can come right in here and take over!

Lucy *(holding out her hand).* These five fingers individually are nothing. But when I curl them together into a single unit, they become a fighting force terrible to behold.

Linus. Which channel do you want? *(He looks at his hand.)* Why can't you guys get organized like that.

Lucy. Linus, do you know what I intend? I intend to be a queen. When I grow up, I'm going to be the biggest queen there ever was, and I'll live in this big palace

---

6. **dispatching:** getting rid of.

with a big front lawn and have lots of beautiful dresses to wear. And when I go out in my coach, all the people . . .

Linus. Lucy.

Lucy. . . . all the people will wave, and I will shout at them, and . . .

Linus. Lucy, I believe "queen" is an inherited title. *(Lucy is silent.)* Yes, I'm quite sure. A person can only become a queen by being born into a royal family of the correct lineage[7] so that she can assume the throne after the death of the reigning monarch. I can't think of any possible way that you could ever become a queen. *(Lucy is still silent.)* I'm sorry, Lucy, but it's true.

Lucy *(silence, and then).* . . . and in the summertime I will go to my summer palace, and I'll wear my crown in swimming and everything, and all the people will cheer, and I will shout at them . . . *(Her vision pops.)* What do you mean I can't be a queen?

Linus. It's true.

Lucy. There must be a loophole. This kind of thing always has a loophole. Nobody should be kept from being a queen if she wants to be one. IT'S UNDEMOCRATIC!

Linus. Good grief.

Lucy. It's usually just a matter of knowing the right people. I'll bet a few pieces of well-placed correspondence and I get to be a queen in no time.

Linus. I think I'll watch television. *(He returns to the set.)*

Lucy. I know what I'll do. If I can't be a queen, then I'll be very rich. I'll work and work until I'm very very rich, and then I will buy myself a queendom.

Linus. Good grief.

Lucy. Yes, I will buy myself a queendom, and then I'll kick out the old queen and take over the whole operation myself. I will be head queen. And when I go out in my coach, all the people will wave, and I will . . . I will . . .

(She has glanced at the TV set and become engrossed. Pretty soon Linus *turns and looks at her.)*

Linus. What happened to your queendom?

Lucy. Huh?

Linus. What happened to your queendom?

Lucy. Oh, that. I've given it up. I've decided to devote my life to cultivating my natural beauty.

(As Linus *looks at her in disbelief, the scene disappears into blessed darkness. Then quick, urgent music is heard, and* Charlie Brown *lurches in from the wings, struggling with an invisible kite on the end of an invisible string. He sings "The Kite.")*

Charlie Brown *(singing).*
Little more speed, little more rope,
Little more wind, little more hope,
Gotta get this stupid kite to fly.
Gotta make sure it doesn't snag,
Doesn't droop, doesn't drag,
Gotta watch out for ev'ry little—whoops!

Little less speed, little more tack,
Little less rise, little more slack,
Gotta keep my wits about me now.
Gotta make sure it doesn't get the best
of me
Till I get it in the air somehow.

---

7. **lineage** (lin′ ē ij): a group of people related as parents and children.

Millions of little kids do it ev'ry day,
They make a kite, and poof, it's in the
  sky.
Leave it to me to have the one fool kite
Who likes to see a little kid cry.

Little less talk, little more skill,
Little less luck, little more will,
Gotta face this fellow eye to eye.
Now that I've seen you chasing moles,
Climbing trees, digging holes,
Wrapping your string on everything
  passing by,
Why not fly?

Wait a minute.
What's it doing?
It isn't on the ground,
It isn't in a tree,
It's in the air.

Look at that, it's caught the breeze now,
It's past the trees now, with room to
  spare.

Oh, what a beautiful sight.
And I'm not such a clumsy guy,
If I really try
I can really fly a . . .

(A terrible rending of paper and wood is heard. Charlie Brown *watches as his imaginary string goes limp. He slumps, heaves a small sigh of resignation, and heads doggedly for the exit as the music chases him out.* Patty *walks pertly onstage with a large pencil and a flat, brightly colored board, which is, of course, a letter she is writing.)*

Patty. Dear Ann Flanders: Last year I sent fifty-two valentines and received seventy-five. This year I sent fifty-eight valentines and only received sixty-one. Am I right in blaming this on the ZIP Code?

(She exits. Charlie Brown *enters, carrying an envelope. He practices presenting it.)*

Charlie Brown. This is for you, Lucy; happy Valentine's Day. That doesn't sound right. Here, Lucy, this is for you; happy Valentine's Day. You can do it if you just don't get nervous. This is for you, Lucy; happy

Valentine's Day. (Lucy *enters.* Charlie Brown *quietly reassures himself.*) OK, just take it easy; you can do it. (*aloud*) This is for you, Lucy. (*He gives her the card.*) Merry Christmas.

(*In an instant he realizes what he's done and collapses with a moan.* Patty *enters, counting valentines. She happens to drop one as she passes* Charlie Brown.)

Patty. Hi, Charlie Brown.

Charlie Brown. Hi, Patty. Oh, wait a minute; you dropped something. Say, what is all this?

Patty. Valentines. They're for all the boys in our class at school that I like.

Charlie Brown. Well, we wouldn't want to lose this one, would we? With the initials C. B. on it.

Patty. No, I guess not. Craig Bowerman would be very disappointed.

Charlie Brown. I can't stand it.

(Patty, Lucy, *and* Schroeder *congregate upstage, exchanging cards.*)

Charlie Brown. Look at them, laughing and enjoying themselves with their valentines. I sent a valentine to everyone I know this Valentine's Day, and did I get any in return? No, not one. I did not get a single valentine. Everybody gets valentines but me. Nobody likes me. I get about as many valentines as a dog. (Snoopy *walks by, counting a large batch of valentines.*) My stomach hurts.

(Charlie Brown *heads for the wings. The others also exit. The lights and music then cheerily accompany* Lucy *as she goes about some sort of business at one corner of the*

stage. *She finally flips a sign in place, reading* The Doctor Is In *and we see that she has set up her booth for psychiatric help.* Charlie Brown *enters, wretched.*)

Charlie Brown. Oh, Lucy, I'm so depressed. Everything is going wrong. I don't know what to do.

Lucy. I'm sorry to hear that, Charlie Brown. Maybe there's something I can do to help. I think what you need most of all is to come right out and admit all the things that are wrong with you.

Charlie Brown. Do you really think that will help, Lucy?

Lucy. Certainly.

Charlie Brown. All right, I'll try.

(*They sing "The Doctor Is In."*)

Charlie Brown (*singing*).

I'm not very handsome or clever or lucid;[8]
I've always been stupid at spelling and
   numbers.
I've never been much playing football or
   baseball
Or stickball or checkers or marbles or
   Ping-Pong.
I'm usually awful at parties and dances;
I stand like a stick, or I cough,
Or I laugh,
Or I don't bring a present,
Or I spill the ice cream,
Or I get so depressed that I
Stand and I scream.
Oh, how could there possibly be
One small person as thoroughly, totally,
   utterly
Blah as me?

---

8. **lucid:** clearheaded.

PEANUTS characters © 1950, 1951, 1952, 1954, 1966 United Feature Syndicate, Inc.

Lucy. Well, that's OK for a starter.

Charlie Brown. A starter?

Lucy. Well, sure. You don't think that mentioning these few <u>superficial</u> failings is going to do any good, do you? Why, Charlie Brown, you really have to delve.[9] *(She sings.)*
You're stupid, self-centered, and moody.

Charlie Brown. I'm moody.

Lucy. You're terribly dull to be with.

Charlie Brown. Yes, I am.
And nobody likes me.
Not Frieda or Shermy or Linus or
Schroeder . . .

Lucy. Or Lucy.

Charlie Brown. Or Lucy.

Lucy. Or Snoopy.

Charlie Brown. Or Sn—

Now, wait a minute. Snoopy likes me.

Lucy. He only pretends to like you because you feed him. That doesn't count.

Charlie Brown. Or Snoopy.
Oh, why was I born just to be
One small person as thoroughly, totally,
utterly . . .

Lucy. Wait.
You're not very much of a person.

Charlie Brown. That's certain.

Lucy. And yet there is reason for hope.

Charlie Brown. There is hope?

Lucy. For although you are no good at
Music, like Schroeder,
Or happy, like Snoopy,
Or lovely, like me,

---

9. **delve:** to dig into something; investigate.

499

You have the <u>distinction</u> to be
No one else but the singular, remarkable,
    unique
Charlie Brown.

Charlie Brown. I'm me!

Lucy. Yes, it's amazingly true.
For whatever it's worth, Charlie Brown,
You're you.

Charlie Brown. Gosh, Lucy, I'm beginning to feel better already. You're a true friend, Lucy, a true friend.

Lucy. That'll be five cents, please.

(The lights dim. Lucy *exits.* Snoopy *is seen seated at one side.* Charlie Brown *greets him weakly before exiting, and one by one the other characters cross the stage, patting* Snoopy's *head or calling their greetings as they go by.)*

Charlie Brown. Hi, Snoopy. How's the fella?

Patty. Hi, Snoopy. Cute doggy.

Schroeder. What d'ya say, tiger!

Lucy. Hi, fuzzy face.

Linus. Hi, Snoopy.

Snoopy *(watches them go, then drags himself offstage, muttering).* Nobody ever calls me sugar lips.

*(A dour musical undercurrent begins, and four gloomy-looking people–*Lucy, Schroeder, Linus, *and* Charlie Brown*–enter with pencils and "notebooks," taking their places at four different parts of the stage.)*

All. Homework. Yeough!

(They sing "The Book Report.")

Lucy. A book report on Peter Rabbit.

Linus. A book report on Peter Rabbit.

Schroeder. A book report on Peter Rabbit.

Charlie Brown. A book report on Peter Rabbit.

Lucy *(thinks briefly, then . . .).*
Peter Rabbit is this stupid book
About this stupid rabbit who steals
Vegetables from other people's gardens.

(She counts the words, one through seventeen.)

Eighty-three to go.

Schroeder. The name of the book about which
This book report is about is
Peter Rabbit, which is about this
Rabbit.
I found it very–

(He crosses out.)

I liked the part where–

(He crosses out.)

It was a–

(Slash!)

It reminded me of *Robin Hood.*
And the part where Little John jumped
    from the rock
To the sheriff of Nottingham's back,
And then Robin and everyone swung
    from the trees
In a sudden surprise attack.
And they captured the sheriff and all of
    his goods,

---

*Words
to Know
and Use* | **distinction** (di stiŋk′ shən) *n.* a mark of honor

And they carried him back to their camp
  in the woods,
And the sheriff was guest at their dinner
  and all,
But he wriggled away and he sounded the
  call,
And his men rushed in and the arrows
  flew—
Peter Rabbit did sort of that kind of thing
  too.

Lucy. The other people's name was Mac-
Gregor.

*(She counts the words from eighteen to twenty-
three.)*

Hmm.

CHARLIE BROWN   © 1950 United Feature Syndicate, Inc.

Linus. In examining a work such as Peter
Rabbit, it is important that the superficial
characteristics of its deceptively simple
plot should not be allowed to blind the
reader to the more substantial fabric of its
deeper motivations. In this report I plan
to discuss the sociological implications of
family pressures so great as to drive an
otherwise moral rabbit to perform acts of
thievery which he consciously knew were
against the law. I also hope to explore the
personality of Mr. MacGregor in his conflicting roles as farmer and humanitarian.
(Charlie Brown begins to sing.) Peter
Rabbit is established from the start as a
benevolent hero, and it is only with the
increase of social pressure that the seams
in his moral fabric . . .

Charlie Brown *(Linus's speech fades as he
begins to sing).*
If I start writing now,
When I'm not really rested,
It could upset my thinking,
Which is not good at all.
I'll get a fresh start tomorrow,
And it's not due till Wednesday,
So I'll have all of Tuesday
Unless something should happen.
Why does this always happen—
I should be outside playing,
Getting fresh air and sunshine;
I work best under pressure,
And there'll be lots of pressure
If I wait till tomorrow;
I should start writing now.
But if I start writing now,
When I'm not really rested,
It could upset my thinking,
Which is not good at all.

Lucy. The name of the rabbit was Peter.
  Twenty-four, twenty-five, twenty-six, twenty-seven,
  Twenty-eight, twenty-nine, thirty.

Schroeder. Down came the staff on his head—smash!
  And Robin fell like a sack full of lead—crash!
  The sheriff laughed and he left him for dead—ha!
  But he was wrong.

Lucy. Thirty-four, thirty-five, thirty-six, thirty-seven,
  Thirty-eight, thirty-nine, forty.

Schroeder. Just then an arrow flew in—whing!

It was the sign for the fight to begin—zing!
And then it looked like the sheriff would win—ah!
But not for long.
Away they ran.
Just like rabbits,
Who run a lot,
As you can tell
From the story
Of *Peter Rabbit,*
Which this report
Is about.

Charlie Brown. How do they expect us to write a book report . . .

Lucy. There were vegetables in the garden . . .

Charlie Brown . . . . of any quality
  In just two days?

Lucy. Such as carrots and spinach and onions and . . .

(Charlie Brown *and* Lucy *sing simultaneously.)*

Charlie Brown. How can they
  Conspire to make life so miserable
  And so effectively
  In so many ways?

Lucy. Lettuce and turnips and
  Parsley and okra and cabbage and string beans and parsnips,
  Tomatoes, potatoes, asparagus,
  Cauliflower, rhubarb, and chives.

Linus. Not to mention the extreme pressure exerted on him by his deeply rooted rivalry with Flopsy, Mopsy, and Cotton-tail.

LUCY   © 1952 United Feature Syndicate, Inc.

(Lucy, Charlie Brown and Schroeder sing simultaneously.)

| **Lucy.** *Peter Rabbit* is this
Stupid book about a
  stupid
Rabbit who steals
Vegetables from other
  people's
Gardens.
   Gardens, gardens.
Seventy-five, seventy-six,
Seventy-seven, seventy-
  eight,
Seventy-nine, eighty,
Eighty-one, eighty-two. | **Charlie Brown.** If I start
writing now, when I'm
Not really
Rested, it could
Upset my thinking,
  which is
Not good at all.
No good at all.
Oh—

First thing after
Dinner I'll start. | **Schroeder.** The name of the
  book
About which this

Book report
Is about is
Peter Rabbit, Peter
  Rabbit.
All for one,
Every man does his part.

Oh— |

Lucy. And they were very, very, very, very,
  Very, very happy to be home.

Schroeder. The end.

Lucy. . . . ninety-four, ninety-five. *(singing)*
  The very, very, very end.

Linus. A-men.

Charlie Brown *(beginning to write)*. A book
  report on *Peter Rabbit.*

(The scene fades. All exit except for Charlie
Brown, *who leaves his "desk" and wanders
dejectedly downstage. He happens to look
up and in doing so sees a single large green
leaf hanging just at the edge of the proscenium.*[10] *He hesitates, then sees the audience
and speaks to them.)*

Charlie Brown. You know, I don't know if
  you'll understand this or not, but sometimes, even when I'm feeling very low, I'll
see some little thing that will somehow
renew my faith. Just something like that
leaf, for instance—clinging to its tree in
spite of wind and storm. You know, that
makes me think that courage and tenacity
are about the greatest values that a man
can have. Suddenly my old confidence is
back, and I know things aren't half as bad
as I make them out to be. Suddenly I
know that with the strength of his convic-
tions a man can move mountains, and I
can proceed with full confidence in the
basic goodness of my fellow man. I know
that now. I know it.

---

10. proscenium (prō sē′ nē əm): the arched wall at the
front of a stage.

(With unfamiliar strength in his step, Charlie Brown turns and makes his way offstage, a glimmer of new hope in his eyes. Then, without even a respectful pause, the leaf promptly drops from its tree and wiggles its way to the ground.)

Curtain

Responding to Reading

First Impressions

1. Which one of the characters stands out most in your mind at this point in the play? Describe your feelings about the character in your journal or on a piece of paper.

Second Thoughts

2. The title of this subunit is "All You Ever Wanted." What do you think Charlie Brown wants out of life?

3. Do you think Charlie Brown can solve his problems, or do you think life will always treat him unfairly? Explain.

4. Based on the dialogue and actions in Act One, what inferences can you make about Lucy's character? Refer to your chart for the details you have recorded.

   Think about
   - her speech about being queen
   - how she treats Linus and Charlie Brown
   - how she feels about Schroeder

5. What do you think Charlie Brown realizes when he says "I'm me!"?

6. How are the book reports on *Peter Rabbit* similar to the characters who write them?

Reading On

At the end of Act One, Charlie Brown expresses a renewed sense of hope and confidence. What do you think will happen to his hopes as the day goes on?

ACT TWO

A throbbing rhythm from the percussion, a hint of "Over There" in the melody, a dimming of the house lights, and Act Two is under way. As the curtain opens, we see a familiar figure silhouetted on the top of his doghouse, seated bolt upright, his arms outstretched before him, a scarf around his neck, and the goggles of his leather helmet pulled down firmly over his eyes. The music and lights help Snoopy *throughout in telling his story of bravery and heroism.*

Snoopy. Here's the World War One flying acc high over France in his Sopwith Camel,[11] searching for the infamous Red Baron.[12] I must bring him down. Suddenly antiaircraft fire—archie we call it—begins to burst beneath my plane. The Red Baron has spotted me. Nyahh, nyahh, nyahh! You can't hit me. *(parenthetically)* Actually, tough flying aces never say, "Nyahh, nyahh." I was just, uh . . . . *(back to business)* Drat this fog. It's bad enough to have to fight the Red Baron without having to fly in weather like this. All right, Red Baron! Come on out. You can't hide from

---

11. Sopwith Camel: a British fighter plane of World War I.

12. Red Baron: Baron Manfred von Richthofen, the top German military pilot of World War I; called the Red Baron because he flew a red airplane.

me forever. Ah! The sun has broken through. I can see the woods of Montsec[13] below. But what's this? It's a Fokker triplane.[14] Ha, I've got you. You can't escape from me this time, Red Baron! Augh! He's diving down out of the sun. He's tricked me again. I've got to run. Come on, Sopwith Camel, let's go. Go, Camel, go! I can't shake him. He's riddling my plane with bullets. Curse you, Red Baron! Curse you and your kind! Curse the evil that causes this unhappiness. *(The tempo changes.* Snoopy *relaxes, removing his goggles and scarf.)* Here's the World War One flying ace back at the aerodrome[15] in France. He is exhausted and yet he does not sleep, for one thought continues to throb in his brain: someday, someday I'll get you, Red Baron!

(He reclines in noble leisure as the music crashes to its final chords. Patty *enters, skipping rope. She circles the doghouse with exuberant energy.)*

Patty. All right, everybody out for rabbit chasing.

Snoopy. Oh, good grief.

Patty. Let's go, Snoopy; up and at 'em. It's a magnificent day for chasing rabbits. The air is clear; the sun is shining; the fields and woodlands lie open and inviting.

Snoopy. If it's such a magnificent day, why spoil it for the rabbits?

Patty. Come on, Snoopy. Where's that old thrill of the chase? Where's your spirit of adventure? What kind of a dog are you, anyway?

Snoopy. I am a sleeping dog. You take it from there.

Patty. You should be ashamed of yourself, wasting a perfect day like this. The scent is fresh. The trail is clear. Let's get out there and track us down a big ol' rabbit.

Snoopy. Well, I get the feeling she's determined. OK, if that's what she wants, she might as well get her money's worth.

Patty. Atta boy, Snoopy. I predict we'll see lots of game today. (Snoopy *takes a deep breath, scrambles from his doghouse, and, with* Patty *following behind, gives a short, furious, and highly convincing display of "dog tracking down rabbit." He ends up panting in front of* Patty.) Well, I guess we're not going to find anything today, Snoopy. But at least you tried. Even though you've failed, it always makes you feel better when you know you've done your best. *(She exits.)*

Snoopy. I'd hate to disillusion her, but I don't even know what a rabbit smells like.

*(Snoopy *retires to his house. Charlie Brown enters, wearing a baseball cap and glove. He assumes his place on the pitcher's mound and begins his speech, in spite of the unnerving fact that no one is there to speak to.)*

Charlie Brown. All right, gang. I want this game to be our biggest and best game of the season, and I want everyone out there playing with everything he's . . .

*(Lucy *comes onstage and approaches him.)*

---

13. **woods of Montsec** (mŏn sek): a forest in northern France.
14. **Fokker** (fäk′ ər) **triplane:** a three-winged German fighter plane of the type flown by the Red Baron.
15. **aerodrome** (er′ ō drōm′): an airfield.

Charlie Brown. The thing we have to remember is spirit and teamwork. If we all really grit our teeth and bear down, I'm sure we can finish off this season with . . .

(Schroeder *comes onstage and approaches* Charlie Brown. *The whole gang is now onstage, each wearing a baseball cap and glove.*)

Schroeder. Charlie Brown, is Lucy going to pitch again? Because if she is, I quit. Do you know what she does? She's always calling me out for conferences on the mound. I go out there, see? I go out there for a secret conference on the mound, and do you know what she does? She kisses me on the nose.

Charlie Brown. If we really grit our teeth and bear down, I'm sure we could finish this season . . .

Linus. Perhaps you shouldn't be a playing manager, Charlie Brown. Perhaps you should be a bench manager.

Patty. That's a good idea. You'd be a great bench manager, Charlie Brown. You could say, "Bench, do this" or "Bench, do that." You could even be in charge of where we put the bench. When we get to the playing field, you could say, "Let's put the bench here" or "Let's put the bench there."

Charlie Brown. I can't stand it.

Lucy. What's the sense of our playing when we know we're going to lose? If there was even a million-to-one chance we might win, it would make some sense.

Snoopy and Charlie Brown in a production of the play. Photofest.

Lucy. Charlie Brown, I thought up some new strategy for you. Why don't you tell the other team that we're going to meet them at a certain place, only it isn't the real place, and then when they don't show up, we'll win by forfeit.[16] Isn't that good strategy? (Charlie Brown *is silent.* Lucy *starts to leave.*) I don't understand these managers who don't want to use good strategy.

---

16. win by forfeit: to win a game because the opposing team or player fails to compete.

Charlie Brown. Well, there may not be a million-to-one chance, but I'm sure there's at least a billion-to-one chance. Now come on, gimme a *T*.

All. T!

Charlie Brown. Gimme an *E*.

All. E!

Charlie Brown. Gimme an *A*.

All. A!

Charlie Brown. Gimme an *M*.

All. M!

Charlie Brown. Whaddaya got?

All. TEAM!

CHARLIE BROWN © 1950 United Feature Syndicate, Inc.

(They burst into "The Baseball Game.")

All *(singing)*.
There is no team like the best team,
Which is our team right here.
We will show you we're the best team
 In the very little league this year.
And in no time we'll be big time,
With the big-league baseball stars,
For all we have to do is win just one
   more game
And the championship is ours.

(Charlie Brown is now on the opposite side of the stage from the rest of the team, who have frozen into a tableau of baseball pandemonium.[17] He writes.)

Charlie Brown. Dear Pen Pal . . . *(singing)*.
You'll never guess what happened today
At the baseball game;
It's hard to believe what happened today
At the baseball game.
I was the manager,
Schroeder was catcher,
And all of the team was the same
As always, but
Somehow or other disaster struck
At the baseball game.

All *(except* Charlie Brown*)*.
There is no team like the best team,
Which is our team right here.
We will show you we're the best team
In the very little league this year.
And in no time we'll be big time,
With the big-league baseball stars,
For all we have to do is win just one
   more game
And the championship is ours.

---

17. pandemonium (pan´ də mō´ nē əm): confusion; disorder.

Charlie Brown. Three balls, two strikes, the bases were loaded
With two men out.
I pitched my curve, but somehow he hit it
A good strong clout.
"Lucy," I hollered, "it's coming right to you."
She caught it as easy as pie—then dropped it;
I don't think it's good for a team's morale
To see their manager cry.
Snoopy helped out by biting a runner
And catching the ball in his teeth.
Linus caught flies from a third-story window
By holding his blanket beneath.
Yes, we had fortitude;
No one could argue with that.
And one run would win us the game as I came up to bat.

Lucy *(speaking, as the others repeat their fight song).* All right, Charlie Brown, we're all behind you—sort of. Now get a hit, Charlie Brown. This guy can't pitch. He pitches like my grandmother. We know you can do it if you just grit your teeth and bear down. Please, Charlie Brown, please . . . .

All. For all we have to do is win just one more game.

Lucy. And the championship is ours!

Charlie Brown. Two men were on with two outs, and me with
One strike to go;
Then I saw her, this cute little redheaded Girl I know.
Firmly I vowed I would win it for her,
And I shouldered the bat, and I swung . . . .
Dear Pen Pal, I'm told where you live is

Really quite far.
Would you please send directions on
How I can get where you are?

Your friend,
Charlie Brown

(The stage slowly darkens as the players drag themselves off. Then Schroeder *and* Lucy *reenter upstage, minus their baseball equipment.)*

Schroeder. I'm sorry to have to say it right to your face, Lucy, but it's true. You're a very crabby person. I know your crabbiness has probably become so natural to you now that you're not even aware when you're being crabby, but it's true just the same. You're a very crabby person, and you're crabby to just about everyone you meet. (Lucy *remains silent—just barely.*) Now, I hope you don't mind my saying this, Lucy, and I hope you'll take it in the spirit that it's meant. I think we should all be open to any opportunity to learn more about ourselves. I think Socrates[18] was very right when he said that one of the first rules for anyone in life is "Know thyself." (Lucy *has begun whistling quietly to herself.*) Well, I guess I've said about enough. I hope I haven't offended you or anything. *(He makes an awkward exit.)*

Lucy *(sits in silence, then shouts offstage at* Schroeder*).* Well, what's Socrates got to do with it anyway, huh? Who was *he* anyway? Did he ever get to be king, huh! Answer me that; did he ever get to be king! *(suddenly to herself, a real question) Did* he ever get to be king? *(She shouts offstage,*

---

18. Socrates (säk′ rə tēz′): a philosopher of ancient Greece.

now a question.) Who *was* Socrates, anyway? *(She gives up the rampage and plunks herself down.)* "Know thyself," hmph.

(She thinks a moment, then makes a silent resolution to herself, exits, and quickly returns with a clipboard and pencil. Charlie Brown and Snoopy have entered, still with baseball equipment.)

Charlie Brown. Hey, Snoopy, you want to help me get my arm back in shape? Watch out for this one, it's a new fastball.

Lucy. Excuse me a moment, Charlie Brown, but I was wondering if you'd mind answering a few questions.

Charlie Brown. Not at all, Lucy. What kind of questions are they?

Lucy. Well, I'm conducting a survey to enable me to know myself better, and first of all I'd like to ask, On a scale of zero to one hundred, using a standard of fifty as average, seventy-five as above average, and ninety as exceptional, where would you rate me with regard to crabbiness?

Charlie Brown *(stands in silence for a moment, hesitating).* Well, Lucy, I . . .

Lucy. Your ballots need not be signed, and all answers will be held in strictest confidence.

Charlie Brown. Well, still, Lucy, that's a very hard question to answer.

Lucy. You may have a few moments to think it over if you want, or we can come back to that question later.

Charlie Brown. I think I'd like to come back to it if you don't mind.

Lucy. Certainly. This next question deals with certain character traits you may have observed. Regarding personality, would you say that mine is *A,* forceful; *B,* pleasing; or *C,* objectionable? Would that be *A, B,* or *C?* What would your answer be to that, Charlie Brown—forceful, pleasing or objectionable—which one would you say, hmm? Charlie Brown, hmm?

Charlie Brown. Well, I guess I'd have to say forceful, Lucy, but . . .

Lucy. Forceful. Well, we'll make a check mark at the letter *A* then. Now, would you rate my ability to get along with other people as poor, fair, good, or excellent?

Charlie Brown. I think that depends a lot on what you mean by "get along with other people."

Lucy. You know—make friends, sparkle in a crowd, that sort of thing.

Charlie Brown. Do you have a place for abstention?[19]

Lucy. Certainly. I'll just put a check mark at "None of the above." The next question deals with physical appearance. In referring to my beauty, would you say that I was stunning, mysterious, or intoxicating?

Charlie Brown *(squirming).* Well, gee, I don't know, Lucy. You look just fine to me.

Lucy *(making a check on the page).* Stunning. All right, Charlie Brown, I think we should get back to that first question. On a scale of zero to one hundred, using a standard of fifty as average, seventy-five as . . .

Charlie Brown *(loud interruption).* I . . . *(quieter)* . . . remember the question, Lucy.

Lucy. Well?

---

19. **abstention:** a refusal to vote on an issue.

Charlie Brown (*tentatively*). Fifty-one?

Lucy (*noting it down*). Fifty-one is your crabbiness rating for me. Very well then, that about does it. Thank you very much for helping with this survey, Charlie Brown. Your cooperation has been greatly appreciated. (*She shakes hands with Charlie Brown.*)

Charlie Brown (*flustered*). It was a pleasure, Lucy, any time. Come on, Snoopy.

Lucy. Oh, just a minute, there is one more question. Would you answer "Yes" or "No" to the question, Is Lucy Van Pelt the sort of person that you would like to have as president of your club or civic organization?

Charlie Brown. Oh, yes, by all means, Lucy.

Lucy (*making note*). Yes. Well, thank you very much. That about does it, I think. (*Charlie Brown exits, but Snoopy pauses, turns, and strikes a dramatic "thumbs down" pose to Lucy.*) WELL, WHO ASKED YOU! (*Snoopy makes a hasty exit. Lucy stands center stage, figuring to herself on the clipboard and mumbling.*) Now, let's see. That's a fifty-one, "None of the above," and . . . (*She looks up.*) Schroeder was right. I can already feel myself being filled with the glow of self-awareness. (*Patty enters. She is heading for the other side of the stage when Lucy stops her.*) Oh, Patty, I'm conducting a survey, and I wonder if . . .

Patty. A hundred and ten, C, "Poor," "None of the above," "No," and what are you going to do about the dent you made in my bicycle!

(*Patty storms off. Lucy watches her go, then looks at the audience.*)

Lucy. It's amazing how fast word of these surveys gets around.

(*Linus wanders in and plunks himself down in front of the TV. Lucy crosses to him, still figuring.*)

Lucy. Oh, Linus, I'm glad you're here. I'm conducting a survey, and there are a few questions I'd like to ask you.

Linus. Sure, go ahead.

Lucy. The first question is, On a scale of zero to one hundred, with a standard of fifty as average, seventy-five as above average, and ninety as exceptional, where would you rate me with regard to crabbiness?

Linus (*slowly turns his head to look at her, then turns back to the TV*). You're my big sister.

Lucy. That's not the question.

Linus. No, but that's the answer.

Lucy. Come on, Linus, answer the question.

Linus (*getting up and facing Lucy*). Look, Lucy, I know very well that if I give any sort of honest answer to that question, you're going to slug me.

Lucy. Linus. A survey that is not based on honest answers is like a house that is built on a foundation of sand. Would I be spending my time to conduct this survey if I didn't expect complete candor[20] in all the responses? I promise not to slug you. Now what number would you give me as your crabbiness rating?

Linus (*after a few moments of interior struggle*). Ninety-five. (*Lucy sends a straight jab to his jaw, which lays him out flat.*)

---

20. **candor:** honesty.

Lucy. No decent person could be expected to keep her word with a rating over ninety. *(She stalks off, busily figuring away on her clipboard.)* Now, I add these two columns, and that gives me my answer. *(She figures energetically, then finally sits up with satisfaction.)* There, it's all done. Now, let's see what we've got. *(She begins to scan the page. A look of trouble skims over her face. She rechecks the figures. Her eternal look of self-confidence wavers, then crumbles.)* It's true. I'm a crabby person. I'm a very crabby person and everybody knows it. I've been spreading crabbiness wherever I go. I'm a supercrab. It's a wonder anyone will still talk to me. It's a wonder I have any friends at all *(She looks at the figures on the paper.)* or even associates. I've done nothing but make life miserable for everyone. I've done nothing but breed unhappiness and resentment. Where did I go wrong? How could I be so selfish? How could . . .

(Linus has been listening. He comes and sits near her.)

Linus. What's wrong, Lucy?

Lucy. Don't talk to me, Linus. I don't deserve to be spoken to. I don't deserve to breathe the air I breathe. I'm no good, Linus. I'm no good.

Linus. That's not true, Lucy.

Lucy. Yes it is. I'm no good, and there's no reason at all why I should go on living on the face of this earth.

Linus. Yes there is.

Lucy. Name one. Just tell me one single reason why I should still deserve to go on living on this planet.

Linus. Well, for one thing, you have a little brother who loves you. *(Lucy looks at him. She is silent. Then she breaks into a great sobbing "Wah!")* Every now and then I say the right thing.

(Lucy continues sobbing as she and Linus exit. A brief musical interlude, a change of light, and Schroeder and Patty come onstage.)

Schroeder. Of course it's surprising, but I'm sure Lucy knows now that she just can't be crabby anymore. Where is everybody? I told them to be here. If we don't rehearse, we can't sing at the assembly tomorrow. *(Calling off.)* Charlie Brown, Linus, Lu—

Lucy *(offstage).* Gimme that pencil, you blockhead!

Linus *(coming onstage).* No! Not until you give me back my crayons.

Lucy *(coming onstage).* That's my best pencil, you block— *(She sees Patty.)* If you don't give me that pencil, I'll tell Patty what you said about her!

Schroeder. Stop that. We've got to rehearse. You're late. *(He arranges them in a row with Linus between Patty and Lucy.)*

Patty. What did you say about me, Linus?

Lucy. He said . . .

Linus. Lucy!

Schroeder. Stop that!

Charlie Brown *(running onstage).* I'm sorry I'm late, but Snoopy and I were . . . *(Snoopy enters behind him.)*

Schroeder. There's no time to be sorry.

Patty. What did he say?

Lucy. He said . . .

Schroeder. Quiet! Now remember, this is a mood piece. We must paint a picture with music and words. And concentrate. *(He takes position as conductor and blows a note on his pitch pipe.)* Remember, *adagio con brio.*[21]

(They perform "The Glee Club Rehearsal." The subplot is carried on with a minimum of gesture and display, and those not directly involved in it are unaware that anything unusual is happening. Schroeder, for instance, is oblivious of anything wrong until the very end. "Home, Home on the Range" is sung throughout; the other lines are sung simultaneously.)

All *(singing).*
   Oh, give me a home
   Where the buffalo roam,
   Where the deer and the antelope play,

Lucy. Give me my pencil.

All. Where seldom is heard
   A discouraging word,

Linus. Not on your life.

All. And the skies are not cloudy all day.

(Patty and Lucy sing simultaneously.)

Patty. If you don't tell me what you told Lucy, I'm just going to scream!

Lucy. Gimme my pencil, you blockhead!

All. Home,
   Home on the range,

Lucy *(sings alone).*
   Give me my pencil.

(Linus and all the other characters sing together)

All. Where the deer and the antelope play,

Linus. No!
   Not until you promise not to tell her.

Lucy. What are you trying to do? Stifle my freedom of speech?

All. Where seldom is heard

Lucy. Give me my pencil.

All. A discouraging word,

Linus. No promise, no pencil.

All. And the skies are not
   Cloudy all day.

Patty. What pencil?

Linus *(looks at his hands and sees he is no longer holding the pencil).* No!

(Patty victoriously holds up the pencil she has managed to sneak away from him. Linus looks horrified at it.)

All. Oh, give me a land

Linus. Give me that pencil! *(He grabs it back.)*

(Patty and all the other characters sing.)

All. Where the bright diamond sand

Patty. Linus, it just isn't fair!

Schroeder. Sing!

All *(with vigor).* Flows leisurely down the stream,

Charlie Brown *(leaning forward and whispering to Linus).* Why did you take Patty's pencil?

Linus. Aaugh!

(He stomps offstage in desperation.)

---

21. **adagio con brio** (ə dä′ jō kän brē′ ō): a musical direction, Italian for "slowly, with spirit."

All. Where the graceful white swan
   Goes gliding along

Patty (*to* Lucy). What did he call me?

(Lucy *and all the other characters sing together.*)

Lucy. He said—
   He said you were—
   an enigma.
All. Like a maid in a heavenly dream.

Patty. An enigma?

Charlie Brown. An enigma?

Snoopy. An enigma?

(Patty *and all the other characters sing together.*)

Patty. Boy, that makes me—
   What a terrible thing to call a—
   What's an enigma?
   Never mind.
All. Home,
   Home on the range,

(Patty *stomps off after* Linus. Lucy *and all the other characters sing together.*)

Lucy. What's an enigma?
All. Where the deer

(Charlie Brown *and all other characters sing together.*)

Charlie Brown. What's an enigma?
All. And the antelope play,

Snoopy. What's an enigma?

Lucy. Hey, he's still got my pencil! (*She exits.*)

All. Where seldom is heard
   A discouraging word,

(Charlie Brown *has become curious and slips out to follow the others.*)

Schroeder. And the skies are not cloudy all day.

(Schroeder *discovers toward the middle of this line that he is the only one left singing except for the mournful, harmonic howls of the dog. As he watches in despair, Snoopy finishes up the song, then tosses a congratulatory kiss to his conductor. Schroeder makes a hasty, explosive exit. Snoopy retires to his doghouse.*)

Snoopy. Now why is it I always have my supper in the red dish and my drinking water in the yellow dish? One of these days I'm going to have my supper in the yellow dish and my drinking water in the red dish. Life is just too short not to live it up a little.

(Schroeder *and* Linus *enter.*)

Schroeder. Linus, did you fill out all those forms that Miss Othmar gave us in school today?

Linus. Uh huh. I put down my name and address and our telephone number.

Schroeder. Well, what did you put where it says "family doctor"?

Linus. I wasn't too sure, so I put down Dr. Seuss.

(Linus *exits.* Schroeder *sits.*)

Snoopy. My teeth are tingling again. I feel like I've just got to bite somebody before sundown or I shall go stark raving mad. And yet I know that society frowns on such an action. So what happens? I'm stuck with tingly teeth.

(Lucy *enters and casually approaches* Schroeder.)

Lucy. Psst. Hooray for Irving Berlin![22] (Lucy *is off and running with* Schroeder *right behind her.*)

Snoopy. I hate cats. To me, cats are the crab-grass on the lawn of life. I am a cat hater, a cat despiser, and a cat loather. *(A burst of cats' yowling is heard offstage.)* I'm also scared to death of them.

(Linus *comes onstage with his blanket.* Lucy *and* Patty *come onstage from another side and see him.*)

Lucy. Oh, here comes my little baby brother, Linus, with his little blanket.

Patty. There's your little baby brother with his silly little blanket.

Lucy. Well, you know how babies are with their baby blankets.

Linus *(flinging the blanket cape-style around his shoulders).* I am Count Dracula from Transylvania.

(Lucy *and* Patty *immediately burst into screams and run offstage.* Linus *happily skips off in another direction.* Snoopy *is left.*)

Snoopy. Sometimes I think I'll just pull up stakes and move out of here. Broaden my horizons, meet new people. But something holds me here. Something binds me to this spot. *(He heaves a great sigh.)* That old supper dish.

(The lights begin doing somersaults as the music swings into a bright and energetic rhythm. Lucy *comes onstage, pulling* Linus *along by the hand. They meet* Charlie Brown *and proceed into the song "Little-Known Facts.")*

Charlie Brown. Hi, Linus. Where are you going?

Linus. Lucy's teaching me, Charlie Brown. She says a sister is responsible for the education of her little brother, so she's teaching me. Boy, is she intelligent.

Lucy. Come along, Linus. *(She sings.)*
Do you see this tree?
It is a fir tree.
It's called a fir tree
Because it gives us fur,
For coats.
It also gives us wool in the wintertime.

Linus. I never knew that before. That's very interesting.

Lucy. This is an elm tree.
It's very little,
But it will grow up
Into a giant tree,
An oak.
You can tell how old it is by counting its leaves.

Linus. Gosh, Lucy, that's fascinating.

Charlie Brown *(speaking).* Now, wait a minute, Lucy. I don't mean to interfere, but . . .

Lucy. And way up there,
Those fluffy little white things,
Those are clouds; they make the wind blow.

---

22. **Irving Berlin:** a famous U.S. composer of popular songs.

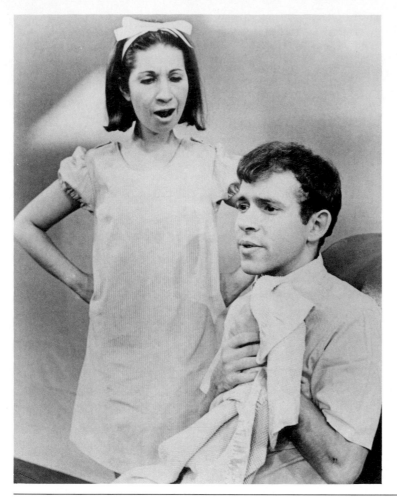

And way down there,
Those tiny little black things,
Those are bugs.
They make the grass grow.

Linus. Is that so?

Lucy. That's right. They run around all day long, tugging and tugging at each tiny seedling until it grows into a great tall blade of grass.

Linus. Boy, that's amazing.

Charlie Brown. Oh, good grief.

Lucy *(singing).* And this thing here,
It's called a hydrant.
They grow all over,

And no one seems to know just how
A little thing like that gives so much water.

Do you see that bird?
It's called an eagle.
But since it's little,
It has another name, a sparrow.
On Christmas and Thanksgiving we
    eat them.

Charlie Brown. Lucy, how can you say that! I'm sorry, but I just can't stand idly by and listen to you . . .

Lucy. And way up there,
The little stars and planets
Make the rain that falls in showers.

And when it's cold and winter is upon us,
The snow comes up,
Just like the flowers.

Charlie Brown. Now, Lucy, I know that's wrong. Snow doesn't come up, it comes down.

Lucy. After it comes up, the wind blows it around so it looks like it's coming down, but actually it comes up out of the ground like grass. It comes up, Charlie Brown; snow comes up!

Charlie Brown. Oh, good grief. (*He makes an agonized rush for the wings.*)

Linus. Lucy, why is Charlie Brown banging his head against a tree?

Lucy. To loosen the bark so the tree will grow faster. Come along, Linus.

(*They exit, the music flitting along behind them. Then a change. The atmosphere grays, and a heavy, tired phrase repeats itself in the orchestra.* Snoopy *is prone on his house.*)

Snoopy. My stomach clock just went off. It's supper time, and Charlie Brown has forgotten to feed me. Here I lie, a withering hollow shell of a dog, and there sits my supper dish, empty. But that's all right. He'll remember. When no furry friend comes to greet him after school, *then* he'll remember. And he'll rush out here to the doghouse, but it will be too late. There will be nothing left but the dried carcass of his former friend who used to run and play so happily with him. Nothing left but the bleached bones of . . .

(Charlie Brown *has come onstage and is standing with* Snoopy's *supper dish.*)

Charlie Brown. Hey, Snoopy. Are you asleep or something? I've been standing here for a whole minute with your supper, and you haven't even noticed. It's supper time. (*He sets the dish down. In an instant* Snoopy *is alert.*)

Snoopy. Supper time? Supper time! (*He strikes a magnificent pose on his rooftop and sings with a grand show of operatic fervor.*)
Behold the brimming bowl of meat and
    meal
Which is brought forth to ease our
    hunger.
Behold the flowing flagon moist and
    sweet
Which has been sent to slake our thirst.

Charlie Brown. OK, there's no need for a big production. Just get down off your doghouse and eat.

(Charlie Brown *exits.* Snoopy *slithers off his perch and proceeds into the song "Supper Time.")*

Snoopy (*singing*).
Supper time.
Yes, it's supper time,
Ooh, it's sup-sup-supper time,
Very best time of day.
Supper time.
Yeah, it's supper time,
And when supper time comes
Can supper be far away?

Bring on the soup dish,
Bring on the cup,
Bring on the bacon,
And fill me up, 'cause it's
Supper, supper, supper, supper time.

(*He fancyfoots with delight around the dish.*)

Br-r-ing on the dog food,
Bring on the bone,
Bring on the barrel, and

Roll me home, 'cause it's
Supper, supper, supper, supper.
Supper, super pepper-upper,
Supper, super-duper supper time.

Wintertime's nice with the ice and snow,
Summertime's nice with a place to go,
Bedtime, overtime, halftime too,
But they just can't hold a candle to
My supper time.
Oh yeah.

Br-r-ing on the hamburg,
Bring in the bun,
Pappy's little puppy loves everyone,
'Cause it's
Supper, supper, supper, supper,
Supper, super pepper-upper,
Supper, super-duper-dupper,
Dupa dupa dipa dapa, dipa dapa
 dupa dapa.

(Snoopy breaks into a wild, ecstatic dance, nearly bowling over Charlie Brown as he comes onstage.)

Charlie Brown. Now, wait a minute, Snoopy. Hey, you'll spill it all over. NOW, CUT THAT OUT! *(Dog, music, action, all stop in midphrase.)* Why can't you eat your meal quietly and calmly like any normal dog? *(He exits.)*

Snoopy *(watches him go, then picks up his supper dish).* So what's wrong with making mealtime a joyous occasion? *(He sings, quietly.)* Doo doo doo, doo-de doo-doo doo.

(He disappears behind his house. The mood changes. The scene is dimmed and spotted with evening colors, and airy music is heard. Linus and Lucy wander on, looking at the sky.)

Lucy. Well, I don't know, Linus; it looks like an airplane to me, the way the lights are blinking on and off. *(Schroeder and Patty enter from the opposite side of the stage.)* Schroeder, is that an airplane or a star?

Schroeder. I believe that is a star. But it could be a planet, you know. Or maybe even a satellite.

Patty. It could be a satellite. I wonder.

Linus. Well, we'll never find out by just sitting here. *(He crosses toward the front of the stage.)*

Lucy. Where are you going?

Linus. I'm going over here to get a closer look.

(They all settle to enjoy the evening. Snoopy climbs up on his doghouse, his empty supper dish in his mouth.)

Snoopy. I like to sit up here after supper and listen to the sounds of the night. But somehow something seems to be missing. *(He lets forth a mournful howl.)* In my opinion, that's exactly what was needed.

(Charlie Brown comes onstage, staring at a pencil in his hands, his face wide with wonder.)

Charlie Brown. That little redheaded girl dropped her pencil. It has teeth marks all over it. She nibbles her pencil. She's human! Gosh, it hasn't been such a bad day after all.

(He and the others sing "Happiness.")

Charlie Brown. Happiness is finding a pencil.

Snoopy. Sleeping in moonlight.

Linus. Telling the time.

Schroeder. Happiness is learning to whistle.

Linus. Tying your shoe
For the very first time.

Patty. Happiness is playing the drum
In your own school band.

Charlie Brown. And happiness is walking
hand in hand.
Happiness is two kinds of ice cream.

Lucy. Knowing a secret.

Schroeder. Climbing a tree.

Charlie Brown. Happiness is five different
crayons.

Schroeder. Catching a firefly.

Linus. Setting him free.

Charlie Brown. Happiness is being alone
every now and then.

All. And happiness is coming home again.

Charlie Brown. Happiness is morning
and evening,
Daytime and nighttime too.
For happiness is anyone and anything
at all
That's loved by you.

Linus. Happiness is having a sister.

Lucy. Sharing a sandwich.

Lucy and Linus. Getting along.

All. Happiness is singing together
When day is through,
And happiness is those who sing
with you.
Happiness is morning and evening,
Daytime and nighttime too.

Charlie Brown. For happiness is anyone
and anything at all
That's loved by you.

(Slowly the group gets up and leaves, nodding silent good nights to each other.

Finally, only Charlie Brown *and* Lucy *are left—except for* Snoopy, *asleep on his house.* Lucy *has been watching* Charlie Brown. *At last she rises, walks resolutely toward him and extends her hand to him. Tentatively, almost fearfully,* Charlie Brown *takes it and receives a firm, definitive handshake.)*

Lucy. You're a good man, Charlie Brown.

(That's as much tenderness as Lucy *can allow herself. She quickly turns and makes her way offstage, leaving* Charlie Brown *to mull it over and perhaps even to arrive at a faint, glad smile as the curtains close.)*

EXPLAIN

Responding to Reading

First Impressions

1. How do you feel about the ending of the play? Describe your feelings in your journal or on a sheet of paper.

Second Thoughts

2. Do you think Lucy gathers accurate information from her friends in her survey? Why or why not?

   Think about
   • the words of the survey and how Lucy conducted it
   • why Charlie Brown answers the way he does
   • how other characters respond and what the results reveal

3. How would you describe Snoopy's attitude toward life?

4. What do you learn about the characters from their words and actions during the baseball game?

5. Do you think Linus believes Lucy's lessons about trees, clouds, and insects? Why or why not?

Broader Connections

6. Look at the characters' definitions of happiness at the end of the play. How do they compare to the answers you collected for the survey, page 486, before you read the play?

Literary Concept: Soliloquy

In drama, a **soliloquy** is a speech in which a character speaks thoughts aloud. Generally, the character is on the stage alone, not speaking to other characters, or even to the audience. A soliloquy by Shakespeare begins with Hamlet saying the famous line, "To be or not to be." Find two of Charlie Brown's soliloquies in Act One and explain what they reveal about him.

Concept Review: Humor Much of the humor in this play occurs in the last lines of scenes. This could be compared to the punch lines of jokes or comic strips. Choose a scene from the play that you find funny and try to explain what makes it funny. Is it *what* the characters do or say, or is it *how* they do and say it?

Writing Options

1. If Charlie Brown could discuss his feelings about his life with you as he does with Lucy, what advice would you give him? Imagine that Charlie Brown is your pen pal and write him a **letter of advice** on how to improve his life.

2. How would characters from other selections in this book complete the sentence "Happiness is . . . ."? Create a **booklet** in which you write the responses of five different characters to this incomplete sentence.

3. Write a **scene** that you could add to one of the acts of this play. Use *Peanuts* comic strips or your own imagination to supply the idea for the scene.

4. Imagine that you have just seen this drama performed on stage. Evaluate the play in a **review** for your newspaper. What do you think of the dialogue? To what audience does the play appeal? Do you think the play captures the humor of Charles Schulz's comics?

Vocabulary Practice

Exercise   On your paper, write the word from the list that matches the meaning of the boldfaced word or phrase.

1. Lucy tries to help Charlie Brown get over his feelings of **being less important than everyone else.**

2. Patty sometimes gives **shallow** answers to deep questions.

3. According to Linus, Patty is a(n) **mystery.**

4. Charlie Brown is likeable because he shows **modesty and seems aware of his faults.**

5. Snoopy has the **one-of-a-kind honor** of being the only animal in the play.

6. Linus's blanket provides a **shelter** that makes him feel safe and secure.

7. By continuing in spite of difficulty and disappointment, Charlie Brown shows his **quality of stubbornly refusing to give up hope.**

8. Linus tries to convince Lucy that she cannot be queen, but his efforts are **useless.**

9. Schroeder admires Charlie Brown's **reliable, never-changing character:** he can always count on Charlie Brown to lose.

10. Although he is just an ordinary boy, Charlie Brown still has a **quality of greatness and dignity** about him.

Options for Learning

1 • *Peanuts* Everywhere! Each year nearly 1 billion dollars worth of *Peanuts* merchandise is sold. Find as many products as you can on which the *Peanuts* characters appear and present your findings in an oral or written report.

2 • The World's a Stage Design the set, the costumes, and the props for *You're a Good Man, Charlie Brown*. Use everyday clothing and objects and simple stages to reflect the scenes in the play.

Clark Gesner   1938–

As a writer and composer, Clark Gesner has contributed to such television shows as *Captain Kangaroo, Sesame Street,* and *Electric Company,* as well as many other TV shows. Gesner says that when *You're a Good Man, Charlie Brown* began rehearsals, none of the actors had a script yet. The play started to take shape, however, as Gesner and the actors worked with ten years' worth of Charles Schultz's cartoons to come up with scenes and songs. Each person contributed something, and the play turned out to be a big hit.

Gesner graduated from Princeton University in 1960, served in the Army for two years, and has pursued composing and lyric writing since 1963.

Charles M. Schulz   1922–

Charles Schulz enjoyed drawing from the time he was a little boy and shared his father's love for the comics. After time in the army during World War II, Schulz was hired as an instructor at his former art school. "I was also using some of my spare time to draw cartoons for magazines," he says, "but nobody was interested." Finally, in 1950, *Peanuts* appeared in seven newspapers.

About Charlie Brown, Schulz says, "I like to think that all of my readers can sympathize with him since everybody has had experiences in losing." In fact, every time *It's the Great Pumpkin, Charlie Brown* or *Be My Valentine, Charlie Brown* is shown on television, people all over the country send candy or valentines to Schulz for him to give to Charlie Brown. Schulz reminds us that "most of us are much more acquainted with losing than we are with winning. Winning is great, but it isn't funny."

WRITER'S WORKSHOP

INFORMATIVE WRITING

What would you like to know about the Wild West, the game of cricket, or the civil-rights movement? After Jesse Watkins read "Carrying the Running-Aways," he wondered how the Underground Railroad got started, how it worked, and who the people were who ran it. In this workshop you'll have a chance to find out more about a topic that interests you. Then you'll have a chance to write a report and share your knowledge with others.

USE INFORMATIVE WRITING FOR

reports
articles
biographies
essays
speeches

GUIDED ASSIGNMENT: RESEARCH REPORT

Research and write an informative report on a subject that is related to one of the selections in this book.

Here is one writer's PASSkey to this assignment.

PURPOSE: To learn and to inform
AUDIENCE: My teacher and classmates
SUBJECT: Heroes of the Underground Railroad
STRUCTURE: Research report

Three Heroes of the Underground Railroad
by Jesse Watkins

The Underground Railroad was not a real railroad, and it wasn't underground. Instead, the Underground Railroad was a secret system made up of people who helped the slaves as they traveled north to freedom. Who were the people who made the Underground Railroad work?

The Underground Railroad provided slaves with places to stay, wagons and carts for transportation, food, clothing, and friends who would help the slaves get from place to place. Blacks who had never been slaves, as well as former slaves and whites who opposed slavery, helped with the Underground

STUDENT MODEL

Before you write, read the beginning and the conclusion of one student's report. The introduction clearly states the topic and lets the reader know what the writer plans to do.

This paragraph explores the first main idea.

Railroad. Both men and women took part. Even slaves who were not free helped with the Underground Railroad. According to <u>The World Book Encyclopedia,</u> "A large part of its work was done by southern slaves who, though unable to escape themselves, helped runaways with food, clothing, and directions."

One of the former slaves who helped was John Mason. Mason escaped from slavery, but then he returned to the South to help others. He was even captured once, but he escaped again. Throughout his life, Mason helped guide 1,300 runaways to freedom, including 265 people that he took to Canada in a year and a half. . . .

In conclusion, it is important to remember that the Underground Railroad was made up of many generous people. These people helped thousands of slaves to escape before the Civil War. Former slaves, such as John Mason and Harriet Tubman, and white people who were against slavery, such as Calvin Fairbanks, did not worry about themselves but thought of the people they could help. With their courage, they helped end slavery in the United States.

List of Sources

Donald, David Herbert. "Underground Railroad." <u>The World Book Encyclopedia.</u> 1988 ed.

Evitts, William. <u>Captive Bodies, Free Spirits.</u> New York: Messner, 1985.

Lester, Julius. <u>To Be a Slave.</u> New York: Dial, 1968.

The words "According to" introduce the quote. This shows the reader the source of the information.

This paragraph discusses the second main idea.

Ellipses (a set of dots) indicate that part of this report is not shown.

The conclusion summarizes the main ideas and ends with Jesse's evaluation.

Jesse's list of sources is given in alphabetical order by author.

Prewrite and Explore

1 **Find a fascinating topic** Thumb through the table of contents in this book. Let the selections trigger topic ideas. Brainstorm a list of topics, then choose the one that interests you most.

2 **Trim your topic**   After you have chosen your topic, create a word web with the topic in the middle. What subtopics does your general topic bring to mind? Select one of these more specific topics for your report.

◀ **KEEP YOUR FOCUS**
. . . .
Remember, this is a short research report. If your topic is too broad, there is no room for interesting details. Focus on a specific topic and two or three main ideas.

GATHERING INFORMATION

Check the card catalog or the computer catalog in the library to find books on your topic. Use the *Readers' Guide to Periodical Literature* to locate magazine articles. You can also look for articles in encyclopedias and other reference books.

On a separate index card write down publication information for each of your sources. Number each card to use as a reference when you take notes. To create a list of sources for the end of your report, make sure you have the following information on each source card:

Book—author, title, city of publication, publisher, copyright date
Magazine—author, title of article, name and date of magazine, page numbers
Encyclopedia—author, title of article, name of encyclopedia, year of edition

Take notes on index cards. Use one card for each piece of information. Do not copy information word for word. Summarize the information or jot down phrases as Jesse did on the note card below.

```
[Topic]          [Source Number]      [Page Number]
John Mason             1                   85

--slave from Kentucky who returned to South

--helped 265 slaves reach Canada in 18 months

--captured and escaped a second time

--total people helped--about 1,300
```

◀ **COMPUTER TIP**
. . . .
List your information sources in a computer document rather than on paper. Later you can alphabetize this list and attach it to your finished report.

◀ **WATCH WHAT YOU COPY!**
. . . .
You *must* enclose what an author says word for word in quotation marks and give credit to the person who wrote the words. If you leave the quotation marks out, you are guilty of plagiarism (plā′ jə riz′ əm), or stealing someone else's words. Don't do it!

---

3 **Organize your notes**   Review your notes. Separate your note cards into stacks according to main idea. Then decide on two or three main ideas to include in your report. For example, Jesse separated his notes into stacks for each of the people he discusses, as well as for the Underground Railroad in general.

Draft and Discover

REMINDER

An outline is a guide for writing, not a straitjacket that you can't get free of. If you start to write your report and discover your outline doesn't work, toss it out or create a new one.

1 **Make an outline** Use your groups of note cards to help you prepare an outline. First, arrange your main idea groups in logical order. Then turn each group into a major division of your outline. Write the main ideas as outline headings. To see how to create an outline, see page 647 in the Writer's Handbook.

2 **Draft the body** Start by writing any part of the report. In Jesse's case, he wrote the section on Harriet Tubman first because he had the most information about her. However, you may want to follow your outline, using a new paragraph for each major division.

3 **Wrap it up** Draft a conclusion that sums up all the ideas you've presented. This last paragraph should provide a clear, definite finish—without being dull or simply repeating what you've already said. Last but not least, you need to tell what sources you used for the report. Write the list of sources in alphabetical order according to the authors' last names. If no author was given, list the title of the article or book first.

NEED HELP?

For information on how to list your sources, see pages 646–647 in the Writer's Handbook.

Revise Your Writing

1 **Is your report well organized?** Check to see that you covered all the points in your outline. Make sure that each paragraph deals with only one main idea, that your supporting details are clear, and that you have used signal words like *first, next,* and *finally* to link ideas. Try changing the order of your paragraphs or adding details.

2 **Use a peer reader** Ask a peer reader to review your report and respond to it. Use the following questions.

Revision Questions

For You	For a Peer Reader
1. Does my introduction grab your attention?	**1.** Is the tone lively enough to interest you?
2. Are the ideas in each paragraph fully developed?	**2.** Is any information unclear?

Proofread

Proofread your report for incorrect punctuation, spelling, capitalization, and grammar. Dates, names, and direct quotes are places where mistakes can easily slip in. Double check!

◀ **NEED MORE HELP?**
See the Language Workshop that follows (pages 528–530) and Section 6 in the Language Handbook.

THE EDITOR'S EYE: VERB TENSES

When you write, be sure to keep your verbs in the proper tense.

The **present tense** describes an action that is happening now.

As we *study* slavery, we *learn* many important things.

The **past tense** describes an action that was completed in the past.

As we *studied* slavery, we *learned* many important things.

Incorrect   Mason escaped from slavery, but then he *returns* to the South to help others.

Correct   Mason escaped from slavery, but then he *returned* to the South to help others.

Publish and Present

Here is a suggestion for sharing your work with others.

A Topic a Day   As a class, group your reports into general topics. Each day, have a different group of students read reports on their related topics. After the presentations, the "panel of experts" can answer questions asked by the other students.

Reflect on Your Writing

Write brief answers to the questions below. Attach your answers to your report and put both in your writing portfolio.

◀ **FOR YOUR PORTFOLIO**

1. How can the process of report writing help you with other assignments?
2. What have you learned about your topic? What else would you like to find out?

LANGUAGE
· · · · · · · · WORKSHOP

UNDERSTANDING VERB TENSES

> Verbs use different forms to show changes in time. These forms are called the **tenses** of a verb.

REMINDER
Verbs are words that tell about an action or state that something *is*.

▶ Verbs do double duty in sentences. Besides describing the action of the subject, the verb also tells you when the action is happening—in the past, the present, or the future.

Forming the Present Tense

The **present tense** of a verb tells about an action or a state of being that is happening now.

I *laugh.* I *am* a comedian. I *can tell* jokes.

When the subject is plural, use the basic form of the verb. Use the basic form of the verb with the pronouns *I* and *you*. Add *-s* or *-es* to the basic form when the subject is singular.

We *laugh.* They *laugh.* I *laugh.* You *laugh.* He *laughs.*

Forming the Past Tense

The **past tense** describes an action or a state of being that was completed in the past.

I *laughed.* I *was* the star of our comedy show.

Add *-ed* to form the past tense of most verbs. Verbs that form the past tense by adding *-ed* to the basic form of the verb are called **regular verbs.**

laugh   laugh*ed*   walk   walk*ed*

IRREGULAR VERBS
For a list of common irregular verbs, see the Language Handbook, Section 6.

▶ **Irregular verbs** change their spelling in a way different from regular verbs to show the past tense.

sing   *sang*   think   *thought*   do   *did*

Forming the Future Tense

The **future tense** tells about an action or a state of being that will happen in the future.

Tomorrow I *will practice.* I *will sing.*

To form the future tense, use the helping verb *will* or *shall* with the present tense.

write   *will write*   read   *shall read*

◀ SHALL WE DANCE? · · · · · · · · · · · · · · · ·
The helping verb *shall* is rarely used in declarative sentences. *Shall* is most often used in questions.

Exercise 1   Concept Review   Write the verb form asked for in each sentence.

1. Our class (future of *read*) a book about Harriet Tubman.
2. I (past of *learn*) about Miss Tubman in social studies.
3. She (past of *work*) for the Underground Railroad.
4. Harriet Tubman (past of *guide*) many slaves to freedom.
5. My family (future of *visit*) her memorial in Auburn, New York.
6. Dad (present of *enjoy*) taking us to historical sites.
7. Last year we (past of *go*) to Abraham Lincoln's birthplace in Kentucky.
8. Of all our presidents, I (present of *admire*) Lincoln most.
9. Someday I (future of *see*) the Lincoln Memorial in Washington, D.C.
10. My father (present of *say*) that's our next trip.

Keeping Verbs in the Same Tense

Keep your verbs in the same tense when you write about actions taking place at the same time. Do not switch from past to present or present to past.

When you write about actions that occur in the same time period, use the same verb tense. For example, if you write about an event that happened yesterday, you should use only the past tense.

Incorrect   I finished my report and *check* it for errors.

Correct   I finished my report and *checked* it for errors.

Use only the present tense when you describe action that is happening now. If you write about something that will happen in the future, use only the future tense.

Incorrect	Our class will perform the play, and the other classes _watch_ us.
Correct	Our class will perform the play, and the other classes _will watch_ us.

LISTEN FOR MISTAKES
Not sure you've used the right verb tenses? Read your writing aloud. Listen carefully for shifts in verb tenses.

▶ Should you ever change tenses? Yes! You should change tenses to indicate that parts of the sentence take place at different times.

When you use time words like _yesterday, before, last year_, or _long ago_, your verbs should be in the past tense. Use the present tense with words such as _today_ and _now_. Use the future tense with words like _tomorrow, next week_, or _someday_.

Exercise 2   Concept Review   Rewrite each sentence. Correct shifts in verb tense. Some of the verbs do not need to be changed.

1. Charles Schulz is born in 1922 and grew up in Minnesota.
2. When he is thirteen, he was given a black and white dog.
3. In high school Charles was gawky and is not good at sports.
4. Although he will hate football, Schulz loved drawing, and he still loves drawing today.
5. Yesterday, our class performed _You're a Good Man, Charlie Brown_, and it will be a big hit.
6. Our audience was another sixth grade class, and they give us a standing ovation.
7. Next week we performed the play again.
8. Our props were ordinary objects such as a card table and a dog dish; we wear ordinary clothes, not costumes.
9. It took a lot of time, but we memorize all the lines.
10. After we gave the last performance, we have a pizza party.

Exercise 3   Looking at Style   At the beginning of Act Two of _You're a Good Man, Charlie Brown_, Snoopy talks about being a World War I flying ace. World War I took place in the past, and yet Snoopy describes his actions in the present tense. Why do you think the author has Snoopy describe his actions as if he were performing them now?

LANGUAGE HANDBOOK
For review and practice: Section 6, Using Verbs.

Exercise 4   Revising Your Writing   Look over your report and lightly underline each verb. Did you use the correct verb tense? Are there any unnecessary shifts in tense? Correct any mistakes in verb tense that you find.

Reader's Workshop

SUMMARIZING

When you **summarize,** you briefly restate the main points of a passage. Summarizing comes in handy when you're gathering information and preparing notes for a report. Summarizing is also a good way for you to help yourself understand what you're reading.

To write a summary, follow these four steps:

Step 1   Skim   To skim, move your eyes rapidly over the page. Glance at titles, topic sentences, highlighted words or phrases, and graphic aids. Skimming gives you a general idea of what the material is about.

Step 2   Reread   Now that you are familiar with the material, reread it slowly and carefully. Make sure you understand the **main idea** of the passage.

Step 3   Make brief notes   Jot down the most important points from the material. These should include the main idea and key facts. Leave out any minor or unnecessary details.

Step 4   Write your summary   Write a few short sentences that sum up the information in your notes. Remember, your summary *must be in your own words*. It should state the main idea of the original reading passage, as well as important facts.

Exercise   Summarize the passage below in your own words.

> From the 1890s through the 1920s, American comic strips mainly gave humorous, exaggerated views of life in the United States. The first comic strip to become popular with a wide audience was called *Hogan's Alley;* it appeared in 1895 in the Sunday edition of *The World,* a newspaper in New York City. The strip related the mischief of a little boy named Mickey Dugan. In 1897 the *New York Journal* began to run a comic strip, *The Katzenjammer Kids,* about a group of children whose everyday pranks amused and delighted readers.
>
> In the 1930s, however, adventure comic strips became a popular trend. Strips such as *Flash Gordon, Buck Rogers,* and *Brick Bradford* told about science fiction adventures. *Dick Tracy,* created in 1931, followed the exploits of a daring detective. Other adventurous heroes were introduced in strips such as *Superman, Captain Easy,* and *Prince Valiant.*

◀ **IN OTHER CLASSES**
Summarizing is especially useful in social studies, science, or any class where you need to use only a few sentences to present the main information from a piece of writing.

◀ **TIP**
Include important names and dates in a summary. Double check each date and the spelling of each name before you return the reference source you are using.

Reading on Your Own

Suggested Novels for Unit Five

"What Matters Most," the Unit Five theme, is asked and answered in the novels introduced on these pages.

ISLAND OF THE BLUE DOLPHINS

SCOTT O'DELL ©1960

Twelve-year-old Karana is stranded on the island that the rest of her tribe has hastily abandoned. No stranger to hardship, the Native American girl takes up the task of gathering food and water to sustain herself. She builds a shelter, defends herself against a pack of wild dogs, and even tames and befriends the pack's leader. The island, known for the dolphins in its surrounding waters, holds other challenges and wonders for Karana. Yet the days of waiting blend into seasons, and the seasons become years. The rescue she hopes for seems out of reach. As you read Karana's story, which is based on the true experience of a girl in the 1800s, think about . . .

- the animals Karana encounters and what she learns from them

- how her early life on the island might have prepared her for her experience

- the attitude Karana seems to have about her successes and failures

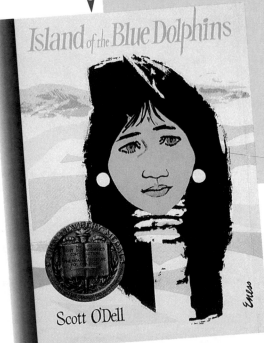

Island of the Blue Dolphins

Scott O'Dell

532

A WRINKLE IN TIME

MADELEINE L'ENGLE ©1962

When Mrs. Whatsit casually mentions that "there is such a thing as a tesseract," Mrs. Murry is shocked. How could this stranger know the scientific concept Mrs. Murry and her husband had explored before his mysterious disappearance? Mrs. Whatsit reveals much more to Meg and Charles Wallace, the Murrys' children, and to Calvin, Meg's friend, before "tessering" with them across time and space on an amazing rescue mission. As you read this science fiction novel, let its ideas challenge your imagination. Think about these questions:

• What extraordinary traits does Charles Wallace possess that set him apart from others?

• What personal traits can Meg use to battle the forces that oppose the rescuers?

• What does the evil power IT have in store for the children?

DRAGONWINGS

LAURENCE YEP ©1975

Leaving his mother behind in China, Moon Shadow journeys to the United States in 1903 to join his father who had left long ago in search of work. Some call the boy's destination the "Land of the Golden Mountain," a land where gold is plentiful. Others call it the "Land of the Demons," where Chinese laborers must endure great hardship for even a tiny fortune. When Moon Shadow arrives in San Francisco's Chinatown, his father, now called Windrider, presents him with a beautiful, handmade kite and a dream of building a flying machine. As you read this historical novel, think about . . .

• the parts several people—including the Wright Brothers—play in helping the father and son

• what causes Moon Shadow's attitudes about the United States to change

• how the San Francisco earthquake of 1906 affects the lives of Windrider and Moon Shadow

Other Recommended Books

Zeely by Virginia Hamilton (©1967). In this novel, eleven-year-old Geeder meets a neighbor whom she imagines to be a Watusi queen. As she gets to know Miss Zeely Tayber, Geeder makes important discoveries about herself and others.

The Root Cellar by Janet Lunn (©1983). Rose, a lonely, modern-day girl in this time-travel fantasy, goes back to the 1860s. The friendships she finds survive the test of time.

The Land I Lost: Adventures of a Boy in Vietnam by Huynh Quang Nhuong (©1982). Cherished memories are shared by a Vietnamese American in this autobiography. The author describes what Vietnam was like before war destroyed his country and changed his boyhood dreams.

Little Town on the Prairie by Laura Ingalls Wilder (©1941). This historical novel is part of a classic series about a pioneer family in the late 1800s. The author based her stories on childhood memories. This book centers on Laura's efforts to send her sister Mary to a college for the blind.

THEMES IN WORLD FOLKLORE

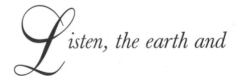

isten, the earth and

its power and people

are singing.

Simon J. Ortiz

CORTÈGE DE CERFS EN RUT
(The Stag's Wedding)
1959   Ivan Generalic.

UNIT PREVIEW

The unit you are about to read is set apart from the other units in two ways.

Folklore All the selections in this unit are classified as folklore—traditional literature that was passed along by word of mouth before being written down. You will learn more about such literature in Elements of Folklore on pages 538–539.

Thematic Links to Previous Units The folklore in this unit is divided into five groups. The selections in each group relate to the theme of a previous unit in this book. For example, the first group of folklore selections extends the theme of Unit One, "With Open Eyes." The second group links to the selections in Unit Two, "Rising to the Challenge," and so on.

You may read each group along with its matching unit, or you may read all the folklore together as a separate unit.

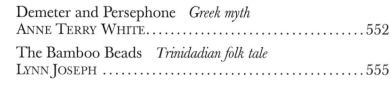

Elements of FOLKLORE

Folklore includes everything from the legends, myths, and folk tales of long ago to the jump-rope rhymes, folk songs, and proverbs that are part of every culture, from the heroes of old legends to the superheroes of today. **Folklore** can be defined as all the traditions, customs, and stories that are passed along by word of mouth in a culture.

All the stories of folklore began as spoken, not written, language. Because these stories are passed along from teller to teller and from generation to generation, their starting point cannot be traced to any one person. A single story may change often as each storyteller adds his or her special touch. Typically, the stories are collected and written down only after they have been told for many years, perhaps centuries. The stories you will read in this unit were not created by the authors named but were retold or translated by them.

These tales—whether woven in the distant past or in modern times—offer more than just entertainment. Folklore helps **keep the past alive,** introducing young people to the history, beliefs, and religion of their society. The stories **teach lessons about human behavior** and **show the qualities that are valued by the society,** such as kindness and courage. They also **reveal negative qualities,** like selfishness and overconfidence.

Very often, the same basic story appears in different cultures. The similarities in these stories point to values that many cultures have in common.

Folklore stories can be grouped into four major categories: myths, folk tales, fables, and legends.

Myths

Myths are stories that were created to answer basic questions about the world, the gods, and human life. Myths tell about events in the distant past and are considered truthful and often sacred by the societies that create them.

Many myths offer explanations of natural events. For example, you will read Greek myths that explain the changes of the seasons and the origin of the first spider. Almost all cultures have **creation myths,** which explain how the world came into being or how humans were created.

Myths usually tell about the adventures of gods or of human beings who come into contact with them. These gods and goddesses have extraordinary powers. The gods of ancient Greece, for instance, were all immortal—they could not die. Each god or goddess had his or her own special areas of power. Yet divine powers were not unlimited. Even Zeus, the ruler of the Greek gods, could not always get his way.

In the myths of many cultures, the gods possess all the emotions and personality traits of human beings. Greek myths tell about the jealousy of Hera, the impatience of Poseidon, and the kindness of Demeter. Like human beings, the gods usually combine a mixture of traits.

Folk Tales

In contrast to myths, folk tales are not about the gods, nor are they about the origins of the world. Told primarily for entertainment, folk tales are not taken as truthful or factual by their audience.

The characters in folk tales are ordinary humans or animals that act like humans. Often, the humans are peasants or other people of the lower classes; they are frequently portrayed as having better values than the rich and powerful.

These tales are told in a simple style, with each character representing one human trait (greed, curiosity, kindness, and so on). Magic and enchantment may play a key role in these stories, as they do in "The Living Kuan-yin" from China (page 571).

The themes of the tales are usually simple—the reward of good, the punishment of evil, the exposing of a fool.

Many folk tales are comical and poke fun at human weaknesses. Among these are the **trickster tales** found in most cultures. In a trickster tale a smart person or animal outwits or takes advantage of some fool. "Why Monkeys Live in Trees" from Africa (page 546) is a good example of a humorous trickster tale.

Fables

A fable is a very short tale that illustrates a clear, often directly stated, **moral**—a principle of right behavior. The characters are often animals that act like humans. "The Disobedient Child" (page 585) is a fable that features a human character with a lesson to learn.

Legends

Legends are considered factual by those who tell them, and many have some basis in historical fact. For example, the legends surrounding Robin Hood are based upon an outlaw who actually existed. These stories tend to be set in a past more recent than that of myths. Legends often include elements of magic and the supernatural.

Strategies for Reading Folklore

1. **Enjoy the tale.** These stories are fun to read because they are filled with action and adventure. As you read, imagine how the stories were told over and over through many generations.

2. **Think about the purpose** of the story. Is its purpose to explain a mystery of nature, to teach a lesson, or to poke fun at human weaknesses?

3. **Look for values and customs** of the culture from which the story comes. What is virtuous behavior, and how is it rewarded? What traits are admired and respected? Which ones are seen as negative?

4. **Decide who holds the power** in the story. Do humans control their own fate, or is some supernatural power in charge?

5. **Compare the story** with others that you know about, perhaps from other cultures. What do the stories have in common? How are they different?

E X P L O R E

With Open Eyes

Examine What You Know

Think back to the nonscientific stories you used to explain natural events, such as thunder, snow, and the sunrise when you were younger. Share one of these stories with your class.

Expand Your Knowledge

"The Gods and Goddesses of Mount Olympus" presents an introduction to the ancient Greek world of gods and goddesses. Exploring Greek myths opens our eyes to a past culture that has influenced Western culture in many ways. In this selection you will discover some of the stories that the Greeks invented to explain the mysteries of nature.

"Yhi Brings the Earth to Life" is a creation myth that tells how life began on the earth. The story represents the beliefs of Australian aborigines, the earliest known inhabitants of Australia.

"Why Monkeys Live in Trees," an African folk tale, is a "why" tale that explains an animal's characteristics. The people who listen to and tell folk tales do not really believe the stories in a literal sense. Nevertheless, folk tales are enjoyed because they often show what a particular culture sees in the workings of nature.

Write Before You Read

■ *Author biographies on Extend page and on page 589 for Olivia Coolidge.*

Make a list of events or forces of nature that you don't understand or that seem mysterious to you. Choose one of these and write a brief explanation of it. As you read, compare your explanation with the explanations presented in the stories.

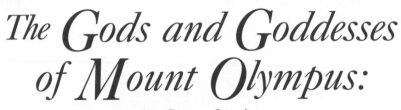

The Gods and Goddesses of Mount Olympus:

An Introduction

OLIVIA COOLIDGE

Greek legends have been favorite stories for many centuries. They are mentioned so often by famous writers that it has become impossible to read widely in English or in many other literatures without knowing what the best of these tales are about. Even though we no longer believe in the Greek gods, we enjoy hearing of them because they appeal to our imagination.

The Greeks thought all the forces of nature were spirits, so that the whole earth was filled with gods. Each river, each woodland, even each great tree had its own god or nymph.[1] In the woods lived the satyrs,[2] who had pointed ears and the shaggy legs of goats. In the sea danced more than three thousand, green-haired, white-limbed maidens. In the air rode wind gods, cloud nymphs, and the golden chariot of the sun. All these spirits, like the forces of nature, were beautiful and strong but sometimes unreliable and unfair. Above all, however, the Greeks felt that they were tremendously interested in mankind.

From very early times, the Greeks began to invent stories to account for the things that went on—the change of seasons, the sudden storms, the good and bad fortune of the farmer's year. These tales were spread by travelers from one valley to another. They were put together and <u>altered</u> by poets and musicians, until at last a great body of legends arose from the whole of Greece. These did not agree with one another in details but, on the whole, gave a clear picture of who the chief gods were, how men should behave to please them, and what their relationships had been with heroes of the past.

The ruler of all the gods was Zeus, the sky god, titled by courtesy "Father of gods and men." He lived in the clouds with most of the great gods in a palace on the top of Mount Olympus, the tallest mountain in Greece. Lightning was the weapon of Zeus, thunder was the rolling of his chariot, and when he nodded his head, the whole earth shook.

---

1. **nymph:** a minor nature goddess, represented as a young, beautiful woman.
2. **satyrs** (sat′ ərz): minor woodland gods.

Words to Know and Use | **alter** (ôl′ tər) v. to change

Zeus, though the ruler of the world, was not the eldest of the gods. First had come a race of monsters with fifty heads and a hundred arms each. Next followed elder gods called Titans, the leader of whom, Cronus, had reigned before Zeus. Then arose mighty Giants, and finally Zeus and the Olympians. Zeus, in a series of wars, succeeded in banishing the Titans and imprisoning the Giants in various ways. One huge monster, Typhon, lay imprisoned under the volcano of Aetna, which spouted fire when he struggled. Atlas, one of the Titans, was forced to stand holding the heavens on his shoulders so that they should not fall upon the earth.

HEAD OF ZEUS   Vatican Museum   Rome, Italy
Art Resource, New York.

Almost as powerful as Zeus were his two brothers, who did not live on Olympus: Poseidon, ruler of the sea, and Hades, gloomy king of the underworld, where the spirits of the dead belong. Queen of the gods was blue-eyed, majestic Hera. Aphrodite, the laughing, sea-born goddess, was queen of love and most beautiful of all.

Apollo and Artemis were twins, god of the sun and goddess of the moon. Apollo was the more important. Every day he rode the heavens in a golden chariot from dawn to sunset. The sun's rays could be gentle and healing, or they could be terrible. Apollo, therefore, was a great healer and the father of the god of medicine. At the same time, he was a famous archer, and the arrows from his golden bow were arrows of infection and death. Apollo was also god of poetry and song; his instrument was a golden lyre,[3] and the nine Muses, goddesses of music and the arts, were his attendants. He was the ideal of young manhood and the patron of athletes.

Apollo was also god of prophecy. There were temples of Apollo, known as oracles, at which a man could ask questions about the future. The priestesses of Apollo, inspired by the god, gave him an answer, often in the form of a riddle which was hard to understand. Nevertheless, the Greeks believed that if a man could interpret the words of the oracle, he would find the answer to his problem.

---

3. lyre (līr): a small stringed instrument related to the harp.

Artemis, the silver moon goddess, was goddess of unmarried girls and a huntress of wild beasts in the mountains. She also could send deadly arrows from her silver bow.

Gray-eyed Athene, the goddess of wisdom, was patron of Athens. She was queen of the <u>domestic</u> arts, particularly spinning and weaving. Athene was warlike too; she wore helmet and breastplate and carried a spear. Ares, however, was the real god of war, and the maker of weapons was Hephaestus, the lame smith and metalworker.

One more god who lived on Olympus was Hermes, the messenger. He wore golden winged sandals which carried him dry-shod over sea and land. He darted down from the peaks of Olympus like a kingfisher dropping to catch a fish or came running down the sloping sunbeams bearing messages from Zeus to men. Mortal eyes were too weak to behold the dazzling beauty of the <u>immortals</u>; consequently, the messages of Zeus usually came in dreams. Hermes was therefore also a god of sleep, and of thieves because they prowl by night. Healing was another of his powers. His rod, a staff entwined[4] by two snakes, is commonly used as a symbol of medicine.

The Greeks have left us so many stories about their gods that it hardly would be possible for everyone to know them all. We can still enjoy them because they are good stories. In spite of their great age, we can still understand them because they are about nature and about people. We still need them to enrich our knowledge of our own language and of the great masterpieces of literature. ❧

---

4. **entwined:** woven about.

*R*esponding to Reading

1. How do you feel about the world of gods and goddesses that the ancient Greeks created? Jot down your response in your journal or on a sheet of paper.

2. Why do you think the stories of the Greek gods and goddesses are still enjoyed today?
   Think about
   • the qualities the gods and goddesses possess
   • what the stories help explain

3. In your opinion, which story provides the best explanation for a mystery of nature?

4. Which of the gods or goddesses do you find most interesting? Why?

543

Yhi Brings the Earth to Life

ERIC AND TESSA HADLEY

There were no stars, no sun, no moon. The earth lay waiting, silent in the darkness. Nothing moved, no wind blew across the barren plain or the bare bones of the mountains. There was neither heat nor cold, alive or dead . . . nothing . . . waiting. Who knows how long?

Beyond the earth, Yhi[1] lay waiting too, sleeping the long sleep. It was Baiame,[2] the great spirit, who broke that sleep.

In the beginning, there was the sound of Baiame whispering across the universe:

"Yhi, awake."

His whisper invaded her dreams.

"Yhi, awake."

Her limbs stirred, her eyelids flickered and opened, and light shone from her eyes, flooding across the plain and the mountains.

Yhi stepped down to earth, and from that moment, where there had been nothing, there was everything—sound, movement, light.

The earth felt all these things; it woke at that first footstep. At each new step Yhi took, it showed what it had dreamed throughout that long, dark time. Flowers, trees, shrubs, and grasses sprang up wherever she walked, and when she finally stopped to rest, the barren plain was lost under a sea of blooms.

As she rested, Baiame whispered to her again:

"This is the beginning. The earth has shown you its beauty, but without the dance of life, it will not be complete. Take your light into the caves beneath the earth and see what will happen."

The old darkness still ruled under the earth. There were no seeds here to spring into life at her footstep. Instead, her light reflected from metallic veins and sparkling opal[3] points in the shadowy rock forms. As she moved, the darkness reformed behind her, and voices boomed and echoed:

"No, no, no! Let us sleep, sleep, sleep."

But Yhi never faltered, and soon there were new sounds—faint clicks, scrapings, and scratchings which grew louder and louder as the insects crept, flew, and swarmed from every dark corner. Yhi's warmth coaxed them out, and she led them up into the plain, into the waiting grass and leaves and flowers where their buzzing and chirruping drowned the dark wailing from below the earth.

This time Yhi did not pause. She strode

---

1. **Yhi** (ē′ hē): a sun goddess of Australia.
2. **Baiame** (bī′ ä mä): a sky god of Australia.
3. **opal:** gemstone with sparkling, rainbowlike colors.

across the plain while Baiame whispered:

"The ice caves in the mountains—take your light there."

It seemed that Yhi had met her match in the cold, blank silence. But somewhere there began the steady drip, drip, drip of water, free at last. Then, a cracking and crashing as great slabs of ice lost their freezing hold on the cave walls. The surface of the ice lakes splintered, and new shapes broke through. These shapes flowed and wavered, unlike the dead ice lumps, and fish, snakes, and reptiles were swept out to join the living earth outside as the lakes overflowed.

Yhi pressed on deeper, but this time as she moved from cave to cave, it was not solid, resisting ice she met but the touch of fur and feather. Birds and animals gathered

UNTITLED: LANDSCAPE WITH ROCKS   Trevor Nickolls
With permission of the artist. Collection of the Flinders University
Art Museum.   Adelaide, South Australia.

to her, and she led them out to add their voices to the new world.

"It is good. My world is alive," Baiame said. ❧

*R*esponding to Reading

1. As you finished reading this creation myth, what image stood out in your mind? In your journal or on a sheet of paper, describe the image and its effect on you.

2. Think of the effects of Yhi's presence on the earth. What words would you use to describe her?

3. What kind of people do you think created this myth?
   Think about
   • the description of the creation of living things
   • Baiame's words

Why Monkeys Live in Trees

JULIUS LESTER

One day Leopard was looking at his reflection in a pool of water. Looking at himself was Leopard's favorite thing in the world to do. Leopard gazed, wanting to be sure that every hair was straight and that all his spots were where they were supposed to be. This took many hours of looking at his reflection, which Leopard did not mind at all.

Finally he was satisfied that nothing was disturbing his handsomeness, and he turned away from the pool of water. At that exact moment, one of Leopard's children ran up to him.

"Daddy! Daddy! Are you going to be in the contest?"

"What contest?" Leopard wanted to know. If it was a beauty contest, of course he was going to be in it.

"I don't know. Crow the Messenger just flew by. She said that King Gorilla said there was going to be a contest."

Without another word, Leopard set off. He went north-by-northeast, made a right turn at the mulberry bush, and traveled east-by-south-by-west until he came to a hole in the ground. He went around in a circle five times and headed north-by-somersault until he came to a big clearing in the middle of the jungle, and that's where King Gorilla was.

King Gorilla sat at one end of the clearing on his throne. Opposite him, at the other side of the clearing, all the animals sat in a semicircle. In the middle, between King Gorilla and the animals, was a huge mound of what looked like black dust.

Leopard looked around with calm dignity. Then he strode regally[1] over to his friend, Lion.

"What's that?" he asked, pointing to the mound of black dust.

"Don't know," Lion replied. "King Gorilla said he will give a pot of gold to whoever can eat it in one day. I can eat it in an hour."

Leopard laughed. "I'll eat it in a half-hour."

It was Hippopotamus's turn to laugh. "As big as my mouth is, I'll eat that mound in one gulp."

The time came for the contest. King Gorilla had the animals pick numbers to see who would go in what order. To everybody's dismay, Hippopotamus drew Number 1.

---

1. strode regally: walked with long steps in a grand manner, like a king or queen.

THE MONKEY 1912 Franz Marc
Courtesy, Stadtische Galerie im
Lembachhaus Munich, Germany.

Hippopotamus walked over to the mound of black dust. It was bigger than he had thought. It was much too big to eat in one gulp. Nonetheless, Hippopotamus opened his mouth as wide as he could, and that was very wide indeed, and took a mouthful of the black dust.

He started chewing. Suddenly he leaped straight into the air and screamed. He screamed so loudly that it knocked the ears off the chickens, and that's why to this day chickens don't have ears.

Hippopotamus screamed and Hippopotamus yelled. Hippopotamus roared and Hippopotamus bellowed. Then he started sneezing and crying, and tears rolled down his face like he was standing in the shower. Hippopotamus ran to the river and drank as much water as he could, and that was very much, indeed, to cool his mouth and tongue and throat.

The animals didn't understand what had happened to Hippopotamus, but they didn't care. They were happy because they still had a chance to win the pot of gold. Of course, if they had known that the mound of black dust was really a mound of black pepper, maybe they wouldn't have wanted the gold.

Nobody was more happy than Leopard because he had drawn Number 2. He walked up to the black mound and sniffed at it.

"AAAAAAAAACHOOOOOOO!" Leopard didn't like that, but then he remembered the pot of gold. He opened his mouth wide, took a mouthful, and started chewing and swallowing.

Leopard leaped straight into the air, did a back double flip, and screamed. He yelled and he roared and he bellowed and, finally, he started sneezing and crying, tears rolling down his face like a waterfall. Leopard ran to the river and washed out his mouth and throat and tongue.

Lion was next, and the same thing happened to him as it did to all the animals. Finally only Monkey remained.

Monkey approached King Gorilla. "I know I can eat all of whatever that is, but after each mouthful, I'll need to lie down in the tall grasses and rest."

King Gorilla said that was OK.

Monkey went to the mound, took a tiny bit of pepper on his tongue, swallowed, and went into the tall grasses. A few minutes later, Monkey came out, took a little more, swallowed it, and went into the tall grasses.

Soon the pile was almost gone. The animals were astonished to see Monkey doing what they had not been able to do. Leopard couldn't believe it either. He climbed a tree and stretched out on a sturdy limb to get a better view. From his limb high in the tree, Leopard could see into the tall grasses where Monkey went to rest. Wait a minute! Leopard thought something was suddenly wrong with his eyes because he thought he saw a hundred monkeys hiding in the tall grasses.

He rubbed his eyes and looked another look. There wasn't anything wrong with his eyes. There *were* a hundred monkeys in the tall grasses, and they all looked alike!

Just then, there was the sound of loud applause. King Gorilla announced that Monkey had won the contest and the pot of gold.

Leopard growled a growl so scary that even King Gorilla was frightened. Leopard wasn't thinking about anybody except the monkeys. He took a long and beautiful leap from the tree right smack into the middle of the tall grasses where the monkeys were hiding.

The monkeys ran in all directions. When the other animals saw monkeys running from the grasses, they realized that the monkeys had tricked them and starting chasing them. Even King Gorilla joined in the chase. He wanted his gold back.

The only way the monkeys could escape was to climb to the very tops of the tallest trees where no one else, not even Leopard, could climb.

And that's why monkeys live in trees to this very day. 🐾

*R*esponding to Reading

1. What was your reaction to Leopard's discovery about Monkey? Record your reaction in your journal or on a sheet of paper.

2. What words would you use to describe Leopard?

3. In your opinion, what qualities help Monkey win the contest?

4. What might one of the animals who failed to swallow the "black dust" have done to succeed?

E X P L A I N

Responding to Reading

Comparing the Selections

1. Choose a character from the selections you have just read and explain why he or she is a good example of the theme "With Open Eyes."

2. How do the explanations of nature in the selections compare with the explanation you described in Examine What You Know?

Broader Connections

3. Greek myths are still widely read and studied in Western culture. What value, if any, do you think these stories have for people who no longer see them as literally true?

Literary Concept: Myth

Myths usually include superhuman beings as well as heroic and ordinary men and women. In some myths the gods have both superhuman and human qualities. Choose one of the Greek gods or goddesses in "The Gods and Goddesses of Mount Olympus" and list his or her human and superhuman qualities.

Writing Options

1. Create your own **myth** about why something occurs in nature.

2. Write the **dialogue** a modern scientist might have with someone from ancient Greece about some event in nature.

Vocabulary Practice

Exercise   Write one word from the list to fill in each blank below.

The ancient Greeks worshiped beings who they thought were __(1)__, or able to live forever. Greek gods and goddesses had the power to __(2)__ their appearance. For instance, the goddess who was the __(3)__ of the __(4)__ arts might turn herself into a weaver in order to deliver a __(5)__ to a human weaver.

Words to Know and Use

alter
domestic
immortal
patron
prophecy

*O*ptions for Learning

1 • **A Jungle Book** Turn the folk tale "Why Monkeys Live in Trees" or the myth "Yhi Brings the Earth to Life" into a comic book. Draw pictures and create dialogue or captions for the story.

2 • **When Zeus Was a Rookie** Design trading cards of the Greek gods and goddesses. Add to your collection as you discover more characters from Greek mythology.

*E*ric Hadley and Tessa Hadley
1945–   1956–

"Yhi Brings the Earth to Life" is from a book by Eric and Tessa Hadley, titled *Legends of Earth, Air, Fire, and Water*. To write the book, the Hadleys researched hundreds of stories and myths.

The Hadleys' interest in writing grew out of teaching children. "Stories," says Tessa Hadley, "are the way through which we try to understand the strange life we are born into. You tell stories about the sun and the moon to try to explain and celebrate the phenomena."

Both Eric and Tessa Hadley, who are husband and wife, were born in England and attended Cambridge University. They now live in Cardiff, Wales, and are currently working on two new books. Their first book of folklore is called *Legends of the Sun and Moon*.

*J*ulius Lester   1939–

When Julius Lester became a father, he began to feel the need to write the sort of books that were unavailable during his childhood.

Lester connects his interest in folklore to his father, who was a minister and a good storyteller. Lester says, "As a child, I loved it when my father got together with other ministers on a summer evening, because I knew that I would be treated to stories for as long as I was allowed to stay up, which was never long enough."

Lester's best-known books are *To Be a Slave* and *The Long Journey Home: Stories from Black History*. The selection you have read is from the book *How Many Spots Does a Leopard Have?*, which contains tales that reflect both African and Jewish story traditions.

Rising to the Challenge

*Links to
Unit Two*

Demeter and Persephone   ANNE TERRY WHITE
The Bamboo Beads   LYNN JOSEPH

*E*xamine What You Know

These selections describe characters who rise to the challenge of accepting certain duties or responsibilities. What duties do your family members, your teachers, or others count on you to perform? In your journal, make a list of the duties and responsibilities that you have.

*E*xpand Your Knowledge

The Greek myth "Demeter and Persephone" presents many gods and goddesses performing their duties. As you will see, a conflict between Hades, the ruler of the underworld, and Demeter, the goddess of the harvest, challenges the patience of the gods and endangers the survival of humans.

"The Bamboo Beads," a folk tale from Trinidad, features Papa Bois, one of Trinidad's most popular folklore characters. His duty is to protect the trees and animals of the woods, but Papa Bois sometimes chooses to make contact with humans. In this tale you will see how one young girl meets the challenge of responding to a strange being with mysterious powers.

*W*rite Before You Read

Think of a challenging duty that you have had to fulfill. In your journal, describe the duty and tell why it was a challenge for you. Were you willing or unwilling to accept it? As you read, compare your duty with the duties of the characters in the selections.

■ *Author biographies on Extend page*

Demeter and Persephone

ANNE TERRY WHITE

Deep under Mount Etna,[1] the gods had buried alive a number of fearful, fire-breathing giants. The monsters heaved and struggled to get free. And so mightily did they shake the earth that Hades, the king of the underworld, was alarmed.

"They may tear the rocks asunder and leave the <u>realm</u> of the dead open to the light of day," he thought. And mounting his golden chariot, he went up to see what damage had been done.

Now the goddess of love and beauty, fair Aphrodite, was sitting on a mountainside playing with her son, Eros.[2] She saw Hades as he drove around with his coal-black horses, and she said:

"My son, there is one who defies your power and mine. Quick! Take up your darts! Send an arrow into the breast of that dark monarch. Let him, too, feel the pangs[3] of love. Why should he alone escape them?"

At his mother's words, Eros leaped lightly to his feet. He chose from his quiver his sharpest and truest arrow, fitted it to his bow, drew the string, and shot straight into Hades's heart.

The <u>grim</u> king had seen fair maids enough in the gloomy underworld over which he ruled. But never had his heart been touched.

Now an unaccustomed warmth stole through his veins. His stern eyes softened. Before him was a blossoming valley, and along its edge a charming girl was gathering flowers. She was Persephone,[4] daughter of Demeter, goddess of the harvest. She had strayed from her companions, and now that her basket overflowed with blossoms, she was filling her apron with lilies and violets. The god looked at Persephone and loved her at once. With one sweep of his arm, he caught her up and drove swiftly away.

"Mother!" she screamed, while the flowers fell from her apron and strewed the ground. "Mother!"

And she called on her companions by name. But already they were out of sight, so fast did Hades urge the horses on. In a few moments they were at the River Cyane.[5] Persephone struggled, her loosened girdle[6] fell to the ground, but the god held her tight. He struck the bank with his trident.[7] The earth opened, and darkness swallowed them

---

1. **Mount Etna:** a volcano on the island of Sicily.
2. **Eros** (er′ äs′): the Greek god of love.
3. **pangs:** sudden sharp pains.
4. **Persephone** (pər sef′ ə nē): the daughter of the Greek goddess Demeter.
5. **River Cyane** (sī′ ə nē): a river of Sicily.
6. **girdle:** a belt or sash for the waist.
7. **trident:** a three-pronged spear.

Words to Know and Use

realm (relm) *n.* a kingdom
grim (grim) *adj.* stern or harsh in appearance

all—horses, chariot, Hades, and weeping Persephone.

From end to end of the earth, Demeter sought her daughter. But none could tell her where Persephone was. At last, worn out and despairing, the goddess returned to Sicily. She stood by the River Cyane, where Hades had cleft[8] the earth and gone down into his own dominions.

Now a river nymph had seen him carry off his prize. She wanted to tell Demeter where her daughter was, but fear of Hades kept her dumb. Yet she had picked up the girdle Persephone had dropped, and this the nymph wafted[9] on the waves to the feet of Demeter.

The goddess knew then that her daughter was gone indeed, but she did not suspect Hades of carrying her off. She laid the blame on the innocent land.

"Ungrateful soil!" she said. "I made you fertile. I clothed you in grass and nourishing grain, and this is how you reward me. No more shall you enjoy my favors!"

That year was the most cruel mankind had ever known. Nothing prospered, nothing grew. The cattle died, the seed would not come up, men and oxen <u>toiled</u> in vain. There was too much sun. There was too much rain. Thistles and weeds were the only things that grew. It seemed that all mankind would die of hunger.

"This cannot go on," said mighty Zeus. "I see that I must <u>intervene</u>." And one by one, he sent the gods and goddesses to plead with Demeter.

WINDFLOWERS   J. W. Waterhouse, R.A.   Private collection.

But she had the same answer for all: "Not till I see my daughter shall the earth bear fruit again."

Zeus, of course, knew well where Persephone was. He did not like to take from his brother the one joyful thing in his life, but he saw that he must if the race of man was to be preserved. So he called Hermes to him and said:

"Descend to the underworld, my son. Bid

---

8. **cleft:** split.
9. **wafted:** floated lightly.

Hades release his bride. Provided she has not tasted food in the realm of the dead, she may return to her mother forever."

Down sped Hermes on his winged feet, and there in the dim palace of the king, he found Persephone by Hades's side. She was pale and joyless. Not all the glittering treasures of the underworld could bring a smile to her lips.

"You have no flowers here," she would say to her husband when he pressed gems upon her. "Jewels have no fragrance. I do not want them."

When she saw Hermes and heard his message, her heart leaped within her. Her cheeks grew rosy and her eyes sparkled, for she knew that Hades would not dare to disobey his brother's command. She sprang up, ready to go at once. Only one thing troubled her—that she could not leave the underworld forever. For she had accepted a pomegranate[10] from Hades and sucked the sweet pulp from four of the seeds.

With a heavy heart, Hades made ready his golden car. He helped Persephone in while Hermes took up the reins.

"Dear wife," said the king, and his voice trembled as he spoke, "think kindly of me, I pray you. For indeed I love you truly. It will be lonely here these eight months you are away. And if you think mine is a gloomy palace to return to, at least remember that your husband is great among the immortals. So fare you well—and get your fill of flowers!"

Straight to the temple of Demeter at Eleusis,[11] Hermes drove the black horses. The goddess heard the chariot wheels, and as a deer bounds over the hills, she ran out swiftly to meet her daughter. Persephone flew to her mother's arms. And the sad tale of each turned into joy in the telling.

So it is to this day. One third of the year Persephone spends in the gloomy abode[12] of Hades—one month for each seed that she tasted. Then Nature dies, the leaves fall, the earth stops bringing forth. In spring Persephone returns, and with her come the flowers, followed by summer's fruitfulness and the rich harvest of fall. ❧

---

10. **pomegranate:** a round fruit containing many seeds.
11. **Eleusis** (ē lōō′ sis): a Greek city, the center of the worship of Demeter.
12. **abode:** home.

*R*esponding to *Reading*

1. What do you think of this explanation of the seasons? Jot down your thoughts about this famous myth in your journal.

2. How did you feel about Demeter's reaction to the disappearance of her daughter?

3. Do you think Persephone will adjust to the portion of the year she must spend underground? Why or why not?

4. Who in this story do you think took his or her duty the most seriously? Give reasons for your answer.

The Bamboo Beads

LYNN JOSEPH

Last year during the planting season, I helped Mama plant seeds on our hill. "One seed for each of my brothers and sisters," she said, and she covered up seven seeds with dark dirt. Mama's family lives on the other side of the island, so we hardly ever see them.

Each day I watched Mama water the dark mounds of dirt and weed around them. Soon, flowers grew up. They were red as the evening sun. But one day the floods came and swept them to the sea.

"Poor Mama," I said.

"They'll grow again," she replied.

She looked at her gardening gloves hanging on a nail. "If they don't grow back, we'll plant some more." And she smiled.

That night the moon was round and white as my Sunday hat. I told Daddy how Mama's flowers had drowned in the flood rains. He said, "Did I ever show you how *I* count my brothers and sisters?"

"No," I answered.

Then Daddy showed me the fisherman stars. "They point fishermen to the way home," he said. "There are eight of them. I named one each for my brothers and sisters."

"How do you know which is which?" I asked.

Daddy pointed again to the bright stars. "Well, there's Rupert and Hazel, Anthony and Derek, Peter, Janet, and Neil."

"You forgot Auntie Sonia," I said.

Daddy smiled and pointed to a tiny star. "That one's her."

I nodded my head as Daddy moved his finger around, although I couldn't tell which star was who.

After that, Daddy and I looked for the fisherman stars each night. Some nights when the sea breezes blew dark clouds in the sky, we couldn't see them. But Daddy would say, "They'll come back." And he'd smile.

"I wish I had brothers and sisters to plant flowers for or to count stars on," I told Mama and Daddy one day. "I'm tired of having only myself."

"What about all your cousins?" asked Mama.

"You can count them on something," said Daddy.

"What can I count them on?" I wondered.

"Maybe Tantie can help find you something," said Mama. "She's the one who keeps track of all yuh."

So, the next time Tantie came to visit, I said, "Tantie, Mama said you keep track of me and my cousins."

"That's right, chile," said Tantie. "And is plenty of all yuh to keep track of, too."

"I know," I said, "but how you do it? I want something that I can name after each one of my cousins. Something I can count them on. Like Mama has flowers and Daddy has his fisherman stars."

Well, Tantie looked me in the eye for a long time. Then from underneath the neck of her dress she pulled out a brown string full of bright, colorful beads.

"Tantie, where you get those pretty beads from?" I asked.

"These, my dear, is a story by itself, and if you have de time to listen, I'll tell it to you."

I nodded and sat down on the porch swing next to Tantie. As Tantie told her story, I kept trying to push the swing with my foot. But Tantie was too heavy. The swing sat quiet quiet. The only sound was Tantie's voice.

"A long, long time ago," she began, "when I was in my bare feet still, I went to market with a basket of bread and red-currant buns to sell. Market day was de busiest time. There was plenty to see as I set up my little stall and tucked cloths around de bread and buns so de flies wouldn't get them.

"I hadn't sold one thing yet when an old man came up. His clothes were ragged, and he didn't have on no shoes. His feet didn't look like no ordinary feet. They looked like cow hooves. I didn't stare, though, because it rude to do that.

"He asked for a piece of bread. Well, I remember Mama telling me that morning to get good prices for de bread, but I was sure Mama hadn't meant from this man too. So, I cut off a hunk of bread, wrapped it in brown paper, and handed it to him. He looked so hungry that I reached for a bun and gave him that too. De man smiled and bowed his head at me. Then he went his way.

"After that I was busy selling bread. De buns went even faster. By afternoon, I had sold them all. Then I saw de old man coming over again. He didn't look so ragged anymore. His hair was combed, and he had on a new shirt.

"'I'm sorry,' I said. 'No more bread left.'

"He didn't answer. Instead he handed me something. It was a piece of brown string. It looked like an ordinary old string, but I didn't tell him that.

"'Thank you for de bread, child,' he said. Then he <u>shuffled</u> off and was gone.

"I looked at de string for a while. I could use it to tie up my bread cloths, I thought. Or I could use it as a hair ribbon. But I decided I would put de string around my neck and wear it like a necklace."

"This de same string, Tantie?" I asked, fingering Tantie's bead necklace.

"De very same," she answered.

"Well, that evening, Mama was so proud I had sold all de bread that she gave me a treat. It was a small blue bamboo bead. It was de exact color of Mama's best blue head scarf.

"'Where you get this bead, Mama?' I asked.

"'Found it in de yard,' she replied.

"I wondered how it got there, but it didn't matter. I pulled out my brown string and untied it. Then I slipped de blue bead on and tied it around my neck again. It looked like a real necklace now that it had Mama's bead on it."

"Is this your mama's bead?" I asked, touching a bright blue bead on Tantie's string.

Words
to Know
and Use

shuffle (shŭf′ əl) v. to walk with a dragging step

"Yes, that's it, chile," said Tantie. "And it shines more now than de day I got it.

"Two days later, Daddy found a smooth black bead down by de sea. He brought it home in his pocket.

"'I thought you might like this,' he said and handed it to me. It sparkled like a black sun. I untied my necklace and slipped it on next to de blue bead. Now my string was beautiful with Mama's and Daddy's bamboo beads on it.

"During de next few days, Mama and Daddy and I kept finding shiny bamboo beads in de strangest places. I found a red one under de bed. Mama found a green one in de garden, and Daddy found a yellow one in his shoe. Mama and Daddy didn't think nothing of it, but as I added each new bead to my necklace, I got a strange, trembly feeling.

"De next week when I took Mama's bread and currant buns to market, I saw de old man who had given me my string. His clothes were still ragged, and he clumped around on his hooves.

"'Hello, mister,' I said when he came over. I wrapped up a chunk of bread and two buns this time and gave them to him. He smiled and shuffled off.

"Again my day of selling flew by. Before lunch time I had sold everything. Mama hugged me hard when I got home. But then she sat down at de kitchen table and looked serious.

"'What's wrong?' I asked.

"'Look,' she said, pointing to a bowl on the table. I looked inside and there were de most beautiful, shiny bamboo beads I'd ever seen. Lots and lots of them. I put my hand in and touched de smooth wood.

"'Where they come from?' I asked.

"'Don't know,' said Mama. 'They were here when I turned around from de sink this morning. I thought you might know something about them, since you're collecting beads.'

THE BAMBOO BEADS   557

"'No,' I said. 'I don't know about these.'

"Then Mama said, 'Let me see that string of beads around your neck, girl.'

"I showed it to Mama. She looked and looked at de beads and tugged on de string until I thought she'd break it. Then she looked at me and said, 'You've met Papa Bois.'[1]

"'Papa who?'

"'Papa Bois,' she murmured. 'He lives in de forest and protects de trees and forest animals from hunters. He spends his time whittling bamboo beads from fallen bamboo shoots. He's de only one who could make these beads. They're priceless.'

"Mama looked at me and gave me back de necklace. 'Have you met an old man without any feet?' she asked.

"I immediately thought of de old man from de market. 'Yes, Mama, I met him last week at de market. An old man in ragged clothes and no feet. He had cow hooves instead.'

"Mama closed her eyes and nodded her head. 'That's Papa Bois,' she said. 'He can be dangerous. Once he meets someone, he keeps track of them by counting their sins, their blessings, even their teeth, on his whittled beads. You never know with Papa Bois just what he's counting for you. The last time Papa Bois gave someone beads, the beads represented de number of days he had left to live. These beads on de table must be for you. He's counting something for you.'"

"'What?' I whispered, almost too frightened to speak.

"'We won't know till he's ready to say. Were you kind or mean to him?'

"'I gave him some bread to eat because he looked hungry,' I said.

"'Good,' said Mama, and she pulled me into her arms. 'That was very kind. Now you might as well put de beads on de string and wait until Papa Bois comes back and tells you what he's counting.'

"I put de pretty beads on de string. I didn't think they would all fit, but no matter how many I put on, de string never filled up. When every bead was on, I counted thirty-three beads. Then I tied it around my neck once more. It wasn't any heavier than when I wore de string empty.

"As de days passed, Mama, Daddy, and I kept our eyes open for Papa Bois. We thought he might come by any time. I wondered over and over what Papa Bois could be counting on my beads."

"Were you scared, Tantie?" I interrupted.

"A little," she answered. "But I knew I had been kind to Papa Bois, and that was all that mattered.

"De next time I went to market for Mama, she wanted to come with me. I told her Papa Bois might not come to our stall if she was there.

At the stall I laid de bread and buns out nicely and covered them with cloths. I saw de old man shuffling up to my table.

"'*Bonjour, vieux Papa,*'[2] I said. Mama had told me that to say hello in French was de polite way to greet Papa Bois. She also said not to look at his feet no matter what.

"'*Bonjour,*' said de old man.

"'Would you like some bread?' I asked. Papa Bois nodded.

"As I cut him a chunk of bread, I said, 'Thank you for de pretty necklace.'

---

1. **Papa Bois** (pä pä′ bwä) *French:* Father Forest.
2. ***Bonjour, vieux Papa*** (bōn zhōōr′ vyö pä pä′) *French:* Hello, old Father.

"'It's for you to wear always,' he said. 'Until you find someone who should wear it instead.'

"Papa Bois's eyes looked kind in his wrinkled face. I decided I go ask him what de beads were for.

"'De beads,' he answered, 'are for all de little children you'll one day have.'

"'Thirty-three children?' I asked.

"'Yes, they'll be yours, but they won't be yours,' he said mysteriously. But then he smiled a big smile.

"'All right,' I said, and I handed him de bread and buns.

"That was de last time I ever see Papa Bois. Mama said he only comes out of his forest when he's lonely for human company. Otherwise his friends are de deer, de squirrels, and de trees. The first person he meets when he leaves his forest early in de morning is de one who counts. If that person stares at his feet or laughs at him—watch out!"

"But Tantie, what happen to de thirty-three children?" I asked.

"You're one of them," she said. "Ever since your oldest cousin Jarise was born, I been de one helping to take care of all yuh. I have thirty grandnieces and nephews now. That mean three more to come. And all yuh are *my* children, just like Papa Bois said."

Tantie reached up and unhooked her bamboo bead necklace. Then she laid it in my hands.

"Oh," I said, looking at Tantie's necklace again. "I'd like to be de red bead."

Tantie took the necklace out of my hands and put it around my neck. She tied the string. The necklace felt cool and smooth against my skin.

"I wish I had a mirror," I said.

"It looking beautiful," said Tantie. "And it for you now. You can count your cousins on them beads."

"You're giving this to me, Tantie?" I asked, not believing what I had heard.

"Papa Bois said I go find someone who should wear it."

"Thank you," I said. I ran my fingers over the bamboo smoothness of the beads and admired the pretty colors.

"And since you wear Papa Bois's beads, you can start helping me tell these stories," said Tantie. "I been doing de work alone for too long."

Tantie reached over and adjusted the bead string on my neck.

I looked down at the shiny red bead that was me and smiled and smiled. ❧

*R*esponding to Reading

1. How did you react to the character of Papa Bois? Take a minute to describe this reaction in your journal.

2. Compare and contrast the narrator and Tantie. In what ways are they similar? different?

3. Do you think the narrator will be able to rise to the challenge that Tantie gives her at the end of the tale? Explain why or why not.

4. How might this story have turned out if Tantie had not given bread to Papa Bois?

*R*esponding to Reading

Comparing the Selections

1. Which story did you like better? Why?

2. In what ways are the **characters** of Demeter and Papa Bois similar? In what ways are they different?

3. Describe how the personal qualities of a character in one of the selections help that character rise to a challenge.

Broader Connections

4. In both the myth and the folk tale, characters try to find ways to stay connected to members of their family. How do families today try to stay connected when they live far apart?

*L*iterary Concept: Folk Tale

Folk tales are simple stories about humans or animals, stories that have been handed down by word of mouth from one generation to the next. Folk tales are usually set in the distant past. Folk tales often teach values or practical lessons. Identify some of the values or lessons that could be learned from "The Bamboo Beads." Explain why they might be important values or lessons to teach.

*W*riting Options

1. Write a **poem** based on one of these selections.

2. Create a **folk tale** about a special object that was given to you by someone in your family.

*V*ocabulary Practice

Exercise Write the paragraph below, replacing the boldfaced words with words from the list.

There once was a **stern** king who forced his subjects to **work hard** day and night. His queen, watching people **move wearily** out of their homes, decided to **interfere** by imprisoning the king and taking control of the **kingdom.**

Words to Know and Use

grim
intervene
realm
shuffle
toil

EXTEND

Options for Learning

1 • Reasons for Seasons What is the scientific explanation for changes in the seasons? In what areas of the world do the seasons change? Present a science report on the seasons to your class. Use charts, maps, and other props to add interest to your report.

2 • Add-a-Bead Necklace Tell a class of younger students the story that Tantie shared in "The Bamboo Beads." Demonstrate how to make a beaded necklace or bracelet. Show them how they too can use beads to keep track of something important to them.

Anne Terry White 1896–1980

The first two books Anne Terry White wrote were about Old Testament figures and William Shakespeare. Writing the books was her way of introducing her daughters to great works of literature in a manner they would find both entertaining and easy to understand.

White came to the United States from the Ukraine when she was eight years old. She grew up in New England and attended Brown and Stanford Universities. In addition to writing books for children, White worked as a teacher and a social worker.

Her books range from nonfiction on a wide range of topics to retellings of myths, legends, and Russian folk tales. Her works include *Lost Worlds* (a book about archaeology) and *Myths and Legends*.

Lynn Joseph

Lynn Joseph recalls, "When I was a little girl in Trinidad, I could not imagine anywhere else but my beautiful island, with its tall coconut trees, sandy beaches, and happy sounds of steel-band music. I've lived in many other places since then, but I've never forgotten the smells, sounds, and foods of my island."

Joseph moved from Trinidad to the United States with her family and graduated from the University of Colorado. She currently lives in New York City, where she attends law school. Joseph says that she has always wanted to be a writer and remembers listening to stories like "The Bamboo Beads" when she was growing up. She has written two books about Trinidad: *A Wave in Her Pocket* (from which the selection "The Bamboo Beads" was taken) and *Coconut Kind of Day: Island Poems*.

Face to Face

Links to
Unit Three

Wings   JANE YOLEN
The Living Kuan-yin   CAROL KENDALL AND YAO—WEN LI (you' wen lē')
The White Buffalo Calf Woman
and the Sacred Pipe   JOSEPH BRUCHAC (brōō shak')

Examine What You Know

Treating people you meet with kindness and respect is an important theme in tales throughout the world. In small groups list stories you know in which characters who treat people kindly or unkindly are rewarded or punished. Then write the moral, or lesson, that each story teaches.

Expand Your Knowledge

Wings retells the Greek myth of a brilliant inventor named Daedalus and his son Icarus. Daedalus is described as clever but not always kind. According to this version of the story, "The gods always punish such a man."

"The Living Kuan-yin" is a Chinese folk tale about a man named Chin Po-wan whose generosity gets him into trouble. The tale describes his journey to an all-merciful goddess named Kuan-yin and his reactions to people who request his help along the way.

"The White Buffalo Calf Woman and the Sacred Pipe" is a Lakota Sioux legend about a face-to-face meeting between two young men and a holy person named the White Buffalo Calf Woman. The Lakota Sioux are Native Americans from the plains of Nebraska and the Dakotas. Each of the young men responds differently to this representative of the spirit world and is treated accordingly.

Write Before You Read

In your experience, do people who treat others with kindness and compassion get rewarded? Do people who treat other people unkindly get punished? Write down your thoughts on this topic in your journal and compare them with the themes expressed in these selections.

■ *Author biographies*
on Extend page

Wings

JANE YOLEN

Once in ancient Greece, when the gods dwelt on a high mountain overseeing the world, there lived a man named Daedalus[1] who was known for the things he made.

He invented the axe, the bevel,[2] and the awl.[3] He built statues that were so lifelike they seemed ready to move. He designed a <u>maze</u> whose winding passages opened one into another as if without beginning, as if without end.

But Daedalus never understood the labyrinth[4] of his own heart. He was clever, but he was not always kind. He was full of pride, but he did not give others praise. He was a maker—but he was a taker, too.

The gods always punish such a man.

Athens was the queen of cities, and she had her princes. Daedalus was one. He was a prince and he was an artist, and he was proud of being both.

The very elements were his friends, and the people of Athens praised him.

"The gods will love you forever, Daedalus," they cried out to him as he walked through the city streets.

The gods listened and did not like to be told what to do.

A man who hears only praise becomes deaf. A man who sees no rival to his art becomes blind. Though he grew rich and he grew famous in the city, Daedalus also grew lazy and careless. And one day, without thought for the <u>consequences</u>, he caused the death of his young nephew, Prince Talos,[5] who fell from a tall temple.

Even a prince cannot kill a prince. The king of Athens punished Daedalus by sending him away, away from all he loved: away from the colorful pillars of the temples, away from the noisy, winding streets, away from the bustling shops and stalls, away from his smithy, away from the sound of the dark sea. He would never be allowed to return.

And the gods watched the <u>exile</u> from on high.

---

1. **Daedalus** (ded′ ′l əs): a legendary craftsman.
2. **bevel:** a tool for measuring and marking angles.
3. **awl:** a pointed tool for making holes in materials.
4. **labyrinth** (lab′ ə rinth): a maze.
5. **Prince Talos** (tā′ läs′): a nobleman and inventor.

Words to Know and Use

maze (māz) *n.* a confusing network of winding pathways
consequence (kän′ si kwens′) *n.* a result or outcome
exile (eks′ īl′) *n.* a person forced to live outside his or her native country

563

Many days and nights Daedalus fled from his past. He crossed strange lands. He crossed strange seas. All he carried with him was a goatskin flask, the clothes on his back, and the knowledge in his hands. All he carried with him was grief that he had caused a child's death and grief that Athens was now dead to him.

He traveled a year and a day until he came at last to the island of Crete, where the powerful King Minos[6] ruled.

The sands of Crete were different from his beloved Athens, the trees in the meadow were different, the flowers and the houses and the little dark-eyed people were different. Only the birds seemed the same to Daedalus, and the sky—the vast, open, empty road of the sky.

But the gods found nothing below them strange.

Daedalus knew nothing of Crete, but Crete knew much of Daedalus, for his reputation had flown on wings before him. King Minos did not care that Daedalus was an exile or that he had been judged guilty of a terrible crime.

"You are the world's greatest builder, Daedalus," King Minos said. "Build me a labyrinth in which to hide a beast."

"A cage would be simpler," said Daedalus.

"This is no ordinary beast," said the king. "This is a monster. This is a prince. His name is Minotaur,[7] and he is my wife's own son. He has a bull's head but a man's body. He eats human flesh. I cannot kill the queen's child. Even a king cannot kill a prince. And I cannot put him in a cage. But in a maze such as you might build, I could keep him hidden forever."

Daedalus bowed his head, but he smiled at the king's praise. He built a labyrinth for the king with countless corridors and winding ways. He devised such cunning[8] passages that only he knew the secret pathway to its heart—he and the Minotaur who lived there.

Yet the gods marked the secret way as well.

For many years Daedalus lived on the island of Crete, delighting in the praise he received from king and court. He made hundreds of new things for them. He made dolls with moving parts and a dancing floor inlaid with wood and stone for the princess Ariadne.[9] He made iron gates for the king and queen, wrought with cunning designs. He grew fond of the little dark-eyed islanders, and he married a Cretan wife. A son was born to them whom Daedalus named Icarus.[10] The boy was small like his mother, but he had his father's quick, bright ways.

Daedalus taught Icarus many things, yet the one Daedalus valued most was the language of his lost Athens. Though he had a grand house and servants to do his bidding, though he had a wife he loved and a son he adored, Daedalus was not entirely happy. His heart still lay in Athens, the land of his youth, and the words he spoke with his son helped keep the memory of Athens alive.

One night a handsome young man came to Daedalus's house, led by a lovesick

---

6. **King Minos** (mī′ näs′): a legendary king of Crete.
7. **Minotaur** (min′ ə tôr′).
8. **cunning:** made with skill and imagination.
9. **Ariadne** (ar′ ē ad′ nē): the daughter of King Minos.
10. **Icarus** (ik′ ə rəs): the son of Daedalus.

Princess Ariadne. The young man spoke with Daedalus in that Athenian tongue.

"I am Theseus,[11] a prince of Athens, where your name is still remembered with praise. It is said that Daedalus was more than a prince, that he had the gods in his hands. Surely such a man has not forgotten Athens."

Daedalus shook his head. "I thought Athens had forgotten me."

"Athens remembers and Athens needs your help, O prince," said Theseus.

"Help? What help can I give Athens when I am so far from home?"

"Then you do not know . . . ," Theseus began.

"Know what?"

"That every seven years Athens must send a tribute[12] of boys and girls to King Minos. He puts them into the labyrinth you devised, and the monster Minotaur <u>devours</u> them there."

Horrified, Daedalus thought of the bright-eyed boys and girls he had known in Athens. He thought of his own dark-eyed son, asleep in his cot. He remembered his nephew, Talos, whose eyes had been closed by death. "How can I help?"

"Only you know the way through the maze," said Theseus. "Show me the way that I may slay the monster."

"I will show you," said Daedalus thoughtfully, "but Princess Ariadne must go as well. The Minotaur is her half brother. He will not hurt her. She will be able to lead you to him, right into the heart of the maze."

The gods listened to the plan and nodded gravely.

Illustrations from *Wings* by Jane Yolen. Illustration copyright © 1991 by Dennis Nolan, reprinted by permission of Harcourt Brace Jovanovich, Inc.

---

11. **Theseus** (thē′ sē əs): a legendary Greek hero.
12. **tribute:** a forced payment.

Daedalus drew them a map and gave Princess Ariadne a thread to tie at her waist, that she might unwind it as they went and so find the way back out of the twisting corridors.

Hand in hand, Theseus and Ariadne left, and Daedalus went into his son's room. He looked down at the sleeping boy.

"I am a prince of Athens," he whispered. "I did what must be done."

If Icarus heard his father's voice, he did not stir. He was dreaming still as Ariadne and Theseus threaded their way to the very center of the maze. And before he awakened, they had killed the Minotaur and fled from Crete, taking the boys and girls of Athens with them. They took all hope of Daedalus's safety as well.

Then the gods looked thoughtful, and they did not smile.

When King Minos heard that the Minotaur had been slain and Ariadne taken, he guessed that Daedalus had betrayed him, for no one else knew the secret of the maze. He ordered Daedalus thrown into a high prison tower.

"Thus do kings reward traitors!" cried Minos. Then he added, "See that you care for your own son better than you cared for my wife's unfortunate child." He threw Icarus into the tower, too, and slammed the great iron gate shut with his own hand.

The tiny tower room, with its single window overlooking the sea, was Daedalus's home now. Gone was Athens, where he had been a prince; gone was Crete, where he had been a rich man. All he had left was one small room with a wooden bench and straw pallets[13] on the floor.

Day after day, young Icarus stood on the bench and watched through the window as the sea birds dipped and soared over the waves.

"Father!" Icarus called each day. "Come and watch the birds."

But Daedalus would not. Day after day, he leaned against the wall or lay on a pallet, bemoaning[14] his fate and cursing the gods who had done this thing to him.

The gods heard his curses, and they grew angry.

One bright day Icarus took his father by the hand, leading him to the window.

"Look, Father," he said, pointing to the birds. "See how beautiful their wings are. See how easily they fly."

Just to please the boy, Daedalus looked. Then he clapped his hands to his eyes. "What a fool I have been," he whispered. "What a fool. Minos may have forbidden me sea and land, but he has left me the air. Oh, my son, though the king is ever so great and powerful, he does not rule the sky. It is the gods' own road, and I am a favorite of the gods. To think a child has shown me the way!"

Every day after that, Daedalus and Icarus coaxed the birds to their windows with bread crumbs saved from their meager meals. And every day gulls, gannets, and petrels, cormorants and pelicans, shearwaters and grebes, came to the sill. Daedalus stroked the feeding birds with his clever

---

13. pallets: thin mattresses laid directly on the floor.
14. bemoaning: complaining about.

hands and harvested handfuls of feathers. And Icarus, as if playing a game, grouped the feathers on the floor in order of size, just as his father instructed.

But it was no game. Soon the small piles of feathers became big piles; the big piles, great heaps. Then clever Daedalus, using a needle he had shaped from a bit of bone left over from dinner and thread pulled out of his own shirt, sewed together small feathers, overlapping them with the larger, gently curving them in great arcs. He fastened the ends with molded candle wax and made straps with the leather from their sandals.

At last Icarus understood. "Wings, Father!" he cried, clapping his hands together in delight. "Wings!"

At that the gods laughed, and it was thunder over water.

They made four wings in all, a pair for each of them. Icarus had the smaller pair, for he was still a boy. They practiced for days in the tower, slipping their arms through the straps, raising and lowering the wings, until their arms had grown strong and used to the weight. They hid the wings beneath their pallets whenever the guards came by.

At last they were ready. Daedalus kneeled before his son.

"Your arms are strong now, Icarus," he said, "but do not forget my warning."

The boy nodded solemnly, his dark eyes wide. "I must not fly too low or the water will soak the feathers. I must not fly too high or the sun will melt the wax."

"Remember," his father said. "Remember."

The gods trembled, causing birds to fall through the bright air.

D aedalus climbed onto the sill. The wings made him clumsy, but he did not fall. He helped Icarus up.

First the child, then the man, leaped out into the air. They pumped once and then twice with their arms. The wind caught the feathers of the wings and pushed them upward into the Cretan sky.

Wingtip to wingtip they flew, writing the lines of their escape on the air. Some watchers below took them for eagles. Most took them for gods.

As they flew, Daedalus concentrated on long, steady strokes. He remembered earlier days, when the elements had been his friends: fire and water and air. Now, it seemed, they were his friends once more.

But young Icarus had no such memories to steady his wings. He beat them with abandon,[15] glorying in his freedom. He slipped away from his father's careful pattern along a wild stream of wind.

"Icarus, my son—remember!" Daedalus cried out.

But Icarus spiraled higher and higher and higher still. He did not hear his father's voice. He heard only the music of the wind; he heard only the sighing of the gods.

He passed the birds. He passed the clouds. He passed into the realm of the sun. Too late he felt the wax run down his arms; too late he smelled the singe of feathers. Surprised, he hung solid in the air. Then, like a star in nova,[16] he tumbled from the sky, down, down, down into the waiting sea.

And the gods wept bitterly for the child.

W here are you, my son?" Daedalus called. He circled the water, looking desperately for some sign. All he saw were seven feathers afloat on the sea, spinning into different patterns with each passing wave.

Weeping, he flew away over the dark sea to the isle of Sicily. There he built a temple to the god Apollo, for Apollo stood for life and light and never grew old but remained a beautiful boy forever. On the temple walls Daedalus hung up his beautiful wings as an offering to the bitter wisdom of the gods.

---

15. abandon: a wildness.
16. a star in nova: a star that fades away after a period of unusual brilliance.

So Daedalus's story ended—and yet it did not. For in Sicily he was received kindly by King Cocalus,[17] who was well pleased with his skills.

Meanwhile, back in Crete, enraged at his prisoners' escape, King Minos was determined to find and punish them. He proclaimed a great reward for anyone skilled enough to pass a silken thread through the closed spiral of a seashell. He knew that if Daedalus was alive, he could not resist the lure of such a game.

Daedalus was sure he could easily solve the puzzle. He bored a small hole in one end of a shell, moistened it with a bit of honey, then closed up the hole. Fastening a thread to an ant, he put the insect into the shell. The ant scurried through the twisting labyrinth toward the sweet smell, running as easily as Princess Ariadne had run through the maze with the thread unwinding at her waist. When the ant emerged from the other end, it had pulled the silken thread through the spirals of the shell.

Though he used a false name to claim the prize, Daedalus did not fool King Minos. Minos knew the winner was his old enemy. So, with a mighty army, Minos sailed to Sicily to bring Daedalus back.

But King Cocalus would not give up Daedalus to the foreign invaders, and a great battle was fought. With Daedalus's help, King Cocalus was victorious and King Minos was killed. Minos was clever, but he was not kind. He had a heart scabbed over with old remembered wounds.

The gods always punish such a man. 🐦

---

17. **King Cocalus** (käk′ ə ləs): a legendary king of Sicily.

Responding to Reading

1. What was your reaction to the ending of the story? Record your thoughts in your journal or on a sheet of paper.

2. What does the description of how the wings were constructed reveal about the cleverness of Daedalus?

3. In your opinion, do the gods treat Daedalus fairly or unfairly?

   Think about
   • why Daedalus helps Theseus through the maze
   • the reactions of the gods to what they see and hear
   • why Daedalus considers himself the favorite of the gods

Words to Know and Use

proclaim (prō klām′) *v.* to announce officially
scurry (skʉr′ ē) *v.* to run quickly; scamper

The Living Kuan-yin

CAROL KENDALL AND YAO-WEN LI

Even though the family name Chin means "gold," it does not signify that everyone of that name is rich. Long ago, in the province of Chekiang, however, there was a certain wealthy Chin family of whom it was popularly said that its fortune was as great as its name. It seemed quite fitting, then, when a son was born to the family, that he should be called Po-wan, "Million," for he was certain to be worth a million pieces of gold when he came of age.

With such a happy circumstance of names, Po-wan himself never doubted that he would have a never-ending supply of money chinking through his fingers, and he spent it accordingly—not on himself, but on any unfortunate who came to his attention. He had a deep sense of compassion for anyone in distress of body or spirit: a poor man had only to hold out his hand, and Po-wan poured gold into it; if a destitute[1] widow and her brood of starvelings[2] but lifted sorrowful eyes to his, he provided them with food and lodging and friendship for the rest of their days.

In such wise did he live, that even a million gold pieces were not enough to support him. His resources so dwindled that finally he scarcely had enough food for himself, his clothes flapped threadbare[3] on his wasted frame, and the cold seeped into his bone marrow[4] for lack of a fire. Still he gave away the little money that came to him.

One day, as he scraped out half of his bowl of rice for a beggar even hungrier than he, he began to ponder on his destitute state.

"Why am I so poor?" he wondered. "I have never spent extravagantly. I have never, from the day of my birth, done an evil deed. Why then am I, whose very name is A Million Pieces of Gold, no longer able to find even a copper to give this unfortunate creature, and have only a bowl of rice to share with him?"

What has happened to Po-wan?

review

He thought long about his situation and at last determined to go without delay to the South Sea. Therein, it was told, dwelt the all-merciful goddess, the Living Kuan-yin,[5]

---

1. **destitute**: poor.
2. **brood of starvelings**: family of starving children.
3. **threadbare**: so worn down that the threads show.
4. **marrow**: the soft tissue that fills the middle of most bones.
5. **Kuan-yin** (gwän' yin'): the Chinese goddess of mercy.

Words to Know and Use

compassion (kəm pash' ən) *n.* a feeling of sorrow for the suffering of others; pity
dwindle (dwin' dəl) *v.* to decrease or shrink
extravagantly (ek strav' ə gənt lē) *adv.* excessively; too much

571

who could tell the past and future. He would put his question to her, and she would tell him the answer.

Soon he had left his home country behind and traveled for many weeks in unfamiliar lands. One day he found his way barred by a wide and furiously flowing river. As he stood first on one foot and then on the other, wondering how he could possibly get across, he heard a commanding voice calling from the top of an overhanging cliff.

"Chin Po-wan!" the voice said, "if you are going to the South Sea, please ask the Living Kuan-yin a question for me!"

"Yes, yes, of course," Po-wan agreed at once, for he had never in his life refused a request made of him. In any case, the Living Kuan-yin permitted each person who approached her three questions, and he had but one of his own to ask.

Craning his head toward the voice coming from above, he suddenly began to tremble, for the speaker was a gigantic snake with a body as large as a temple column. Po-wan was glad he had agreed so readily to the request.

"Ask her, then," said the snake, "why I am not yet a dragon, even though I have practiced self-denial[6] for more than one thousand years."

"That I will do, and gl-gladly," stammered Po-wan, hoping that the snake would continue to practice self-denial just a bit longer. "But, your . . . your Snakery . . . or your Serpentry, perhaps I should say . . . that is . . . you see, don't you . . . first I must cross this raging river, and I know not how."

"That is no problem at all," said the snake. "I shall carry you across, of course."

"Of course," Po-wan echoed weakly. Overcoming his fear and his reluctance to touch the slippery-slithery scales, Chin Po-wan climbed onto the snake's back and rode across quite safely. Politely, and just a bit hurriedly, he thanked the self-denying serpent and bade him goodbye. Then he continued on his way to the South Sea.

By noon he was very hungry. Fortunately, a nearby inn offered meals at a price he could afford. While waiting for his bowl of rice, he chatted with the innkeeper and told him of the Snake of the Cliff, which the innkeeper knew well and respected, for the serpent always denied bandits the crossing of the river. Inadvertently,[7] during the exchange of stories, Po-wan revealed the purpose of his journey.

"Why then," cried the innkeeper, "let me prevail upon your generosity to ask a word for me." He laid an appealing hand on Po-wan's ragged sleeve. "I have a beautiful daughter," he said, "wonderfully amiable and pleasing of disposition. But although she is in her twentieth year, she has never in all her life uttered a single word. I should be very much obliged if you would ask the Living Kuan-yin why she is unable to speak."

Po-wan, much moved by the innkeeper's plea for his mute daughter, of course promised to do so. For after all, the Living Kuan-yin allowed each person three questions, and he had but one of his own to ask.

Nightfall found him far from any inn, but there were houses in the neighborhood, and he asked for lodging at the largest. The owner, a man obviously of great wealth, was

---

6. **self-denial:** giving up one's own desires or pleasures.
7. **inadvertently:** by mistake.

pleased to offer him a bed in a fine chamber but first begged him to partake of a hot meal and good drink. Po-wan ate well, slept soundly, and, much refreshed, was about to depart the following morning when his good host, having learned that Po-wan was journeying to the South Sea, asked if he would be kind enough to put a question for him to the Living Kuan-yin.

"For twenty years," he said, "from the time this house was built, my garden has been cultivated with the utmost care; yet in all those years, not one tree, not one small plant, has bloomed or borne fruit, and because of this, no bird comes to sing, nor bee to gather nectar. I don't like to put you to a bother, Chin Po-wan, but as you are going to the South Sea anyway, perhaps you would not mind seeking out the Living Kuan-yin and asking her why the plants in my garden don't bloom."

"I shall be delighted to put the question to her," said Po-wan. For after all, the Living Kuan-yin allowed each person three questions, and he had but . . . .

Traveling onward, Po-wan examined the quandary[8] in which he found himself. The Living Kuan-yin allowed but three questions, and he had somehow, without quite knowing how, accumulated four questions.

One of them would have to go unasked, but which? If he left out his own question, his whole journey would have been in vain. If, on the other hand, he left out the question of the snake or the innkeeper or the kind host, he would break his promise and betray their faith in him.

Which question will Po-wan leave out?

predict

"A promise should never be made if it cannot be kept," he told himself. "I made the promises and therefore I must keep them. Besides, the journey will not be in vain, for at least some of these problems will be solved by the Living Kuan-yin. Furthermore, assisting others must certainly be counted as a good deed, and the more good deeds abroad in the land, the better for everyone, including me."

At last he came into the presence of the Living Kuan-yin.

First, he asked the serpent's question: "Why is the Snake of the Cliff not yet a dragon, although he has practiced self-denial for more than one thousand years?"

---

8. **quandary:** a confusing situation.

Words to Know and Use | **vain** (vān) *n.* (after *in*) without purpose; useless

573

And the Living Kuan-yin answered: "On his head are seven bright pearls. If he removes six of them, he can become a dragon."

Next, Po-wan asked the innkeeper's question: "Why is the innkeeper's daughter unable to speak, although she is in the twentieth year of her life?"

And the Living Kuan-yin answered: "It is her fate to remain mute until she sees the man destined to be her husband."

Last, Po-wan asked the kind host's question: "Why are there never blossoms in the rich man's garden, although it has been carefully cultivated for twenty years?"

And the Living Kuan-yin answered: "Buried in the garden are seven big jars filled with silver and gold. The flowers will bloom if the owner will rid himself of half the treasure."

Then Chin Po-wan thanked the Living Kuan-yin and bade her goodbye.

On his return journey, he stopped first at the rich man's house to give him the Living Kuan-yin's answer. In gratitude the rich man gave him half the buried treasure.

Next Po-wan went to the inn. As he approached, the innkeeper's daughter saw him from the window and called out, "Chin Po-wan! Back already! What did the Living Kuan-yin say?"

Upon hearing his daughter speak at long last, the joyful innkeeper gave her in marriage to Chin Po-wan.

Lastly, Po-wan went to the cliffs by the furiously flowing river to tell the snake what the Living Kuan-yin had said. The grateful snake immediately gave him six of the bright pearls and promptly turned into a magnificent dragon, the remaining pearl in his forehead lighting the headland like a great beacon.

And so it was that Chin Po-wan, that generous and good man, was once more worth a million pieces of gold. ❧

---

*R*esponding to Reading

1. What was your reaction when Po-wan decided to ask the three other questions instead of his own? Record your thoughts in your journal or on a sheet of paper.

2. Besides generosity, what other traits characterize Po-wan?

3. How would you describe the **theme** of the story, or its message about life?

   Think about
   • what happens to Po-wan as a result of his behavior
   • the traits demonstrated by the snake, the innkeeper, and the rich man

4. Do you think Po-wan will remain rich once he returns home? Explain.

The White Buffalo Calf Woman and the Sacred Pipe

JOSEPH BRUCHAC

It was a time when there was little food left in the camp and the people were hungry.

Two young men were sent out to scout for game. They went on foot, for this was a time long before the horses, the great Spirit Dogs, were given to the people. The two young men hunted a long time but had no luck. Finally, they climbed to the top of a hill and looked to the west.

"What is that?" said one of the young men.

"I cannot tell, but it is coming toward us," said the other.

And so it was. At first they thought that it was an animal, but as the shape drew closer, they saw it was a woman. She was dressed in white buffalo skin and carried something in her hands. She walked so lightly that it seemed as if she was not walking at all but floating with her feet barely touching the Earth.

Then the first young man realized that she must be a Holy Person, and his mind filled with good thoughts. But the second young man did not see her that way. He saw her only as a beautiful young woman, and his mind filled with bad thoughts. She was now very close, and he reached out to grab her. As soon as he did so, though, there was a sound of lightning, and the young man was covered by a cloud. When it cleared away, there was nothing left of the second young man but a skeleton.

Then the White Buffalo Calf Woman spoke. "Go to your people," she said, holding up the bundle in her hands so that the first young man could see it. "Tell your people that it is a good thing I am bringing. I am bringing a holy thing to your nation, a message from the Buffalo People. Put up a medicine lodge[1] for me and make it ready. I will come there after four days have passed."

The first young man did as he was told. He went back to his people and gave them the message. Then the crier went through the camp and told all the people that something sacred was coming and that all things should be made ready. They built the

---

1. **medicine lodge:** a building used by Native Americans for religious rituals.

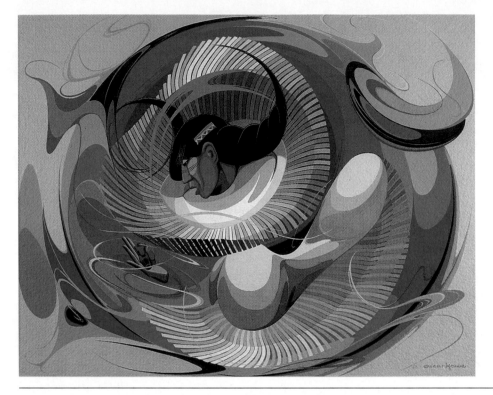

BUFFALO CALF WOMAN   Oscar Howe   Collection, U.S. Department of the Interior, Indian Arts and
Crafts Board, Sioux Indian Museum and Crafts Center, Rapid City, South Dakota.

medicine lodge and made an earth altar which faced the west.

Four days passed, and then the people saw something coming toward them. When it came closer, they saw it was the White Buffalo Calf Woman. In her hands she carried the bundle and a bunch of sacred sage.[2] The people welcomed her into the medicine lodge and gave her the seat of honor. Then she unwrapped the bundle to show them what was inside. It was the Sacred Pipe. As she held it out to them, she told them what it meant.

"The bowl of the Pipe," she said, "is made of the red stone. It represents the flesh and blood of the Buffalo People and all other Peoples. The wooden stem of the Pipe repre-sents all the trees and plants, all the things green and growing on this Earth. The smoke that passes through the Pipe repre-sents the sacred wind, the breath that carries prayers up to Wakan Tanka, the Creator."

When she finished showing them the Pipe, she told the people how to hold it and how to offer it to Earth and Sky and the Four Sacred Directions. She told them many things to remember.

"The Sacred Pipe," said the White Buffalo Calf Woman, "will show you the Good Red Road. Follow it, and it will take you in the

---

2. **sage:** an herb having a strong pinelike odor.

right direction. Now," she said, "I am going to leave, but you will see me again."

Then she began to walk toward the setting sun. The people watched her as she went, and they saw her stop and roll once on the Earth. When she stood up, she was a black buffalo. Then she went farther and rolled again on the Earth. This time when she stood up, she was a brown buffalo. She went farther and rolled a third time and stood up. Now the people saw that she was a red buffalo. Again she walked farther, and for a fourth and final time she rolled upon the Earth. This time she became a white buffalo calf and continued to walk until she disappeared over the horizon.

As soon as the White Buffalo Calf Woman was gone, herds of buffalo were seen all around the camp. The people were able to hunt them, and they gave thanks with the Sacred Pipe for the blessings they had been given. As long as they followed the Good Red Road of the Sacred Pipe and remembered, as the White Buffalo Calf Woman had taught them, that all things were as connected as parts of the Pipe, they lived happily and well. 🐾

*R*esponding to *Reading*

1. What image remains in your mind after reading this legend? Describe the image in your journal or on a sheet of paper.

2. Why do you think the White Buffalo Calf Woman gives the Sacred Pipe to the people?

3. What do you think it means to follow "the Good Red Road of the Sacred Pipe" and to remember that all things are "as connected as parts of the Pipe"?

   Think about
   • the relationship of humans to the Creator
   • the connections among all people and all things

EXPLAIN

Responding to Reading

Comparing the Selections

1. Compare the selections' ideas about the costs of giving and receiving.

2. What is the relationship between the god or goddess figure(s) and the people in each story?

Broader Connections

3. These ancient stories reflect the values and beliefs of a different culture. Do you think the values encouraged by each story are important in the culture you live in today? Explain your answer.

Literary Concept: Legend

Legends are often a mix of fact and fiction and reflect the values of the people who tell them. What values of the Lakota Sioux people do you think are reflected in the legend on page 575?

Writing Options

1. Write a different **ending** for one of the selections.

2. Imagine that one of the characters has applied for a job in today's society. Write a **letter of recommendation** for the person.

Vocabulary Practice

Exercise   Identify each pair of words as either *Synonyms* or *Antonyms*.

1. proclaim—announce
2. consequence—cause
3. devour—gobble
4. compassion—sympathy
5. extravagantly—cheaply

6. vain—useful
7. exile—outcast
8. scurry—hurry
9. dwindle—increase
10. maze—puzzle

Words to Know and Use

compassion
consequence
devour
dwindle
exile
extravagantly
maze
proclaim
scurry
vain

*O*ptions for Learning

1 • **Puppet Presentation** Make stick puppets of the characters in one of the selections. With classmates, use the puppets to perform the story as it is read.

2 • **Ancient Builder** Design and build a scale model of the labyrinth Daedalus built for the Minotaur or the medicine lodge the Lakotas built for the White Buffalo Calf Woman.

*J*ane Yolen   1939–

Jane Yolen's style is to give modern twists to familiar stories or to create original stories based on the feel and structure of classic tales. Yolen is best known for her folk and fairy tales. *Wings,* her version of the story of Daedalus and Icarus, won a 1992 Children's Choice award. Yolen is also known for her science fiction and fantasy stories, such as *Dragon's Blood,* the first volume of a three-part fantasy about dragons.

*C*arol Kendall and Yao-wen Li
1917–   1924–

Carol Kendall says the things she likes to do best are writing, reading, studying Chinese, and "climbing to the tops of things." Kendall is best known for *The Gammage Cup,* a 1960 Newbery Honor Book. She now lives in Lawrence, Kansas.

Yao-wen Li was born and raised in Canton, China. She left China in 1947 and has lived in the United States ever since. She has coauthored two books of Chinese tales with Carol Kendall: *Sweet and Sour* and *Cinnamon Moon.*

*J*oseph Bruchac   1942–

Award-winning poet, novelist, and storyteller Joseph Bruchac began hearing Native American legends as a small child. Bruchac says he likes to share stories from Native American traditions because "they have messages, sometimes very subtle, which can help show young people the good paths to follow." Other Native American tales shared by the writer can be found in *The Wind Eagle and Other Abenaki Folk Stories.*

In and Out of Control

**Links to
Unit Four**

Arachne   OLIVIA COOLIDGE
The Disobedient Child   VICTOR MONTEJO (môn te' hồ)

Examine What You Know

People who disobey rules or ignore the advice of their elders are often testing the limits of control. With a small group of classmates, list some of the limits that are placed on you by authorities such as parents, teachers, and the police. What kinds of limits are important and necessary? Why?

Expand Your Knowledge

Many myths are about characters who do not pay attention to limits or who ignore warnings given by their elders or the gods. "Arachne" is a Greek myth that tells the story of a weaver who boasts that her skill is equal to that of the gods. Unwilling to see her own shortcomings, Arachne pits herself against Athena, the goddess of wisdom and of all crafts, particularly weaving.

"The Disobedient Child" is about another character who tests limits. Like Arachne, the boy in this Guatemalan fable disregards warnings about the limits set by someone who is truly in control. Also like Arachne, the boy seems unteachable and is put to the test by someone with supernatural powers.

Write Before You Read

■ *Author biographies
on Extend page*

Think about a time when you got in trouble by disregarding a warning that someone in authority gave you. What were the consequences of your behavior, and what did you learn? In your journal or on a sheet of paper, describe this incident.

Arachne

OLIVIA COOLIDGE

Arachne[1] was a maiden who became famous throughout Greece, though she was neither well-born nor beautiful and came from no great city. She lived in an obscure little village, and her father was a humble dyer of wool. In this he was very skillful, producing many varied shades, while above all he was famous for the clear, bright scarlet which is made from shellfish and which was the most glorious of all the colors used in ancient Greece. Even more skillful than her father was Arachne. It was her task to spin the fleecy wool into a fine, soft thread and to weave it into cloth on the high-standing loom[2] within the cottage. Arachne was small and pale from much working. Her eyes were light, and her hair was a dusty brown; yet she was quick and graceful, and her fingers, roughened as they were, went so fast that it was hard to follow their flickering movements. So soft and even was her thread, so fine her cloth, so gorgeous her embroidery, that soon her products were known all over Greece. No one had ever seen the like of them before.

At last Arachne's fame became so great that people used to come from far and wide to watch her working. Even the graceful nymphs would steal in from stream or forest and peep shyly through the dark doorway, watching in wonder the white arms of Arachne as she stood at the loom and threw the shuttle[3] from hand to hand between the hanging threads or drew out the long wool, fine as a hair, from the distaff[4] as she sat spinning. "Surely Athena herself must have taught her," people would murmur to one another. "Who else could know the secret of such marvelous skill?"

Arachne was used to being wondered at, and she was immensely proud of the skill that had brought so many to look on her. Praise was all she lived for, and it displeased her greatly that people should think anyone, even a goddess, could teach her anything. Therefore, when she heard them murmur, she would stop her work and turn around indignantly[5] to say, "With my own ten fingers I gained this skill, and by hard practice from early morning till night. I never had time to stand looking, as you people do, while another maiden worked. Nor if I had, would I give Athena credit because the girl was more skillful than I. As for Athena's weaving, how could there be finer cloth or more beautiful embroidery than mine? If

---

1. Arachne (ə rak′ nē): a legendary Greek girl.

2. high-standing loom: an upright frame used to hold threads in a vertical position as other threads are woven through horizontally.

3. shuttle: a piece of wood holding the thread that is to be woven horizontally through the threads on a loom.

4. distaff: a short rod for holding wool that is to be spun into thread.

5. indignantly: in a way that expresses anger and scorn.

From *Favorite Greek Myths,*
illustrated by Troy Howell.

Athena herself were to come down and compete with me, she could do no better than I."

What do you think of Arachne's pride?

One day when Arachne turned around with such words, an old woman answered her, a gray old woman, bent and very poor, who stood leaning on a staff and peering at Arachne amid the crowd of onlookers. "Reckless girl," she said, "how dare you claim to be equal to the immortal gods themselves? I am an old woman and have seen much. Take my advice and ask pardon of Athena for your words. Rest content with your fame of being the best spinner and weaver that mortal eyes have ever beheld."

"Stupid old woman," said Arachne indignantly, "who gave you a right to speak in this way to me? It is easy to see that you were never good for anything in your day, or you would not come here in poverty and rags to gaze at my skill. If Athena <u>resents</u> my words, let her answer them herself. I have challenged her to a contest, but she, of course, will not come. It is easy for the gods to avoid matching their skill with that of men."

At these words the old woman threw down her staff and stood <u>erect.</u> The wondering onlookers saw her grow tall and fair and stand clad in long robes of dazzling white. They were terribly afraid as they realized that they stood in the presence of Athena. Arachne herself flushed red for a moment, for she had never really believed that the goddess would hear her. Before the group that was gathered there, she would not give in; so pressing her pale lips together in obstinacy[6] and pride, she led the goddess to one of the great looms and set herself before the other. Without a word both began to thread the long woolen strands that hung from the rollers and between which the shuttle would move back and forth. Many skeins[7] lay heaped beside them to use, bleached white, and gold, and scarlet, and other shades, varied as the rainbow. Arachne had never thought of giving credit for her success to her father's skill in dyeing, though in actual truth the colors were as remarkable as the cloth itself.

Soon there was no sound in the room but the breathing of the onlookers, the whirring of the shuttles, and the creaking of the wooden frames as each pressed the thread up into place or tightened the pegs by which the whole was held straight. The excited crowd in the doorway began to see that the skill of both, in truth, was very nearly equal but that, however the cloth might turn out, the goddess was the quicker of the two. A pattern of many pictures was growing on her loom. There was a border of twined branches of the olive, Athena's favorite tree, while in the middle, figures began to appear. As they looked at the glowing colors, the spectators realized that Athena was weaving into her pattern a last warning to Arachne. The central figure was the goddess herself, competing with Poseidon for possession of the city of Athens; but in the four corners were mortals who had tried to strive with gods and pictures of the awful <u>fate</u> that had overtaken them. The goddess ended a little before Arachne and stood back from her marvelous work to see what the maiden was doing.

How do you think the weaving contest will end?   *predict*

Never before had Arachne been matched against anyone whose skill was equal, or even nearly equal, to her own. As she stole glances from time to time at Athena and saw the goddess working swiftly, calmly, and always a little faster than herself, she became angry instead of frightened, and an evil thought came into her head. Thus as Athena

---

6. **obstinacy** (äb′ stə nə sē): stubbornness.
7. **skeins** (skānz): coils of thread or yarn.

Words to Know and Use | **resent** (ri zent′) *v.* to feel angry and hurt
erect (ē rekt′) *adj.* straight up
fate (fāt) *n.* an outcome or end

583

stepped back a pace to watch Arachne finishing her work, she saw that the maiden had taken for her design a pattern of scenes which showed evil or unworthy actions of the gods, how they had <u>deceived</u> fair maidens, resorted to trickery, and appeared on earth from time to time in the form of poor and humble people. When the goddess saw this insult glowing in bright colors on Arachne's loom, she did not wait while the cloth was judged but stepped forward, her gray eyes blazing with anger, and tore Arachne's work across. Then she struck Arachne across the face. Arachne stood there a moment, struggling with anger, fear, and pride. "I will not live under this insult," she cried, and seizing a rope from the wall, she made a noose and would have hanged herself.

The goddess touched the rope and touched the maiden. "Live on, wicked girl," she said. "Live on and spin, both you and your <u>descendants.</u> When men look at you, they may remember that it is not wise to strive with Athena." At that the body of Arachne shriveled up; and her legs grew tiny, spindly, and <u>distorted.</u> There, before the eyes of the spectators, hung a little dusty brown spider on a slender thread.

All spiders descend from Arachne, and as the Greeks watched them spinning their thread wonderfully fine, they remembered the contest with Athena and thought that it was not right for even the best of men to claim equality with the gods. ❧

*R*esponding to Reading

1. What adjectives would you use to describe Arachne? Write down these adjectives in your journal or notebook.

2. What are your impressions of the goddess Athena?

   Think about
   • the ways she tries to warn Arachne
   • why she gets so upset at Arachne's weaving
   • her choice of punishment

3. What does the outcome of the **conflict** between Athena and Arachne suggest about the relationship between the Greek gods and humans?

4. Why do you think Arachne is so determined to test her limits?

The Disobedient Child

VICTOR MONTEJO

In old times in *Xaqla'* Jacaltenango,[1] there was a very disobedient child who often disappointed his parents. No matter how hard they tried to teach him, he never changed.

One afternoon the boy ran away from home, looking for someone who would tolerate his mischief. Walking through the woods, he discovered a lonely little house and ran up to it. On the porch of the straw-covered house sat an old man, smoking peacefully. The boy stood before him without saying hello or any other word of greeting.

When the old man noticed the boy's presence, he stopped smoking and asked him, "Where do you want to go, boy?"

"I am looking for someone who can give me something to eat," the boy answered.

The wise old man, who already knew the boy's story, said, "No one will love you if you continue being so bad."

The boy did not respond except to laugh.

Then the old man smiled and said, "You can stay with me. We will eat together."

The boy accepted his offer and stayed in the old man's house. On the following day, before going to work, the old man told the boy: "You should stay in the house, and the only duty you will have is to put the beans to cook during the afternoon. But listen well. You should only throw thirteen beans in the pot and no more. Do you understand?"

The boy nodded that he understood the directions very well. Later, when the time arrived to cook the beans, the boy put the clay pot on the fire and threw in thirteen beans as he had been directed. But once he had done that, he began to think that thirteen beans weren't very many for such a big pot. So, disobeying his orders, he threw in several more little fistfuls.

No one will love you if you continue being so bad.

When the beans began to boil over the fire, the pot started to fill up, and it filled up until it overflowed. Very surprised, the boy quickly took an empty pot and divided the beans between the two pots. But the beans

---

1. *Xaqla'* **Jacaltenango** (chäk lä häk' äl te näŋ' ō): a town in the mountains of Guatemala.

overflowed the new pot, too. Beans were pouring out of both pots.

When the old man returned home, he found piles of beans, and the two clay pots lay broken on the floor.

"Why did you disobey my orders and cook more than I told you to?" the old man asked angrily.

The boy hung his head and said nothing. The old man then gave him instructions for the next day. "Tomorrow you will again cook the beans as I have told you. What's more, I forbid you to open that little door over there. Do you understand?"

The boy indicated that he understood very well.

The next day the old man left the house after warning the boy to take care to do exactly what he had been told. During the afternoon the boy put the beans on the fire to cook. Then he was filled with curiosity. What was behind the little door he had been forbidden to open?

Without any fear the boy opened the door and discovered in the room three enormous covered water jars. Then he found three capes inside a large trunk. There was one green cape, one yellow cape, and one red cape. Not satisfied with these discoveries, the boy took the top off the first water jar to see what it contained.

Immediately the water jar began to emit great clouds that quickly hid the sky. Frightened and shivering with cold, the boy opened the trunk and put on the red cape.

At that instant a clap of thunder exploded in the house. The boy was turned into thunder and lifted to the sky, where he unleashed a great storm.

When the old man heard the thunder, he guessed that something extraordinary had happened at home, and he hurried in that direction. There he discovered that the forbidden door was open and the top was off the jar of clouds, from which churning mists still rose toward the sky. The old man covered the jar and then approached the trunk with the capes. The red cape, the cape of storms, was missing. Quickly the old man put on the green cape and regained control over the sky, calming the great storm. Little by little the storm subsided, and soon the man returned to the house, carrying the unconscious boy in his arms.

A little while later the old man uncapped the same jar, and the clouds which had blackened the sky returned to their resting

Words to Know and Use | **indicate** (in′ di kāt′) *v.* to show
churning (chʉrn′ iŋ) *adj.* stirring with a forceful motion **churn** *v.*
subside (səb sīd′) *v.* to become weaker; decline

place, leaving the heavens bright and blue again. When he had done this, the old man capped the jar again and put away the red and green capes.

Through all of this the boy remained stunned and soaked with the rains until the kind old man restored his spirit and brought him back to normal. When the boy was alert again and his fear had left, the old man said, "Your disobedience has almost killed you. You were lucky that I heard the storm and came to help. Otherwise you would have been lost forever among the clouds."

The boy was quiet, and the old man continued.

"I am Qich Mam,[2] the first father of all people and founder of *Xaqla*, he who controls the rain and waters the community's fields when they are dry. Understand, then, that I wish you no harm, and I forgive what you have done. Promise me that in the future you will not disobey your parents."

The boy smiled happily and answered, "I promise, Qich Mam, I promise." Qich Mam patted him gently and said, "Then return to your home and be useful to your parents and to your people."

From that time on the boy behaved differently. He was very grateful for the kindness of the old man who held the secret of the clouds, the rains, the wind, and the storms in his hands. ❧

---

2. **Qich Mam** (kēch mäm): a thunder spirit of the Mayan people.

*R*esponding to Reading

1. What thoughts went through your mind as the boy started to misbehave the second time? Record your thoughts in your journal or on a sheet of paper.

2. Besides disobedience, what other qualities does the boy have?

3. In your opinion, does the boy deserve what happens to him in this story? Why or why not?

   Think about
   • why you might have added more beans to the pot
   • the boy's reasons for looking in the closet
   • the difficulty his parents had in controlling him

4. How do you feel about the way Qich Mam treats the boy?

*R*esponding to Reading

Comparing the Selections

1. Compare and contrast Athena and Qich Mam. Which character do you think does a better job of teaching respect for limits? Explain.

2. What do the myth and the fable reveal about the qualities admired by the Guatemalans and by the ancient Greeks?

Broader Connections

3. In your opinion, what is the best way to control behavior such as boastfulness, stubbornness, and disobedience in young people?

*L*iterary Concept: Fable

A **fable** is a brief story, often with animal characters, that teaches a lesson about human nature. This lesson is often called the **moral.** What lesson, or moral, might appear at the end of "The Disobedient Child"?

*W*riting Options

1. What might Qich Mam have done to try to change Arachne's attitude? Rewrite the **myth,** replacing Athena with Qich Mam.

2. Write your own **fable** about a character who is out of control.

*V*ocabulary Practice

Exercise   Copy the paragraph below, replacing each boldfaced word or phrase with a word from the list.

Athena is a direct **offspring** of Zeus. She does not **allow** disrespect and seems to **strongly dislike** Arachne's boastfulness. To **show** her anger with Arachne, Athena decides to **trick** Arachne by disguising herself as an old woman with a **twisted** posture. Even after Athena stands **up straight** and reveals her true identity, Arachne's competitive spirit does not **decrease.** Anger and pride begin **swirling forcefully** within her. In the end, Arachne's **destiny** is to live the rest of her life as a spider.

> *Words to Know and Use*
>
> churning
> deceive
> descendant
> distorted
> erect
> fate
> indicate
> resent
> subside
> tolerate

Options for Learning

1 • **A Pattern for Living** Draw the scenes Arachne and Athena wove into their cloth. To draw Athena's picture, research Athena's life story and the stories of mortals who tried to strive with the gods. For Arachne's picture, research some of the unworthy actions and mischief created by the Greek gods.

2 • **Act Too** With a group of your classmates, dramatize one of these selections. Create a script for a narrator or dialogue for the characters. Include props and sound effects. Present your drama to the class and let your classmates comment on which dramatizations were most effective and why.

Olivia Coolidge   1908–

Olivia Coolidge grew up in England, where her father was a journalist and historian. After completing her studies at Oxford University, Coolidge came to the United States and taught English for several years. She is interested in history as well as in the classics of Greek and Latin literature. Coolidge has written a number of biographies for young people in which she needed to carefully separate facts from opinions. As Coolidge says, "Facts are the bricks with which a biographer builds. . . . The more facts I have to work with, the freer I am to design my own book." Coolidge carefully researches her subjects and then forms her own opinions. Her many books include *Greek Myths, Gandhi,* and *The Apprenticeship of Abraham Lincoln.*

Victor Montejo   1952–

Victor Montejo was born and raised in rural Guatemala. He later taught primary school in Jacaltenango, the setting of "The Disobedient Child." Unfortunately, because of political differences, Montejo was threatened with death by the Guatemalan government. He fled to the United States in 1982. Since then, he has published a number of stories, fables, and poems. Montejo has worked as a writer-in-residence at Bucknell University, where he was able to write stories and have discussions with students. Montejo is currently completing his doctoral studies in anthropology at the University of Connecticut. "The Disobedient Child" is from his book *The Bird Who Cleans the World.*

EXPLORE

What Matters Most

Links to Unit Five

Damon and Pythias: A Drama   FAN KISSEN
King Thrushbeard   THE BROTHERS GRIMM
The Three Wishes   RICARDO E. ALEGRÍA (rē kär' dô ä le grē' ä)

Examine What You Know

How many answers are there to the question, What matters most? With your class create a list of answers to this question. Rank your answers from most to least important, with number 1 being what the class as a whole considers most important. As you read, see how the things that matter most to the people in your class compare with what matters most to the characters in these three tales from long ago and far away.

Expand Your Knowledge

Damon and Pythias is a Greek legend about the value of friendship. According to legend, Damon and Pythias lived in the city of Syracuse, on the island of Sicily, in the fourth century B.C. Syracuse, one of the most powerful cities in the ancient Greek world, was ruled at the time by an unjust ruler named Dionysius.

"King Thrushbeard" tells the story of a proud princess who finds fault with all the men who want to marry her. It is only through hardship that she comes to recognize the most valuable qualities of a person. This tale was written by the famous brothers Grimm, who in the early 1800s collected and recorded the stories that had been told orally in Germany for generations.

"The Three Wishes," like many folk tales that involve the granting of wishes, deals with what is most important in life and what brings the greatest happiness. This tale comes from the island of Puerto Rico, and it takes place in the forest of a distant past.

Write Before You Read

■ *Author biographies on Extend page*

What would you ask for if you were granted three wishes? In your journal describe the three things you would wish for and explain why you made these choices.

Damon and Pythias:

A Drama

FAN KISSEN

CAST

Damon	**First Robber**	**First Voice**
Pythias	**Second Robber**	**Second Voice**
King	**Mother**	**Third Voice**
Soldier	**Narrator**	

(Sound: Iron door opens and shuts. Key in lock.)
(Music: Up full and out.)

Narrator. Long, long ago there lived on the island of Sicily two young men named Damon and Pythias.[1] They were known far and wide for the strong friendship each had for the other. Their names have come down to our own times to mean true friendship. You may hear it said of two persons:

First Voice. Those two? Why, they're like Damon and Pythias!

Narrator. The king of that country was a cruel <u>tyrant</u>. He made cruel laws, and he showed no mercy toward anyone who broke his laws. Now, you might very well wonder:

Second Voice. Why didn't the people rebel?

Narrator. Well, the people didn't dare rebel because they feared the king's great and powerful army. No one dared say a word against the king or his laws—except Damon and Pythias. One day a soldier overheard Pythias speaking against a new law the king had proclaimed.

Soldier. Ho, there! Who are you that dares to speak so about our king?

Pythias *(unafraid).* I am called Pythias.

Soldier. Don't you know it is a crime to speak against the king or his laws? You are under arrest! Come and tell this opinion of yours to the king's face!

---

1. **Damon** (dā′ mən) **and Pythias** (pith′ ē əs): legendary friends.

Words to Know and Use

tyrant (tī′ rənt) *n.* a harsh, unjust ruler

(Music: A few short bars in and out.)

Narrator. When Pythias was brought before the king, he showed no fear. He stood straight and quiet before the throne.

King (*hard, cruel*). So, Pythias! They tell me you do not approve of the laws I make.

Pythias. I am not alone, your Majesty, in thinking your laws are cruel. But you rule the people with such an iron hand that they dare not complain.

King (*angry*). But *you* have the daring to complain *for* them! Have they appointed you their champion?[2]

Pythias. No, your Majesty. I speak for myself alone. I have no wish to make trouble for anyone. But I am not afraid to tell you that the people are suffering under your rule. They want to have a voice in making the laws for themselves. You do not allow them to speak up for themselves.

King. In other words, you are calling me a tyrant! Well, you shall learn for yourself how a tyrant treats a rebel! Soldier! Throw this man into prison!

Soldier. At once, your Majesty! Don't try to resist, Pythias!

Pythias. I know better than to try to resist a soldier of the king! And for how long am I to remain in prison, your Majesty, merely for speaking out for the people?

King (*cruel*). Not for very long, Pythias. Two weeks from today at noon, you shall be put to death in the public square as an example to anyone else who may dare to question my laws or acts. Off to prison with him, soldier!

(Music: In briefly and out.)

Narrator. When Damon heard that his friend Pythias had been thrown into prison, and about the severe punishment that was to follow, he was heartbroken. He rushed to the prison and persuaded the guard to let him speak to his friend.

Damon. Oh, Pythias! How terrible to find you here! I wish I could do something to save you!

Pythias. Nothing can save me, Damon, my dear friend. I am prepared to die. But there is one thought that troubles me greatly.

Damon. What is it? I will do anything to help you.

Pythias. I'm worried about what will happen to my mother and my sister when I'm gone.

Damon. I'll take care of them, Pythias, as if they were my own mother and sister.

Pythias. Thank you, Damon. I have money to leave them. But there are other things I must arrange. If only I could go to see

---

2. **champion:** one who fights on behalf of a person or group.

them before I die! But they live two days' journey from here, you know.

Damon. I'll go to the king and beg him to give you your freedom for a few days. You'll give your word to return at the end of that time. Everyone in Sicily knows you for a man who has never broken his word.

Pythias. Do you believe for one moment that the king would let me leave this prison, no matter how good my word may have been all my life?

Damon. I'll tell him that *I* shall take your place in this prison cell. I'll tell him that if you do not return by the appointed day, he may kill *me* in your place!

Pythias. No, no, Damon! You must not do such a foolish thing! I cannot—I *will* not—let you do this! Damon! Damon! Don't go! *(to himself)* Damon, my friend! You may find yourself in a cell beside me!

(Music: In briefly and out.)

Damon *(begging)*. Your Majesty! I beg of you! Let Pythias go home for a few days to bid farewell to his mother and sister. He gives his word that he will return at your appointed time. Everyone knows that his word can be trusted.

King. In ordinary business affairs—perhaps. But he is now a man under sentence of death. To free him even for a few days would strain his honesty—*any* man's honesty—too far. Pythias would never return here! I consider him a traitor, but I'm certain he's no fool.

Damon. Your Majesty! I will take his place in the prison until he comes back. If he does not return, then you may take *my* life in his place.

King *(astonished)*. What did you say, Damon?

Damon. I'm so certain of Pythias that I am offering to die in his place if he fails to return on time.

King. I can't believe you mean it!

Damon. I do mean it, your Majesty.

King. You make me very curious, Damon, so curious that I'm willing to put you and Pythias to the test. This exchange of prisoners will be made. But Pythias must be back two weeks from today, at noon.

Damon. Thank you, your Majesty!

King. The order with my <u>official</u> seal shall go by your own hand, Damon. But I warn you, if your friend does not return on time, you shall surely die in his place! I shall show no mercy.

Words to Know and Use | **official** (ə fish′ əl) *adj.* belonging to a person of authority

(Music: In briefly and out.)

Narrator. Pythias did not like the king's bargain with Damon. He did not like to leave his friend in prison with the chance that he might lose his life if something went wrong. But at last Damon persuaded him to leave, and Pythias set out for his home. More than a week went by. The day set for the death sentence drew near. Pythias did not return. Everyone in the city knew of the condition on which the king had permitted Pythias to go home. Everywhere people met, the talk was sure to turn to the two friends.

First Voice. Do you suppose Pythias will come back?

Second Voice. Why should he stick his head under the king's ax once he's escaped?

Third Voice. Still, would an honorable man like Pythias let such a good friend die for him?

First Voice. There's no telling what a man will do when it's a question of his own life against another's.

Second Voice. But if Pythias doesn't come back before the time is up, he will be killing his friend.

Third Voice. Well, there's still a few days' time. I, for one, am certain that Pythias *will* return in time.

Second Voice. And *I* am just as certain that he will *not*. Friendship is friendship, but a man's own life is something stronger, *I* say!

Narrator. Two days before the time was up, the king himself visited Damon in his prison cell.

(Sound: Iron door unlocked and opened.)

King *(mocking)*. You see now, Damon, that you were a fool to make this bargain. Your friend has tricked you! He will not come back here to be killed! He has deserted you.

Damon *(calm and firm)*. I have faith in my friend. I know he will return.

King *(mocking)*. We shall see!

(Sound: Iron door shut and locked.)

Narrator. Meanwhile, when Pythias reached the home of his family, he arranged his business affairs so that his mother and sister would be able to live comfortably for the rest of their years. Then he said a last farewell to them before starting back to the city.

TRIUMPH OF JUNIUS BASSUS   Palazzo Vecchio Florence, Italy   Scala/Art Resource.

Mother (*in tears*). Pythias, it will take you only two days to get back. Stay another day, I beg you!

Pythias. I dare not stay longer, Mother. Remember, Damon is locked up in my prison cell while I'm gone. Please don't make it any harder for me! Farewell! Don't weep for me. My death may help to bring better days for all our people.

Narrator. So Pythias began his journey in plenty of time. But bad luck struck him on the very first day. At twilight, as he walked along a lonely stretch of woodland, a rough voice called:

First Robber. Not so fast there, young man! Stop!

Pythias (*startled*). Oh! What is it? What do you want?

Second Robber. Your money bags.

Pythias. My money bags? I have only this small bag of coins. I shall need them for some favors, perhaps, before I die.

First Robber. What do you mean, before you die? We don't mean to kill you, only take your money.

Pythias. I'll give you my money, only don't delay me any longer. I am to die by the king's order three days from now. If I don't return to prison on time, my friend must die in my place.

First Robber. A likely story! What man would be fool enough to go back to prison ready to die.

Second Robber. And what man would be fool enough to die *for* you?

First Robber. We'll take your money, all right. And we'll tie you up while we get away.

Pythias (*begging*). No! No! I must get back to free my friend! (*fade*) I must go back!

Narrator. But the two robbers took Pythias's money, tied him to a tree, and went off as fast as they could. Pythias struggled to free himself. He cried out for help as loud as he could for a long time. But no one traveled through that lonesome woodland after dark. The sun had been up for many hours before he finally managed to free himself from the ropes that had tied him to the tree. He lay on the ground, hardly able to breathe.

(*Music: In briefly and out.*)

Narrator. After a while Pythias got to his feet. Weak and dizzy from hunger and thirst and his struggle to free himself, he set off again. Day and night he traveled without stopping, desperately trying to reach the city in time to save Damon's life.

(*Music: up and out.*)

Narrator. On the last day, half an hour before noon, Damon's hands were tied behind his back, and he was taken into the public square. The people muttered angrily as Damon was led in by the jailer. Then the king entered and seated himself on a high platform.

(*Sound: Crowd voices in and hold under single voices.*)

Soldier (*loud*). Long live the king!

First Voice (*low*). The longer he lives, the more miserable our lives will be!

King (*loud, mocking*). Well, Damon, your lifetime is nearly up. Where is your good friend Pythias now?

Damon (*firm*). I have faith in my friend. If he has not returned, I'm certain it is through no fault of his own.

King (*mocking*). The sun is almost overhead. The shadow is almost at the noon mark. And still your friend has not returned to give you back your life!

Damon (*quiet*). I am ready and happy to die in his place.

King (*harsh*). And you shall, Damon! Jailer, lead the prisoner to the—

(*Sound: Crowd voices up to a roar, then under.*)

First Voice (*over noise*). Look! It's Pythias!

Second Voice (*over noise*). Pythias has come back!

Pythias (*breathless*). Let me through! Damon!

Damon. Pythias!

Pythias. Thank the gods I'm not too late!

Damon (*quiet, sincere*). I would have died for you gladly, my friend.

Crowd Voices (*loud, demanding*). Set them free! Set them both free!

King (*loud*). People of the city! (*crowd voices out*) Never in all my life have I seen such faith and friendship, such loyalty between men. There are many among you who call me harsh and cruel. But I cannot kill *any* man who proves such strong and true friendship for another. Damon and Pythias, I set you both free. (*roar of approval from crowd*) I am king. I command a great army. I have stores of gold and precious jewels. But I would give all my money and power for one friend like Damon or Pythias.

(*Sound: Roar of approval from crowd up briefly and out.*)

(*Music: Up and out.*) ❧

Responding to Reading

1. What was the strongest emotion you felt as you read this story? Write about this emotion in your journal.

2. Why do you think the robbers do not believe Pythias's story?

3. Do you think Damon goes too far in supporting his friend? Why or why not?

King Thrushbeard

THE BROTHERS GRIMM

A king had a daughter who was unequaled for beauty, but she was so proud and thought so much of herself that no suitor[1] was good enough for her. She rejected one after another and, to make matters worse, poked fun at them. Once the king gave a great feast and invited all the marriageable young men from far and near. They were all lined up in the order of their rank: first came the kings, then the dukes, princes, counts, and barons, and last of all the knights. The king's daughter was led down the line, but to each suitor she had some objection. One was too fat, and she called him a "wine barrel." The next was too tall: "Tall and skinny, that's a ninny." The third was short: "Short and thick won't do the trick." The fourth was too pale: "As pale as death." The fifth too red: "A turkey." The sixth wasn't straight enough: "Green wood, dried behind the stove." She found some fault with every one of them, but she made the most fun of a kindly king who was standing at the head of the line and whose chin was slightly crooked. "Heavens above!" she cried. "He's got a chin like a thrush's bill!" And from then on he was known as Thrushbeard.

When the old king saw that his daughter did nothing but make fun of people and rejected all the suitors who had come to the feast, he flew into a rage and swore to make her marry the first beggar who came to his door. A few days later, a wandering minstrel came and sang under the window in the hope of earning a few coins. When the king heard him, he said, "Send him up." The minstrel appeared in his ragged, dirty clothes, sang for the king and his daughter, and asked for a gift when he had finished. The king said, "Your singing has pleased me so well that I'll give you my daughter for your wife." The princess was horrified, but the king said, "I swore I'd give you to the first beggar who came by, and I'm going to abide by my oath."

I'll give you my daughter for your wife.

All her pleading was in vain; the priest was called, and she was married to the minstrel then and there. After the ceremony the king said, "Now that you're a beggar woman, I can't have you living in my palace. You can just go away with your husband."

---

1. **suitor** (sōot′ ər): a man seeking to marry a woman.

THE ROSE   1845–1847   Moritz Ludwig von Schwind
Staatliche Gemaeldegalerie (Nationalgalerie) Berlin.   Bridgeman/Art Resource, New York.

The beggar took her by the hand and led her out of the palace, and she had to go with him on foot. They came to a large forest, and she asked:

"Who does that lovely forest belong to?"

"That forest belongs to King Thrushbeard. If you'd taken him, you could call it your own."

"Alas, poor me, if I'd only known. If only I'd taken King Thrushbeard!"

Next they came to a meadow, and she asked:

"Who does that lovely green meadow belong to?"

"That meadow belongs to King Thrushbeard. If you'd taken him, you could call it your own."

"Alas, poor me, if I'd only known. If only I'd taken King Thrushbeard!"

Then they passed through a big city, and she asked:

"Who does this beautiful city belong to?"

"This city belongs to King Thrushbeard. If you'd taken him, you could call it your own."

"Alas, poor me, if only I'd known. If only I'd taken King Thrushbeard!"

"You give me a pain," said the minstrel, "always wishing for another husband. I suppose I'm not good enough for you!"

At last they came to a tiny little house, and she said:

"Heavens, this shack is a disgrace! Who could own such a wretched place?"

The minstrel answered, "It's my house and yours, where we shall live together." The king's daughter had to bend down to get through the low doorway. "Where are the servants?" she asked. "Servants, my foot!" answered the beggar. "If you want something done, you'll have to do it for yourself. And now make a fire and put on water for my supper because I'm dead tired." But the king's daughter didn't know the first thing about fires or cooking, and the beggar had to help her or he wouldn't have had any supper at all. When they had eaten what little there was, they went to bed. But bright and early the next morning, he made her get up and clean the house.

They worried along for a few days, but then their provisions were gone, and the man said, "Wife, we can't go on like this, eating and drinking and earning nothing. You'll have to weave baskets." He went out and cut willow withes[2] and brought them home. She began to weave, but the hard withes bruised her tender hands. "I see that won't do," said the man. "Try spinning; maybe you'll be better at it." She sat down and tried to spin, but the hard thread soon cut her soft fingers and drew blood. "Well, well!" said the man. "You're no good for any work. I've made a bad bargain. But now I think I'll buy up some earthenware pots and dishes. All you'll have to do is sit in the marketplace and sell them."

You're no good for any work. I've made a bad bargain.

"Goodness gracious!" she thought. "If somebody from my father's kingdom goes to the marketplace and sees me sitting there selling pots, how they'll laugh at me!" But there was no help for it; she had to give in or they would have starved.

The first day, all went well: people were glad to buy her wares because she was beautiful; they paid whatever she asked, and some didn't even trouble to take the pots they had paid for. The two of them lived on

---

2. **willow withes** (withs): tough, bendable twigs from willow trees.

the proceeds as long as the stock held out, and then the husband bought up a fresh supply of crockery. She took a place at the edge of the market, set out her wares around her, and offered them for sale. All of a sudden a drunken hussar[3] came galloping through, upset her pots, and smashed them all into a thousand pieces. She began to cry; she was worried sick. "Oh!" she wailed. "What will become of me? What will my husband say?" She ran home and told him what had happened. "What did you expect?" he said. "Setting out earthenware pots at the edge of the market! But stop crying. I can see you're no good for any sensible work. Today I was at our king's palace. I asked if they could use a kitchenmaid, and they said they'd take you. They'll give you your meals."

So the king's daughter became a kitchenmaid and had to help the cook and do the most disagreeable work. She carried little jars in both her pockets, to take home the leftovers they gave her, and that's what she and her husband lived on.

It so happened that the marriage of the king's eldest son was about to be celebrated. The poor woman went upstairs and stood in the doorway of the great hall, looking on. When the candles were lit and the courtiers[4] began coming in, each more magnificent than the last, and everything was so bright and full of splendor, she was sad at heart. She thought of her miserable life and cursed the pride and arrogance that had brought her so low and made her so poor.

Succulent[5] dishes were being carried in and out, and the smell drifted over to her. Now and then a servant tossed her a few scraps, and she put them into her little jars to take home. And then the king's son appeared; he was dressed in silk and velvet and had gold chains around his neck. When he saw the beautiful woman in the doorway, he took her by the hand and asked her to dance with him, but she refused. She was terrified, for she saw it was King Thrushbeard, who had courted her and whom she had laughed at and rejected. She tried to resist, but he drew her into the hall. Then the string that kept her pockets in place snapped, the jars fell to the floor, the soup spilled, and the scraps came tumbling out. The courtiers all began to laugh and jeer, and she would sooner have been a hundred fathoms under the earth. She bounded through the door and tried to escape, but on the stairs a man caught her and brought her back; and when she looked at him, she saw it was King Thrushbeard again. He spoke kindly to her and said, "Don't be afraid. I am the minstrel you've been living with in that wretched shack; I disguised myself for love of you, and I was also the hussar who rode in and smashed your crockery. I did all that to humble your pride and punish you for the insolent way you laughed at me." Then she

---

3. **hussar** (hoo zär′): a cavalry soldier.
4. **courtiers** (kôrt′ ē ərz): attendants at a royal palace.
5. **succulent** (suk′ yoo lənt): tasty; appetizing.

Words to Know and Use | **insolent** (in′ sə lənt) *adj.* rude

wept bitterly and said, "I've been very wicked, and I'm not worthy to be your wife." But he said, "Don't cry, the hard days are over; now we shall celebrate our wedding." The maids came and dressed her magnificently, her father arrived with his whole court and congratulated her on her marriage to King Thrushbeard, and it was then that the feast became really joyful. I wish you and I had been there. 🐦

*R*esponding to Reading

1. What is your opinion of King Thrushbeard? State your thoughts in your journal.

2. What seems to matter most to the king's daughter?

   Think about
   • what matters most to her before she marries the minstrel
   • how she feels as she travels to the shack
   • how she feels at the end of the story

3. Do you think the king's daughter is treated fairly in this story? Why or why not?

4. Given her past personality and her recent experiences, what kind of wife and ruler do you think Thrushbeard's bride will be?

The Three Wishes

RICARDO E. ALEGRÍA

Many years ago, in the days when the saints walked on earth, there lived a woodsman and his wife. They were very poor but very happy in their little house in the forest. Poor as they were, they were always ready to share what little they had with anyone who came to their door. They loved each other very much and were quite content with their life together. Each evening, before eating, they gave thanks to God for their happiness.

One day, while the husband was working far off in the woods, an old man came to the little house and said that he had lost his way in the forest and had eaten nothing for many days. The woodsman's wife had little to eat herself, but, as was her custom, she gave a large portion of it to the old man. After he had eaten everything she gave him, he told the woman that he had been sent by God to test her and that as a reward for the kindness she and her husband showed to all who came to their house, they would be granted a special <u>grace</u>. This pleased the woman, and she asked what the special grace was.

The old man answered, "Beginning immediately, any three wishes you or your husband may wish will come true."

When she heard these words, the woman was overjoyed and exclaimed, "Oh, if my husband were only here to hear what you say!"

The last word had scarcely left her lips when the woodsman appeared in the little house with the ax still in his hands. The first wish had come true.

The woodsman couldn't understand it at all. How did it happen that he, who had been cutting wood in the forest, found himself here in his house? His wife explained it all as she embraced him. The woodsman just stood there, thinking over what his wife had said. He looked at the old man who stood quietly, too, saying nothing.

Suddenly he realized that his wife, without stopping to think, had used one of the three wishes, and he became very annoyed when he remembered all of the useful things she might have asked for with the first wish. For the first time, he became angry with his wife. The desire for riches had turned his head, and he scolded his wife, shouting at her, among other things, "It doesn't seem possible that you could be so stupid! You've wasted one of our wishes, and now we have only two left! May you grow ears of a donkey!"

He had no sooner said the words than his wife's ears began to grow, and they contin-

Words to Know and Use | **grace** (grās) *n.* a gift from God

LA CLAIRIÈRE (The Clearing)   Dominique-Paul Peyronnet
Private collection.   The Granger Collection, New York.

ued to grow until they changed into the pointed, furry ears of a donkey.

When the woman put her hand up and felt them, she knew what had happened and began to cry. Her husband was very ashamed and sorry, indeed, for what he had done in his temper, and he went to his wife to comfort her.

The old man, who had stood by silently, now came to them and said, "Until now, you have known happiness together and have never quarreled with each other. Nevertheless, the mere knowledge that you could have riches and power has changed you both. Remember, you have only one wish left. What do you want? Riches? Beautiful clothes? Servants? Power?"

The woodsman tightened his arm about his wife, looked at the old man, and said, "We want only the happiness and joy we knew before my wife grew donkey's ears."

No sooner had he said these words than the donkey ears disappeared. The woodsman and his wife fell upon their knees to ask God's forgiveness for having acted, if only for a moment, out of covetousness[1] and greed. Then they gave thanks for all the happiness God had given them.

The old man left, but before going, he told them that they had undergone this test in order to learn that there can be happiness in poverty just as there can be unhappiness in riches. As a reward for their repentance, the old man said that he would bestow upon them the greatest happiness a married couple can know. Months later, a son was born to them. The family lived happily all the rest of their lives. 🐦

---

1. **covetousness** (kuv' ət əs nis): a desire for wealth or possessions.

Responding to Reading

1. Did you like this story? Jot down your response to it in your journal.

2. Since the husband and wife have always been kind to others and happy with their life, what do you think this experience teaches them about themselves?

3. What, if anything, do you think the couple would wish for if they could have three more wishes?

4. According to the story, what matters most?

Words to Know and Use | **repentance** (ri pen' təns) *n.* sorrow for wrongdoing

Responding to Reading

Comparing the Selections

1. Which character in the three stories do you admire the most? Why?

2. How do the **conflicts** in the stories help teach the characters about what is most important?

Broader Connections

3. Think about the values that are taught in these three selections. Are they still important in today's world? Explain why or why not.

Literary Concept: Theme

The **theme** of a work of literature is the work's main idea. Often the theme is a message about human nature. Think about the desirable and undesirable human qualities each of these three tales portrays. Then state each tale's theme in one sentence.

Writing Options

1. Write a **news update** on conditions in Sicily one year after Damon and Pythias are freed.

2. Imagine you are the television host of *Brothers Grimm Theater*. Write an **introduction** to the show's feature presentation of "King Thrushbeard."

Vocabulary Practice

Exercise   For each pair write *S* if the words are *synonyms* or *A* if they are *antonyms*.

1. insolent—polite

2. grace—punishment

3. repentance—sorrow

4. tyrant—dictator

5. official—informal

Words to Know and Use

**grace
insolent
official
repentance
tyrant**

EXTEND

Options for Learning

1 • **How Grim Is Grimm?** Find and read other Grimm fairy tales. Create a comic book version of one of these to share with your class. Write up-to-date dialogue for your comic book.

2 • **Puppet Show** Present one of the selections as a puppet show for younger children. Make puppets for each character and backdrops for the settings. Rehearse the story and present it on a puppet stage.

Fan Kissen   1904–

For seventeen years, Fan Kissen was a radio scriptwriter. Her plays, which are written as radio scripts, always include instructions for music and sound effects. Kissen has also been an elementary school teacher in her hometown of New York City. In addition to writing plays, she also writes biographies for young people. Her books include *The Crowded House and Other Tales* and *They Helped Make America.*

Jakob and Wilhelm Grimm
1785–1863   1786–1859

The brothers Grimm, born in Hanau, Germany, trained to be lawyers. However, Jakob and Wilhelm were much more interested in collecting local folk tales than they were in practicing law.

The two brothers were always very close, and as Jakob wrote, "Up to the very end we worked in two rooms next to each other, always under one roof." *Grimm's Fairy Tales* has remained popular to this day.

Ricardo E. Alegría   1921–

Ricardo Alegría lives and writes in the city in which he was born—San Juan, Puerto Rico. "The Three Wishes" is taken from Alegría's collection of Puerto Rican folk tales, also called *The Three Wishes.* In addition, Alegría is the author of several other books and articles on folklore, history, and archaeology (the study of ancient remains). Alegría is a history professor at the University of Puerto Rico, and he has served as the director of the Institute of Puerto Rican Culture.

WRITER'S
WORKSHOP

WRITER'S CHOICE

From ancient Greece to the island of Trinidad in the present day, this unit explores many lands and their folklore. Now you are going to do some exploring of your own. In this workshop you will choose one writing assignment from a range of familiar formats. You will create your own PASSkey and your own writing steps. So get ready to pick an assignment, pack up your imagination, and push off into new territory.

A. Narrative Writing: A Myth or Folk Tale for Today

Though most of the selections in this unit are tales from long ago, the selections contain characters and teach lessons that people of any time can understand. Rewrite one of these myths or folk tales in your own words. Use a familiar setting and write dialogue that reflects the way people talk today.

Prewrite and Explore   Think about how you could update some of the selections in this unit by using modern settings and characters. For example, could Daedalus be a mad scientist in a laboratory? Could his invention be something that destroys the people he is trying to save? Could the beautiful but proud princess in "King Thrushbeard" be a high school beauty queen who thinks only of herself? What experience could force her to change? Reread the myth or tale carefully before you begin drafting your version.

Draft and Discover   Keep your plot simple by using chronological order and focusing on one main event. Even if the original myth or tale is not humorous, you may enjoy using a humorous tone in your version.

Revise Your Writing   Look at the Revision Questions on page 210 and at the Language Workshop on punctuating dialogue, pages 212-214. Make sure that your story remains true to the characters or lesson of the original myth or tale.

B. Descriptive/Personal Writing: A Letter from the Past

Suppose you were able to hop into a time-and-space machine and visit the setting of any selection in this unit. Which setting would you

NEED MORE HELP?

Myths and **folk tales** are narratives. For more about narrative writing, see the Writer's Workshop on pages 207–211.

TWO OR MORE HEADS ARE BETTER THAN ONE

If you have trouble thinking of ways to do this assignment, brainstorm with a group of your classmates. One idea will often spark another. Let your ideas flow freely.

like to visit? What might you see and experience? Imagine yourself in that setting and write a letter to your best friend back home. Describe the setting, the people or animals you've met, and the experiences you've had.

Prewrite and Explore   Which setting will you visit? Look at the table of contents on pages 536–537 and jot down some possibilities. Will you journey to present-day Trinidad or to the China of long ago? After you have chosen the setting, find additional information in an encyclopedia, an atlas, or another reference book.

Draft and Discover   Keep your audience in mind as you write. What would your best friend enjoy hearing about? The scenery? An encounter with the people or creatures of the region? A humorous or exciting adventure that you have had? As you write, organize your ideas clearly.

Revise Your Writing   Use the checklists on page 151 to help you revise your writing. Ask a friend to read your draft and respond to it.

◀ NEED HELP?
For more about writing letters, see the Writer's Workshop on pages 58–62.

C. Informative Writing: What's the Real Story?

Some of the myths and folk tales in this unit give far-fetched explanations of natural phenomena. For example, "Why Monkeys Live in Trees" tells why monkeys live high in the jungle and why chickens don't have ears. However, what are the real facts? Choose one nonscientific explanation from a selection in this unit and research the scientific explanation of the same phenomenon. Write a report that details your findings.

◀ NEED MORE HELP?
For more about writing a report, see the Writer's Workshop on pages 523–527.

Prewrite and Explore   The first selection in this unit, "The Gods and Goddesses of Mount Olympus," is an overview of important Greek myths. How thunder and lightning came to be, why volcanoes explode, and how day and night occur are just a few of the aspects of nature that Greek myths tried to explain. Look at this selection and others in the unit. Then choose the topic that you think would be most interesting to research and explain.

Draft and Discover   Collect information about your topic from sources such as encyclopedias, magazines, science textbooks, and other nonfiction books. Organize your draft so that it presents your information clearly. Include an introduction, a body, and a conclusion in your report. Use signal words and phrases to guide your readers through your explanation.

Revise Your Writing   Use the checklists on page 526 as a revision guide. Ask a classmate to read your report. Does your explanation make sense? Is it understandable?

D. Persuasive Writing: Wrap It Up

Which of the selections in this unit would make a good children's book? Choose a selection and write the copy for a book jacket that will convince people to buy the book.

NEED MORE HELP?

For more about persuasive writing, see the Writer's Workshops on pages 376–380 and 421–425.

▶ **Prewrite and Explore**   Read the copy on the jackets of children's books in your school or public library. Then choose from this unit a selection that you like and that you think younger children would like. Reread the selection and list reasons why children might enjoy reading it. Find supporting details for your reasons. Search the selection for one or two quotations that could help "hook" someone into wanting to read it.

BOOK SUMMARIES

For examples of how to summarize the plot or main idea of a book, see Reading on Your Own at the end of each unit.

▶ **Draft and Discover**   Consider beginning with an interesting summary of the selection. Keep your audience in mind. "The White Buffalo Calf Woman and the Sacred Pipe" might interest someone who wanted to understand the Lakota Sioux and their culture. Write the reasons you think someone might find the selection humorous or exciting or heartwarming. Use quotations from the story that would attract readers.

Revise Your Writing   Have a classmate read your book-jacket copy. Ask him or her whether the copy does a good job of summarizing the selection and whether it would get readers interested.

E. Writing About Literature: Who's Your Hero?

In this unit you have come across characters who are powerful, tricky, brilliant, stubborn, kind, and wise. Which character do you admire the most? Write an essay explaining your choice.

NEED HELP?

For more on writing about literature, see the Writer's Workshop on pages 476–480.

▶ **Prewrite and Explore**   Make a list of characters in this unit. Next to each name write an adjective or two that describes this character. Ask yourself questions such as these: What are the qualities of a hero? (This is a personal list; each person may consider different characters heroic.) How does this character act? What are the results of his or her actions?

Draft and Discover   You might start with a paragraph that states your overall opinion of the hero you have chosen. Then you can give specific details to support your opinion. You could also begin with supporting details and give your overall opinion at the end. Back up your opinions with direct quotations and references from the selection.

Revise Your Writing   Look at the Revision Questions on page 479. Use any appropriate questions from these lists to help you revise your paper.

◄ WHAT'S YOUR MAIN POINT?

Choose an overall point that you want to make. Is your hero the smartest, the kindest, the wisest? Why do you admire this particular quality?

F. Narrative Writing: Keeping Stories Alive

Every family has stories. Interview a member of your family or an older neighbor and write your interview as an oral history.

Prewrite and Explore   Find someone with a good story to tell. Arrange a time and date to interview this person. Make a list of open-ended questions to ask. Avoid asking questions that can be answered yes or no. For example, you might say, "Tell me about the time when. . . ." You may want to use a tape recorder so that you don't have to worry about taking notes during the interview.

◄ NEED HELP?

For more help in describing someone you know, see the Writer's Workshop on pages 148–152.

Draft and Discover   Listen to your tape or review your notes. Decide on a focus. Draft an introduction in which you give any necessary background information on the person. You can write your report as a question-and-answer interview or as a narrative told by you or the person you interviewed.

Revise Your Writing   The best person to comment on your oral history is the person you interviewed. Let that person read your paper. Make additions or corrections as needed.

Final Revision

No matter which assignment you chose, be sure to give your draft another look. Before you proofread for errors in grammar, spelling, punctuation, and capitalization, look for ways you can add life to your writing. Try varying sentence beginnings, as shown in the box at the top of the next page.

NEED MORE HELP?
See the Language
Workshop on pages
612–614.

THE EDITOR'S EYE: SENTENCE COMBINING

Your writing can sound dull when you repeat the same words from one sentence to the next. Try combining sentences that express closely related ideas. Use the words *and, but,* and *or* to join parts of the sentences.

Problem   "King Thrushbeard" has many plot twists. It has many surprises.

Revised   "King Thrushbeard" has many plot twists and surprises.

Publish and Present

Here is a suggestion for sharing your work with others.

An Oral Tradition Book   As a class, group your papers by types of writing. Organize the six types of writing into chapters to create an oral-tradition book for your class. Ask volunteers to design a cover and to create simple illustrations for some of the selections. Prepare a copy of the book for each class member.

Reflect on Your Writing

FOR YOUR PORTFOLIO

Briefly answer the following questions. Include your answers with your paper when you put it in your writing portfolio.

1. What do you like most about the type of writing you chose for your paper?
2. What other uses might you find for the different types of writing discussed in this workshop?

WRITER'S WORKSHOP

SELF-ASSESSMENT

Portfolio Review

Guided Assignment   Write a one-page evaluation of your achievements as a writer this year.

Prewrite and Explore   Read through your writing portfolio. Jot down notes that answer these questions:

1. What is my best piece of writing? What do I like most about it?
2. What assignment would I do differently now?
3. Where do I see the most improvement? Where do I need to work harder?
4. What do my revisions tell me about the way I write?

Draft and Discover   Use your notes to help you draft your evaluation. Organize your comments in a logical way. For example, you may want to proceed chronologically through the year, or you may want to describe the high points of your writing experience first and then the low points.

Revise Your Writing   Reread your draft, checking to see that your main points are clear. Be sure to include an introduction and a conclusion. As you review your writing, ask yourself, Will readers understand how I feel about my writing? Can I add any examples to make my main points easier to understand?

Proofread   Check your draft for errors in grammar, punctuation, capitalization, and spelling. Correct any mistakes that you find.

Publish and Present   Share your writing with a small group of classmates. As a group, discuss your writing goals for the coming school year.

LANGUAGE WORKSHOP

SENTENCE COMBINING

> You can combine sentences with **conjunctions.** The words *and, but,* and *or* are conjunctions. You can also combine related ideas within a sentence.

Combining Sentences with Conjunctions

When you revise your writing, you may come across sentences that are closely related and could be combined. Sentences that contain similar ideas can be combined with the word *and.*

> One storyteller began the tale. The second one finished it.

REMINDER
When you join two complete sentences with a conjunction, don't forget to add a comma before the conjunction.

▶ One storyteller began the tale**, and** the second one finished it.

Use the word *but* to combine sentences that are on the same topic but contain contrasting ideas.

> The food looked delicious. It tasted terrible.

> The food looked delicious**, but** it tasted terrible.

Sometimes related sentences show a choice between ideas. Use the word *or* to combine these sentences.

> Did Matthew cheat? Did he win the contest fairly?

> Did Matthew cheat **or** did he win the contest fairly?

Joining Sentence Parts

COMMA OR NOT
No comma is needed when you join sentence parts.

▶ Sometimes ideas in two sentences are so closely related that words are repeated. Use conjunctions to combine such sentences. Leave out words or ideas that are repeated.

> Tiffany plays the drums. *Tiffany plays* the piano.

> Tiffany plays the drums **and** the piano.

Ahmad writes the words. *He does* not *write* the music.

Ahmad writes the words **but** not the music.

Exercise 1   Concept Check   Combine each pair of sentences with *and, but,* or *or.* Leave out any words in italics. Use commas where needed.

1. Was Aesop a real person? Was he a fictitious figure?
2. There are many stories about Aesop. They may be untrue.
3. He was supposedly a former slave. *He was supposedly* a writer.
4. Some say Aesop came from the island of Samos. Others say he came from Thrace.
5. He may have lived in the fifth *century. He may have lived in* the sixth century B.C.
6. Birds are characters in Aesop's fables. Beasts *are characters in his fables.*
7. These characters are not human. They have many human traits.
8. Each fable has a message. *Each fable has* a moral.
9. Jamal wrote a fable. Keisha illustrated it.
10. My favorite fable may be "The Fox and the Crow." *My favorite may be* "The Tortoise and the Hare."

Adding Words to Sentences

Sometimes in your writing you may find a sentence that mainly repeats the one before it. There might be only one word in the second sentence that is really important. Look at this example:

Po-wan went on a journey. *The journey was* long.

You can add the important word, *long,* to the first sentence and drop the rest of the second sentence. Notice that all the words in italics were dropped.

Po-wan went on a **long** journey.

In some cases you can combine several sentences this way.

The innkeeper had a daughter. *The innkeeper was* friendly. *His daughter was* beautiful.

The **friendly** innkeeper had a **beautiful** daughter.

Exercise 2 Concept Check   Combine each set of sentences. Add the important word in the second sentence (and in the third sentence where there is one) to the first. Omit any words in italics and add commas when necessary.

1. The folklore of the United States tells of many heroes. *These heroes are* legendary.
2. Johnny Appleseed planted trees. *He planted* apple *trees.*
3. Davy Crockett was a frontiersman. *He was* daring. *He was* fearless.
4. Paul Bunyan is the hero of many tall tales. *The tales are* colorful.
5. Paul had a blue ox named Babe. *She was a* loyal *ox.*
6. Babe drank rivers dry. *She did it* easily. *The rivers were* huge.
7. A ballad tells the story of John Henry. *The ballad is* Southern. *The story is* famous.
8. John competed against a steam drill in a tunnel-digging race. *He competed* successfully.
9. John used his hands and a large hammer. *The hammer was* heavy.
10. John Henry won the race but perished from his efforts. *The race was* exhausting. *His effort was* brave.

▶ **Exercise 3 Revision Skill**   Revise the paragraph below, using techniques from this Workshop. Then share your work with classmates.

> The Trojan horse was a huge structure. It was a wooden structure. Soldiers hid inside the horse. The soldiers were Greek. The horse was offered as a gift to the people of Troy. It was really a trick. The Trojans brought the horse into the city. They were baffled. At night the Greek soldiers crept out of the horse. They unlocked the city doors. The Trojans finally realized what was going on. They were too late. The Greeks conquered Troy.

Exercise 4 Looking at Style   The following passage has three compound sentences, joined by the conjunction *but*. Rewrite the sentences as several shorter sentences. Compare your version to the original. Which version do you prefer? Why might Yolen have chosen to combine these sentences?

▶ He was clever, but he was not always kind. He was full of pride, but he did not give others praise. He was a maker—but he was a taker, too.

Exercise 5 Revising Your Writing   Review the paper you wrote for this unit's Writer's Workshop. Look for sentences that repeat ideas or words. Wherever possible, combine these sentences.

DON'T GO OVERBOARD!
When you write, you don't need to join *all* your sentences. Combine some sentences to make them longer and more interesting. For variety, keep some sentences short.

LITERARY MODEL
From *Wings* by Jane Yolen

LANGUAGE HANDBOOK
For review and practice: Section 2, Understanding Sentences.

VOCABULARY
WORKSHOP

WORD ORIGINS

The English language may be the world's biggest borrower. English has borrowed words from Greek, Latin, and many other languages. Tracing the origins and histories of these words is like going on a fascinating archaeological dig.

Look at this dictionary entry for the word *arachnid*. The origin of the word appears in brackets at the end of the entry.

> **arachnid** (ə rak' nid) *n.* any of a group of insectlike animals that have eight legs and a body divided into two parts. Spiders and scorpions are arachnids. [Latin *Arachnida,* class name, from Greek *arakhnē,* spider.]

This entry tells you that *arachnid* is derived from *arakhnē,* the Greek word for spider. Like many words, *arachnid* was used in another language—Latin—before it entered English. *Arachnid* should already sound familiar to you, though. In this unit you read a myth called "Arachne," in which the title character is turned into a spider. A number of modern words, in fact, come from the names in Greek and Roman myths.

About 85 percent of the words in the English language have been borrowed from such languages as Latin, German, and Russian. We are still borrowing words from other languages. Here are some examples.

Language	Word	Language	Word
Bantu	chimpanzee	Hindi	shampoo
Chinese	tea	Italian	macaroni
Dutch	waffle	Japanese	kimono
French	blouse	Persian	caravan
German	hamburger	Spanish	coyote

Exercise   Look up the following words in a dictionary. Write an explanation of each word's origin.

1. music	**6.** banana	**11.** patio
2. robot	**7.** skunk	**12.** algebra
3. sofa	**8.** cafeteria	**13.** canyon
4. palomino	**9.** flower	**14.** kindergarten
5. turkey	**10.** tornado	**15.** spaghetti

> **TIP**
> Word origins usually appear in brackets in dictionary entries. Many dictionaries use abbreviations for names of languages, such as *Gr* for "Greek" and *Sp* for "Spanish." Look in the front of the dictionary to find a list of these abbreviations.

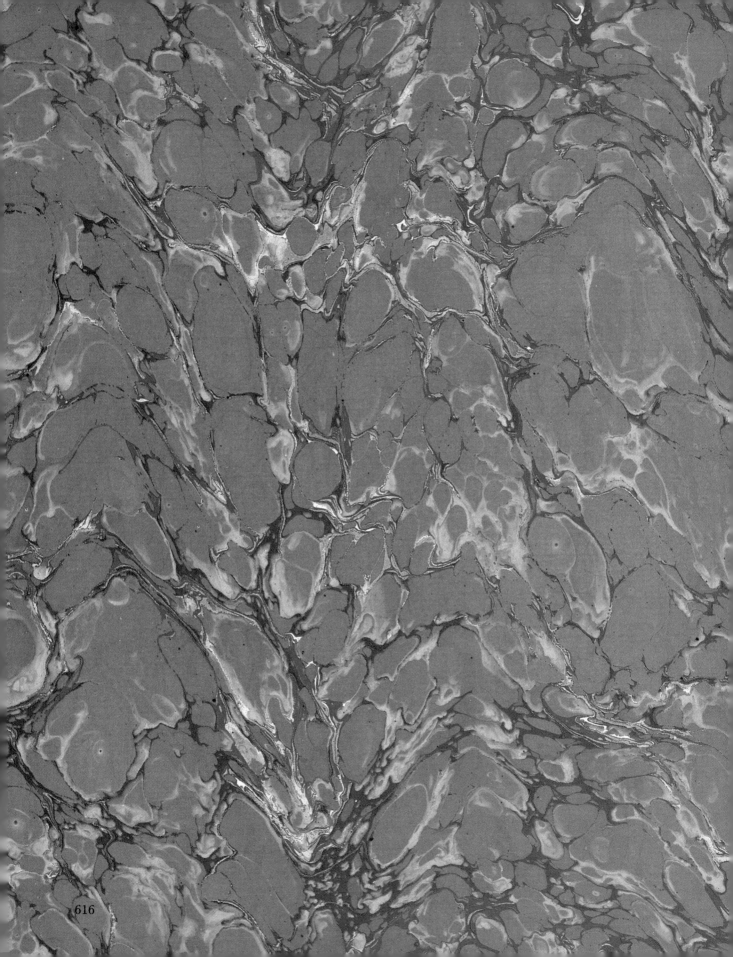

Handbook Contents

READER'S HANDBOOK

GLOSSARY

The **glossary** is an alphabetical listing of words from the selections, with meanings. The glossary gives the following information:

1. **The entry word broken into syllables.**

2. **The pronunciation of each word.** The **respelling** is shown in parentheses. The Pronunciation Key below shows the symbols for the sounds of letters and key words that contain those sounds.

A **primary accent** ' is placed after the syllable that is stressed the most when the word is spoken. A **secondary accent** ' is placed after a syllable that has a lighter stress.

3. **The part of speech of the word.** These abbreviations are used:

   n. noun   *v.* verb   *adj.* adjective   *adv.* adverb

4. **The meaning of the word.** The definitions listed in the glossary apply to selected ways a word is used in these selections.

5. **Related forms.** Words with suffixes such as *-ing, -ed, -ness,* and *-ly* are often listed under the base word.

1. entry word		2. respelling
	def er en tial (def′ ər en′ shəl)	
3. part of speech	*adj.* showing courteous regard or respect	4. meaning

Pronunciation Key

Symbol	Key Words	Symbol	Key Words	Symbol	Key Words	Symbol	Key Words
a	at gas	ōō	tool, crew	ə ⎰ a	in ago	ch	chin
ā	ape, day	oo	look, pull	e	in agent	sh	she
ä	car, lot	yōō	use, cute, few	i	in insanity	th	thin
e	elf, ten	yoo	cure	o	in comply	*th*	then
ē	even, me	oi	oil, coin	u	in focus	zh	leisure
i	is, hit	ou	out, sour			ŋ	ring
ī	bite, fire	u	up, cut			'	ab**le** (ā′b′l)
ō	own, go	ʉr	fur, bird				
ô	law, horn	er	perhaps, murder				

Foreign Symbols

à	salle	*n*	mon
ë	coer	ð	abuelos
ö	feu	*r*	gringos
ü	rue		

A

a bun dance (ə bun′ dəns) *n.* wealth

ac qui si tion (ak′ wə zish′ ən) *n.* something that has been obtained

ad o ra tion (ad′ ə rā′ shən) *n.* great love

a gi tat ed (aj′ i tāt′ id) *adj.* excited, nervous

al ma nac (ôl′ mə nak′) *n.* a book that is published yearly, containing a calendar, weather forecasts, and other information

al ter (ôl′ tər) *v.* to change

a nal y sis (ə nal′ ə sis) *n.* a detailed investigation

an guish (aŋ′ gwish) *n.* suffering; pain

anx ious (aŋk′ shəs) *adj.* worried

ap pren tice ship (ə pren′ tis ship′) *n.* the learning of a trade by helping a skilled craftsperson

au di ble (ô′ də bəl) *adj.* able to be heard

B

ban ish (ban′ ish) *v.* to send away

ba zaar (bə zär′) *n.* in Middle Eastern countries, an outdoor market of small shops

bi as (bī′ əs) *n.* an unreasonable judgment

bick er ing (bik′ ər iŋ) *n.* quarreling; arguing **bick er** *v.*

bliss ful (blis′ fəl) *adj.* very happy

bond age (bän′ dij) *n.* slavery

C

cal cu la tion (kal′ kyo͞o lā′ shən) *n.* a carefully thought-out decision

ca tas tro phe (kə tas′ trə fē) *n.* an extreme misfortune; disaster

cease less (sēs′ lis) *adj.* constant; never ending

cha os (kā′ äs′) *n.* a state of total disorder

char i ta ble (char′ i tə bəl) *adj.* generous in giving

churn ing (chʉrn′ iŋ) *adj.* stirring with a forceful motion **churn** *v.*

clam or (klam′ ər) *n.* a loud noise; uproar

clan (klan) *n.* a family group or tribe

co ma (kō′ mə) *n.* a condition of deep unconsciousness caused by injury or illness

com pas sion (kəm pash′ ən) *n.* a feeling of sorrow for the suffering of others; pity

com pul so ry (kəm pul′ sə rē) *adj.* required

con firm (kən fʉrm′) *v.* to make certain

con front ed (kən frunt′ id) *adj.* met face to face

con gen ial (kən jēn′ yəl) *adj.* friendly

con se quence (kän′ si kwens′) *n.* a result or outcome

con sis ten cy (kən sis′ tən sē) *n.* the condition of always behaving in the same way

con sole (kən sōl′) *v.* to cheer up; comfort

cope (kōp) *v.* to deal with difficulties

coun ter (kount′ ər) *v.* to respond to another's action

co-work er (kō′ wʉrk′ ər) *n.* a fellow worker

crest (krest) *n.* the highest point; top

cul vert (kul′ vərt) *n.* a gutter or tunnel that runs along or under a road

cur ren cy (kʉr′ ən sē) *n.* money

cus toms (kus′ təmz) *adj.* collecting duties or taxes on imported goods

D

de ceive (dē sēv′) *v.* to fool or trick

de cree (dē krē′) *n.* an official order

de fi ance (dē fī′ əns) *n.* an open resistance to authority

de mer it (dē mer′ it) *n.* a mark in a student's record for poor work or for misbehavior

de scend ant (dē sen′ dənt) *n.* a child, grandchild, or more distant offspring

des ti tute (des′ tə to͞ot′) *n.* people lacking the necessities of life

de vour (di vour′) *v.* to eat greedily

dig ni fied (dig′ nə fīd′) *adj.* majestic and restrained

dis charge (dis chärj′) *v.* to release; give permission to leave

dis creet (di skrēt′) *adj.* careful about what one says or does

dis tinc tion (di stiŋk′ shən) *n.* a mark of honor

dis tort ed (di stôrt′ id) *adj.* twisted out of shape **dis tort** *v.*

di vert (də vʉrt′) *v.* to change the direction of

do mes tic (dō mes′ tik) *adj.* having to do with the home or family

dras ti cal ly (dras′ tik lē) *adv.* in a severe way

drone (drōn) *v.* to talk on and on in a low, dull way

drought (drout) *n.* a long period of little or no rain

dumb found ed (dum′ found′ əd) *adj.* made speechless by shocking; astonish

dune (do͞on) *n.* a rounded hill

dwin dle (dwin' dəl) *v.* to decrease or shrink

dy nas ty (dī' nəs tē) *n.* a series of rulers who are members of the same family

E

ec stat i cal ly (ek stat' ik lē) *adv.* with great joy

el e gant (el' ə gənt) *adj.* tasteful and dignified

em brace (em brās') *v.* to clasp affectionately; hug

em er ald (em' ər əld) *adj.* bright green

e merge (ē murj') *v.* to come into sight

e nig ma (ə nig' mə) *n.* a puzzle; mystery

e rect (ē rekt') *adj.* straight up

e ro sion (ē rō' zhən) *n.* the wearing away of something

es sen tial ly (ə sen' shəl ē) *adv.* basically

et i quette (et' i kit) *n.* the rules of proper social behavior

e va sive (ē vā' siv) *adj.* not straightforward

e vict ed (ē vict' id) *adj.* legally removed from a rented house or apartment **e vict** *v.*

ex ile (eks' īl') *n.* a person forced to live outside his or her native country

ex trav a gant ly (ek strav' ə gənt lē) *adv.* excessively; too much

F

fa nat i cal (fə nat' i cəl) *adj.* extreme

fate (fāt) *n.* an outcome or end

fidg et y (fij' it ē) *adj.* moving restlessly

fi na le (fə nal' ē) *n.* the last scene of a performance

flair (fler) *n.* a sense of style

flour ish (flʉr' ish) *n.* a sweeping gesture

fren zied (fren' zēd) *adj.* wild; frantic **fren zy** *n.*

fu gi tive (fyo͞o' ji tiv) *n.* a person who runs away

fume (fyo͞om) *v.* to show anger

fu mi gate (fyo͞o' mə gāt') *v.* to use smoke or gas to destroy pests

fu tile (fyo͞ot' 'l) *adj.* useless

G

gloat (glōt) *v.* to show pleasure in another's trouble

grace (grās) *n.* a gift from God

grim (grim) *adj.* stern or harsh in appearance

H

hu mil i ty (hyo͞o mil' ə tē) *n.* a lack of pride

I

il lit er ate (il lit' ər it) *adj.* not able to read or write

il lu mi nate (i lo͞o' mə nāt') *v.* to light up

im mi grate (im' ə grāt') *v.* to move to a new country

im mor tal (im môrt' 'l) *n.* a being who lives forever

in di cate (in' di kāt') *v.* to show

in dif fer ence (in dif' ər əns) *n.* lack of interest

in fe ri or i ty (in fir' ē ôr' ə tē) *n.* a lack of worth or excellence

in fu ri at ed (in fyo͞or' ē āt' id) *adj.* very angry **in fu ri ate** *v.*

in gen ious (in jēn' yəs) *adj.* clever and inventive

in hab it ant (in hab' i tənt) *n.* a permanent resident

in so lent (in' sə lənt) *adj.* rude

in sta bil i ty (in' stə bil' ə tē) *n.* a state of being out of control

in te grate (in' tə grāt') *v.* to make available to people of all races

in ter ject (in' tər jekt') *v.* to say as an interruption

in ter vene (in' tər vēn') *v.* to interfere; use one's influence to settle something

in tim i date (in tim' ə dāt') *v.* to make nervous and uncertain

in ven to ry (in' vən tôr' ē) *n.* a detailed list of items owned or in stock

L

lav ish ly (lav' ish lē) *adv.* in an abundant way

le thal (lē' thəl) *adj.* deadly

M

mal ice (mal' is) *n.* a desire to cause harm; ill will

ma neu ver (mə no͞o' vər) *v.* to move or guide something

mar gin (mär' jən) *n.* an amount to spare

maze (māz) *n.* a confusing network of winding pathways

me di a (mē' dē ə) *n.* the forms of mass communication

mel an chol y (mel′ ən käl′ ē) *adj.* sad

men ace (men′ əs) *n.* threat; danger

mid riff (mid′ rif) *n.* the upper part of the stomach

mi nor i ty (mī nôr′ ə tē) *adj.* having people who are not part of the most common racial or ethnic group

mock (mäk) *v.* to make fun of; jeer

mor tal (môr′ təl) *adj.* of the earth; not a spirit

N

no bil i ty (nō bil′ ə tē) *n.* a greatness of character

nov el ty (näv′ əl tē) *n.* something new or different

O

ob liv i ous (ə bliv′ ē əs) *adj.* not aware or attentive

of fense (ə fens′) *n.* a violation of a rule

of fi cial (ə fish′ əl) *adj.* belonging to a person of authority

om i nous (äm′ ə nəs) *adj.* threatening harm or evil

P

pa tron (pā′ trən) *n.* a helper or protector

peal (pēl) *n.* a long-lasting, loud sound

ped i greed (ped′ ə grēd′) *adj.* having papers showing that all of the animal's ancestors were the same breed

pen ance (pen′ əns) *n.* an act done to make up for wrongdoing

pe ri od i cal ly (pir′ ē äd′ i kəl ē) *adv.* from time to time

per sist (pər sist′) *v.* to remain or continue

phi lo soph i cal ly (fil′ ō säf′ ik lē) *adv.* in a calm and sensible way

plague (plāg) *n.* a deadly disease that spreads widely

pledge (plej) *n.* something given to guarantee fulfillment of a promise

pon der (pän′ dər) *v.* to think carefully about

pre cise (prē sīs′) *adj.* exact

pred a tor (pred′ ə tər) *n.* an animal that kills other animals for food

pro ce dure (prō sē′ jər) *n.* a course of action

pro ces sion (prō sesh′ ən) *n.* a group of people moving along in an orderly way

pro claim (prō klām′) *v.* to announce officially

proph e cy (präf′ ə sē) *n.* the predicting of the future

pros per (präs′ pər) *v.* to be successful; thrive

pro vi sion (prō vizh′ ən) *n.* a supplying of needs

pur sue (pər so͞o′) *v.* to chase after

Q

que ry (kwir′ ē) *n.* a question

R

ram bunc tious (ram buŋk′ shəs) *adj.* wild; difficult to control

ran dom (ran′ dəm) *adj.* without a clear purpose

realm (relm) *n.* a kingdom

re as sur ance (rē′ ə sho͞or′ əns) *n.* a restoring of confidence

re bel lious (ri bel′ yəs) *adj.* disobedient

rec om men da tion (rek′ ə mən dā′ shən) *n.* a suggestion

reign (rān) *n.* the period during which someone rules

re luc tant (ri luk′ tənt) *adj.* unwilling

re morse (ri môrs′) *n.* regret for a wrongdoing

ren di tion (ren dish′ ən) *n.* a performance; version

ren e gade (ren′ ə gād′) *n.* a person who rejects lawful behavior

re pent ance (ri pen′ təns) sorrow for wrongdoing

re sent (ri zent′) *v.* to feel angry and hurt

res er va tion (rez′ ər vā′ shən) *n.* a limitation or doubt

re solve (ri zälv′) *v.* to make a firm decision

re store (ri stôr′) *v.* to bring back to an original condition; repair

re sume (ri zo͞om′) *v.* to begin again

rev e la tion (rev′ ə lā′ shən) *n.* something made known to others

re vul sion (ri vul′ shən) *n.* a feeling of disgust or horror

rig id (rij′ id) *adj.* stiff; not moving

rum mage (rum′ ij) *v.* to sort or search through

S

sanc tu ar y (saŋk' chōō er' ē) *n.* a shelter

saun ter (sôn' tər) *v.* to walk leisurely

scav enge (skav' inj) *v.* to take things left by others

scorn ful (skôrn' fəl) *adj.* full of disgust

scur ry (skʉr' ē) *v.* to run quickly; scamper

shod dy (shäd' ē) *adj.* poorly made

shud der (shud' ər) *v.* to tremble violently

shuf fle (shuf' əl) *v.* to walk with a dragging step

skir mish (skʉr' mish) *n.* a minor conflict

slink (sliŋk) *v.* to creep along quietly

sod den (säd' 'n) *adj.* thoroughly wet

sol i tude (säl' ə tōōd') *n.* the state of being alone

so phis ti cat ed (sə fis' tə kāt' id) *adj.* based on much study or knowledge

stag ger (stag' ər) *v.* to stand or move unsteadily

sta tus (stat' əs) *n.* standing; rank

stench (stench) *n.* a strong, offensive odor

stock y (stäk' ē) *adj.* built solidly; sturdy

stoop (stōōp) *n.* a small porch outside the door to a house

stuc co (stuk' ō) *n.* a plaster or cement covering for walls

stu pen dous (stōō pen' dəs) *adj.* tremendous; marvelous

stu por (stōō' pər) *n.* a state of mental dullness; a daze

sub side (səb sīd') *v.* to become weaker; decline

sul len (sul' ən) *adj.* sad and grumpy; sulky

su per fi cial (sōō' pər fish' əl) *adj.* on the surface

sur plus (sʉr' plus') *adj.* extra; more than is needed

sus pend (sə spend') *v.* to keep a person from going to school for a period of time as a punishment

sus tain (sə stān') *v.* to keep alive

syn on y mous (si nän' ə məs) *adj.* having the same meaning

sys tem at ic (sis' tə mat' ik) *adj.* precise and orderly

T

te nac i ty (tə nas' ə tē) *n.* a refusal to give up; persistence

ten e ment (ten' ə mənt) *n.* an apartment building in a run-down, crowded city area

thrash (thrash) *v.* to move wildly

toil (toil) *v.* to work hard and steadily; labor

tol er ate (täl' ər āt') *v.* to put up with

to paz (tō' paz') *adj.* yellow-gold, like the topaz stone

tox ic (täks' ik) *adj.* poisonous

trans fu sion (trans fyōō' zhən) *n.* an addition of blood into the bloodstream, usually done with tubes and an injection needle

tran si tion (tran zish' ən) *n.* a passage from one activity to another

trek (trek) *n.* a slow, difficult journey

tu mult (tōō' mult') *n.* noisy uproar

tu nic (tōō' nik) *n.* a loose, knee-length garment like that worn in ancient Greece and Rome

tur moil (tʉr' moil') *n.* a state of confusion; commotion

tu tor (tōōt' ər) *v.* to give additional instruction

ty rant (tī' rənt) *n.* a harsh, unjust ruler

U

u ni son (yōōn' ə sən) *n.* a speaking of the same words at the same time

V

vain (vān) *n.* (after *in*) without purpose; useless

venge ance (ven' jəns) *n.* a greater force than necessary

W

wel fare (wel' fer') *n.* well-being

wheeze (hwēz) *v.* to make a whistling, breathy sound

wretch ed (rech' id) *adj.* awful

LITERARY AND READING TERMS

Act   An act is a major unit of action in a play. *You're a Good Man, Charlie Brown* is divided into two acts. Each act may have several smaller units of action called **scenes**.

See *Drama* and *Scene*.

Alliteration   The repeating of consonant sounds at the beginnings of two or more words is called alliteration. Poets and songwriters use alliteration to emphasize certain words. Alliteration can also add a musical beat to a work. Note the repetition of the l and r sounds in these lines from "The Cremation of Sam McGee":

In the long, long night, by the lone firelight,
    while the huskies, round in a ring,

Analysis   Analysis is the process in which something is broken down into its parts. Each part is then studied individually to see how it works with other parts. For example, in analyzing a poem, one looks at such elements as form, rhyme, rhythm, figurative language, imagery, mood, and theme.

Anecdote   A short and entertaining account about a person or an event is called an anecdote. Anecdotes are often included in larger works to amuse or to make a point and are often told about a particular person. Gary Paulsen uses an anecdote in his book *Woodsong* to point out that humans must respect the wildness of nature.

Audience   In literature, audience refers to the particular group of people to whom an author is writing. Authors consider their audience when choosing subject matter, a purpose for writing, and the particular style in which they will write.

Author's Purpose   Authors write for many reasons. An author might write to entertain, to inform, or to express an opinion. Authors also write to persuade the reader to do or believe something. The author may combine two or three purposes, but one is usually the most important.

Autobiography   An autobiography is the story of a person's life, written by that person. Autobiographies are normally written in the first-person point of view. Because an autobiography is written about a real person and real events, it is a form of nonfiction. *Woodsong* and *Sweet Summer* are examples of autobiographies.

See *Nonfiction*.

Biography   A biography is the story of a person's life written by another person. Biographies are written in the third-person point of view. "The Real McCoy" is an example of biography.

See *Nonfiction*.

Cast of Characters   A list of the names of the characters in a play is called the cast of characters. The list is presented at the beginning of the script, with characters usually listed in order of appearance. For example, note the cast of characters at the beginning of *A Shipment of Mute Fate*.

See *Drama*.

Cause and Effect   Events are often related by cause and effect. One event brings about, or causes, a second event. The event that happens first is the cause. The second event is the effect. Writers sometimes use clue words or phrases to signal a cause-and-effect relationship. Some of these clue words and phrases are *because, next, therefore, since, so that,* and *in order that.* The following sentence from "The Gold Coin" shows cause and effect: "Because he spent his time either hiding or sneaking about, his body had become shriveled and bent."

Character   Each person, animal, or imaginary creature in a work of literature is called a character. The most important characters are called **main characters**. Less important characters are called **minor characters**. In "Lob's Girl," Sandy and her dog Lob are the main characters. The others in the story are minor characters.

Characterization The way a writer creates and develops a character's personality is called characterization. Writers develop characters in four basic ways: (1) a physical description of the character; (2) the character's thoughts, speech, and actions; (3) the thoughts, speech, and actions of other characters; and (4) direct comments on a character's nature.

Chronological Order Chronological order is the order in which events happen in time. "A Secret for Two" follows chronological order, beginning with the meeting of Pierre and Joseph.

Climax The climax is the high point of interest in the plot of a story. At the climax, the outcome of the story becomes clear. The climax of "Tuesday of the Other June," for example, occurs when June T. says "No" to the other June with such forceful determination that the astonished bully leaves her alone.
   See *Plot*.

Comparison To point out what two or more different things have in common is to make a comparison. Writers use comparisons to make certain ideas or details clearer to the reader. For example, in "Unfolding Bud," a poem is compared to the unfolding bud of a water-lily.

Concrete Poetry See *Form*.

Conflict A struggle between opposing forces is called conflict. The struggle faced by a character creates the conflict that is important to every story and play. Conflict may be external or internal. **External conflict** often occurs between a character and an outside force such as society, a force in nature, or even another character. For example, in the excerpt from *Woodsong*, Gary Paulsen faces an external conflict with a bear. **Internal conflict** is a struggle within a character's mind. An internal conflict often occurs when a character has to make a difficult decision or deal with opposing feelings. In "Cricket in the Road," Selo experiences internal conflict over whether or not to make up with his friends.

Connecting When readers relate the content of a literary work to what they already know or have experienced, they are making connections. Connecting helps the reader identify with the experiences of the characters. For example, when they read the story "Eleven" by Sandra Cisneros, readers may remember times they were embarrassed or falsely accused.

Context Clues Readers can pick up context clues from the words or phrases before or after an unfamiliar word in a sentence. Context clues may define the word, give a synonym or an example, or provide comparisons or contrasts, to help a reader infer the meaning.

Contrast To contrast means to point out the differences between two or more things. Note how the narrator in "The All-American Slurp" contrasts Chinese and American eating habits in the following sentence: "In fact we didn't use individual plates at all but picked food from the platters in the middle of the table and brought it directly to our rice bowls."

Description In description, a writer creates a picture of a scene, an event, or a character. Writers choose details carefully to create descriptions. These details usually appeal to a reader's sense of sight, sound, smell, touch, or taste. Note the details in these sentences from "My Friend Flicka" in which Mary O'Hara describes the view outside Kennie's window.

> The hill opposite the house, covered with arrow-straight jack pines, was sharply etched in the thin air of the eight-thousand-foot altitude. Where it fell away, vivid green grass ran up to meet it; and over range and upland poured the strong Wyoming sunlight that stung everything into burning color.

Dialect Language that is spoken in a particular place by a certain group or class of people is called a dialect. A dialect may have different pronunciations and grammatical rules than the standard form of language. Written dialect is usually spelled as it is pronounced. Note the dialect that

Gus, the Swedish ranch hand in "My Friend Flicka," uses as he tells how Kennie and Flicka might have spent their night in the stream. "All night dat boy sits dere and says, 'Hold on, Flicka, Ay'm here wid you.'"

Dialogue   A conversation between two or more characters is called dialogue. Dialogue moves the story forward and reveals the personalities of the characters. Dialogue is usually set off with quotation marks. In a play, however, dialogue is the main way the writer tells the story. No quotation marks are used for dialogue in plays.

Drama   A drama, or play, is a form of literature meant to be performed before an audience. The story is presented through the dialogue and the actions of the characters. The written form of the play is known as the **script**. The script usually includes the **dialogue**, the **cast of characters**, and the **stage directions**, which give specific instructions about performing the play.

See *Act, Cast of Characters, Dialogue, Scene,* and *Stage Directions.*

Evaluating   The process of judging the worth of something or someone is called evaluating. To evaluate a literary work, look closely at the elements found in that type of literature. For example, in fiction you might study plot, setting, character, and theme. You might also evaluate literature by comparing and contrasting it with similar works.

External Conflict   See *Conflict.*

Fable   A brief story that teaches a lesson about life is called a fable. The characters in fables may be humans, or they may be animals that act and speak like humans. Fables often end with a moral, a statement that summarizes the story's lesson. "The Disobedient Child" is an example of a fable.

Fact and Opinion   A fact is a statement that can be proved, such as "Mars is the fourth planet from the sun." In contrast, an opinion is a statement that expresses a person's feelings, such as "Mars is the most beautiful planet." Opinions cannot be proved.

Fiction   Literature that tells about imaginary people, places, or events is called fiction. Writers of fiction may make up an entire story, or they may base part of a story on real people or events. Fiction includes both short stories and novels. Short stories can usually be read in one sitting. Novels are longer and tend to be more complex.

Figurative Language   Language that expresses something more than the dictionary meaning of words is called figurative language. Figurative language paints vivid images in the minds of readers. Three kinds of figurative language are **simile, metaphor**, and **personification.** In "The Circuit," figurative language helps create a picture of working in the fields.

> The sun kept beating down. The buzzing insects, the wet sweat, and the hot, dry dust made the afternoon seem to last forever. Finally the mountains around the valley reached out and swallowed the sun.

See *Simile, Metaphor,* and *Personification.*

Flashback   A flashback is an interruption in the events of a story to present an event that took place before the story's beginning. The information that a flashback provides about the past helps to explain the present actions or attitudes of characters. For example, in *A Shipment of Mute Fate*, a flashback explains how the snake was captured.

Folk Tale   A folk tale is a simple story that has been handed down by word of mouth from one generation to another. Folk tales are usually about humans, animals, or occurrences in nature and are usually set in a time long past. Folk tale plots often include supernatural elements, such as the talking animals in "Why Monkeys Live in Trees" or the granting of wishes in "The Three Wishes."

Foreshadowing   A hint about an event that will occur later in a story is called foreshadowing. Note that in the opening lines of *A Shipment of Mute Fate,* the main character, Chris, warns the reader that a disturbing event will take place: "But all at once in the midst of those peaceful surroundings, a cold chill gripped me, and I shivered with sudden dread—dread of the thing I was doing, and was about to do!"

Form   The shape of the words and lines of a poem on the page is called form. Occasionally, a poet uses the form of a poem to emphasize the poem's meaning. In **concrete poetry**, for example, the shape of the poem reflects the ideas expressed in the poem. Note how the form of Mel Glenn's poem "Crystal Rowe (Track Star)" resembles the parts of a race.
See *Poetry.*

Free Verse   Poetry with no regular patterns of rhyme, rhythm, or line length is called free verse. Free verse often sounds like conversation. Myra Cohn Livingston's poem "74th Street" is written in free verse.
See *Poetry.*

Generalization   A statement made about a whole group is called a generalization. For example, in "The All-American Slurp," the character Meg makes a generalization when she says, "All Americans slurp." The word *all* in this generalization makes the statement untrue. Many generalizations are too broad and are not based on fact.

Genre   Literature is normally divided into four main categories, or genres. These four genres are **fiction, nonfiction, poetry,** and **drama.**
See *Fiction, Nonfiction, Poetry,* and *Drama.*

Haiku   Haiku is a traditional form of Japanese poetry that describes a single moment, feeling, or thing. A haiku normally has three lines. Traditionally, the first line has a total of five syllables, the second line has seven syllables, and the third line has five syllables.

Humor   The quality that makes writing funny or amusing to the reader is called humor. Writers can create humor by using exaggeration, amusing descriptions, sarcasm, witty dialogue, and other devices. For example, Ann Cameron uses more than one meaning for the words *beating* and *whipping* to create humor in "The Pudding Like a Night on the Sea."

Imagery   Words and phrases that appeal to the reader's senses are referred to as imagery. Writers describe characters, places, and events in ways that help the reader imagine how they look, feel, smell, sound, or taste. Note the imagery in these lines from "Mama Is a Sunrise."

When she comes sweet-talking in the room,
    she warms us
    like grits and gravy,
    and we rise up shining.

See *Sensory Details.*

Inference   An inference is a logical guess based on facts or evidence. Readers make inferences or draw conclusions as they read. They infer, or figure out, more than the words say. The evidence may be facts the writer provides, or it may be experiences from the reader's life. For example, based on your own experiences with brothers or sisters and this dialogue from *You're a Good Man, Charlie Brown,* you can infer that Linus knows when to let Lucy have her way.

Lucy. OK, switch channels.
Linus. Are you kidding? What makes you think you can come right in here and take over!
Lucy (*holding out her hand*). These five fingers individually are nothing. But when I curl them together into a single unit, they become a fighting force terrible to behold.
Linus. Which channel do you want?

Internal Conflict   See *Conflict.*

Interview   A meeting in which one person is asked about personal matters, professional matters, or both is called an interview. Interviews may be written, recorded, or filmed. The excerpt from *How It Feels When Parents Divorce* is an example of an interview that was first recorded and then later transcribed into print.

Legend   A legend is a story handed down from the past that explains something that really happened or tells about someone who really lived. Legends often mix fact and fiction. "The White Buffalo Calf Woman and the Sacred Pipe" is an example of a Native American legend.

Main Idea   The main idea is the central idea that a writer is trying to get across. The main idea may refer to the central idea of the entire work or simply to the topic sentence of a paragraph. Topic sentences may be found at the beginning, middle, or end of a paragraph. A writer may need to use more than one paragraph to develop a main idea. In the following paragraph from *Save the Earth,* the main idea is stated in a topic sentence at the beginning of the paragraph.

The earth is always changing. Storms and fires, winds and droughts, earthquakes and floods, and the slow, strong force of water over rock change the land and seas and the climate around them. Over long periods of time these natural changes have affected all life on earth.

Metaphor   A comparison of two different things that have something in common is called a metaphor. A metaphor does not use words such as *like, as, than,* or *resembles.* For example, in *A Shipment of Mute Fate,* Chris uses the following metaphor: "Fear was a heavy fog in the lungs of all of us."
See *Figurative Language.*

Minor Character   See *Character.*

Mood   Mood is the feeling that the writer wants the reader to get from a work of literature. Writers carefully choose words and phrases to create such feelings as sadness, excitement, or anger. For example, a mood of deep sadness is created in "My Friend Flicka" when it appears that Flicka will die in the stream.

Motive   The motive is the reason a character says or does something. For example, in "Flowers and Freckle Cream," the young girl's motive for buying freckle cream is her desire to get rid of her freckles.

Myth   A myth is a traditional story that explains how something came to be. Myths may explain such things as human behavior or the origins of the world and people. They may also explain certain elements of nature or social customs.

Because myths have been handed down from one generation to the next for a long time, the original authors are unknown. The characters in myths are often gods and human heroes with supernatural abilities. The selection *Wings* is a retelling of a myth of ancient Greece.

Narrative   Writing that tells a story is called a narrative. The events in a narrative may be real or imagined. Fictional narratives include myths, short stories, novels, and narrative poems. Narratives that deal with real events include autobiographies and biographies.

Narrative Poetry   Narrative poetry is poetry that tells a story. Like all stories, narrative poetry has a setting, characters, and a plot. Like much poetry, narrative poems may also have rhyme, rhythm, imagery, and figurative language. "The Walrus and the Carpenter" is an example of narrative poetry.
See *Poetry.*

Narrator   The teller of a story is called the narrator. In some stories the narrator is a character who takes part in the action. At other times the narrator is an outside voice created by the author. For example, the narrator of "The Scribe" is James, the main character, while the narrator for "Two Dreamers" is an outside voice.
See *Point of View.*

Nonfiction   Nonfiction is writing that tells about real people, places, and events. There are two broad types of nonfiction. Informative nonfiction provides factual information. Examples include newspaper or magazine articles, pamphlets, history and science textbooks, and encyclopedia articles. Literary nonfiction reads much like fiction, except that the characters, setting, and plot are real rather than imaginary. Autobiographies, biographies, memoirs, journals, and diaries are examples of literary nonfiction.

Novel   A novel is a work of fiction that is longer and more complex than a short story. The setting, plot, and characters of a novel are developed in detail. The plot usually focuses on the actions and personalities of a group of characters.

Onomatopoeia   The use of words to imitate sounds is called onomatopoeia. The words *bang* and *hiss* are examples of onomatopoeia. Notice the onomatopoetic words in this passage from "Yhi Brings the Earth to Life."

> But somewhere there began the steady *drip, drip, drip* of water, free at last. Then, a *cracking* and *crashing* as great slabs of ice lost their freezing hold on the cave walls.

Personification   Personification is the giving of human qualities to an animal, object, or idea. In "Why Monkeys Live in Trees," Julius Lester uses personification by having the animals act and speak like humans.

Persuasion   Writing that is meant to change a reader's feelings, beliefs, or actions is called persuasion. Persuasive writing usually contains both facts and opinions. In this way the writer can appeal to both the mind and the emotions of the reader. The excerpt from *Save the Earth* is an example of persuasive writing.

Play   See *Drama*.

Plot   The series of events in a story is called the plot. The plot usually centers around a conflict—a problem faced by the main character. Most plots follow a regular pattern. The action that the characters take to solve the problem builds toward the **climax**, or turning point of the story. At this point, or shortly thereafter, the problem is solved and the story ends.
See *Climax* and *Conflict*.

Poetry   Poetry is a type of literature that often uses a few words to express ideas, images, and feelings. The language of poetry is imaginative and musical. Poets carefully select words for their sounds and meanings. They combine these words in unusual ways to present different feelings, pictures, experiences, and themes. The images in poetry appeal to the reader's senses. Poems may also possess elements of sound, such as alliteration, rhythm, or rhyme. Normally, poetry is written in lines, which are sometimes grouped into stanzas.
See *Alliteration, Figurative Language, Form, Imagery, Narrative Poetry, Rhyme, Rhyme Scheme, Rhythm,* and *Stanza.*

Point of View   Point of view refers to how a writer tells a story. Most stories are told from either the first-person or third-person points of view. In the first-person point of view, the narrator is a character in the story and uses pronouns like *I, me,* and *we.* For example, "Eleven" by Sandra Cisneros is written in the first-person point of view.

In the third-person point of view, the narrator is outside the story and uses pronouns such as *he, she,* and *they.* "Aaron's Gift" by Myron Levoy is written in the third-person point of view.
See *Narrator.*

Predicting   Predicting means guessing what might happen in the future, on the basis of what you already know. Good readers gather information as they read. They combine that information with their own experiences to predict what might happen next in a story.

Questioning   The process of asking questions when reading is called questioning. Good readers ask questions in order to understand what is happening in a piece of literature. As they read on, they look for answers to their questions.

Radio Play   A radio play is a form of drama that is written specifically to be broadcast over the radio. Because the audience cannot see the play, sound effects are used to help listeners imagine the setting and action. These sound effects appear in the stage directions of the script. *A Shipment of Mute Fate* by Les Crutchfield is an example of a radio play.

Refrain   A word, phrase, line, or group of lines that is repeated regularly in a poem or song is called a refrain.

Repetition   Repetition is the use of a word or phrase over and over again in a literary work. Writers use repetition to bring certain ideas, sounds, or feelings to the reader's attention. In the poem "Forgotten Language," Shel Silverstein uses repetition for emphasis.

Reviewing   Reviewing means pausing while reading a story and thinking about the events that have already taken place. Readers check their understanding when reviewing by reflecting on what they have found out about certain characters in the story. This information is used to infer what is happening and to better understand the selection.

Rhyme   Rhyme is the repetition of sounds at the ends of words. In poetry, words can rhyme either within lines or at the ends of lines. Rhyme that occurs within a line is called **internal rhyme**. Rhyme that occurs at the ends of lines is called **end rhyme**. Note both the internal rhyme and end rhyme in these lines from "The Cremation of Sam McGee."

> Now a promise *made* is a debt *unpaid*,
>   and the trail has its own stern *code*.
> In the days to *come*, though my lips were *dumb*,
>   in my heart how I cursed that *load!*

> See *Poetry*.

Rhyme Scheme   The pattern of rhyme at the ends of lines of poetry is called the rhyme scheme. A rhyme scheme is noted by assigning letters of the alphabet to the lines of a poem. The letters show which lines end with the same sounds.

Note the rhyme scheme below of the first four lines of Eleanor Farjeon's "The Quarrel."

I quarreled with my *brother*	a
I don't know what *about*	b
One thing led to *another*	a
And somehow we fell *out*.	b

Rhythm   In poetry, the pattern of stressed and unstressed syllables is called rhythm. Poems with a regular, even beat have a musical sound. Note the regular rhythm in these lines from Kaye Starbird's "The Spelling Test." The stressed syllables are marked with a ∕. The unstressed syllables are marked with a ◡.

> One morning in a spelling test
> The teacher said to Hugh:
> "I have a word for you to spell
> The word is 'kangaroo.'"

> See *Poetry*.

Scene   A scene is a unit in a play that takes place in one setting. A scene changes in a play when the story calls for a change in time or place. The play *A Christmas Carol*, for example, has six scenes.

See *Drama*.

Science Fiction   Fiction that is based on real or possible scientific developments is called science fiction. The setting of science fiction is often in the future, though the problems that characters face may be similar to real problems people face today. "Playing for Keeps," a story about an invasion by aliens from outer space, is an example of science fiction.

Sensory Details   Words and phrases that help the reader see, hear, taste, smell, and feel what the writer is describing are called sensory details. Note the sensory details that describe the flight of Icarus in this passage from *Wings*.

> He passed into the realm of the sun. Too late he felt the wax run down his arms; too late he smelled the singe of feathers. Surprised, he hung solid in the air. Then, like a star in nova, he tumbled from the sky down, down, down into the waiting sea.

Sequence   Sequence refers to the order in which events occur or ideas are presented. In a story, events are usually presented in time order, or the order in which they happened. Writers use clue words and phrases such as *then, until, after a while*, and *finally* to show the reader the sequence of events.

Setting   Setting is the time and place in which a story happens. The time may be past, present, or future. The place can be real or imaginary. In some stories, including many fables, the setting may not be clearly defined. In other stories, however, the setting plays an important part. For example, the seaside setting of "Lob's Girl" plays an important part in the story's action.

See *Fiction.*

Setting a Purpose   The process of establishing specific reasons to read a selection is called setting a purpose. Readers can use such information as the title of a selection, headings and subheadings, and illustrations to guess what a selection may be about. Readers then use their guesses to guide their reading, discovering whether their ideas match the actual content of the selection.

Short Story   A short story is a work of fiction that can generally be read in one sitting. Like other works of fiction, short stories have characters, plot, setting, and theme. The plot of a short story usually involves one main conflict. "The Secret of the Wall" is an example of a short story.

See *Fiction.*

Simile   A comparison of two different things that have something in common is called a simile. Similes contain such words as *like, as, resembles,* or *than.* Writers use these comparisons to help the reader see things in new ways. Note the following simile from "The Bamboo Beads": "That night the moon was round and white as my Sunday hat."

See *Figurative Language.*

Skimming   Skimming is reading quickly to get the general idea of a piece of writing. When you skim you read titles, headings, words in special print, and the first sentence in paragraphs.

Slang   Very informal, everyday speech that is outside the standard version of a language is called slang. Slang is usually spoken by a particular group of people at a particular time. Many slang terms are either new words or old words that have taken on a new meaning. For example, *cool* is a slang term that has come to mean "good" or "neat." Slang words and phrases often go out-of-date very quickly.

Slave Narrative   A true story told by a former slave is called a slave narrative. "Carrying the Running-Aways" by Virginia Hamilton is an example of a slave narrative.

Soliloquy   In drama, a soliloquy is a speech in which a character speaks his thoughts aloud. People in the audience feel as if they are overhearing a character talking to himself or herself. In *You're a Good Man, Charlie Brown,* Charlie Brown delivers a soliloquy as he talks about lunchtime, loneliness, and the cute little redheaded girl.

Speaker   The speaker in a poem is the voice that talks to the reader. The speaker in a poem is like the narrator in a work of fiction. The poet is not necessarily the same as the speaker in a poem; however, the speaker may express the feelings of the poet.

See *Poetry.*

Stage Directions   Instructions that help the performers, director, and stage crew present a play are called stage directions. These instructions usually appear in italics within parentheses in the script of a play. Stage directions provide suggestions about such things as scenery, lighting, music, and sound effects. They may also tell performers how to move or speak their lines. Note the following stage directions from *Damon and Pythias.*

> **Damon** (*calm and firm*). I have faith in my
>   friend. I know he will return.
> **King** (*mocking*). We shall see!
>   *Sound: (Iron door shut and locked.)*
> See *Drama.*

Stanza   In poetry, a group of lines is called a stanza. A stanza is somewhat like a paragraph in a story. The poem "The Walrus and the Carpenter," for example, has eighteen stanzas.

See *Poetry.*

Summarizing   To summarize means to tell briefly in your own words the main idea of a piece of writing. When you summarize, you condense your ideas or those of the writer into precise statements. You omit unimportant details.

Suspense   Suspense is the growing feeling of tension and excitement that makes a reader curious about the outcome of a story or an event within a story. For example, suspense occurs in "The Secret of the Wall" when Carlos is suddenly trapped within the walls of an old house.

Symbol   A symbol is a person, a place, or an object that stands for something outside of itself. In literature, objects and images are used to symbolize things that cannot actually be seen, such as an idea or a feeling. In "Flowers and Freckle Cream," for example, the tiger lily Elizabeth receives from her grandfather may symbolize the beauty he sees in her freckled appearance.

Theme   The theme is the message about life or human nature that the writer presents to the reader.

Some themes are stated directly. Most often, however, the reader must figure out a theme. Any lessons learned by the main character can be clues to a theme. For example, a theme of "The Scribe" might be that helping people is not a simple matter.

Tone   A writer's attitude toward his or her subject is called tone. The tone may reflect one strong feeling, such as the tone of admiration in "Mama Is a Sunrise." On the other hand, the tone in a story may consist of several emotions. In "Fire!" for example, the tone toward the main character, the grandfather, seems to be a mixture of fear, wonder, and respect.

Visualizing   Forming a mental picture from a written description is called visualizing. Readers use details of sight, sound, touch, taste, and feeling to visualize the characters, settings, and events in a work of literature. Mentally picturing a writer's descriptions makes reading more enjoyable and memorable.

BIOGRAPHIES OF THE AUTHORS

Alma Flor Ada

Alma Flor Ada *(1938–   )* was inspired to write "The Gold Coin" by an encounter with migrant workers. She was touched by the dignity with which they carried out their hard daily labor. Raised in Cuba and now a professor in the United States, Ada has created stories in Spanish and in English for young people. She is a recipient of the Christopher Award.

Art Buchwald *(1925–   )* is one of America's most famous writers of humor. He often pokes fun at a part of American life—as he does in "Love and the Cabbie"—by presenting a conversation between himself and someone who is an "expert" observer of human behavior. Buchwald's popular newspaper column appears twice weekly around the world.

Ann Cameron *(1943–   )* grew up in northern Wisconsin. She wrote the book *The Stories Julian Tells,* from which "The Pudding Like a Night on the Sea" comes, after hearing stories a South African friend shared about his childhood. In the tale of the forbidden pudding, Cameron saw an experience that everyone could identify with, based on the idea that "just a *little* bit won't hurt."

Arthur Cavanaugh

Arthur Cavanaugh *(1926–   )* is a native of Woodhaven, New York, who now lives in New York City. He has created television plays, short stories (one of which earned an O. Henry Award), and four novels. "Miss Awful" is based on the experiences of his son, who attended a school in the Greenwich Village section of New York City.

Sandra Cisneros *(1954–   )* remembers moving frequently as a child, particularly between Chicago—her birthplace—and Mexico. "I didn't like school because we moved so much, and I was always new and funny looking," she says. It was her out-of-class reading that sparked her interest in writing. Cisneros has won praise both in this country and abroad for her writings about Mexican Americans.

© Layle Silbert

Lucille Clifton

Lucille Clifton *(1936–   )* was the poet laureate, the official poet, of Maryland from 1979 to 1982. An author of nonfiction and fiction as well as poetry, Clifton often portrays family life in urban communities. In 1984 she won the Coretta Scott King Award for her children's book *Everett Anderson's Goodbye.*

Elizabeth Ellis *(1943–   )* was a children's librarian before becoming a full-time professional storyteller in 1979. She is a native of the Appalachian mountain region of Tennessee. The story "Flowers and Freckle Cream" is based on experiences she had while spending summers with her grandfather in Kentucky. Ellis credits her grandfather with giving her a love of stories and an ability to see the beauty in everyone.

Eleanor Farjeon *(1881–1965)* had a career as a writer that spanned seventy years. Her poetry, plays, and fantasies reveal the joy she took in living. Farjeon was the first children's writer to receive the Hans Christian Andersen Award. The Children's Book Circle in England established the Eleanor Farjeon Award in her memory.

James Cross Giblin *(1933–   )*, a children's-book editor and author, enjoys writing books filled with facts. Giblin says, "I try to write books that I would have enjoyed reading when I was the age of my readers." His book *From Hand to Mouth: Or, How We Invented Knives, Forks, Spoons, and Chopsticks and the Table Manners to Go with Them* has won numerous awards.

Mel Glenn *(1943–   )* became a writer as a result of his interest in teaching. He has worked as a teacher in Sierra Leone, West Africa, as well as in his hometown of Brooklyn, New York. Glenn's collection of poems, *Class Dismissed! High School Poems*, was selected as a Best Book for Young Adults by the American Library Association.

Harriett Starleaf Gumbs   lives on the Shinnecock Indian Reservation on Long Island, New York, and can trace her roots there through thirteen generations. An elder of her tribe, she has fought to protect the tribe's land, saying, "We only ask to survive so that we can remain who and what we are." Harriett Starleaf Gumbs has also taken a part in the struggle of Shinnecock women to gain the right to vote within their tribe.

Jack C. Haldeman II *(1941–   )* specializes in a unique kind of science fiction that deals with sports of the future. He says that to create his stories, "I often draw on my scientific background as well as my sense of humor." Haldeman's short stories have appeared in the magazines *Omni, Twilight Zone,* and *Isaac Asimov's Science Fiction.*

Virginia Hamilton *(1936–   )* is the first writer in history to have a novel, *M.C. Higgins, the Great,* win both a Newbery Medal and a National Book Award. Hamilton grew up on a small farm in Ohio, listening to stories told by her relatives. Much of her work, which includes realistic fiction, fantasies, biographies, and folk tales, is influenced by her childhood and incorporates elements of history.

LANGSTON HUGHES

Langston Hughes *(1902–1967)* did not have children in mind when he wrote his poems; however, the intelligent simplicity of his language has appealed to the young for several decades. Hughes's basic goal was to portray the joys and sorrows of African-American life. His writings often featured the ordinary people of Harlem, a section of New York City.

Evelyn Tooley Hunt *(1904–)* graduated from William Smith College, where she edited its literary magazine. Her first poetry collection, *Look Again, Adam,* published in 1961, won the Sidney Lanier Memorial Award. Hunt's interest in different cultures is apparent in her writing, particularly in her variations of haiku, a form of Japanese poetry.

Kristin Hunter *(1931–)* is known for her realistic descriptions of urban life; many of her books are set in cities similar to the one described in "The Scribe." At fourteen she was a teen columnist and feature writer for the Philadelphia edition of the *Pittsburgh Courier.* Hunter has produced novels, short stories, poems, and magazine articles for a wide audience.

JILL KREMENTZ

Jill Krementz *(1940–)* explores children's innermost feelings during emotional crises in the books *How It Feels to Be Adopted, How It Feels When a Parent Dies,* and *How It Feels When Parents Divorce.* Whether she is photographing children or interviewing them, Krementz has, as one critic said, "an uncanny gift for bringing out the best in all her subjects."

John D. MacDonald *(1916–1986)* was a best-selling mystery writer who created a popular series of detective novels featuring the character Travis McGee. Over 70 million copies of his books have been sold worldwide. Many of MacDonald's works, which include short stories, science fiction, and nonfiction, have become television shows and movies.

Toshi Maruki *(1912–)* is an author and highly regarded artist. She based her book *Hiroshima No Pika* on the story of a survivor of the attack on Hiroshima whom she met at an exhibit of her paintings dealing with the atomic bomb. Maruki herself was a witness to the effects of the bomb; she went into Hiroshima to help the survivors. Since the end of World War II, she has campaigned for nuclear disarmament and world peace.

TOSHI MARUKI

Lillian Morrison *(1917–)* is a poet, librarian, and compiler of anthologies—a selector of other people's writings for publication. She spent nearly ten years researching and collecting poems about almost every kind of sport to produce a book called *Sprints and Distances: Sports in Poetry and Poetry in Sport.*

Abiodun Oyewole reflects in his poetry his deep commitment to young people, his sensitivity to the cultural heritage of African Americans, and his love of life. Oyewole has also created plays and songs and has led a jazz group called *Griot* (named for a type of African storyteller).

Dudley Randall *(1914–   )* has contributed to literature not only as a poet but as the founder of Detroit's Broadside Press, which has published the work of many African-American poets. For his achievements, Randall was named the first poet laureate of Detroit, Michigan, in 1981.

DUDLEY RANDALL

Quentin Reynolds *(1902–1965)* became famous as a war correspondent during World War II. He presented emotional and vivid reports of battles in North Africa and Europe. In addition to his articles and short stories, Reynolds wrote twenty-four books, including an autobiography that focuses on his experiences during the war.

Cynthia Rylant *(1954–   )* lacked money for books as a child growing up in West Virginia but was captured by the wonder of children's books as an adult, while working in a library. In her career she has produced award-winning poetry, picture books, short stories, and novels for children and young adults.

Gary Soto *(1952–   )* often writes about the experiences of Mexican Americans. Although the Fresno, California, native first earned recognition for his poetry, it was his collection of autobiographical essays, *Living up the Street: Narrative Recollections,* that won an American Book Award in 1985. *Baseball in April and Other Stories,* from which "Two Dreamers" is taken, is a collection of short stories for young people.

GARY SOTO

Kaye Starbird *(1916–   )* says she draws her ideas from personal experience and from her "galloping imagination." She started writing at the age of eight and began publishing poetry in magazines while still in college. Starbird, who also writes under the name C. S. Jennison, has written books for children and adults.

May Swenson *(1919–1989)* experimented with constucting poems in which the words are arranged in the shapes of the poems' subjects. This award-winning poet has been praised for the imaginative quality of her observations. Her book *Poems to Solve* presents thirty-five poems that contain riddles, unusual metaphors, hidden meanings, and ideas to puzzle and challenge the reader.

MAY SWENSON

THE WRITING PROCESS

Writing is a process—a series of steps taken to create a finished product. The process a writer uses is unique to him or her and may not be the same for every writing experience. You need to develop your own writing process, one that works best for you.

Many writers focus their thinking and writing in stages similar to the ones outlined on these pages and shown in the graphic below. Use these stages as a guide, but feel free to go backward or forward in the procedure and to shorten or even skip some stages if you are comfortable doing so.

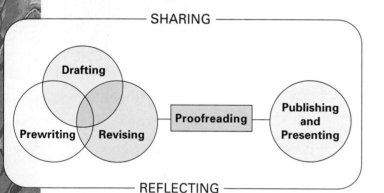

Prewriting and Exploring

Before you write, you think and plan. The following steps might help you get started:

1. Clarify the Assignment

When you are given a writing assignment, make sure you understand what you are being asked to write. To clarify your task, fill out as much of a PASSkey as you can for the assignment by answering the following questions:

P = Purpose

Is the purpose stated in the assignment?
Do I want to express ideas or feelings? to inform? to entertain? to analyze? to persuade?

A = Audience

Who will read my writing?
How much about the subject do my readers know?
How much more do they need to know?
What might they find interesting?
How do I want my audience to respond?

S = Subject

Has a topic been assigned?
What topic do I know about or want to explore?
What topic can I handle well in the length of time that has been assigned?

S = Structure

Has a structure or form been assigned?
What organization would help me accomplish my purpose?
What should the final product look like?

2. Get Ideas for a Topic

Try some of these different ways of finding topics:

Recalling   Remember events and scenes from your past. Look through family photo albums, scrapbooks, diaries, or your journal to jog your memory. Talk to family members or old friends. Think of the first time you did something.

Brainstorming   With a partner or a small group of classmates, think of and jot down as many ideas as possible. One person's ideas will spur another's. Keep the atmosphere positive and don't stop to evaluate. Ideas should be generated, not judged.

Listing   Write a topic or category at the top of a page and list every idea you can think of that relates to it. Go in as many different directions as your imagination will allow.

Freewriting   Choose a topic you want to explore and write the first thing that pops into your head. For about three minutes, keep writing everything that comes into your mind. Don't worry about grammar, spelling, or punctuation, and don't stop to read what you've written. After a few minutes, stop writing, read what you wrote, and pick out any ideas that you want to explore further.

Webbing   Write a central idea in the middle of your page and circle it. Outside the circle write related ideas. Circle each and draw a line connecting it to the central idea. Do the same for each related idea, as in the idea web below.

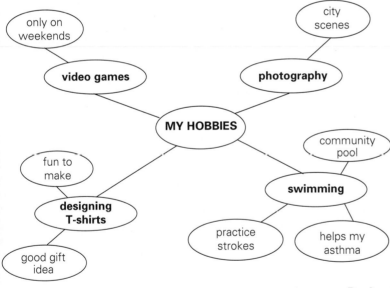

3. Choose and Limit Your Topic

Choose a topic that excites you—one you know about or would like to learn about. Narrow your topic to a size you can deal with in the length of your paper. For example, "my family" is too broad a topic to cover in a short composition, but a topic like "my brother's funny habits" could be handled easily.

4. Gather Information

Although different kinds of writing require you to gather information in different ways, most writing involves doing some research and/or using your imagination. If you write an informative or persuasive paper, you must do research to get facts and statistics. If you write about your own experience, you will delve into your memory. If you create fiction or drama, you will use your imagination, but you might do research as well. When you write about literature, you study the literary work itself. For whatever type of writing you do, make notes on a piece of paper, index cards, or a computer screen to record your thoughts .

5. Organize Your Ideas

After you have all the information and ideas you need, organize your notes into the order in which you wish to present your ideas. You can organize by outlining, numbering, using graphic devices, arranging index cards, or moving sections of notes around on a computer screen.

Draft and Discover

When you draft, you begin to put your ideas on paper, following any notes, graphics, or outlines you have made. Drafting is a time to let ideas flow without concern for spelling and punctuation. Errors can be corrected later.

Revise Your Writing

When you revise, you judge the strengths and weaknesses of your paper. You can do this by yourself or with a peer reader. Try to improve what you said and how you said it.

Look for ways you can improve your writing by asking yourself questions about the content. The revision questions on the next page will help you get started.

When you are satisfied with the content of your writing, check for mistakes in grammar, usage, capitalization, punctuation, and spelling. Use proofreading symbols to mark these errors. Then make a clean, corrected copy of your paper.

Proofreading Symbols

Symbol	Meaning	Example
∧	insert	leson
≡	capitalize	douglass
/	lowercase	History
∿	transpose	veiw
ℐ	take out	lots of
¶	paragraph	¶The
⊙	add a period	slavery⊙
⌃	add a comma	Finally⌄

Publish and Present

You communicate with others by sharing your writing. Here are a few possible ways to do this.

- Read your writing aloud to classmates.

- Trade papers with a classmate so that you can read each other's work.

- Publish everyone's work in your own magazine.

- Submit your writing to a school newspaper.

- Tape-record a reading of your work.

- Videotape classmates acting out your writing.

Reflect on Your Writing

After you have completed your writing, think about it and the process you went through to complete it. What have you discovered about your own writing process? Should you change your method the next time around? By learning from what you do each time, you will constantly improve your personal writing process.

TIPS FOR BETTER PARAGRAPHS

Paragraphs are the building blocks of writing. Whether a paragraph stands by itself or is part of a longer composition, such as an essay or a story, it needs to be solidly constructed.

The following information will help you understand paragraphs and give you tips for constructing better paragraphs.

What Is a Paragraph?

A **paragraph** is a group of related sentences that work together to develop a main idea or accomplish a single purpose. Each paragraph that follows has a single main idea or purpose. In the model below, the first sentence states the main idea.

> We have bear trouble. Because we feed processed meat to the dogs, there is always the smell of meat over the kennel. In the summer it can be a bit high because the dogs like to "save" their food sometimes for a day or two or four—burying it to dig up later. We live on the edge of wilderness, and consequently the meat smell brings any number of visitors from the woods.
>
> Gary Paulsen, from *Woodsong*

In the next model paragraph, no one sentence states the main idea. Instead, all the sentences work together for a single purpose—to describe aliens from outer space.

> The aliens stood about eight feet tall with thick, stocky bodies. Their four arms had too many elbows and not enough fingers. Folds of wrinkled green skin covered their neckless heads, and their three unblinking eyes held what could only be interpreted as malice and contempt for the entire human race.
>
> Jack C. Haldeman II, "Playing for Keeps"

Unity and Coherence

Well-written paragraphs, such as the previous models, reflect two characteristics: unity and coherence. A paragraph has **unity** when all the sentences tell about one main idea or serve a single purpose. In the example below, one of the sentences strays from the topic. Can you tell which one?

> I thought my grandmother's college graduation would be boring. I was wrong. Everyone there seemed excited to see her achieve a goal that had been out of reach for so many years. A news crew from a local TV station videotaped the moment when Grandma crossed the stage to get her degree. It must take hard work to become a TV reporter. The entire auditorium cheered for Grandma.

The sentence "It must take hard work to become a TV reporter" has nothing to do with the description of the graduation. The sentence breaks the unity of the paragraph. It strays from the point and may confuse readers.

A paragraph has **coherence** when the sentences flow smoothly and logically from beginning to end. In a well-written paragraph, the relationship between the sentences is clear to the reader. Compare the following two paragraphs. Which has more coherence?

> The origins of the bicycle can be traced back over two thousand years. The bicycle was used in Egypt and Italy. It did not look much like the ones riders now use. The bicycle of long ago looked like a modern-day scooter. It could only be moved by pushing one's foot against the ground. It could not be steered. The early bicycle appeared not to be practical or safe.

> The origins of the bicycle can be traced back over two thousand years. *Originally,* the bicycle was used in ancient Egypt and Italy. *However,* it did not look much like the ones

riders now use. *On the contrary,* the bicycle of long ago looked like a modern-day scooter. *Similarly,* it could only be moved by pushing one's foot against the ground. It could not be steered, *unlike* today's scooter. The early bicycle, *therefore,* appeared to be *neither* practical *nor* safe.

The second paragraph in the pair is more coherent because it makes use of **transitions,** the words in italic type. Transitions are the connecting words that let readers know how the details in a paragraph are related.

Some common transitions show relationships of time and space. Others point out comparison and contrast and other logical relationships.

When you revise your paragraphs, check to make sure that your sentences are clearly connected to one another. When necessary, add transition words to help make the relationships clearer.

The chart below lists words and phrases commonly used as transitions.

Transition Words and Phrases

Time Order	before then during	after meanwhile first	then yesterday second
Spatial Order	above around inside	below to the left outside	behind on top of in front of
Order of Importance	first second third	most important less important least important	strongest most significant weakest
Comparison	as similarly neither/nor	than in the same way either/ or	like by comparison also
Contrast	yet unlike nevertheless	but instead on the contrary	however in contrast on the other hand
Cause and Effect	because if/then as a result	therefore thus since	for this reason so due to

Making Your Main Idea Clear

There are two ways of getting across the main idea of your paragraph. One way is to come right out and state your main idea in a **topic sentence.** A topic sentence identifies your topic and tells what you want to say about it. Often, writing that explains or persuades makes use of topic sentences.

The topic sentence may be the first sentence of the paragraph, as in the example below.

> Thinking globally is like looking at a whole forest and seeing beyond the beauty of the trees. It means thinking about the forest's history, its wildlife, the resources it provides, the people it supports. When you think globally, you think about the forest's effect on the climate around it, about over-logging, acid rain, and soil erosion. You think about worldwide action to preserve forests and provide jobs for people who depend on them for a living. That's taking a global view.
>
> Betty Miles, from *Save the Earth*

A topic sentence may appear elsewhere in a paragraph. Sometimes, the second sentence in a paragraph serves as the topic sentence. At other times, it may be the last sentence of the paragraph.

A good topic sentence does more than state the main idea of a paragraph. It also catches readers' interest and makes them want to read on. Compare the following topic sentences.

> I am going to explain the second reason our school should broadcast over cable TV.

> Besides helping students to learn media skills, broadcasting over cable TV would link our school to the entire community.

The second sentence is more interesting and more specific than the first. It tells readers what the paragraph will be about and makes them curious to find out more. Use the checklist below to improve your own topic sentences.

Topic Sentence Checklist

1. Does the sentence tell what the paragraph is about?

2. Is the main idea stated clearly?

3. Is the sentence interesting enough to catch the reader's attention?

4. Is the main idea narrow enough to be developed in one paragraph?

5. Does the sentence cover all the related ideas in the paragraph?

Another way of getting across main ideas is to use an **implied main idea.** Unlike a topic sentence, an implied main idea is not stated directly but is communicated by all the paragraph's sentences working together.

Narrative and descriptive writing often make use of implied main ideas. In the following model, all the sentences work together to describe the distress felt by Roger, the main character in the story.

> Roger's head spun dizzily around. He gaped at the monstrous tweed figure in dismay. Book bags were being clicked open, notebooks drawn out—what was he to do? He had gone to his room after the outing in the park yesterday, but alas, it had not been to complete his assignment. He watched, horrified, as the tweed figure proceeded among the aisles and inspected notebooks. What had she said her name was? Awful— was that it? Miss Awful! Biting his lip, he listened to her scathing comments.
>
> Arthur Cavanaugh, "Miss Awful"

Elaboration

A well-constructed paragraph needs details that support its main idea or help to accomplish its purpose. The chart below lists some common types of **elaboration,** or ways of adding supporting details, that you might use to develop your paragraphs.

A well-developed paragraph feels complete. It doesn't leave out important information or state ideas without explaining them. Do you think the following paragraph is well developed?

> A spectator who is unfamiliar with sumo wrestling, Japan's national sport, might not easily see the skills used in competing. Yet there are actual strategies and moves that the athletes use.

This paragraph leaves too many questions unanswered. What are the strategies that sumo wrestlers use? What kind of skills do they need? Now read another version of the paragraph, one with more elaboration.

> A spectator who is unfamiliar with sumo wrestling, Japan's national sport, might not easily see the skills used in competing. When opponents collide with each other in a match, it might seem that only the heftier one can stay within the ring and win. Yet there are actual strategies and moves that athletes use. Since the average weight of a sumo wrestler is four hundred pounds, maintaining balance is an important skill. Wrestlers must master various ways of keeping as steady as possible in the ring.

When you revise your paragraphs, look for places where you need more information or details.

Types of Elaboration

Type	Definition	Example
Facts/Statistics	Statements that can be proved	Milk contains calcium.
Sensory Details	Words that appeal to the five senses	Squealing with delight, a child in shiny, yellow rainboots leaped from the curb and splashed into a puddle.
Reasons	Logical statements to support an idea	Our park needs more trees. Last spring, violent storms destroyed all the maple trees near the bandstand. Several elm trees at the park's entrance are infected with disease.
Examples	Specific cases or instances that illustrate a main idea	Chin-ups, sit-ups, and jumping jacks are three exercises that promote physical fitness.
Quotations	Someone's exact words	"I felt very comfortable being in space," said astronaut Mae Jemison.

Paragraphing

When you begin drafting, you often do not know how many paragraphs you will write or what the main idea of each paragraph will be. The following guidelines will help you organize your ideas into effective paragraphs.

Guidelines for Paragraphing

As you draft:

- **Look for related details.**
  Group them together as a paragraph.

- **Look for changes in main ideas.**
  Start a new paragraph with each new idea.

- **Recognize changes in setting or speaker.**
  Whenever the setting or speaker changes, begin a new paragraph.

As you revise:

- **Look for overloaded or overly long paragraphs.**
  Break these down into smaller paragraphs, each focusing on one main idea.

- **Look for strings of short paragraphs.**
  These paragraphs may need to be grouped together or need further elaboration.

- **Make sure each paragraph has a main idea or clear purpose.**
  If you can't tell what the main idea is, how will your reader be able to?

- **Watch out for paragraphs that overlap one another.**
  If two paragraphs cover the same topic, revise one or both of them.

RESEARCH AND REPORT WRITING

This section gives you a brief overview of the steps involved in writing research papers and reports. For further help in this area, consult the Writer's Workshop on Informative Writing on page 523.

Finding a Topic

These tips on finding an idea can make writing easier:

1. Choose a topic that truly interests you. That way you won't get bored and your work will be easier to finish.

2. Check the library. See whether there are enough books and articles available for you to adequately research your subject.

3. Limit your topic. Many topic ideas start out too big. A topic like ecology may be too large because there is simply too much to say. Choose a smaller topic, such as the importance of rain forests or how rain forests can be saved. A smaller topic makes a report more manageable.

4. Jot down major points you think you might cover in your report. You may need to look through books to get some general ideas for what you might write about. These general ideas will help you focus your research.

Using the Library

After choosing and focusing your topic, begin your search for information. Like most researchers, you will probably begin with the resources in the library. However, research can also include interviews, TV programs, and many other nonprint sources.

The Card Catalog The card catalog lists all the materials in the library and tells you where to find them. There are three cards for every book: a **title card,** an **author card,** and a **subject card.** Begin by looking up your subject, but don't panic if you can't find what you want right away. You may need to look under a different heading.

Computerized Catalogs Most public libraries now have computerized catalogs. Instructions for using them are usually posted next to the terminals. Generally, you type in your subject; the title of the book; or the last name, then first name, of the author.

Call Numbers Most libraries arrange nonfiction books according to the Dewey Decimal System. The Dewey Decimal System assigns every book a number in one of ten categories. This **call numbe**r is usually printed on the spine of the book. The books are then arranged on the library shelves in numerical order. When you use a card catalog or computer, you are given the call numbers to help you locate the book. Find the area of the library containing those numbers, and search for your book.

Reference Section

The reference section of your library contains all kinds of books that provide facts and statistics, including the different types of materials mentioned below. Ask the librarian for help if you have trouble finding any source.

Readers' Guide to Periodical Literature This journal lists, by subject, articles in current magazines and newspapers. Find the most current *Readers' Guide* and look up the subject of your report. After you find an article that looks promising, write the name and date of the magazine and the page number. Then go to the magazine area and ask the librarian for the issue of the magazine you need.

General Encyclopedias Encyclopedias are often a good place to start your research, since they give a general overview of a subject. Beware of depending on them, however. If you use only an encyclopedia entry, you haven't done any serious research. You need to find more current and detailed information by using other sources as well.

Specialized Dictionaries and Encyclopedias These books focus on a particular area of knowledge. You can find dictionaries for ballet, biographies, and slang, for example, and encyclopedias on science, sports, and so on.

Almanacs and Yearbooks Since these books are published yearly, they have up-to-date facts and statistics. Check the table of contents and the index of the most current almanac to find your subject.

Atlases These books of maps also contain information on other geographical topics, such as population, temperature, and weather.

Parts of a Book

With the help of a card catalog or computer, you will find many nonfiction books on your topic. By scanning the parts of a book, you can decide immediately whether the book will be useful to you or not.

Title Page This page gives the full title of a book, the place of publication, and the names of authors, editors, and publishers.

Copyright Page This page has the publication date, so you can decide how current the information in the book is. A 1972 book on Russia, for instance, will not discuss the breakup of the Soviet Union.

Foreword, Preface, or Introduction These pages contain important background information, such as the author's purpose for writing or the method used to collect the information.

Table of Contents This is a summary of the contents of the book, arranged in order of appearance. These pages are especially important because they may quickly show you whether the book discusses your topic and whether the coverage is detailed enough for your purposes.

Text This is the body of the book. A quick look can help you decide whether the book is too simple or too technical for your needs.

Glossary This is a dictionary at the back of the book that defines technical terms used in the text.

Index Found at the back of the book, this is an alphabetical list of the subjects in the book, together with the page numbers where they can be found. Check the index to see how many pages are devoted to your topic.

Taking Notes

When you find facts and details you can use, take notes. Using index cards can make note-taking easy for you.

Begin by recording important information about each source you use on a **source card** or **bibliography card.** Include the author or editor, last name first; the title of the book or name of the article (for magazines and encyclopedias); the city and publisher; the year (or date for a magazine) of publication; and the library call number (for nonfiction books). You will use the information on these cards later, when you compile your **bibliography** or list of **works cited.** Notice the example below.

Source Card

```
                                    x574.5264
                                         M.


Mutel, Cornelia F., and Mary M. Rodgers.
     Tropical Rain Forests. Minneapolis:
     Lerner, 1991.
```

Then use one note card for each fact or idea you might want to include in your report. On the first line, write the title of the source. On the second line, write the page numbers. Then write the fact. You will use these cards to organize your outline and write your paper. To see how note cards look, see the example below.

Note Card

<u>Tropical Rain Forests</u>	**Title**
14–15	**Pages**
	Information

Many species of plants and animals in rain forests cannot be found in other areas of the world.

When to Take a Note As you read, keep your topic in mind. When you find information that will help you get your ideas across, stop and take a note. Look for the following:

- details about the main ideas you plan to cover in your paper
- important dates and facts
- important people
- interesting events or examples
- conflicting opinions
- special terms or jargon

Summarizing and Quoting Whenever you can, summarize information in your own words. If you want to include someone else's idea, be sure you say whose idea it is. You might choose to quote someone's exact words because they are clever, famous, or memorable. If so, copy the quotation word for word, and mark the beginning and end with quotation marks.

Remember that **plagiarism** is the use of someone else's words or ideas without giving

that person credit. Plagiarism is against the law. Always give credit to your sources.

If your teacher requires you to credit sources within your report, put the source in parentheses at the end of the passage that contains someone else's words or ideas. Use these guidelines:

Crediting Sources Within Your Paper

- **Work by one author** At the end of your sentence, put the author's last name and the page number in parentheses.
(George 20)

- **Work by more than one author** Put all the last names and the page number in parentheses.
(Mutel and Rodgers 37)

- **Works with no author** Put the title or a shortened version of the title and the page number in parentheses.
("Rain Forest" 30)

- **Nonprint works** Put the name of the person interviewed, the television program, or other nonprint work in parentheses.
(Ortiz)

Outlining

An outline helps you organize your main points and supporting details in logical order. Begin by reviewing your note cards. Group the cards into separate piles, putting together those that are about similar ideas. Then review the groups, thinking about what they have in common. Your groups can help you organize your outline into headings and subheadings.

In a topic outline, use phrases, not complete sentences, in a form similar to that shown on the next page.

Outline

Title ⟶ Tropical Rain Forests

Roman numeral ⟶ I.   Exploring rain forests

Capital letter ⟶   A. Their importance to Earth

Arabic numeral ⟶   1. How they protect air and soil

Capitalize each line   2. How their resources help us as well as
⟶   people of the rain forests

   B. Their locations

Indent each subdivision ⟶   1. Africa

      2. Asia and Australia

      3. South and Central America

Lowercase letter ⟶   a. Has world's largest rain forest

        b. How the Amazon River affects it

II. Saving Rain Forests

Guidelines for Listing Works Cited

On a separate sheet of paper at the end of your report, you must list the sources you used while writing. This list is sometimes called a **bibliography.** You can compile the information from your source cards. List sources in alphabetical order by the name of the author. The guidelines and examples below show the correct format and punctuation for several different kinds of sources. Remember to underline any information that appears in italics.

Books   Author or editor, last name first; book title; city and publisher; year of publication

> George, Jean Craighead. *One Day in the Tropical Rain Forest.* New York: Crowell, 1990.

> Mutel, Cornelia F., and Mary M. Rodgers. *Tropical Rain Forests.* Minneapolis: Lerner, 1991.

Magazine articles   Author, if one is named; article title; name and date of magazine; page numbers

> "Rain Forest Mailbag" *National Geographic World* Sept. 1991:30–31.

Encyclopedia articles   Author, if listed; title of the entry; encyclopedia name; year of publication

> Lovejoy, Thomas E., "Tropical Rain Forest." *The World Book Encyclopedia.* 1988 ed.

Interviews   Name of person interviewed; type of interview (personal or telephone); date

> Ortiz, Victor. Personal interview. June 10, 1992.

Television programs   Name of program; narrator or other person providing information; name of series; network; local station; date

> "A Desert Blooming." Writ. Marshall Riggan. *Living Wild.* PBS. WTTW, Chicago. 29 Apr. 1984.

Recordings   Artist; title of work; title of recording; type of recording; manufacturer; catalog number; year

> U2. "MLK." *The Unforgettable Fire.* Audiocassette. RCA, 90231-4, 1984.

WRITING LETTERS

Business Letters

A business letter is written for a specific purpose—for example, requesting information or ordering a product. It requires a formal writing style and a specific format. Business letters have six parts: the **heading,** the **inside address,** the **salutation,** the **body,** the **closing,** and the **signature.** These six parts can be arranged in either **block form** or **modified block form.**

Block Form and Modified Block Form

For any business letter, use plain white 8½" X 11" paper, whether you type the letter or write it by hand. In **block form** all parts begin at the left margin. Use this form only when you type a letter. In **modified block form** the heading, the closing, and the signature are aligned near the right margin, and the other parts are at the left margin. With this form new paragraphs may be indented.

BLOCK FORM

```
37254 Breezeway Terrace
Spokane, Washington 99208          Heading
October 8, 19—


United States Forest Service
Gifford Pinchot National Forest
P.O. Box 8944                      Inside
Vancouver, Washington 98668        Address

Dear Sir or Madam:                 Salutation

                                   Body
During my vacation I spoke with
Ms. Julie Pizarro, a ranger stationed
in the Gifford Pinchot National Forest.
I told her that I was interested in a
career in the Forest Service in your
area. She suggested that I write to you
for information.

Please send me any material you have
that describes the qualifications I
would need to join the Forest Service.
Thank you for your time and attention.

Yours truly,                       Closing

Maya Garber
Maya Garber                        Signature
```

MODIFIED BLOCK FORM

```
                    451 Pine Street
Heading             Ames, Iowa 50010
                    June 6, 19—


Credit Manager
Threads Express, Inc.
P.O. Box 14367              Inside Address
Ithaca, New York 14851

Dear Sir or Madam:         Salutation

                           Body
  I shop regularly at one of your
stores, and I saw a report on our local
television news about your new credit
line for young people.

  Please send me an application form
for your special "Kid's Charge" card.
I understand that my parents must
cosign the application. Thank you for
your prompt response.

Closing           Sincerely,

Signature         Mark O'Neill
                  Mark O'Neill
```

Heading The heading of a letter tells where and when you are writing. It gives your street address on the first line; your city, state, and ZIP code on the second line; and the month, day, and year on the third line. The heading should be placed about an inch below the top of the page.

Inside Address The inside address tells to whom the letter is being sent. Place the inside address at the left margin at least four lines below the heading. On the first line you should place the name of the receiver (if you know the person's name). If there is room, place the person's title on the same line, separated from the name by a comma. Otherwise, place the title on the next line. If you do not know the name of the person who will receive the letter, use the person's title or the name of the department. On the following lines, place the name and address of the organization or company, including the city, state, and ZIP code.

Salutation The salutation of a business letter is the way you greet the person to whom you are writing. The salutation should be positioned two lines below the inside address. Begin with the word *Dear,* follow it by the name of the person, and end with a colon. Use only the person's last name, preceded by a title such as *Mr., Mrs., Ms., Dr.,* or *Professor.* If you do not know the person's name, use a general salutation such as *Ladies and Gentlemen.* Another alternative is to write to a department or to a position within a company. The following forms are acceptable:

Dear Mr. Allen: Dear Sir or Madam:
Dear Ms. Kreutzer: Dear Customer
Dear Mrs. Jackson: Service Department:
                    Dear Editor:

Body The body, the main part of the letter in which you write your message, begins two spaces below the salutation. The body may contain a single paragraph or several paragraphs. Leave a space between each paragraph.

Closing The closing is placed two lines below the body, in line with the heading. Closings commonly used for business letters include *Sincerely, Sincerely yours,* and *Very truly yours.* Note that only the first word is capitalized and that the closing ends with a comma.

Signature Type or print your name four spaces below the closing, and sign your name in the space between.

Friendly Letters

A friendly letter has all the parts of a business letter except the inside address. Notice that a friendly letter is not formal in tone; its salutation might read *Hey Susie!* or *Howdy, John,* while its closing might read *Your pal* or *Missing you.* Notice that the salutation is followed by a comma instead of the colon that is used in a business letter. Indent each paragraph, and write clearly so that your reader can follow what you are saying.

Heading   813 King Drive, #2
                    Dallas, Texas 75215
                    March 12, 19—

Dear José,   **Salutation**
                      Body

   I am very sorry I can't accept your invitation to visit you at your summer place in Michigan. I have already signed up to go to scuba-diving camp during that week in June! Maybe you could go to the camp with me, and we could go to Michigan from there. Could you ask your parents? Hurry and write me back to tell me what they say.

Closing   Take it easy,
Signature   Stan

USING THE LANGUAGE HANDBOOK

You can use this handbook as a guide when you need help in understanding the rules of the English language. The handbook explains the most common parts of English. It teaches you how to avoid many common errors so that you can improve your writing, your reading, and your speaking.

SECTION 1: PARTS OF SPEECH PREVIEW

All words in the English language are classified into eight different groups called the *parts of speech*.

Your knowledge of the parts of speech will allow you to discuss what you read and what you write. The examples below define and give examples of the major parts of speech.

Noun   A noun is a word that names a person, a place, a thing, or an idea.

> Examples: violin   apple   Ithaca   lunch   freedom
> An *apple* that we picked in *Ithaca* became our *lunch.*

Pronoun   A pronoun is a word used in place of a noun or another pronoun.

> Examples: we   ourselves   nobody   I   him   her
> If *we* don't respect *ourselves, nobody* will.

Verb   A verb is a word that tells about an action or about a state of being.

> Examples: dug   built   dance   believes   is
> Marina *dug* clams and *built* sand castles. I *was* happy.

Adjective   An adjective is a word that modifies, or defines by describing, a noun or a pronoun. Adjectives tell *which one, how many, what kind,* or *how much.*

> Examples: two   big   red   round   the
> *Two big red* cars pulled into *the* driveway.

Adverb   An adverb is a word that modifies, or defines by describing, a verb, an adjective, or another adverb.

> Examples: quickly   very   carefully   always
> They *quickly* packed their suitcases and placed them *very carefully* in the trunk of the car.

Preposition   A preposition is a word used with a noun or a pronoun to show how the noun or pronoun is related to some other word in the sentence. Prepositions often show direction, position, or relation in time.

> Examples: over   through   to   in   of   by   before
> We walked *over* the bridge and *through* the woods *to* the campsite.

Conjunction   A conjunction is a word that connects words or groups of words.

> Examples: and   or   nor   for   but   so   because   if
> Tamara can cook the greens, *but* I will fry the chicken.

Interjection   An interjection is a word or group of words that shows strong feeling.

> Examples: Oh no!   Help!   Hey!   Wow!
> *Oh no!* There goes the bus!

Parts of Speech at a Glance

The various parts of speech are used together to make sentences, as the following graphic shows.

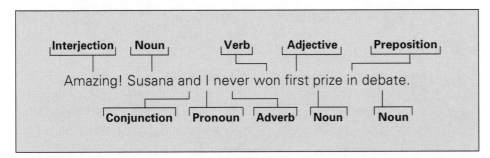

The rest of this handbook describes in detail the parts of speech and their many uses. The following exercises will help you review the parts of speech.

Exercise 1   Concept Check

Identifying Parts of Speech   Write the part of speech of each italicized word.

1. Most *large* cities *in* the United States have Chinese restaurants.
2. *You* can also buy Chinese foods in most grocery *stores.*
3. My favorite supermarket *carries* bean sprouts, sesame oil, *and* pea pods.
4. My *mother received* a wok for her birthday last year.
5. *Now* she uses it several times each *week.*
6. *Wow!* I *really* love her fried wonton!
7. *Traditional* Chinese families do not have knives *at* their tables.
8. The cook cuts everything *into* small *pieces.*
9. Small pieces of food *cook* quickly *and* evenly in a wok.
10. *I* can pick up the pieces easily *with* my chopsticks.

Exercise 2   Application in Literature

Parts of Speech   Write the part of speech of each italicized word.

LITERARY MODEL
· · · · · · · · · · · · · ·
from "The
All-American Slurp"
by Lensey Namioka

(1) The day came when my parents *announced* that they wanted to give a dinner party. (2) *We* had invited Chinese (3) *friends* to eat (4) with us *before,* but this dinner was going to be different. (5) In addition to a Chinese-American *family,* we were going to invite the Gleasons. (6) *"Gee,* I can hardly wait to have dinner (7) *at* your house," Meg said to me. (8) "I just *love* Chinese food."

(9) That was a relief. Mother was a *good* cook, (10) *but* I wasn't sure if people who ate sour cream would also eat chicken gizzards stewed in soy sauce.

Exercise 3   Drafting Skill

Adding Words   On your paper, write words to complete the following sentences. Choose the most interesting words you can think of, but be sure to use the parts of speech indicated in the blanks.

One night our peace was disturbed by a (1) __(noun)__ outside our house. My mother (2) __(verb)__ to the window to see what it was. (3) __(adverb)__ her face went pale. What (4) __(adjective)__ sight greeted her eyes? (5) __(preposition)__ the street stood a man (6) __(conjunction)__ a (7) __(noun)__ . (8) " __(interjection)__ !" she screamed. "Now (9) __(pronoun)__ must (10) __(verb)__ !"

SECTION 2: UNDERSTANDING SENTENCES

A *sentence* is a group of words that expresses a complete thought. A sentence must have a *subject* and a *predicate*.

Subjects and Predicates

The **subject** tells whom or what a sentence is about. The **predicate** tells what the subject does or is. A sentence can be divided into two main parts. These two parts are the complete subject and the complete predicate. Together, these two parts contain all the words in the sentence.

Complete Subject	Complete Predicate
Quentin Jackson	organized the meeting.
The car	spun around the corner on two wheels.
His old friend	appeared in a dream.

Simple Subjects and Verbs

The **simple subject** is the key word in the complete subject. The **simple predicate** is the most important word in the complete predicate. The simple predicate is also called the **verb.** Look at the following sentence:

A scrawny black-and-white *cat*   *clung* to the tree.

Cat is the key word in the complete subject. It tells what the sentence is about. The other words in the complete subject give additional information about the cat. *Clung* is the key word in the complete predicate. It tells what the cat did. *Clung* is the verb.

Subjects and Verbs at a Glance

The **complete subject** includes all the words that identify the person, place, thing, or idea the sentence is about.	The **complete predicate** includes all the words that tell or ask something about the subject.

The talented young **trumpeter won** the audience's hearts.

The **simple subject** tells specifically what the sentence is about. It may be one word or a group of words, but it does not include words that modify, or describe.	The **simple predicate,** or **verb,** tells what the subject does or is. It may be one word or several, but it does not include modifying words.

Exercise 1 Concept Check

Subjects and Predicates Copy each sentence below. Draw a line to separate the complete subject from the complete predicate. Circle the simple subject, and draw two lines under the verb.

1. My brother collects masks.
2. He owns dozens of them.
3. My favorite mask has many colors.
4. A Native American craftsperson made this mask.
5. The mask-making Kwakiutl tribe lives in British Columbia.
6. Their fancier masks have movable parts.
7. A medicine man wore the mask.
8. Strings moved the parts.
9. My brother's beautiful mask is red, green, and white.
10. Some historical museums display colorful masks.

Finding the Verb

A verb can express an action, state that something exists, or link the subject to a word that describes it.

Here are some guidelines to help you find the verb in a sentence.

An **action verb** tells what the subject of the sentence does. The action may or may not be something you can see.

> The jaguar *leaped* from the tree.
> Shana *thinks* quickly.

Other types of verbs may tell that something *is,* or they may link the subject with some other words that describe it. These are called **state-of-being verbs** or **linking verbs.**

> The party *is* over (state of being)
> William Weld *is* the governor. (links *William Weld* with *governor*)

The following are some common state of being or linking verbs: *am, are, were, being, is, was, be, been, look, appear, seem, become, remain, feel, sound, taste, grow, smell.* Some linking verbs can also be used as action verbs.

> Dean *smells* the barbecue. (action verb)
> The barbecue *smells* good. (linking verb)

Helping Verbs and Main Verbs

When there are two or more words in the verb, the last word is the **main verb.** Other verbs are **helping verbs.** A **verb phrase** is made up of a main verb and its helping verbs.

> He *was asked* a question.　　*Has* Sally *finished?*

Usually, the words in a verb phrase are next to one another. Sometimes, however, the parts of a verb phrase are separated by words that are not part of the verb phrase.

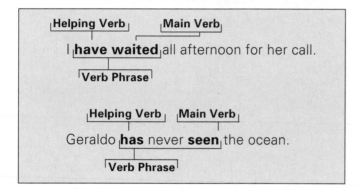

Helping Verb　Main Verb

I **have waited** all afternoon for her call.

Verb Phrase

Helping Verb　Main Verb

Geraldo **has** never **seen** the ocean.

Verb Phrase

QUICK TIP　Use these steps to find the verb of a sentence:

1. Find the word that tells the main action, expresses a state of being, or links the subject with a description.
2. Look for helping verbs. Here are some examples: *am, are, is, was, were, do, did, does, shall, will, should, would,* and *could.*
3. Find all the verbs that make up the verb phrase.

Exercise 2　Concept Check

Identifying Verbs　Write the verb or verb phrase in each of the following sentences. Tell whether the verb or verb phrase expresses an action or a state of being. Be sure to include any helping verbs.

1. James Banning was a young African American in the early 1900s.
2. He had always loved airplanes.
3. However, no flight schools accepted black people at that time.
4. Banning grew more determined.

5. He had met an army officer in Iowa.
6. Lieutenant Fischer was a pilot.
7. Soon he and Banning were copilots.
8. Banning would later become a stunt pilot.
9. Stunt pilots perform tricks with airplanes.
10. In 1932, Banning and another man flew all the way across the United States.

Compound Sentence Parts

A *compound subject* or a *compound predicate* has two or more parts.

This sentence has a compound subject:

> *Harvey* and *Max* competed in the swim meet.

This sentence has a compound predicate:

> Harvey *swam* daily and *lifted* weights three times a week at the YMCA.

QUICK TIP You can eliminate the choppy sound of two short sentences that differ only in their subject or verb. Simply combine the sentences by using a compound subject or a compound predicate.

Choppy Marty prepared our lunch. Marty brought it to us.

Improved Marty prepared our lunch and brought it to us.

Exercise 3 Concept Check

Compound Subjects and Verbs Write the compound subject or compound verb in each of the following sentences. Tell whether it is a compound subject or a compound verb.

1. Lois visited Japan and stayed in Tokyo for two weeks.
2. She and I took subway trains everywhere.
3. The trains run frequently and carry millions of commuters.
4. Maps and color-coded trains help travelers.
5. We stopped at Akihabara and shopped for hours.

Exercise 4   Revision Skill

Combining Sentences   Combine each pair of sentences to form a single sentence with either a compound subject or a compound verb. You may add, change, or delete words if necessary.

> **Example**   At 4:30 A.M. we packed our bags. We left the hotel.
> **Answer**   At 4:30 A.M. we packed our bags and left the hotel.

1. Lois and I traveled to Tsukiji. Lois and I arrived at 5:00.
2. Lois heard a noise. I heard it too.
3. A signal always sounds at 5:00. It announces the start of the fish auction.
4. Truckers drive to the area. They unload hundreds of kinds of fish.
5. Shrimp pour out of the trucks. Tuna pour out too.
6. Buyers look at the fish in the bins. Then the buyers start bidding.
7. People shout at the auctioneer. They wave their hands in the air.
8. Workers spray the floor with water. Workers keep the floor clean.
9. Many buyers wear boots. Some visitors also wear boots.
10. The auction continues for more than an hour. The auction ends at about 6:30.

Kinds of Sentences

You write different kinds of sentences for different purposes. Sentences can be grouped into four basic categories.

A *declarative sentence* makes a statement.

> Chicago has been called the Windy City.

An *interrogative sentence* asks a question.

> Why was that nickname given to Chicago?

An *imperative sentence* makes a request or commands someone to do something.

> Ask a politician, not a weather forecaster, about Chicago's nickname.

An *exclamatory sentence* expresses strong feeling.

> Wow! It was "windy" politicians that gave Chicago its nickname!

Notice the **end marks** that are used at the end of the preceding examples. A period (**.**) marks the end of either a declarative or an imperative sentence. A question mark (**?**) marks the end of an interrogative sentence. An exclamation point (**!**) marks the end of an exclamatory sentence.

Exercise 5   Concept Check

Kinds of Sentences   On your paper, write *Declarative, Interrogative, Imperative,* or *Exclamatory* to show what kind each sentence is. Then write the correct punctuation mark.

1. Yikes, it is cold today
2. Look at that little bird sitting on the telephone pole
3. Why does it seem so fat
4. The feathers are all fluffed up
5. Birds fluff up their feathers in very cold weather
6. How does that help to keep birds warm
7. Think about the warm air that is trapped between the feathers
8. Does that air keep the birds warm
9. That's incredible
10. A dog's thick winter fur traps warm air in a similar way

Exercise 6   Revision Skill

Revising Sentences   Rewrite each sentence in Exercise 5 as a different kind of sentence. Tell whether the new sentence is *Declarative, Interrogative, Imperative,* or *Exclamatory*. Add or delete words as necessary.

Avoiding Sentence Fragments

A *sentence fragment* is a group of words that does not express a complete idea.

Sentence fragments are confusing because they do not express complete thoughts. A sentence fragment may be missing a subject, a verb, or both.

Fragment   Climbed the mountain. (The subject is missing.)

Sentence   Jacques climbed the mountain.

Fragment   Hank, the yellow Labrador retriever. (The verb is missing.)

Sentence   Hank, the yellow Labrador retriever, was barking.

Exercise 7 Concept Check

Identifying Fragments   Write *Sentence* or *Fragment* on your paper for each of the following. Then change all the fragments to complete sentences.

1. Three basic kinds of rocks.
2. One kind forms from magma or lava.
3. This kind of rock is called igneous rock.
4. Rocks can change form.
5. Wind, water, heat, and pressure.
6. Rocks are made from various minerals.
7. Quartz is a very common mineral.
8. May be white, pink, or purple.
9. Quartz, a hard, brilliant mineral.
10. Often occurs in hexagonal crystals.

Exercise 8 Proofreading Skill

Correcting Fragments   Rewrite the following paragraph, turning any fragments into complete sentences. Add the correct punctuation.

> (1) There are a number of different kinds of igneous rocks that come from the earth's center (2) Obsidian and pumice, for example, are formed from lava (3) Obsidian a glassy black rock formed from quick-cooling lava (4) Pumice is light in color (5) Looks like a sponge because it contains air bubbles (6) Sometimes called feather rock (7) Can actually float on water

Avoiding Run-on Sentences

A *run-on sentence* occurs when two or more sentences are written as one.

Run-on sentences are often created when writers are in a hurry. Instead of showing where one sentence ends and another begins, a writer may write two sentences as one. Sometimes the writer uses a comma instead of an end mark. This error is known as a **comma splice.**

Run-on (comma splice)	The lion escaped from the zoo, it hid in the old garage.
Corrected	The lion escaped from the zoo. It hid in the old garage.

To correct run-on sentences, use one of the methods described below.

Correcting Run-on Sentences

- Add an end mark to the first sentence. Begin the second sentence with a capital letter.
- Add a semicolon after the first sentence.
- Add a comma after the first sentence and use a conjunction, such as *and, or, nor, for, but, so,* or *yet* to join the two parts of the sentence.

Run-on   Beijing is the capital of China, it used to be called Peking.

Corrected   Beijing is the capital of China. It used to be called Peking.

Corrected   Beijing is the capital of China; it used to be called Peking.

Corrected   Beijing is the capital of China, but it used to be called Peking.

Exercise 9   Concept Check

Run-ons   Decide if each of the following is a correct sentence or a run-on. If it is correct, write *Correct* on your paper. If it is a run-on, rewrite it correctly.

1. Long ago, the Aztec people ruled what is now Mexico City, they watched with fear two mountains near the city.
2. Sometimes a river of fire came out of one mountain; it flowed through the land.
3. People whispered about the mountain, they said that a fire giant lived there.
4. The Aztec people gave the mountains names, they named them after a legendary princess, Ixtacihuatl, and the warrior who loved her, Popocatépetl.
5. Today we know about such mountains, we call them volcanoes.

Exercise 10   Revision Skill

Correcting Run-ons   Each sentence below is a run-on. Correct each sentence in two different ways.

Example   One giant grew angry, he threatened our village.

Separate   One giant grew angry. He threatened our village.

Combined   One giant grew angry, and he threatened our village.

1. The king made a promise, he promised a bride for the angry fire giant.
2. A young woman was chosen to be the bride, she was the king's daughter.
3. The king was frightened, he called for Tavadan.
4. Tavadan promised to help, he tricked the fire giant.
5. The fire giant went to sleep, he slept for a thousand years.

Exercise 11   Revision Skill

Sentence Review   Rewrite the following paragraph, correcting all sentence fragments and run-ons.

(1) Little Rosa Bonheur loved to draw animals, she drew them everywhere. (2) Wanted to go to art school. (3) This was in the 1800s, girls at that time did not attend art school. (4) Rosa's father was an artist, he knew she had talent. (5) At fourteen she studied at the Louvre in Paris, she was the only female student. (6) Gave her first art show at the age of nineteen. (7) She still loved animals, she painted them frequently. (8) Also created sculptures of animals. (9) She made more than a thousand paintings during her life, they are quite realistic. (10) Was awarded the Grand Cross of the Legion of Honor in 1865.

SECTION 3: PREPOSITIONS, CONJUNCTIONS, AND INTERJECTIONS

Prepositions show how a word is related to another part of a sentence. Conjunctions connect words. Interjections express emotion.

Three Parts of Speech at a Glance

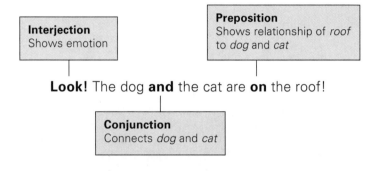

Interjection
Shows emotion

Preposition
Shows relationship of *roof* to *dog* and *cat*

Look! The dog **and** the cat are **on** the roof!

Conjunction
Connects *dog* and *cat*

Prepositions and Prepositional Phrases

A *preposition* is a word that shows the relationship of its object to some other word in the sentence.

Prepositions relate the words following them to other words in sentences. The noun or pronoun following a preposition is called the **object of the preposition**. Together, a preposition, its object, and any words modifying the object make up a **prepositional phrase.** Look at the prepositional phrases below.

to the park (*To* is a preposition; *park* is its object.)

among the friends (*Among* is a preposition; *friends* is its object.)

Many prepositional phrases tell where something happens: *by the river, in the house, across the bridge.* Many other prepositional phrases tell when something happens: *before daybreak, during the war, at noon.*

Eloise walked *to the park on Sunday.* (*To the park* tells where Eloise walked. *On Sunday* tells when she walked.)

The chart on the next page lists some of the most commonly used prepositions.

Words Often Used as Prepositions

about	below	from	past
above	beneath	in	through
across	beside	inside	to
after	between	into	toward
against	beyond	near	under
along	but (except)	of	underneath
among	by	off	until
around	down	on	up
as	during	out	with
before	except	outside	within
behind	for	over	without

Quick Tip In your writing make sure that your prepositional phrases are close to the words they tell about. A sentence with a misplaced prepositional phrase may communicate something that you did not intend. Study the following examples.

Confusing Maxwell climbed the rope ladder *with a fierce grin*. (Does the ladder have a fierce grin? The prepositional phrase *with a fierce grin* is misplaced.)

Clear *With a fierce grin,* Maxwell climbed the rope ladder. (Now the prepositional phrase is close to the word it modifies, *Maxwell.*)

Exercise 1   Concept Check

Prepositional Phrases Write the prepositional phrases that appear in the following sentences. Draw one line under each preposition. Draw two lines under its object. There may be more than one phrase in a sentence.

Example   I found this poem in a book of African poems.
Answer   in a book   of African poems

1. Nadine Gordimer was born in South Africa.
2. She lived in a small town.
3. Many people around her worked in the mines.

◀ WHAT'S PROPER
A proper noun can be made up of one or more words. Capitalize all important words in a proper noun.
Ohio River
North Dakota

4. Few people had very much money except the Gordimers.
5. Gordimer was born into a rich family.
6. She began writing during her childhood.
7. One of her short stories was published before her sixteenth birthday.
8. Gordimer writes about the people of South Africa.
9. She won the Nobel Prize for her work.
10. The store down the street from me sells her books.

Exercise 2   Drafting Skill

Using Prepositional Phrases   Complete the following story by writing prepositional phrases to fit the blanks.

(1) When I have a free afternoon, I like to go ___?___. (2) Last Saturday my sister and I walked ___?___. (3) ___?___ we took our time. (4) We enjoyed looking ___?___ and talking ___?___. (5) My sister got tired and rested ___?___. (6) I had more energy and explored ___?___. (7) I was amazed to find myself ___?___. (8) ___?___ I suddenly remembered my sister. (9) Would she be waiting ___?___? (10) Fortunately, I found her ___?___.

Conjunctions and Interjections

A *conjunction* is a word that connects words or groups of words.

An *interjection* is a word or short group of words used to express a feeling such as anger, fear, joy, or surprise.

When you want to combine sentences or sentence parts, you can use conjunctions.

Two Sentences	James seems unhappy. James seems disappointed.
Combined Sentences	James seems unhappy, *and* he seems disappointed.
Combined Sentence Parts	James seems unhappy *and* disappointed.

Common conjunctions include *and, or, nor, for, but, so,* and *yet.*

Interjections express emotion. Use an exclamation point after an interjection that shows a strong emotion. Use a comma after an

TIP
· · · ·
Sometimes other parts of speech are used as interjections. Look at the following examples:
Noun   Boy!
Verb   Help!
Adjective   Great!
Adverb   Not!
Conjunction   So!

interjection that shows a mild emotion.

> *Hooray!* Here comes the parade! (strong emotion)
> *Well*, I hope the rain does not start again. (mild emotion)

Common interjections include *ah, hey, hooray, no, oh, oops, ouch, ugh, uh-oh, well, whew*, and *wow*.

Exercise 3   Concept Check

Conjunctions and Interjections   Write the conjunctions and the interjections in the following sentences. Identify each word by writing *Conjunction* or *Interjection*.

1. Hey, I was just reading about an interesting place.
2. It's a cave, but the walls have been carved into rock sculptures.
3. Wow! Look at the beautiful Buddha in the middle.
4. These sculptures are religious figures, and people come here to worship.
5. Yeah, there are many such shrines in east central India.

Exercise 4   Revision Skill

Adding Interest to Your Writing   Rewrite the following paragraph. Make it more lively by adding prepositional phrases, conjunctions, and interjections. Underline each addition you make, and in the margin of your paper, identify what kind of addition it is. You may combine sentences and add words if necessary.

The United States has many caves. Most of them are rather ordinary. Some caves are famous. Kentucky has many well-known caves. One cave is in a national park. It is called Mammoth Cave. It is the largest cave system in the world. It extends more than 200 miles. Imagine how long it would take to walk that distance. Mammoth Cave has been a tourist attraction since 1816. The earliest visitors had to carry lights. They had to climb over rocks. Today's visitor can walk on paths and ride in boats.

SECTION 4: USING NOUNS

A *noun* is a word that names a person, a place, a thing, or an idea.

Persons	programmer, acrobat, President Clinton, Aunt Sue
Places	forest, Saturn, temple, city
Things	lamp, sky, backpack, helmet
Ideas	love, determination, fun, liberty

QUICK TIP To find out whether a word is a noun, simply see if it makes sense in one of these blanks:

	_____ is	_____ are
Nouns	*Brazil* is	*comets* are
Not Nouns	*great* is	*daily* are

Types of Nouns

A noun that names a particular person, place, thing, or idea is called a *proper noun.*

Eiffel Tower	Napoleon	Arkansas
Kristi Yamaguchi	Tom Sawyer	Islam

A noun that names a kind of person, place, thing, or idea is a *common noun.*

structure	leader	state
skater	character	religion

A noun made up of more than one word is called a *compound noun.*

Some nouns, like *storyteller, Annie Oakley,* and *volleyball* are made up of more than one word.

outfield	sweatshirt	Yankee Stadium
solar system	Fred Flintstone	Gulf War

QUICK TIP A compound noun might be spelled as one word, like *earthworm;* with a hyphen, like *warm-up;* or as two words, like *air shaft.*

Exercise 1   Application in Literature

Types of Nouns   Write the italicized nouns in the following passage. Label each noun as *Proper* or *Common*. Add the label *Compound* for the four compound nouns.

(1) *Elijah McCoy* (1843–1929) was born on *May* 2, 1843, in *Ontario*, *Canada*, the *son* of two runaway *slaves*, *fugitives* who had escaped from *Kentucky* by *way* of the *Underground Railroad*. (2) After the *Civil War*, *Elijah* and his *parents* returned to the *United States*, settling down in *Ypsilanti*, *Michigan*. (3) There *Elijah* attended *school* and worked in a machine *shop*.

◀ LITERARY MODEL
from "The Real McCoy" by Jim Haskins

Exercise 2   Concept Check

Proper Nouns   On your paper write a proper noun that is an example of each common noun.

Example   city   **Possible Answer**   Paris

1. street   **5.** state   **8.** singer
2. month   **6.** country   **9.** holiday
3. pet   **7.** building   **10.** president
4. student

Using Nouns

In sentences nouns can be used as *subjects*, *direct objects*, *predicate nouns*, and *objects of prepositions*.

Think of the **subject** as naming the actor in a sentence—whom or what the sentence is about. The **direct object** names the thing or person who *receives* the action.

Carl sent the *letter*.

Carl names the actor, so it is the subject. To determine the direct object, ask yourself what he sent. The direct object is *letter*.

When a noun after the verb refers to the subject, it is called a **predicate noun.**

Marci is an *artist*.

Since *artist* renames the subject *Marci*, *artist* is a predicate noun. It is a noun in the predicate that refers to the same person, place, thing, or idea as the subject.

TRADING PLACES
One way to see if a noun is a predicate noun is to reverse its position with the subject of the sentence. The sentence should still have the same meaning.

Paquito is the singer. The singer is Paquito. (*Singer* is a predicate noun.)

Paquito loves pizza. Pizza loves Paquito. (*Pizza* is not a predicate noun.)

You may remember that a preposition takes an object. A noun can function as the **object of a preposition.**

Marci is the best artist in our *school.*

School is the object of the preposition *in.*

Uses of Nouns at a Glance

The **subject** is the person, place, thing, or idea that the sentence is about.

The **direct object** tells who or what receives the action of the verb.

Li Hua served the **volleyball.**

A **predicate noun** comes after a linking verb such as *is, are,* or *seems.* It describes or renames the subject.

The **object of a preposition** comes after a preposition such as *of, at, on, to,* or *for.*

Li Hua is a new **student** in our **class.**

Exercise 3   Concept Check

Uses of Nouns   Decide what job each italicized noun is doing in the sentence. Write *Subject, Direct Object, Object of a Preposition,* or *Predicate Noun.*

1. *Mel* is my *partner* in social studies.
2. Our *class* is studying *South America.*
3. *Mel* drew a *picture* of Lake Maracaibo.
4. All the students must write *reports* about *South America.*
5. The topic of our *report* is *Bolivia.*

Exercise 4   Drafting Skill

Nouns in Sentences   Think of an interesting noun that can be used to complete each sentence. Write the noun on a sheet of paper. Then identify the noun as *Subject, Direct Object, Object of a Preposition,* or *Predicate Noun.*

Example   ____?____ took me to see a monster truck race.
Possible answer   Mom, Subject

1. The truck race was a big ____?____ in our town.
2. The ____?____ of a monster truck is amazing.

3. An announcer stood on a _____?_____.
4. A clown gave free _____?_____ to the children.
5. The truck drivers were_____?_____ who raced their machines for a living.
6. The _____?_____ was covered with dirt ramps and junk cars.
7. The huge trucks tore around the _____?_____.
8. The blue truck won the _____?_____ by only one second!
9. Our seats were by the _____?_____.
10. Mom took a _____?_____ of me standing beside the winning truck.

Using Plural Forms of Nouns

A noun that names one person, place, thing, or idea is a *singular* noun. A noun that names more than one person, place, thing, or idea is a *plural* noun.

1. To form the plural of most nouns, add -*s*.

squirrel	kilometer	astronaut
squirrels	*kilometers*	*astronauts*

2. When the singular ends in *s, sh, ch, x,* or *z,* add -*es*.

sandwich	ax	waltz
sandwiches	*axes*	*waltzes*

3. For most singular nouns ending in *o,* add -*s*.

patio	silo	auto
patios	*silos*	*autos*

For some nouns that end in *o* preceded by a consonant, add -*es*.

potato	echo	hero
potatoes	*echoes*	*heroes*

4. When the singular noun ends in *y* preceded by a consonant, change the *y* to *i* and add -*es*.

party	quality	ruby
parties	qualities	rubies

If the *y* is preceded by a vowel, do not change the *y* to *i*. Just add -*s* to the singular.

bay	decoy	guy
bays	decoys	guys

5. For some nouns ending in *f*, add -*s*.

cliff	reef	puff
cliffs	*reefs*	*puffs*

For other nouns ending in *f* or *fe*, change the *f* to *v* and add -*es* or -*s*.

shelf	half	wife
shelves	*halves*	*wives*

6. Some nouns are spelled the same in the singular and in the plural.

Sioux	moose	aircraft

7. Some nouns form their plurals in unusual ways.

child	goose	man
children	*geese*	*men*

8. For a compound noun written as one word, form the plural by changing the last word in the compound to its plural form.

stepmother	raincoat	dragonfly
stepmothers	*raincoats*	*dragonflies*

LOOK IT UP
. . . .
A dictionary entry usually shows the plurals of nouns when the plurals are formed in unusual ways. The plural form usually appears in boldfaced type near the pronunciation of the word.

Exercise 5   Concept Check

Plural Nouns   Write the correct plural form of each noun.

1. piano	**8.** mattress	**15.** wax
2. speech	**9.** tomato	**16.** fish
3. proof	**10.** moose	**17.** grandmother
4. table	**11.** leaf	**18.** pioneer
5. valley	**12.** loudspeaker	**19.** goose
6. tooth	**13.** butterfly	**20.** melody
7. fingernail	**14.** dish	

Exercise 6   Revision Skill

Revising Sentences   Rewrite the following sentences. Change the italicized singular nouns to their correct plural forms.

1. My grandparents talked about the *life* people led in the 1940s.

2. They both owned *radio* then but no televisions.

3. Grandfather remembers hearing many *speech* by President Franklin D. Roosevelt.

4. People who lived in *valley* could only get a few radio stations.

5. Few *family* owned televisions until the 1950s.

6. They told us about the early *day* of television.

7. One appliance store lined up several *couch* in front of its TV set.

8. Many *shopper* would come in just to see this new machine.

9. Grandpa named some of the early actors and *actress*.

10. Today the United States has more than 1200 TV *station!*

Using Possessive Nouns

To show ownership or belonging, use a *possessive noun.*

1. If a noun is singular, add -'s to form the possessive.

Kara's homework   Rufus's briefcase

2. If a noun is plural and already ends in *s,* add only the apostrophe.

the roses' scent   two countries' leaders

3. If a noun is plural and does not end in *s,* add 's.

the children's idea   some deer's trails

Exercise 7   Concept Check

Possessive Nouns   On a separate piece of paper, write the possessive forms of these nouns.

1. actor	**6.** hostess	**11.** person
2. fox	**7.** deer	**12.** Detroit
3. mice	**8.** Carlos	**13.** women
4. calves	**9.** nurses	**14.** custodians
5. lawyer	**10.** chief	**15.** hero

Exercise 8   Revision Skill

Possessive Nouns   Rewrite the following sentences. Change the italicized nouns to their correct possessive forms.

1. Margaret *Roberts* birthplace was Grantham, England.

2. The *girl* father was a grocer.

3. Her father was also the *town* mayor.

4. Denis *Thatcher* marriage to Margaret took place in 1951.

5. Margaret Thatcher finished her law studies just in time for her *twins* birth.

6. In 1979 she was her *country* choice for Prime Minister.

7. Reelected twice, she became one of the *world* most powerful women.

8. She became one of President Ronald *Reagan* friends.

9. Later, some *people* opinions about her changed.

10. Thatcher gave in to her party *members* pressure and resigned in 1990.

Exercise 9   Revision Skill

Noun Usage Review   Each sentence below has one error in the form of a plural or possessive noun. Find the error and write the correct word on your paper.

1. Childrenses' mouths have fewer teeth than adults' mouths.

2. A tooth's covering is one of the bodies hardest materials.

3. A baby's first tooth usually appears when the baby is about six month's old.

4. A childs' permanent teeth start coming in at about age six.

5. Many people get their last molars' at age thirteen.

6. Look at the photoes in Jess's science book.

7. The teeth with the boxs drawn around them are called wisdom teeth.

8. They are called wisdom teeth because people get them later in their lifes.

9. Sometimes these molars don't have enough space to come in properly; then these tooth must be removed.

10. My dentist gives us new toothbrushs every time we visit her.

11. After this years checkup, I will see a different dentist.

12. My dentist's patients are children, and I won't need a childrens' dentist anymore.

13. Several dentist's offices are in the same building.

14. My toothbrush's handle is long, and my two sister's toothbrush handles are short.

15. I don't have any cavitys in my teeth, but I'm not sure about my little brother's teeth.

NEW NOUNS
. . . .
New nouns become part of the English language every year. Look in a dictionary and see if you can find these new nouns: *pixel, space shuttle, spin doctor, hard drive,* and *flextime.*

SECTION 5: USING PRONOUNS

A *pronoun* is a word that is used in place of a noun or another pronoun.

Noun	*Clark Kent* was really Superman.
Pronoun	*He* was really Superman.
Nouns	*Lois Lane* fell in love with *Superman*.
Pronouns	*She* fell in love with *him*.

Personal Pronouns

A *personal pronoun* can refer to a person, a place, a thing, or an idea.

Like a noun, a personal pronoun can have different jobs in different sentences. It can be a **subject**, an **object**, or a **possessive.**

> They ordered crab cakes for lunch. (subject)
> Mom invited them. (object)
> The station wagon is theirs. (possessive)

As you can see in the three sentences above, the pronoun takes a form that depends on its job. There are three forms of personal pronouns: **subject**, **object**, and **possessive**.

The following chart shows all the personal pronouns in English.

Forms of Personal Pronouns

	Subject	Object	Possessive
Singular	I	me	my, mine
	you	you	your, yours
	he, she, it	her, him, it	her, hers, his, its
Plural	we	us	our, ours
	you	you	your, yours
	they	them	their, theirs

Personal Pronouns at a Glance

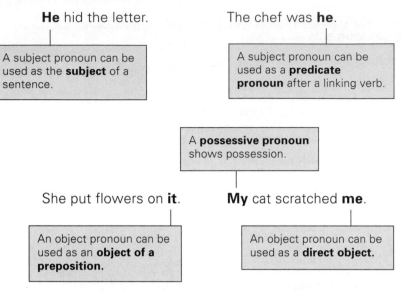

He hid the letter.

A subject pronoun can be used as the **subject** of a sentence.

The chef was **he**.

A subject pronoun can be used as a **predicate pronoun** after a linking verb.

A **possessive pronoun** shows possession.

She put flowers on **it**.

An object pronoun can be used as an **object of a preposition.**

My cat scratched **me**.

An object pronoun can be used as a **direct object.**

Exercise 1   Application in Literature

Identifying Pronoun Forms   Write the italicized personal pronouns in the following passage. Then write *S* above each subject pronoun, *O* above each object pronoun, and *P* above each possessive pronoun.

LITERARY MODEL
from "Nadia the Willful" by Sue Alexander

▶ (1) *She* went to where the shepherds tended the flock and spoke of Hamed. (2) The shepherds ran from *her* in fear and hid behind the sheep. But Nadia went on speaking. (3) *She* told of Hamed's love for the little black lamb and how *he* had taught *it* to leap at *his* whistle. (4) Soon the shepherds left off *their* hiding and came to listen. (5) Then *they* told *their* own stories of Hamed and the little black lamb.

Using the Subject Form

Use the subject form of a pronoun (*I, you, he, she, it, we,* or *they*) when the pronoun acts as the subject of a sentence or as a predicate pronoun. A **predicate pronoun** follows a linking verb and renames or describes the subject of a sentence.

Subject	**Predicate Pronoun**
She raked the beach.	The caretaker was *she*.
They kept the kitten.	The owners were *they*.

Using the Object Form

Use the object form of a pronoun (*me, you, him, her, it, us,* and *them*) when the pronoun acts as the object of a preposition or as a direct object.

Direct Object	Simon Bolívar liberated *them*.
Object of Preposition	Please write a letter to *me*.

Exercise 2   Concept Check

Using Subject and Object Pronouns   Write the correct pronoun.

1. In the museum (we, us) looked at an ancient Egyptian game.
2. My friend told (I, me) about the game called snake.
3. Lia explained the board game to all of (we, us).
4. (She, Her) pointed out the shape of a coiled green snake.
5. Lia and (I, me) talked about how old the game board was.
6. (We, Us) talked about Horus, a god whose picture appears on the board.
7. A hawk is the hieroglyphic sign for (he, him).
8. Later, Lia challenged (I, me) to a modern game of snake.
9. After two hours of playing, the winner was (she, her).
10. The Egyptians' game was fun for (they, them) and fun for (we, us).

Exercise 3   Proofreading Skill

Correcting Pronoun Forms   Rewrite the following paragraph, correcting all pronoun errors.

> (1) Us were curious about the food of the ancient Egyptians. (2) Mr. Taglione, the librarian, showed a typical Egyptian menu to I. (3) Melon, beef, onions, pita bread, dates, and figs were common foods for they. (4) Him and Ms. Woo read a list of other Egyptian foods. (5) Joy thought that wild celery and pomegranates would taste good to she. (6) After a while, the hungriest girl in the library was her.

Using the Possessive Form

Possessive pronouns show ownership. Unlike possessive nouns, possessive pronouns do not contain apostrophes.

Possessive Nouns	Marco's	women's
Possessive Pronouns	his	their

A **contraction** is a word that takes the place of two words. In contractions, apostrophes are used to signal missing letters. Three of the possessive pronouns are often confused with three contractions that sound like them. If you remember that possessive pronouns never have apostrophes, you won't confuse these words.

Possessive Pronouns	**Contractions**
its	it's (it is)
your	you're (you are)
their	they're (they are)

Exercise 4   Revision Skill

Pronouns and Contractions   Rewrite each sentence, correcting errors in the use of pronouns and contractions. If a sentence is already correct, write *Correct*.

1. Have you ever seen an animal try to keep it's balance on a floating log?
2. Well, people try to keep they're balance on logs too.
3. Your about to learn about a sport called logrolling.
4. "Logrolling" is its common name, but its also called birling.
5. Two logrollers stand on a log and spin it with they're feet.
6. Their goal is to make their opponents fall off the log.
7. Its an exciting sport with plenty of action.
8. If your lucky, you will get to watch a competition one day.
9. It's not unusual for a competition to last thirty minutes.
10. You might even try some logrolling of you're own!

Pronouns and Their Antecedents

The word to which a pronoun refers is its *antecedent*.

You can almost always find the word that a pronoun is replacing by looking back over the words before it in the sentence or paragraph.

> Do you know how *Calcutta* was named? *It* may have been named for the Hindu goddess Kali. (The antecedent of *it* is *Calcutta.*)

> *Kali* is known for *her* anger. (*Kali* is the antecedent of *her.*)

When you use a pronoun, make sure that the pronoun agrees with its antecedent. A singular antecedent takes a singular pronoun; a plural antecedent takes a plural pronoun.

Antecedent   Pronoun

The *singers* kept *their* voices low at the beginning of the song.

Exercise 5   Concept Check

Pronouns and Their Antecedents   Write the pronouns in the following sentences. Then write the antecedent of each pronoun.

Example   Every country has its heroes.
Answer   its, country

1. Franklin Delano Roosevelt is an American hero; many people admire him.
2. Roosevelt gave the country the New Deal. It included benefits for the unemployed, for farmers, and for laborers.
3. Franklin and Eleanor Roosevelt worked tirelessly. They are remembered fondly and with great respect.
4. Roosevelt was also president during World War II, when people counted on him to defeat the Germans and the Japanese.
5. Eleanor was a friend of the poor; she helped them in many ways.

Indefinite Pronouns

An *indefinite pronoun* is a pronoun that does not refer to a particular person or thing.

The following chart lists singular and plural indefinite pronouns.

Singular Indefinite Pronouns

another	each	everything	nothing
anybody	either	neither	one
anyone	everybody	nobody	somebody
anything	everyone	no one	someone

Plural Indefinite Pronouns

both	few	many	several

Pronouns that have indefinite pronouns as their antecedents must agree in number with the antecedents.

NONSEXIST LANGUAGE

Today we no longer use the masculine pronouns *he, him,* and *his* to refer to all people. We now use *he or she* or *his or her* as a way of referring to a situation where the antecedent could be either a male or female. Example: A mayor should keep *his or her* budget balanced.

▶ Someone is flying in (his or her, their) balloon. (The indefinite pronoun *Someone* is singular. Therefore, the singular *his or her* is correct.)

Many wish (he or she, they) could fly with him. (The indefinite pronoun *Many* is plural. Therefore, the plural pronoun *they* is correct.)

Exercise 6   Revision Skill

Agreement with Indefinite Antecedents   Write the correct possessive pronouns.

1. Each of the girls in our class must write (her, their) research paper on China.
2. Many of the girls will write (our, their) reports on the Great Wall.
3. One of the twins will do (her, their) research about the emperor who built the wall, Shi Huangdi.
4. Because China was often attacked by outside invaders, the people lived in fear of losing (his or her, their) lives.
5. Emperor Shi Huangdi planned the wall; neither he nor his successors saw the completion of (his, their) labors.
6. Each of the sections has (its, their) own history.
7. Many Chinese people hoped the wall would guarantee (its, their) safety.
8. Few realized that (his or her, their) wall could be broken through.
9. Anyone would want to spend (his or her, their) time seeing this structure.
10. Each of my uncles has extended (his, their) vacation to China in order to see the Great Wall.

Exercise 7   Revision Skill

Pronoun Usage   Most of the following sentences contain errors in the use of pronouns, contractions, or pronoun agreement. Rewrite the sentences that need correction. If a sentence has no error, write *Correct.*

1. Both Martin and Andrea have studied they're notes about American folk heroes.
2. Their busy writing a report on Paul Bunyan, Johnny Appleseed, and other folk heroes.
3. Long ago, many learned in their history classes that Betsy Ross sewed the first U.S. flag.
4. There is actually no proof that the flag was sewn by she.
5. Another folk hero is Davy Crockett; there are many frontier legends about he.
6. Its fun to read stories about Jesse James, a robber of banks and trains.
7. Legends about Jesse James have made he an American folk hero.
8. Is there anyone who hasn't seen a picture of Uncle Sam in one of their history books?
9. Although Uncle Sam is a figure that represents the United States, him was not a real person.
10. Their reading legends about the origins of Uncle Sam.
11. Carrie and me hope to learn more about how the legend of Uncle Sam came about.
12. You're poetry book contains a poem about Barbara Frietchie.
13. According to some, she was a brave and patriotic Union woman.
14. Was the woman who waved the Union flag at Confederate troops really her?
15. Many of the folk-hero legends are based on truth, but their not all true.

SECTION 6: USING VERBS

A *verb* expresses an action or a state of being.

> Kendra *grabbed* the can from the shelf.
> His songs *are* funny and popular.
> She *was* home yesterday.

An *action verb* is a verb that tells what a subject does.

> Gabriela *clapped* her hands.   The audience *talked* loudly.

A *linking verb* connects the subject of a sentence to a word that renames or describes the subject.

> Sue *is* intelligent.   Her hand *felt* cold.
> Allan *was* the champion.   The water *looks* choppy.

All the forms of the verb *be* are linking verbs. These include *am, is, are, was, were, be, been,* and *being.* Other common linking verbs are *appear, become, feel, grow, look, seem, smell, sound,* and *taste.*

QUICK TIP   Some words can be either action verbs or linking verbs. To see whether a verb is a linking verb, try replacing it with a form of *be.* If the sentence still makes sense, the verb is a linking verb. If it does not, the verb is an action verb.

> The fresh-cut grass *smelled* sweet. ("The fresh-cut grass is sweet" makes sense, so *smelled* is a linking verb here. *Sweet* describes the *fresh-cut grass.*)

> The young child smelled the white rose. ("The young child is the white rose" does not make sense. *Smelled* is an action verb here.)

Exercise 1   Concept Check

Types of Verbs   Write the verbs in the following sentences. After each verb, write *A* for *action* or *L* for *linking.*

1. Maya Angelou gave a reading in New York City yesterday.
2. I saw her on television.
3. She is a wonderful speaker and writer.
4. Angelou spent much of her early life in Stamps, Arkansas.
5. Her grandmother was very important in Maya's early life.
6. Her autobiography, *I Know Why the Caged Bird Sings,* was a bestseller.

7. She also writes wonderful poems.
8. Much of Maya Angelou's work seems inspirational.
9. President Jimmy Carter appointed her to a commission on women's rights.
10. Angelou also read a poem at President Bill Clinton's inauguration.

Verb Phrases

A *verb phrase* consists of a main verb and one or more helping verbs.

Often the **main verb** of a sentence is accompanied by one or more **helping verbs.** A main verb with one or more helping verbs is called a **verb phrase.** Notice the helping verbs in italics below.

will run   *could be* prevented   *has been* searching

Helping Verbs	
Forms of *be*	am, is, are, was, were, be, been, being
Forms of *do*	do, does, did
Forms of *have*	have, has, had
Other Verbs	can will shall may must could would should might

Verbs at a Glance

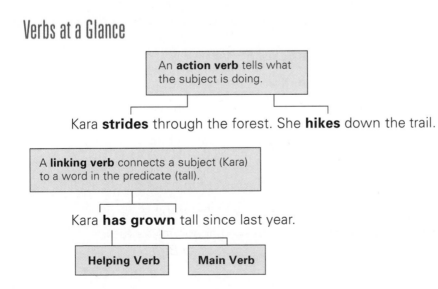

An **action verb** tells what the subject is doing.

Kara **strides** through the forest. She **hikes** down the trail.

A **linking verb** connects a subject (Kara) to a word in the predicate (tall).

Kara **has grown** tall since last year.

Helping Verb   Main Verb

Exercise 2   Concept Check

Types of Verbs   Write the verb phrase in each sentence. Underline the helping verb once and the main verb twice.

1. Everyone must know some of the legends about King Arthur.
2. We have been reading many stories about this medieval king.
3. He has been called the most famous king in the history of England.
4. Arthur had named his knights the knights of the Round Table.
5. Storytellers might have added bits and pieces to this legend about a king and his knights.

Exercise 3   Drafting Skill

Helping Verbs   Add a helping verb to complete the meaning of each sentence.

1. Joel __?__ been a reader of the Arthur legends for many years.
2. He __?__ know the answer to your question about the Lady of the Lake.
3. He __?__ read about the sword in the stone many times.
4. Joel __?__ know the story of Guinevere and Lancelot too.
5. When it comes to legends, he __?__ be the most knowledgeable person in our class.

Verb Tense

Every verb has several different forms that are used to refer to different times. These forms are called the *tenses* of the verb.

Tenses of Verbs

Present   Shows an action that is happening now or that happens regularly or constantly

> Now: Joaquim *looks* happy.
> Regularly: The gardener *plants* bulbs each fall.
> Constantly: The human heart *contains* four chambers.

Past   Shows an action that was completed in the past

> The tide *came* in at 6:37 last night.

Future   Shows an action that will happen in the future

> Dorinda *will* join us tomorrow.

TENSE CHANGES

The tense of a verb can be changed in three ways: (1) by a change in ending—*look, looked*; (2) by a change in spelling—*know, knew;* (3) by a change in helping verb—*will play, has played.*

Exercise 4   Concept Check

Identifying Tenses   Identify the verb and its tense in each sentence.

1. This book discusses legends of ancient Rome.
2. Ms. Carrera will tell us about the founding of the city.
3. The story is about Romulus and Remus, the twin sons of the war god.
4. Together they established Rome on the banks of the Tiber River.
5. Later, Romulus killed his brother.

Exercise 5   Drafting Skill

Using Tenses   Complete the following sentences with the verb forms described in parentheses. Write the complete sentences.

1. Today we (future of *learn*) about the early lives of Romulus and Remus.
2. This (present of *be*) the most interesting part of their history.
3. A jealous uncle (past tense of *throw*) them into the Tiber River.
4. A female wolf (past tense of *save*) the young twins.
5. A statue of this famous wolf now (present tense of *stand*) in a museum in Rome.

Principal Parts of Verbs

Every verb has four principal parts. The principal parts of verbs are the *present*, the *present participle*, the *past*, and the *past participle*.

The principal parts of verbs are used to make the verb tenses. Most verbs are regular, like those in the chart below. **Regular verbs** are those in which *-ed* or *-d* is added to the present form to show the past tense. The past form never has a helping verb. The past participle is the same as the past form, but it always has a helping verb.

Regular Verbs			
Present	**Present Participle**	**Past**	**Past Participle**
help	(is) helping	helped	(have) helped
lift	(is) lifting	lifted	(have) lifted
wait	(is) waiting	waited	(have) waited

Verbs whose past tense is not formed by adding *-ed* or *-d* are called **irregular verbs.** In some cases the past and the past participle are the same, but in many cases they are not. Learn as many of the irregular forms in the following chart as you can.

Irregular Verbs

Present	Past	Past Participle	Present	Past	Past Participle
become	became	(has) become	rise	rose	(has) risen
blow	blew	(has) blown	run	ran	(has) run
break	broke	(has) broken	say	said	(has) said
bring	brought	(has) brought	see	saw	(has) seen
build	built	(has) built	shake	shook	(has) shaken
choose	chose	(has) chosen	shrink	shrank	(has) shrunk
come	came	(has) come	sing	sang	(has) sung
do	did	(has) done	sink	sank	(has) sunk
draw	drew	(has) drawn	sleep	slept	(has) slept
drink	drank	(has) drunk	speak	spoke	(has) spoken
drive	drove	(has) driven	spend	spent	(has) spent
eat	ate	(has) eaten	spring	sprang	(has) sprung
fall	fell	(has) fallen	stand	stood	(has) stood
fly	flew	(has) flown	steal	stole	(has) stolen
give	gave	(has) given	swear	swore	(has) sworn
go	went	(has) gone	swim	swam	(has) swum
grow	grew	(has) grown	take	took	(has) taken
keep	kept	(has) kept	teach	taught	(has) taught
know	knew	(has) known	think	thought	(has) thought
lead	led	(has) led	throw	threw	(has) thrown
leave	left	(has) left	wear	wore	(has) worn
meet	met	(has) met	write	wrote	(has) written
ride	rode	(has) ridden			

Exercise 6   Concept Check

Irregular Verbs   Write the correct verb form.

1. We have (came, come) to the unit about metals in our science books.
2. Ancient people (knew, knowed) about several different metals.
3. Many ancient people (think, thought) silver was more valuable than gold because it was rarer.
4. Copper and iron (became, become) the most commonly used metals.

5. Engineers have (took, taken) the main ingredient of steel, the metal iron, from iron ore.

6. Since about 1000 B.C., iron has (met, meet) people's need for strong tools.

7. Modern builders have (chose, chosen) steel for its strength.

8. Many of the engineering advances of modern civilization have (rose, risen) out of the knowledge of how to make steel.

9. In structures all over the world, steel has supported great weight and has not (wore, worn) out.

10. Today, however, supplies of iron ore have (shrank, shrunk).

11. The shortage of iron has (led, lead) engineers to replace steel with aluminum.

12. The use of aluminum has (grew, grown) dramatically.

13. Many new cars, for example, are (build, built) with aluminum.

14. Like steel, aluminum does not (break, broke) easily if it is thick.

15. Experts have (spoke, spoken) about the need to find other uses of aluminum.

Confusing Verb Pairs

The following verb pairs are sometimes confused.

Let means "to permit or allow." *Leave* means "to cause or allow to remain."

> *Let* me take your bags.
> *Leave* your keys on the hook.

Lie means "to rest in a flat position." *Lie* never takes a direct object. *Lay* means "to place." It almost always takes a direct object.

> The cat will sometimes *lie* in front of the fireplace.
> *Lay* your coat down on the bed.

Sit means "to occupy a seat." *Sit* never takes a direct object. *Set* means "to place." *Set* almost always takes a direct object.

> Su Lin and Leah will *sit* together at lunch today.
> Why don't we *set* the lilacs on the table?

Rise means "to go upward." It never takes a direct object. *Raise* means "to lift" or "to make something go up." It usually has a direct object.

> The sun will *rise* at six o'clock tomorrow morning.
> If you *raise* the lid of the box, you'll see the surprise.

	Present	Past	Past Participle
Let and **Leave**	let	let	(has) let
	leave	left	(has) left
Lie and **Lay**	lie	lay	(has) lain
	lay	laid	(has) laid
Sit and **Set**	sit	sat	(has) sat
	set	set	(has) set
Rise and **Raise**	rise	rose	(has) risen
	raise	raised	(has) raised

Two other verbs that are sometimes confused are *can* and *may*. *Can* means "to be able." *May* means "to be allowed" or "to be permitted."

Belia *can* sing loudest.
You *may* leave the room.

Exercise 7   Concept Check

Confusing Verbs   Write the correct verb form.

1. "(Can, May) we look at some paintings of life in colonial America?" Shira asked.
2. (Lie, Lay) the art book on the table in front of us.
3. "(Sit, Set) down for a moment and look at this," she said.
4. "I know you (can, may) find *The Peaceable Kingdom* in here," she told us.
5. In this painting many different animals are sent to (lay, lie) peacefully on the ground together.
6. In the center of the painting (sit, set) two young children.
7. Another child seems to (rise, raise) up from the animals in the background.
8. The painter Edward Hicks (sat, set) forth an idea of peace in the New World.
9. The wolf (lies, lays) down with the lamb, and Native Americans and European colonists exist peacefully together.
10. The painting shows how Quakers had (raised, risen) their hopes about living peacefully among all creatures in the New World.

Exercise 8   Proofreading Skill

Verb Review   Each of the following sentences contains one error in verb usage. Write the correct verb.

1. Many people have wrote about the building called Hagia Sophia in Istanbul, Turkey.
2. It were a beautiful Christian church built by a Roman emperor.
3. Have you ever saw pictures of this beautiful building?
4. I will sit some photographs out on this table for you.
5. Leave me show you its huge dome in this photograph.
6. The dome raises majestically to a height of 180 feet.
7. The dome has gave an inspiring quality to the inside of the building throughout its history.
8. Today Arabic is wrote on some parts of the walls.
9. Muslims taked over the church and added to its beauty.
10. Did Christians really lie the foundations of a Muslim house of worship?

Exercise 9   Revision Skill

Verb Usage Review   Rewrite the following paragraph, correcting any errors in verb usage.

(1) The whole class set down together to talk about the story of Aladdin. (2) People have tell this story for generations. (3) In the story Aladdin come upon a genie in a magic lamp. (4) The lamp had laid in a secret place, untouched for hundreds of years. (5) Only a worthy individual could have brung that lamp out of its hiding place. (6) Although he was poor, Aladdin raised to the challenge. (7) The class decided that the story teached them a lesson. (8) With a pure heart and courage, anyone may do extraordinary things.

SECTION 7: USING ADJECTIVES AND ADVERBS

Understanding Adjectives

An *adjective* is a word that modifies a noun or a pronoun.

clean air   *unbroken* chain   *scratchy* blanket
peaceful music   *angry* bee   *open* door

Articles

Three little words used in many sentences are *a, an,* and *the.* These special adjectives are called **articles.** *The,* which is sometimes called the **definite article,** points to a specific person, place, thing, or group.

the governor   *the* tortilla   *the* Pacific

A and *an,* which are sometimes called **indefinite articles,** indicate kinds of items, rather than specific ones. *A* is used before a consonant or consonant sound. *An* is used before a vowel or a vowel sound.

▶   *an* owl   *a* tablecloth   *a* hedge   *an* honor

SILENT *H*
. . . .
The silent *h* in words such as *honor* and *hour* should be preceded by *an* rather than *a.*

Proper and Common Adjectives

Adjectives formed from proper nouns are known as *proper adjectives.*

A proper adjective is an adjective formed from a proper noun. A proper noun names a specific person, place, thing, or idea.

Notice that some proper nouns, such as *New Hampshire,* do not change form when they become proper adjectives.

Proper Noun	Proper Adjective	Example
Guatemala	Guatemalan	Guatemalan folktale
Switzerland	Swiss	Swiss cheese
New Hampshire	New Hampshire	New Hampshire granite
Jamaica	Jamaican	Jamaican music
Hawaii	Hawaiian	Hawaiian luau

When an adjective is not an article or a proper adjective, it is called a **common adjective.** Here are some examples: *warm, rough, shiny, yellow, sweet, kind,* and *indignant.*

Exercise 1 Concept Check

Identifying Adjectives Write the adjectives in the following sentences on your paper. Then label each one *P* for *proper adjective* or *C* for *common adjective.* Ignore the articles.

Example	What do the Asian elephant and the blue whale have in common?
Answer	Asian, P blue, C

1. A large number of animals disappear every year.
2. What Australian birds are on the endangered list?
3. There are long lists of animals that are in serious danger.
4. Other animals that are in danger are the Florida cougar, the California condor, and the humpback whale.
5. Few people who live in America have seen an American crocodile.
6. Many rare plants are also in danger.
7. People have destroyed sections of tropical forests.
8. Environmental groups identify new animals in trouble.
9. The various organizations concern themselves with water pollution and air pollution as well as with animals in danger.
10. Higher standards for clean air and water might help us solve environmental problems.

Predicate Adjectives

A *linking verb* can connect an adjective to the noun it modifies. An adjective used this way is called a *predicate adjective.*

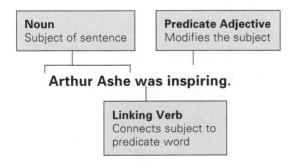

Here are some commonly used linking verbs: *am, are, be, been, being, is, was, were, become, feel, grow, look, appear, seem, smell,* and *taste.*

Exercise 2 Concept Check

Predicate Adjectives Write each sentence on your paper. Circle the linking verb. Underline the subject once. Then underline the predicate adjective or adjectives twice.

1. Liberty Island is popular as a New York tourist attraction.
2. The statue on this island was important to many immigrants arriving in the United States by boat.
3. The Statue of Liberty looks magnificent in New York Harbor.
4. It appears especially beautiful at night.
5. Lady Liberty is not dainty; she weighs 225 tons.
6. Her 150-foot-high pedestal is huge.
7. Many people feel inspired reading the poem on the pedestal.
8. Emma Lazarus is famous for writing the poem, called "The New Colossus."
9. The statue seems both kind and mighty in this poem.
10. It would be terrific to visit the island someday.

Understanding Adverbs

An *adverb* can modify a verb, an adjective, or another adverb. Many adverbs end in *-ly.*

Modifying Verbs	runs *quickly,* plays *well,* smiled *shyly*
Modifying Adjectives	*very* angry, *quite* healthy, *extremely* pleased
Modifying Adverbs:	*too* slowly, *quite* recently, *so* happily

Exercise 3 Concept Check

Finding Adjectives and Adverbs Make two columns on your paper. In the first column write all the adjectives (except articles) you find in the following paragraph. Write all the adverbs in the second column.

(1) Ancient Roman merchants traded indirectly with Chinese merchants. (2) European people wanted the valuable and unusual fabric called silk. (3) The Chinese people closely guarded the secret of making this precious cloth. (4) What was the trade route between Europe and China commonly called? (5) Travel was unsafe

along the route, so Roman merchants avoided traveling the entire distance from Europe to China. (6) Traders went back and forth between marketplaces along the route.

Adjective or Adverb?

Adjectives and adverbs are the two parts of speech that modify, or change, the meanings of other words.

Adjective   He is a *happy* child. (*Happy* is an adjective that changes the meaning of the noun *child*.)

Adverb   She seems *slightly* nervous. (*Slightly* is an adverb that changes the meaning of the adjective *nervous*.)

Adjectives and adverbs modify different kinds of words. An adjective always modifies a noun or a pronoun. An adverb always modifies a verb, an adjective, or another adverb.

A linking verb connects a noun or a pronoun to a word that modifies or renames it. You always need an adjective, not an adverb, to modify a noun or a pronoun. Do not use an adverb after a linking verb.

Incorrect   She became *happily.*

Correct   She became *happy.*

On the other hand, you always need an adverb, not an adjective, to modify a verb, an adjective, or an adverb.

Incorrect   Suzana danced *good.*

Correct   Suzana danced *well.*

Exercise 4   Concept Check

Choosing the Correct Modifier   Write the modifier that is correct.

1. The effect of smells on humans is (real, really) interesting.
2. The smell of (fresh, freshly) cookies can make people happy.
3. Sometimes machines in shopping malls release delightful smells to make people feel (secure, securely) and encourage them to shop.
4. Some garbage bags never smell (bad, badly) because pleasant aromas are added to the plastic.
5. A new-car smell is even added to some cars to be released (slow, slowly) over time.

IT'S REALLY REAL
. . . .
The word *real* is an adjective, while *really* is an adverb. Notice how the following sentence requires an adverb to modify *sweet.*
Incorrect
That ice cream tastes *real* sweet.
Correct
That ice cream tastes *really* sweet.

Exercise 5   Proofreading Skill

Using Modifiers Correctly   Decide whether the italicized modifiers in the following paragraph are used correctly. If the modifier is correct, write *Correct* on your paper. If the modifier needs to be changed, write the correct form on your paper.

(1) Does an idea called Smell-O-Vision sound *crazily* to you? (2) The idea didn't seem *bad* to some moviegoers in 1959. (3) Back then, a Smell-O-Vision movie called *The Scent of Mystery* featured smells piped *direct* to every seat in the theater. (4) The audience smelled more than forty fragrances that were *closely* related to the events in the film. (5) Obviously, Smell-O-Vision did not catch on very *good*.

Avoiding Double Negatives

Do not use two negative words together in the same sentence.

Some adverbs are negative words. Here are some of them: *not, never, hardly, scarcely,* and *rarely.* Words like *no, none,* and *nothing* are also negatives. So are contractions that contain *not,* such as *don't* (do not). If you use two negative words when only one is needed, the result is an error called a **double negative.**

Double Negative	I have *never* seen *no* blackbirds around here.
Correct	I have never seen any blackbirds around here.
Correct	I have seen no blackbirds around here.
Double Negative	We *don't* have *no* umbrellas.
Correct	We don't have any umbrellas.
Correct	We have no umbrellas.
Double Negative	She *wouldn't never* upset her friend.
Correct	She wouldn't ever upset her friend.
Correct	She would never upset her friend.

Exercise 6   Proofreading Skill

Correcting Double Negatives   Rewrite the following sentences, correcting all double negatives.

1. Some people don't know nothing about the contributions of Italian Americans to our country.

2. I have scarcely heard nothing about the accomplishments of Italian Americans.

3. There is hardly no female U.S. politician more famous than Geraldine Ferraro, who was once a candidate for vice-president.

4. Haven't you ever heard nothing about the Nobel Prize winner Renato Dulbecco?

5. Haven't you never heard of Lee Iacocca, one of America's most famous businessmen?

6. At first I didn't want to write no report on Fiorello La Guardia, the former mayor of New York.

7. If I hadn't written the report, I wouldn't have learned nothing about this great man.

8. I wouldn't never have known that he was the first Italian American in the U.S. House of Representatives.

9. Haven't you never heard of these famous Italian Americans: Frank Sinatra, Sylvester Stallone, and Madonna?

10. Governor Mario Cuomo has considered running for the U.S. presidency, but he wasn't never an actual candidate.

Adjectives and Adverbs in Comparisons

Many modifiers have special forms that are used to compare the qualities of two or more things. A *comparative form* compares a person or thing with one other person or thing. A *superlative form* compares a person or thing with two or more persons or things.

	Adjective
Modifier	I have a *bad* cold.
Comparative	Your cold is *worse* than mine.
Superlative	Bob has the *worst* cold.

	Adverb
Modifier	I work *diligently.*
Comparative	Sheila works more *diligently* than I do.
Superlative	Tom works most *diligently* of all.

For many short adjectives and adverbs, the comparative is formed by adding *-er,* and the superlative is formed by adding *-est.* Sometimes, slight spelling changes are required when these suffixes are added.

Modifier	Comparative	Superlative
shy	shyer	shyest
hot	hotter	hottest
happy	happier	happiest
cloudy	cloudier	cloudiest

For many longer modifiers, the comparative is formed by adding *more,* and the superlative is formed by adding *most.*

Modifier	Comparative	Superlative
colorful	more colorful	most colorful
beautiful	more beautiful	most beautiful
clearly	more clearly	most clearly
carefully	more carefully	most carefully

A **double comparison** occurs when *-er* is used with *more* or *-est* is used with *most.* A double comparison, like a double negative, is an error.

| **Incorrect** | more better | most quietest |
| **Correct** | better | most quiet |

Exercise 7   Revision Skill

Comparison of Modifiers   Find the errors in adjective and adverb forms in the following sentences. Write the correct forms on your paper.

1. Of popcorn, ice cream, and potato chips, which do you think is the healthier snack?
2. Potato chips seem like the greasier of all the snack foods.
3. Regular microwave popcorn has a more higher percentage of fat than regular ice cream.
4. Buttered and salted microwave popcorn is not the healthier snack choice you can make.
5. Popcorn popped on a stove or in a popping machine, without butter, has fewest calories than microwave popcorn.
6. Some people think that microwave popcorn with salt and butter is the most flavorfulest kind of popcorn.
7. Microwave popcorn may be the easier of all popcorns to prepare.

8. Popcorn sold in jars or bags is cheapest than the varieties packaged for microwaves.
9. I also find that popping popcorn on the stove is more funner than making microwave popcorn.
10. Most dentists say that eating any kind of popcorn is smartest than eating sugary snacks.

Unusual Comparative and Superlative Forms

Some modifiers do not use *-er, -est, more,* or *most* in comparisons. They change form completely.

Modifier	Comparative	Superlative
bad	worse	worst
good	better	best
little	less	least
many	more	most
much	more	most
well	better	best

Exercise 8   Concept Check

Unusual Forms   Find the errors in modifier forms in the following sentences. Write the modifiers correctly.

1. The goodest book I have read lately is a collection of stories from Trinidad, called *A Wave in Her Pocket.*
2. I like "The Bamboo Beads" most than any other story in the book.
3. Its interesting plot makes it the better story in the collection.
4. Another story, "The Graveyard Jumbies," is the one I liked the less of all.
5. I thought it was worser than the story we had to read for homework last night.
6. Tantie, who tells all the stories, is the bestest storyteller ever.
7. More stories that she tells come from West Africa or Trinidad.
8. I think this book is gooder than *Where the Red Fern Grows.*
9. For a while I wanted to own that novel in the worse way.
10. Now I have lesser interest in it than in *A Wave in Her Pocket.*

Using Demonstrative Adjectives

This, that, these, and *those* can be used either as **demonstrative pronouns** or as **demonstrative adjectives.** When they are used as demonstrative pronouns, they point out specific persons or things but do not modify other words.

> Please give me *that.*

When they are used as demonstrative adjectives, these words modify other words—nouns or pronouns.

> Please give me *that* fan.

Use *this* and *that* to modify singular nouns. Use *these* and *those* to modify plural nouns.

this train	*these* trains
that collar	*those* collars

Exercise 9 Revision Skill

Demonstrative Adjectives   Rewrite the following paragraph, correcting the errors that you find. If a sentence has no errors, write *Correct.*

(1) Today I want to show you some examples of space spinoffs—things used every day that were invented for the space program. (2) This Mylar blankets are an example. (3) So are those there freeze-dried foods. (4) This kinds of objects were first used in the U.S. space program. (5) That there material in the car seat and dentist's chair is the same material that makes an astronaut's ride in space more comfortable. (6) These hand-held vacuum cleaner is based on technology that was used to collect rocks on the moon. (7) These athletic shoe, which absorbs shock better and lasts longer than a traditional shoe, uses ideas that were developed for making spacesuits. (8) That sorts of uses of space technology are getting to be very common.

Exercise 10   Revision Skill

Modifier Review   All of the following sentences contain errors in the use of modifiers. Rewrite the sentences correctly.

1. Some weather on the earth can be real extreme.
2. I don't never want to spend time at Commonwealth Bay, Antarctica.
3. It is one of the most windiest places on earth.

IT TAKES ALL KINDS
(AND SORTS)
. . . .
Use the singular demonstrative adjectives *this* and *that* with the singular nouns *kind* and *sort.* Use the plural adjectives *these* and *those* with the plural nouns *kinds* and *sorts.*

Singular	**Plural**
this kind	these kinds
that sort	those sorts

HERE AND THERE
. . . .
Do not use *here* and *there* with demonstrative adjectives.
Incorrect
This here cat needs to go outside.
Correct
This cat needs to go outside.

4. Those there winds can blow at speeds of 200 miles per hour.
5. Maybe being at Commonwealth Bay is more better than living in Al Azizyah, Libya.
6. On September 13, 1922, it had the hotter temperature ever recorded in the world.
7. Even if you like hot weather, 136 degrees Fahrenheit is extreme hot.
8. This kinds of extremes in weather can be just as unpleasant when they involve rain and snow.
9. The more rain received by any place during twelve months—1,042 inches—fell in the town of Cherrapunji, India.
10. I can't hardly imagine getting almost eighty-seven feet of rain in a year.
11. Maybe the worse weather of all is a big snowstorm.
12. Silver Lake, Colorado, got the mostest snow in twenty-four hours when seventy-six inches fell there in April of 1921.
13. For more people who lived there, that snowstorm must have been amazing.
14. I think I am most happiest living where it is not too windy, too hot, too rainy, or too snowy.
15. I don't never want to leave my home in Elizabeth, New Jersey.

SECTION 8: SUBJECT—VERB AGREEMENT

Singular and Plural

Singular means "one" and **plural** means "more than one." A **singular** noun or pronoun names one person, place, thing, or idea. A **plural** noun or pronoun names more than one.

Singular	Plural
kitten	kittens
farm	farms
shop	shops

Verbs also have singular and plural forms. The following table shows the present tense forms of the verb "to know."

	Singular	Plural
First person	I know	we know
Second person	you know	you know
Third person	he, she, or it knows	they know

The verb form remains the same in each of the six positions except in the third-person singular. In the present tense, an *-s* is added to the end of third-person singular verbs.

A few verbs have special singular and plural forms, as shown by the following examples.

	Be	Have	Do
Singular Forms	is, am, was	has, had	does, did
Plural Forms	are, were	have, had	do, did

Exercise 1   Concept Check

Identifying Singular and Plural Words   Tell whether the italicized word in each sentence is singular or plural.

1. Arlene Jefferson *does* research on termites.
2. *People* often think of termites simply as destructive insects.
3. The termite *is* both a fantastic builder and a talented destroyer.
4. These tiny *insects* build mounds as high as thirty feet.
5. Tunnels *connect* the spaces inside these huge mounds.
6. A termite *colony* takes as long as eight years to build such a huge mound.
7. Besides being great builders, termites also *have* huge appetites.

8. They *damage* forests and also cause wooden beams to collapse.

9. This full-time eating *machine* inflicts its damage silently and steadily.

10. As a result, homeowners *fear* these tiny creatures.

Agreement of Subject and Verb

A verb and its subject must agree in number.

A singular subject takes a singular verb. A plural subject takes a plural verb.

> In developing countries, many <u>people</u> <u>suffer</u> blindness. (*People* is plural, so it takes the plural verb *suffer.*)

> <u>Glaucoma</u> <u>is</u> one cause of blindness that is preventable. (*Glaucoma* is singular, so it takes the singular verb *is.*)

QUICK TIP   Sometimes a prepositional phrase separates a verb from its subject. The verb must still agree with its subject. The object of the prepositional phrase is *not* the subject of the verb.

Incorrect: The <u>cup</u> with the flowers <u>are</u> mine.
(The verb incorrectly agrees with the object of the preposition, *flowers,* instead of with its subject, *cup.*)

Correct: The <u>cup</u> with the flowers <u>is</u> mine.
(The verb correctly agrees with its subject, *cup.*)

Exercise 2   Drafting Skill

Making Subjects and Verbs Agree   Write the correct verbs.

1. This book (tell, tells) about the travels of Marco Polo.

2. We (look, looks) at some of Polo's books from time to time.

3. Marco (was, were) a member of a family of adventurers.

4. At that time in Europe, journeys to the East (was, were) not common.

5. Marco Polo's character traits (make, makes) him a memorable figure in world history.

6. Marco Polo's books (contain, contains) both fact and fiction.

7. The books also (explain, explains) in great detail much of what he experienced.

8. The stories of his trip (was, were) not believable to many Europeans of that time.

9. His adventures at the court of Kublai Khan (is, are) recorded for the world to read.

10. Our class (enjoy, enjoys) his descriptions of oil, coal, crocodiles, yaks, and coconuts.

Agreement with Compound Subjects

When two or more subjects share the same verb, they are known as a *compound subject*.

A compound subject that has parts joined by *and* takes a plural verb.

Compound Subject	<u>Carnivals and circuses</u> <u>are</u> part of our country's heritage.

A compound subject that has parts joined by *or* or *nor* takes a verb that agrees with the subject closest to the verb.

Compound Subject	Neither <u>Sam nor his friends</u> <u>have</u> a basketball. (The verb *have* agrees with the nearer subject, *friends*.)
Compound Subject	Either the <u>pineapple or the apricots</u> <u>make</u> a nice dessert. (The verb *make* agrees with the nearer subject, *apricots*.)

Exercise 3   Drafting Skill

Choosing the Correct Verb   Write the correct verb.

1. Animals and veterinary students (fill, fills) the Lifeline for Wildlife, a veterinary clinic in New York.

2. Neither wild animals nor tame ones (is, are) turned away from the clinic.

3. Neither peace nor quiet (reign, reigns) in this busy clinic.

4. Inside the cages, either a squirrel or two baby muskrats (screams, scream) in fright.

5. Neither the birds nor the injured raccoon (understand, understands) that the veterinarians are there to help.

6. A sparrow and a pelican (needs, need) to have someone clean oil from their feathers.

7. Neither the baby opossums nor the fawn (seem, seems) to be healing fast.

8. Shari and Valerie (clean, cleans) the cages as often as they can.
9. Either tubes or bottles (is used, are used) to feed the babies.
10. Both adults and children (thank, thanks) the doctors for saving creatures' lives.

Agreement with Indefinite Pronouns

Singular indefinite pronouns take singular verbs.

Each apple is washed carefully.

Plural indefinite pronouns take plural verbs.

Many swimmers are strong.

Some indefinite pronouns can be either singular or plural.

These indefinite pronouns are plural in some sentences and singular in others: *all, any, most, none,* and *some.* You can decide whether they are singular or plural by looking at the rest of the sentence.

All of the cake is gone. (*All* is singular because *cake* is singular.)

All of the Jackson girls got A's in chemistry. (*All* is plural because *girls* is plural)

Indefinite Pronouns			
Singular	another	anybody	anyone	anything
	each	either	everybody	everyone
	everything	neither	nobody	no one
	one	somebody	someone	
Plural	both	few	many	several
Singular or Plural	all	most	none	some
	any			

Agreement with Indefinite Pronouns   Rewrite the following paragraph, choosing the verb that agrees with each subject.

(1) Milo and Temos (lives, live) in Pompeii. (2) Most of their friends (attends, attend) private school with them. (3) Everyone in the town (hears, hear) Mt. Vesuvius roar occasionally. (4) Few (worries, worry) about its rumbling. (5) No one (believes, believe) that anything will happen. (6) Neither the teacher nor the boys (pays, pay) much attention to the volcano.

Agreement with I and You

Although *you* can refer to one person or more than one person, it always takes a plural verb.

You *were* the best artist in the competition. (one person)
You *were* the best wrestlers at the meet. (more than one)

Although the pronoun *I* refers to one person, it uses the plural form of the verb.

I *do* a lot of reading at night.
I *have* a long reading list.
I *plan* my reading time carefully.

Exception: With the verb "to be," *I* takes a singular form.

I *am* eager to be in the tournament.
I *was* the champion chess player last year.

Making Subjects and Verbs Agree   Write the correct verb.

1. I (was reading, were reading) about the Black Hawk War yesterday.
2. I (am, is) eager to learn more about Black Hawk himself.
3. Today you (find, finds) information about the Treaty of 1804 in many history books.
4. I (think, thinks) the treaty was unfair to the Sauks, who traded their land for very little money.
5. You (say, says) that William Henry Harrison made this treaty with five chiefs.
6. I (read, reads) that the Sauks traded a large part of their land in what is now Illinois, Missouri, and Wisconsin.

7. You (tell, tells) me they received a little more than two thousand dollars for their land.
8. I (was, were) sure that they also got a small yearly income.
9. You (mention, mentions) how angry Black Hawk was about this treaty.
10. I (agree, agrees) that the Sauks traded a great deal to get very little in return.

Exercise 6   Drafting Skill

Review of Subject-Verb Agreement   Write the correct verb.

1. My brother and I often (wonders, wonder) about our ancestry.
2. Either Benin or Songhai (is, are) the kingdom that my ancestors came from.
3. Neither my mother nor my other relatives (know, knows) for sure.
4. Our grandparents (tells, tell) us what they were told.
5. You must sometimes (listens, listen) to hear your own history.
6. I (am, is) sure some people have written records of their ancestors.
7. Many African Americans in my neighborhood (believe, believes) that their ancestors came from Benin.
8. Everybody (is, are) certain that their ancestors came from what was called the slave coast.
9. We (likes, like) to read books from the library about Benin and Songhai.
10. I (has, have) an interest in the art and religion of the people who lived there.
11. Many beliefs, songs, and dances (was brought, were brought) by slaves from that region to the United States.
12. The people of these kingdoms (was, were) farmers, traders, craftspeople, merchants, and servants.
13. I now (knows, know) that both of these kingdoms were in northwestern Africa.
14. My family and others in our neighborhood (hope, hopes) to travel to this area one day.
15. You (needs, need) to find out about your own ancestors.

SECTION 9: CAPITALIZATION

Proper Nouns and Proper Adjectives

Capitalize proper nouns and proper adjectives.

A **common noun** is the name of a kind of person, place, thing, or idea. An example of a common noun is the word *country.* Common nouns are not capitalized. A **proper noun** is the name of a particular person, place, thing, or idea. An example of a proper noun is the word *England.* Proper nouns are capitalized. A **proper adjective** is an adjective made from a proper noun. An example of a proper adjective is the word *English.* Proper adjectives are capitalized.

Common Noun	drama	music
Proper Noun	Elizabeth	Brazil
Common Adjective	dramatic	musical
Proper Adjective	Elizabethan	Brazilian

Names and Titles of People

Capitalize names of persons and initials that stand for names.

Edward Carlson   Norma Landa Flores   A. D. Barnhart

Capitalize titles and abbreviations of titles when they appear before people's names. Capitalize abbreviations, such as *Jr.,* that appear after names.

Rev. Hudgens   Dr. Ngoni Kunonga   Harry Smith, Jr.

Capitalize a word such as *mother, father, aunt,* or *uncle* when the word is used as a name or when it comes just before a name.

Hey, Dad, where are we going?
We're going to Uncle Fred's for dinner.
Good, I like Aunt Diane's cooking.

Do not capitalize a word that names a family member when the word is preceded by a possessive, such as *your* or *my,* or by an article, such as *a* or *the.*

My dad is a carpenter.   I have an uncle who is a carpenter.

The Pronoun I

Capitalize the pronoun *I*.

Marsha and **I** kicked the leaves as we walked.

Religions, Sacred Beings, and Sacred Writings

Capitalize words that name religions, sacred beings, or religious scriptures. Also capitalize most adjectives formed from these names.

the **K**oran	**J**ehovah	the **T**orah	the **B**ible
Krishna	**I**sis	the **N**ew Testament	the **H**oly **S**pirit
Hinduism	**I**slam	the **L**ord	**A**llah

Races, Ethnic Groups, Languages, and Nationalities

Capitalize the names of races, ethnic groups, languages, and nationalities. Also capitalize adjectives formed from such names.

Nepalese	**C**herokee	**G**erman
Navajo language	**S**omali	**C**olombian coffee
Swahili	**J**ordanian food	**Y**iddish

Exercise 1   Concept Check

Using Capital Letters   Write the following sentences, using correct capitalization.

1. My aunt rowena and i have become interested in islamic traditions and beliefs.
2. Today i plan to read some selections from the koran.
3. Is reading the koran similar to reading the bible or the torah?
4. According to ms. donnelly, there are common themes in the jewish, christian, and muslim traditions.
5. Because my father is iranian, i learned a lot about the koran.
6. Someday i would like to study other sacred writings, like the vedas and upanishads.
7. Many chinese people are buddhists.
8. Some of the people in india are hindus, muslims, christians, and sikhs.
9. Is the official language of india hindi or english?
10. Was there any british influence on indian religions?

Geographical Names

Capitalize each important word in a geographical name. Do not capitalize prepositions, such as *in* or *of*, or the articles *a, an,* or *the.*

Geographical Names	Amazon River, Red Sea, South America, Cape of Good Hope, Mount Everest
Cities, States, and Countries	New York City, Wyoming, Italy, Peru
Parks and Bridges	Halibut State Park, San Francisco Bay Bridge, Tappan Zee Bridge
Highways and Streets	Kennedy Expressway, Route 66, Greentree Lane
World Regions	the South Pacific, the Middle East, Southeast Asia

Directions and Sections

Capitalize names of sections of the United States or the world. Also capitalize adjectives made from these names.

The **W**est is a popular setting for movies.

Antarctica and **A**ustralia are in the **S**outhern **H**emisphere.

Do not capitalize nouns or adjectives that merely refer to compass directions.

Turn **n**orth at the corner of the park to get to my house.

Organizations, Institutions, and Buildings

Capitalize all important words in the names of organizations, institutions, and buildings.

Organizations and Institutions	Daughters of the American Revolution, Amnesty International
Buildings	the Sears Tower, the Empire State Building

Months, Days, and Holidays

Capitalize the names of months, days, and holidays, but not the names of seasons.

August   **T**hursday   **M**other's **D**ay   **w**inter

Exercise 2   Concept Check

Using Capital Letters   Write the words that should be capitalized in the following sentences. Capitalize them correctly.

1. Last september, the boy scouts sponsored a summer camping trip over labor day weekend.
2. As we started south into san francisco across the golden gate bridge, we waved goodbye to our parents.
3. We wouldn't see the transamerica building or the pacific ocean again for three days.
4. From route 80 we turned southeast for a long ride to yosemite national park.
5. We traveled toward the sierra nevada, east of the california coast.
6. Towns like los angeles and sacramento don't seem like the west, but the little towns in the country do.
7. One street of a little town, murphy street, could have come right out of a TV movie about the west.
8. One of the boys in our troop grew up in guatemala; he said he had always wanted to see a cowboy town.
9. Finally, we got to the park and pulled up to a campground near bridalveil fall.
10. No wonder the sierra club does its best to preserve the beauty of this magnificent place.

Sentences and Poetry

Capitalize the first word of every sentence.

Rowena talked about animals a lot.

Capitalize the first word of every line of poetry.

The curved shadows under lips and eyes,
Promise a laugh, but then she cries.
                                        —Mary Longhorn

Quotations

Capitalize the first word of a direct quotation that is a sentence.

> Abraham Lincoln said, "**Y**ou can't fool all of the people all of the time."

Do not capitalize the second part of an interrupted quotation, or **divided quotation,** unless the second part starts a new sentence.

> "Let's go," suggested Carla, "**t**o the comedy show at the Chinese restaurant."

> "Let's go to the comedy show," suggested Carla. "**T**he review I read said that it was hilarious."

Parts of a Letter

In the greeting of a letter, capitalize all important words.

> **D**ear **M**r. **P**erez: **D**ear **J**osh, **D**ear **S**ir or **M**adam:

In the closing of a letter, capitalize only the first word.

> **S**incerely yours, **Y**ours truly,

Outlines and Titles

Capitalize the first word of each item in an outline and the letters that introduce major subsections.

> I. **S**chools
>   A. **P**ublic schools
>   1. **C**ity schools
>   2. **S**uburban schools
>   3. **R**ural schools
>   B. **P**rivate schools

Capitalize the first word, the last word, and all other important words in titles.

Book	*The Red Pony*
Newspaper	*The Dallas Morning News*
Play	*A Shipment of Mute Fate*
Television Series	*Mystery!*
Short Story	"The White Umbrella"

Song	"This **L**and **I**s **Y**our Land"
Work of Art	*The Scream*

The word *the* at the beginning of a title and the word *magazine* are capitalized only when they are part of the formal name.

the *Merlyn's Pen* **m**agazine on the couch
The New York Times **M**agazine
Newsweek **m**agazine

Exercise 3   Concept Check

Using Capital Letters   Copy the following letter, correcting each error in capitalization.

4554 ocean boulevard
brooklyn, NY 11224
march 14, 19—

dear rodrigo,

My grandmother is coming to visit this Saturday, so I won't be able to work on the report on Clyde Tombaugh with you. Here is some information I got from a magazine called *odyssey* and outlined for you.

I. early career
   a. becomes astronomer at Lowell observatory
   b. makes his first telescope mirror
II. search for Planet X
   a. discovery
      1. first sighting
      2. follow-up
   b. announcement of discovery of pluto

The end of the article sums up why this discovery was important. It says, "only three planets—Uranus, Neptune, and Pluto—have been discovered since the telescope was invented almost four hundred years ago."
I hope you can use some of my work in the report.

your friend,
alonso

Exercise 4 Proofreading Skill

Using Capital Letters Write the following sentences with correct capitalization.

1. on tuesday i finished reading a truly wonderful book.
2. it is called *child of the owl*, and it is written by laurence yep.
3. Wasn't mr. yep raised in the chinese-american section of san francisco?
4. i wonder if he ever walked down grant avenue, one of chinatown's biggest streets.
5. there are also chinatowns in new york city, seattle, los angeles, boston, chicago, and washington, d.c.
6. yesterday ms. hryniewich explained, "areas called chinatown exist for many reasons."
7. like italians, jews, germans, swedes, poles, and mexicans, chinese people wanted to preserve their culture.
8. Not knowing english was not as great a problem when one lived in a chinese community.
9. discrimination against asian-american people also caused people to create chinatowns.
10. one of the great events in every chinatown is chinese new year.
11. my aunt said that this holiday is always celebrated in the winter.
12. she and i discovered that it always falls between january 20 and february 19.
13. there is a good description of preparations for the holiday in the book called *in the year of the boar and jackie robinson*.
14. Last week, uncle frank said, "you will enjoy any book by bette bao lord."
15. I. history of queue, a traditional hairstyle
        a. began in china in 1645
        b. custom for generations of chinese men
    II. queue in america
        a. american reaction
            1. jokes and insults
            2. violence
            3. laws
        b. custom ends

SECTION 10: PUNCTUATION

When you read, you need punctuation marks. It would be very difficult to read without them because you wouldn't know where one idea ended and another began. Because it's so important for a writer to show where ideas end and begin, end marks are one of the most important kinds of punctuation.

End Marks

End marks show where sentences end. The three end marks are the period, the question mark, and the exclamation point.

The Period

Periods are used in the following places:

- at the end of a **declarative** sentence
- at the end of most **imperative** sentences
- after an **indirect question**
- after an **abbreviation** or an **initial**
- after each **number** or **letter** that shows a division of an outline or an item in a list

A **declarative sentence** makes a statement.

> Flagstaff is a city in the mountains of Arizona.

An **imperative sentence** is one that gives a command or that makes a request.

> Turn left at the library.

An **abbreviation** is a shortened version of a word.

Sat. (Saturday)	Dr. (Doctor)
Gov. (Governor)	Co. (Company)
B.C. (before Christ)	Penn. (Pennsylvania)

> The Qin Dynasty was established in 221 B.C.

An **initial** is the first letter of a name, used by itself.
> Nicolas J. Shepherd   R. K. O'Donnell

◄ **ONE IS ENOUGH**
When you use an abbreviation at the end of a sentence, you only need one period, not two.

An **outline** or a **list** uses periods to mark divisions or items.

I. Girls' Sports	Party List
A. Softball	1. Send invitations
B. Soccer	2. Decorate basement
C. Basketball	3. Buy refreshments
D. Volleyball	4. Organize music

Exercise 1   Concept Check

Using Periods Correctly   Copy the following items, adding periods where needed.

1. Grand Teton Park is one of the most spectacular parks in the world
2. Visit this park if you ever get the chance
3. Ms Domblewski told us about her recent trip there
4. She also showed slides of her hike to Hidden Falls on Aug 1, 1993
5. The park is located near Jackson Hole, Wyo, and it borders Yellowstone National Park
6. I Attractions
      A Mountains
      B Wildlife
7.   1 Antelope
         a Physical features
         b Habitat
       2 Buffalo
       3 Elk
8. The original 30,000 acres was purchased by John D Rockefeller, Jr
9. He presented the land to the government of the U S in 1926
10. Find out who was president at that time

The Question Mark and the Exclamation Point

Use a question mark at the end of an interrogative sentence.

An **interrogative sentence** asks a question.

> How many sisters does Joelle have**?**
> What is the capital of West Virginia**?**

Use an exclamation point at the end of an exclamatory sentence.

An **exclamatory sentence** expresses strong feelings.

> Keep away from that live wire**!**

Use an exclamation point at the end of an imperative sentence that expresses excitement. Other imperative sentences should be followed by a period.

Use an exclamation point after a strong interjection.

Yikes!   Look out!   What a game!

Exercise 2   Concept Check

Using Questions Marks and Exclamation Points   Copy the following sentences and add the proper end marks.

1. The Aztec empire was at its peak in the fifteenth century
2. Didn't the Aztecs settle on the swamps in central Mexico
3. How did the Aztecs manage to build such large cities
4. Imagine the number of workers it took to construct palaces of stone
5. What an amazing feat to create solid ground out of swamp
6. How beautiful their palaces of silver and gold were
7. The Aztecs were an agricultural community
8. Didn't they also develop systems for irrigation
9. By the fifteenth century the Aztecs controlled south-central Mexico
10. Wow I would like to know more about the Aztecs

Commas That Separate Ideas

Use commas to separate items in a series.

Commas keep readers from running together words or ideas that should be kept separate. A series is a list of three or more words or phrases. Use a comma after each item in the series except the last item.

The hardware store sells paint, brushes, and rollers.
The children learned to paste, cut, and draw at preschool.
My brother Nicolas made a paper chain, drew a clown, and painted a cut-out figure.

When using *and, but,* or *or* to combine sentences, put a comma before these words.

Buy your movie tickets at the booth before 6 P.M.**, or** you will have to pay the full price.
Martine had a terrible temper**, and** she stormed out of the room.

Exercise 3   Proofreading Skill

Commas in a Series and in Combining Sentences   Rewrite the following paragraph, adding commas where needed.

(1) Marisa Jason and Morgan read about funny moments in sports history. (2) Here is a story that always results in sighs groans and giggles. (3) Snooks Dowd was once a major-league baseball player but this story is about football. (4) One day, Dowd picked up a fumble and he ran seventy yards with it. (5) Cheers, laughter and shouts came from the stands. (6) Soon, Snooks realized he was running in the wrong direction so he ran the other way. (7) Amazingly enough, he made it all the way to the goal line and he scored a touchdown. (8) All together, he ran more than two hundred yards scored six points and set a very amusing record.

Commas with Introductory Elements and Interrupters

Use a comma to separate an introductory word or phrase from the rest of a sentence.

All right, I'm packed and ready to go.
With no sense of humor, a person can be pretty dull.

> **QUICK TIP**   After a single introductory prepositional phrase, you may not need a comma.
>
> In the corner the mouse crouched.
>
> A comma is necessary after two or more introductory prepositional phrases.
>
> In the corner of the kitchen, the mouse crouched.

Use a comma to set off the names of people who are being addressed, or spoken to, directly.

Roberto, do you know why Joan is laughing?
Yes, Amy, we just heard a funny story.

Use a comma to set off an appositive. An appositive is a word or group of words that renames something.

Mahatma Gandhi, a hero of nonviolence, was a person of great kindness and humility.

Exercise 4 Concept Check

Using Commas Correctly Copy the following sentences, adding commas where needed.

1. Well I never realized that people knew the history of bananas.
2. Mrs. Campanella will you tell us what you learned about them?
3. Yes the banana probably first appeared in the Indus Valley four thousand years ago.
4. The banana a delicate fruit was not introduced to other lands for many years.
5. Did you know Lauren that Arabs first brought bananas from the valley to northern Egypt?
6. In the Koran the holy book of Islam the banana was the forbidden fruit
7. That is the first time Mrs. Campanella that I heard that fact.
8. The first bananas in the Western Hemisphere were planted on Hispaniola a Caribbean island.
9. In fact the banana came to the United States three hundred years later.
10. The banana an unusual-looking fruit was quite a curiosity when it first arrived in this country.

Commas with Quotations

Use a comma to set off a direct quotation from the rest of a sentence.

A **direct quotation** gives the exact words of a speaker. Explanatory words, such as *he whispered* or *Margie said,* may come before, after, or in the middle of the quotation. A comma separates the explanatory words from the direct quotation. When the explanatory words begin the sentence, place a comma after the last explanatory word.

> Namid said, "My father and mother are both Cherokee."

When the explanatory words are at the end of the sentence, place the comma before the first explanatory word but inside the quotation mark.

> "My name is an English Gypsy name," replied Tem.

Sometimes a quotation has two parts. Use a comma after the last word of the first part and after the last explanatory word.

> "Some names appear in different languages," said Che, "and my name is a Spanish form of the name Joe."

Commas with Dates, Locations, and Letters

Use commas to separate the parts of dates and locations.

A comma separates the day of the month and the year. However, no comma is needed if only the month and year are given.

Comma Needed	On Friday, February 5, 1993, we celebrated Mexico's Constitution Day.
No Comma Needed	Some friends in New Orleans celebrated Mardi Gras in February 1993.

A comma separates the name of a city and its state or country.

Our friends live in Denver, Colorado.
The plane landed in Quito, Ecuador.

Use a comma after the greeting of a friendly letter and after the closing of any letter.

Sincerely yours,   Always,   Dear Dwayne,

Exercise 5   Concept Check

Correct Comma Usage   Copy the following sentences, adding commas where needed.

1. Lily was looking for silly headlines in newspapers dated November 8 1991 and earlier.
2. She found a funny one in an old newspaper printed in Chicago Illinois.
3. "Most on death row here" the headline read "were appealing."
4. Zach found an even funnier headline in an old newspaper printed in New York New York.
5. "A grateful nation buries its leader" it read.
6. "This next headline" said Lily "is funny because of a spelling error."
7. It says "Man booked for wreckless driving."
8. Some editors in Baton Rouge Louisiana must be embarrassed about that one!
9. "Do you think the newspaper editors in Atlanta Georgia have let silly headlines get by them?" asked Lily.
10. "Let's look at these newspapers from May 1993" said Zach "to see if they have."

Exercise 6　Proofreading Skill

Checking for Comma Errors　Write the following letter, correcting all errors in comma usage.

(1)

(2)

                          4431 Meridian Street
                          Indianapolis Indiana 46208
                          February 6 1993

(3) Dear Carol

(4) Well I found the information you wanted about newspapers. (5) The first regular newspaper was published in Roman times but the Chinese also published one of the world's earliest newspapers. (6) When I asked Mr. Greeley the head librarian he said the Chinese newspaper was controlled by the government. (7) "One of the first true newspapers with freedom of expression was read by European traders" he said. (8) "The readers included people in Antwerp Holland and Venice Italy." (9) I hope this information helps you with your report on magazines newspapers and pamphlets.

                      (10)　　Yours truly
                              Aunt Millie

Exercise 7　Revision Skill

Using Commas and End Marks　Copy the following sentences, adding end marks and commas as needed.

1. "Clayton" I said "what an amazing article this is."
2. The article was from the January 26 1993 issue of the *New York Times.*
3. "It explains how space exploration used to be based on competition" I told him.
4. When the Soviet Union launched the *Sputnik* satellite on October 4 1957 a space race began.
5. U.S. scientists tried to keep up with everything the Soviets did
6. "Didn't the Soviets" asked Clayton" also try to keep up with everything the Americans did"
7. What a lot of time money and effort was poured into that competition
8. On July 20 1969 people first walked on the moon.
9. "Today many countries cooperate on space research" I said
10. "The world will always benefit" Clayton said "when nations cooperate."

The Semicolon

Use a semicolon (;) to join parts of a compound sentence if no coordinating conjunction is used.

> Let's wash the car after school today; we can ask Mom for a bucket and sponge.

The Colon

Use a colon (:) after the salutation of a business letter.

> Dear Sir or Madam:

When figures are used for hours and minutes, separate the figures with a colon.

> 1:00 A.M.   3:30 P.M.

Exercise 8   Concept Check

Using Semicolons and Colons Read each sentence. If the sentence needs a semicolon or a colon, write the sentence correctly.

1. Every day Marcia turns on her favorite soap opera at 300 P.M.
2. A soap opera is a story that continues the story is told in sections or parts.
3. The idea of the soap opera was not invented for television the idea existed long before that.
4. Marcia learned about the first continuing stories on a show about English writers it was called "The Soap Opera Novel."
5. Dear Producers

    Please send me a bibliography of the English writers featured on "The Soap Opera Novel."

    > Sincerely yours,
    > Marcia Knight

6. The show was on at 800 P.M. last night and will be shown again at 1100 A.M. on Tuesday.
7. It told about Dickens, Trollope, and Thackeray they all wrote during the nineteenth century.
8. These novelists gave their publishers a chapter of a book as soon as the chapter was written these chapters were printed in popular magazines.
9. Charles Dickens's work was very popular eager readers awaited each monthly installment of his novels.

10. Sometimes Dickens would create endings for his stories in response to his readers' pleas otherwise, he used his own ideas.

The Hyphen

Use a hyphen (-) to show word breaks at the end of a line. Be sure to break words between syllables.

> After the hike, we dropped our heavy backpacks and col-
> lapsed in exhaustion.

Use hyphens in some compound words.

> baby-sit   full-time   house-raising

Use a hyphen in compound numbers from twenty-one to ninety-nine.

> twenty-seven students   forty-six elephants

Use a hyphen in fractions.

> three-tenths   two-thirds   one-half

Exercise 9   Concept Check

Using Hyphens   Write the words that need hyphens in the following sentences, adding the hyphens that are needed.

1. Our class has spent the past twenty one days studying the planet earth.
2. Three fourths of the earth's surface is covered with water.
3. Our earth is covered by a thick blanket of air called the atmos phere.
4. Earth is constantly spinning on its axis, and each complete spin takes twenty four hours.
5. One half of the earth always faces the sun; but the other half is always turned away from it.
6. The part of the earth facing away from the sun experiences dark ness.
7. Earth has four seasons, and each lasts one fourth of the year.
8. For example, spring lasts approximately ninety one days.
9. Are all of our seasons caused by a change in sunlight on one partic ular side of earth?
10. Earth's southern half gets plenty of bright sunlight in Decem ber, and its northern half gets plenty of sunlight in June.

The Apostrophe

Use an apostrophe (') to make the possessive form of a noun.

Make the possessive of a singular noun by adding an apostrophe and an *s,* even if the noun already ends with an *s.*

the glass**'s**   a coat**'s**   Tina**'s**

Make the possessive of a plural noun that ends with an *s* by adding only an apostrophe.

the cities**'** problems   the girls**'** swim team

Make the possessive of a plural noun that does not end with an *s* by adding an apostrophe and *s.*

the cattle**'s** markings   the men**'s** choir

Use an apostrophe in a contraction to show that one or more letters have been left out.

don't (do not)   we'll (we will)

Exercise 10   Concept Check

Using Apostrophes   Write the words that need apostrophes in the following sentences. Add the needed apostrophes.

1. The Martinsville Womens Club will feature discussions of African wildlife.
2. This weeks topic is the hippopotamus, whose name comes from the Greek word for "river horse."
3. The hippopotamus is one of the worlds largest land mammals.
4. There couldnt be an animal less graceful in appearance.
5. Yet, a hippos features allow it to swim fluidly and with great ease.
6. Because of its great weight, the hippo can stay beneath the waters surface and even walk on the bottom of lakes.
7. Jamess mother has studied the behavior of these animals in zoos.
8. She described the hippopotamuss ability to use its tusks, or teeth, as weapons.
9. There arent many animals with teeth that weigh up to four pounds each!
10. Like other animal babies, the calves job is to learn how to survive.

Exercise 11   Proofreading Skill

Using Punctuation Correctly   Write correctly any sentences that need additional punctuation in the following paragraph. If a sentence needs no additional punctuation, write *Correct.*

(1) At 300 this afternoon we will watch a show about the mountain lion. (2) It is the largest purring cat in North America it is also called the puma, panther, and cougar. (3) An adult mountain lion has a large hunting range and may run twenty one miles in a single day. (4) The mountain lions territory once included almost the entire United States, but legal hunting changed that. (5) Hunters were paid to kill mountain lions as recently as twenty five years ago. (6) The animals didnt survive in the eastern states, but they are making a comeback in the West. (7) Although mountain lions don't normally attack people, scientists methods for handling them involve using extreme care. (8) The animals are first tranquilized; they are then fitted with radio collars. (9) This allows the scientists to gather information on what the animals do and where they go. (10) The TV sequel to this program will be shown next Saturday at 200 P.M.

Quotation Marks

Use quotation marks (" ") at the beginning and end of a direct quotation.

"Are you going swimming next week?" asked Robb.

Use quotation marks around both parts of a divided quotation.

"Call the YMCA," said Dad, "and ask if they offer a
CPR course."

Capitalize the first word of a quotation.

"Oh," replied Marcia.

The second part of a divided quotation is not capitalized if it is not a complete sentence.

"Take the cards to the post office," said Carlos," and mail them
for me, please."

A comma or period before a quotation comes before the quotation marks. A comma or period after a quotation goes inside the quotation marks.

> Lamar said, "I like to practice piano after school."
> Candice frowned. "I like to play piano in the morning," she replied.

A question mark or an exclamation point goes inside the quotation marks if it is part of the quotation and outside the quotation marks if it is not part of the quotation.

> Carlos asked, "Could I help you make the pizza?"
> Did you say, "The pizza is already cooked"?

Punctuating Dialogue

When punctuating dialogue, begin a new paragraph to indicate a new speaker.

> "Marilyn, would you like to be responsible for leading the discussion on this chapter?" asked Ms. Robb.
> "Yes, I would, Ms. Robb," replied Marilyn.

Exercise 12 Concept Check

Using Quotation Marks and Other Punctuation   Write the following sentences, adding quotation marks and other punctuation as needed.

1. Would you like to be a weather pilot asked Jill
2. Well said Roberto that's not exactly my idea of a safe or easy job
3. Don't weather pilots sometimes fly above the center of hurricanes asked Roberto
4. They do said Mr. Chin and they often experience terrible bumping and shaking
5. The winds of a hurricane can pull trees out of the ground, can't they asked Jill
6. Mr. Chin replied They often do severe damage
7. Weather pilots he explained gather information about many kinds of storms
8. Sometimes he added their planes are struck by lightning during the storms
9. You wouldn't catch me being a weather pilot exclaimed Roberto
10. I think I would like to try doing an important job like that said Jill

Exercise 13   Revision Skill

Punctuating Dialogue   Rewrite the following passage by using correct paragraphing and punctuation.

Who do you think asked Sarah was the better pilot, Jamie Amelia Earhart or Ruth Rowland Nichols. Well Jamie replied Earhart was the first woman to fly across the Atlantic alone in 1932 But during the same year Ruth Rowland Nichols held three international records for speed, distance, and altitude She was also the first woman airline pilot Sarah said. They were both pretty important women in the history of flight Yes said Jamie but Earhart is definitely more famous

Punctuating Titles

Use quotation marks to set off the titles of short stories, poems, essays, magazine articles, chapters, television episodes, reports, and songs.

Short story	"The White Umbrella"
Poem	"The Walrus and The Carpenter"
Essay	"Love and the Cabbie"
Song	"We Are the World"
Television Episode	"The Civil War, Episode I"

Underline or italicize the titles of books, newspapers, magazines, movies, television series, plays, works of art, and long musical compositions.

Book	*Children of the Wild West*
Newspaper	*Washington Post*
Movie	*Home Alone*
Painting	*American Gothic*
Long Musical Composition	*The Magic Flute*

Underline or italicize the names of ships, trains, and aircraft.

Queen Mary
The Spirit of St. Louis
Apollo 11

Exercise 14   Concept Check

Punctuating Titles   Write the titles given in the following sentences. Underline them or use quotation marks as needed.

1. I am searching for ideas for a short story I am writing called Star Walker.
2. I had been watching reruns of Star Trek before I brainstormed for ideas.
3. I like the characters and adventures on the starship Enterprise.
4. I might also read the book called Hitchhiker's Guide to the Galaxy.
5. I plan to look for ideas in the articles and pictures in Omni magazine.
6. When I saw the movie called Brother from Another Planet, I decided to make my story humorous.
7. If my story turns out to be long, I will use chapters, and the first one will be called Star Gate.
8. If I illustrate my story, I will draw skies like those in the Van Gogh painting called The Starry Night.
9. Maybe someday I will sell the script to a television show, and they will make an episode called Star Walker.
10. Also maybe I could publish the story in Merlyn's Pen, a magazine for young writers and artists.

Exercise 15 Proofreading Skill

Using Quotation Marks and Punctuating Titles   Rewrite the following passage, correcting any errors in punctuation or paragraphing that you find. If a sentence has no errors, write *Correct.*

(1) "Did you read about the Harlem Renaissance in "Cobblestone" magazine?" Ana asked. (2) She urged her friend Ryan to read the article called Entertainers of the Renaissance. (3) Ryan replied, I already read it. It was about some great stars from that period. (4) Ryan went on to explain that the article included information about Fats Waller, the composer of the song "Honeysuckle Rose." (5) It also told about the all-black Broadway hit play Shuffle Along. (6) One of the famous writers of the Harlem Renaissance Ana said was Langston Hughes. (7) He wrote a collection of poems called "The Weary Blues." (8) Many of his first poems were published in an African-American magazine called *The Crisis*.

Exercise 16   Revision Skill

Using Punctuation Marks Correctly   Write the following sentences, correcting any errors in punctuation.

1. I read about eclipses in an article called *The Makings of a Prize Eclipse.*
2. It appeared in the July 1991 issue of "Sky and Telescope" magazine.
3. Eclipses occur when the sun moon and earth are in a straight line
4. During eclipses of the sun animals often think its nighttime.
5. Crickets chirp frogs start to croak mosquitoes bite and birds roost just as they do at night.
6. On March 24 1992 I saw an episode of the "Nova" tele vision series.
7. It had been filmed in Hawaii it was called Eclipse of the Century.
8. "Did it show an eclipse while it was happening asked Jennie."
9. Yes it did said Elaine and it also explained why eclipses occur
10. How strange it must feel to experience nighttime in the middle of the day exclaimed Jennie
11. I doubt that even one half of the people in the world ever do experience that replied Elaine.
12. Scientists can predict eclipses said Jennie but many people never have the chance to see a total eclipse.
13. This may be because eclipses dont often occur over heavily popu lated areas.
14. The next total eclipse of the sun will occur on August 21 2017 in the United States.
15. Wow cried Jennie I'll mark that date on my calendar

Index of Fine Art

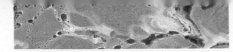

Index of Skills

Literary Terms

Action, 210, 365
Acts, 188, 623
Alliteration, 233, 623
American slave tales, 452, 630
    dialect in, 452
Anecdote, 316, 623
Atmosphere. *See* Mood
Audience, 340, 623
Author's purpose, 55, 90, 145, 340, 623
Autobiography, 48, 49, 50, 373, 623
    diaries, 48
    journals, 48
    memoirs, 48
Biographer, 48
Biography, 48, 49, 145, 245, 623
Cast of characters, 188, 206, 623
Cause and effect, 623
Characterization, 180, 624
Characters, 15, 45, 48, 82, 91, 96, 97, 138, 167, 188, 189, 208, 245, 486, 623
    development of, 45, 292, 473
    in drama, 188, 486
    main, 15, 45, 73, 208, 623
    minor, 15, 623, 627
Chronological order, 49, 395, 624
Climax, 15, 624, 628
Comparison, 624
Concrete poetry, 230, 233, 400, 624, 626
Conflict, 15, 26, 123, 189, 204, 209, 473, 604, 624
    external, 123, 357, 624
    internal, 123, 624
Description, 68, 210, 245, 624
Dialect, 29, 624–25
    in American slave tale, 452
Dialogue, 91, 188, 208, 210, 248, 486, 625
Diaries, 48
Drama, 188–89, 625
    action in, 188
    acts of, 188, 623
    cast of characters for, 188, 206, 623, 625

characters in, 188, 486
conflict in, 189, 204
dialogue in, 188, 206, 248, 486, 625
elements of, 188–89
performing, 189
plot in, 188, 189, 206
props for, 188, 522
radio play, 190, 628
reading, strategies for, 189
scenery for, 188, 522
scenes of, 188, 623, 629
script for, 188, 625
setting in, 188, 248
soliloquy in, 520, 630
sound effects for, 190, 206
stage directions for, 188, 189, 190, 206, 248, 254, 625, 630
End rhyme, 138, 629
Essay, 48, 56, 103–107, 131, 205, 317
    formal, 48
    informal, 48
    persuasive, 48
Exposition, 15
External conflict, 123, 357, 624
Fables, 539, 580, 588, 625
    moral in, 539, 588
    themes in, 539, 580
Fact, 379, 484
    vs. opinion, 49, 283, 333, 625
Fantasy, 91
Fiction, 625
    characterization in, 180, 624
    characters in, 15, 45, 48, 82, 91, 138, 167, 189, 208, 245, 623
    climax in, 15, 624, 628
    complications in, 15
    conflict in, 15, 26, 123, 189, 208, 357, 473, 604, 624
    elements of, 15–16, 91
    exposition in, 15
    flashback in, 272, 625
    narrator in, 45, 72, 627
    novel, 15, 627
    plot in, 15, 26, 48, 82, 91, 209, 418, 628

Reading and Critical Thinking Skills

Grammar, Usage, and Mechanics

Writing Skills, Modes, and Formats

Vocabulary Skills

Research and Study Skills

Speaking, Listening, and Viewing

Index of Titles and Authors

Page numbers that appear in italics refer to biographical information.

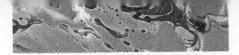

Acknowledgments

(continued from page iv)

The Christian Science Monitor: "Unfolding Bud" by Naoshi Koriyama. Copyright © 1957 by The Christian Science Publishing Society. All rights reserved. Reprinted by permission of *The Christian Science Monitor*.

Ruth Cohen, Inc., Literary Agent: "The All-American Slurp" by Lensey Namioka. Copyright © 1987 by Lensey Namioka. Reprinted by permission of Ruth Cohen, Inc., Literary Agent.

Collins/Angus & Robertson Publishers, Australia: Excerpt from *Australia's Kakadu Man* by Big Bill Neidjie, Stephen Davis, and Allen Fox. Copyright © 1986 by Resource Managers Pty. Ltd. Reprinted by permission of Collins/Angus & Robertson Publishers, Australia.

Don Congdon Associates, Inc.: "The Scribe," from *Guests in the Promised Land* by Kristin Hunter. Copyright © 1972 by Kristin E. Hunter. Reprinted by permission of Don Congdon Associates, Inc.

Ray Pierre Corsini and Elizabeth Borton de Treviño: "The Secret of the Wall" by Elizabeth Borton de Treviño. Copyright © 1966 by Elizabeth Borton de Treviño. Reprinted by permission of the author and Ray Pierre Corsini, agent for the author.

Curbstone Press: "The Disobedient Child," from *The Bird Who Cleans the World and Other Mayan Fables* by Victor Montejo, translated by Wallace Kaufman. Copyright © 1991 by Curbstone Press. Reprinted by permission of the publisher.

Dell Books and A. M. Heath & Company Limited, London: "Lob's Girl," from *A Whisper in the Night* by Joan Aiken. Copyright © 1984 by Joan Aiken. Used by permission of Delacorte Press, a division of Bantam Doubleday Dell Publishing Group, Inc., and A. M. Heath & Company Limited, London, agents for the author.

Andre Deutsch Ltd., London: "Cricket in the Road," from *Cricket in the Road* by Michael Anthony. Copyright © 1973 by Michael Anthony. Reprinted by permission of Andre Deutsch Ltd., London.

Diskant & Associates: "Fire!" by John D. MacDonald, originally published under the title "Wild, Wonderful Old Man." Copyright © 1964 by United Newspapers Magazine Corporation. Copyright renewed © 1992 by Maynard MacDonald. Reprinted by permission of Diskant & Associates.

Doubleday: "King Thrushbeard," from *Grimm's Tales for Young and Old* by Jakob and Wilhelm Grimm. Copyright © 1977 by Ralph Manheim. Used by permission of Doubleday, a division of Bantam Doubleday Dell Publishing Group, Inc.

Elizabeth Ellis and the National Association for the Preservation and Perpetuation of Storytelling: "Flowers and Freckle Cream" by Elizabeth Ellis of Dallas, Texas, from *Best-Loved Stories Told at the National Storytelling Festival*, edited by Jimmy Neil Smith. Copyright © 1991 by the National Association for the Preservation and Perpetuation of Storytelling, publisher. Reprinted by permission of the author and publisher.

Fulcrum Publishing: "The White Buffalo Calf Woman and the Sacred Pipe," from *Native American Stories* told by Joseph Bruchac. Copyright © 1991 by Joseph Bruchac. Reprinted by permission of Fulcrum Publishing, 350 Indiana Street #350, Golden, CO 80401, telephone 303-277-1623. Reprinted by permission of the publisher.

Maxine Groffsky Literary Agency: "The White Umbrella" by Gish Jen. Copyright © 1984 by Gish Jen. First published in *The Yale Review*. Reprinted by permission of the author through her agent, Maxine Groffsky Literary Agency.

Jack C. Haldeman II: "Playing for Keeps" by Jack C. Haldeman II. Copyright © 1982 by Davis Publications, Inc. Reprinted by permission of the author.

Harcourt Brace Jovanovich, Inc.: Excerpt from "To Look at Any Thing," from *The Living Seed* by John Moffitt. Copyright © 1962 by John Moffitt and renewed © 1990 by Henry Moffitt. "Two Dreamers," from *Baseball in April and Other Stories* by Gary Soto. Copyright © 1990 by Gary Soto. "Fog," from *Chicago Poems* by Carl Sandburg. Copyright 1916 by Harcourt Brace Jovanovich, Inc., and renewed 1944 by Carl Sandburg. Entire text of *Wings* by Jane Yolen. Copyright © 1991 by Jane Yolen. Reprinted by permission of Harcourt Brace Jovanovich, Inc.

HarperCollins Publishers: "The Quarrel," from *Eleanor Farjeon's Poems for Children* by Eleanor Farjeon, originally appeared in *Over the Garden Wall* by Eleanor Farjeon. Copyright 1933, renewed © 1961 by Eleanor Farjeon. "Abd al-Rahman Ibrahima," from *Now Is Your Time: The African-American Struggle for Freedom* by Walter Dean Myers. Copyright © 1991 by Walter Dean Myers. "Aaron's Gift," from *The Witch of Fourth Street and Other Stories* by Myron Levoy. Text copyright © 1972 by Myron Levoy. "Forgotten Language," from *Where the Sidewalk Ends* by Shel Silverstein. Copyright © 1974 by Evil Eye Music, Inc. Excerpt from *From Hand to Mouth: Or, How We Invented Knives, Forks, Spoons, and Chopsticks and the Table Manners to Go with Them* by James Cross Giblin. Copyright © 1987 by James Cross Giblin. Reprinted by permission of HarperCollins Publishers.

John Hawkins & Associates, Inc.: "My Friend Flicka" by Mary O'Hara, published in *Story Magazine,* 1941. Copyright 1941 by Mary O'Hara. Reprinted by permission of John Hawkins & Associates, Inc.

Houghton Mifflin Company: "Damon and Pythias," from *The Bag of Fire and Other Plays* by Fan Kissen. Copyright © 1964 by Fan Kissen. "Arachne" and "Introduction," retitled as "The Gods and Goddesses of Mount Olympus," from *Greek Myths* by Olivia Coolidge. Copyright 1949 and renewed © 1977 by Olivia E. Coolidge. Reprinted by permission of Houghton Mifflin Company. All rights reserved. Excerpt from *Children of the Wild West* by Russell Freedman. Copyright © 1983 by Russell Freedman. "The Bamboo Beads," from *A Wave in Her Pocket* by Lynn Joseph. Text copyright © 1991 by Lynn Joseph. "Crystal Rowe (Track Star)," from *Class Dismissed II* by Mel Glenn. Text copyright © 1986 by Mel Glenn. Reprinted by permission of Clarion Books, a Houghton Mifflin Company imprint. All rights reserved.

Houghton Mifflin Company and Random Century Group, London: "The Living Kuan-yin," from *Sweet and Sour: Tales from China* by Carol Kendall and Yao-wen Li. Text copyright © 1980 by Carol Kendall and Yao-wen Li. Reprinted by permission of Clarion Books, a Houghton Mifflin Company imprint, and Random Century Group, London.

Evelyn Tooley Hunt: "Mama Is a Sunrise," from *The Lyric* by Evelyn Tooley Hunt. Reprinted by permission of the author.

Francisco Jiménez: "The Circuit" by Francisco Jiménez, from *Arizona Quarterly,* Autumn 1973. Reprinted by permission of the author.

Macmillan Publishing Company: "Little Short Legs," from *Waiting to Waltz.* Copyright © 1984 by Cynthia Rylant. Excerpt from *Woodsong* by Gary Paulsen. Text copyright © 1990 by Gary Paulsen. Reprinted with permission of Bradbury Press, an Affiliate of Macmillan, Inc. "The Spelling Test," from *The Covered Bridge House and Other Poems* by Kaye Starbird. Copyright © 1979 by Kaye Starbird Jennison. Reprinted with permission of Four Winds Press, an imprint of Macmillan Publishing Company. Entire text of *The Gold Coin* by Alma Flor Ada, translated from the Spanish by Bernice Randall. Text copyright © 1991 by Alma Flor Ada. Reprinted with permission of Atheneum Publishers, an imprint of Macmillan Publishing Company.

Elaine Markson Literary Agency, Inc.: "Tuesday of the Other June" by Norma Fox Mazer. Copyright © 1986 by Norma Fox Mazer. Reprinted by permission of the author.

Jean Merrill and Ronni Solbert: Three haiku from *A Few Flies and I: Haiku by Issa,* selected by Jean Merrill and Ronni Solbert from translations by R. H. Blyth and Nobuyuki Yuasa (Pantheon Books). Copyright © 1969 by Jean Merrill. Reprinted by permission of Jean Merrill and Ronni Solbert.

William Morrow & Company: Text only of *Hiroshima No Pika* by Toshi Maruki. English translation rights arranged with Komine Shoten through Kurita-Bando Literary Agency. First published in Japan in 1980 by Komine Shoten Co., Ltd. Copyright © 1980 by Toshi Maruki. Reprinted by permission of Lothrop, Lee & Shepard Books, a division of William Morrow & Company, Inc.

New Directions Publishing Corporation: "The Secret," from *O Taste and See* by Denise Levertov. Copyright © 1964 by Denise Levertov Goodman. Reprinted by permission of New Directions Publishing Corporation.

Abiodun Oyewole: "Another Mountain," from *Rooted in the Soil,* 1st edition. Reprinted by permission of the author.

The Putnam Publishing Group: Excerpt from *Sweet Summer* by Bebe Moore Campbell. Copyright © 1989 by Bebe Moore Campbell. Reprinted by permission of The Putnam Publishing Group.

The Putnam Publishing Group and Feinman & Krasilovsky: "The Cremation of Sam McGee," from *The Collected Poems of Robert Service.* Copyright 1910 by Dodd, Mead & Company. Reprinted by permission of The Putnam Publishing Group and the Estate of Robert Service.

Dudley Randall: "Ancestors," from *After the Killing* by Dudley Randall (Broadside Press). Copyright © 1973 by Dudley Randall. Reprinted by permission of the author.

Random House, Inc./Alfred A. Knopf, Inc.: *You're a Good Man, Charlie Brown* by Clark Gesner. Copyright © 1967 by Clark Gesner. Copyright © 1965, 1966, 1967 by Jeremy Music, Inc. Reprinted by permission of Random House, Inc. Professionals and amateurs are hereby warned that *You're a Good Man, Charlie Brown* is fully protected under the Universal Copyright Convention, Berne Convention, and Pan-American Copyright Convention and is subject to royalty. All rights are strictly reserved including professional, amateur, motion picture, television, radio, recitation, lecturing, public reading, and foreign translation, and none such rights can be exercised or used without written permission from the copyright holder. All inquiries for licenses or permissions for stock and amateur uses should be addressed to Tams-Witmark Music Library, 560 Lexington Avenue, New York, NY 10022. *Nadia the Willful* by Sue Alexander. Copyright © 1983 by Sue Alexander. "The Pudding Like a Night on the Sea," from *The Stories Julian Tells* by Ann Cameron. Text copyright © 1981 by Ann Cameron. Reprinted by permission of Pantheon Books, a division of Random House, Inc. "Life Doesn't Frighten Me," from *And Still I Rise* by Maya Angelou. Copyright © 1978 by Maya Angelou. Reprinted by permission of Random House, Inc. "Carrying the Running-Aways," from *The People Could Fly: American Black Folktales,* told by Virginia Hamilton. Text copyright © 1985 by Virginia Hamilton. "Words Like Freedom," from *The Panther and the Lash* by Langston Hughes. Copyright 1947 by Langston Hughes. Excerpt from *How It Feels When Parents Divorce* by Jill Krementz. Copyright © 1984 by Jill Krementz. Excerpts from *Save the Earth: An Action Handbook for Kids* by Betty Miles. Text copyright © 1974, 1991 by Betty Miles. Excerpt from "The Dream Keeper," from *The Dream Keeper and Other Poems* by Langston Hughes. Copyright 1932 and renewed © 1960 by Langston Hughes. Reprinted by permission of Alfred A. Knopf, Inc.

Marian Reiner, Permissions Consultant: "74th Street," from *The Malibu and Other Poems* by Myra Cohn Livingston. Copyright © 1972 by Myra Cohn Livingston. "The Sprinters," from *Sprints and Distances* by Lillian Morrison. Copyright © 1965 by Lillian Morrison. Reprinted by permission of Marian Reiner for the authors.

The Estate of Quentin Reynolds: "A Secret for Two" by Quentin Reynolds. Copyright 1936 by Crowell-Collier Publishing Company. Reprinted by permission of the Estate of Quentin Reynolds.

Scholastic, Inc.: "Why Monkeys Live in Trees," from *How Many Spots Does a Leopard Have?* by Julius Lester. Copyright © 1989 by Julius Lester. Reprinted by permission of Scholastic, Inc.

The Literary Estate of May Swenson: "Southbound on the Freeway" by May Swenson. Copyright © 1963 by May Swenson and renewed © 1991. First appeared in *The New Yorker.* Reprinted by permission of the Literary Estate of May Swenson.

University of Minnesota Press: *A Christmas Carol,* adapted from the novel by Charles Dickens by Frederick Gaines, from *Five Plays from the Children's Theatre Company of Minneapolis,* edited by John Clark Donahue and Linda Walsh Jenkins. Copyright © 1975 by the University of Minnesota. All rights reserved. Reprinted by permission of the University of Minnesota Press. Professionals and amateurs are hereby cautioned that *A Christmas Carol* and the musical score thereto are fully protected under the copyright laws of the United States of America and of all other contracting states of the Universal Copyright Convention. The sale or purchase of this volume does not constitute authorization to perform, read publicly, televise, or adapt for television, film or adapt for motion picture, record, broadcast, translate into other languages, or reproduce the play or the score, wholly or in part, in any other manner, all such rights being strictly reserved. Inquiries regarding the play or the score should be addressed to the Children's Theatre Company, 2400 3rd Avenue South, Minneapolis, MN 55404.

Walker and Company: "The Real McCoy," from *Outward Dreams: Black Inventors and Their Inventions* by Jim Haskins. Copyright © 1991 by Jim Haskins. Reprinted with permission of Walker and Company.

Western Publishing Company, Inc.: "The Bride of Pluto," retitled as "Demeter and Persephone," retold by Anne Terry White, adapted from *Golden Treasury of Myths and Legends*. Copyright © 1959 by Western Publishing Company, Inc. Used by permission of Western Publishing Company, Inc.

The authors and editors have made every effort to trace the ownership of all copyrighted selections found in this book and to make full acknowledgment for their use.

Illustrations

Jerry Nelson: 15, 46, 89, 188, 538.   Robert Voigts: 29, 73, 117, 132, 167, 190, 395, 406, 435, 541, 544, 546, 552, 555, 563, 571, 571, 575, 581, 591, 597, 602.

Author Photographs

AP/Wide World Pictures: Shel Silverstein 405, Charles Schulz 522.   APA Photo Agency, Singapore: Toshi Maruki 634.   Courtesy, Arte Publico Press: Pat Mora 405.   Photo by Jerry Bauer: Gish Jen 47.   Joseph Bruchac 579 Photo by Martin Benjamin.   Courtesy, CBS Photography: Les Crutchfield 206.   Courtesy, Clarion Books: Russell Freedman 318.   Photo by Cox Studios: Virginia Hamilton 633.   Culver Pictures: Robert W. Service 139, Charles Dickens 274.   Photo by Gene Golden: Bebe Campbell 375.   The Granger Collection, New York: Lewis Carroll 97, Brothers Grimm 605, Langston Hughes 634.   Courtesy, HarperCollins Publishers: Walter Dean Myers 247.   Courtesy, Heibonsha Ltd., Tokyo: Issa 102.   Photo by Bill Heyes: Michael Anthony 36.   Historical Pictures/Stock Montage: Carl Sandburg 102.   Photo by George Janoff: Norma Fox Mazer 28.   © Tony Kent: Jill Krementz 634.   Photo by Willy Leon, courtesy, Random House: Sue Alexander 125.   Photograph by Ed Lettars: Arthur Cavanaugh 632.   The Luce Studio: Denise Levertov 187.   Photo by Richard McNamee: Lensey Namioka 304.   Photo by Mel Rosenthal: Victor Montejo 589.   Photo by Louis Melancon: Elizabeth Borton de Treviño 182.   Photo by Ed Scott: Lynn Joseph 561.   University Communications, Santa Clara University: Francisco Jiménez 442   UPI/Bettmann: 364 Maya Angelou.

Miscellaneous Art Credits

viii SUMMER SONG Rod Frederick The Greenwich Workshop.   x ©1986 Robert Cunningham.   xii THE COTTAGE HOME 1891 William H. Snape Courtesy, Christopher Wood Gallery, London.   xiv FOOTBALL 1979 Graciela Rodo Boulanger Oil on canvas, 1.62 x 1.30 m.   xvi Madonna 1983 Brenda Joysmith Courtesy of the artist. xviii CORTÈGE DE CERFS EN RUT 1959 Ivan Generalic.   4 SIRI 1970 Andrew Wyeth Tempera on panel 30 x 30 1/2 (76.2 x 77.5 cm) © Collection of the Brandywine River Museum. Photo courtesy of the Brandywine River Museum.   5, top 69 From *A Collector's Guide to Nesting Dolls* by Michele Lyons Lefkovitz. © 1989 Books Americana.   5, bottom CUADRILLAS Edmundo Otoniel Mejia Courtesy, Galleria 123, Middleburg, Virginia. 14 RAIN, LOS ANGELES 1983 William Clutz. Collection of Janice C. Oresman.   17 © 1988 Bill Binzen/The Stock Market.   31 From *Caribbean Canvas,* MacMillan Press, Ltd.   33 LES ENFANTS 1937 Balthus Musee Louvre, Paris. Giraudon/Art Resource, New York. 67, 100 FLOWERS AND INSECTS (detail) 17th century, Qing dynasty, Kangxi period (1622–1722), Chai Zhengyi and Chai Jingyi, Handscroll, ink and color on paper, 27.9 x 430.6 cm. © 1992 The Art Institute of Chicago, S. M. Nickerson Fund, 1954.104 view #2. 68 Courtesy, Hirschl and Adler Modern, New York.   81 © Angelo Lomeo and Sonja Bullatty/The Image Bank.   85 Illustration by Michael Deas.   87 From *How It Feels When Parents Divorce* by Jill Krementz © 1984 by Jill Krementz. Reprinted by permission of Alfred A. Knopf, Inc.   91 Courtesy, William Morrow and Company.   92, 93, 95, 183, 248 The

Granger Collection, New York.   98 CAT Kohei Aida from the book *Japanese Brush Painting*, Courtesy, Japan Publications Trading Co., Tokyo.   112 *Shiloh* by Phyllis Naylor Reynolds. Cover reprinted with permission of Macmillan Publishing Company and Dilys Evans.   113 Jacket illustration by Natalie Babbitt from *Tuck Everlasting* by Natalie Babbitt. Copyright © 1975 by Natalie Babbitt. Reprinted by permission of Farrar, Straus & Giroux, Inc.   113 Reprinted with permission of Charles Scribner's Sons, an imprint of Macmillan Publishing Company from *Hawk, I'm Your Brother* by Byrd Baylor, illustrated by Peter Parnall. Jacket illustration copyright © 1976 Peter Parnall.   116 WINTER NIGHT IN RONDANE (detail) 1914 Harald Sohlberg. Nasjongalleriet, Oslo, Norway. Photo J. Lathion © 1992 NG.   117 © M. Thonig/H. Armstrong Roberts.   132 Culver Pictures. 142 Anacostia Museum Smithsonian Institution, Washington, D.C. Harold Dorwin, photographer.   140 © Superstock.   157 WINTER: CAT ON A CUSHION (detail) Théophile-Alexandre Steinlen. The Metropolitan Museum of Art, New York Gift of Henry J. Plantin, 1950.   158 Illustration by Mark Corcoran.   216 *The Lion, the Witch and the Wardrobe* by C.S. Lewis. Cover reprinted with permission of Macmillan Publishing Company.   217 *Shoebag* by Mary James: Copyright 1990 by Mary James. Reprinted by permission of Scholastic, Inc.   217 From *Anthony Burns: The Defeat and Triumph of a Fugitive Slave* by Virginia Hamilton. Jacket illustration copyright © 1988 by Leo and Diane Dillon. Jacket illustration by Leo and Diane Dillon. Reprinted by permission of Alfred A. Knopf, Inc.   220 Illustration by Denise Chapman Crawford/Repertoire.   221 © Leo de Wys.   230 The Bettmann Archive.   234 The Wedgwood Museum, Barlaston, England. 284 Illustration by David Cunningham.   285 Courtesy, Contemporary Books, Chicago. 293 © Barry O'Rourke/The Stock Market.   301 © 1991 Naideau/The Stock Market.   305 DYING GIANTS 1990 Michael L. Scott Courtesy, Sherry French Gallery, New York   311 The Kansas State Historical Society, Topeka.   328 Reprinted with permission of Macmillan Publishing Company from *Call it Courage* by Armstrong Sperry. Copyright © 1940 Macmillan Publishing Company; copyright renewed © 1968 Armstrong Sperry.   329 *Hide and Seek* by Ida Vos, © 1991, published by Houghton Mifflin Company.   329 Reprinted with the permission of Atheneum Publishers, an imprint of Macmillan Publishing Company from *Shadow of a Bull* by Maia Wojciechowska, drawings by Alvin Smith. Jacket design by Alvin Smith. Copyright © 1964 Maia Wojciechowska.   332 ROLLERSKATES (detail) © Roy Lichtenstein.   333 Larry Lee/H. Armstrong Roberts. 339 © Superstock.   359 © S. Feld/H. Armstrong Roberts.   365, 386, 401 Camerique/H. Armstrong Roberts.   385 © 1988 Michael Garland/The Image Bank.   393 Fred Conrad/ Leo de Wys   430 *Bridge to Terabithia* by Katherine Patterson. Cover reprinted by permission of HarperCollins Publishers.   431 *The Whipping Boy* by Sid Fleischman. Jacket illustration © 1986 by Peter Sis. By permission of Greenwillow Books, a division of William Morrow & Company, Inc.   431 *Sweetgrass* by Jan Hudson. Reprinted by permission of Philomel Books, a divison of Putnam.   434 THE WILD ONES (detail) Frank C. McCarthy From the limited edition book *The Art of Frank C. McCarthy* © The Greenwich Workshop, Inc. Trumbull Ct.   440 © Bob Daemmrich/Stock Boston.   446 DAYBREAK (DAYLILIES) 1985 © Gary Bukovnik. Watercolor over pencil on two sheets of paper, overall 29 1/2 x 83. Collection, Brian Lewis, Los Gatos, California. Reproduced courtesy of Harry N. Abrams, Inc., Publishers, New York.   448 Ronnie Kaufman/The Stock Market. 452 The Underground Railroad 1982 Oberlin Senior Citizens, Inc., Oberlin, Ohio.   455 American Numismantic Society, New York.   457 © 1989 Jan Oswald/The Stock Broker. 486 AP/Wide World Photos.   532 *Island of the Blue Dolphins* by Scott O'Dell. © 1960. Reprinted with permission of Houghton Mifflin Company.   533 Jacket illustration by Leo and Diane Dillon from *A Wrinkle in Time* by Madeleine L'Engle. Jacket illustration copyright © 1979 by Leo and Diane Dillon. Reprinted by permission Farrar, Staus & Giroux, Inc. 533 *Dragonwings* by Laurence Yep. Cover reprinted by permission of HarperCollins Publishers.   536, 540 The Stock Market.   536, 551 Demeter running Museum of Greece, Eleusis Scala/Art Resource, New York.   537,562 From *Chinese Papercuts* by Florence Temko (China Books, 1982)   537, 580 © Stephanie Stokes/The Stock Market. 537, 590 Thonig/H. Armstrong Roberts.   573 An Imperial badge of office embroidered with a dragon, probably 19th century, Chinese silk embroidery on silk. Werner Forman Archive. Private collection.   582 From *Favorite Greek Myths* retold by Mary Pope Osborne, illustrated by Troy Howell. Illustrations copyright © by Troy Howell. Reprinted by permission of Scholastic, Inc.   586 Museo Sylvanus G. Morley, Tikal, Guatemala. 592, 593 Portrait Busts early 1st century A.D. The J. Paul Getty Museum, Malibu, California.